Neill
of Summerhill

Neill
of Summerhill
The Permanent Rebel

Jonathan Croall

Routledge & Kegan Paul
London, Melbourne and Henley

First published in 1983
by Routledge & Kegan Paul plc
39 Store Street, London WC1E 7DD,
296 Beaconsfield Parade, Middle Park,
Melbourne, 3206, Australia, and
Broadway House, Newtown Road,
Henley-on-Thames, Oxon RG9 1EN
Set in Linotron Sabon by
Input Typesetting Ltd, London
and printed in Great Britain by
T. J. Press (Padstow) Ltd
Padstow, Cornwall

British Library Cataloguing in Publication Data

Croall, Jonathan
Neill of Summerhill
1. Neill, A S   2. Summerhill School—
Biography   3. Teachers—Great Britain
Biography
I. Title
371.2'012'0924   LF796.L6

ISBN 0–7100–9300–4

For Jan, Ben and Julius, with love and thanks

Contents

Contents

Illustrations

European beginnings: the International School in Hellerau, Germany, and its second home on Sonntagsberg, Austria

Edwin Muir in Vienna during the time he stayed with Neill, 1923–4 (The Literary Estate of Willa Muir/The Hogarth Press)

The young Willa Muir as Neill first knew her, at St Andrews University (The Literary Estate of Willa Muir/The Hogarth Press)

Wilhelm Stekel, Neill's analyst and friend (Mary Evans/Sigmund Freud Copyrights)

Summerhill at Lyme Regis, Dorset, 1924–7 (Mervyn Corkhill)

Neill with a group of staff and children at Lyme, 1925 (Margaret McCance)

Neill and Mrs Lins in the early years at Leiston (Mervyn Corkhill)

Neill's allies on the left wing of the progressive school movement: Bill Curry (Richard Rushton), Dora Russell (Dora Russell) and Bertrand Russell (Camera Press)

Neill, George Corkhill and Summerhill children on a camping holiday in Scotland, 1932 (Roger Anscombe)

Neill at work – as craftsman (Leslie and Vivien Morton), labourer (Leslie Thomson), storyteller (Claude Ferrière) and writer (Antoine Obert)

Neill at play – escaping from visitors on the golf course (Jacky Monty); taking a leading role in his own play, *One of the Family* (Leslie and Vivien Morton)

Summerhill parents: J. D. Bernal (Ramsey & Muspratt: Nicholas Lee), Ivor Montagu (Ivor Montagu), Miles Malleson (S. & G. Press Agency), Ethel Mannin and her daughter Jean, 1929 (Mansell Collection)

Summerhill at Ffestiniog, 1940–5 (Joan Phelan)

Ena Wood, Neill's second wife (Jacky Monty)

Neill's daughter Zoë: on the cover of *Picture Post*, and with her father (Report: Elisabeth Chat)

Neill with his therapist and great friend Wilhelm Reich (Antoine Obert)

Neill en route to the USA, 1948 (Jacky Monty)

Life in Summerhill – teaching, attending the weekly meeting, handing out pocket money (Report: Alan Vines/John Bulmer Camera Press/Report: Alan Vines)

Henry Miller in 1969 (Popperfoto)

Anti-Polaris protest on the Dunoon ferry, May 1961 (John Topham Picture Library)

Neill receiving one of his three honorary degrees, University of Exeter, 1968 (*The Times*)

Neill in old age, with his dog Biscuit (Libby Hall)

Text illustrations

The Quest for Neill

> I would go almost as far as to put a ban on the biography of any
> great man. . . if we want to keep our illusions.
>
> *The Free Child,* 1953

When first I began to consider the idea of writing Neill's life, there were
some who suggested that the exercise would be a pointless one. Surely,
their argument ran, Neill himself, in his many lectures, books, newspaper
articles and interviews, had told us all we might want to know about his
life and work. This seemed to me extremely unlikely, but nevertheless a
point of view I would have to bear in mind before committing myself to
the task. I decided to look into what would undoubtedly be my primary
source, *Neill! Neill! Orange Peel!,* the first half of which contained Neill's
account of his pre-Summerhill years. As I read this wonderfully vivid and
poignant evocation of his childhood and youth in Scotland, of his struggles
as an impoverished university student, his attempts to break into journalism, his discovery of Homer Lane and the Little Commonwealth, his wanderings in Europe in search of a country where he would be free to run his
experimental school – so I wondered if there *would* be very much point in
attempting to compile a biography.

Yet when I looked at the book a second time, I began to realise that
Neill had been selective in what he had put down. Here and there he
referred to other books he had written, and to these I now turned: the
delightful 'Dominie' series, and the famous 'Problem' books, which did so
much to introduce his ideas to a wider audience. These did indeed help to
fill in certain gaps; but they also introduced a problem of a different kind.

I soon discovered that Neill was not always careful to keep fiction separate from fact. I also found that he was by no means as reliable a witness of his own intentions and behaviour as his apparently frank and self-deprecating writing might suggest. I was pleased to discover, in support of my growing scepticism on this score, that Neill himself had taken a similar view of his early memoir. 'I wish I had the moral courage to write an Autobiography telling everything,' he confessed in 1940. 'I wrote one last summer but it was so half true that I refrained from publishing it.' The first half of the book – which was not to be published until the very end of his life – had, it transpired, been written at a moment of personal crisis, during which he had undergone a course of analysis which had had a profound effect on his later life.

But it was only when I turned from documents to people that I became truly convinced of the need for an objective biography. As I started to gather opinions and memories from people who had known Neill – as pupils, staff or parents of Summerhill, as friends or visitors, critics or admirers – I wondered if they were all talking about the same man. Naturally, most of us present different sides of ourselves to different people, depending on circumstances, mood, the nature of the other person concerned and other factors. But with Neill the contrasts were particularly startling. While one person recalled his warmth, humour and fundamental gaiety, the next would speak of a remote and grumpy Scot, a shy and withdrawn pessimist, who preferred – often literally – to cultivate his garden than to have contact with the adults around him. Some former Summerhill pupils recalled his genius in handling their emotional problems; others the crudity and ineffectiveness of his idiosyncratic brand of Freudian analysis. To one, Neill was the very centre of the community; to another, he was a remote, almost unnoticed figure. This latter view found its ultimate expression in the comment of one 6-year-old boy. While staying with his aunt during a school holiday, he talked to her about the adults at Summerhill, and then added that there was also a chap there called Neill, 'who tells stories'.

Neill, I soon realised, was a complex man, who found it hard to operate in the adult world, and was in general much more at ease amongst children. Yet I saw that I would have to be particularly cautious in making use of the recollections of his former pupils. A significant number of them, without any prompting, felt that Neill had been a 'father-figure' to them in their childhood – and in some cases in their adult lives too. He was indeed a surrogate father to many, a man who bestowed on them much love and affection – which he preferred to call approval – without demanding anything in return. Many of them were not used to this kind of adult, having previously gone through unhappy and sometimes traumatic childhood experiences. Some felt that Neill had changed their lives, and that it was principally due to him that they could now function as normal adults. It was therefore very hard, perhaps impossible, for them to be objective, and to distinguish between their feelings at the time as children and their later adult perceptions.

As my researches progressed, I was faced with another problem encountered by most biographers: the unevenness of the oral and written evidence I was accumulating. For the pre-Summerhill period of his life, I was evidently going to have to rely very substantially on Neill's version of events. True, I was fortunately able to track down a small number of men and women who had been taught by him in Bonnyrigg, Kettle, Newport and Gretna. But here again I was having to rely on the testimony of those who had known him only as children, in some cases as much as seventy-five years previously. The same problem arose concerning his years at King Alfred School in London. Not until Neill was joined by Willa and Edwin Muir in Germany when he was nearing 40 was I able to make use of any *adult* evidence for his actions and opinions, and for the way he was developing as a person.

For the Summerhill period, on the other hand, I was able to unearth an abundance of material. Neill's 'dreadful school' has probably been the subject of more media attention than any other this century. Newspaper accounts vary, from the ludicrously sensational and distorted to the calm and reasonably accurate. Often they tell us as much about contemporary attitudes as about what Neill was doing at Summerhill. Letters, in contrast, are more reliable sources of information, though of course they too must be read with a sceptical eye. Neill's letters, of which I managed to gather some 900, provided invaluable evidence of his private hopes and regrets, his changing moods, and his real feelings and opinions of the people around him. Yet, of this substantial collection, no more than three belong to the period before Neill brought Summerhill to Lyme Regis in 1924. How different might this book have been if the proportions had been reversed?

Like thousands of others before me, I found Neill's best books a delight to read. Fresh, humorous, provocative, they were often inspiring in their profound common sense. Yet Neill could also be infuriatingly simple-minded or evasive when tackling certain issues. I had constantly to bear in mind the fact that, though he was in many respects a brilliant publicist for his own ideas, he was also a propagandist, intent on convincing an often puzzled or hostile world of the value and practicality of his revolutionary ideas about children. A pioneer is reluctant to give hostages to fortune, and it is easy to forget how thoroughly shocking parts of Neill's philosophy were during the 1920s, when he first began to work with problem children. So it came as no real surprise to find that many of the anecdotes he related, and which made his books so eminently readable, were not always accurate in the detail, though their essence was true enough. Perhaps they should be treated as parables: in setting them down or telling them to his lecture audiences, he was doing what Orwell once observed in Dickens's work, 'telling small lies in order to emphasise what he regards as a big truth'. Over the years he would tell the same story in different ways; often he would retell an anecdote of twenty years' standing as if it had happened the day before; and he was not above manufacturing certain details in order to make a story more startling or complete.

While trying to get to the heart of Neill himself, I gradually realised that, almost without meaning to, I was building up a picture of what it was like to live and work and play at Summerhill. Needless to say, the private reality was quite unlike the public image. The popular idea of the school was of a place where anarchy prevailed, since everything and anything was permitted; or of a model community pervaded by peace and love, a blueprint for Utopia where children were free to be happy and happy to be free. The picture I was being shown was of a much more complex, structured and constantly changing community, in which both adults and children were frequently subject to very much the same kind of hardships, crises, satisfactions, and delights as others living in tightly-knit communities. Nevertheless, there were important differences in attitudes and behaviour, which made Summerhill unique. In trying to get Neill's work as well as his personality into perspective, it seemed important to try to reproduce this picture as faithfully as possible.

There was one matter that I was forced to consider time and again, since it clearly interested so many people. This was the question of whether a school like Summerhill could succeed without the presence of Neill himself. In one sense the question has already been answered: under Ena Neill the school has continued to be run on the same principles ever since Neill died and when she retires Neill's daughter Zoë will take over her position. Of course Summerhill can never be *quite* the same without Neill. A community that depended so much for its spirit and purpose on the personality and temperament of its creator is bound to alter when he is no longer there. But the question has a wider importance, since it asks whether the particular type of freedom that Neill made possible at Summerhill can be emulated in other communities, run by men and women with different qualities from those which he possessed.

It is perhaps premature even to try to formulate an answer to the question, since so few people have made any serious and whole-hearted attempt to put his ideas to the test. Perhaps this account of his life will make it a little easier to see how Neill achieved what he did with his remarkable experiment, and why, when he died, *The Times* was moved to begin its obituary with the words: 'If children anywhere are happier nowadays in school than their elders sometimes were, it is due in no small measure to this craggy, lovable Scot.'

PART ONE

The Road to Summerhill

CHAPTER 1

The Problem Child

My father did not care for me when I was a boy.
Neill! Neill! Orange Peel!, 1972

George Neill was accustomed to handling children: he was the village school teacher – or 'dominie', as they were called in Scotland. It had not been an easy matter for him to reach a position of such relative respectability. The MacNeill clan came originally from the island of Barra. After George's birth, in 1852, his family settled in Tranent, a village near Edinburgh, where both his father and his brothers worked down the mines. As a boy he was very fond of his mother, and was shattered when she died of cholera when he was 14. He cried for a fortnight, he later told his children, and her death nearly broke his heart. He went to live with an aunt, and was brought up with his cousins, who decided they would call him just Neill. He had a flair for learning, and though there were no grants then, and the family could ill afford the fees, he was sent to college to train as a teacher. At this time the professions were closed to working-class families, but schoolmastering, though less lucrative and of a lower status, was certainly an occupation that a bright village boy could aspire to. After qualifying, George Neill went to teach in a school in Edinburgh.

One of his fellow-teachers there was Mary Sutherland. For her, too, it had been a struggle to qualify. Her mother, Clunes Sinclair, came from a farming family in the Shetlands. Mary, born in 1854, was the only one of twenty children not to die of tuberculosis. Her mother became a servant girl after she left school, moving to Leith on the edge of Edinburgh, where she met and married Neil Sutherland, a worker in the local dockyards. One night he was found drowned, and his widow had to take in washing to support her family. Somehow, she managed to send her only daughter, Mary, to training college, holding out the possibility of her becoming an assistant in one of the local schools.

However, this idea soon had to be set aside. She met George Neill, and after a year's courtship they decided to marry. No married women were allowed to teach in Scottish schools at this time; they had to hand in their resignation one month before their wedding. Although George Neill's qualifications were no more than moderate – at college he received a third-class certificate – his career developed quite rapidly. At the age of 24, after working for a while as an assistant teacher in the village school at Inveriarty, in the county of Angus in Lowland Scotland, he took up the post of head teacher of the school in the nearby village of Kingsmuir in 1876. The village was two miles from the county town of Forfar, and in November 1880, just a fortnight before the birth of their first child, the Neills moved in to a seven-roomed top-storey flat in Forfar's East High Street.

Until shortly before they came there, Forfar had remained much as one traveller described it in 1760, 'a poor, ill-built town of small farmers, innkeepers and linen manufacturers'. Then jute came to Dundee from India, several local manufacturers made the switch from linen, and also made their fortunes. Forfar became prosperous, libraries and halls being built to cater for the growing population. Farming, though, still remained crucial to the town – whether it was dairy, cattle, arable or fruit farming. On Mondays the farmers would drive their cattle through the town; and on the Saturday market days they would arrive with their gigs and ponies to trade, hire labourers, and gossip. The drink flowed freely, ploughmen and their employers often being taken home in a stupor by their driverless gigs. Such occasions, with the attendant hobby horses, swing boats, boxing booths, sweet stalls and town bands, offered local children a rare chance for excitement.

No one took more delight in the chance of a day's outing than the Neills' third son, Alexander Sutherland. Born on 17 October 1883, he was in fact the fourth boy in the family; the second, Hamish, had died the year before, aged 2. Allie's two brothers were Willie, four years his senior, and Neilie, some two and a half years older than him; and thirteen months after his birth, the Neills' first girl, Clunes St Clair, was born. The two older boys became close companions, leaving Allie and Clunie to enjoy the market days together, and to become firm friends.* They would wander the streets together, searching the gutters for any treasure left by the departing farmers, or marching along behind the town band. Some of the farmers' children had half a crown to spend for the day; the Neills, being poor, had no more than sixpence, and would try to increase it by looking after a farmer's horse, then a popular way of making some extra pocket

---

*Alexander was shortened to 'Alec', but Clunie as a child could only say 'Allie', and this name stuck.

money. On a lucky day, they could pick up a few extra halfpennies, or a gift in kind, such as a piece of bread and jam.

However, such good fortune had to be kept from their mother, who had forbidden them to accept money or food from others under any circumstances. Punishment was swift if ever she caught them doing this, as Allie discovered: 'One day when I proudly told Mother that I had refused such a tempting dainty, she smiled and told me I was a good boy. "Of course, you said you weren't hungry, didn't you?" "No," I said with confidence, "just, 'Thank you, but my ma says I mustn't take it.' " And she slapped me hard.' After that, he was careful to accept any gifts surreptitiously.

Mary Neill was a proud and ambitious woman, anxious that her children should 'better' themselves. Yet her husband's salary of £120 a year tied her to a modest standard of living which made it difficult to keep up appearances. Her efforts to do this were made more difficult when, some time after Allie's sixth birthday, the family moved yet again. A schoolhouse had been recently built across the road from the school in Kingsmuir, where George Neill had been the 'dominie' for some thirteen years. An attractively proportioned house with oriel and gabled windows in its high-sloping roof, it consisted of a parlour, a dining room, a kitchen and five bedrooms. There was no indoor lavatory, but simply an earth closet at the end of the garden, on to which the children could look out from their bedroom windows at the back of the house.

Kingsmuir in the last decade of the nineteenth century was no more than a hamlet, made up of a few houses built either side of the road running through the village from Forfar to Carnoustie, and a number of farms scattered about the parish. The residents were mostly farm workers and their families, together with a small number of craftsmen – a joiner, a blacksmith, a tailor. There was no church or pub, and only two small shops, which sold sweets and a few basic commodities. Milk and eggs could be had from the local farms; other provisions necessitated a two-mile walk along the lanes into Forfar, with only a slim chance of getting a ride from a farmer's gig or a milkcart. Although bicycles were then just beginning to come into fashion, traffic through the village was almost non-existent: the children could play safely in the road, indulging in the latest crazes for marbles, hoops or tops, or using a tin can for a makeshift football game.

What communal life there was invariably took place in the schoolroom – an occasional concert, lantern-slide show or performance by an itinerant juggler or conjuror, the annual prize-giving ceremony, and a weekly prayer meeting. On Saturday nights the ploughmen would assemble at the bridge, to sit and gossip the time away, or throw insults at passers by. The villagers' lives were also enlivened by the annual picnic, and by the occasional wedding or funeral. Some of the marriages were 'forced' ones between the ploughmen and the servant girls, a fact mostly accepted by working families, amongst whom illegitimate children were comparatively common. The farmers, some of them prosperous, or anyone else with aspirations to status or gentility, made sure of regular attendance at the church in Forfar. They treated Sundays as holy days, when only necessary work could be done, and no books other than the Bible or other 'improving' volumes could be read. Class divisions were marked out by language, dress and behaviour, and were particularly to be seen in attendance at the 'kirk'. The traditional hierarchy of a Scottish village would find the dominie ranked below the 'laird', the minister and the doctor: in Kingsmuir, which lacked any of these, George Neill was 'head mon' of the village, and his wife made strenuous efforts to ensure that the family lived up to this position. 'We didn't keep up with the Joneses; we *were* the Joneses,' Neill observed later.

Mary Neill was a small, plump and homely woman, who devoted her life to her family. She gave birth to thirteen children in all, of whom one was still-born, four died in infancy, and eight survived into adulthood. This was not untypical of a period in which, when a baby was born, people would sometimes ask: 'Has it come to stay?' Mary Neill was philosophical about her large family: 'I took what my Maker gave me,' she told her children later. Her life was almost entirely circumscribed by her domestic tasks. She had what amounted to an obsession about cleanliness, spending many hours at the washtub to get her linen white, or wielding a charcoal iron over the ironing board. She was proud to be the only woman in the village able to make her strawberry jam 'firm'. She made all her own clothes, grew her own vegetables in the garden, and earned extra money by dyeing and curling the ostrich feathers then fashionable for hats and boas. Once she had set up house, she tried to keep both her own and her husband's relatives at arm's length – she found it particularly hard to tolerate her father-in-law's dress and manner, which betrayed his humble origins.

She also kept her children on a tight rein, doing all she could to prevent them from mixing with the rough and ragged children of the local ploughmen and farm hands. She refused to let them join the other children in bringing in the potato harvest or gathering the strawberry crop; years later Neill still remembered vividly an occasion when he had not been allowed on a picnic with the others. She also, her daughter May recalls, made a distinction between her sons and daughters: 'Ma treated the boys like gods, while the girls had to be the domestic servants, and clean, polish and wax our brothers' shoes. It was most unfair: eventually I told Allie I would only go on doing his if he gave me sixpence – which of course he never had. So that was the last of the shoe cleaning.' In summer, while other children ran about barefoot, the Neill children had to put up with the discomfort of stockings and boots; they were also forced to wear stiff collars throughout the week. And on Sunday their mother poured them into their best clothes for the two visits to church that day: Allie and the other boys in their well-brushed clothes, starched collars and cuffs, and oiled hair, the girls in their carefully ironed dresses. 'She was a proud wee woman,' Neill remembered. 'She was a snob, and she made us snobs.'

Tall and thin, with a moustache that seemed to fit his military bearing, George Neill would lead the family group on the two-mile walk to Forfar, dressed in a chimney hat, frock coat and starched shirt – though more in deference to his wife's wishes than to public opinion. Though he was as concerned as she was that their children should succeed in life, he neither shared her snobbery nor her preoccupation with outward form. He never bothered to say the traditional grace before a meal unless she was present, when a firm 'Now George. . .' would remind him of his duty. Once he expressed a desire to join in a game of quoits with other men in the village, but submitted to her injunction not to 'lower himself' in this fashion. Often he would give way to his wife simply for the sake of peace. Later Neill wrote with evident feeling: 'It is the mother who makes the Scots home an uneasy place, in which one has to think three times before one speaks.'

To the inhabitants of Kingsmuir, George Neill seemed in all respects a model citizen. Conscientious and hard-working, he never had a day off school, except to assist at a funeral. He was generous with his time and knowledge, and the community invariably turned to him on matters both great and small. Most of the adults in the village had a bare minimum of education, and many looked to him for advice about their children's future. In the evenings he gave extra tuition in French and Latin to those who wanted to study for the university or civil service – a traditional part of a village dominie's role. He organised concerts in the schoolroom, and held services there on Sunday afternoons, delivering a short sermon without the need for notes. If there was a death in a family, he would 'coffin' the body – it was the custom for the deceased to be put in the coffin during rather than before the service. He also sat on the parish council, and was an elder in the church in Forfar.

Yet in his inner life he seems to have been less than happy. At one stage during his tenure of the Kingsmuir job he failed a medical because of being highly strung, though his own doctor gave him a certificate saying it was only 'his nerves'. There is some evidence that he resented his wife's insistence on maintaining a respectable image. Other dominies in the area would play bowls at the weekend, or go drinking together. According to some members of the family, George Neill did not drink, and was anyway too involved in looking after his children to join them. However, this is contradicted by Neill himself who, though never mentioning the matter in print, did later talk freely about the fact that his father was a 'dipsomaniac'. Whether this drinking was covert, or known only within the Neill household, is not clear; but there is a memory in Kingsmuir that the dominie maltreated his wife. (Another memory, impossible now to verify, was that he 'interfered' with young girls.)

None of this darker side of his personality can now be substantiated. It is clear, though, that his life was a hard one, not least in the financial sphere. To their first four children the Neills added a further four: three girls, May, Ada and Hilda, and one boy, the youngest in the family, Percy. This large family had to be fed, clothed and looked after on an annual salary of £120, though this was occasionally supplemented by some small income from Mary Neill's dyeing work. 'My parents never went anywhere,' remembers their daughter May, 'they just sacrificed their lives for their family.' Not surprisingly, George Neill became preoccupied with the fortunes of his children – and it was Allie who caused him the greatest distress.

The third of the Neill children was in many respects an unprepossessing boy. 'There was something amiss with Allie – he was big and soft,' is how Fred McFarlane, a Kingsmuir man who knew the whole family, remembers him. With his turned-in feet, his sticking-out ears – which brought him the nickname 'Saucers' – and his clumsy manner, he came in for his share of bullying from other children. When they came to pick sides for a game of football, he was usually the last to be chosen. He received a similar humiliation at home, as he later recalled: 'If there was a particularly hard and unappetising heel of a loaf, my father would cut it off with a flourish; with another flourish, he would toss it over the table in my direction, saying: "It'll do for Allie." ' His father, as his sister May recalls, 'acted the policeman about the house'. It was Allie who tended to get the harshest treatment – a hard pinch on the cheek, or a painful squeeze on the arm. As an adult, Neill wrote: 'My father did not care for me as a boy. Often he was cruel to me, and I acquired a definite fear of him.'

His fear of his father was reinforced by a natural timidity and gentleness, recalled later by his sister May, some six years his junior: 'I would have done anything for him, because he was such a nice soul. He was very meek and mild, and everybody loved him. My grandmother thought there was nobody like him, and used to say to my mother, "He'll be your best son, mark my words." He never fell out with you, you never had a fight with him.' Unlike Allie, May did speak out against their parents, although 'I got hammered for it'. On the other hand Willie, the eldest son, full of energy and exceptionally bright, was able to escape punishment for all kinds of escapades. His academic ability brought him into favour with his father. The boy had a prodigious memory, and by the age of 2 was able to read parts of the Old Testament. He read everything he could lay hands on, needing no one to drive him to his books. At the age of 8 he was second in the arithmetic class in school, and only a year later entered for the St Andrews University Local Exams Prelims. To his father, as to many other parents in Scotland, advancement in life meant advancement in learning. There was never one moment's doubt about Willie's brilliance as a scholar, his capacity to shine in an educational system which put such emphasis on the retention and repetition of information. Clearly he was destined for academic distinction, and the social approval that would come in its wake.

Allie was a complete contrast. In temperament and interests he seemed closer to the village children destined to work on the land. His early heroes were the local ploughmen, whose rolling walk he imitated. He was deeply upset when his mother refused to make a pair of breeches for him in ploughman style – she said they were common, and considered the flies on male trousers indecent. Such carefree hours that he had were mostly spent well away from home or school. With other village children he went birds' nesting; caught minnows in the streams around the village; plundered the dovecotes in the local farms; put farthings on the railway line, in the hope they would turn into pennies. There were occasional fights with the children from the nearby villages of Letham and Lunanhead. In the evenings, Allie and his friends dug for skeletons and treasure in the ruins of Restenneth Priory nearby. The Neill children became friendly with the Adam family, who owned Ladenford Farm just south of Kingsmuir: the farm became one of their favourite playgrounds, where they could climb on walls, or search for birds' nests around the estate.

Maggie Adam, one of the children living there at the time, remembers the frequent visits of Allie and Clunie, and also Allie's 'devilment'. This quality, which was to be well in evidence in later life, had to be firmly suppressed once Allie came back under his own roof. Indeed, after a while he was compelled to live two lives. Around the village and the fields he was the country urchin; once back in the house he had to adjust his behaviour to that expected of the son of the 'head mon' of the village. Nowhere was this distinction more apparent than in the question of speech, about which his mother in particular had very firm views. As a result, Allie became adept at switching from the strong Broad Scots Forfar dialect he used with his friends to the correct English expected of him at home. Such early lessons in the need to cultivate respectability had a profound effect on his later outlook on life.

The tension was also highlighted by a ritual that became familiar in Kingsmuir. At 8.30 every weekday evening the dominie would blow a dog whistle, and the Neill children, in contrast to others in the village, would have to break off from their games and settle down to their evening homework. 'Time for the dogs to go home' would be the cry from the village children, much to Allie's resentment. It was here that he came into direct conflict with his father, because of his total inability to grasp the essentials of Allen's *Latin Grammar* or, on Sunday, to commit to memory verses of a Psalm. Typically, he would be the last to finish, sitting tearfully at his meaningless task while the other children in the family returned to play with the village children.

Allie's attitude to book learning was intimately bound up with his fear of his father, so it was unfortunate that he should, like the rest of the family, have to attend the village school run by George Neill. As pupil number 557 of Kingsmuir School, he joined the roll on 29 June 1888, at the age of four and a half, before the family moved to Kingsmuir. Only a few of the wealthy farmers could afford gigs in those days, and bicycles, though becoming popular, would have been an undignified method of transport for the dominie. So, every day, morning and night, Allie and his father would cover the two miles between Forfar and Kingsmuir. George Neill was a very fast walker who would jump over the puddles as he went; one of Allie's earliest memories of these trips with his father was of being 'merely a drag who made him late for school. . .I still see myself falling behind and whimpering in dread of being left'. It was a harsh introduction to the world of learning.

The school stands in the middle of the single straight road running through the village, opposite the schoolhouse where the Neills lived. It is a simple stone building, much as it was after improvements were made in the 1880s to cope with the growing numbers of children. In 1982 it had only 17; when George Neill took over in 1876 there were 55; and by the end of Allie's first term the numbers had risen to 109. By then the school had two rooms, which were used in the traditional fashion of the time. The dominie took the top three classes (standards) in the larger room, while the assistant teacher (the 'Missy') taught the younger children in the smaller room. The larger room at Kingsmuir was a mere 31 by 24 feet, conditions which made teaching and learning extraordinarily difficult. Much of the school day was spent on mechanical tasks, as the children sat in their long rows of desks, while different standards tackled different subjects within the same room. The teacher could only attend to one of the standards at a time, and few children did any work when they were not being directly instructed. David Adam, a contemporary of the younger Neill children, recalls their father's method: 'It was a system of learning things off by heart rather than understanding them. For instance, if he was talking about geography, it would be "Leeds, Bradford, Halifax, Huddersfield, Dewsbury, Wakefield" – the textile group; or I can remember having to learn the river entrances to the sea, as they occurred when read in a clockwise direction.'

Each school day would start with a scripture lesson, consisting of a reading from the Bible and a prayer, which the children had to learn the previous night. In arithmetic, they had to grapple with the propositions of Euclid or the mysteries of algebra. On the slates which were then still in use, they calculated sums involving acres, roods and poles, or groats – already extinct – which had to be converted into half-crowns. 'Writing and figuring' meant copying exercises from the blackboard in order to improve their penmanship. There was also parsing and analysis, a subject that seems to have held a lot of interest for Allie's father – Neill recalls him having an inconclusive argument with another dominie about the parsing of the word 'what' in the sentence: 'What with the bother of packing I was late for the train.' Other subjects included grammar, spelling, reading and repetition, numeration and notation, Latin, singing (from notes) and ear exercises (or tests). The only practical subjects in the curriculum were map drawing and needlework, the latter being confined to girls.

Allie was never quite the 'dunce' of the class – he enjoyed the 'intelligence' class, which involved explaining the meaning of words and phrases in the Reader. Once he even won a prize for arithmetic. But in general he was deeply unhappy with his lessons, which appeared to have little to do with what seemed to him useful or interesting. He was unable to master spelling for many years, until he became a keen reader. He developed a passion for objects and materials, for activities involving his hands, showing considerably more interest in the contents of his pockets than in the official offerings of the school. Later, one of the most persistent memories of his schooldays was of sitting fiddling with a nut and bolt beneath his desk. In *Carroty Broon*, an autobiographical story he wrote some twenty-five years later, he painted a self-portrait in his description of the young hero's attitude to school:

He turned his attention to the blackboard with its tiresome requests
to find the Lowest Common Denominator, but his interest was
elsewhere; he was wrong in every sum, because his interest lay in a
folding pair of nail scissors he had found in the gutter in Tarby.
They were very rusty, and his whole soul longed for a free hour and
a sheet of emery-cloth, with bath-brick to finish up with.

Allie's soul similarly yearned for excitement outside the formal curriculum. 'He was not too great a scholar, he was more of a mischief than
anything else,' recalls David Adam. Another contemporary remembers that
'he was a great one for not paying attention: he liked to turn the world
into a joke.' Truancy, of course, was not an option he could consider, but
as he moved up the school, he developed a reputation for being 'a bit of a
wag'. He smuggled white mice into class in his pocket, and was sent out
when his father discovered them. He seldom read a book, though one type
of literature did catch his imagination – the adventure story. He liked
especially the 'Century Reader' used in the school, with its stories about
the Burning of Moscow, and the deeds of pirates and Red Indians. The
stories of Guy Boothby, with their arresting openings – 'Hands up, or I
fire!' – were particular favourites. He became absorbed in the tales full of
crime and passion to be found in the immensely popular 'penny dreadfuls',
which he read surreptitiously under the desk while his father was preoccupied with one of the other classes. He revelled in the exploits of Frank
Reade and Dare Devil Dick, in the stories of trips around the world in
airships or submarines, in which our heroes invariably escaped at the last
moment from being captured and burnt alive by marauding tribes. It was
a type of literature he never really lost his taste for, to such an extent that
he later made his own use of the genre. Yet not all of the bloodcurdling
tales came out of books. Next door to the schoolhouse lived a man who
had served as an officer in the Indian Mutiny of 1857, who enthralled Allie
with his exaggerated tales of bravery and butchery.

His father was profoundly disappointed with Allie's performance as a
pupil – though not just because he was his son. The educational achievement of the children was of critical significance to a dominie. Both Scottish
and English schooling were still dominated by the system which came to
be known as 'payments by results', though before the century was out the
system was to be officially ended. Introduced in 1862 because of the
expense incurred during the Crimean War, it provoked great hostility
between teachers and inspectors. An annual grant was given by the government to the managers of each school, who in turn paid the teacher. This
grant was dependent on the results of tests administered by Her Majesty's
Inspectors to the 'standard five' class, as well as on the rate of attendance
by the children. The literary critic and poet Matthew Arnold, who was a
schools inspector in England for thirty-five years, summed up the growing
criticism of the system when he wrote in a report in 1869: 'As long as the
whole grant-earning examination turns on results precisely and literally
specified by the Department beforehand, so long the inspection will be

mechanical and unintelligent, and it will inevitably draw the teaching after it.'

In Kingsmuir the inspector, a Mr Calder, would note down his thoughts in a pocket diary. He would call for the school logbook, and report on whether it had been properly kept. It was the duty of the head to make at least one entry a week, detailing the pupils' progress, and noting facts about attendance, illness and discipline. According to the New Scottish Education Code of May 1873, 'Personal opinions or reflections, such as "Unpleasant visit from ——, who gave me much impertinence," are not permitted, and may cause forfeiture of certificate.' The head had also to copy verbatim into the logbook a summary of the inspector's report, and any remarks made upon it by the Education Department. The system was so severe that sometimes the mere failure to inform the Department of the takeover date by a new head resulted in the forfeit of part or the whole of the grant for the school.

Allie's arrival at the school came at a time of anxiety for his father. In 1885 the inspector had declared: 'This school can hardly be said to be in a satisfactory condition at present. In the lower classes there are more failures than usual, and many of those that passed did so with difficulty.' Only the year before George Neill's salary had been reduced. Three weeks after Allie started, Mr Calder made some stringent observations on his father's performance with the younger children: 'The work of the two lower standards is susceptible of considerable improvement. Their reading is monotonous: Mental Arithmetic has not been sufficiently practised, and fingering is too common. The writing and figuring of the infants should be neater and more carefully formed.' A year later he commented: 'The children should be questioned on the General Meaning of their reading lessons, so as to awake their intelligence and interest them.' And in 1890 he noticed that 'the senior pupils are better trained in order and good manners than the junior.' As a result of these reports, the grant for Kingsmuir School was reduced from £95 5s in 1888 to £92 12s the following year, to £89 6s in 1890, and right down to £79 15s 6d for 1891 – though in the following years it slowly rose again.

The annual inspection was an agonising occasion for the dominie. He would peer anxiously out of the window of the school, his face white and strained, awaiting the arrival of Mr Calder. Mary Neill would prepare the inspector's favourite pudding for the lunch he would be offered in the schoolhouse. The children were never allowed at table at these critical times, though Allie remembers Mr Calder as 'a sour, unfriendly man'. There were stories that the outcome of a report could be influenced by the quality of the whisky which a dominie could provide for the inspector. In England, a few headteachers managed to play the system by obtaining in advance the test cards on which the inspectors' questions were printed, and coaching the children to learn the answers. But it is unlikely that George Neill, a highly conscientious as well as nervous man, attempted either of these ploys. Instead, he tended to take his anxieties out on the children;

and his fear of the school authorities was transmitted to the young Allie, with significant consequences for his later life.

Children in Scotland were kept under tight control by the threat of the tawse, a leather strap used by teachers to beat any who showed the merest signs of indiscipline or laziness. 'Well, have you had your licks today?' was a commonplace query for an adult to put to a child. Allie's father was certainly not as harsh as some dominies of the period: the children in Kingsmuir were allowed a certain amount of leeway to talk in the classroom, and were not, as others were, compelled to march in and out of school in military fashion. In other respects, though, George Neill relied on the conventional method of punishment. According to the daughter of one woman who was a pupil teacher under his direction, he was 'a bit of a curmudgeon'. One ex-pupil remembers him walking about the schoolroom with the tawse on his shoulder; another, that 'he couldna do with backsliding. He'd give them one or two then, to keep them going.' A third recollects that 'he used to burn the little thongs on the end of the tawse, to make them harder'; and another that 'he'd set a group of us to do some sums, and you had to put up your hand when you'd finished. The last one'd get the strap – and you'd have a strapping for any you got wrong, and all.' At this time some children from the slums of Glasgow had been 'farmed out' in the Forfar area, and there is some suggestion that Allie's father was more inclined to beat these newcomers than the others. There is also a distinct memory that he was hardest on his own children, a belief that Neill later confirmed: 'I came in for more than my fair share when the strappings were given for noise or mischief.' His father, he recalled, 'strapped often and hard' – perhaps partly to avoid showing any signs of favouritism.

Both at home and school then, the threat of punishment hung heavily over Allie's head; he would, his father told him continually, 'come to nothing'. This amounted to a moral as much as an intellectual criticism. For more than 300 years the dark shadow of John Calvin had lain across the lives of the Scots people, turning them into a God-fearing rather than a God-loving nation. Calvin's God was remote and all-powerful, while man was corrupt and powerless. Only a chosen few could hope for salvation – through effort, work and austere living; the rest could expect eternal damnation. The Bible was the source of all truth; the Word of God could be heard and read in the fulminations of the Old Testament. In this cold and hard system of belief, the schools played a key part: education was a means of keeping children from sinning, and for those who transgressed, through failure or moral laxity, chastisement was quickly to hand.

In line with these doctrines, Sundays were looked upon with special reverence. Any activity – especially one which might be enjoyed – was forbidden, as 'profaning God's day'. So the children were firmly prevented from playing games and, in the Neill household, compelled to stay in and memorise Psalms or verses from the Bible. In the evening there was always the same ritual: their father would read a chapter from the Bible, sing a Psalm, and then offer a blessing. Sometimes the children found it hard to behave with the expected solemnity, and would only just succeed in suppressing their giggles. Allie himself, though mostly 'obedience personified', occasionally found the courage to break the moral code: within the covers of an 'improving' book he would lose himself in one of his 'penny dreadfuls'.

Sometimes his ruse was noticed, and he was duly punished for his profane behaviour. The keenest-eyed adult in such incidents was Clunes Sinclair, his maternal grandmother, who lived with the family throughout Allie's schooldays, and was for him a major source of both love and terror. He was her favourite grandchild: when Allie was left alone with his books in the evening, his grandmother would demonstrate her affection by giving him a kiss, transferring a peppermint from her mouth to his as she did so. On the other hand, she was excessively religious, more so than Allie's mother and father. She was also psychic, as Allie's sister May recalls: 'She really had second sight. She knew when anybody was going to die: she saw visions and things. I used to be scared. We got our own breakfast, and she used to come down in the morning – wearing a cap and frills, as old ladies did then – and she would say, "I dreamed of old so and so last night," and I used to sit and wonder if she had dreamt of me.' Allie, being of a more fearful disposition than May, was absolutely terrified by his grandmother's religious fervour. She made the children read aloud to her from books of sermons, notably Boston's *Fourfold State*. This book contained one particular description which became imprinted on Allie's mind. 'If you want to know what the torments of hell are like,' it ran, 'just light a candle and hold your finger in the flame.' His grandmother drew his attention to this passage when she discovered that, at the age of 7, he was familiar with the word 'bugger'. For years afterwards, convinced that he had sinned beyond redemption, this image caused him much anguish. Death came to mean 'a kind of grand "school inspection", which I, for one, expected to fail, for my copybook was all blots.'

Yet religion was not the only source of his childhood terrors. Like his father and grandfather before him, Allie was afraid of the dark, and this served to arouse other fears. For a while he believed that a man with a cheesecutter bonnet wielding a knife was waiting for him whenever he took the Forfar–Kingsmuir road, ran an errand in the village, or went to use the dry earth closet at the top of the garden. Superstitions abounded in the village. It was said that the human heart was made up of strings as thin as hairs, and that if one string snapped, sudden death would follow. To Allie this prospect was appalling, since there would certainly then be no hope of being 'saved'. He was impressed by the story of a servant girl, who cried, 'May God strike me dead if I have stolen the silver spoons,' and fell at once to the floor as the spoons fell out of her dress. He was terrified by the Biblical story of the children who were eaten by bears. Granny Sinclair told him that thunder represented the wrathful voice of God: this made thunderstorms a terrifying experience for him. When he was 9, a local woman told his mother that Allie had death written all over his face, and that he wouldn't live long. 'That remark haunted my life for years,' he later wrote.

When he eventually learned to read, he took to consulting books such as *The Doctor at Home*, and imagined that he had contracted most of the diseases described there. Yet neither Willie, Neilie nor Clunie appears to have had the fear of God so thoroughly put into them as Allie had. Willie in particular ridiculed some of the dogma, and once stood out in a thunderstorm, defying the Almighty to do His worst. Clunie scoffed at Allie's capacity to believe all the tales of hellfire and damnation. He did, indeed, seem to be more gullible than the others, with his strong imagination and essentially timid and gentle temperament.

This gullibility also extended to sex, where once again Allie was caught between two opposing moralities. Amongst the village children with whom he liked to play, sex was a matter for earthy if not always well-informed comment. Some were born out of wedlock, and had attended their own parents' subsequent wedding. Childish fumblings were commonplace, half-truths about conception and birth passed around with alacrity. However, the Neills treated any remotely sexual activity or curiosity as a cardinal sin. 'My parents never mentioned masturbation when I was a boy,' Neill remembered later. 'You just felt that it was against God, that God wouldn't approve of it.' For a while Allie shared a bed with Clunie, and many times their mutual explorations brought a beating. In school, George Neill reserved his most savage punishment for any misdemeanours of a sexual nature. Neither sex nor reproduction were ever mentioned in the home, and Allie was left to glean his knowledge from the animals on the nearby farms, and the stories of the other children. This caused him immense confusion. He found he could not come to terms with his own birth: since sex was wicked, how could his parents, who beat him for showing interest in the matter, have been guilty of committing such an unforgivable sin?

The dilemma caused him to remain in wonderful ignorance of very basic facts. His mother told him that babies were brought by the doctor, and he accepted this, even as she gradually added to her family. When he heard of the man's part in conceiving a child, he just could not believe it: 'My parents were pure and holy, they could never do a thing like that.' His ignorance about the female sex was such that, until around the age of 12, he believed that women were immortal – when he read that a woman had been killed in a train accident, he believed the report must be untrue. There was nothing especially unusual about such adult attitudes to sex in Victorian Britain, nor such attempts to keep children in ignorance. But the association of sex not just with sin but with dire punishment created great difficulties for Allie. It gave him a very unreal picture of the nature of women, which the presence of four sisters seems to have done nothing to change. When, aged 12, he came across some love letters his father had once written to his mother, he was shocked by their erotic quality, and assumed that his mother must have felt the same.

Allie was very attached to his mother in his early years, though the relationship was one of dependence as much as love. Later Neill quoted with implicit acceptance a remark of a friend, who observed: 'Scots mothers seem to bind their sons to them with steel apron wires.' Holidays at the

seaside at Easthaven on the east coast of Scotland provided some rare
moments of happiness for the Neill children. There they would play among
the rock pools, search for shells, lobsters and agate pebbles, free momen-
tarily to forget the trials of home and school life. But even here Allie
experienced fear. Though she loved the water, his mother had never learned
to swim; her father's death by drowning had left an anxiety which she
quickly transmitted to her son. If she went too far out to sea, he stood
fearfully at the water's edge, screaming for her to return. Her ill-health
aroused even greater apprehension in him. She was often in agony from
gallstones, and suffered bilious attacks which turned her face a jaundiced
yellow. Allie saw the pain in her eyes, and was unable to play, fearing that
she would die. He brooded about what kind of horrendous stepmother
might take control of his life. More acutely, he dreaded the thought of his
parents being in heaven whilst he, convinced of his sinfulness, would be
subject to the torments of hellfire in quite another place. Once he tackled
his mother about the awfulness of this separation. She told him that 'God
will change our hearts so that we won't care' – an answer that merely
increased his anxiety.

Plagued by fears and anxieties, Allie often found reassurance in the
company of Clunie. She was, her sister May recalls, 'the keenest and
brightest, a very clever person', and though younger than Allie, she was
clearly the dominant force in their relationship. If he admired and worshipped his eldest brother Willie, it was Clunie who inspired affection by
her kindness and sympathy. Once, when he gullibly lost all his pocket
money to a swindler at the local fair, she gave him half of hers. She could
also get indignant at the way Allie was treated by their parents, protesting
vigorously, for instance, when he was told he would have to make do with
some of Willie's cast-off clothes. Unlike Allie, she was quick to see through
the superstitions prevalent in the village, and soon concluded, well before
her brother felt able to do so, that there was certainly no such place as
heaven or hell, and possibly no God either. It was her and Willie's scepticism which helped to sow doubts in Allie's mind about the religious doctrines to which he had been subjected.

Both Allie and Clunie were imaginative children, delighting in creating
their own fantasies – while playing at Laidenford Farm, or on the beach at
Easthaven, where tales of skullduggery, buried treasure and mysterious
corpses could be conjured up. Allie's own fantasies were often connected
with death: sometimes he would imagine his own funeral, and how sorry
his parents would be that he had died. Here *Carroty Broon* has some
revealing passages. Peter, red-haired like Allie, has a father who is 'a
good-natured sort of man who took life easily. He did not ask much from
life; a dram on Saturday night, kirk on Sunday morning, and the *People's
Journal* on Sunday afternoon.' Later, in a dream sequence full of images of
death and disease, Peter imagines he has become a mad dog: 'He pictured
himself going to school on all fours. "Maybe I'll bite the Mester," he
thought, and the thought made him cheerier.' And in a further episode, he

imagines a day when he can get his revenge on the severe and insensitive village dominie:

> Scene – Garlie. Time – twenty years hence.
> Sir Peter Brown drives up in his carriage and pair to the school. He knocks, and Dominie Dakers comes to the door. Dominie starts, and then bows reverently.
> *Dominie*: Welcome, Sir Peter!
> *Sir Peter*: Do you mind yon day when you thrashed me out o' the schule?
> *Dominie* (*bowing his head*): I've regretted it a thousand times.
> *Sir Peter*: I'll forgive you, for you little kent I was to be a great man. Give the bairns a holiday.
> *Dominie*: Yes, my lord! Your humble servant!

However, the real-life 'Carroty Broon' now had to put away childish things, as the time came for him to try to come to terms with the adult world.

CHAPTER 2

Young Teacher

astell round drawn about 1905 or 9.

I did my work with fear in my heart.
The Problem Teacher, 1940

As each of the Neill children reached the age of 14, they moved out of their father's school in Kingsmuir to the nearest elementary school, Forfar Academy. One of the Academy's former pupils had already made a name for himself as a writer. James Barrie was the third son of a well respected member of the small and tightly-knit village of Kirriemuir, some seven miles from Kingsmuir. He too lived in the shadow of a brilliant older brother, and, like Allie, at an early age created a fantasy life, stimulated in part by the blood and thunder of the 'penny dreadfuls'. For a while the Barrie family lived in Forfar, in a house standing close by the turret of Forfar Castle, which once belonged to Malcolm Canmore, the supposed slayer of Macbeth. His parents attended the East Free Chuch a few yards from where Allie was later born, and sent their son to Forfar Academy, where he won two book prizes 'for excellence in English'. These links were to have significance for Allie in later years.

Some twenty years later – by which time Barrie had achieved popular recognition with his portrait of Kirriemuir in *A Window in Thrums* – Willie Neill was enrolled at the Academy. The bright hope of his parents, he came top in most subjects, shared the gold medal, and then got into St Andrews University at the age of 16. It was customary in Scotland for a mother to want her son to become a minister 'wagging his head in the pulpit', and Mary Neill was no exception. George Neill also felt that this was the right career for his brilliant eldest son, and his decisions were usually final – as his daughter May recalls when it came to her turn. 'He said to me, "You're to be a teacher." I said, "I don't want to be a teacher." He said what did I want to be, and I said a typist. "A typist! That's no job for you, if you're married, and left a widow. If you're a teacher you can carry it around with you." He said if I didn't study for my exams, I would go off to domestic service. I believed him; he looked as if he meant it.' She duly went off to study for her teaching certificate, just as Willie before her had been forced by their father, against his wishes, to study divinity at the university.

It became the accepted practice for the Neill children to go to the Academy – with one exception. When it came to Allie's turn, he was sent out to work instead. 'I was obviously the inferior article, the misfit in a tradition of academic success, and automatically I accepted an inferior status,' Neill observed later. His father had repeatedly shouted at him, 'You've no ambition! You'll end in the gutter!' He would quite probably have been unhappy and a failure at the Academy, even away from his father's stern jurisdiction. However, a more pressing reason for his father's decision had no connection with Allie's academic failings. Willie was in his second year at St Andrews, and was already pursuing his real interest, journalism. He wrote light, humorous verse, and for some time edited *College Echoes*, the student magazine. (For many years its cover carried one of his sketches, showing his talent for drawing in pen and ink.) But he also developed a taste for the university social life, going to dinners and dances, joining in the heavy drinking and experiments in table tapping at the stag parties he frequented. Agnes Salmond, a medical student at the university who later became his wife, was already attached to Willie, and often had to take him home in a drunken state at the end of such evenings.

Such a life required money, and Willie took advantage of his parents' fond belief that he could do no wrong. Messages asking for 'more tin' began to arrive, and though his parents at first came up with the necessary, they became increasingly ill-tempered about their son's way of life. Some of this they took out on the children left behind, who would be punished severely for apparently trivial misdemeanours. Allie until now had worshipped his eldest brother like a 'demi-god', believing all the stories he came home with from the university. Now he began to see his more mortal side; and, though he was unaware of it at the time, it was Willie's extravagance which helped to determine the direction his life was now to take. Neilie, who had been at the Academy for a short time, was not making the kind of progress his father had hoped for, so both he and Allie were sent out to work. The family was now complete – the eighth and youngest survivor, Percy, was three by this time – and the Neills were finding it hard to make ends meet. Allie was even allowed to join the other children for the strawberry picking and potato gathering in his last year at school – economic necessity had overridden his mother's snobbery.

The next few months were among the most anguished of Neill's life. At first he welcomed the thought of escaping from the strictures of the schoolroom. About leaving Kingsmuir itself he was less certain; but his father persuaded him to apply for clerical jobs advertised in the *Scotsman*. He had at least learned one skill from his schooldays. His father wrote in a fine copperplate script, a manual skill that Allie took pleasure and pride in emulating. It was a skill that would have been of use in the jobs he now applied for, and may have helped him to be offered, after three months, a junior clerical position with a firm of gas meter manufacturers in Edinburgh. Neilie meanwhile had found a job in a flour mill in Leith, and it was decided that the brothers should lodge together in the capital.

Not yet 14, Allie set out in the late summer of 1897 on the 80-mile journey to Edinburgh. Up to then his life had been almost entirely circumscribed by the village and its surrounding fields and farms; only the very occasional visit with his parents to Easthaven or Dundee had given him a glimpse of the wider world. His one trip to Edinburgh had been just a few months before, when the family took a rare trip by train to attend Granny Sinclair's burial in Leith. Here was his chance to test out his capabilities away from the unremitting severity of his parents' rule.

The firm of W. and B. Cowan was situated at 79 Buccleuch Street on the south side of the city. Through the Georgian side-streets the young Allie could look up to the prominence of Arthur's Seat, the volcanic hill rising above Edinburgh. At its foot stood Holyrood House where, as he had learnt in his history classes, Riccio, the lover of Mary Queen of Scots, had been murdered by her husband's assassins. His own work surroundings, however, were infinitely less magnificent than those that stood nearby. Buccleuch Street wound its narrow way through the city suburb, a place of tall office and factory buildings which contrasted with the wide and airy spaces of other parts of Edinburgh. Allie's job consisted of minor clerical and messenger boy duties, which he hated. Its only redeeming features were the chance to loiter with the workmen when on his message rounds; a kind and sympathetic senior clerk; and the experience of being addressed as 'Mr Neill' by his fellow-clerks. His wages were 6s a week, part of which he probably sent home or set aside for his family's use. Certainly he seems to have lived close to the breadline: he could afford 3d for lunch, but only 1d if he took the horse-drawn tram on the 2-mile journey across the city morning and evening. Again, his continued poverty was to leave its mark.

Edinburgh, therefore, was 'one long misery'. Within a few weeks Neilie lost his job, and returned home to Kingsmuir. Allie became desperately homesick, and wrote tear-drenched letters to his parents. His mother came for a brief visit, but refused to allow him to return with her, though he clung tearfully to her and implored her to do so. Eventually, one of his letters touched a chord with his father. Allie wrote to suggest that, as prospects at Cowan's seemed to be nil, he should study for the Boy Clerks' Competitive Examination. George Neill recognised the futility of his son's existence in Edinburgh and, after seven months, Allie was allowed to return home. 'Thae Neills canna bide at nithing,' remarked a local farmer, to Allie's intense shame and embarrassment.

'From the hell that was Edinbugh, sitting in Kingsmuir schoolhouse all day long seemed like paradise,' Neill later wrote. It is perhaps difficult to conjure up a much more dismal vision of paradise. But, whatever his intentions, once he found himself in front of the textbooks he needed to study for the exam, the old reactions set in. Neither he nor Neilie – who was now also studying for the civil service – could apply themselves. In despair their father flung their books at the pair of them, declaring to his wife: 'They're just fit for nothing, Mary!' He determined to fix them up with employment near to hand, and soon found them apprenticeships in Forfar. Once again Allie was given no choice: while Neilie was fixed up at Johnson's the chemists, Allie was taken on as an apprentice draper at Anderson & Sturrock, whose shop was only a few yards from the house where he had been born fifteen years before. In more than one sense, he had not come far.

Drapery proved to be scarcely less agonising than clerical work, even though he was living at home. The hours were from 8 in the morning to 8 at night, extended to 10 on Saturdays; and the work was menial and undemanding. He had to open up the shop, sweep the floor, and deliver parcels to customers in and around the town. The work he found hateful – and he was horribly aware that retail trade was an occupation well below his family's expectations. Yet once again he showed no signs of rebellion, and was only saved from what might have been years of drudgery by a lucky chance. Because of his unusually large feet he had to wear special boots. Being on his feet most of the day, and having a 2-mile walk to and from Kingsmuir every weekday, he found his big-toe joints becoming inflamed, and then stiff – a condition that remained with him for life. Painful though this was, it did allow him to give up the drapery business. It was presumably with the idea of a sedentary job in mind that his father then agreed to allow him to study yet again, this time for the civil service proper. Yet, once again, when he sat down with the dreaded books, he was incapable of putting his mind to them.

Allie's interests and ambitions lay in a totally different direction. A year before he left school, he had decided that his future lay in being an inventor. Bicycles were still at a very rudimentary stage of development at the time, though they were fast becoming popular and cheap enough to be within the range of working families. Allie was given one of his own, and took to dismantling it to see how he could improve the design. With considerable ingenuity and imagination for a boy of his age, he experimented with a new form of brake; with a homespun method of creating more pedal power; and with a bizarre idea for a bicycle which could be driven by compressed air. All these schemes were shown to be impractical, but they had caught his imagination, brought out an enthusiasm and a persistence which had not been in evidence in the schoolroom, and left him with a life-long curiosity about how mechanical objects worked.

Allie was caught between his innate interest in objects and handwork, and his father's insistence that he should find some job requiring mental application. George Neill was in despair about his son's future. Clearly he had no aptitude for study, which immediately narrowed his choice considerably. Manual or labouring work of any kind would have been a social embarrassment – his brother Neilie's desire to be a shepherd had been hastily put down by his parents. Allie himself was equally gloomy, wondering if he even had the ability to succeeed as an ordinary ploughman. It was now that his mother stepped in with an idea that she saw as being of benefit to both father and son. As her husband had more than enough classes to deal with in the school, she suggested he should take Allie on as a pupil teacher. His father replied, apparently without irony, 'It's about all he's fit for!'

The remark indicates the low regard in which George Neill held his son. He was at first reluctant to agree to the suggestion, perhaps still entertaining a residue of hope that Allie would find some success in another sphere. But Mary Neill, who seemed to be able to get her way when she really wanted to, must by now have realised that Allie was certainly no candidate for the ministry. Seeing the idea as solving two problems at a stroke, she kept on at her husband, and eventually won the day. And so, on 2 May 1899, Alexander Sutherland Neill, aged 15 years, started work in Kingsmuir Village School, first as a monitor, and then as a pupil teacher. It was, as it turned out, his first step on the road to Summerhill.

The system of pupil teachers, then in force both in Scotland and England, allowed youngsters both to work in the classroom and, in some cases, to study at the same time for the further qualifications they might need to enter the teaching profession. In England they were known as 'improvers'; their job was to pass on what they themselves had just learned to children often no more than a year or so younger. In Allie's case the post seemed to be exclusively concerned with teaching. His father up to then had been compelled to have four classes in his charge. Now he was able to give Allie responsibility for the lower infant class, while he concentrated on the senior standards sitting at their long benches in the main room. As there was only a blackboard between the two rooms, Allie felt himself to be under constant scrutiny by his father and George Neill took no trouble to hide his disappointment with his son.

Yet Allie seems to have been generally liked in his new role. Because of his age, he was able to establish informal contact with the children, many of whom would have known him in his urchin guise out of school hours. David Adam remembers that, when the dominie went over to the schoolhouse for his coffee break, Allie would offer to sketch any of the pupils who would sit for him. Maggie Adam, another of his pupils, remembers 'sitting in a chair in the "minutes" [morning break] and he would sketch me. Black and white, you know, just with a pencil. Oh, he was quite an artist.' Yet he was in an awkward position as a provider rather than consumer of education. At 15 he was still essentially a child, lacking in confidence, self-conscious about his appearance, and living in daily fear of his father. It could not have been easy to assume the authority that his father might have required of a pupil teacher. So it is hardly surprising that, at the end of his first year, the inspector described the teaching of the lower infants as 'barely fair', while that for the classes above was seen to be 'pretty satisfactory'. The following year the inspector became more personal in his criticism: 'This candidate is warned that his work all round is weak.' The same report shows his sister May as being amongst those who gained a merit certificate for her work. It also makes it clear that George Neill was pulling the school into a better shape than before, at least according to the values of the time. Allie, to his father's shame, was once again letting the family down.

Allie's backwardness in the academic sphere was highlighted by the kind of literature he was reading in these formative years. While Clunie, a year younger than him, was getting eagerly into *Jane Eyre*, Dickens and Thackeray, he remained an avid consumer of the 'penny dreadfuls', supplied to him by the boy who delivered milk to the Neills' house, who in turn had stolen them from the newsagents. When, through Willie and Clunie, he did move on to more established fiction, he retained a distinct preference for tales of adventure. Among his favourites at the adolescent stage were Rider Haggard's *She* and *King Solomon's Mines*, Anthony Hope's *The Prisoner of Zenda*, Walter Scott's *Ivanhoe* (he skipped the descriptions of scenery), and the short stories of W. W. Jacobs and the young H. G. Wells. He also 'devoured in secret' *Tess of the D'Urbevilles* – but principally because his parents forbade him to read the novel which had so upset Victorian notions of decency. And then, on the shelves of the Meffan Library in Forfar, he came across the writings of J. M. Barrie.

The settings of Barrie's early stories – *Margaret Ogilvie, A Window in Thrums, Sentimental Tommy* – would have been familiar to Allie, as would the passages of Scots dialect with which they were filled. At first, he was swept along by the stories. He read *Sentimental Tommy* again and again, identifying fiercely with the boy hero. Given his own failure in the academic sphere, it is easy to see the attraction the book held for him, beyond the familiarity of the settings and the speech forms. His teacher's summary of Tommy's nature – 'There is something inside him, or so I think at times, that is his master, and rebels against book-learning' – could equally well have applied to Allie. He would have undoubtedly reacted favourably to Tommy's explanation that 'there are two kinds of cleverness, that kind you learn from books and a kind that is inside yourself'. Barrie was the first of his literary heroes, and for a time he revelled in his stories.

During his pupil-teacher days, Allie began to make some forays into unfamiliar territory. Following up his interest in drawing, he and Neilie joined the Forfar Graphic Arts Club. Here they experimented with life drawing, learning to use charcoal. This new hobby led to an invitation from one of the other club members to her house 'for croquet and supper'. It was a world where social status, as defined by income, counted for much. As the child of a dominie, Allie was not accepted by the families of jute manufacturers, lawyers or shopkeepers, all of whom considered 'the son of a little schoolhouse' to be out of place in their circle. He tried nevertheless to master the art of survival in this world of finger bowls, whist, afternoon tea and Chopin on the piano, very conscious that he himself could not in turn 'entertain' at home.

He was ashamed to realise the extent of his ignorance of music and literature, and of the conventions of social behaviour in these genteel surroundings. He determined to do something about it. In music, as with schooling at the Academy, he was the odd one out in his family: all the other children received music tuition. Twice during this period he made serious efforts to learn the piano, but never got beyond picking out the notes laboriously for the mnemonic 'Every Good Boy Deserves Favour'. He attended a concert, and clapped at the end of the first movement of a symphony, believing it to be the end. It was the custom at evenings out for guests to perform in some way – a song, a piano piece, a card trick. Allie worked up some recitations for such occasions, in particular the poem *The Dream of Eugene Aram*, which caused him particular social anguish when performed to one gathering. He even bought a book of etiquette, but found it to be principally concerned with telling the reader how to address bishops and princes, by no means everyday phenomena in the Forfar of 1900. In general, his efforts to work up the accomplishments necessary for acceptance in local society met with failure, and he remained, and was very conscious of being, an outsider.

Occasionally Allie did find some companionship. Sometimes he would cycle across to Kirriemuir, to visit the low white-washed cottage where his hero Barrie was born, and try to re-create in his mind the characters from his books. Just beyond Kirriemuir, in a neo-Georgian manse, lived a family known as 'the wild Craigs of Memus'. The father was a Presbyterian minister and the son of a gypsy who, in most unconventional fashion, allowed his four daughters and four sons to grow up pretty much as they liked. However, his wife did insist on certain rules: no one was allowed into the manse except by invitation – 'I married you, not your congregation,' she told her husband. The rule extended to the young admirers of the daughters, who had to do their courting at the manse gate. Willie became interested in the oldest girl, Elizabeth, who would play truant from Forfar Academy in order to go out into the countryside with him. Willie, it seemed, divided the female sex into those you had to be introduced to, and those you picked up. The Craigs undoubtedly came into the first category. In the vacations from St Andrews Willie would cycle up to the manse. Elizabeth Craig remembers his boldness and spirit, his passion for writing and drawing – after each of their meetings he would send her a coloured sketch to mark the event. Sometimes, she recalls, he would bring his two younger and less adventurous brothers along: 'Allie was interested in my sister Carrie, but she was engaged to a neighbouring farmer, so there was no development there. He was a tall, lean, good-looking young man, rather shy and gangly.' Neill later remembered the Craig girls as 'an original, unconventional lot, gaily flirting but always keeping out of reach. . .they were good companions rather than love objects.'

It was the sort of relationship that he seemed to be most comfortable with at this age, since anything with any sexual flavour put him in a dilemma. His natural inclination was to share the open and frank attitude to sex of the ploughmen and farmers' children; but under his parents' severe eye and because of the guilt which he came to associate with sex, he developed a highly idealistic view of the opposite sex. His trips to church now focused on the girls in the choir rather than the tedium of the sermon or the hardness of the benches. When delivering parcels during his months at the drapers, he would make a special detour in order to catch just a glimpse of the current object of his dreams. The girls were from families with status in the town, pupils at the private school for girls rather than the Forfar Academy. At the other extreme, he was still able to have a number of what he later described as 'quite earthy adventures with village girls whose feet did not turn the daisies into roses'. More often than not it was Willie who provided the opportunities of this kind; Allie later spoke of his brother's capacity to 'tumble farmers' daughters in the hay'. The Neill boys would cycle to Carnoustie or Kirriemuir during the summer season, and try their luck with the local girls. Normally, both Willie and Neilie would claim the better looking of any pair they encountered, though just occasionally Allie was able to get in first. In general, the Neill boys were looked upon as country upstarts, and only rarely achieved even a restricted kiss-and-cuddle in the dusk of the streets or on the sea promenade. In Allie's case it was gay and unfettered companionship, rather than any directly sexual relationship, that he seemed to be seeking.

During the time he was making these ridiculous and abortive efforts to improve his status locally, he plodded on with his duties in the Kingsmuir schoolroom. From his early months, when he started to teach the infants to read by the 'look-and-say' method, he moved slowly up the standards as he gained experience, and eventually taught all the subjects. He began to find that he could learn a little more easily – perhaps, as he came to believe, 'the best way to learn anything is to teach it'. He took some private maths lessons from the maths teacher at Forfar Academy, Ben Thomson, who is remembered locally as an inspirational teacher. Certainly he awoke Allie's interest in the subject – and was generous enough to refuse any payment from his impoverished pupil. 'He made mathematics live for me,' Neill wrote later. 'I think he had a genius for teaching; I have never seen a teacher who took so much pains with his pupils. I know that I was a dull pupil, but he sacrificed hours of his time to make me understand.' It was his first encounter with a teacher outside the uncongenial conditions of the Scottish schoolroom, and it gave him a lifelong interest in mathematics.

Allie's apprenticeship came to an end on 30 June 1903, and on 17 July, at the end of the summer term, he left Kingsmuir School for good. It had been in many respects a difficult four years, working under the constant scrutiny of his father, who made no attempt to hide his continuing disappointment with him. George Neill treated him more as a pupil than a pupil teacher, though it seems he did refrain from criticising him in front of the children in the classroom. Now approaching his twentieth year, Allie nevertheless remained in fear of his father. Later he wrote about the difficulties of working alongside him: 'I had to be on the side of authority before my own desire to play had been lived out. It was the role of a boy pretending to be a man.' Now, however, he was at last to have the opportunity of leaving behind his boyhood, and striking out on his own. It was the beginning of a phase in his life which was to bring him considerable emotional distress and some economic hardship. But it also saw him beginning to take the first tentative steps in his growing revolt against some of the received educational and cultural ideas of the time.*

At the end of his time as a pupil teacher, as was the custom, Neill sat the examination for entry into a teacher training college. The result was a disaster: out of 104 candidates, he found himself in 103rd position, with all hopes of a college place in Glasgow or Edinburgh vanished. This must have been a terrible blow to what small amount of self-esteem he may have developed in the previous four years. It certainly helped to shape his bitter antagonism in later years to the examination system in general. It was a humiliation that he felt keenly at the time, recalling later 'sitting in our conspicuous pew the next Sunday wondering if the congregation knew what a dunce I was'. His father compounded his shame by pointing out a girl in the church choir who had been placed in the first class in the examination. His sister Clunie's response to his failure was equally characteristic: she reminded him of all the great men who had failed their examinations in their youth.

Neill was now simply an 'Ex-Pupil Teacher', the lowest worm in the educational garden. Why then did he continue to pursue a teaching career? In the first place, despite his difficulties in sorting out his role with his father in the Kingsmuir schoolroom, he had clearly not found the work of a teacher wholly distasteful. He had been able to establish good relations with some of the children, and discover a certain capacity to learn which must have given him some measure of confidence previously lacking. In addition, it was still possible to improve his status by taking the ordinary certificate examination, a pass in which would raise him to the status of 'authorised teacher', though he would remain untrained. Finally, and perhaps most compellingly, there must have seemed to his father no other alternative open to him; and Neill was as yet showing no sign of rebelling against his father's authority.

His first taste of a Scottish schoolroom other than his father's was brief, illuminating and extremely unpleasant. He applied, no doubt under pressure from his father, for a number of teaching jobs, and was soon appointed to a post in Bonnyrigg, a small town a few miles south of Edinburgh. The Durham School in Bonnyrigg had been started in 1868 as a girls' school, though by this time it was also taking in boys. It was known locally as 'the Jane McKinley School', after the formidable woman who had been headteacher there for 35 years. By the time Neill came to the school she was crippled with arthritis, and would arrive at school in a wheelchair, directing two boys and two girls to go in before her to arrange the books and equipment. 'You heard about it if you weren't tidy,' remembers one pupil, Mary Stewart. Another recalls: 'Woe betide any who did

*It was also the beginning of the metamorphosis of the boy 'Allie' into the young 'Mr Neill' and, eventually, just plain 'Neill'. I have used this last, more familiar, label from here on.

wrong, the strap was thrown at the culprit, and they had to go to her to take their punishment.' Neill was horrified to learn that he had to beat any child who so much as dared whisper in class. He was too afraid of Miss McKinley to question this rule; indeed, he was not yet questioning the wisdom of corporal punishment.

Both in Scotland and England at this time, a few individual teachers and administrators were beginning to criticise this system, which relied on fear as an encouragement for children to learn. But as yet the huge majority of children being compulsorily schooled by the state had to endure the sort of experience which the writer V. S. Pritchett set down in his autobiographical memoir, *A Cab at the Door*. In his school in Camberwell Green in London,

> A couple of hundred boys from seven to fourteen were in this sooty churchy building, and sat in one great unvarnished hall. The teachers stood in a row before us unruly cattle; the headmaster, a little man with a long white beard, stood in the middle of the school on a dais. . . . In most schools such a crowd was kept in order by the cane. Girls got it as much as the boys and snivelled afterwards. To talk in class was a crime, to leave one's desk inconceivable. Discipline was meant to encourage subservience, and to squash rebellion.

Failure was also a matter for chastisement, as the writer Robert Roberts remembers from his pre-war schooling in Salford:

> Our chorus mistress didn't guide or conduct, but as we made a 'joyful' sound she stalked tall among us, suddenly ducking an ear to within an inch of a child's mouth and, if no note came forth, she brought the lad out and caned him.

Many of the children who passed briefly across Neill's life during the next five years were successfully drilled in the values of the system in Scotland. Most now look back at their schooldays with a peculiar ambivalence. They will simultaneously criticise and approve of the severity of the headteachers' regime: 'strict' and 'good' are often interchangeable terms. So it was with Miss McKinley: the eagle-faced, tawse-wielding headteacher was nevertheless 'well liked and loved'; 'a very good teacher and very just'; and 'many a pupil had reason to be thankful for her strict ways and teaching'. Neill, however, felt no such ambivalence. He was shocked to find himself in a place which made his father's school seem a haven of kindness, and was absolutely terrified of Miss McKinley. He stood it for just eight weeks, and then resigned, moving straightaway to Kingskettle School in Fife, where he began teaching on 12 November 1903 at a salary of £60.

On the day on which he arrived the attendance was low, since many of the children were helping with the potato harvest. Kettle was principally a farming area, and by law children over 12 could be hired by the farmers during harvesting and the potato-lifting seasons and taken off the roll. But many under 12 were also taken on illegally, a worrying fact for the headteacher, whose grant depended on attendance as well as results. Not all the pupils were local children, however. As in Kingsmuir during Neill's pupil-teacher period, the village went in for 'baby farming', several of the families taking in infants from Leith, Edinburgh and Dundee. Most of the pupils would, nevertheless, be destined for manual work or domestic service; and not all the farmers looked on attendance at school as a priority.

If he had thought to improve his working conditions by fleeing from Miss McKinley, Neill had made the wrong decision. The Kettle dominie, James Calder, had been in charge since 1881, and was, in the words of one former pupil, James Dewar, 'what some people call a brutal tyrant'. A small, stern-faced and unhealthy man, he ran the school like a military operation, and no insubordination, from pupils or teachers, was tolerated. He persistently made cruel jokes at the children's expense, which terrified the younger children. Isabella Skinner, another pupil, remembers: 'A look from Mr Calder was equal to the strap, when anything was not pleasing to him. He would have discipline, no matter the hardship the class went through.' Every day the class had to march in and out like soldiers, to sit in hushed rows while the dominie, decked out in his frock coat, wrote out essays and maths problems on the blackboard, which they then had to copy into their books. Like George Neill, James Calder had a fine copper-plate hand. Much emphasis was placed on this skill, and the children, whatever else some may have failed in, could all write well, a feat that would bring commendation from the inspector.

Margaret Boyle, another Kettle pupil, remembers James Calder as 'a very stern, strict teacher, always ready to use the tawse on any who didn't learn their homework. . . . He took no excuse, out came the tawse from his coat pocket, and he used it with all his strength on the boys' hands, which left its mark right up their arms. Some of the boys would draw in their hand, and that made him very angry, as it used to come down on his leg. Then he would hold their hand and give them extra strokes.' Few, even of the older children, dared to stand up to this treatment, though on one occasion a boy did get some small revenge for the punishments he had endured. This boy, having discovered the precise moment of his birth, waited until he was a few minutes older than the school-leaving age of 14, and then bundled up his books in preparation for leaving. James Calder bellowed at him to sit down, to which he replied, 'Calder, I'm 14 now, and you can't touch me. You can go to hell!', and swept out of the classroom, leaving the dominie with his mouth wide open.

The cruel behaviour of James Calder made its mark on Neill, and reinforced his already fearful attitude towards authority. Some thirty-five years later he could recall clearly the extreme severity of the headteacher's punishments: 'One lad who was dull was strapped regularly every morning because he could not learn the Shorter Catechism. His right hand was always raw and red, as were his eyes. The law was that the Shorter Catechism had to be learned, and there was no defence, no extenuation.' Not only did Neill have to witness such incidents; he was compelled to use the strap himself. He had a perpetual fear that the class would get beyond his control. 'I did my work with fear in my heart,' he wrote later. 'I had to be the sternest of taskmasters.' The dominie kept a very tight watch on his staff. Their attendance, as well as the pupils', was rigorously noted every week in the logbook. He was in the habit of suddenly announcing that he would take over one teacher's class for a morning, while they took his. Neill himself was in a worse position than the other two teachers: James Calder's classroom and his own were separated only by a glass partition, through which the head could see everything that was going on.

The only respite from this harsh regime came when James Calder was away through ill-health. Then Neill was in charge of the school, and he found that discipline could be relaxed to some extent. The children would take advantage of the head's absence, but Neill did not report their misdemeanours. This gave the pupils a chance to see behind the authoritarian mask that he had donned with such misgivings. Margaret Boyle, another Kettle pupil, recalls that, 'Mr Neill was loved by his pupils, being kind, but strict and firm. He had a charming personality.' Isabella Skinner is quite fulsome in her recollection, remembering 'a tall, handsome gentleman, slim built, with a lovely complexion, pink cheeks, and a lovely head of dark brown hair. A proper gentleman in every way, with a lovely nature, and very slow to anger. He always saw the humorous side of everything, and was adored by all the pupils. . . .He was a jewel of a teacher.'

This description suggests that the gauche and timid adolescent had by now turned into a more easygoing young man, with some attractive features more in evidence. Despite his unhappy situation at work, he was beginning to make a life for himself outside the classroom. Socially he remained isolated, finding it hard to get to know the village families – with one exception. He was lucky enough to find lodgings with the Tod family, who owned Idolkettle Farm, about a mile from the school. They were quiet, reserved people, who mixed little with others, but treated their lodger as one of the family. Mr Tod, a gentleman farmer and a member of the Tory Party, talked politics with Neill, and got him enthusiastic about the speeches of A. J. Balfour, a Scot who became Prime Minister the year before Neill moved to the village. At the subsequent general election in 1906, Neill proudly wore the blue Tory favours on polling day, and joined in the barracking of Herbert Asquith, who had been Member of Parliament for East Fife for twenty years.

The Tods had three children, and Neill enjoyed the musical evenings round the piano, though he felt unable to join in himself. He made one or two attempts at his recitations, his repertoire now having expanded to include a piece in which he imitated the pianist Rubinstein. The reception was less than fervent. Neill derived rather more pleasure from a surprising new interest. Through Walter Tod, the youngest son, he joined the army volunteers. He learned to play the bugle; visited a rifle range, where he eventually won a prize for shooting; went on regular camping expeditions; and took part in a parade in front of King Edward VII in a massive review of volunteers in Queen's Park, Edinburgh. Initially it was the comradeship that drew him to the volunteers; he revelled in being one of 'such a jolly

lot', who didn't take their military duties very seriously. But he did ultimately become quite interested in the soldier's life. He bought and studied
the latest edition of the infantry training manual, and actually passed the
sergeant's exam – a novel experience for someone who clearly thought he
was born to fail.

Through the Tods, Neill made friends with the first of a number of
men who became his 'mentors', and whose ideas and personalities, temporarily or permanently, affected his development and the course of his
life. The Reverend Aeneas Gunn Gordon was by all accounts a fairly
remarkable man. A Canadian from Nova Scotia, he had come to Kingskettle
in 1873, and was to remain a minister for the parish for 54 years. Tall,
well built, handsome and bearded, he was immensely popular with his
parishioners. He was a great reader, and a fine Greek and Latin scholar –
it was said that he twice turned down a university professorship in order
to stay in the village. He tutored adults for professional jobs or for entrance
to the university, without any payment. Such a system of self-help was part
of the Scottish way of life; and Neill now entered the tradition by becoming
one of Gordon's pupils. For a short time he had thought about entering
the ministry, though more with the idea of dazzling the congregation with
brilliant sermons, than from any inherent religious feelings. Gordon un-
dertook to teach him Greek for one hour every day, before school began,
on condition that Neill attended church on Sunday and respected the
Sabbath. Neill duly attended. Before long he was reading the first two
books of Homer's *Odyssey*, and was able to cope with parts of Herodotus.

It was a learning experience of a kind quite different from any he had
undergone before, except when Ben Thomson had taught him mathematics.
His progress was probably helped by the personality of his teacher, and by
the fact that the two men soon became good friends – Neill was later best
man at Gordon's wedding. Though he found the minister's sermons dull
and his conversation commonplace, Neill responded to his kind and charitable nature; he was 'a man whose kindness helped me greatly during an
unhappy period', he wrote later. Gordon once asked a working man to
lunch at the 'manse' and, when his guest began to shovel his mince in with
his knife, at once followed suit; Neill, impressed, did the same. On another
occasion the two men were in a crowd in nearby Cupar, listening to the
announcement of Herbert Asquith's victory in the general election. A workman swore vigorously, saw the minister standing behind him, and apolo-
gised. Gordon merely told him to carry on, as he was expressing his own
feelings perfectly.

It was from Gordon that Neill developed an interest in literature
beyond the level of the adventure story. He began to appreciate Milton's
poetry, and that of Dante and Tasso, and found himself 'gripped' by
Macaulay's essays. His ambition to get in to the ministry receded as a
different possibility began to emerge – that of getting in to the university.
St Andrews seemed the obvious choice; Neill had visited his elder brother
there, and liked what he saw of the social life. To get in, he would have to
pass a preliminary examination in four subjects, the first part consisting of

English and maths. Gordon encouraged him by lending him books from his own library; and his old tutor Ben Thomson coached him by post for the mathematics paper. From Kettle he cycled over to St Andrews and, helped by his first ever brandy-and-soda in the lunch break, passed in both subjects.

This was his first real taste of academic success in any form, and it came, significantly, from his own desire to learn rather than as a response to compulsory pressures. Not long afterwards, he also passed the first part of his acting teacher's certificate. It was perhaps through a growing sense of his own potential, which these results confirmed, that Neill decided that three years of James Calder was enough. There is some evidence that, despite his harrowing emotional experience, he had made some impact on the academic quality of the pupils' learning, even if at the same time he abhorred the system. The school had a good reputation – which cynics attributed to the quality of the whisky offered to the inspector. The report by the inspector for 11 May 1904 noted: 'The school is in an advanced state of efficiency in the Senior Division and Penmanship and Arithmetic and Coloured Design are of quite exceptional merit.' Neill was in charge of the third class, and the inspector found the geography 'poor'. A year later he noted, among points needing attention, 'Word-Building and Derivation in Senior Class III, a markedly provincial pronunciation of the vowels.' However, by Neill's third year, he thought that, 'Class III in particular acquits itself with conspicuous success.' Evidently Neill's comparatively relaxed attitude towards the pupils, especially when James Calder was absent, had not resulted in any deterioration in results. He had survived three hard years, which would have proved something to his father. It certainly gave him a very clear and intimate picture of the system which he was now beginning to question, not just emotionally, but intellectually.

He left Kettle School on Friday 23 November 1906, and on the following Monday began work as an assistant master at Newport Public School in Fife. A small, residential town, Newport stood on the banks of the River Tay. Across the water, joined by the 'Old Fife' ferryboat, and the railway bridge which had replaced that destroyed in the Tay Bridge Disaster in 1879, lay the industrial city of Dundee. Here was the other side of Scotland, and one that was quite unfamiliar to Neill: extremes of poverty, slum housing conditions, squalor and disease. The manufacturing of jute had brought prosperity to many in the town; but to the labouring classes it had meant low wages, one- or at best two-roomed dwellings, a lack of privacy, and minimum sanitation. In times of slump unemployment was chronic. Child labour was still normal: in the year Neill arrived in Newport, 13-year-olds in Dundee often worked a twelve-hour day in the jute mills, and then attended evening classes for two hours on four evenings a week. Women would give birth in beds swarming with lice, while other children lay sleeping in the same room. Little of this impinged on Neill at the time; he was much more concerned with making his mark in respectable Newport 'society', where making and spending money appeared to be paramount. Matters of class, dress and status were well defined and stringently observed; and he soon realised that teachers could and did mix with the sons and daughters of the rich. He determined to join them.

One teacher who was already moving in these circles was Harry Willsher, who just a few weeks before Neill's arrival had moved up from first assistant to become head of Newport School. Aged 26, and only three years Neill's senior, he was thought to be 'a coming man in education'. For the first time, Neill was able to be on friendly terms with the head of a school in which he was working; 'he was a companion rather than a master,' he later recalled warmly. Musically very gifted, Willsher had written a textbook on Elizabethan music, and was music critic for the *Dundee Evening Telegraph*. He had a passion for Gilbert and Sullivan, believing everyone should have a knowledge of their work as a basic part of their mental equipment. Though he was unable to convince Neill on this score, in other respects he became his musical 'mentor', and in general helped him to widen his cultural horizons.

Newport Public School, built in 1878, stood on a slope amidst residential streets, only a few yards from the shore of the Tay, and in close proximity to the local Congregational and Episcopal churches. The 290 children, mostly of lower-middle-class and working-class families, had little space in which to learn and play; during break time, in these pre-motor car days, they were allowed to spill out into the road running alongside the school railings. It was, it seems, a well run school, and some of the teachers were genuinely interested in the children. Again, former pupils remember their teachers with a mixture of respect and, in most cases, affection. But one or two dissented from the general approval. Jack Anderson recalls: 'I feared and disliked most of them in the lower grades. They were, male and female alike, bullies, prone to resort to the strap at the least provocation. One of them, a Mr Brice, a sadist, used a strap of rawhide, which really hurt.' Another pupil, Flora Scrymgeour, remembers 'hard-faced Miss Jeffrey leathering away'.

The tawse hung on the walls of many homes at this time in both Scotland and England. 'For bad boys a yard of strap is worth a mile of talk,' a Manchester mother told her children. So it needed someone with either strong convictions or a powerful personality to be able to give up Scotland's favourite traditional weapon of discipline. From the recollections of several Newport pupils, it appears that Neill avoided actually using the strap, though not the threat of it: 'He once threatened to use it on me when I had forgotten for two successive days to bring my Latin book,' recalls James Wannan, another pupil taught by Neill. Willsher, despite his friendliness to Neill, could still be very harsh with the children, and made regular use of the tawse. One boy, Jimmy Don, was given '20 lines' by Neill as a punishment for some misdemeanour; when he presented his exercise book next day to him, with 20 neatly ruled lines, Neill sent him to the head for a strapping.

Yet, within his own classroom, he now for the first time had some measure of freedom to teach in his own way, and to try to establish more informal relations with his pupils. Both his personality and his teaching had an impact on many of the children. One of those who was very taken with Neill was James Scrymgeour, who has vivid memories of his time at Newport School, and who was 11 when Neill first taught there. 'He had an original mind, and put things in a different way. He was slightly ahead of his time, and ready to try new methods. He used original, arresting phrases, and his lessons were very enjoyable. He imputed as much intelligence to his pupils at that juncture as he had himself – that was part of his charm and success. The pupils recognised in him a person who was willing to "upgrade" them, and they responded to it. He communicated with sincere enthusiasm, and was very popular.' Jack Anderson has a similar view of Neill: 'Above all, he was a friend to his classes; his most important attribute as a teacher was that he never talked down to his students.' Inevitably, there were some who made fun of this rather unorthodox adult, but this seems to have been something Neill was now able to endure – and possibly even encourage. Certainly it was now that he really began to break down the conventional adult-child barriers that most teachers insisted upon. He had taken lodgings with a widow in Queen Street, only a couple of minutes' walk from the school; often, at the end of the day, he could be seen coming along the street surrounded by a group of boys.

Neill soon instituted an unusual addition to the curriculum, which provided a further opportunity to get on easier terms with the children. Any pupils who were interested were invited to come, after school, on what were variously known as 'nature walks', 'geography explorations' or 'botanising walks'. The countryside was within easy reach of the school, and they would ramble out of the town, up on to Causeway Head, Inverdouit, overlooking St Andrews Bay and Newport itself, or across to a local landmark, Willie Washer's Pond. Neill would amble along, arm in arm with the children, encouraging them to observe nature at first hand. He suggested they each buy a notebook and write up the day's temperature, the wind direction, the shape and appearance of the clouds. He also encouraged them to draw and paint what they saw, showing them how to work with pencil and brush.

Neill clearly began to relish his new-found role of unconventional teacher. Once he sent a pupil down to the grocer's store for a bunch of grapes, then ate them sitting cross-legged on his desk in front of the class. In matters of dress he also began to cultivate what then passed for eccentricity. He was one of the first men in the town to go hatless, a gesture which caused some to think him crazy, since some kind of headgear was considered compulsory. He found a fancy green waistcoat which had belonged to his mother's father, and took to wearing it with a fashionable gold watch chain; at other times he would wear a sports jacket rather than a conventional suit and tie. He was, though, careful to keep his appearance within the bounds of decency, especially as he began to gain a toehold in Newport society. He became tutor for a year to Arnold Leng, the son of Sir John Leng, whose family founded the Dundee newspaper industry. In characteristic manner, Neill entered his first dance in Newport at the Lengs' house in a suit thrown together by a tailor in Kingsmuir, out of material

that was too heavy, and to measurements that didn't match up to his body.
After this preliminary gaffe he made some headway, took some dancing
lessons, and began to feel more at ease on such occasions.

In the middle of this social whirl, Neill became enraptured with one
of his pupils. Margaret Ritchie, the daughter of a jute merchant, was 16,
and generally reckoned to be the beauty of Newport. She had grey eyes,
long lashes, fair hair and a creamy complexion, and Neill, who was rapidly
becoming susceptible to this kind of beauty, became totally infatuated:

> Her voice struck me as the essence of sweetness. To me, she was all
> that was lovely. . . .I found that I could not look at her when she
> looked at me. She personified the whole school for me: if she
> happened to be absent, the day was dark, long and dreary; when she
> was present, the day was always far too short.

His feelings only seemed to grow stronger as she made her indifference
clear. Though she was friendly enough to him, she was already interested
in a boy of her own age, to whom she later became engaged. Though Neill
used to visit her at her house, and talk with her father, he never made any
'advances'. It was perhaps because of this that she made such a lasting
impression on him.

However, Margaret Ritchie's eyelashes did not put all thoughts of
other women out of his mind. He courted another Newport girl for a time,
but found that she was shocked when he arrived once to take her out
dressed in a full-length coat. He actually proposed marriage to one pupil
at the school, Janet Sturrock, but she would have nothing to do with him.
(Her sister, who was devoted to Neill, feels she herself might have given a
different answer.) He also claimed later that the father of one 16-year-old
labelled him 'a seducer of innocence', after he had lent her a copy of H. G.
Wells' novel *Marriage*. But since this was not published until well after he
left Newport, and caused much less of a stir than another of Wells' stories
of an Emancipated Woman, *Ann Veronica*, Neill clearly had in mind the
wrong book – or else the wrong girl.

Neill took no notice of political or social questions during his time in
Newport, despite the fact that he occasionally accompanied Neilie, who
was about to qualify as a doctor, on his rounds among some of the Dundee
hovels. But he did develop what became an abiding interest in the theatre
and music. At 12 he had been taken to the theatre in Edinburgh; at 19 he
had watched in ecstasy as Henry Irving tore his hair in front of the footlights
in his famous melodrama *The Bells*. Now he was able to see two of the
most celebrated Hamlets of the day, Martin Harvey and Forbes-Robertson,
playing the part at Her Majesty's Theatre in Dundee. Here too he discovered Wagner for the first time, when a touring company performed *Loh-
engrin*. He also attended a series of shilling concerts given by, among
others, Jan Paderewski. Perhaps it was one of these occasions which
prompted a gesture remembered by his sister May: 'I learned the piano for
three years, and would have liked to have carried on if my parents had
been able to afford it. Allie was just beginning to teach, and had no money,

but he paid for me to have an extra year. I remember he bought me a big book of Chopin, and he said: "Now, May, practise that before I come back." I was so fond of him that I used to practise, and he would sit down beside the piano and listen to me.' It was a generous gift for someone with little money to spare.

Despite his fuller and more varied life, Neill was still intent on getting in to university – not necessarily just out of an unadulterated love of learning, but also for the status it would bring, and because his two idols, Willie and J. M. Barrie, had taken the same path. Barrie had been a student in Edinburgh, and this may have been one of the reasons why Neill now switched his attention to that University. Since he was still quite unclear what line of work he wanted to pursue, he again allowed his father to make a key decision for him. A former Kingsmuir pupil had made a visit to the village, and spoke of the possibilities in the colonies for men with a degree in agriculture. George Neill thought this would be just the career for his son – in itself a further indicator of his failure to understand Neill's particular abilities. Neill had no interest in agriculture whatsoever, and 'accepting it as a career meant as much as accepting an invitation to play tennis, because I had no wish to do anything else at the moment.'

During his final weeks in Newport he passed the second half of both his university entrance examination, in Latin and physics, and the acting teacher's certificate. Thus he was finally qualified at the very moment when he decided to move out of teaching. In some ways it was a peculiar decision. In Newport there was more scope for creative teaching than he had encountered before, as the inspector's report for the higher grade at the end of his first year makes clear: 'The Department is full of promise. The work is intelligently and thoughtfully planned, and the pupils are bright and responsive. In English in particular the choice of books has been made with taste and judgement, and the teachers have been remarkably successful in arousing a genuine interest in and feeling for the literature.' On the other hand, he may have already sensed that the rigours of the Scottish system were alien to his temperament. There is a suggestion that, however tolerant Harry Willsher may have been, other staff were not so happy about their colleague's unusual ideas. Even Harry Willsher occasionally came into conflict with Neill, as James Scrymgeour recalls: 'Mr Neill regarded as false modesty children being taught to whisper in a grown-up's ear, "I want to go to the Houses of Parliament." He indicated this was the only useful function that Parliament performed. This observation did not meet with Mr Willsher's approval.' 'The other teachers didn't think much of him,' recalls Janet Sturrock. The university at least offered him the chance of wider horizons, with the possibility of finding his real niche at the end of three years.

He left Newport at the end of the summer term of 1908. The night before, the normally cool Margaret Ritchie threw her arms around his neck, and said: 'Mr Neill, you are a dear.' He left both the school and the town with mixed feelings.

CHAPTER 3

Journey to Fleet Street

Canongate Tolbooth

One is bound to admit that it marks a new tendency in university journalism.
Editorial in Edinburgh University *Student* magazine, June 1912

'In a big city you are one of thousands, you see life, you have a wide field of vision; you become urbane and snobbish in address, and, incidentally, dress. You must of necessity stand alone, and you become a fighter unconsciously.' Neill began his four years as a student in Edinburgh very conscious of being a newcomer to metropolitan life. By the time he wrote these words in the middle of his final year, he had entered into much of the university's social life, and had to a great extent overcome his initial isolation.

He was helped in this by his appointment as editor of the *Student* magazine. This position not only confirmed in him a growing feeling that he should take up journalism, but gave him a forum in which he could develop his skills as artist, reviewer, fiction writer, sub-editor and social critic. Into his editorials he poured his feelings about issues of the day, as well as more personal observations, mixing anecdote, polemic and confession in a manner that was soon to gain him a much wider readership. Above all, for the first time outside a school setting, he began to challenge accepted notions about education, and wrote some fulminating paragraphs about the defects of Scotland's university system. From being a lukewarm follower of the Tory Party, he began to find considerable sympathy with socialist ideas and the writers who expounded them. His rebellion was beginning in earnest.

As a city, Edinburgh had already acquired its label of the 'Athens of the North'. The beauties of its architecture, its rich political and literary history, provided an awesome backdrop for the still immature young man accustomed to provincial ways. The university itself, over 400 years old, was dominated by its celebrated faculties of divinity, law and medicine, which attracted the cream of students from all over the world, many of them from wealthy and distinguished backgrounds. Neill, on the other hand, found himself stuck with a subject he had no real interest in, and living at a level of subsistence little better than that which he had endured in the city ten years before, during his seven miserable months with Cowan's in Buccleuch Street. This time he was given some assistance by the Carnegie Trust, which helped poorer students with their fees; but he still had to pay for his examinations, as well as food and board. He was consequently forced to live frugally, in a way that markedly affected his life as a student.

Though there was beginning to be pressure in Edinburgh for halls of residence, students still had to live in lodgings, often miles from the university itself. Neill found some cheap rooms off Clerk Street, living initially with his brother Neilie, who was in his last year as a medical student. The brothers found they had 3*d* a day to cover their regular lunch in the Students' Union – a sandwich, a bun and a glass of milk. Sometimes they could not even afford this, and had to rely solely on the breakfast and high tea supplied by a kindly landlady. Survival had become marginally easier during Neill's second year: he won £40 in a Sunday newspaper competition, a sum which he used sparingly for his keep throughout that year, with enough left over to buy an overcoat. Yet it was not just poverty that made life difficult, but his own feelings of shame about it. He had to refuse invitations to functions because he could not afford to send his one dress shirt to the laundry. Unable to afford to go to the music hall for his first three years, he pretended to a dislike of such entertainment.

Despite these handicaps, Neill slowly began to build a life for himself. He started to contribute short stories and pen-and-ink sketches to the *Student*. As in Kingskettle, he joined the volunteers, and again became something of a marksman. He not only took up golf, but – perhaps through economic necessity – designed and made his own clubs. He even dared to revive his recitations for a fresh audience, and took part in some musical activities. He gained a reputation for being a raconteur – notably of 'blue' stories. The university offered its students a full range of clubs and societies, from the normal political ones through the subject-based variety, to some more recently founded such as the Fabian Society, the Tariff Reform League and the Women's Suffrage Society. Neill took little interest in these, being more interested in student affairs in general – in his last year he was the Union representative for his year on the Arts Committee of the Student Representative Council, and was convenor of the Standing Committee dealing with matters affecting the *Student*.

It was his editorship of the student magazine that allowed his social and intellectual horizons to widen significantly. One of the 'perks' of the job was a free dress-circle ticket every Monday evening to the city's four theatres, the Lyceum, the Theatre Royal, the Kings and the Empire. There was a rich and diverse number of entertainments on offer: Vesta Tilley, Little Tich, Harry Tate and George Formby were some of the music-hall stars who appeared at the Kings and Empire in the course of that year. Neill enjoyed these evenings, and met one or two of the comedians further down the bill. He also commissioned himself to review the Christmas pantomine, devoting much of the article to descriptions of the charms of the principal ladies – Daisy West Collins 'is a fair maid – literally fair – and her eyes are full of fun'; Nora Guy 'is dark, and has eyes that seem to be everywhere. If you are a susceptible youth, Miss Guy will disconcert you. . . .She sings her plaintive song, and you can do nothing afterwards but cheer and cheer again.'

Cinema was the newest form of entertainment to be popular amongst the students: the Cinema House offered 'thrills, pathos and screaming farce', featuring cowboy drama such as *The Dearest Claim*, billed as 'a stirring tale of love and horsemanship'. Neill undoubtedly welcomed the chance to see the 'penny dreadful' type of story before his very eyes, and made sure that the *Student* gave regular coverage to the week's programme. Drama and music were also given their place: plays by Wilde and Pinero, evenings of acting by Forbes-Robertson and Laurence Irving; seasons of opera given by the Carl Rosa and Ernest Denhof companies. In one week there were performances of *Die Meistersinger, Orpheus, Elektra, The Flying Dutchman* and *Tristan und Isolde*. Neill attended them all, solving the problem of dress by chalking his one shirt every night, and sneaking in illegally a second time to *Die Meistersinger* when the press tickets ran out. It was this opera which, he wrote later, 'knocked me over. I had never heard such music. To me it was the purest of gold.' He left no record of his feelings at the time; but when the great dancer Anna Pavlova came for two nights to the Lyceum in December 1911, Neill was transported, and said so at length in his magazine:

> It is on such an occasion as this that we realise our mediocrity; we
> have seen Pavlova and our ecstasy is out of proportion to our
> command of expression. . . . She is the spirit of transcendent joy; you
> watch her as she moves, and you are carried far beyond anything
> base, anything mundane; you are carried to the bar of heaven. The
> greatest joys are pure; you see Pavlova interpret the brief life of a
> butterfly in the sun, and you forget everything in the supremacy of
> an ecstatic joy. You forget to think of her movements; you know in
> a vague sort of way that every part of her beautiful body is dancing
> – her eyes most of all; you forget that she is the greatest living
> dancer. . . . As you go out into the night the banality of things
> earthly comes to you like a chilling wind, and you realise that you
> have been in a dream-paradise. But dreams are the only substantial
> things, for in them one *lives*: in Dreamland there is nothing gross,
> nothing impure.

This review is interesting, in that its style is more effusive, its feeling more passionate, than most of Neill's later writing. It also shows the extent of his susceptibility to female beauty, perhaps all the more deeply felt for being 'untouchable'. Certainly the reference to the purity of dreams, the implied grossness of everyday life in comparison, suggest that he was still in considerable confusion about the nature of women. This is borne out by the very different encounters with them that he had during his student years, few of which brought him any lasting happiness. Until this time, his relations with women had almost certainly been Platonic – though not necessarily because he wanted them to be so. It was perhaps his diffidence as much as his need to idealise women from afar that led to this situation – and the two traits would tend to reinforce each other. In Edinburgh many students, in particular the boys from English public schools, would pick up and sleep with shop assistants and other working-class girls, the 'nice' girls supposedly being taboo. One night Neill made love to one of these girls on Blackford Hill, just outside Edinburgh. Afterwards she cried, and, when Neill asked her the reason for her tears, she replied: 'It isn't fair. You students take us out, and we like your manners and educated speech, but you never marry us. I'll have to marry some workman who can only talk about football and beer.' That was the last time he picked up a shop girl. He had, it seems, found these occasions degrading anyway, and suffered feelings of guilt – enough to make him temporarily impotent on more than one occasion. He was still a long way from exorcising the belief that sex was synonymous with sin.*

Yet by now Neill felt that there could perhaps be a middle way, that it was possible to find women who were not just sex objects, or idols to be revered. In the *Student* he wrote in May 1912: 'Personally we believe that there *can* be a real chumminess between a man and a woman without danger of a drifting into deeper waters. . . .When there is such a friendship it is a glorious thing, and the man is happy who has known the sweet sympathy, the warm friendliness of a good, true woman.' He then declared that 'the most natural and chummy girls in the world are professional actresses.' He had by now met one such person who seems to have come near his ideal, an actress called Dorothy, who had performed in Edinburgh. Pretty and mischievous, but with the capacity to be serious, the two of them were, Neill later observed, 'too much of the pal to each other for emotion to enter'. Perhaps it was his emotional confusion that drew him towards this type of woman, the 'good sport' whose natural warmth would help to keep sex and emotion at bay.

Once, during a summer vacation, Neill did become entangled emotionally, this time with a farm girl from Ayrshire. He fell in love with 'Beatrice', and seriously considered marriage. She was, however, a very shy girl, and had no desire to leave the family farm. This, Neill recognised, would condemn him to life as a country headmaster, exactly the position he had striven most to avoid in coming to Edinburgh. He felt torn between

---

*Many years later, when asked what he regretted most in life, he replied 'that I hadn't sinned enough when young, thanks to Scots Calvinson and hell fire'.

his feelings and his ambition, and tried, unsuccessfully, to interest Beatrice in the books and ideas which were now absorbing his attention. He remembered a saying of his mother's: 'Marriage hinders a man, because it forces him to think of bread and butter.' The class and cultural gap, and Neill's attempts to narrow it, may have been one of the reasons why Beatrice decided to marry someone else while Neill was hesitating. He himself later offered a further explanation, though it is difficult to know how far it reflected his own feelings at the time. 'I lost Beatrice, warm and dear as she was, because – without knowing it – I was looking for the ideal that my mother's sinful notion of sex had compelled me to form.'

Certainly, Neill was searching for a warmth and acceptance in women that his mother had never provided. And it was approval and self-confidence that he gained from another friendship of this period, this time with someone on his own intellectual level. May Baxter was in his class at the university. On long walks and in lengthy letters, she and Neill discussed themselves, literary matters, Neill's abilities as a writer: 'her belief in me supplied much that I needed,' he recalled later. The friendship foundered over social matters. She mixed in aristocratic circles, and though Neill was attracted to what he saw as the glamour of such a social set, he grew increasingly resentful of her attempts to make him conform to the manners and customs of her associates.

Though he was still in many respects a snob himself, Neill made several attacks on the snobbery within the student body at Edinburgh, chiefly on the grounds that it killed all hope of what he saw as a highly desirable commodity, good fellowship. With feeling, he wrote about students to be found in the Union who, 'if you ask them for a match, look at you in a way that seems to say, "I *beg* your pardon, I don't know you." ' Snobbery was at its worst in Princes Street, where women would parade in their furs and men in their latest spats, tacitly joining 'in the inglorious worship of wealth', when as students, Neill argued, 'we should be Bohemians, amongst us there should be the comradeship that exists in theatrical circles'. He pointed to the campaign for electing a Rector, which occurred every three years, as a rare moment for the cliques in the university to forget their differences: 'For once the blood forgot his snobbishness, for once the swot forgot his books; all men were equal for the time being.'

Although it was certainly a matter that concerned Neill, he gave no coverage in the *Student* to a very different social question. There were many 'coloured' students studying in Edinburgh at the time, as well as a significant number of white students who came from the colonies, and who would be returning there as administrators when their course was completed. There was a good deal of overt colour prejudice in the university: the 'coloured' students were openly known as 'niggers', and were treated as inferiors by those who had been brought up to think this normal. Neill neither shared nor endorsed such attitudes, but neither did he appear to take up any position on the issue in his editorial role. Clearly the class issue was of more personal significance than the colour question – and was also perhaps an easier matter to deal with at the time. Neill hinted at this five years later when he looked back at his student self: 'I regret very much that I had not the moral courage to chum up with the coloured man at the university: prejudices leave one after one has left the university.'

Many of his editorial outpourings in the *Student* seem more of a cry for help than a balanced consideration of the topic in hand. And, although he complained vigorously about the hostility between groups of students, he also had plenty to say about contacts between students and professors. Here again his words arise from his own experience, and his growing conviction that not only the school system, but also Scotland's renowned university education, was 'really a ramming in' rather than a 'leading out'. His view of the system was undoubtedly affected by the professors under whom he studied. For his degree in agriculture he was required to take chemistry, and to attend lectures given by Sir James Walker. Lectures were the dominant method of teaching, and Neill spent many hours copying out notes from them. He did however find some solace in the practical laboratory work. He enjoyed trying to analyse inks and dyes, finding a good solder for aluminium – and making use of the department's supply of chloroform to clean the pipe he had recently taken to smoking. The other half of the course, natural philosophy (dynamics, physics, sound and light), he found excessively difficult, and the lectures by Professor MacGregor quite incomprehensible. Later he remembered the professor 'mumbling into his beard as he wrote mysterious formulae on the blackboard, while we passed the time cat-calling and tramping tunes with our feet. . . .MacGregor never seemed to mind; I wonder if he ever heard us?'*

The thought of grappling with the mysteries of sulphuric acid and relative velocity for another three years was finally too much for him. Despite doing unexpectedly well in passing his first-year exams, at the end of the year he switched to the Honours English course. Once again he was following directly in Barrie's footsteps. Here, though, the frustrations were of a different kind. The professor, George Saintsbury, had the reputation of being the best-read man in Europe on English literature. He had written numerous books, including the standard work, *A Shorter History of English Literature*. In his view, a literary work should be judged on its execution rather than its content, though his own style, full of digressions and parentheses, was hardly a model of precision.

Since Saintsbury's thoughts about the key figures in English Literature could all be found in his books, Neill, along with many others, spent his time in the lecture hall in what he felt were more purposeful ways, writing letters and doing his pen-and-ink sketching. But his hostility to the course did not derive solely from the inadequacies of the lecture stystem. Aside from having to learn Anglo-Saxon and Middle English, neither of which he mastered, Neill had to study the works of major poets such as Chaucer, Spenser, Pope, Dryden, Keats, Tennyson; playwrights such as Shakespeare,

*Similar unruly scenes in university classes have been described by two of Neill's literary heroes: George Douglas Brown in *The House with the Green Shutters*, and J. M. Barrie in *An Edinburgh Eleven: Pencil Portraits of College Life*.

Marlowe and other Elizabethans, Congreve, Sheridan and Wycherley; and, in the prose field, Dr Johnson, Thomas Browne, Coleridge, Hazlitt and others. Yet he had to concentrate exclusively on tracing influences and movements, and to read the recommended books *about* these writers, rather than develop his own ideas about their works. 'I was compelled to concentrate on whether a blank-verse line had elision or not, or whether one could trace the rhythm of *Christabel* in *The Lotus Eaters*. It was all piddling stuff, like taking Milan Cathedral to pieces stone by stone to discover where the beauty lay.'

By his fourth year, Neill had become disenchanted with both the substance and the method of his university education, and used the *Student* to make an attack on the system. In March he penned two successive editorials on the subject, with the titles 'The Cursed Exam System' and 'In Which we Criticise our Professors'. Drawing on his own experience of the system, on his capacity to store and regurgitate for his natural philosophy exam a mass of information which he had already forgotten, he suggested that

> most exams test knowledge, not thinking ability. Indeed,
> independent thinking is discouraged; there are professors who view
> with displeasure any opinion that runs contrary to their own. . . .The
> exam system is responsible for the parochial idea that medals signify
> brains; sometimes they do, more often they signify great memory
> and lack of originality. . . .With the exception of a few swots, we are
> all apathetic and disinterested. Our profs are not to blame, we are
> not to blame; the faults lies at the door of the antiquated system
> which is termed the Examination System.

He went on to suggest that exams in certain subjects should be abolished. He cited the liberal attitude of one of the young lecturers in the English Department, Blyth Webster. For the Old English papers he allowed the students an indefinite time, the chance to bring textbooks into the examination, and the opportunity to see the exam papers some weeks in advance. In his second editorial Neill decided that, on reflection, the professors were far from blameless after all. They were chosen for their great knowledge of their subject, but, he thought, 'a great authority is often a bad teacher'. He then extended this criticism to make a point that became one of the cornerstones of his later critique of the school system:

> Our Profs are many of them disqualified as teachers, for a teacher
> must first make friends with his pupils before they will listen to
> him. . . . If you go to them after a class to consult them, they stand
> upon their dignity and their whole attitude says, "I don't want any
> of your familiarity. I am a Professor; my duty is lecturing, not
> advising. Go to your Official Adviser." As a result you do not
> respect them; you must like a man before you can respect him.

The solution, Neill felt, was for the professors to become teachers in the way in which they worked in schools, 'for then there will be complete sympathy between teacher and taught'. Finally, he proposed that no man should be made a professor until he had undergone an apprenticeship as a schoolteacher.

Neill was still wrestling with the question of the role of authority, and his attacks on the aloofness and dignity of the university lecturer clearly reflect his earlier difficulties with his father. Respect and dignity, those archetypal Victorian qualities which had caused him to suffer in his childhood, were to him loathsome ideas, and were always to remain so. An incident in Edinburgh reveals both the problem, and an indication that Neill was beginning to tackle his own timidity. During a history lecture given by Sir Richard Lodge, Neill was wrongfully blamed for a disturbance, and was angrily dismissed from the classroom. Afterwards, he came to Lodge's private room to explain what had really happened. The professor – a tall man with a moustache, not unlike his father in appearance – appeared unconvinced. Neill, uncharacteristically, was roused:

> Suddenly I lost all my fear of authority, and my temper as well. 'Look here, sir,' I said, 'I had to work for years to save up enough money to come to the university. I am years older than the average student. Do you think, in the circumstances, I came to Edinburgh to behave like a raw schoolboy?' His eyebrows went up in surprise. Then he smiled, held out his hand and apologised.

Not only was Neill now beginning to stand up for himself, but also for the first time to take an interest in politics, in social questions, and in some of the new writers whose work could only be read outside the formal syllabus of the Honours English course. Three such figures helped to shift his politics towards socialism, and had a permanent influence upon his philosophy of life: H. G. Wells, George Bernard Shaw and Henrik Ibsen.

Wells and Shaw probably had more influence on the young than any other writers during the first two decades of the century: as Rebecca West put it, they 'hung about the houses of our minds like uncles'. As a youth, Neill had read and enjoyed some of Wells's scientific short stories. During his second year in Edinburgh Wells published *Ann Veronica*, a novel concerned with women's freedom which caused an uproar, and was used by certain moral crusaders to launch a counter-attack against what they saw as Edwardian permissiveness. Neill read both this novel and *Marriage*, which came out just as he was leaving university. Yet he retained a special affection for the more autobiographical works such as *The History of Mr Polly* and *Kipps*. Here it seems to have been Wells's sharply ironical observation of the shabby-genteel world of 'trade', rather than his ideas about free love, religion or politics, which struck a chord with Neill. The masterly evocation in *Kipps* of the apprentice draper's life, of the 'inflamed ankles and sore feet that form a normal incident in the business of the making of an English draper', echoes Neill's earlier experience in Forfar, as do some of the themes of the scenes of Kipps's childhood. Sundays appeared to Kipps as terrible gaps of inactivity, no work, no play, a dreary expanse of time with the mystery of church twice, and plum duff once in the middle. . . . It was from the difference between this day and common days that Kipps derived his first definite conception of the nature of God and heaven.

The novel also dealt with the issue of class, with obvious parallels to Neill's tribulations in Kingsmuir: Kipps's aunt 'would appear at door and window to interrupt interesting conversations with children who on unknown grounds were considered "low" and undesirable'. And Wells's hero, like the young Neill, 'never ready any newspapers except occasionally *Tit Bits* or a ha'penny comic'.

If Wells's novels, with their perky humour, and their characters' search for happiness, provided a mirror of Neill's own youth, Shaw's appeal lay elsewhere. His devastating and mischievously brilliant attacks on the most cherished institutions of English society – the Church, the Law, Marriage, the Family, Schools – articulated Neill's own still confused but deeply felt antipathy to the values of conventional society. Until now its superficial attractions, his snobbery and desire to be accepted, had over-ridden his sense of unease about manners, good form, hypocrisy. Shaw, however, brought the social critic in Neill to the surface, and for a while he became a thoroughgoing Shavian. 'When I first discovered his plays and prefaces in my student days, a new world was opened to me. He was the oracle,' he wrote later. Neill was able to hear the oracle speak at first hand: on 25 November 1908 Shaw made his first public appearance in Edinburgh, when he addressed the University Fabian Society for an hour and a half in the Synod Hall. Neill was in the audience: 'I recall trembling with fear when I got up to ask a question, and blushing with shame when the answer poked a little fun at me. . . . I don't expect that I am the only one to feel himself a country bumpkin in the presence of his wit and wisdom.' Nevertheless the great man's image remained intact; Neill had noticed his kindly, twinkling eyes.

Hesketh Pearson, in his biography of Shaw, has suggested:

> The qualities in him that specially appealed to youth were his
> irreverence for tradition and office, his indifference to vested interests
> and inflated reputations, his contempt for current morality, his
> championship of unpopular causes and persecuted people, his vitality
> and humour, and above all his inability to take solemn people
> seriously.

His ideas now brought out some of these qualities in Neill himself, and gave them much sharper focus. When Neill wrote an attack on the lack of camaraderie in university life, he was reprimanded by a reader in the following issue of the *Student*: 'Do you imply that our university is filled with rotters? Who are you, that you should take upon yourself to hang out the University's dirty linen in full view of the world at large?' Neill's reply is marked by wit, sense and forthrightness, a combination that was to be much in evidence in his later writing:

> I like your letter, it is forcible and to the point, but, you know, it *is* somewhat heated. . . .You do not realise that great reformers like Shaw and myself have to use hyperbole. . . .Don't you see that a journalist must be forcible if he is to be read. . . .The *Student* is for students, not students' parents, and I see no cogent reason for continually asking, 'How will the folks at home take this?' There are many men who require a little plain speaking, and to suggest that the blood who talks about 'Carnegie men' is a narrow-minded snob, may lead that man to be a little less aggressive in his bearing towards poorer men. I am an idealist: I detest warfare of any kind, and I want to see a Varsity where all men are brothers.

Neill's hero-worship of Shaw is discernible both in the choice of subject for his editorials, and some of their style and content. In November he defended Shaw, Wells, Galsworthy and Sidney Webb for stimulating debate on issues that went beyond party politics:

> From an intellectual point of view, there is infinitely much more food for thought in questions like Eugenics, The Superman, The Marriage Laws, Land Nationalisation, Town Planning, than in subjects like Home Rule or Tariff Reform.

And, in rather pompous vein, he began to see himself as a social reformer along Shavian lines:

> One correspondent asks what right we have to preach against evils or supposed evils. We give answer thus. We always seek for truth, because hypocrisy is destroyed by sunlight. We may be on the wrong track, but our protestant spirit says to us: 'You are satisfied that some evils exist. You have the chance to attack them; perhaps you may do some good.'

One medium that Shaw used most effectively to preach against social evils was of course the drama. The theatre, he believed, could be 'a factory of thought, a prompter of conscience, an elucidator of social conduct, an armoury against despair and dullness'. Neill was already attracted to the theatre for its glamour and colour; Shaw's plays gave his interest a new dimension. But it was the drama of Ibsen that really took Neill by storm. It was Shaw as much as anyone who had helped to establish Ibsen's reputation in England, just as he had championed the music and philosophy of Wagner and Nietzsche – in both of whom Neill became interested around this time. Through the translations of William Archer, Shaw had helped to get Ibsen's plays performed in England during the 1890s. *Hedda Gabler, Ghosts* and *A Doll's House*, with their breaking of taboos, had scandalised public and critics alike. For the student Neill, Ibsen's plays were of infinitely greater interest than the classical drama he had to study for his degree course. His preference led to a clash with George Saintsbury, who believed the students, in order to avoid controversy, should not concern themselves with anything more modern than the poetry of Walter Pater. Neill wrote a humorously critical essay on *Much Ado About Nothing*, suggesting in essence that Shakespeare could pick up a few hints from a study of Ibsen's plays. Saintsbury was very angry, and told him not to do it again, reinforcing Neill's contempt for the English course.

As with Barrie and Wells, there are some interesting parallels between Ibsen and Neill. Both were brought up in small, isolated communities, where the outlook on life was narrow, the conditions impoverished. Both went late to the university, after some years' work followed by self-motivated study, and both edited the student magazine. Ibsen even taught for a very short period at a workers' Sunday school; and he had some Scots blood in him. Neill showed a special interest in Ibsen's heroes, strong individuals who stand out against convention, and often rail against the majority: Dr Stockmann, in *An Enemy of the People*, was a figure that he had particular sympathy with. During Neill's first year, *Peer Gynt* was given its first British performance in Edinburgh. The city also played host to a touring company specialising in Ibsen's plays. In his enthusiasm, and making use of his position as editor of the *Student*, Neill obtained an invitation to a supper party in their honour, and was horribly disillusioned to discover that the leading actress had no real interest in the playwright.

His acquaintance with and liking for theatre people, and his passion for Shaw and Ibsen, led him for a brief moment to consider trying to fashion a career for himself as an actor. But a more substantial ambition soon put this idea in the shade. During his early teaching days he had taken to doing pen-and-ink drawings, under the influence of Joseph Pennell and Herbert Railton. He continued to pursue this hobby in Edinburgh, and before he became its editor had submitted some of these to the *Student*. When – after at least one rejection – they began to publish them, he tried his hand at short comic sketches, which initially were rejected. A friend suggested that he try one out on the *Glasgow Herald*, and Neill was astonished to see it printed there only a few days later. 'It seemed incredible, wonderful, glorious,' he wrote later. 'I trod on air all that day.' The sketch tells of a man who walks by mistake on to a public platform, is mistaken for the speaker, and has to try and convince a hostile audience that he knows what he is talking about. It is a jolly, contrived little tale, which conveys in a knockabout way the boisterousness of a public meeting. It was written in a style that Neill was to use in some of his early books; but it had none of the growing power and assurance of his polemical leaders in the *Student*.

Neill threw himself wholeheartedly into his editorial work, perhaps now experiencing for the first time a real sense of vocation. Apart from his weekly editorials, he wrote six more light-hearted pieces entitled 'Letter to a Fresher', signing himself 'Sandy' – a nickname that his red hair had now brought him; seven sketches, three of which featured a girl called Margaret who, unlike in real life, landed up in the young hero's arms; half a dozen pen-and-ink drawings of Edinburgh scenes; some book and theatre reviews;

a parody of George Saintsbury's lecture technique; and a number of short and mostly excruciating jokes ('X: I say, old man, I've got an awful cold in my head; what'll I do for it? Y: Take it out and warm it.'). He also occasionally invented letters for the correspondence columns when there was a dearth of student reponse to his efforts. His enthusiasm for the job was reinforced by a long weekend spent in St Andrews as part of the Edinburgh delegation to the annual Inter-University Conference. There he met up with fellow student editors from Glasgow, Aberdeen and St Andrews. They lit their pipes, 'and talked journalism of all colours. It was a serious talk, and we each gained much. . . it was an enlightening comparing of notes. . . a gathering of four kindred spirits; from the first we were all brothers.' The editor of the St Andrews *College Echoes*, to which Neill's brother had contributed some years before, was J. B. Salmond. Neill described him at the time as 'a typical St Andrews man, a clean, straight, decent fellow, with huge biceps and a soft heart. . . .He will succeed as an editor, for he is absolutely clean, honest, just and a shrewd critic.' It was the start of a close friendship between the two men.

On 5 July 1912, Neill graduated from Edinburgh, becoming a Master of Arts with Second Class Honours in English. Eight weeks previously, a note had appeared in the *Student*, revealing that 'The Editor is trying to cram a year's work into three weeks, and absolutely refuses to interview spring poets or pained women students'. In the circumstances his results were very satisfactory, and took Neill himself by surprise – he had expected a Third Class pass, the lowest possible. However, the degree seemed of little practical use in itself, since 'All I knew was that I didn't want to teach: to think of going on all my life as an English master in some provincial secondary school or academy made me shiver. No, teaching would be the last resort, if every other line failed.'

Nevertheless, his four years in Edinburgh were by no means wasted. He had taken considerable advantage of the cultural life of the city. He may have been contemptuous of his degree course, but at least he had now been right through the celebrated Scots system of education, and could base his criticisms on real experiences as pupil, pupil teacher, assistant teacher and student. Socially he had come through a great deal of loneliness, to a position where he could count on the friendship of several fellow-students, a few of whom he kept in touch with afterwards. Politically he had found socialism, and embraced it warmly, though without much interest in the party political aspect. Intellectually he had felt himself challenged by Shaw, Nietzsche, Ibsen and others, who provided some compensation for the dreariness of Dryden and Sir Thomas Browne. And his year on the *Student* had given him a platform for his views, a chance to develop his writing skills, and the hope of avoiding the dreaded 'last resort' of the teaching profession.

After the exams, Neill wrote a final editorial, and reflected on his success and failure as an editor. He felt he had perhaps neglected certain areas because of his preoccupation with 'forcible expression'. He argued that he had tried to keep the magazine as light as possible, 'and many contributors were very, very serious'. He boasted of his disregard for precedent – 'I seldom, if ever, asked myself the question, "Did previous editors do this?" ' – and for public opinion – 'I have never thought of the folks at home: if the word "damn" came along I printed it in full.' He defended his alleged obsession with snobbery by declaring it to be 'one of the great forces of life'; and to those who accused him of lowering the tone of the magazine, he replied; 'the *Student* never had any dignity, and if it ever has any it will be damned. . . .Young people have nothing to do with dignity, and the *Student* is for young people.' He made one last attack on the university – 'You can say anything to our Varsity and no one bothers to contradict you.' And then he took a sentimental farewell: 'I am very, very sorry that my "crowded hour of glorious life" is over, for I have given to the *Student* practically all my time. . . the magazine becomes a treasure, and its editor's heart is always with that treasure.'

A week before graduation day, his successor defined his achievement and his personality, deciding that he

> has produced an excellent volume both from the literary and from the financial point of view. His editorials have frequently been a diatribe against some particular class of people, but he has on no occasion stooped to gratify private spleen. It takes a strong man to refrain from this. In private life he is quiet, and somewhat inclined to be shy on first acquaintance, but when one gets to know him better he opens out considerably.

By now Neill had decided to try his luck in journalism. Having at last a sense of purpose was a step in the right direction for him; translating this into a real-life job outside the university was quite another matter. His first few job applications to Fleet Street made no impression at all – not one editor bothered to reply – and he was forced to lower his sights for a while. A university friend, R. Scott Stevenson, helped him to get a job in Edinburgh, editing a one-volume encyclopedia for the publishers T. C. and E. Jacks. It was something of a hack job: many of the contributors sent in their material in illegible longhand; other pieces that he commissioned were well over length, and he had to learn to prune them ruthlessly; some were so poor that he had to scrap them altogether and, with the help of existing encyclopaedias, write them himself. Though he found the work tedious, it did give him an understanding of the value of precision in writing, a lesson that he was to find useful for his own writing.

At Jacks Neill worked for their editor and literary advisor H. C. O'Neill, who had previously been on the *Daily Mail*. O'Neill persuaded the directors of the firm that they should have their editorial office in London, a prospect that Neill found 'both wonderful and inevitable'. Though by now his early ardour for Barrie's fiction had cooled, he still saw him as a model in other respects. Neville Cardus, in his autobiography, recalls Barrie's attraction for potential young journalists:

> All my earliest aspirations towards journalism had been kindled by reading Barrie's *When a Man's Single* and *My Lady Nicotine*; during

the early 1900s he symbolised a young man's most romantic notions about freelance work in Fleet Street, pipe-smoking, and lodgings in London, and letters from editors commanding more and more articles.

At this particular time, Neill was very conscious of following in Barrie's footsteps, as indeed he had been doing for a while. Barrie too had suffered poverty in his university days in Edinburgh, existing on oatmeal porridge, penny rolls and glasses of milk. While there he had read Honours English, and become the freelance dramatic critic of the *Edinburgh Courant*, qualifying, as did Neill later, for free theatre tickets. After Edinburgh he had worked on the *Nottingham Journal* before coming to London, and fame. And, in Neill's second year, the celebrated Scot had been given an honorary degree by Edinburgh University, and had called the city 'the most romantic on earth'.

Now approaching thirty, Neill arrived at King's Cross station one Sunday morning in the autumn of 1913. He would undoubtedly have opted for the kind of reception his fellow-Scot had received on arrival in London, in preference to that of his other two literary mentors. While Shaw arrived in 1876 without work or money and spent several penniless years writing novels which he detested, and while Wells came there with enough money to live for a month at subsistence level, and took eight years to make it as a writer, Barrie got off the night train from Kirriemuir in 1885 to find that one of his first stories had been printed in the *St James Gazette* the previous evening. Neill at least had a job and a salary, and immediately found himself some lodgings just off Hammersmith Broadway in west London.

Yet he very quickly came up against the very same problem he had encountered in his first year at Edinburgh – loneliness. He spent Christmas with the O'Neill family, evidently having nowhere else to go. The only person he knew in London, his actress friend Dorothy, had left to go on tour a week after he arrived. 'For the first time in my life, I learned the truth of the platitude that a man can be loneliest in a crowd. When my work was over I had no one to speak to.' Still in many respects shy and unforthcoming with strangers, he took to going for long walks out into the suburbs, or hiring a skiff on the river at Richmond, hoping to have some romantic meeting that would end his isolation. Another disappointment was Fleet Street itself: the streets were meaner than he had expected; and he never bumped into the editors of the national newspapers, as he had half expected to do. (In Barrie's *When a Man's Single*, the newcomer to Fleet Street 'could not resist looking into the faces of the persons who passed him and wondering if they edited *The Times*'.) For a while he settled into what an earlier literary hopeful, Thomas Hardy, defined as 'the fitful yet mechanical and monotonous existence that befalls many a young man in London lodgings'.

Two events then effected a change in his life. His brother Neilie, who had spent eighteen months as a ship's doctor travelling along the coast of South America, now returned to London and secured an appointment at

Rochester Hospital. The brothers moved in to a studio flat, where they were joined by J. B. Salmond, who was now a sub-editor on the *Daily Mail* having written for the *Boys' Own Paper*. The three lived on sardines and tinned salmon, and Neill began to associate with 'carefree lads from the Northcliffe Press'. He tried his hand at writing a serial for a woman's weekly, in the hope of increasing his income: the result, when read out loud by Salmond, was greeted with hoots of derision by his friends. He became interested in boxing, again through Salmond, who fought a number of amateur fights. Neill acted as his sparring partner, and went with him to his contests. His social life developed to such an extent that he had an affair with the wife of a well-known musician, and was lucky not to be named as co-respondent in the subsequent divorce proceedings.

The other major change was in his work. Once the encyclopaedia was completed, O'Neill suggested and was put in charge of another project by Jacks: a *Popular Educator*. This type of book was much in vogue during this period: *Harmsworth's Self-Educator* and Arthur Mee's *Book of Knowledge* were two of the better known examples. Neill was asked to compile the English Literature, Language and Mathematics sections, and spent many days in the Reading Room of the British Museum, ploughing through volumes of literary criticism in search of second-hand opinions about Great Authors, many of whose works he had never read. The end result included some bizarre statements, which have nothing of Neill's personal stamp on them. He wrote, for instance, that 'Blake was a philosopher with ideas ahead of his time; consequently he was known to a coterie only. Burns, as a man of his time, a keen observer, a graphic describer, a malignant laugher, a sweet singer, was lionised in Edinburgh. His idea of freedom is platitudinous; a man who prided himself on being a Jacobite was not a democrat.' He dismissed Burns as 'artistically hardly more than inarticulate', while Shakespeare, Neill concluded, was 'no innovator. . .he appears to have no definite criterion for life. . . his outlook is frankly that of a hedonist'. Some sections, however, were less derivative. That on literary style, for instance, shows that he was already interested in matters of language, and how best to write briefly and without verbosity: ' "Lucy in vain sought the dreamy realms of Morpheus, but the dismal wail of feline wanderers kept recalling her to the stern realities of a grim world." This is merely a flowery way of writing: "Lucy could not sleep because of a cat's concert on the tiles." '

Neill then moved on to the section on Drawing, for which he used his own illustrations (this section did not appear in the final version), after which his job came to an end. Though he was now mingling with journalists, there seemed little prospect of breaking into the world of newspapers and journals. He got as far as an interview with a daily paper, to be told by one of the staff that he should conceal his degree qualification if he wanted to have any chance of getting the job. Whether he did this or not, he was not appointed. An evening paper invited him to apply for the job of drama critic, and gave him a trial. Again he didn't get the job: the editor, Neill recalls, was not impressed by his desire to analyse the play and its characters. But then his luck changed. In the *Morning Post* he saw an advertisement for an art editor for a new magazine. To his astonishment he got the job, even though two very experienced art editors were also in for it. The editor had apparently been intrigued by his frivolous application, and offered him a salary of £150 a year.

At last he had his foot in the door. From Long Acre in Covent Garden, where Jacks had their offices, Neill moved across to Fleet Street itself. The *Piccadilly Magazine* had rooms in number 40, a solid, six-storey block close to the junction with Fetter Lane. From the French windows and balcony, Neill could look across to other familiar newspaper offices: the *People's Journal*, the *People's Friend*, the *Sunday Post* and, just to remind him of home, the *Dundee Courier*. He soon found that his new job was something more than would normally be expected of an art editor. He did commission drawings for short stories, suggesting to the artists the scenes which might be most worthy of illustration. But the editor, a Mr Vincent, also allowed him to help in the initial sifting of material submitted – Alec Waugh and Horace Vachell were among those who sent in stories. He even gave Neill the responsibility of rejecting contributions. One rejection gave him particular pleasure: 'When returning a serial to H. G. Wells' agent as unsuitable, I felt myself grow inches higher,' he recalled later.

Even this didn't fully occupy his time, and he was asked to do interviews with celebrities of the day. One was George Robey, whose comic act Neill had already seen in the music halls: 'I had never met so solemn and pessimistic a man.' Another was the champion jockey Steve Donaghue, whom he met while working on a piece on the human behaviour of animals. He also interviewed Bombardier Billy Wells, the British boxing heavyweight champion, for a symposium on the controversial issue, 'Should the Knock-Out Be Abolished?'

It was probably while working on the new magazine, though not necessarily in his role as reporter, that Neill visited the criminal courts in Bow Street near to the *Piccadilly* offices. There he saw men and women being tried and sentenced, sometimes for relatively trivial crimes – in one case a homeless child was sent to prison for stealing a pair of boots. Scenes such as these made an impression on him, and contributed to his growing conviction that such forms of punishment were both unjust and damaging. A year later he wrote that 'a criminal cannot help himself; heredity and environment make a man good or bad'. He referred to 'the environment that makes millions of children diseased morally and physically'; and 'the law that punishes a man for the sins of the community'. He concluded that 'there should be no prisons; if a man is a murderer he is not responsible for his actions, and he must be confined. . . but not in prison. Our present system is not justice; it is vengeance.' Already he was showing a general interest in the social aspect of crime and punishment, though there was nothing exceptional in this sort of viewpoint among social reformers of the day; in 1905, in the preface to his play *Major Barbara*, Shaw had described imprisonment as 'an act of diabolical cruelty'. It was still a little while before Neill was to become preoccupied with the motives of *individuals* who behaved in an anti-social or criminal manner.

It may also have been Shaw whose example prompted Neill while he was in London to embark on a brief and initially unsuccessful career as a public speaker. Thirty years before, Shaw had preached the gospel of Marxism from a cart at Speaker's Corner in Hyde Park. When he in his turn came to London, Neill, now saturated with the socialist ideas he had absorbed at university, joined the Westminster Labour Party, and in his enthusiasm attended small meetings in St James, 'to talk and plan a new world'. He too 'talked socialism' in Hyde Park: together with two fellow-students from Edinburgh, he tested out with a live audience some of the ideas he had put forward in print in the *Student*. On one occasion he was thoroughly humiliated in debate, when an articulate post office worker demolished his argument that the post office provided a fine example of socialism in action. Later Neill recalled the episode ruefully: 'My ignorance of politics and economics was profound,' he wrote. The experience did, at least, give him his first taste of a hostile audience, though of a rather different kind than those which he was to meet later. The mere fact that he felt able to stand up on his soapbox also suggests a gradual growth in confidence, as well as a developing interest in politics.

Soon, however, political matters of infinitely greater moment than the structure of the post office occupied his attention. The first issue of the *Piccadilly Magazine*, which included an article entitled 'The Real German Danger – The Crown Prince!', was scheduled to appear at the end of August 1914. The international events which prevented it from doing so brought yet another abrupt change to the course of Neill's life.

CHAPTER 4

A Dominie in Doubt

Many a night I feel disheartened. I feel that I am on the side of the bairns.

A Dominie's Log, 1916

At the eleventh stroke of the clock, the crowd. . . burst with one accord into 'God Save the King'. . . .The great crowd rapidly dispersed in all directions, most of them running to get home quickly, and as they ran, they cried aloud rather hysterically, 'War! War! War!'

This was the scene in Parliament Square in London on Tuesday 4 August 1914, observed by a reporter from *The Times*, as Britain's ultimatum to Germany to withdraw from Belgium expired. It captures the mood of fervent enthusiasm which the huge majority of the population felt for what H. G. Wells misguidedly called 'The War that Will End War'. Even the Labour Party dropped their opposition at the last moment – Ramsay Macdonald and a few other lone radical voices were the only ones in Parliament to dissent from the general view that the Germans should be 'taught a lesson'. The *Journal of Education* declared, 'No one in England, except a few cranks or professional jesters like G.B.S., now needs convincing that our cause is just.'* Many men joined up immediately war was

---

*Shaw's pamphlet 'Common Sense about the War' brought down almost universal abuse upon his head. In it he suggested that the violation of Belgian neutrality was a trumped-up excuse for British intervention, and that the soldiers of all armies should shoot their officers and return to their home countries.

declared; and when Lord Kitchener, the Secretary for War, asked for a further hundred thousand, he found himself with nearly double that number of recruits in the first week of September alone.

One of the very first casualties of the war was the *Piccadilly Magazine*, whose first issue had been due to appear at the end of August. Once war was certain the magazine was abruptly closed, leaving Neill's journalistic ambitions frustrated. He was still in London on the night the war began, staying in Windsor with an old university friend, D. G. Watson, who was now a doctor and, like Neill, a socialist. As they sat up late discussing the coming war, they could hear the Life Guards celebrating noisily nearby. Later Neill recalled: 'Like most people, we were quite vague about the question, and the only thing we strongly agreed upon was that Germany had asked for it, and was going to get it too.' He seems to have been less enthusiastic than most about joining up, but ready to do so with reluctance. However, his friend Watson advised him that an inflammation of the leg – which had caused him to have an operation a few months before – would disqualify him from acceptance. Neill returned to Scotland in some perturbation, evidently with some guilt feelings about this let-out, though his leg was swollen and numb and a second doctor had confirmed Watson's opinion. Once again he was back home, without a job, with the prospect of that 'last resort' becoming a reality again.

He didn't have long to wait. After a few weeks he received two job offers in Scotland by the same post: that of English teacher at Tain Academy in the north-east beyond Inverness; and the Headship of Gretna Public School in the south-west, near the English border. The opportunity to be in charge of a school seemed to him preferable to being a subordinate yet again. His decision is reflected in the Gretna school's logbook entry for 15 October: 'I, A. S. Neill, entered upon duties as Interim Headmaster of this school.' His label underlines the common feeling at the time that the war would be over in a matter of weeks, perhaps even by Christmas. Neill's predecessor, Thomas Blackburn, had been a member of the Territorial Army, and as soon as the war started had been granted a temporary commission in the King's Own Scottish Borderers 'for the duration'. His last logbook entry as headteacher ended with the comment: 'I have left "hints" for future guidance.' Whatever these hints were, it soon became abundantly clear that the new Interim Head was going to run the school in his own way, and in a thoroughly unconventional fashion.

Gretna was then little more than a hamlet, with thatched cottages grouped around a green, where men halted for the night with their droves of cattle on their way over the border to the English market towns. The life of the community was marked by events similar to those which Neill had experienced in his youth at Forfar: market days, fairs, church services. Social events at the village hall included dances, whist drives and concerts, and soirées given by the Temperance Band of Hope. There was also the occasional cinema show, where some of the early silent films were shown. The villagers themselves worked as signalmen, platelayers, clerks and porters on the railway; as 'fee'd' labourers on the surrounding farms; or as

workers in the peat industry. Gretna of course had its share of artisans too
– a clogger, a joiner, a blacksmith. It was the latter's shop at Headless
Cross which gave the village a reputation well beyond the parish boundaries: couples eloped there from England in order to go through a clandes-
tine marriage, usually in defiance of one of the parents concerned. By the
time Neill arrived the laws had been amended, though it was still possible
for couples to get married there if they fulfilled certain conditions. However,
the Blacksmith's Shop was mostly in use for other purposes, as hundreds
of tourists came to inspect the registers for traces of their ancestors' acts of
defiance.

Whether because of this, or some innate characteristic of these bor-
derland people, Gretna had a reputation for being, as the *Imperial Gazette*
noted in 1865, 'the most outstandingly demoralised and uncivilised parish
in broad Scotland'. Certainly Neill's predecessor had had some battles to
fight when he took over in 1909, even though he had been brought up in
the village, and was both organist and choirmaster. A man of athletic build,
with a dark, heavy beard, and a good amateur boxer, he had, as a family
friend Forbes McGregor recalls, many conflicts 'with a parsimonious parish
school board and a strictly independent community with a tradition of
successful defiant outlawry behind them'. The 1872 Act which made education in Scotland compulsory had not prevented many families from keeping their children off school for days or even weeks, so they could help on
the farm or with whatever work their parents were engaged in. According
to his daughter Jean, Thomas Blackburn 'pulled the school up from what
had been a fairly mediocre concern to one of real progress, discipline and
learning'. In listing the improvements she felt he made, she described her
father as a disciplinarian at school matters, 'as well as life in general'. One
pupil, Walter Roan, remembers him as 'a strict teacher. . . most pupils were
afraid of his tawse.' Another of his pupils, Barbara Johnson, disliked 'his
way of embarrassing people in the class. There was one very shy lass, and
he would imitate her.' A third, David Davis, recalls: 'He used to look out
of the window, and point to the stick he wanted to go and cut out of the
hedge to use as a tawse.' This behaviour was characteristic of the dominies
of the time, though some were harsher than others. Such methods were
already anathema to Neill: but would the children, and indeed their parents
and the community as a whole, accept any other way?

The school itself, a small, red-stone building, and the schoolhouse
alongside it, were situated in a lane on the edge of Gretna, and close to the
adjoining village of Springfield. It was surrounded by fields, with views of
the Solway Moss, Langholme Hills and the Cumberland Fells. In the middle
distance ran the railway line from Glasgow to Carlisle. Perhaps because he
saw the job as only a temporary appointment, Neill lived not in the schoolhouse, but in one of a group of three cottages at The Hill on the Glasgow
Road, about a mile from the school. His landlady, Mrs Craig, soon became
aware of her new tenant applying himself to his typewriter during the
evenings, and often well into the early hours of the morning. Neill felt the
isolation keenly after Fleet Street: 'When my landlady brought in my par-

affin lamp of an evening, and drew the blind of the small window, I felt
that I was separated from the whole world,' he wrote later. Early in his
first year, probably around Christmas time, Neill decided that, while he
would dutifully record in the official logbook of the school 'all the futile,
never-to-be-seen piffle about Mary Brown's being laid up with the measles',
he would in a private log 'write down my thoughts on education'. For the
next two terms he did precisely that, mixing anecdote and reflection, incident and theory: the result was subsequently published as his first book, *A
Dominie's Log*. This was not, as has been suggested, a work of fiction, but
an authentic account of Neill's initial efforts to change 'a hard-working
school into a playground': many ex-pupils were able to identify individual
incidents and characters as being drawn from real life. It also, he soon
found, fulfilled another purpose: 'I began these log-notes in order to discover my philosophy of education, and I find that I am discovering myself.'

For a brief moment, from training rather than instinct, Neill attempted
to play the role of the conventional dominie. On his second day, sensing
that the children were testing him out, he strapped one of the boys, for
'insolence'. He wanted to get rid of the tawse, noting early in the *Log*: 'I
have not used the strap all this week, and. . . I hope to abolish it altogether. . . . I see that it is only the weak man that requires the strap.' One
day he put it in the stove that heated the school, vowed never to use it
again, and kept his word. 'It was difficult, because they had been accustomed to being beaten up. Still, I got over it,' he remembered later. It was
a gesture that brought him considerable relief: 'When I lost my leather
tawse for ever I lost my fear of my pupils and they lost their fear of me,'
he recollected. Having thrown away the traditional symbol of authority,
he proceeded to divest himself of many of its other accoutrements.

Walter Roan, who stayed on for one term under Neill, recollects his
'easy-going manner – he used no punishment, yet maintained perfect control. . .the pupils relaxed into an easygoing freeness which was unknown
prior to his taking over.' Neill's chief aim was to allow the children to have
as much freedom as possible: 'I want a bairn to be human, and I try to be
human myself.' To achieve this, he took down most of the barriers that
normally existed between pupil and teacher. He summoned the children to
school by playing a bugle; his rendering of 'Come to the Cookhouse Door,
Boys' could be heard right across the fields around the village. He found
that he didn't mind if they talked during lessons, and let them do so. 'We
never asked to leave the room, we just up and went,' remembers one of his
pupils, Elizabeth Sword. He began to allow them to break away from the
normal lesson plan. 'His method of teaching was very simple; we just did
what we liked', she recalls. 'For instance, I was good at arithmetic, so I did
nothing else.' Soon the pupils were allowed one 'free' day, when they could
choose their own activity entirely. The older ones were allowed to spend
the whole day in the 'manual' room, or to take the books outside into the
fields. During the winter Neill would help them make a snowman instead
of a lesson, or extend playtime so that both he and the children could have
an extra half-hour on the playground slide. 'He was a kind, gentle man,

and we all loved him, especially the girls,' was the recollection of another pupil, Agnes Macdonald. The children held tea parties on Friday afternoons in the cookery room, and Neill and his two female assistant teachers would be invited. He joined in some of their games with a will, as Barbara Johnson remembers: 'In one game, Mr Neill and me were supposed to elope, and we went into the joinery, and he put a curl from my hair round my finger, and the boy in the joinery was supposed to be my husband, and so he and Neill pretended to have a stand-up fight.' Again, as in Newport, there were nature walks and sketching rambles, which often ended up as kite-flying expeditions or races, or culminated in a quick dip in the nearby Solway Firth. He widened the nature study activities by building a pigeon-house, and a pond in the playground into which he put some fish.

In shedding his dignity in this manner, Neill was perhaps looking for the carefree childhood that he had never been allowed. But his motives for changing the school lives of his 'bairns' were not merely a result of his own experience. In his *Log* he confessed: 'My work is hopeless, for education should aim at bringing up a new generation that will be better than the old. The present system is to produce the same kind of man as we see today. And how hopeless he is.' He thought despairingly of the fact that, whatever he did, the boys in Gretna would end up as farmhands, the girls as servants or factory workers, wage slaves who would simply accept society as it was. But, another day, in more optimistic vein, he declares that 'I shall lead my bairns to doubt everything'. He decides that he will 'help them to find an attitude. Most of the stuff I teach them will be forgotten in a year or two, but an attitude remains with one throughout life. I want these boys and girls to acquire the habit of looking honestly at life.'

Neill was determined that his pupils should be allowed to behave in a natural manner in school, and not be required to learn and employ the formalities that traditionally passed between children and adults. His predecessor, Thomas Blackburn, had told the children: 'Always remember that manners will carry you through this world.' Neill took a completely opposite view, noting in his *Log*: 'No, I do not teach manners. If a boy "Sirs" me, he does so of his own free will. I believe that you cannot teach manners; taught manners are always forced, always overdone.' In what is probably a reference to his tortured experience under James Calder at Kingskettle School, he went on: 'I once was in a school where manners were taught religiously. I whacked a boy one day. He said: "Thank you." ' Now he was actually in charge of a school he was able to a great extent to set the tone, and to positively encourage the children to treat him as a friend rather than an awesome adult to whom deference was due. In this he was lucky enough to have the willing support of his assistant teachers, May Macdonald, Bell Duncan and Christine Wilson, who seem to have welcomed the loosening up in the running of the school.

In an effort to get his pupils 'looking honestly at life', Neill made some radical changes, both to the content and the style of their lessons. He took to reading the war news from the paper to them in the mornings, trying to make them think about the conflict. 'I find it difficult to discuss the causes of the war with the bairns. I refuse to accept the usual tags about going to the assistance of a weak neighbour whom we agreed to protect. We all want to think we are fighting for Belgium, but are we?' He read Ibsen's *An Enemy of the People* to them, and tried to draw some parallels with a hypothetical situation, in which Gretna suddenly became a health resort faced with a similar civic dilemma. The question of Votes for Women was in the air, so he also introduced this topic to the children:

> I tried to show them that the Women's Movement was a much bigger thing than a fight for political power. It was a protest against the system that made sons doctors and ministers, and daughters typists and shopgirls, that made girls black their idle brothers' boots, that offered £60 to a lady teacher who was doing as good work as the man in the next room with his £130.

Many schools in Britain were encouraging children to contribute to the war effort, by starting a school garden, sending parcels to prisoners of war, making sandbags, knitting socks and mufflers. They were encouraged to write essays on Patriotism, to sing the national anthems of Britain's allies, and to salute the flag on Empire Day. Neill appears to have had no interest in any of this, concentrating instead on getting the children to question ideas and conventions, and trying to create an environment in which their own personalities would be allowed to develop.

The result was a dramatic change in almost every subject. Neill was compelled to give religious instruction, though he felt this was really the duty of the local ministers, and that he was hardly the most appropriate person to tackle the job: 'I am just enough of a Nietzschean to protest against teaching children to be meek and lowly', he wrote in his *Log*. So he confined the lessons to having the children read from the Gospels, and meanwhile introduced discussions about the scientific views of creation. He tried, too, to show that there were other religions that should be considered, 'that Muhammudans and Buddhists are not necessarily stupid folk who know no better'. Occasionally he would make the RI period into a singing one, inserting *Onward Christian Soldiers* 'to save my face, or maybe to salve my conscience'.

He found much to criticise in the textbooks available, especially the children's Readers, filled with excerpts from authors such as Fielding, Hawthorne, Borrow and Dickens. Neill's view was that children liked complete stories, filled with bright dialogue and rich in incident. He scrapped the existing Readers, and brought in a number of 'sevenpennies', stories by Jack London, Anthony Hope, Rider Haggard and Wells that he had enjoyed as a young boy. He abolished homework, preferring to sit alongside children to show them their mistakes, and refused to teach spelling as was normally expected: 'Mistakes in spelling and grammar are minor matters, what I look for are ideas,' he wrote in the *Log*. In composition he suggested they write autobiographies – not of themselves, but of inanimate objects: a hat, a boot, an old penny, a nose. Barbara Johnson remembers a variation of this idea: 'He was a great one for autobiographies. There was a pond in the school yard, and a shed there too. So the conversation had to be between the shed and the pond. That was his way of getting us to learn inverted commas.' He also invited the children to write their own obituaries; to tell the story of waking after a thousand-year sleep; to write about being invisible; to imagine they were 'the last man alive'; to describe the arrival of a hen in the kirk. The suggestions emphasise his own style of humour and liking for the absurd, as well as his intention to encourage the children to use their imagination, which he saw as the source of ideals.

He also believed that mathematics, his own favourite subject, should appeal to the imagination, that it was an art as much as a science. So he scrapped the rural arithmetic book he had inherited: 'It is full of the sums of the How-much-will-it-take-to-paper-a-room? type', he wrote scornfully. 'This cursed utilitarianism in education riles me. Who wants to know what it will take to paper a room? Personally I should call in the painter, and take my meals on the parlour piano for a day or two.' His disgust with the mechanical nature of traditional learning was reinforced when he got hold of the examination papers for the previous year's bursary competition for Annan Academy, the neighbouring secondary school. A typical question in the English paper was: 'Name the poem to which each of the following lines belongs, and add, if you can, the next line in each case.' Neill noticed that, with his Honours English degree, he could only name six of the ten poems. A further question asked for 'an essay of twenty lines or so on any one of these subjects: School, Holidays, Examinations, Bursaries, Books'. He thought the examiners could have added 'a few other bright interesting topics such as Truth, Morals, Faith, Courage'.

He was also critical of the history section, which offered such questions as 'Name an important event in British History for each of any eight of the following years: 1314, 1688, 1759, etc.'; and observed wryly in his *Log*, 'and Wells says that teaching is the most creative profession of all!' History, he believed, should be making children think, instead of forcing them to digest and repeat mere incident. He disliked the nationalistic bias of most textbooks, recalling how he had been misled as a child: 'My early impression of the Indian Mutiny was one of very noble English people being massacred by hell-fiends.' He felt the normal school history book was 'a piece of snobbery; it can't keep away from the topic of kings and queens. They don't matter; history should tell the story of the people and their gradual progress from serfdom to... sweating.' He looked ahead to the way in which the war would be presented to pupils in the future: while school histories would talk merely of the treaties and blame it all on the Kaiser, 'the real historians will be searching for deeper causes; they will be analysing the national characteristics, the economical needs, the diplomatic methods of the nations... they will relegate the Kaiser to a footnote.'

In his determination to 'tear all the rags of hypocrisy from the facts of life', to 'form minds that will question and destroy and rebuild', Neill was treading a difficult path. By now he was a convinced socialist, heavily influenced by Shaw, enthused by William Morris's ideas of Utopia, flirting with Nietzsche and Schopenhauer, and a regular reader of radical journals such as the *New Statesman* and the *New Age*. The latter journal particularly took his fancy: 'The magazine is pulsating with life and youth,' he wrote approvingly. 'Every contributor is so cock-sure of himself. It is the only fearless journal I know.' The *New Age* was edited by A. P. Orage, a former member of the Fabian Society then dominated by Shaw and Beatrice and Sidney Webb. His 'Notes of the Week' Neill thought to be 'easily the best commentary on the war I have seen', and he embraced with enthusiasm the particular brand of socialism advocated by Orage, known as Guild Socialism. Under this system, the workers would have a say in the production of goods, the idea being that 'the productive life of the country should be run and organised by self-governing democratic guilds, each embracing all workers in a service or industry'. The guilds would handle the organisation, giving the workers both status and responsibility, while the state provided the capital.

Neill was for a while attracted to these ideals. In an imaginary encounter between a trade union official and the dominie which Neill put in to his second book, *A Dominie Dismissed*, published in 1917, the dominie – 'the only socialist in the village' – urges the unions to destroy capitalism by taking over the state and running it on Guild Socialism lines:

> At present we are selling our labour to the highest bidder, and in the process we are selling our souls along with our bodies. Each industry will conduct its own business, not for profit but for social service; no shareholders will live on our labour; we shall give our members pay instead of wages.

But he also felt that the workers would be hopeless without their managers, arguing: 'What can you expect from a section of the community that has never been educated?' Already his Utopian leanings were tempered by his endorsement of Ibsen's phrase in *An Enemy of the People*, 'The majority *never* has right on its side.' This conviction was to be strengthened rather than weakened in the years to come.

In opening out his lessons, and inviting children to question and argue with him, Neill seems to have found it hard not to assume the role of preacher as much as teacher. On the one hand, he felt that 'I do not preach morality for I hardly know what morality is. . . . I judge not, and I mean to school my bairns into judging not.' This belief, which was soon to be strengthened, that adults should not impose their values on a child, was both an emotional and intellectual conviction. Yet, in practice, he was not able to remain totally objective in his presentation of issues such as punishment, capitalism, the press. Nor was he able to shake off a certain didacticism in his teaching style. Much of his teaching, though doubtless entertaining or surprising to children schooled in the old ways, seems to be a matter of speaking out loud his own beliefs, doubts and uncertainties. Similarly, his choice of materials, topics and activities reflect his own likes and dislikes, as he himself acknowledged in his *Log*: 'My theories on education are purely personal; if *I* don't like a thing I presume that my bairns dislike it. And the strange thing is that my presumptions are nearly always right.'

Nevertheless, many of his lessons consist of his inveighing against the iniquities of life under capitalism, as he strives 'to convey some idea of my ideal to my bairns'. One early entry in the *Log* suggests that the Gretna children were by no means the recipients of 'child-centred' education:

> I have been image-breaking today, and I feel happy. It began with
> patent medicines, but how I got to them I cannot recollect.
> I remember commencing a lesson on George Washington. The word
> hatchet led naturally to Women's Suffrage; then ducks came up. . . .
> Heaven only knows how, and the word quack brought me to Beans
> for Bibulous Britons. I told how most of these medicines cost half a
> farthing to make, and I explained that the manufacturer was
> spending a good part of the shilling profit in advertising. Then I told
> of the utter waste of material and energy in advertising, and went on
> to thunder against the hideous yellow tyre signs on the roadside. At
> dinner time I read in my paper that some knight had received his
> knighthood because of his interest in the Territorial Movement.
> 'Much more likely that he gave a few thousands to the party funds,'
> I said to my wondering bairns. Then I cursed the cash values that
> attach to almost everything.

Those of the 'wondering bairns' who look back on Neill's time in Gretna give no hint that they felt 'got at' in any way. On the contrary, they remember above all Neill's informality, and his refusal to compel them to learn. Elizabeth Sword remembers him as 'a kind man, he never strapped a girl, in fact he used the strap very little, and we all loved him'. Barbara Johnson recalls that 'He used to use silly tricks with us when it was our birthday, he would take us over his lap, and "dip the flaps" [spank them] by however many years we were. We really liked him very much.' She felt, though, that 'he was really a bit too soft with the classes; we rather got a bit of our own way'. This last point is echoed by Gladys Parker, whose mother, Isobella Cartner, helped her own parents in the general store in Springfield, and became a firm friend of Neill's.* 'The school was absolute chaos. . .He was very charming, and the kids liked him because he didn't give them lessons.' Ray Hemmings, when researching his book *Fifty Years of Freedom*, talked to some of Neill's former pupils fifty-five years after their schooldays. He found that Neill was

> remembered now with affection and some admiration by several of
> the people still living in the neighbourhood, who as children were in
> his class or who had friends or brothers or sisters there. . . .It is
> generally an amused pleasure that lights the faces of these people
> when they are reminded of this distant dominie. . . there is no doubt

*It was she who helped Neill to fulfil a local ambition: a couple who arrived at the Blacksmith Shop were short of witnesses, and Neill was called from the school to fill one of the two vacancies.

that those who were his pupils thought him 'the cat's whisker' (as one of them put it).

In general, the children's parents do not seem to have been especially disturbed by Neill's easygoing methods. This is surprising in view of the difficulties almost any state school teacher had in breaking away from the expected pattern of discipline. While Neill was working in Gretna, a London teacher, Dorothy Mackenzie, touched on this dilemma:

> It is very difficult to know what to do. I am an elementary teacher, and every class in the school but mine is disciplined by a military method. I have to work as it were by stealth, disguising my ideas as much as possible.

Around the same time, a class teacher in a school in Dulwich was attempting a similar shake-up to Neill, and was soon in trouble. The writer V. S. Pritchett was one of his pupils:

> He never used the cane. Since we could make as much noise as we liked, he got silence easily when he wanted it. . . . I said good-bye to Stephen and Matilda and the capes and rivers of England, the dreary sing-song. We were no longer foredoomed servants but found our freedom. Mr Bartlett's methods were spacious. A history lesson might go on for days. . . .He set us tasks in threes and fours; we were allowed to talk to each other, to wander about for consultations: we acted short scenes from books at a sudden order.

Even an innovator in the celebrated English public schools, where eccentricity at least was often tolerated and enjoyed, could find himself in trouble, as Robert Graves remembers in the case of one of his teachers at Charterhouse, the mountaineer George Mallory:

> He tried to treat his class in a friendly way, which puzzled and offended them, because of the school tradition of concealed warfare between boys and masters. . . . I always called him by his Christian name. . . .This lack of dignity put him beyond the pale with most boys, and all masters. . .yet he always managed to find four or five boys who were, like him, out of their element, befriending and making life tolerable for them.

Dignity and aloofness were still considered essential qualities in the 'good' teacher.

A few Gretna parents did object to Neill's approach, anxious lest their children should fail the exams required to go on to secondary school. Some moved their children when another school was opened on the other side of the village, though this may in some cases simply have been prompted by overcrowding in Neill's school. But there is no evidence of fierce or widespread revolt amongst the parents. There are, though, hints of some dissatisfaction amongst the members of the school board, though Neill later wrote that they 'did not care very much what I was doing'. Agnes Macdonald believes that Neill 'tried then to do what they are trying to do in schools today; he was a man before his time; but the Dumfriesshire education committee did not appreciate it.' One of the school board members was the minister of the local church, the Reverend John Stafford, who, she remembers, 'disapproved of A. S. Neill. Over the years when I met him, he always said to me, "Yes, Agnes, you were one of *Neill*'s pupils" – which was as much as to say that I was no good.' Yet Neill's own recollection is of someone who was personally kind to him, found him his lodgings, and generally welcomed him to Gretna – though he heard that the minister disapproved of his typing on Sundays. John Stafford himself does not appear to have been the most conventional member of the small community. He rode around on a strange green bicycle, which had a hammock in place of a saddle; he invariably had a cigarette in his mouth; and though he talked about the evils of drink in the pulpit on Sunday, he was not averse to 'a wee dram' during the week. It is perhaps difficult to see such a man taking up arms against Neill's highly individual teaching style.*

Neill's only battle of substance seems to have been over the physical conditions in which he had to teach. During his second winter in Gretna the allusions in the official logbook to the state of the school increase both in number and asperity. In December 1915 Neill noted: 'No woodwork or cookery owing to burst pipes and boiler'; 'Closed school this morning owing to fact that fire was not on: no kindling'; 'No marking in morning: no coal and school cold'. In the following term the school cleaner resigned, and five of the girls took over her duties. 'Result – work not properly done. I object to dust in a badly-ventilated room, and I am taking the school in late and closing early.' In March the matter came to a head: 'I asked the Chairman of Board for permission to close school tonight until it has been cleaned. He replied verbally by messenger that he had nothing to do with the cleaning of school. I at once acted. I told scholars that there would be no school tomorrow.' In his unofficial *Log* he was more forthright about the board's imperfections:

> if the School Board would yield to my importunities and lay a few
> loads of gravel on the muddy path commonly known as the
> playground I should almost die of surprise and joy. One learns to be
> content with small mercies when one is serving those ratepayers who
> control the rates.

He also reported that: 'Broken windows stand for months; the plaster of the ceiling came down months ago, and the lathes are still showing. The sanitary arrangements are a disgrace to a long-suffering nation. Nothing is done.'

*This more private aspect of the minister's life was mentioned by a man who, as a boy, did odd jobs for him, until relieved of his duties for having taught the family parrot to swear. It is impossible to be sure whether it was the Reverend John Stafford, Aeneas Gunn Gordon or some other representative of the faith that Neill had in mind when he wrote later: 'When young I got most of my best dirty stories from clergymen, who, when they preached on Sundays, appeared to be holy men.'

Sometimes this tone creeps in to the official logbook, despite his aim to keep the two separate. The administrative side of his job caused him intense irritation. The Education Department would insist on sending back forms that he had filled in incorrectly; the sight of these bits of paper gave him a splitting headache. Form 9b gave him particular trouble, with demands for information which Neill dismissed later as 'The Average Age of the Average Number of Children who have completed God knows what'. Another demand from the Department provoked a terse entry on 24 February: 'SED had demanded last year's registers – attendance and admission, summary, and manual work. The registers have been forwarded with pleasurable indifference, but no reply has been received.' If there is a hint here that someone wanted to take a closer look at what Neill was up to, there is no indication that any significant follow-up occurred. There was of course the annual examination by His Majesty's Inspectors, but even this, though certainly double-edged, was cautiously approving. Neill entered the 1915 Report in the logbook on 9 July:

> Under the present Headmaster the work of the school is being carried on with much earnestness, and the results on the whole are pretty satisfactory in the circumstances. The pupils in the Senior Division are intelligent and bright under oral examination, and make an exceedingly good appearance in the class subjects. More attention, however, should be paid to neatness of method and penmanship in copies and jotters. In the Junior Division spelling is a weak subject. The Infant Division is in capable hands, and the pupils generally do well in all their subjects. Discipline, which is kindly, might be firmer, especially in the Senior Division, so as to prevent a tendency to talk on the part of the pupils whenever opportunity occurs.

The entry ends there; but in his private *Log* Neill ponders on the inspector's words:

> I scratch my head thoughtfully. If the inspector finds the bairns intelligent and bright, why does he want them to be silent in school?. . . I freely admit to myself that the jotters are not neat, but I want to know why they should be. . . I find that my bairns do neat work on an examination paper. The truth is that I am incapable of teaching neatness. . . . I object to my report. I hate to be the victim of a man I can't reply to, even when he says nice things.

He determined to take no notice of the inspector's ideas about discipline.

Neill's earnestness and kindliness clearly made an impression on the inspector, just as it did on the children. Indeed it was perhaps his personality which in part enabled him to go as far as he did in his classroom reforms: he was seen in the village as an amusing oddity rather than a dangerous revolutionary figure. One evening he gave a lecture in the village hall on the subject of 'Children and their Parents'. Despite his generally hostile comments about parents, those who came treated the affair as a huge joke. Opinions about him would have been perhaps based as much upon his appearance as anything else. Sometimes he dressed fairly scruffily, in an old jersey and corduroy trousers, looking, as one pupil put it, 'more like a farmer than a headmaster'. At other times he wore tweeds, or grey flannel Oxford bags and smart ties, of a style quite unknown in the village. 'He was very smart and sophisticated for Gretna,' Gladys Parker remembers. 'He was the only one to smoke Craven A, the other men smoked thick black or brown tobacco.' This slightly bohemian image was reinforced by one of his spare-time activities. He would sit out of doors with an easel, bristol board and a small table, turning out pen-and-ink drawings of the Blacksmith's Shop, Gretna House and other local landmarks. 'According to general opinion among the villagers,' Neill wroter later, 'I was quite a nice chap, but half daft.'

Neill did cause a commotion in one Gretna home, but paradoxically this was as a direct result of an act of kindness on his part, and one that was associated with the traditional role of a village dominie. Barbara Johnson remembers the episode, which had a marked affect on her future life, and also underlined the different ways in which parents treated their sons and their daughters: 'There were one or two of us in the school who were poor, and Mr Neill wanted to help bring us forward, so we could go to Annan Academy. He kept us in at night time to do that. But when my father got to hear of this, he said, "Forget it, you're going to have to look after the house" – we had no mother then. Mr Neill thought that was an awful pity, because he said he would have helped me in every way. I had to leave in the summer when I was 13, to look after the house. So that was my schooling done.' It may have been this episode which prompted Neill to muse on the lack of opportunity for girls, as exemplified in the case of 'Margaret Steel'. In his *Log* he wrote:

> Poor Margaret! When she is fourteen she will go out to the fields, and in three years she will be an ignorant country bumpkin. Our education system is futile because it does not go far enough. The State should see to it that each child has the best of chances. Margaret should be sent to a secondary school and to a University free of charge. Her food and clothes and books and train fares should be free by right. The lassie has brains. . . and that is argument enough.

The bleak future awaiting almost all of his 'bairns' is a theme that Neill touches on several times in the course of the book: he was now able to see at close hand the result of the inequalities between rich and poor with which Shaw and others were concerning themselves.

There is one notable and curious omission from both the logs which Neill kept during his headship. Everyone in Gretna who was in the village on 22 May 1915 remembers that day. At 6.45 in the morning there was a loud explosion from the main railway line across the field from the school. The postman rushed through the village, with the news that a train had been bombed by a German Zeppelin. The truth was slightly different. A troop train, carrying members of the 1st Battalion of the 7th Royal Scots to Liverpool to embark for overseas service, had crashed into a goods train in Quintinshill Siding, and had in turn been hit by an express train. Gladys Parker remembers the sight: 'Mother and I were first on the scene. The smell of flesh was everywhere, the bodies were roasting.' The steam engine had caught fire, ammunition was exploding, fire crept along the wreckage. Neill was woken by his landlady and, with the rest of the village, ran across the cornfield to the accident. Later he remembered the day:

> Men were lying dead or dying; one soldier with both legs torn off asked me for a cigarette, and he grinned as I lit it for him. 'May as well lose them here as in France,' he said lightly. He died before the cigarette was half smoked.

Neill joined a rescue party working under the blazing sun. The dead were put in one field, the injured in another. Many had to have their legs amputated on the spot; others asked their officers to shoot them. Some of the women acted as stretcher bearers, while Neill's pupils ran to fetch water from a nearby cottage. A roll call was held in the field, to find out who had survived. The dead totalled 164, of which nearly half could not be identified; a further 200 were injured. 'It was worse than any sight seen in Flanders,' one soldier said.

To his bewilderment, Neill found that he felt no emotion during those terrible hours of rescue work, not even pity. He was comforted to find that night that the minister had had the same experience. 'We apparently had assumed the attitude doctors and nurses have.' In contrast, he experienced real grief that same evening when, at the mother's request, he went to see the body of one of his pupils, who had been killed by a passing motor-bike on his way to the scene of the accident. He was also distressed to discover that one of the three signalmen whose negligence had caused the accident, and who was imprisoned as a result, was already known to him. 'I had his sons in school, and liked them, as well as their father. To me, imprisoning him was only one of the many signs of barbarity in our legal code.' The incident may have been too overwhelming to have seemed appropriate for either his private *Log* or the school version; the next entry, on 4 June, simply says: 'Today I examined Miss Wilson's classes, and was satisfied with the progress shown.'

By this time Neill seems to have decided that his stay in Gretna was not to be a purely temporary one. In France trench warfare had brought the opposing sides to a virtual halt, the filth and monotony broken by the occasional futile effort, made at appalling cost, to gain a few yards of enemy mud. Thomas Blackburn was still with his battalion; in September he was injured at the Battle of Loos, and taken to a prisoner-of-war camp. Neill decided to hold an Evening School in the winter: his work with the younger children sometimes left him gloomy. One day he noted in his *Log*: 'I feel that I am merely pouring water into a sieve. I almost feel that to meddle with education is to begin at the wrong end. I may have an ideal, but I cannot carry it out because I am up against all the forces of society.' In particular, he found that he was having to come into conflict with parents who still believed in the traditional way of training and punishing a child. 'Many a night I feel disheartened. I find that I am on the side of the bairns. I am against law and discipline; I am all for freedom of action.' An Evening School would give him a chance to carry on preaching his gospel to an older age group. 'I shall have the lads and lassies of sixteen to nineteen in my classroom twice a week, and I guess that I'll tell them things about citizenship they won't forget.'

One of the lassies who enrolled for his evening classes was Jessie Irving, who lived at Springfield Farm, just down the lane from Gretna Public School. The fourth child in a family of eight, she was 16 when Neill arrived in Gretna. An attractive and innocent girl with a merry way about her, she had a talent for mimicry, a fine singing voice, and attracted a number of young men who saw themselves as potential suitors. But she was not the only one being assessed in the village. Walter Roan remembers that 'Neill was watched carefully by prospective young ladies in the district.' 'All the girls were in love with him,' is how Gladys Parker puts it. His relationships with the 'lassies' of Gretna seem to have been affectionate and playful, both in and out of school. As in his student days, he had a basic yearning for friendship; but 'real companionship between the sexes was almost impossible then'. With Jessie Irving he was evidently hoping for something different: the two of them became engaged.

The relationship soon hit trouble, though those who recall the engagement are reluctant to talk in detail about the reasons for this. Evidently Neill took his fiancée at least once to visit his parents in Kingsmuir, where his father was still in charge of the village school. But it seems to have been the Irving family who were unhappy with the match, in particular Jessie's mother, a very forceful woman. It was she, according to one member of the family, who actually broke off the engagement, though there is a suggestion that it was already beginning to cool in some way by then. Neill much later recalled that 'the gulf between our interests was too great.' The difference in their backgrounds evidently played a part. 'She was brought up in the farm, and had only known farm work,' one villager recalls. 'She knew that she would never have fitted in with his people.' Neill suggested that if she came to London with him she would begin to develop in other ways. As one member of the family observed, 'In a little village this would be taken as an insult'. Whatever the details, the break appeared to affect her more than it did Neill. Her brother felt that 'our Jess was never the same after Neill; the gaiety of youth had gone'; later, on the eve of her wedding, she 'still hankered after him'. Later in the war, after Neill had left Gretna, he begged her to write him just one letter, but she refused. He came back at least twice on visits to Gretna and may have had some contact. He kept in touch for a while; and much later, when she was living as a widow in Gretna during the Second World War, he came to visit her again. On that occasion, Neill complained to the friend who drove him there that she had spent most of the visit complaining about his earlier attempts to seduce her, which seemed to have been unsuccessful. Of this period Neill later wrote: 'The red light was sex. . . but in my youth young women did not give the amber and green go-ahead signal so easily.' This may have been a further complicating factor.

In *A Dominie Dismissed*, his second book but a work of fiction, Neill describes a love affair which ends in marriage between the dominie and 'Margaret Thomson', a young girl who 'attended my evening class last winter'. Though the ending is in contrast to the real-life version of events, the portrait of the heroine was, according to Jessie Irving's son Alan, 'my mother to a T'. Given his earlier conflict between his emotions and his ambition, it is hard not to feel that some of the key scenes between the pair in the book reflect the nature of the difficulties that arose between Neill and the country girl fifteen years his junior. The dominie is attracted physically to Margaret, but spends a great deal of time lecturing her, provoking her to reply that she doesn't understand half of what he's saying. She also criticises him for not being like other men, for always analysing and criticising. One night she tells him: 'I am not clever; I am only an ordinary farmer's daughter working in the dairy and the fields. . . .We have nothing in common, and if you met me in London you wouldn't be interested in me at all. You will bring clever women to the house and I – I will sit in a corner and say nothing, for I won't understand the things that you talk about. . . I will stay here, but you must go to your work and your clever friends.' The dominie, musing on the possibility of marrying Margaret, tells himself: 'She knows nothing about music or painting or literature. Unless we are ragging each other we have not a single topic of common interest; we should certainly bore each other during the first-class honeymoon journey south.' Neill dedicated the book 'To the Original of Margaret', and in writing it may have been able to come to terms with the break more easily than he was able to do in the case of Margaret Ritchie.

Despite his involvement with his school, Neill had not lost sight of his intention to return to journalism. The *New Age*, to which he subscribed by post, printed a short sketch of his called 'The Lunatic' in February 1915. A slight and rather feeble tale, it describes the trial of a man who has inserted an advertisement in a paper saying: 'Scot, author and humourist, offers to help any society girl, tired of tangos and futile functions, to find her soul.' This distinctly autobiographical character defends himself against the magistrate's charge that he is involved in white slavery, but is certified as insane for wanting to save women's souls in this manner. The story was not up to the standard of his earlier attempts at light fiction in the *Student*, but publication by a London paper must have given him some confidence. Not long after, he sent the first four chapters of *A Dominie's Log* to the *Scottish Educational News*, which accepted them for publication. Encouraged by this, and by letters both complimentary and hostile that he received from teachers, he submitted the full version of the *Log* to the publisher John Lane at the Bodley Head.* There it landed on the desk of a young

---

*One of those correspondents may have been the publisher Victor Gollancz, who taught at Repton for two years during the war, and later recalled that he had had 'a good deal of correspondence with A. S. Neill'. According to his biographer, Ruth Dudley Edwards, Gollancz was inclined to exaggerate somewhat; but he would probably have been in sympathy with Neill, having been sacked in 1918 for being too innovative at Repton.

editor called Herbert Jenkins, who was on the point of setting up on his own as a publisher. He thought the work too radical for Lane, and offered to take Neill on to his own list.

The book was published in November 1915, and caused considerable interest. Neill was thrilled to see the book published, delighted at the mostly favourable reviews, but also depressed by the critical ones. The popular *Weekly Dispatch* printed a selection of his more provocative remarks, and declared the book to be 'one of the wittiest, one of the most human and one of the most refreshing books that have been written for many a year'. It also suggested that Neill was running his school on 'no-discipline' lines – an inaccurate label with which Neill was soon to become familiar. The more serious papers and journals, such as *The Times*, the *Sunday Times*, the *Daily Telegraph*, the *Scotsman*, the *Clarion* and the *Bookman*, all reviewed it with approval, and before the month was out Neill was honoured with a spirited parody of his style in the humorous magazine *Punch*. The magazine was provoked by the *Weekly Dispatch*'s remark that Neill had displayed 'tremendous courage' in running his school 'on the no-discipline lines', and offered their own extracts from the *Log*. A characteristic paragraph runs:

> I object to age and experience; I am all for youth and empiricism. The duty of a schoolmaster is not to teach, but to preserve the youthfulness of his pupils by adopting their standpoint, and dress. I always wear short, thick pants.

A paragraph from the book was also quoted in the *New Age*'s column called 'Current Cant', and drew this rejoinder from Neill a fortnight later:

> I take it that cant means hypocrisy, and most people take it thus. If the compiler of your column sees any attempt at hypocrisy in the passage quoted, I should not be surprised if he looks upon the Sermon on the Mount as an advocacy of polygamy and vegetarianism.

Perhaps stung by this rejoinder, the paper waited four months before reviewing the book itself, and then scolded Neill on a number of points:

> His heart is in the right place, but where, oh where, is his head?. . . he is trying to make a merit of mere revolt. . . .There is no real reason why his new-found sympathy with children should be made offensive to adults, and Mr Neill must be told not to prejudice his case by an apparent preference for anarchy. . . . He is not quite alone in the world, and there is no good reason why he should appear before it deliberately déshabillé of thought and style.

Neill however was determined to have the last word. In a letter published the following week he wrote:

> I hold that revolt is urgently needed. Every advance in ideas is a revolt against something, and when your reviewer says there is no real reason why my views should be offensive to parents, I marvel. . .

> I set out to tell my scholars the truth that our teachers ignore. . . I
> offend the reactionary parties.

The exchanges mark the beginning of a debate with an often uncomprehending or hostile press and public that was to last the rest of Neill's life.*
 'I began to think about education for the first time in Gretna,' Neill wrote many years later. *A Dominie's Log*, which covers less than a year of his time in charge of the school, reveals, as the reviewer in the *Times Educational Supplement* put it, 'the soul of a teacher struggling to emancipate himself from the shackles of formalism and tradition'. Certainly the chance to organise a school, in a way that allowed for what he saw as the innate goodness of a child's nature, appears to have renewed his interest in teaching as an occupation he might pursue. Yet there are already hints that, if he is to practise his beliefs to the full, he will have to move away from the state system. How, for example, can he break what he sees as the conspiracy of silence about sex?

> In reality I can do nothing. If I mentioned sex in school I should be
> dismissed at once. But if a philanthropist would come along and
> offer me a private school to run as I pleased, then I should introduce
> sex into my scheme of education.

A few days later he records the thought: 'When I am sacked. . . and I half expect to be some day soon. . . I shall wander round the schools of Scotland collecting the folk-songs.' And, shortly after, in a discussion about manners, he acknowledges the need to compromise in his present situation: 'Were I to carry my convictions to their natural conclusion I should be an outcast. . . and an outcast is of no value to the community.' It was an early sign of his awareness of the need to compromise in order to fulfil his aims.
 Neill was also unhappy about the changes that the war was bringing to the village. When Lloyd George took over from Asquith as Prime Minister, he instituted a crash programme to provide the country with the munitions needed for the war. New factories were hastily built, many in rural areas; and one of the largest, to manufacture cordite, was sited on the edge of Gretna. Many of the workers' children came to Neill's school for a few months, until the completion of the school in the new Gretna Township. At one stage Neill had as many as 200 on the roll, in a school designed to seat 136. He then refused to take any more, noting with unaccustomed ferocity in the school logbook that 'school work is impossible in the horrid atmosphere'. It was not the overcrowding, however, that principally concerned him; the children moved to their new school after Easter 1916 anyway. Thinking in the longer term, Neill was depressed at

---

*The book attracted readers from many different walks of life. In August 1918 the Prime Minister, Herbert Asquith, wrote to a friend: 'I was looking for some books in Bumpus' shop and my eye was suddenly caught by the title *A Dominie's Log*. Without further inspection I bought a copy for you. I hope the contents will bear out the promise of the exterior.'

the thought of the effects of the creeping industrialisation on the countryside:

> I look out at my wee window and I see the town that will be. There will be gin palaces and picture houses and music-halls — none of them bad things in themselves, but in a filthy atmosphere they will be hideous tawdry things with horrid glaring lights. I see rows of brick houses and acres of clay land littered with bricks and stones thrown down any way. Stores will sell cheap boots and frozen meat and patent pills, packmen will lug round their parcels of shoddy and sheen.

He envisages a new school geared solely to the commercial and technical needs of the community: once that is built, 'I shall trek inland and shall seek some rural spot where I can be of some service to the community.'

William Morris's vision of Utopia in *News from Nowhere* had made an impression on him, and this is also reflected in a similar passage from *A Dominie Dismissed*. Neill writes an imaginary letter to the Educational Institute of Scotland, angered by a visit he had made to a city school: 'It had nine hundred pupils, and it was four stories high. The playground was a small concrete corner; the discipline was like prison discipline; the rooms were dingy, soul-destroying cages.' He goes on to suggest that the schools cannot be reformed from within, that what is needed is not a change of management, but a new house altogether:

> You know Dundee?. . .well, Dundee is one of the dirtiest slums in creation. At present it has lots of big grey schools. We are going to knock 'em down. After that we are going to build bonny wee schools out in the country; schools that won't hold more than a hundred pupils. There will be lovely gardens and ponds and rabbit-houses. . . .When we insist on taking the kiddies to bonny wee schools the profiteer will realise with dismay that his factory and his slum-hovels will have to adapt themselves to the new attitude of the kids.

The story of Neill's second book, *A Dominie Dismissed*, revolves around a battle for the hearts and minds of the local children, between MacDonald, the new and traditional dominie, and his Neillian predecessor, who has just been dismissed from the dominie's job for giving the children too much freedom. Although the story was a fictitious one, Neill used elements of his own life in it. One character was based on a real local dominie who Neill used to go and see every Saturday. Though he disliked this man's educational views, he liked his personality — a distinction that Neill was usually able to make once he got to know someone personally. In the book he puts into the mouth of the dismissed dominie ideas and views which are indisputably his own, and which indicate how far his ideas had progressed in a libertarian direction. Teachers, he felt, should be no more than enablers in his ideal school:

I would have classes of not more than a dozen pupils. In the free
school I picture, classes would not in fact exist; if there were a
hundred and twenty scholars there would be ten teachers. They
would act as guides to be consulted when necessary. Each teacher
would learn with his or her pupils.

He felt it should be up to the children whether or not they attended school,
but believed that 'Make their schools playgrounds instead of prisons, and
you'll have no truancy. . . .The whole trend of society is to recognise and
provide for the conscientious objector, and society should certainly recognise the conscientious objector to school-going.' If he had his way, 'no boy
would learn to read a word until he desired to read; no boy would do
anything unless he wanted to do it.' Above all other aims, 'the first thing
a child should learn to be is a rebel'.

Neill was also clear that one of the chief obstacles to the creation of
such a free school was the parents. Though here he undoubtedly exaggerates
their hostility for the purpose of the story — it is they who have provoked
his dismissal — his underlying attitude is clearly not a fictitious one, as was
to be shown later. The dominie ponders on his dilemma: 'If the children
had not been going to homes at night I should have trusted to freedom
alone. As it was the poor bairns were between two fires. I gave them
freedom. . . and their parents cursed me.' He suggests, perhaps not altogether light-heartedly, that a board should be set up 'to enquire into the
upbringing of children. We might call it the Board of Parental Control. It
would bring parents before it and examine them. Parents convicted of
stupidity would be ordered to hand over their children to a Play-yard
School.' He concludes that 'there are only the two kinds of message. . .love
and freedom', and that 'you can't reform the schools from within.'

However, any plans that he might be formulating to start a 'bonny
wee school' of his own had to be set aside for a time. In July 1916 the
Battle of the Somme began. By its conclusion in November it had resulted
in nearly half a million casualties, effectively bringing to an end any remaining enthusiasm for the war. In the trenches the poet Wilfred Owen
wrote to his mother: 'I censored hundreds of letters yesterday, and the
hope of peace was in every one.' In Britain pressure to introduce conscription was building up; it was suggested that perhaps half a million 'shirkers'
were avoiding the call to arms; women presented white feathers on the
street to any who they thought came in to this category. In January 1916,
under a new Military Service Act, all unmarried men between 18 and 41
were 'deemed to have enlisted', unless they could show that they had 'a
conscientious objection to the undertaking of combatant service'. This
clause provoked an outcry, and public opinion was hostile to the 16,000
who invoked it. They had to appear before local tribunals, who were
reluctant to grant exemption even on religious grounds, and asked the
'COs' questions such as 'What would you do if a German attacked your
mother or sister?' Some agreed to undertake non-combatant duties, but
6,000 refused to do even this, usually on political, religious or pacifist

grounds, and were arrested and imprisoned. There, many of them were subject to extremely harsh treatment: 73 died in prison or soon after their release, and 31 went mad.

Neill, like many other socialists, was faced with a moral dilemma. After only a few months any belief he may have had in the justice of the British cause had evaporated. At the same time, he was unhappy to see others joining up, and being wounded or killed. At the outbreak of war, his socialist friend Watson had immediately offered his medical services. He became bored with hospital routine, enlisted in a regiment, and was killed in France. Each of Neill's brothers also took part in the war. Percy, only 19 when the war started, joined within a few weeks, and was subsequently invalided out after being wounded. Neilie joined the Royal Army Medical Corps in 1916, and spent the next two years in German East Africa. As for Willie, he had, against his wishes, duly become a minister, and worked in Kircudbright in Dumfriesshire, and for a while in Mauritius, before settling in Ayrshire. In 1915 he joined the Royal Field Artillery, where he became a bombardier, but suffered from wounds and the effects of gas which permanently damaged his health.

Although Neill had enjoyed playing at soldiers in the volunteers at Kingskettle, he was appalled at the prospect of having to do the real thing. At the same time, as he confessed later to a fellow-soldier, 'I thought of being a CO, but hadn't the moral courage.' That he was aware of the courage shown by those who did refuse to fight is clear from one passage in *A Dominie Dismissed*, in which the Neill-like figure is lecturing his sweetheart 'Margaret'. The village girl asks the dominie what a pacifist is, and he replies:

> A pacifist is a man who loves peace so much that people look up almanacs to see whether his name was Schmidt a generation back, Margaret. He is usually a nervous man with the physical courage of a hen, but he has more moral courage than three army corps. He is usually a Conscientious Objector, and it takes the moral courage of a god to be that.

Clearly Neill had experienced conflicting emotions ever since his earlier decision not to volunteer because of his bad leg. After a year at Gretna he did attempt to join the army, but was rejected, and given a certificate to say he was permanently unfit. In August 1916 he went for another examination by the Medical Board in nearby Dumfries, and this time was passed fit 'for general service' – though with the proviso that he was 'not to be called up for service unless by arrangement between the Education Department and the War Office'. It was a further six months before this took place. On 16 February 1917 he noted in the school logbook: 'I am told that I shall be called up on March 2nd. School is in a very dirty condition as usual. Teachers are all suffering from chronic sore throat.' And on 2 March he signed off in brief and unemotional style: 'I leave the school tonight.' Two of his girl pupils saw him off at the station, and Neill gave them each a small leather workbag as a parting gift. It was, as it turned out, his last day as a teacher in the state system.

Neill's spell in the army was short and inglorious, and contained several elements of farce. He joined the 3rd Battalion of the 'Royal Scots Fusiliers Short Service Regular Army for the Duration of the War'. Initially he spent three months at a training camp at Fort Matilda near Greenock, which he later described as 'just a hell of fear. There was no escape; even if you sat in the latrine all morning, some orderly officer would come round.' William Coutts, then aged 18, was in the same camp: 'I was only a youngster, and thought he was a bit of a cynic. He really loathed the place, his heart wasn't in it. It was rumoured that he gave whisky to the sergeant so that he would get weekend leave.' (The rumour was inaccurate; Neill used cigars for the purpose. They had been sent by Walter Martin, the rich cigar merchant, whose wife had read and liked *A Dominie's Log*.) Neill's life was made a misery by one lance-corporal, who picked on him to do the most unpleasant tasks. He proved to be thoroughly inept at many of the basic drill activities; William Coutts recalls that 'when Neill stood to attention on the parade ground, he looked like a question mark'. Nor was he the most spruce in appearance – his sister May remembers him coming home on leave with 'his puttees out of place – he was the most untidy soldier I have ever seen.'

His discomfort was aggravated by the condition of his feet: after an hour's drill in army boots his ankles were raw flesh, and soon he had to soak his feet every night to try to get rid of the blisters. Fortunately, his condition was noticed by a sympathetic major, who decided to find a better use for him. He was 'considered suitable for an Officer Cadetship RGA and recommended as a special case in view of his mathematical attainments' – a reference to his work compiling the Mathematics section of Jacks's *Popular Educator*. 'That book saved my life,' he commented later. His degree and his status as an author caused some of those who had mocked his military deficiencies to change their attitude to him. However, the class divisions in the army bothered Neill considerably. (William Coutts remembers him as 'one of those well-educated chaps you couldn't aspire to'.) The necessity for privates to act with unquestioning obedience to the orders of their superiors was also anathema to him. His previous experience of authority, both at home and in his working life, had given him a hearty dislike for any form of compulsion.

In June he began his cadet training, and hated it, especially the bayonet practice: 'We were told to regard the sacks as Huns who had just raped our sisters, and were instructed to stab them with fitting fierceness.' To his relief he was eventually excused this activity, and in October was transferred to the Trowbridge Cadet School in Wiltshire. Here, for the first time, he found army life tolerable, even congenial. Later he recalled it as 'a most easy time', even though 'the whole battalion laughed its head off because I shined my boots before a parade and swung my arms shoulder high'. The discipline at Trowbridge was more easygoing; the other men, many of them clerks or teachers, were closer to his own class; life was more 'like a university, easy and academic'.

In March 1918 Neill was appointed to a temporary commission as 2nd Lieutenant in the Royal Garrison Artillery Regular Army, and joined a pool of officers in Aldershot waiting to be drafted for active service in France. That month the German army started to advance across the old Somme battlefield, and made some territorial gains. Douglas Haig, the commander-in-chief of the British army, declared: 'With our backs to the wall, and believing in the justice of our cause, each one of us must fight to the end.' Like many others, Neill had no such belief, and could not have relished the idea of fighting to no apparent good purpose, with a strong likelihood of injury or death. It had been calculated that the ordinary soldier was likely to remain unscathed in the trenches for twice as long as an officer, and that officers between the ages of 23 and 33 could count on a longer 'useful' life there than those younger or older. Neill was now 34. For four months he waited while his fellow-officers were despatched to the fighting. He was surprised and somewhat ashamed to find his name continually omitted from the list of officers to be drafted, and felt 'like the lame boy in the Pied Piper story'. (Later he was given, but could not believe, an explanation for his being overlooked: Walter Martin told him that he had secured his exemption from active service through 'a pull at the War Office'.)

The strain of waiting eventually told on him. In June an epidemic of Spanish flu hit Britain, and affected three-quarters of the population. Neill succumbed, as did many other officers in Aldershot; but then his condition worsened, and he had a complete breakdown, suffering alternately from insomnia and nightmares. The army medical officer ordered him to see a specialist, believing that he was suffering from 'neurasthenia'. This 'illness', more commonly described as 'shellshock', was most common amongst those who had actually fought in the trenches, and was particularly prevalent among officers. One of its more celebrated victims was Wilfred Owen. During the Battle of the Somme a shell had exploded six feet from his head, and he had been sent to Craiglockhart War Hospital in Edinburgh. One of the senior men there specialising in such cases was W. H. R. Rivers, who had previously done pioneering work in neurology and ethnology before turning to the newer field of psychology. According to Owen, at Craiglockhart 'a man could discuss his psychoneurotic symptoms with his doctor, who could diagnose phobias and conflicts and formulate them in scientific terminology. Significant dreams could be noted down, and Rivers could try to remove repressions.'

Rivers saw Neill in London, and asked him about his dreams; Neill obliged by describing one in which a snake that he killed kept coming to life again. Neill knew nothing about psychology, and was most surprised at Rivers's interest. Whatever interpretation he put on the dream, Rivers concluded that if Neill was sent to France he would either win the Victoria Cross or be shot for desertion. He recommended a six months' convalescence. And so, on 25 July 1918, as the war turned in favour of Britain and her allies, Second Lieutenant Neill relinquished his commission 'on account of ill health', and returned yet again to Scotland, to lick his purely psychological wounds. Within less than four months the crowds in London were again calling for the King, to celebrate the news on 11 November that 'fighting has ceased on all fronts'. By Christmas Neill himself had returned to the capital he had left so abruptly in August 1914. This time, however, it was not journalism that had lured him to the city.

CHAPTER 5

Homer Lane

AUTHORITY:

The Fundamental Problem of Society.

SYLLABUS

OF

A Course of Six Lectures

WHICH WILL BE GIVEN BY

Mr. HOMER LANE

(of The Little Commonwealth)

At the Central Hall, Westminster,

every Tuesday, at 8 o'clock,

on February 25th, March 4th,

11th, 18th, 25th, April 1st.

I believe that Lane is right. I also believe that the schools will come to see he is right. . . somewhere about the year 2500.

A Dominie in Doubt, 1921

One weekend in the winter of 1917, while he was still in the Cadet School in Wiltshire, Neill paid a visit to an unusual community near Evershot in Dorset. This was the Little Commonwealth, a home for delinquent boys and girls at Flowers Farm, which belonged to the Earl of Sandwich.

> I arrived in time to see a self-government meeting, and a breezy one it was. The Commonwealth was divided into houses, and one house was attacking another on its disorderliness, saying that the rest of the Commonwealth was kept awake late at nights by the unseemly noise coming from the unsocial house. I forget how the meeting ended: all I remember is my surprise to see a company of delinquent children manage their social affairs so easily and cleverly.

Neill's surprise turned to astonishment when he met the man in charge of the community, Homer Lane. 'I sat up until four in the morning listening to him, to all his cases. I'd never heard anything like it in my life. That was the turning point in my career.'

It was Lane's work with delinquent children which turned Neill's own life in that direction. At Gretna and in his earlier teaching career, he had gradually become critical of the accepted ideas about how children should grow and learn. As yet, his attempts at providing them with a different experience had been pragmatic, instinctive and even confused: he retained a belief that reforms could still be made to the school system. His meeting with Lane, and just a few hours' observation of the way the Little Commonwealth operated, were a revelation to him: 'It was a new world that he opened up to me,' he wrote later. That world was one in which the new psychology played a central part in any attempt to understand children's behaviour; and it was through Lane that Neill first heard about Freud's ideas about the Unconscious which were to play such a significant part in his life's work.*

Homer Lane was eight years older than Neill, and had only come to England four years before. In America, his home country, he had started as a teacher, and then become Superintendent of Playgrounds in the city of Detroit. There he allowed children as much freedom as possible to play their own games. He discovered that it was the playgrounds with the most adult supervision in which the rate of juvenile crime increased: crime, he concluded, was essentially a form of play. Later, on a farm outside Detroit, he ran the Ford Republic, in which twenty delinquent boys were given the opportunity to govern their own lives. Lane wanted them to gain self-respect, a quality which he believed the normal apparatus of courts and reformatories had helped to suppress. One way of developing this was to give the boys a personal stake in the governing of their community. At the Ford Republic Lane instituted a Citizens' Court and a regular self-governing meeting, which enabled the boys to create and enforce laws, and to punish staff as well as children for offences committed against those laws. His work provoked enormous interest amongst penal reformers.

In 1913 Lane was invited to take over the Little Commonwealth by the committee of influential people who had set it up. Lane took in sixteen boys and eleven girls, as well as a small number of infant-age children. His method of 'recruitment' was simple and startling. He attended hearings at a Magistrate's Court in London, and offered to take in some of the more difficult cases. Lane was given to saying that he believed in original goodness, and not original sin. He gave evidence of this by entrusting a new 'citizen' of the Commonwealth with the money to buy a train ticket, or by refusing to use handcuffs. His technique was to try to break down the young delinquents' hostility to authority by avoiding the normal attitude adopted by adults. In his view, 'A man who cannot sympathise enough with a group to become one of the gang will never become a useful teacher.' Lane demonstrated this belief in practical ways. Once, when he was building a wall with some of the boys, and noticed that they were discouraged by his greater skill, he deliberately but secretly spoilt his own part of the wall. And when the boys smashed windows at the Commonwealth, Lane joined in the destruction. He encouraged larder-raids, pillow-fights and other anti-social acts, hoping that by removing the adult sanction against

*In *A Dominie's Log* Neill had written: 'Can it be that my God is my ego?' But this appears to have been no more than an indication of a slight familiarity with some of the vocabulary of psychoanalysis: he had not then read Freud or any of the others in the movement.

them he would remove the element of enjoyment. In a famous incident, he incited one boy to smash some crockery, and then dared him to do the same with his watch. The boy backed down from his aggressive stance, his behaviour changed dramatically, and he later became one of the more able judges of the Citizen's Court at the Little Commonwealth. Lane's aim was to turn the children's attention to more fundamental matters, the need to define in practical living terms the question of right and wrong. The children, at his instigation, discussed the question of schooling, and decided that they should be required to attend for a certain number of hours a week. This decision was subsequently reversed, as was one which required them to attend the local church. The self-government was real, and made for a community in which tumult and conflict was regularly present.

By the end of that memorable weekend at the Little Commonwealth, Neill had decided that he would like to work with Lane once the war was over. He raised the possibility with Lane, who replied that he was about to make the same proposal; and the idea was agreed upon. However, quite unknown to Neill, the community was even then on the point of closure, because of an accusation by two of the girls that Lane had 'had immoral relations with them'. Though they soon after retracted their accusation, a subsequent Home Office inquiry led to the withdrawal of the community's certificate as long as Lane continued to be in charge. The Home Office report on which this decision was based was never published, and there was a feeling in many quarters that the action had arisen chiefly from hostility to Lane's pioneering methods, rather than from any belief that he was guilty of the charges made. But the damage had been done. In July 1918 the Little Commonwealth closed down.*

Coincidentally, Neill's breakdown while waiting to be sent to France had occurred in the same week, and he returned to Scotland to recuperate at his parents' house in Kingsmuir. From there he wrote on 6 August:

> Dear Mr Lane,
> Can money save the Commonwealth? I have interested one of my plutocratic friends in your work, a born advertiser and business man. If it isn't too late I shall try to get him to do something. Meanwhile, apart from above, will you send every pamphlet you have on the L.C. to Mr Martin, Grand Hotel, Frinton-on-Sea, Essex. Yrs sincerely, A. S. Neill.

Lane sent this letter on to Lord Lytton, who the previous month had resigned from the General Committee of the Commonwealth, in protest against the closure. At the foot of the letter Lane wrote: 'From author of "Dominie's Log". Have replied that plans for future are not yet complete and that you are helping.'

---

*The details of this extraordinary episode are to be found in David Wills's excellent biography of Lane. Just before his death in 1980, Wills showed me a letter from the Home Office, written in August 1975, which said that the report had been destroyed 'some years ago'. This was Wills's third or fourth application to see the report: previously he had been told that no one was allowed to see it.

Neill later claimed that it was Lane who 'taught me to get at the motive of the child, and the idea of being on the side of the child'. The first half of the statement is broadly true, but the second half is not. *A Dominie's Log* is, at one level, a description of the life of a teacher who eventually finds it impossible *not* to be 'on the side of the child'. Once or twice in the book he even makes this explicit, and uses the precise phrase which was soon to become a cornerstone of his philosophy and practice. 'If I hit a boy the parents side with him, if I don't hit the boy who hit their boy, they indignantly ask what education is coming to. Many a night I feel disheartened. I find that I am on the side of the bairns.' Yet Lane certainly made Neill aware for the first time of the value of looking at a child's motive for behaviour as much as at the behaviour itself. His opinions about the potential harmfulness to children of imposed adult values also made a strong impression on Neill. Lane believed that 'original sin' was simply the conflict created by adults between what children rightly wanted, and what adults thought they ought to want. He believed the teacher's job was to make children 'natural' again, and not to make them good. 'We believe that children develop bad habits by indulging in them; in reality, children develop bad habits if prevented from indulging in them.'

By the time Neill met him in 1917, Lane was a well-established figure in educational circles. At a conference in Stratford-upon-Avon in September 1915 on 'New Ideals in Education', the American ambassador had noted in introducing him that 'the transformations of character effected in the Little Commonwealth by the deft handling of Mr Lane justify the hope that anything can be done with any child'. The following year, the newly founded *Times Educational Supplement* commented: 'The principles underlying Mr Lane's words will assuredly influence and stimulate the education of tomorrow.' Lane was, indeed, gradually moving beyond the delinquent to an interest in the normal child, and teachers and educationists, as well as those working with 'problem' children, were showing considerable interest in his ideas.

In his lectures, Lane set out many ideas which gave support to and reaffirmed Neill's growing feeling that a new approach to children was required. Lane argued forcibly that the traditional form of education based on fear should be abolished. Teachers must stand down from their position of authority, and let children resolve their own difficulties in an atmosphere of encouragement and freedom. 'Freedom cannot be given,' he stated. 'It is taken by the children. . . .Freedom demands the privilege of conscious wrong-doing.' Schools should re-awaken the play instinct in children, and allow them time to run wild with their friends. Lane attacked the teaching of manners to children, arguing that this gave them a sense of inferiority. Adults, he felt, should both trust and revere the nature of children, and try to understand the processes of their unconscious minds. Such beliefs, derived from Lane's considerable experience of working with children in self-governing communities, came at an opportune moment for Neill: they not only re-awakened his interest in working with children, but provided him with a practical model.

Many of Lane's ideas had a profound and lasting effect on Neill, to such an extent that he incorporated them – sometimes almost down to the precise wording – into his own belief-system. His next dominie book, *A Dominie in Doubt*, reflected the new influence, as he acknowledged in its dedication, written on 12 August 1920: 'To Homer Lane, whose first lecture convinced me that I knew nothing about education. I owe much to him, but I hasten to warn educationists that they must not hold him responsible for the views given in these pages. I never understood him fully enough to expound his wonderful educational theories.' In the book itself, much of which is a debate between 'Macdonald' and the 'Dominie', the latter suggests that the difference between them is that Macdonald 'believes in original sin, while I believe in original virtue', and declares that 'every child is a saint if you treat him as an equal'. He tells Macdonald how to break a child's fear of a teacher:

> By coming down off your pedestal. You must become one of the gang. . . smash a window; chuck books about the room. . . anything to break this idea that you are an exalted being whose eye is like God's, always ready to see evil. . . . I say that anarchy is necessary if these children are to get free from their dependence on you and their fear of you.

He puts juvenile delinquency down to bad education, when schools encourage passivity and bottle up a child's energy: 'No boy who has tools and a bench will express himself by smashing windows. Delinquency is merely misplaced social conduct.' A teacher's best approach when a child is being anti-social is not to intervene himself, but to leave him to his companions: 'The gang is the best disciplinarian,' he concluded.

Perhaps Lane's most important action was to introduce Neill to the revolutionary ideas of Sigmund Freud and his fellow-psychoanalysts in Vienna. Freud's brilliant work in uncovering the unconscious mind, his techniques of free association and dream interpretation, his findings about child sexuality, his discovery of repressions and neuroses – all these had a gradual but ultimately profound effect on people concerned to understand the complexities of human behaviour. Few people in England, even in the professions, then knew of Freud's work: although his *Interpretation of Dreams* was translated into English in 1913, it was not until after the war that his more influential *Introductory Lectures on Psychoanalysis* appeared. Although Lane was in America when Freud lectured there in 1909, it seems unlikely that he came across his work until he arrived in England. In a letter written in 1916 he referred to Ernest Jones, a colleague and disciple of Freud who did much to popularise his work in England. Lane read his *Papers on Psychoanalysis*, and told his correspondent: 'You will find the gist of Freud's psychology in this very readable little book, and see much in it that justifies the Commonwealth.' Freud, in other words, was not Lane's original inspiration, but someone whose ideas generally gave endorsement to his approach. Two years later, after the Commonwealth had been closed, he told one of his former staff: 'I have for a long time been trying to out-Freud Freud. . . .Of course the committee are dreadfully excited about it and deeply prejudiced.' Such a reaction to Freud's revolutionary and often shocking ideas was quite normal for the time – but Lane was by no means a conventional Freudian, as Neill was soon to discover.

It was during his late-night conversation with Lane at the Little Commonwealth that Neill had his first taste of Freud. Initially he was both excited and inspired; yet it was not long before he began to have reservations about certain aspects of Freud's psychoanalytic beliefs. *A Dominie in Doubt* reflects these uncertainties, as well as his increasing doubts about the education system. He confesses that, when he started writing the book, he was 'a more or less complete Freudian', confidently interpreting dreams and behaviour according to the master's doctrines. But by the end he decides that Freud has his limitations, that 'Life is too complex for a "nothing but" psychology'. He finds he cannot accept Freud's view that dreams always represent the fulfilment of wishes; and he thinks Freud has a mistaken belief in 'original sin'. In one passage he sums up what he feels to be the limitations of his insights:

> I am indeed a Dominie in Doubt. What is education striving after?
> I cannot say, for education is life and what the aim of life is no one
> knows. Psycho-analysis can clear up a life; it can release bottled-up
> energy, but it cannot say how the released energy is to be used. The
> analyst cannot advise, because no man can tell another how to live
> his life. Freud clears up the past, but he cannot clear up the future.

Already Neill was moving towards a conviction that education should be an experience in its own right, and not just a preparation for what was to come later. But here it seems he was caught between his desire to let people live their own lives, and a feeling that there should be some formula for living, which could show 'how the released energy is to be used'. It was not long before the former view was to predominate. And, despite his reservations, he remained convinced of the underlying significance of Freud's achievement, as he makes clear in *A Dominie in Doubt*: 'I firmly believe that Freud's discovery will have a greater influence on the evolution of humanity than any discovery of the last ten centuries.' Freud and his co-workers were, he was sure, bringing 'a great message of hope'.

Neill had first heard of Lane when he was teaching in Gretna. A woman who had read *A Dominie's Log* invited him to come to London to visit a school which she was involved with, King Alfred in Hampstead. She also gave him a report of a lecture that Lane had recently given, and introduced him to the head of King Alfred, John Russell. Neill spent half a day in the school, and thought it 'a delightful place'. In *A Dominie Dismissed* he wrote: 'The tone of the school is excellent: the pupils are frankly critical and delightfully self-possessed. And since parents choose this school voluntarily, I presume that the education we call home-life is ideal.' He compared the set-up with his own in Gretna, envying John Russell working with 'children of parents who were intellectual enough to seek a free education for their children in a land where the schools are barracks. "If only I had children like these!" I said to him, but a moment later I thought of my little school up north and I said: "No! Mine need freedom more than these." ' Yet it was perhaps with his own freedom in mind that, once he discovered that the Little Commonwealth no longer existed, Neill wrote to John Russell and got a job in what was then considered by many to be the freest school in England. In December 1918 the King Alfred School magazine reported that 'Ex-Lieutenant A. S. Neill (M.A.Edin.)' would be 'joining the school as a full-time master'.

The school had been started by a group of parents in Hampstead who were dissatisfied with the education available in the neighbourhood. Unusually for the time in England, it was co-educational: such a set-up was thought by many to make the boys 'sissies' and the girls 'tomboys'. It placed emphasis on the 'educational value of personal liberty': there was no religious teaching or observance; the traditional incentives of marks and prizes were ruled out; and the children were encouraged to discuss moral questions freely. There was also a considerable measure of self-government. The Advisory Council consisted of elected representatives from amongst the staff and the older children. It was supposed to act as a forum for discussion, and could both formulate and enforce school rules; the children had a majority on the Council. Most of these ideas were still revolutionary for the time, though Neill by now would have assented to them without hesitation.

Since its founding some twenty years previously, KAS had occupied a large three-storey Victorian house just off Hampstead High Street, built on a slope overlooking the more traditional University College School. On his first morning, Neill was introduced to the children at morning assembly by John Russell, who declared, 'This is Mr Neill, who has more knowledge in his little finger than I have in my head.' This flattering though wildly inappropriate introduction failed to dispel the alarm of some KAS pupils. The reputation of being 'a mad Scots dominie' had preceded Neill; some of the children later told him that they had wondered that first day whether he really was mad, or just a 'crank'. He wore large, unusual shoes, a bow tie and tweeds; and a new set of false teeth made his Scots accent so marked that some of the children found him at first almost unintelligible. One who was there at the time, Patrick Harvey, remembers 'a tall, rather reserved character with a very red face. Whenever he spoke to me, which wasn't often, I could hardly understand a word he said.' Another pupil, R. E. B. Mullins, recalls that: 'We all regarded him as a man from outer space whom one should befriend with caution.' If Neill appeared eccentric and reserved to some pupils, other saw him in a more sympathetic light. Muriel Rocke thought 'he was fun, universally friendly and I think liked by the pupils'. Anthony Horton also has positive memories of Neill: 'He had a rare knack of getting children to talk freely and naturally to him, and would use a smiling, rather abrasive banter. He would often stop a conversation with "Och, awa wi ye, mon." This we loved, and it became a catchword.'

Neill certainly made determined efforts, as he had to a lesser extent in

Gretna, to be 'one of the gang'. He joined in the children's games at playtime, and introduced to them a game from his childhood days, a form of 'tag' or 'he' known as 'Gig or no Gig'. There are glimpses of his determination to allow for, and even encourage, behaviour that would normally be considered anti-social. Peggy van Praagh, whose brother was a pupil at the adjacent University College School, remembers one such incident: 'My brother complained to Neill that we Alfredians were dirty and badly behaved, and used to spit at the boys over the fence of our playground. Neill's answer, delivered in his broad Scots accent, was "Did they aim straight?" ' But his consciously anti-authority stance didn't appeal to everyone. Another pupil, Roderick Garrett, felt that Neill was 'a poseur, always conscious of the impression he made, and thinking it very fine. Once I remarked to him that I wanted to do something, but that I knew I ought not to. Neill's reaction was, "Go on, do it." I refused, and he went on pestering me.'

To most of the children, he was an original and attractive teacher. In English lessons he would set them unusual topics as essay subjects, such as 'Five Minutes to Live' or 'The Autobiography of a Nose' ('When first I began to run', was one boy's opening gambit). He wrote plays to be performed in class, as Patrick Harvey remembers: 'I recall one scene where people were listening to Chopin being played in a drawing room, and were making grimaces; and then the pianist started to play something ultramodern, and everyone's face was wreathed in a smile. I believe it was a satire.' Once he encouraged the 8- and 9-year-olds to write a play, and to produce it themselves for the school concert. Peggy van Praagh, later an eminent name in the ballet world, was in that form: 'Neill was the first person to recognise that I had a talent for theatre production, and to draw it out publicly. I arranged a dance, and taught the others to be Tulip Fairies in the Finale.' Occasionally the children would perform outside the school in a local hall; a member of the audience on one such occasion recalls 'a great, tall lanky young man with rather reddish hair and very short shorts, dressed as a scoutmaster'. Nor was it only in the arts sphere that Neill gave encouragement. He would suggest that children bring in any pebbles they may have collected during their summer holidays, and he would then help them to polish them in the school workshop.

Neill liked the free and easy atmosphere of the school, and found his work in the classroom congenial. However, he soon began to find himself in conflict with the KAS staff. A letter written by one of the parents on 25 February 1919, just a few weeks after Neill arrived at the school, reveals the kind of difficulties he was facing. 'Our poor Mr Neill is having an awful time here in King Alfred's School, where he has just started self-government. Allen [her son] is the chairman of his class and he is in hot water most of the time.' Neill had lost little time in preaching the gospel according to Homer Lane. Although the staff opposed the idea of a form of self-government going beyond what already existed, John Russell, perhaps knowing what the result would be, suggested, after several staff meetings about the idea, that Neill try it within his own class. Neill reflected later on the outcome:

> Naturally, all self-government meant to them was a chance to let off steam in my room for an hour. They made a hell of a row, and teachers in neighbouring rooms got annoyed. At the next staff meeting, they all said it was obvious, of course, that self-government didn't work.

It is not totally clear what Neill's objections to the existing Council were, nor precisely what happened during the self-government meetings within his class. The idea does not seem to have been a total disaster. His class did hold some meetings on their own, and even when such meetings took place with Neill present, he insisted that they should be chaired by a child. On one occasion he refused to be annoyed when a child was reported to have insulted him behind his back. When he was told that staff shouldn't be criticised, his reply was 'Why not?' This encouraged one of the girls to criticise another member of staff, with Neill again being attacked by the children for refusing to intervene or to defend 'Miss Brown'. The wrangle was cut short by the bell for the next lesson; later Neill reflected on the ethics of the issues raised:

> My colleagues when they heard the story agreed with the children; they held that I acted wrongly in listening to an accusation against a colleague. My argument was that I was a guest at a meeting; I had no vote, nor would I have interfered had I been a member of the meeting. I was quite sure that if the bell had not broken up the meeting somebody would have made the discovery that Miss Brown was the proper person to make the accusation to. When they thought that Mary insulted me they sent for me, and I fully expected they would send for Miss Brown. Again I argued that if Miss Brown had favourites the class had a right to criticise her. If she had no favourites let her arraign the class before a meeting of the whole school and accuse them of libel.

From this experience Neill learned two things: that self-government of the kind he favoured required the support in principle of *all* the staff and pupils; and that it was impractical to try to introduce it in a day school, since so much of the children's lives would fall outside the jurisdiction of the meeting. He also found that the school was not quite as 'free' as he had hoped it to be. He was astounded that most of the pupils were quite unfamiliar with the basic swear words – except two of the girls, who had the whole repertoire at their command. He was also disturbed when John Russell gave a long lecture to the children, after a boy of 9 had been discovered kissing a girl of 8. Neill came out of the assembly 'feeling that kissing must be the main sin against the Holy Ghost'. He began to feel that 'I had come to a school whose life attitudes were fundamentally those which had damned my own life in Scotland – moral standards from without.' In essence he put this down to Russell's personality. 'He was God, a

lovable old God, but nevertheless God – and a moralist of great force.'
Neill was especially critical of Russell's view of the school as a place where
'boys and girls are all brothers and sisters', believing that this was an
attempt to repress or ignore normal sexual instincts in the young.

Despite their disagreements, Neill and Russell appear to have remained
on cordial personal terms – and Neill was sufficiently taken with Russell
to imitate his dress, adopting the grey corduroy favoured by the older man.
In the end it seems that it was essentially the self-government issue which
led to Neill's departure after five terms. He related the final break in a letter
to one of Russell's successors at KAS, B. H. Montgomery: 'I wanted more
self-govt; J.R. and staff didn't. J.R. said to me: "Neill, either you or I must
resign." I said: "Me, J.R.; you've been here longer than I have." ' Russell
in fact retired very soon afterwards, and as part of his send-off Neill wrote
a one-act play, called 'The Piper Passes', a version of the Pied Piper story.
Neill himself played the Piper, and seems to have written his own farewell
into the piece. The Piper's music is too sweet for a younger generation of
children, and so, 'Children, I have loved you well, and you have loved me
well, but the time has come when I must away from you.' There is a hint
here that Neill felt it was now time to strike out on his own, and that he
could never adapt himself to a school regime ultimately determined by
others.

It was undoubtedly Lane's influence which was the principal cause of
Neill's inability to see eye to eye with Russell and his staff. Nor was that
influence entirely in the realm of ideas. In October 1918, shortly before
Neill's appointment to KAS, Lane himself came to London. He had no job,
£200 to his name, a wife and three children, and six former 'citizens' of
the Little Commonwealth (two of whom were among his accusers the
previous year). Undismayed by such an unstable position, he rented some
furniture, a house in north London, 36 Highbury Hill, and immediately
took up his second career as a 'lecturer and consultant psychoanalyst'. It
is possible that Neill applied for and accepted the KAS job partly so that
he could be near Lane, whom he knew to be in London. Neill found some
lodgings in the upper part of an attractive late Victorian house, belonging
to Mr and Mrs May, the local greengrocer. Situated at 23 Gayton Road,
just off Hampstead High Street, it was only a short walk from the school,
and within easy reach of Highbury Hill. The Lanes sent two of their
children, Polly and Allen, to KAS because Neill was taking up his appointment there, and the two men re-established contact soon after Neill's arrival
in London at the end of 1918.

Lane soon visited KAS, to give a few talks on psychology to the staff.
There seems to have been mutual hostility: Neill recalls Lane sitting 'with
a face like vinegar', and the staff being 'bloody'. It may be that the hostility
to Neill was transferred on to his friend – it was Neill who, at Russell's
suggestion, had invited Lane to the school. Lane soon suggested that Neill
should come to him for analysis, on the grounds that if he was to work
with children he should be aware of his own Unconscious. Since Lane was
not a qualified analyst, he took 'pupils' rather than 'patients', and called

his sessions with them 'private lessons' – another phrase that Neill was later to take on board. So, every weekday for about a year, when he had done his teaching stint at KAS, Neill changed roles, and became a pupil of Homer Lane. Unlike conventional Freudian analysts, during the 'lessons' Lane did most of the talking, sitting on the fender of the fire in his consulting room, while his pupil sat listening in an easy chair or on the sofa. He would expound his version of the Freudian idea of the Unconscious, and its relation to conscious thought and to moral teaching. He would then interpret his pupil's dreams, using the Freudian technique of 'free association', and discuss his or her symptoms, behaviour and unconscious motives.

Many of those who came to him for help testified to the power of his personality, which gave them a feeling of enormous confidence in his ability. One of his many pupils was J. H. Simpson, a teacher interested in the possibilities of self-government. He recalls the powerful impression made on him by Lane when, in 1913, he came to Gresham's School in Norfolk to talk to the pupils about his work with the boys and girls of the Little Commonwealth: 'As he spoke of their natural and innate goodness, you felt that here was a man who had not only the imagination to understand and sympathise with them, but also an extraordinary capacity for loving those whom he was trying to help, whose love was indeed both the motive and the method of this help. . . . His intuition and largeness of spirit made you feel that with him, rather than with anyone you had ever known, you could discuss the doubts and perplexities that beset your own life. So I for one felt when I first heard Lane, and I know that others felt the same.' Another 'pupil' pinpoints the skills which he displayed during these 'private lessons': 'So many of us were being stifled behind imposed restrictions, bound in intellectual and moral prisons whose locks we could not reach; he had the key which set us all free. His work in life was to break down barriers and release the soul within. . . .To those who knew him only slightly his power of intuition seemed positively uncanny, his penetration magical. How did he know the things which his patients had so carefully concealed, or in many cases were unaware of themselves? How was it that his diagnosis was so accurate, and his unconventional remedies so unfailing?' John Layard, the anthropologist, another who was greatly indebted to Lane, remembers that Lane practised 'a kind of psychic midwifery that set one at one's ease, and banished shame. There was no breaking of resistances. They just vanished. One had the feeling of blossoming.' Layard also recalled that 'his face was a mirror of what one wanted him to be, an elder brother, a younger one, the loving and successful father of a family, an ideal husband, a wise man, one who took life so lightly that he could laugh kindlily at everything, a biting cynic without malice.'

In February 1919, Lane wrote to one of his former colleagues at the Little Commonwealth: 'I only do analysis for certain teachers who are in a position to influence others and a few personal friends who are unhappy in their own unconscious.' Neill, it seems, would probably have qualified on both counts. He was certainly in need of support and guidance at this moment in his life. Towards the end of his second term at KAS, he experienced what he described later as 'a week of a kind of hell that I had never known then and have not known since'. On 16 July 1919 he received a telegram from his parents: 'Clunie gravely ill pneumonia. Come at once.' He left for Scotland immediately. His much-loved sister had for many years suffered from a throat disease; now, within a week of catching pneumonia, she was dying. During her last days Neill sat in anguish at her bedside, in the small room in which as children they had shared a bed. Every morning, he later recalled, he awoke 'feeling that I had been in the deepest pit in Dante's Inferno and that I had been there for a thousand years'. Some of his memories of the days following her death he appears to have put into the final pages of *Carroty Broon*, when Peter's sister Bets is taken ill and dies:

> Night-time was worst of all. When he went to bed he had to think of the yellow box that lay so still in the bed through the wall. Then remorse took violent hold of him. . . .His thoughts seemed as if they would drive him mad, but weeping came to his rescue, and he cried himself to sleep.

Clunie too had gone into teaching, even though she, like Neill, had failed the teacher training college examination. She taught in a village school in Spott, near Edinburgh, and later in Pontefract in Yorkshire. Neill had only seen her occasionally during school holidays, on his increasingly rare visits to Scotland. Yet the bond between brother and sister remained an intensely close one, as Neill recalled later:

> Most men know what it is to have someone who will always understand, someone you naturally turn to in joy or sorrow. To me Clunie was that one: I knew exactly what her reactions would be to anything I said, knew what would make her laugh, what would pain her. I knew also that she was always on my side.

Clunie had clearly supplied him with the kind of understanding, sympathy and support which his parents, whatever their intentions, had signally failed to do. But she had also, according to Neill, made it difficult for him to make a successful close relationship with other women. In Edinburgh during his student days, he later wrote, he and 'Beatrice' 'went through heaven and hell, and I knew that the hell was on account of Clunie. Unconsciously, I compared every girl with Clunie; unconsciously, she hated every girl I loved. While praising them, she subtly made me see their shortcomings.' Similarly, in his only published reference to his relationship with Jessie Irving, Neill described the episode in Gretna as 'a love story – wrecked again on the Clunie fixation'. This psychoanalytical interpretation may have come from Lane: whether it is either helpful or accurate is open to question. Neill recalls that Clunie's death 'killed life in me for months', and there is no doubt at all that he suffered intensely; for several years he dreamt of her again and again. There is less evidence to back his view that it was only after her death that he felt able to have a normal relationship with women.

Clunie's death also had the effect of bringing him a little closer to his parents: for the first time he began to feel some tenderness towards his father. This may partly be explained by the fact that, though he had not quite found his métier, Neill had certainly demonstrated that he was after all 'good for something'. Nevertheless, George Neill was still anxious enough about his son's prospects to offer to help him secure a job as a schools inspector in Australia, through a friend with connections in that country. Neill declined the helping hand. A scene in *Carroty Broon* also suggests that Neill was moved by his father's suffering at Clunie's death:

> But when his father gave a sobbing cry and went quickly from the room, reality forced itself once more into his consciousness. He had never before seen a grown-up man weep, and the sight of his father gave him a strange shock.

Even if he had wanted to, Neill would have found it very hard to conceal his feelings of distress from the perceptive Homer Lane. It comes as no surprise then that the Lane family now took Neill to its bosom: for the next two years he dined every weekend at their house in Highbury Hill. Neill found that he both liked and sympathised with Lane's wife Mabel, a motherly woman who made no emotional or intellectual demands, who simply talked about people and what had happened last week, and was generally overshadowed by her husband's powerful personality.* Neill was, in a sense, to spend much of his adult life looking for the father and mother he had 'lost' in his childhood. In part he found the missing father in the select few 'mentors' that influenced his life, of which Lane was one of the most influential. He also found comfort and even tenderness in his relationships with older women, of which Mabel Lane was an example.

Lane himself Neill found a more complex character to meet socially. At dinner time at Highbury Hill he would sometimes find his host merry, on other occasions laying down the law, on others gloomily silent. At times 'he radiated warmth'; he could be 'charming, always immaculately dressed, genial'. Yet within his own family he could also be dictatorial, as Neill saw more than once. 'I recall the stern hateful face he had on when his son Raymond married the uneducated Evelyn, and how I found Connie, a Little Commonwealth girl of 19, in tears at his home. . . "Daddy has forbidden me to walk out with the postman." I feared him too much to ask him why.'

This last remark indicates how far Neill was the dependent 'pupil' in his relations with Lane. 'I found it hard to be critical because I was so overwhelmed with wonder and joy at his treatment of his Little Commonwealth cases,' he wrote later. 'His attitude to me was a complex one. . . . He liked me, but had an attitude I couldn't fathom. Later a woman patient said that he was jealous of me, but I can't believe that, for I was a nobody, a very weak disciple knowing my inferiority to him.' If Neill was right in detecting ambivalence in Lane's attitude to him, it may have been prompted by Neill's rampant enthusiasm for his ideals. Lane lectured frequently to

---

*'Mabel? She's all right. She just gets on with her knitting,' Lane once remarked.

parents, teachers and other more professional audiences. Neill went to all his lectures, and became a ceaseless quoter of Lane's opinions – to such an extent that Lane described him to another of his patients as 'a bloody sycophant'. Some months after his analysis began, Neill himself gave a lecture on Lane's work at the Little Commonwealth. Lane was furious, accusing Neill of misrepresenting him – as indeed, at this very early stage in his familiarity with Lane's ideas, he may have done. Lane told Neill never to mention his name again in public. Angry at this edict, Neill for a while broke off his analysis with Lane, and took his dreams to Maurice Nicoll, a leading Jungian analyst in London.

Lane's reaction does suggest that he may have seen his 'disciple' as some kind of threat. He was not known for his generosity in acknowledging the achievement of others. When another pioneering educator, Norman MacMunn, sent Lane a copy of one of his books, Neill asked his 'teacher' what he thought of it. 'Its chief fault is that the paper is too stout to use in the WC,' came the reply. Nevertheless, it was Lane who encouraged Neill to do some analytical work of his own. He lent him some books to introduce him to the new ideas in psychology. Oscar Pfister's *The Psychoanalytic Method* was the first, and this got Neill on to Freud's *Interpretation of Dreams*, and then articles by Ernest Jones and other Freudians. By the time he left KAS, Neill's library was dominated by works on psychology and psychoanalysis, dealing with insanity, morbid fears and compulsions, mental conflicts, crowd psychology, the child's unconscious mind, and other similar topics.

Soon Lane suggested that Neill should take on a young woman teacher for analysis – a move that most analysts would have frowned on, but one quite in keeping with Lane's cavalier attitude to professional conventions. Another convention he broke was to become sexually involved with some of his female patients – despite his warning to Neill and others that 'If you kiss one, you'll never be able to analyse her further'. When Neill later left London, Lane took over this young woman's analysis. After Lane's death, she told Neill that, when he was making love to her, Lane often shouted in fury: 'You are not thinking of me, it is Neill you want to sleep with!'

Neill also became a member of a study circle that Lane set up in a house in Regent's Park shortly after he came to London. Here he talked to a number of people, many of them eminent in public life, who were professionally interested in his ideas about analysis. Some of these also came to him as 'pupils'. Lord Lytton, who had been involved with the committee running the Little Commonwealth, regarded him as 'a genius. . .the most original and impressive personality I have ever met', and became his unofficial patron and champion during the crises of his controversial career. Also among his patients were the headmaster of Rugby School, Dr David; H. H. Symonds, who later became the Bishop of Liverpool; the Earl of Sandwich, who had founded the Little Commonwealth; and Dick Sheppard, who initiated the Peace Pledge Union.

With these and other lesser known men and women, Lane effected some remarkable cures for a variety of both mental and physical disorders, and in doing so often bound his pupils to him in a way that made it difficult for them to subsequently break away. His dictum was, 'I want to be like the petrol inside the car, unseen and out of sight'; yet his personality was so magnetic that often the very reverse of this seemed to happen. Indeed, his technique was sometimes quite at variance with this intention: in addressing a person's unconscious mind he often intruded his personality in a highly visible manner. Perhaps the most striking occasion was in his treatment of one inmate of a lunatic asylum who was considered beyond cure. Lane persuaded the governor to allow him to see the man alone in his padded cell, and introduced himself with the words: 'I have been told that you have some skill in curing the insane. I am mad and have come to consult you. Can you help me?' The man responded positively, and after lengthy therapy with Lane was able to leave the asylum.

Neill's testimony as to the effect of Lane the analyst upon him is inconsistent. On the one hand he confesses to having been as mesmerised as many others by Lane the Oracle:

> He made the most extravagant assertions, and we just accepted
> them. He would say something quite outrageous like, for example,
> 'All footballers have a castration complex,' without ever giving any
> reason for it, and it never occurred to us to say, 'What makes you
> think that?' We just accepted it, and told all our friends that of
> course all footballers have a castration complex.

On the other hand, Neill was contemptuous of his abilities as a personal therapist, at least in his own case. Lane, he thought, was 'so keen on his symbolic interpretations that not a bloody thing he ever said to me awakened any emotion whatsoever.' It was, he felt, 'all head stuff', and 'his brilliant analysis of dreams and their symbolism. . . never touched me below the neck'.*

This comment was written many years later, when Neill had come under the influence of a very different analyst. From what he wrote at the time, it is quite clear that Neill *did* have his emotions awakened. Lane evidently explained Neill's anti-authoritarian ideas and behaviour in terms of his attempt to rebel against his father, suggesting that he had shown 'infantile Oedipus Complex traits'. Neill acknowledged some three years later that the private lessons with Lane had forced him 'to face many unpleasant memories', and that the experience of analysis had been a painful one:

> I would sit for two hours listening to the most fascinating (and
> shattering) analysis of my own character, and later when I came
> down the steps I could not recall a single thing the analyst had said.
> If it were not for inner resistances, a person could be fully analysed
> in half an hour.

---

*Neill later recalled one moment from his analysis: 'Homer Lane, analysing a dream, said I had a height phobia. I laughed scornfully and told him I'd prove he was wrong. So I climbed the Monument . . . and shrank back sick at heart.'

Neill's two years as a pupil of Lane gave him both the momentum and the inspiration to clarify his goal, which was now to work with children 'the Little Commonwealth way'. Lane was, in both senses, 'a star' for Neill:

He came along amongst a rather dull set of people with set ideas, people who knew, or thought they knew, what a child should be. . . .He was the first man who simply said, we don't know a damn thing about children, let's observe them, and not force our personalities upon them. That's what I got from Lane.

It was the power of Lane's ideas which lay behind Neill's new conviction that 'the teacher's job is to evoke love. This he can only do by loving.' He now saw clearly that, in dealing with children, 'I can only stand by and give them freedom to unfold.' He asserted that 'The teacher should never try to teach; he should work alongside the children; he should be a co-worker, not a model.' Similarly, 'the only questions asked in a school should be asked by the pupils.' The purpose of education, he emphasised, was 'to make the Unconscious conscious'. And, at a more personal level, Lane seems to have given him the moral strength to break out on his own: 'To live your own life. . . that is the ideal. To discover yourself bravely, to realise yourself fully, to follow truth even if the crowd stone you. That is living. . . but it is dangerous living.'

Neill was soon to be given a graphic illustration of one of the dangers facing the pioneer. In 1925 Lane once again found himself in trouble with the authorities, but this time in full public view. As a result of some concern on the part of the family of one of his private 'pupils', a highly neurotic young woman, the police called at his consulting rooms, and he was charged with the technical offence of failing to register as an alien. The sensational trial that followed made it clear that there were other reasons for the authorities wanting to prevent him from continuing his practice in England. Although a large number of expert and eminent witnesses were lined up in court to speak in his defence, at the last moment he made a deal which enabled him to avoid possible imprisonment by leaving the country voluntarily. He died four months later in Paris, a broken man. For years afterwards Neill had dreams about his former analyst: 'They were unpleasant dreams, the sun did not shine in them,' he wrote. Yet when he read of Lane's death in the newspapers, he caught himself smiling. 'I thought it was hard-heartedness, but later I think I got the true explanation: I was free at last. Up to then I had relied on him. . . what would Homer say? Now I had to stand on my own feet.' But this – perhaps not before time – he was already beginning to do.

CHAPTER 6

The New Era

AN INTERNATIONAL QUARTERLY MAGAZINE FOR THE
PROMOTION OF RECONSTRUCTION IN EDUCATION.

The problem of education is not Continuation Schools, or subjects,
or Time Tables; the problem is morality, or rather how to get rid of
the morality that comes from without.
                        Article on 'Right and Wrong', *New Era*, July 1921

By the time Neill left King Alfred School, he had decided to set up a school
of his own, and begun to take steps to find suitable premises. He looked
around the London suburbs, hoping at first to find a house in Highgate for
what he was determined would be a self-governing community. For a
moment it seemed he might be able to take over an existing school, but the
landlord decided to sell rather than rent the premises. He rationalised his
disappointment by asserting that his school would ideally need to be in the
country 'where there is fresh air and space to grow' – presumably for the
children rather than the buildings. However, even fresh air would cost
money: with his teaching salary now ended, where was he to find the
capital for 'my Utopia'?

He was, of course, earning money as a writer, principally from the
royalties of his books. His first two, *A Dominie's Log* and *A Dominie
Dismissed*, had not only gained him a reputation as a humorous writer and
an educational renegade, but had been successful commercially. Two years
after publication, the *Log* was in its third printing, selling around 13,000
copies in hardback. Its sequel had done even better: published in 1916, it
had reached a printing of 36,000 copies five years later. By 1923 Neill was
referring to his books selling 'by the forty thousand'. The blend of folksy
humour, educational polemic and sentiment had found a market, though

some reviewers were not quite sure whether to treat Ncill as a humorist or an educationist. In *A Dominie Dismissed*, when congratulated on the merry yarns in the earlier book, the Dominie replies: 'The worst of being called a humorist is that everybody seizes on your light bits, and ignores your serious bits.' Neill's efforts to be taken seriously may have been hindered by finding himself on the same list as P. G. Wodehouse, and by the fact that his publisher, Herbert Jenkins, was himself a successful author of light fiction, featuring a Cockney character called Bindle.* Jenkins, like many humorists, was a rather doleful character, who sat in his office seven days a week, and refused to accept a dinner engagement unless mother and sister came too. It seems that he encouraged Neill, somewhat against the latter's inclination, to concentrate on the 'light bits'. His next book, *The Booming of Bunkie*, was a cheerful comic tale about a small Scottish village which had been turned in to a flourishing seaside resort. Into it Neill put some heavy-handed observations on Scottish village life, travelling salesmen, and the habits of golfers. There is, as in *A Dominie Dismissed*, a love story. In the earlier book the heroine was based very closely on Jessie Irving; in *Bunkie* Neill uses her for the purpose of a gentle satire on manners and class, with a pastiche of romantic fiction thrown in – 'Evelyn! Won't you speak to me? Won't you give me some hope? Won't you ——?' etc., etc.

Bunkie had been published in 1919, but Neill soon looked back on it severely, suggesting that it failed to rise above 'a specialised type of humour, or rather wit, the type that undergraduates might appreciate'. It had been started as a comic novel written in 'a merry mood'. It was a very different kind of inspiration which produced his next book, *Carroty Broon*. It seems very probable that it was Clunie's death which prompted him to look back at his childhood and recapture, in only thinly disguised fictional form, much of the feeling and many of the incidents of his early days in Forfar and Kingsmuir. *Carroty Broon* tells the story of a red-headed boy who flees from the reality of his life in a Scottish village into a fantasy world. It is filled with much of the earthy humour and lively action of the two Dominie books, but there are also several sombre, even anguished scenes. Several analytical terms crop up, indicating again the force of Lane's influence.

Among Peter's fantasies, one is of particular interest. A series of 'free associations' connected with punishment, guilt and illness, leads him

> to picture the school without the dominie, and a pleasant picture it
> was. He was now quite sure that he would recover, but the dominie
> would never recover, and he would stay for years and years in the
> asylum with chains round his body, the warders giving him raw

---

*Neill seems to have been Jenkins's third acquisition, after Wodehouse and Robert Baden-Powell, the founder of the Scout Movement. Baden-Powell knew of Neill, and was familiar with attempts at non-traditional schooling, favouring those that trained character rather than the intellect. It may have been Jenkins who once brought Neill and 'B-P' together over the dinner table. Neill asked B-P if he had heard the story about himself in which, at midnight, he realised he hadn't done his 'good deed' for the day, and so opened its cage and gave the canary to the cat. 'I have a vague memory that his polite smile was not genuine,' Neill later remembered.

meat on long pitchforks. Then he turned to the school, and thought of a joyful place where boys and girls did what they liked. It was no wonder that he fell asleep with a smile on his face.

This is the first explicit suggestion from Neill himself of the nature of his feelings about his father, and of the link between those feelings and his desire to create 'a joyful place where boys and girls did what they liked'.

Although it contained more 'serious bits' than his previous book, *Carroty Broon* did no harm to Neill's reputation as an author. The *Pall Mall Gazette* thought it 'a really first-rate story', while the prestigious *Times Literary Supplement* believed that the various episodes in Peter's life 'are all told with a touch of nature', and that Peter was 'a real boy'. The *TLS* reviewer also found 'much psychological insight and a good deal of shrewd (sometimes) biting humour' in the tale. Jenkins, in the blurb printed opposite the title-page of the book, invited a comparison that must have pleased Neill: 'Someone said who had read the manuscript, *Carroty Broon* will rank with *Sentimental Tommy* as one of the finest studies of a boy ever written north of the Tweed – only, *Carroty Broon* is not merely sentimental.' This allusion to Barrie may have seemed extravagant at the time. Yet Neill's book, partly through its avoidance of sentimentality, its more blunt and earthy humour, is perhaps more readable today than the work which acted as one of his earliest inspirations.

As it happened, his next job offered him a rare opportunity both to develop his writing talents further, and to see at first hand experiments in education being carried out by men and women who, like him, were rebelling against traditional methods, structures and principles. When Homer Lane had first come to London, he had rented a room at 6 Tavistock Square, which he used as part office and part consulting rooms. In January 1920, while Neill was still at King Alfred School, the first issue of a new educational magazine was published from 11 Tavistock Square; by the time the third issue was published in July, Neill had been taken on as co-editor of *Education for the New Era: An International Quarterly Journal for the Promotion of Reconstruction in Education*. Its founder and original editor, Beatrice Ensor, was already familiar with the work of Homer Lane, and it may have been through Lane that she got to know of Neill. She invited him to write an article for the new magazine on the subject of co-education – an invitation which Neill declined, on the grounds that such a set-up was quite normal for a Scot, and did not need to be supported by argument.

This spell on the new journal, which was to last for more than a year, gave Neill an invaluable chance to step back from his own teaching, and to find out what other reformers were up to. At first sight it may have seemed that he had found a number of allies and substantial support for his ideas amongst those who subscribed to some or all of the ideals of 'The New Education'. For many, and not only those working in education, the horrors of the war had revealed the awful consequences of blind obedience to authority. The conflict, which had soon lost any moral purpose it may have seemed to have had, had lasted for four years, and had resulted in the death of three quarters of a million men from the United Kingdom. In the immediate aftermath, people looked around for ways to establish a new world, where nations could work for the abolition of war, and for a new spirit of co-operation and trust.

Reflecting this, the first aim of the *New Era* (as it soon came to be known for short) was to

> foster that wider spirit of democratic brotherhood springing to life in so many movements today. . . .We desire that this magazine shall help to bring freedom and tolerance and understanding into all relations, not only between parent and teacher and child, but also one nation and another.

It was also part of the magazine's policy to provide a record of experiments in different countries:

> Pioneers are everywhere endeavouring to apply the New Ideals in education. We wish through these pages to make such pioneers feel that they are members of a widely scattered brotherhood. The principles underlying all these unrecorded experiments are those of self-development, self-government and democracy in education.

Alice Woods, the principal of a training college, who had visited a number of experimental schools, wrote in 1920: 'The cry is almost world-wide for greater freedom in education, and for "the development of individuality".'

In practice, there was a very considerable divergence of opinion, even amongst the 'pioneers', as to what constituted a proper freedom for the child, and how individuality could best be developed. Neill soon began to discover that he differed on most issues from his fellow reformers over matters of philosophy, aims or methods. One conflict was potentially there from the start of his time on the *New Era*, though it was a while before it intruded into its pages. Beatrice Ensor was an immensely energetic woman, with great organising abilities, and a matching enthusiasm for new ideas. During the war she had been the first woman to be appointed as a schools inspector by the Board of Education. She had specialised in reporting on schools for girl delinquents in southern England, and had also found time to inspect the working conditions of women in factories. As a result of her visits, she became highly critical of the regimented and uncreative schooling which the majority of children still had to undergo in the elementary schools.

Her views were reinforced by a book by Edmond Holmes, who on his retirement as chief inspector for elementary education had published in 1911 a forthright attack on the system of 'mechanical obedience' under which Neill and thousands of other children had been educated. In his book *What Is and What Might Be* he wrote:

> The adult who exacts from a child blind faith and literal obedience, and, having secured these, proceeds to tell the child in the fullest detail what he is to do, to say, to think (or pretend to think), to feel

(or pretend to feel), is devitalizing his whole personality. . . .Unless
the child himself – his soul, his self, his ego, call it what you please –
is behind his own actions, they are not really his.

This belief in the value of a child's inner motivations was one that was
shared by many of the pioneers of the time, and Holmes's book, which
was in its eighth impression by 1917, provided them with substantial
encouragement and support.

Both Holmes and Beatrice Ensor were members of a group concerned
with 'New Ideals in Education', which started to meet just before the war.
At their 1915 conference at Stratford-upon-Avon, their president, Lord
Lytton, said that the conference welcomed 'all ideas which represent the
substitution of the freedom and self-expression of the pupil for the imposed
authority of the teacher'. Both Holmes and Homer Lane read papers at the
conference, and it was at this moment, inspired partly by these two men,
that Beatrice Ensor founded the Theosophical Fraternity in Education. The
new group, which met under the umbrella of the New Ideals Conference,
consisted of a number of teachers within the Theosophical Society. Eventually, by 1920, they were big enough to hold their own conference, to
begin publishing their own journal, the *New Era*, and to form an international organisation which became known the following year as the New
Education Fellowship.

The Theosophists believed that there was some divinity in every man
and woman, and that this power should be drawn out and encouraged
wherever possible. Such a belief cut across differences in language, race and
creed; and the Theosophists' internationalism struck a chord with those
who hoped to work for peace and co-operation between nations. However,
there was also a considerable mystical element in theosophy, which was
reflected in the principles of the New Education Fellowship printed in one
of the very early numbers of the *New Era*. These principles underline the
need to 'give free play to a child's innate interest', to respect a child's
individuality, to abolish competition in favour of co-operation, to encourage forms of self-government, to support co-education. If Neill could find
a great deal to agree with in these very generalised sentiments, he was by
no means in tune with the first of the seven principles, which stated: 'The
essential aim of all education is to prepare the child to seek and realize in
his own life the supremacy of the spirit. Whatever other view the educator
may take, education should aim at maintaining and increasing spiritual
energy in the child.' Neill, of course, held no such view about the supremacy
of the spirit; nor did he feel that adults should be the ones to *prepare*
children for anything. Even some of the pioneers whose work he now began
to look at were, he felt, simply exchanging one form of adult 'moulding'
for another.

Neill was soon given the chance to outline his objections to certain
features of the new experimental schools. A note from Beatrice Ensor
appeared in the July 1920 issue of the *New Era*:

Owing to the fact that I have had much to do in my capacity of

Secretary to the Children's Famine Area Committee, the editing of this number has been left entirely to my co-editor Mr A. S. Neill. As his interest is in the psychological side of education the main portion of this issue is devoted to the new psychology.

Neill used the editorial space to attack what he called the 'Crank Schools', the label he used for those pioneer schools which, he believed, imposed adult ideals and tastes on children. He suggested that

> at our crank schools we find too many ideals. Children whose natural liking is for Charlie Chaplin are surrounded with art pictures, portraits of Walt Whitman and Blake; they hear the music of Schumann and Beethoven. . . while they prefer listening to a foxtrot on a gramophone. . . .The psychoanalyst who treats children from a crank school early discovers that all the good taste has simply driven the more earthy part of the child's psyche underground. . . .The ideal of education is to allow a child to express *all* his soul, and Charlie Chaplin is just as necessary in the scheme as Shakespeare.

In the same editorial Neill went on to emphasise some other fundamental beliefs. Self-government, he stated, would 'never succeed unless the teacher believes that all authority is dangerous for the child'. Pointing out that 'psychoanalysis has shown us authority and fear in their true lights', he went on: 'Fear of authority makes the child repress his ego instinct, and a deep hate of authority comes to life in his unconscious.' Obedience, he felt, 'is tolerable only when it is a mutual contract. If the child can order the teacher to do a certain thing the teacher is justified in giving orders to the child. Thus in a good school the teacher would command the noisy boy to be silent, and the children, when bored by a lesson, would cry in one voice: "Shut up!" ' He believed that 'There is no such thing as the Lazy Child. . . .What is called laziness is psychically lack of interest. The child's libido or life-force is bottled up, and if arithmetic or geography fail to provide a release for the libido, the teacher must allow the child to choose his own subject. There are no lazy children in a free school.' Punishment he felt was totally wrong 'because it deals with results and not with causes. It is the greatest enemy of true education, for it introduces Fear, and Fear is fatal to a child. . . .The bad boy ought to be treated as a sick person: the prison and the cat should give way to the analyst.' As for teaching, 'The only way to teach is to love. Love children and your love evokes their love: hate them and your hate evokes their hate.' A teacher should not be out to gain a child's respect: 'To a child respect merely means an attitude which contains an element of fear. Unless your children can talk to you as they talk to each other, calling you "a silly donkey" as occasion arises, you are not fit to be with children. No child can expand in an atmosphere of fear.'

This editorial signifies clearly that Neill had moved beyond the 'groping' of *A Dominie's Log*, and now felt able to lay out a set of beliefs which was to furnish him with a working philosophy for the rest of his life. As was to happen so often later, his provocative opinions made an impact on his readers. Beatrice Ensor took back the editorial column for the October issue of the *New Era*, observing that Neill had 'stirred folk to bless or curse according to their complexes'. After a plea for tolerance of different opinions, which perhaps was addressed as much to Neill as to her readers, she went on: 'Mr Neill does us great service in stressing the danger which may entrap the new idealists in trying to impose their views of life on children who are not ready for them, or are not along that particular line of development.' If this looks like a double-edged remark, her next comment underlined one area where she could not agree with Neill: 'A child who pines for Charlie Chaplin or *Comic Cuts* should undoubtedly have the opportunity to satisfy his craving, but – and this is important – my experience has shown that if the child is supplied with good music, good literature, good drama, good art, and taught to appreciate these, he does not want the bad.'

Practising the tolerance that she preached, Beatrice Ensor allowed Neill some space to reply to critical letters which had been sent as a result of his July editorial; and in doing so he implicitly replied to her remarks as well. One woman had written to ask if Neill thought Charlie Chaplin of more educational value than Shelley. Neill hastened to explain:

> Life is so difficult to understand that I personally cannot claim to settle the relative educational value of anyone. I know a market-gardener who never read Shakespeare, yet I have heard more wisdom from him than from any professor of English Literature I have known. And it is because I am so ignorant about values that I dislike the 'cranks' who rule out Charlie.

Another woman wrote angrily of his advocacy of the abolition of respect, to which Neill replied:

> I do not ask too much of teachers: all I ask is that they should be natural and not try to be models and saints. At the same time I realise that being natural is a vague phrase. It is natural for me to romp with children, to have them call me a silly ass when necessary, but I should think it would not be natural for – say – the Archbishop of Canterbury to accept with indifference a child's calling him a silly ass. And there are scores of teachers who have more dignity than all the bishops of the Anglican church put together.

Neill was beginning to enjoy himself.

In a corner of one page of the same issue Neill inserted a short note: 'In our next issue we shall publish a rousing article by E. F. O'Neill, the Lancashire Village Teacher, perhaps *the* most original village schoolmaster in the world. I have seen his school and it is a pure delight. He is a great man.' Neill had visited his near-name sake in July, and been astounded at what he saw. Two years before, O'Neill, who had been brought up in the slums of Manchester, had become head of Prestolee Village School, at the age of 28. He had abolished the timetable, and allowed the children to initiate their own work programmes to a degree unknown within the state system. He had turned a dreary concrete playground into a living garden, in which the children worked and learned. He had encouraged children to work with rather than against each other, and to use the teachers as 'research workers'. The distinction between work and play had been abolished, and O'Neill himself joined in many of the activities in what had become a thriving educational workshop.

On his visit, Neill was impressed with the lack of visible authority, finding the children busy on their individual tasks with not a teacher in sight. He wanted to tell O'Neill that his school was a pure delight, 'but I couldn't get a word in edgeways. If anything, he was over-explanatory, but I pardoned him, for I realised that the poor man's life must be spent in explaining himself to unbelievers.' Neill thought that O'Neill's greatness lay in the fact that, though he seemed not to have any theoretical knowledge, 'the man seems to know it all by instinct or intuition. To him creation is everything.' He liked his flexibility, and lack of dogma or fixed beliefs about methods of study: 'If the ideal man is the man who is always learning, then O'Neill comes pretty near that ideal. I wish that every teacher in Britain could see his school.'* Neill may have seen in O'Neill's work a more successful reflection of his own efforts in Gretna with another group of working-class children. Certainly such wholehearted approval for another pioneer was a rare thing for Neill to bestow, both then and later: normally he would find some major area of disagreement.

One other teacher that he met at this time did, however, find favour in Neill's eyes. Just prior to his visit to Lancashire, he paid a call on Norman MacMunn, who was running a school for war orphans at Tiptree Hall in Essex. Many of the children were severely repressed, and 'of the poorest class'. MacMunn, whose book *The Path to Freedom in the School*, published in 1914, was another key text for the pioneers of the time, believed that children should have 'no masters and mistresses, no adult imposed laws, no rigid professions or prescriptions'. Neill liked his relaxed style, the fact that he taught with a cigarette in his mouth, that 'his boys filled the room with noisy talk as they worked, and never have I seen children do more work with so much joy. . . .They talk openly and they make jokes and take jokes against themselves gladly and eagerly.' He was also struck by another quality in MacMunn: he was 'a true educationist in that he does not suggest. . . .The secret of teaching is to keep out of the picture.'

MacMunn was one of the New Ideals group; another member who received a visit from Neill was Caldwell Cook. His book, *The Play Way*, had been published in 1917. His principal belief was that learning came best if it was made into a game; and his 'play-way' methods, later termed 'learning by play', were absorbed into the thinking of many English nursery

---

*O'Neill, in his later years, could recall only one detail of Neill's visit: the thickness of the soles of his shoes.

and infant school teachers. Neill thought his book fascinating, 'delightful' and full of good things, and found much to admire when he watched Cook at work at The Perse School in Cambridge. But he criticised him for 'using the play way with an end in view', rather than for its own sake.

Both Cook and MacMunn, like other members of the New Ideals group, were familiar with the work of one figure of major significance with whom Neill soon found himself in disagreement. Maria Montessori had been the first woman to qualify as a doctor in Italy. Working first with mentally defective children, then with slum children in Rome, she observed that children had enormous powers of concentration, preferred work to play, and seemed to have a fundamental need for order and repetition in their activities. To support her theories, she devised a range of 'didactic apparatus', which would allow children to direct their own learning free from the normal coercion of adults. At her school in the Via Giusti in Rome she dispensed with the timetable, and the children were allowed to choose their own activity, following it as far and as long as they wished to. Her book *The Montessori Method* was translated into English in 1912; and, through the instigation of Edmond Holmes, the 1914 New Ideals conference was devoted solely to her ideas and practice. Interest in her methods grew throughout the war. In 1919 she visited England, when a banquet in her honour was given at the Savoy Hotel in London. Interest in the training course she ran was enormous, and many Montessori schools or departments were opened, as teachers saw the practical possibilities of her theories.

Neill welcomed some of Montessori's ideas, in particular her belief that children should be freed from the dominance of adults. But other aspects of her system he found repellent:

Her system is highly intellectual, but sadly lacking in emotionalism. This is seen in her attitude to phantasy. She would probably argue that phantasy is bad for a child, but it is a fact that much of a child's life is lived in phantasy. . . .No, the Montessori world is too scientific for me; it is too orderly, too didactic. The name 'didactic apparatus' frightens me.

Education, he felt, was 'more than matching colours and fitting cylinders into holes'. He was also hostile to her belief in order and silent work: 'every child should be allowed to make a noise, for noise means power to him, and he will use it only as long as it means power to him.' Neill also declared himself to be repelled by her lack of humour and, what was worse, her religious attitude: 'She is a church woman; she has a definite idea of right and wrong. Thus, although she allows children freedom to choose their own occupations, she allows them no freedom to challenge adult morality.'

One of Neill's visits for the *New Era* was to Brackenhill Theosophical Home School in Kent, which had a Montessori Department for the youngest children. He reported his reception with undisguised delight:

I spoke not a word. In five minutes the insets and long stairs were lying neglected in the middle of the floor, and the kiddies were scrambling over me. I felt very guilty, for I feared that if Montessori herself were to walk in she would be indignant. I cannot explain why I affect kiddies in this way. It may be that intuitively they know that I do not inspire fear or respect; it may be that they unconsciously recognise the baby in me.

Montessori tried to control too much of the child's environment for Neill's liking, and he remained suspicious and critical of her ideas throughout his life.

In addition to his work for the *New Era*, Neill was now trying his hand at public speaking. The *Forfar Dispatch* for 21 January 1921 included a notice of a 'Lecture by A. S. Neill Esq', to which 'all interested are cordially invited'. Neill had been lecturing just before in Edinburgh and Dundee where, the *Dispatch* reported, 'his views have provoked a good deal of discussion and comment'. Five years later, in a letter to a fellow-pioneer, he recollected being 'abused' at one lecture by the Dundee Director of Studies. Since he arrived in London some two years before, Neill had gradually made his mark as a lecturer on educational and psychological topics. The previous autumn he had given a course of lectures at the Eustace Miles Restaurant in London, where he had spoken on Mind Mechanisms, Psycho-Analysis, The Unconscious of the child, The Psychology of the Flogger, Self-Government and Crowd Psychology.

George Neill was now nearing 70. He had retired from Kingsmuir School some eighteen months before, after nearly 43 years as headteacher, and kept his hand in by doing some part-time and relief teaching. It would have been strange if he had not been in the 'pretty large and representative audience' which turned out to hear his son speak in the Meffan Hall in Forfar. Neill's lecture was described by the celebrated local journalist 'The Drummer' as an 'interesting, fascinating if at times provocative discourse', while his illustrations and allusions were reckoned to be 'always very telling and luminous'. He concluded his report with the observation that 'Our Forfar author has indeed belied the usual fate of the prophet who is not without honour in his own country.' Neill was later to quarrel with this judgment in connection with his native country; but on this occasion he maintained the formalities: 'Mr Neill expressed his pleasure at standing before his own folk,' the report noted.

Neill's most interesting and substantial contribution to the *New Era* appeared in April 1921. This issue was almost entirely given over, probably at Neill's instigation, to a topic he now considered absolutely crucial – self-government. Since the war a number of schools, or teachers within their own classrooms, had been experimenting with different forms of self-government, and it was clearly a good topic for a journal such as the *New Era* to look at in some detail. A number of contributors, most but not all working in education, were asked to consider three questions: At what age can self-government be given to children? Should it be given suddenly or gradually? Should the teacher set limits? Neill was partly responsible for choosing the contributors, some of whom he had come across in his reporting visits in previous months. One surprising choice was George Lansbury, then editor of the *Daily Herald*, which had been the most widely read and influential of the anti-war journals. Lansbury, who was a greatly loved figure within the new Labour movement, had been a manager of schools, and had children of his own. His opinion was that 'we know so little about children that we ought to proceed along the lines of experiment. . .in my judgement none of us, not even the most clever, have begun to understand how to educate either our children or ourselves'.

Another contributor was Geraldine Coster, head of Wychwood School in Oxford, a small, select but unconventional fee-paying school for upper-class girls, which claimed to be 'self-governing and progressive, but with old-fashioned ideas of courtesy and refinement'. Neill had recently spent a weekend at the school, which had been struggling without great success to find a self-governing formula. The headmistress referred to Neill's visit in her article in the *New Era* symposium: 'Things were at a deadlock when Mr A. S. Neill came down for a weekend. We were in quarantine for mumps, and bored to extinction; and in half an hour he had started a blaze of enthusiasm for "the real thing this time", which is bidding fair to turn into a steady fire at last.' One of those who was enthused at the time, Meriel Cardew, remembers the occasion clearly: 'One evening there came this shock-headed, vital and interesting-looking man to talk about self-government. He sat on the floor like many of the pupils, cross-legged and very eager. "You think it's right to do what you're told," he said, "but why don't you learn to think for yourselves?" It was as if he was instigating a rebellion. We immediately started to have school meetings, and the curriculum went to the dogs, as we had meetings all day trying to hammer out a constitution. Then we began, and it worked, right from the beginning. It induced a sense of self-responsibility: although the school was geared to individuals before, after Neill's visit there was more consciousness of the community.' Geraldine Coster wrote at the time: 'We found on consideration that we disagreed with him in most things, but that merely added fuel to the blaze.' Neill took up the point in his editorial comment:

> I found her girls apathetic. I talked psychology to them for half an hour. . . and in a body they rushed off to institute self-government. And the fact that they disagreed with what I said is delightful. Had they accepted me as an authority, their self-government would have fizzled out in a week. The only thing that mattered was the rousing shock.

Neill was beginning to gain a reputation as a person whose views could have an unsettling effect. Another headteacher, Isobel King, invited him along to 'rouse' her school, St Christopher's, in Letchworth Garden City. The school had been started by the Theosophical Educational Trust, and at this time Beatrice Ensor was heavily involved in the running of it.

By 1920 the school had a well-established 'Moot', a meeting of the whole school which discussed and made judgments on children's behaviour, and decided on sanctions for those who broke the rules. Two of the nine school rules agreed upon by the Moot were 'Our bodies must be kept scrupulously clean and tidy, so as to make the world more beautiful,' and 'Our thoughts must be as scrupulously clean as our bodies.' Children heard to utter the words 'Curse', 'Damn' and even 'Help' had to be silent for a whole school day during school hours (later you could receive half a day's such punishment for 'Hang', 'Dash', 'Blow' and 'Shut Up'). It was this sort of 'crankiness' which Neill was fighting against, labelling people who adopted such attitudes 'High Lifers'. Perhaps for this reason, or because his ideas were more familiar to the staff and children of St Christopher's, Neill seems to have made much less impact than he did upon the refined young ladies at Wychwood.

As he made clear in his comments on the various contributions to the symposium in the *New Era*, Neill was already a wholehearted advocate of self-government. 'Most of our contributors to this issue have declared against a sudden introduction of self-government. I disagree. I am all for the dramatic moment, the abreaction of the repressed emotions.' And at this stage in his thinking he could anticipate no limitations: 'to be successful, self-government must be full and free.' Education, he wrote, 'is release; it is a making of the unconscious conscious'. This last idea, borrowed from Homer Lane, was now one of the keynotes of his philosophy about children, and it was a dispute on this question which eventually led to a break between Neill and Beatrice Ensor.

The tone of many of his book reviews, editorials and reports in the *New Era* suggest that Neill relished the clash of ideas within the editorial office. His memory later was that Beatrice Ensor had similar feelings: 'I soon saw that the more outrageously I attacked pedants and schools the more delighted she was. . . . I liked her and ragged her most of the time. She was about the only theosophist I met who could laugh at theosophy and herself.' Though some people later mentioned rows between these two very different personalities, Neill could remember none. Michael Ensor, Beatrice's son, confirms Neill's recollection: 'I vaguely recall my mother later in life referring to Neill as a person for whom she had an admiration, but whom she could not accompany so far down the road of libertarianism.' Their differences came to a head with the October 1922 issue of the *New Era*. Beatrice Ensor had become a devotee of the new ideas of Coué relating to suggestion and auto-suggestion, which were then having a vogue. In essence, Coué's ideas involved the individual in learning how to will her or himself to act in certain ways. Another enthusiast for Coué's ideas was Norman MacMunn, who wrote a sympathetic notice in the *New Era* of Coué's book on the subject. Neill added a warning footnote to the review: 'Still, MacMunn, I'm afraid of this suggestion business. It is not touching root causes.' Neill feared that suggestion would work against the Unconscious, arguing that the whole point of psychoanalysis as formulated by Freud and his co-workers was to allow patients to find out the truth about themselves. He also thought that the practice of suggestion and auto-suggestion was open to misuse on children, and was therefore potentially 'a crime against humanity'.

Beatrice Ensor, on the other hand, believed that teachers should be preparing the right stimuli for children to develop 'their impulses towards perfection', and that it was 'for the teacher to see that the suggestions that reach the child are the right suggestions'. In the October 1922 issue of the *New Era*, the whole of which was devoted to her new preoccupation, she made, without naming him, an explicit attack on Neill, mentioning the 'extremist in education' who believes in leaving children free to respond to motivation from within. This was too much for Neill, who confessed annoyance that the *New Era* should support such ideas: 'I assert that every suggestionist believes in original sin. . . he tries to make the child better. . . as if God didn't know his job.' The dispute was becoming a more fundamental one, and was perhaps on the point of becoming personal. Beatrice Ensor, who seemed to prefer cordial disagreement to open conflict, decided that Neill's time had come. In the January 1923 issue of her journal she wrote:

> Mr Neill has very definite views on psychology and education, and it is probable that I print many opinions with which he would not agree. This has occurred in connection with my October editorial on Suggestion and Auto-Suggestion, and therefore, in fairness to 'The Dominie', I think his name must be dropped from the magazine as co-editor.

But by this time, 'The Dominie' was one step closer to setting up his own school, where he could put into practice these very definite views on psychology and education. At King Alfred it had been a custom while Neill was there for the children to invite their teachers back home for tea. The last child in his form to ask Neill back was Walter Neustatter, who lived in a large house in Regent's Park, within the sound of the lions' roar from the nearby London Zoo. There Neill found his pupil living with his mother, Lilian, and his aunt Ethel. The two sisters had, in very different ways, struggled hard to get to their present position in this fashionable part of London. They had been brought up together in various country districts of Northern Australia. Their father, Walter Lindsay Richardson, had come from Ireland to set up a practice as a country doctor. A brilliant, bookish man, he deteriorated mentally when the girls were still very young, and, after a prolonged and distressing illness, died of insanity. His widow was determined that her daughters, despite the family's poverty and isolation, should have the opportunity to escape from the small-town life in which they found themselves. She trained and then worked as a postmistress, made all her daughters' clothes herself, and saved money in order to give the girls an education that would allow them to take their places in more 'cultured' society. Her determination paid off: after attending school at the Presbyterian Ladies' College in Melbourne, the two sisters and their mother took the 'escape route' to Europe, where they settled in a flat in Leipzig, one of the musical centres of the Continent.

Ada Lilian Sydney Lindesay, born on 28 April 1871, was the younger by some two years. A girl of gentle disposition, short, round, with wavy hair, she generally followed the lead of her older sister. Ethel Florence was a dark, thin, determined and more self-sufficient girl, with a talent for inventing games and telling stories. The girls enacted scenes from Shakespeare in the backyard of the small, dark tin-roofed homes which their mother's job compelled them to inhabit. Both were introduced to music at an early age, and showed outstanding talent, Lilian on the violin, Ethel on the piano. Lilian hoped to perform professionally, but found that she had a desperate fear of performing in public, which proved impossible to overcome.

Her sister turned to literature as a possible career: in 1903 she married a Scot, George Robertson, an expert in German literature, who later became professor in the subject at London University. Ethel had written her first novel with encouragement from her sister, who read and commented on the manuscript. They also discussed what pen-name she should adopt. Ethel had decided on this course because 'There had been much talk in the press about the ease with which a woman's work could be distinguished from a man's; and I wanted to try out the truth of the assertion'. She eventually decided to use her uncle's name, and in 1908 the first novel written by 'Henry Handel Richardson' was published. *Maurice Guest*, based on the family's life in Leipzig, was a critical success. Two years later Ethel drew on her schooling experience in Melbourne for *The Getting of Wisdom*, a powerful and subtle story of an up-country girl's gradual adaptation to life in the rarefied atmosphere of a girls' city boarding school. After a visit by the sisters to their childhood home, Ethel wrote her celebrated trilogy, *The Fortunes of Richard Mahoney*, of which the first volume, *Australia Felix*, appeared in 1917.

The relationship between the two sisters was an intense one, though not always harmonious; Lilian remained in awe of her older sister, even when they began to lead their separate lives. In Germany she met and married an eye surgeon, Otto Neustatter, and settled in Munich with him. She had been accustomed in Leipzig to a busy and varied social and intellectual life – tennis, music, parties, love affairs. She grew discontented with her new role of *hausfrau*, and joined a circle of friends who entertained each other, went to the theatre and recitals, read and discussed the current literature. Although the two Richardson girls had vowed never to have children, Lilian broke the agreement in 1890, when she gave birth to her son, Walter. In one of her numerous letters to her sister, Lilian told her that the baby 'will learn in its very earliest infancy that its Aunt is the cleverest woman in the world and you will probably become its God and its oracle and have to give the proper answers to its questions'. She looked to her sister for guidance about the growing child: should she, for example, smack him for putting his fingers in his mouth? Mother and child spent an increasing amount of time in England with Ethel. Eventually it was agreed that Walter would go to school in England and live with his aunt.

One of the reasons Lilian Neustatter chose King Alfred's was because she felt a co-educational school would give her son a more sensible attitude towards women. The question of women's rights was a matter of intense debate and action during the pre-war years, with the focus on the issue of whether women should be allowed the vote. The two sisters were both feminist in outlook, but Lilian was the more active in the suffragette movement, joining in protest marches under the Votes for Women banner. She was arrested for smashing a Post Office window with a hammer, and sent for two months to Holloway Gaol for women. There her fellow campaigners, who had been cutting up golf courses, slashing pictures in the National Gallery, firing houses and breaking up meetings to draw attention to their cause, were being subjected to the indignity of force-feeding. Lilian went on hunger strike, but found herself unable to cope with the brutal instruments, or the humiliation of being pinioned down while the tubes were applied. On her release she returned to Dresden, and spent her energy for the cause on writing letters, entertaining sympathisers from England, and preaching the rights of women.

The outbreak of war found her in England, where she decided to stay with Walter while her husband remained in Germany. The decision was an agonising one that was to leave its mark; her sympathies in the conflict lay with the British, despite the fact that her husband would shortly be called up in the German army. The war years were unhappy ones for her. She had to register as an enemy alien, which was a constant anxiety: anti-German feeling ran high for most of the war years. She had little money and no real home. For a while she ran a small restaurant with a friend, though with little success. Later she offered her services as a cleaner, calling on people's doorsteps with one of the newly invented vacuum cleaners. Eventually she was compelled to accept a position as her sister's house-keeper. She was now the poor relation, having to keep unwanted visitors away from her eminent sister, and help her to find the quiet and isolation she insisted on for her work. In the summer, while her sister, in fear of the bombs, stayed in her second house in Lyme Regis in Dorset, Lilian was left in charge of the big house in Regent's Park.

Her life, then, was at a low ebb when this lanky Scot, with strange square shoes and even stranger ideas about children, walked through the door, and changed the course of both their lives. Neill came to tea at 4 o'clock, and stayed talking until 10, pouring out his plans for a new kind of school. He found a very sympathetic listener, and returned to the house several times. Gradually a scheme emerged for the two of them to co-operate on Neill's planned pioneering school, with Lilian Neustatter supplying the practical ideas for running it. She wrote to her husband about the idea, and tried to persuade him to come to England to rejoin her. However, the war was now over, and Otto Neustatter wanted his wife to return to their home in Dresden. Since it proved impossible for she and

Neill to find premises they could afford, she complied with her husband's request.

Yet she did so with considerable reluctance. Neither she nor Neill had by any means given up the idea of starting a school of their own, of realising Carroty Broon's fantasy of 'a joyful place where boys and girls did what they liked'.

CHAPTER 7

The International School

I am only just realising the absolute freedom of my scheme of
education.

A Dominie Abroad, 1923

In August 1921, Mr A. S. Neill, M.A., author of the Dominie books,
joined Mrs Baer-Frissell, an American lady, in the directorship of the
Dalcroze-School Hellerau. . . .The centre of school life will be social
life. There will be no dictatorship from above. Already democratic
government from within has begun, and the school is really a self-
governing body. The pupils and staff had begun to make
constructive experiments in education. . . . Psychologically the school
is founded on the belief that the child is good, and no punishment or
rewards will be given. The school is also founded on the belief that
creation and self-expression are of more importance than mere
learning. The school has no politics: we believe that to teach
pacifism is almost as dangerous as to teach militarism. We mean to
live pacifism by realising that behind nationalism is a common
human nature.

Unable to track down suitable premises in England for his projected school,
and finding himself at odds with not only Beatrice Ensor but most of the
educational pioneers there, Neill had extended his search to other countries.
It had taken him more than a year to find the right setting.

He had begun his search in Holland, only a few months after he joined
the *New Era*. As part of her work for the Famine Area Relief Committee,
Beatrice Ensor was helping to bring 500 children from Vienna to England.

She asked Neill to help her escort them on the last stage of their journey, from Rotterdam to a refugee camp in England. Neill decided to go over to Holland ten days early, and 'look for my Utopia' among the Dutch schools. He certainly liked the country itself, writing to Jessie Irving from Rotterdam: 'Glorious place, Holland. Cigars one penny each. I love the place, so peaceful.' But he was not nearly so satisfied with the educational side of Dutch life. He visited an ordinary state school in Rotterdam and was disappointed to find children sitting silently in rows: 'all I saw was the spoon-feeding we call education in our English board schools.' In The Hague he dropped in on an 'observation house', which held offenders from the juvenile courts pending a decision on their future; and called in on an actual reformatory in Amersfoort. Neither had any form of self-government, and in the reformatory Neill was disturbed by the boys' punishment of being confined in locked rooms. He thought it 'a prison, an airy, clean, cheery sort of prison, but still a prison. The staff seemed to be good-natured, kindly fellows, but that is not enough. The criminal child is not to be reformed by benevolent authority.' He was more impressed by the Humanitaire School in Laren, which he felt had an air of freedom, and where a lot of emphasis was put on handwork. Yet even here he thought there was too much consideration given to instruction, and he noticed that every child seemed to be doing the same thing. 'Benevolent authority again, I said to myself, not true freedom.'

By now the question of authority was of overriding concern to Neill, and it figured prominently in his second trip abroad. One of the ideas behind the launching of the *New Era* was to establish 'an International Fellowship of Teachers, to meet in annual conference'. The first conference, which launched the New Educational Fellowship, was held at the end of July 1921 in Calais, the theme of the main lectures being 'The Creative Self-Expression of the Child'. Neill was invited to participate, and chose as his subject 'The Abolition of Authority'. Some of those in the audience at Calais thought his ideas 'dangerous' and 'anarchic'. He opened in the direct and humorous manner for which he was soon to become celebrated:

> I define authority as the force outside a personality that thwarts the libido of that personality. But then I should define libido, and I don't know if I can. Libido is the life force, the life force that expresses itself as interest. At the present moment part of my libido is directed to the task of making you interested. Last night my libido went into fox-trotting with Miss King down at the Casino. Now you know what libido is.

He went on to mix folksy interpretations of Freudian concepts with earthy anecdotes, and provocative remarks about the harm done to children by 'moralists' – in which mothers, fathers, teachers and clergymen were seen as the principal offenders. He concluded that if the authority of adult over child were to be provisionally abolished, the law would then come 'from the children themselves'.

From Calais – 'the ugliest town on earth I hope' – he travelled through the Bavarian lakes and mountains to Salzburg, to speak a few days later at a conference on Psychology, Education and Politics, organised by the Women's International League for Peace and Freedom. Here the lectures were mostly in French and German, and he spent a good deal of time sightseeing – an object of some curiosity in the street, where he added a pair of green Bavarian braces and a grey velour hat to his Glasgow boots and Edinburgh leggings. His own talk went unreported, even in the *New Era*; but one lecture that did capture his attention was that given by Professor Franz Cizek. In 1898 Cizek had opened free classes for children in the School of Applied Art in Vienna where he worked. The results created a revolution in thinking about children's capacity to be creative artists, and provided the impetus for much of the practice now considered quite normal in schools in many countries. As he always did on such occasions, Cizek illustrated his talk with the children's paintings and drawings, which Neill found 'wonderful': Cizek's discoveries confirmed his growing certainty about the importance of encouraging creativity in children.

From Austria, still on behalf of the *New Era*, Neill moved on to Germany, supposedly to report on the new schools there. However, his own personal plans were now uppermost in his mind, and he was not taking his official assignments too seriously. He sent one report to Beatrice Ensor, which she included in the October 1921 issue with the explanation label, 'All that I have been able to extract from the Co-Editor.' Neill chose to write his piece in letter form, beginning: 'Dear Mrs Ensor, I know that you picture me spending my time running round visiting the schools of Germany. The truth is that I spend the day lying in the sun. . . at the present moment I am much more interested in sunbaths, beer and baccy, than in all the new education experiments.' The garden in which he was so defiantly taking his ease belonged to the Neustatter family: the article went on to describe in enthusiastic terms the Jacques Dalcroze School in Hellerau, a suburb of Dresden where the Neustatters now lived. Neill wrote: 'I have spent a few delightful evenings over at the Dalcroze School. . .and I warn you solemnly that I am not coming back to London until I have taken a full course here.' It was in fact to be three years before he returned to England permanently. Four months after he sent this report to the *New Era*, the Dalcroze School began the January term with Neill as co-director, and Lilian Neustatter as matron. This, in essence, was the beginning of Summerhill.

Hellerau, two miles outside Dresden, was an unusual village. It had been originally planned as a place for artists and craftsmen, and had provided the model for the early English garden cities such as Letchworth. The houses, set well apart from each other, were built in an irregular pattern on a hillside, in the middle of a pine forest stretching for seven miles. At weekends it became a focal point for some of the newer cults and movements that had sprung up in Germany, as the younger generation revolted against the attitudes of their parents, whose militarism had brought them to war. One prominent group was the *Wandervogel*, a youth movement whose members aspired to the 'simple life'. They wore sandals, open-necked shirts and shorts, and spent most of their time in the open air. At night they camped in woods, sang German folk songs, danced, and read poems and legends by the firelight. It was in many respects an austere movement, which preached hardiness and self-control, and renounced the use of alcohol and tobacco.

At the top of the hill on which Hellerau had been built there stood a palatial building. It had been built by a violinist, Wolf Dohrn, who wanted it to become a world centre for 'all that is noblest and best in education'. From the start it was devoted to the teaching of a new branch of dance and movement called Eurythmics, and run by its originator, Jacques Dalcroze. After the war it re-opened under one of his pupils, Christine Baer, the American wife of a Hellerau architect. By the time of Neill's visit the school was well established, with over a hundred pupils from many different countries. The premises included a great hall, which could hold 600 people and was equipped with up-to-date theatre lighting and apparatus. There were sun terraces, shower baths, large playing grounds and tennis courts, practice rooms and lecture halls, all of which were available for use by the Dalcroze students. On each side of the main building was a substantial wing, one of which housed a German school started by a group of parents for the children of the village. Neill had liked what he saw of it during a brief visit: 'No punishment, no rewards, any amount of outside rambles for Geography and Nature Study. In school quite a lot of creation. . . .The staff seems to be composed of young people who are out to find and give freedom.'

According to her son Wally, it was Lilian Neustatter who saw the possibilities for Neill of the other, unused wing, and suggested that he come to Hellerau to see it for himself. However the scheme took shape, she was undoubtedly a prime mover in getting the idea off the ground. According to Neill, he was considering buying a castle in Vienna to open an International School, but was persuaded by Christine Baer that his castle was on his doorstep, and that they should turn the Dalcroze School into an International School. This, after a complicated series of negotiations, is what happened. A limited liability company was formed, and Neill, with the exchange rate greatly in his favour, invested what money he had in the school. Soon the German school was persuaded to join the venture, so that the International School consisted of three divisions: the Eurythmics section under Christine Baer; the German school, part day and part boarding, under its existing head, Dr Theil; and the 'foreign' sector, under Neill.

Five minutes away from the school stood a separate building, in which Neill and some of his pupils lived. Lilian Neustatter had appointed herself housekeeper/matron of this *Schulheim*, and from now on her support was crucial to Neill. The question of her allegiance to both Neill and her husband appeared not to create any significant problems. It seems abundantly clear that, both now and later, her relationship with Neill was a working one, which excluded any romantic or sexual element. One of the few references to the personal side of their relationship was made by Neill at about this time when, in writing about the setting up of the school, he said, 'I compare myself with Aeneas, who had such a struggle to found his city, and bring his household gods into Latium, only, in my labours, there has been no Helen to supply the romantic element'.* His new matron did have plenty of other elements to offer. She had immense practical and organisational abilities of a kind that Neill visibly lacked. She was gregarious, warm and enthusiastic, and soon became a mother-figure to a number of the Eurythmic students, as well as some of Neill's pupils. It was she who dealt with the finance, the children's illnesses, the day-to-day running of the school. She did all this while still running her own home, in which Neill became a guest until he moved into the *Schulheim*. He and Otto Neustatter took to each other on sight. A vast, imposing but genial man, he enjoyed being fussed and mothered, and treated as a mild invalid by his wife. As one who visited their household observed, he 'had to have his bowl of thick sour milk waiting for him in the evening when he came home from his office, or else!' Neill described him at the time as 'the sort of man for whom railway porters always open doors of first-class compartments'. He addressed Neill affectionately as 'Old Beans', and seems to have had no reservations about his wife's dedicated commitment to Neill's dream.

Neill was very attracted both to the idea and the practice of Dalcroze Eurythmics. The ideas were not totally new to him: in the winter of 1912–13 he had seen Dalcroze himself demonstrate his art at the Queen's Hall in London, and while in Gretna he had come across an illustrated article on the Hellerau School. At the time he noted in his *Log*: 'The photographs were beautiful studies in grace; the school appears to be full of Pavlovas. I think I shall try to found a Eurythmics section on the photogaphs.' The idea of teaching children to move to rhythm seemed to him a wonderful antidote to the traditional 'drill' practised in Scottish schools. And when he linked up with Christine Baer in the famous school itself, his initial enthusiasm for Dalcroze's ideas was considerable. Not the least of its attractions for him was its flexibility. 'Among Dalcrozians,' he wrote in the *New Era*, 'there does not appear to be that unfortunate Montessorian habit of waiting for guidance from the Fountain-head. I see Montessorianism becoming a dead, apparatus-ridden system, but I see rhythm extending its influence in all branches of education. Thank heaven, there is no apparatus required for Eurythmics!'

When the school opened, he saw it as part of his job 'to try to link up Rhythm with other departments of education. . . we are experimenting with rhythm and music, trying to find out if they can assist such subjects as drawing, writing, Mathematics.' He was at pains, though, to emphasise that there was no belief in Eurythmics as a panacea: 'To found a school on an ideal is fatal,' he wrote. If he did have an ideal at this time, it was, to judge by his prospectus, certainly a very broad one:

We dream of a school where creation will be the chief object, where

---

*Neill's classical learning was evidently already fading: it was Dido, Queen of Carthage, who fell in love with Aeneas.

the child will do rather than learn, where he will make his own
books instead of reading lesson books. . . because the world has had
too much intellectual education and too much education of the
conscious mind, we concentrate on creative education, that is, the
release of the unconscious. We believe that to make a sketch of a
church is better for a child than to copy a Rembrandt in an art
gallery, that to write a poem is better than to recite *Paradise Lost*.

Down in the real world, Neill soon began to encounter difficulties. He
found a fundamental divergence of philosophies between his own and that
of the staff of the German division. The trouble, he felt, was that they were
interested in education, not children: 'It was really a conflict between
freedom and asceticism.' There was a joint initiative to lay on film shows
for the village children: while Neill argued for silent comedies for the
children, the German teachers pressed for educational features – 'boring
films about travel and shellfish', as he wrote disparagingly. Many of the
Germans belonged to the youth movement: Neill found them often kind,
courteous and honest, but came to mistrust what he saw as their puritanism:

> We differed in fundamentals. . . .They disapproved of tobacco,
> alcohol, foxtrots, cinemas. . . .We, on the other hand, had other
> ideals; we were ordinary folk who drank beer and smoked and
> danced foxtrots. . . .Our intention was to live our own lives while we
> allowed children to live theirs.

He thought they were mistaken in concentrating on educating a child's
conscious mind: 'To read Goethe to a child who would rather be catching
minnows is a psychological mistake.' He chided the head of the German
division for always beginning his talk to parents with the words: 'Here we
work.' Why, Neill asked him, could it not be, 'Here we play'?

Finding suitable staff for his own division was no easy matter either:
even in a place such as Hellerau, where radical or free-thinking individuals
were part of the landscape, he could not find many adults who shared his
ideas about freedom in schools. Now that he had a school of his own he
was quite unprepared to compromise: 'I don't want teachers who say "Yes,
but. . .", I want teachers who say "Yes, yes." ' However, in his search for
such wholehearted enthusiasts, Neill was not always able to pick the right
person, as he himself admitted. 'I fear that I am not a born employer, for
I sum up a candidate by his looks rather than by his attainments or
theories.' This statement was inaccurate, both at the time and later. Neill's
tendency was to pick staff for their attitudes to children, something that he
could often though not always sense instinctively. He was also interested
in what they could do, and to a certain extent in their theories. This is
borne out by one of his appointments at Hellerau. Professor Zutt had been
running a handwork school in Budapest for fifteen years when he joined
the International School. A skilled craftsman in metal and clay, he believed
in the capacity of all children to create objects of beauty, and to do so in
a short time without endless practice work. The aim of handwork was to

give *joy* to a child; he believed you could tell if children were having such an experience by the very sound of their filing and hammering. Neill warmly approved of Zutt's theories as well as his practice: 'What Zutt calls Freude [Joy], I call interest, and although our terms are different, we are completely at one in our attitude to education.' For Neill, Zutt had done for handwork what Cizek had done for painting.

Neill found one of his key teachers in an unusual place – standing at a tram stop in Dresden. Willa Muir, whom Neill had known as Willa Anderson when she was an undergraduate at St Andrews, was at this time travelling around Europe with her husband, the poet Edwin Muir, surviving with difficulty on his literary commissions and their joint translation work. The previous year she had been in charge of the Day Continuation School at Selfridges department store, from which she had been dismissed as a subversive influence. When Neill offered her a job in his school, and Lilian Neustatter promised the couple board and lodging in her own house at a nominal rent, she accepted at once. Edwin Muir took no part in the running of the school, spending much of his time in the pine forest, meditating and reciting the poems of Hölderlin and Kleist. Writing to his sister in December 1922, he noted that Neill's school had 'the usual complement of Communists, vegetarians, simple lifers, and so on'. He told his wife that he thought Neill was silly to criticise schools that played Bach to their pupils before breakfast. Teaching in the school every morning, Willa Muir had ample opportunity to see at first hand the way Neill worked with his pupils. She agreed that 'he was rather inclined to sport chips on his shoulder, and no one paid much attention'; but added that 'it didn't really matter, because whatever theories Neill might air, his practice with children was almost infallible'. She was not to be the last to come to this conclusion.

Later in his life, Neill wrote down his memories of Edwin Muir. Though the observations were made forty years after his time in Hellerau, they do give a glimpse of his life there, as well as throw an interesting light on the contrasting qualities of the two Scotsmen:

> Edwin had a genuine inferiority complex about never having been to a university. . . . You couldn't get inside him, at least I couldn't. We were of different types, well, he lived higher up the mountain, descending, true, for his *Helles Bier* in the local, but even then sitting high. . . . He had a mysticism that was beyond me, I was a pagan, but Edwin always had a kind of spiritualised Orkney puritanism. . . . His humour was receptive; he laughed heartily at jokes, but I can't ever recall his making one or writing humorously in his books. . . . Edwin was a gentleman in both ways, indeed I fancy his gentleness led to his being bored by inferiors. The paradox was that he was both highbrow and lowbrow. . . a merry night at the Waldschenke local and deep talks next day. I never got the impression that he was interested in what was going on around him in Dresden. . . . I cannot recall his ever talking to my pupils in Hellerau. . . . I always thought that he thought too much, that emotionally he remained a frightened

little Scottish boy. If you were taller than he you felt you had to protect him.*

Neill's first group of children was truly international: four English, one Russian, two Belgians, three Yugoslav, and one Norwegian. He also accepted three German pupils who needed psychological treatment, even though by law they were supposed to attend a German school. He hoped to get support from his former school in Hampstead: in October 1921 he wrote to the chairman of the King Alfred School Council: 'Perhaps KAS may be able to help me by sending me its matriculated pupils, for here, today, my youngest pupil is 8, and my oldest 30!' Five of the girls were over 15 and were apparently unable to cope with the comparative freedom they were allowed. This was to be a recurring problem for Neill, taking on children who had during their early years gone through a very different experience of schooling. There were also, inevitably, difficulties over language – though not just with the children, as Neill later remembered:

I wasn't allowed to teach English because I didn't have a degree from a German university. So I had to appoint a German woman. I found her one day asking a pupil 'How is the window?' I told her that if she were to ask me that, I'd say, 'Very well, thank you.' She argued with me that she knew English better than I did. We had a visitor once with a real Irish brogue, and she said: 'That's the kind of English I want to hear – the perfect Oxford accent!'

A key element was the *Schulgemeinde*, the meeting of all staff and pupils which from this point on was to form a crucial part of his school's organisation. For the moment, with such a small group, the meetings were little different from those which might take place in a large family. Anyone could call a meeting at any time; the adults and children would sit round and voice their opinions; and if some kind of vote was necessary, usually in connection with anti-social behaviour, the 'sentence' was decided informally by a show of hands. There were to be many variations in the form of the meeting in later years, but certain elements remained constant from this time: every member of the school had the right to attend the meeting as well as to stay away, to voice their opinion, and to cast a vote where necessary. In the *New Era* issue dealing with self-government, Neill had written: 'It is probable that self-government, in a school moot sense, will not suit children under twelve.' Despite this feeling, there was never any question that children of this age should be excluded or denied a vote.

Neill described a discussion at one meeting in which a younger child,

*Willa Muir's view was that these comments 'tell you more about Neill than about Edwin'. She pointed out that her husband 'was wistfully envious about never having had the fun and companionship I had at St Andrews, but it wasn't an "inferiority complex" '; that 'he could be – and was – very witty, but he didn't tell or remember "funny stories" '; and that 'he was on close terms of friendship with a group of Eurythmic students. He wasn't much interested in Neill's school: he and Neill always regarded each other with a residue of misgiving. Neill was practical in education, Edwin theoretical.'

Wolfgang, played a key part. The incident is interesting in itself, but also for the role played by Neill:

> This meeting was. . . called by Wolfgang. Our science master had found three lizards and thirty grasshoppers in a cardboard box, and he had set them free. Wolfgang argued that the animals were his property, and the master had no right to set them free. The master's contention was that Wolfgang was guilty of animal torture. I defended Wolfgang, and held that the teacher ought to have warned Wolfgang of the cruelty, and at the same time ought to have put the animals in better quarters. The discussion wandered on to pets in general, and the majority of us agreed that animals should not be kept in bedrooms. Then little Eddie, almost in tears, told of his aquarium, which he had had in his bedroom for a year. He said he loved his aquarium, and would be miserable if it were taken away. So the chairman said: 'Is the meeting prepared to make an exception in the case of Eddie's aquarium?' and the meeting in one voice shouted: 'Ja!'

Other meetings were more contentious, and in one Neill came into conflict with the pupils. Lessons were entirely voluntary, as Neill now insisted they should be. There had been complaints that, because he was having trouble in finding suitable staff, the children were getting behind with their work. Neill argued that the children should have welcomed the challenge to show how they could carry on themselves; instead only two of them had come to his English lesson that morning, while the rest of the class 'played football or loafed about the square'. The children replied that they understood they were free to play football if they were not interested in a lesson. Neill suggested that as a group they had shown that they had no desire to help the teachers, and that self-government should be taken away from them, since they were not ripe for it.

The dispute is a difficult one to assess without the evidence of any first-hand witness other than Neill. On the face of it, he appears to be arguing against his own beliefs, as well as confusing the roles of children and staff. If his was a free school, where subjects were supposed to be of little importance, why should the children be expected to help him with his staffing problems? Did they or did they not have the right to work only when they felt like it? Who was it that wanted to tell the parents, 'Here we play'? There are two possible explanations for Neill's behaviour. One is that he wanted to provoke the children into discussion for its own sake, as he was to do so often later. The other, and more likely explanation, was that he was genuinely annoyed and frustrated, despite all his beliefs, that children should be 'loafing around' and enjoying themselves, when he was struggling to find teachers, weeding the garden, cleaning the premises and generally trying to get the school on a firm footing. In fact, at this stage, he could still see a role for adults in a child's school life: 'I think that children ought not to be left to themselves. They must have a director who sees their problems, and continually shoves forward new problems to be solved.' It was not a view he was to hold for much longer.

One boy who spoke in the meeting concerning pets was Derrick Boyd, whom Neill had brought to Germany three months before. He was his first original pupil, his first 'problem child', and also the first of many children whose parents were attracted to Neill's school because of his ideas about the deficiencies of conventional education. Stanley Boyd, Derrick's father, was a doctor, who had read Freud, Jung and Alder, and was interested in the psychosomatic causes of illness. He had also read some of Neill's 'Dominie' books. He and his wife had brought their boys up strictly, had then changed their minds, and given Derrick virtually total freedom. As a result, their son's behaviour was quite unrestrained, as Neill found when he escorted him from Harwich to Hellerau. He talked to everybody on the train and boat, climbed up and over everything in sight, and exposed himself to critical comment on several European platforms. Neill's patience and tolerance were tested to the limit.

When they reached Hellerau Neill started to sort out Derrick's problem. He found that the boy had many fears, including dreams of ghosts, and others linked to the Bible, which he kept by his bedside. He had no conception of private property, and was soon in amongst Neill's tools, bookbinding equipment and other possessions. His demand for attention was continuous, his temper often uncontrollable. Neill aimed to get him to express his fears, which at first remained hidden. He talked to him about his dreams and, using symbols and associations, traced much of his behaviour to a fear of his father. He teased his fears out of him with a combination of humour, affection, and a firm indication that he was interested in the reasons for Derrick's behaviour. At one moment he made a solemn and apparently binding peace treaty with the boy, defining in humorous vein the boundaries of their mutual relationship and the rights of property involved.

As the 'treatment' continued, Neill played an active part in helping Derrick to explore his fantasies. They wrote a shipwreck story together, Neill typing on his new Underwood Portable machine to Derrick's dictation. On another day he helped Derrick to draw his own version of Africa in the sand behind the schoolhouse, and assisted him with his fantasy explorations. Slowly, Neill's efforts began to bear fruit, and people began to notice that Derrick was becoming more sociable. Having walked out of lessons on the very first day, he had eventually come back of his own accord, and begun to take a positive interest in certain subjects – a pattern that was to be often repeated with later children who came to Neill's school. Neill believed that it was not just his own sessions with Derrick that had altered his behaviour:

> I am willing to give much credit to the influence of his free
> environment. Indeed, I have much more faith in that than in
> psychological treatment, and if he were not such a difficult problem,
> I should certainly allow the environment to do all the work.

Gradually, Neill became more and more absorbed in his psychological work, first with Derrick and subsequently with other children. He decided that treating children in a consulting room was hopeless: 'The only satisfactory way is to live with children, to study the workings of their unconscious minds, and then to adapt their environment to their special needs.' He noticed that, as his fascination with treating children grew, he became bored with teaching English; and concluded that he ought to take on someone else to be in charge of the running of the educational side of the school: 'The life I fancy is to go round with a pipe in my mouth, speaking to individual pupils who are in any way unusually interesting psychologically.'* He began to give lectures on Psychology one evening a week, and found that his ideas about the Unconscious provoked great interest among the older students in his International section and in the Eurythmics division. Some of these girls, in their late teens or early twenties, came to him afterwards and began to ask him questions, especially about their dreams. Neill found that a few were badly in need of help, and allowed them to come to his room in the school house, so beginning the Private Lessons (PLs) that were to become such a feature of Summerhill life.

Neill listened to their fears and doubts, and tried to interpret and resolve their difficulties. He had some success with one or two, but found the work more difficult than that with the younger children. His German was still comparatively rough and ready, which made the discussions more difficult. He was also anxious about the possibility of 'transference', where the girl might offload her hate or love of some other adult on to him. One Russian girl, whom Neill scarcely knew, came into his office one day and declared that she loved him, that her husband had found this out, and that he was coming to shoot him. Fortunately, the idea remained in the realms of fantasy; but the incident alerted Neill to the risks of his informal analytical technique. Mixing socially with the pupils and being a friend to everyone, he could not adopt the normal detached and objective stance of the professional analyst – even if he had been temperamentally capable of doing so. As it was, there were some problems of the kind he anticipated, as Willa Muir recalled: 'Neill was to some extent a father-figure for all of them, but he and a handsome young Bavarian assistant in the German school, the only two bachelors among so many girls, became also emotional centres for the "hopeless passions" which young girls seem to need for practice.'

Whatever difficulties he experienced in his emotional and working life, Neill was enormously excited by the cultural life of Germany. Symphony concerts and operas, especially those of his beloved Wagner, were on offer at the Dresden Opera House, once the finest in Germany. He was taken to see Strindberg's *Dance of Death* in Berlin, and without knowing the language was absorbed by its intensity. For the first time he found himself living amongst people who took a passionate interest in the arts. He was

---

*A report in a Berlin newspaper at this time referred to 'a mad Engländer who smokes in the classroom while he teaches'.

astonished to find that the Neustatters' domestic help not only spent her afternoon off at the Dresden Opera House, but knew the whole Wagner repertoire by heart. Some of the best artists in Europe came to Hellerau. Neill listened to painters talking of their work, musicians discussing the new compositions of Béla Bartók. The dancer Isadora Duncan paid a visit while he was there; Upton Sinclair came to the Dalcroze division to sample the atmosphere for use in his novel *World's End*. Though Neill was fascinated by this cultural bonanza, he remained conscious of his own limitations: 'Here I was with my Honours English degree, having to sit silent when the talk was of art and music and philosophy.' However, there was plenty else to do besides sitting passively and feeling ignorant. Neill indulged a new passion for bookbinding to add to his other practical pursuits. He bought a cornet and tried to master the technique of playing it, though with little success. During the day he joined in swimming expeditions to Meritzburg Lake. In the evenings he went with the staff and some of the older pupils to the local inn, dancing foxtrots and one-steps, singing German folk-songs, and drinking beer. One day, with a party that included Edwin and Willa Muir, Neill went to see the famous Passion Play, which was performed every ten years at Oberammergau. This particular event was memorable for another reason, for Neill took two guests with him – his mother and father. It was perhaps a measure of his increasing confidence in his own achievement that he felt able to invite his parents to Germany, and to see his school. They greatly enjoyed the trip to Oberammergau, and talked about it for years afterwards. Because of the favourable currency rates they were able to travel cheaply during their visit of several weeks and stay in the best hotels in Germany. (The cost of both items were clearly a matter of some awe, and passed into family legend.) For Mary Neill, now in her seventieth year, it was her first trip outside Scotland, and Neill found her outlook a little parochial – when he took her to see Nuremburg, he was irritated by her insistence on 'rhapsodising about the beauties of Edinburgh'. Nevertheless, the trip marked a further step in the softening of Neill's attitude towards his parents. He was perhaps beginning to understand some of the cultural and personal factors which had moved them to bring him up in the way that they did.

Neill also found time in Hellerau to continue with his writing. *A Dominie Abroad*, published in 1923 by Herbert Jenkins, was, like most of the books in the series, an informal diary of his life, interspersed with both humorous and serious observations on people and places, incidents and journeys. It included affectionate portraits of Otto Neustatter and others in Hellerau, though there are only fleeting references to Lilian Neustatter. For the first time the 'Dominie' is explicitly acknowledged to be the same person as the author, rather than, if only nominally, a separate character.

The two years he spent in Hellerau opened up a number of horizons for Neill. They brought him into contact with people of many nationalities, both in and outside the school, increasing his distrust of nationalism which he, and many others, now recognised as one of the prime causes of the recent war. 'When I look at the decent young lads I meet here, and think that three years ago the press had almost persuaded me that such men were criminals, I sadden and blush for myself and the press of England.'* Some thirty years later Edwin Muir captured part of the spirit of the time and place:

> We lived. . . in a climate of 'new ideas', and looked forward to a 'new life' which would be brought about by the simple exercise of freedom, a freedom such as had never been formulated before in any terms, since it was too new. We were, or thought we were, without 'prejudices'. We accepted everything, no matter what it might be. We were interested in psychoanalysis, not as a scientific method but as a magical process which would deliver us from our inhibitions and leave us with a freedom all the dearer because it was beyond our imagining.

If such a description fitted the more bohemian souls in Hellerau, amongst whom Muir spent much of his time, it certainly didn't take account of Neill's essential independence and thoroughly *un*cranky pragmatism. Though he could be swayed by an individual's ideas or actions, he was never one to join a movement or follow a crowd. He was also prepared to translate his international outlook into deeds. In 1923 the French government, eager to force the Germans to pay the war 'reparations' agreed on in the Treaty of Versailles, occupied the Ruhr, a move bitterly resented in Germany. The mark began to drop drastically in value. In Dresden prices were altering two or three times in an hour. Men could be seen rushing out with their week's wages crammed into a suitcase, to buy enough food for the family meal.

Neill was concerned about the deprivation being suffered by many families. In order to help alleviate their situation, German children were charged lower fees than others, and were effectively subsidised by families from countries who had benefitted from the currency turmoil. Neill also made an appeal to *New Era* readers in the April 1923 issue:

> Many children are suffering from the Ruhr Occupation, especially the children of officials and others who are out of work for obvious reasons – as protest, for instance. Our International School in Hellerau has started a fund to aid these children and already generous donations have reached us from home.

The money collected was distributed to German and Belgian families alike. Such philanthropy, cutting across alliances, got Neill into trouble. The District Chief of Police in Dresden tried to deport three of his Belgian pupils. Neill pointed out that German children were being subsidised by other nationals, and threatened to close the school if such an action were taken. The official changed his mind, and no more was heard of the matter.

Neill had been a comparatively wealthy man in Hellerau, though his

---

*Neill's internationalism clearly preceded his spell in Hellerau: in 1920 he acted as sponsor for a German girl who wanted to be naturalised.

life remained a simple one, since most of his money was invested in the school venture. Now he found that every pound that he had changed into marks for this purpose was worth a halfpenny. To make the situation more desperate, a Communist 'putsch' now occurred in Saxony. Many of the students in the Eurythmics division were from Jewish families, as were some of Neill's own pupils, and the increasing evidence of anti-semitism made the situation even grimmer. Several parents removed their children from the school, and the German division was forced to close down. When street fighting broke out in Dresden, and parents from England began to wire Neill anxiously about bringing the children home, he decided it was time to leave, and the school broke up.

Although this was a blow to Neill, he might have soon moved on anyway without prompting from outside events. He found the formality of German manners and customs oppressive.* He had a number of brushes with officialdom – over the hours of schooling a child should have, over questions such as whether he himself should be allowed to teach English in the German division. He was also conscious of the watchful eye that German parents were keeping on their children's progress in the conventional school subjects. He noticed that when he entered the school he always turned unconsciously to the left side to the Dalcroze division, and decided that this meant 'I am incapable of running a school of learning. It means that I want a school of creation, a school where plays are written, dances invented, copper designs carried out, an out and out "doing" school.' There is also a small piece of evidence to suggest that, though Hellerau itself was a free-thinking and cosmopolitan place, and in that respect an ideal setting for Neill to get his school off the ground, the people of Dresden were less inclined to accept his unorthodox ways. Not long after Neill was forced to leave Hellerau, a correspondent in a Scottish newspaper wrote: 'I had a letter recently from a friend in Germany, who says the Dresden people were glad to see the last of Neill and his school. . . as they considered the liberty given to the young lady pupils was excessive, and set a bad example to the girls of the town.' In general, though, relations with the outside community appear to have been much calmer than they were to be in the place in which Neill next found himself.

Although he now had a number of English pupils in his school, Neill still saw Continental Europe as a more suitable place than England in which to continue his experiment. Christine Baer had transferred the Eurythmics division to Schloss Laxenburg, near Vienna, and Neill now travelled to the Austrian capital in search of premises. After several weeks he met Oscar Bock, secretary of Das Akademische WohlfahrtsWerk, a youth movement which had been given a hostel by the government. They only needed part of the building for themselves, and offered Neill the rest. It

---

*Later he also recalled 'a woeful lack of humour in German kids. On a hot July day I put a notice on the board . . . Ski laufen Ausflug Morgen um Acht Uhr. Neill. [Ski outing at eight o'clock in the morning. Neill] The whole bloody lot came to me . . . Es Gibt keinen Schnee! [There was no snow!]'

stood right at the top of a 2,500-foot mountain called Sonntagsberg, the last small summit in a range of mountains which curved round the Danube basin. Neill was given the use of two floors of the wing of what used to be a monastery. Right next to this yellow-stuccoed building stood a huge twin-towered Baroque church, designed by the architect of Melk Abbey, Jackob Prandtauer. The hostel contained 200 beds, although no baths had yet been installed; the walls of the rooms were thick and bare, cut here and there into alcoves and arches. The view across the valley was a stupendous one: the mountain top was often *above* the clouds. When they cleared, Neill and his group could from the top floor of the hostel see right across the Danube basin, and watch the vivid sunsets and violent storms which were a feature of the region.

While Neill returned to England to collect some of the pupils, Lilian Neustatter prepared the school for their arrival. It had been a relatively easy decision for her to decide to come with Neill, rather than remain in Hellerau. She was still on good terms with her husband, but their wartime separation had lessened the bond between them. By now she was convinced of the importance of Neill's venture, and that her place was with him: henceforth, it was to be 'their' school. They were joined on the mountain top by others from Hellerau, so that it remained a genuine International School. Edwin and Willa Muir, after further wanderings around Europe, had found themselves homeless, and received a warm invitation from Neill to rejoin their community. In May 1924 Edwin Muir wrote to a friend: 'We do not teach in the school here, which is run by a delightful Scotsman, a friend of my wife. We are boarders and friends of the dominie, to whom we are very attached.' Willa Muir was equally grateful to Neill and Lilian Neustatter: 'what I did to help in the school was no sufficient return for their kindness.' Her brother, Willie Anderson, now joined the community. Also from Hellerau came a young Italian carpenter, Giuseppe, a first-rate piano player. The assistant matron was an elderly Polish woman, the cook a German, the waiter and maid both Austrian. There were also other semi-permanent guests staying in the hostel: Gustav Mattson, a Swedish violin teacher, who later became involved with the New Education Fellowship, and his wife, also a teacher; Jean Lancaster, a young analytical chemist from Lancashire; and, together with his wife and baby son, the writer Edward Loving, then a travelling correspondent for a number of American periodicals. This cosmopolitan group was soon joined by a young Welsh woman, who appeared on the mountain top one day with a rucksack on her back, and stayed with Neill for several years. Bronwen Jones, who became known as 'Jonesie', was a maths graduate who had taught for a couple of years in Cambridge. While on holiday in Vienna she had attended a series of lectures on Freud's new analytical theories. She had a wide variety of interests, teaching astronomy and photography as well as mathematics, and was the first adult to join the school as a teacher.

On Monday 24 January 1924 Neill set out from Victoria Station in London with five of his English pupils. Derrick Boyd had been joined by his brother Donald, who with his parents had visited Hellerau, and asked to be allowed to join the school. Another pupil was Geoffrey Carter from Oxford, and Neill had also taken on his brother Neilie's 8-year-old son – also called Neilie. The fifth boy was a typical example of the kind of child that Neill took in during the years that followed. Angus Murray was an intelligent boy – while in Vienna his IQ was measured at a phenomenal 189. He had previously been at the Bridge of Allen, a school in St Andrews in Scotland, where he received the kind of treatment that Neill had so disliked in his early teaching days. He had been frequently beaten and had his ears boxed, with the result that he became slightly deaf, and was constantly running away from school. Eventually his parents were recommended to try Neill, who provided him with a very different experience.

It was Neill's intention to continue to help those German families who had been affected by the turmoil in their country. In the January 1924 issue of the *New Era* he wrote a terse paragraph: 'I want to take as many hungry German children with me as possible. Twelve shillings a week will feed one child. We provide housing and schooling free. Help for these children is asked for. The children of Germany are really starving.' Little money must have come in, for only one German child came to Sonntagsberg: Walter Erhardt, a 6-year-old boy whose mother was the school's cook. Others who came from Hellerau were Nushy Roth, a strikingly beautiful girl from Budapest who had been in the Eurythmics division, and Mary Artner, whose parents lived in Vienna. A friend of her family, Inge Foerstel, completed the pupil community.*

Life for the children was for much of the time a great adventure. Four hours' train journey away from Vienna, they were comparatively cut off from the outside world; even to climb up the gently winding road to the top of the mountain took more than an hour, though on skis or a toboggan you could descend in six minutes. Provisions had to be dragged up by oxen or mule; the postman came only twice a week; newspapers arrived approximately once a month. Nevertheless, the children found plenty to interest them. They became adept at skiing, and were able to bathe in the village pond near the school. A farm nearby, with pigs, oxen and mules, gave them an opportunity to care for animals. In the pond they found some newts, and started a vivarium to observe their development. Occasionally there were excursions down the mountainside to a nearby town, Waldhofen-an-der-Ybbs, where they feasted on fresh trout and wild strawberries. They played games such as Hare and Hounds, or created elaborate treasure hunts in the nearby pine woods on the mountain's slopes.

Neill and the other adults joined in many of these activities: there was indeed even less separation between them and the children than there had been in Hellerau, and the line between teachers and guests was similarly blurred. Angus Murray remembers: 'There were no formal lessons at all. When we were interested we just asked how things were done, and a group would be formed.' There were few of the normal facilities to be found in the school, so that such groups had to a great extent to improvise. Jonesie

*I have retained the 'maiden' name of all female pupils who came to Neill's school.

used her bedroom to show the children how to develop photographic plates and make pinhole cameras: with no tap to hand, the room was crowded with buckets and basins of water for the developing work. To get some pottery going, they dug clay out of a bank near the pond; to make vegetable dyes they made use of the flowers and plants around.

Gustav Mattson, who had spent a couple of weeks at Neill's school in Hellerau, remembers the spirit of the Sonntagsberg period, and provides an early testimony to the effect of Neill's personality on the children around him. He also underlines, as many others were to do, the crucial role of Lilian Neustatter – or 'Frau Doktor', as she was called in Austria: 'Neill, Frau Doktor, their friends and the children became one large family. Frau Doktor was a most remarkable woman, almost like a mother to most of us, without any favourites, but with a good understanding – Neill's great support and indefatigable co-operator. I don't think he could have carried through his enormous task without her. Neill himself had a deep insight into the minds of young people, of children with very complicated problems. His tolerance seemed almost unbelievable, but without any weakness. I might say there was no distance between him and the children: I believe they loved him dearly and admired him. It is strange perhaps to use the word authority about someone who, if anything, was completely anti-authoritarian, yet that is also a word that comes into my mind.'

Neill now had something that was beginning to approximate to the 'out and out "doing" school' which he desired. Aside from any value this may have had for the children, it also gave him ample opportunity to indulge in his own creative pastimes. His woodwork tools had been brought on from Hellerau, and he began experimenting with metals for inlaying and fret-cutting. Using celluloid toothbrushes and shaving-brush handles, he cut monograms and other motifs, which he would rivet to small shields cut from copper. He used the lathe to carry on another hobby, polishing and 'buffing up' a variety of objects. Much of his belief in the value of creative work for children came from the pleasure which he himself derived from this type of practical activity; both now and later he spent countless hours in his favourite room in the school, the workshop.

There was a lot of musical activity at Sonntagsberg. In the evenings the adults and children would get together for a communal sing-song, or an impromptu concert. On one occasion Neill sang and played the cornet, Willa Muir gave a rendering of 'Lord Randolph, My Son', and a comic version of the ballad of 'Romeo and Juliet' ('Lovers I warn you all to be wary/Don't stab yourself through the left pulmonary'), Angus Murray recited 'How Horatius Kept the Bridge', Gustav Mattson played the violin, and Giuseppe and Lilian Neustatter the piano. Sometimes there would be poetry sessions which, at Neill's instigation, would turn before long into limerick sessions. A characteristically bawdy favourite of his ran:

> There was a young lady from Gloucester
> Whose parents once thought they had loucester
> Til they found in the grass

> The mark of her arse
> And the knees of the fellow that croucester.

In Hellerau Neill had acquired a taste for dancing. This he was able to indulge again in Austria, especially the new foxtrots and tangoes which he especially liked. He went dancing in Vienna, and developed 'a sentimental attachment to anything Austrian'. His romantic view of Viennese society was reinforced by the first German book he read, *A Young Girl's Diary*, an account of her life in Vienna in the late 1890s by a middle-class adolescent girl. Neill enjoyed 'its after-glow from the days of the Strauss waltzes, the *Rosenkavalier*, and the gaiety of the city with its *Gemütlichkeit*, its Schlag Seine [coffee with whipped cream] and its Wiener Schnitzels'. He found the book easy to read, and learned from it many Viennese words, which he used constantly in later years. He also found the book interesting psychologically, seeing it as a wonderful story of a girl's sex repressions and sex ignorance, a book on which Freud might have based his whole sexual philosophy. The book in fact became a matter of considerable interest and curiosity among analysts and psychologists; Freud, who wrote a preface for the English translation, called it a 'jewel'. Neill was convinced that the psychologist Cyril Burt was wrong in suggesting that the book was a fake; no adult, he argued, 'could have pictured the misery alternating with the joy of a young girl'.*

Life, however, was not all tangoes and whipped cream for Neill. The problem children he had with him took up a lot of his time and energy. One, who tried to burn down the house by making a fire in the cellar, needed to be kept under close scrutiny the entire time. Derrick Boyd, though he had evidently now settled into the community, was still not the easiest of children. His brother Donald needed and received sensitive treatment for his particular problem, as he recalls: 'Neill helped me a lot. I was enuretic, and it was his analysis that cured me. He was able to determine the fears that were causing the difficulty, and get in touch with my father, who was able to reassure me over these fears. After that I had no further trouble. To me Neill was a sense of security. When I was about 4 I needed security from almost everybody I met.' Angus Murray found Neill a delightful contrast to the authority figures he had met in St Andrews: 'He used to call me his "little Harry Lauder". And you could call *him* anything you liked.' His only unhappy recollection of Sonntagsberg was when a young puppy that he was playing with fell from a second-storey window and had to be destroyed. The boy suffered a traumatic shock, and Neill decided to take him into Vienna to see an eminent analyst with whom he had recently made contact.

Wilhem Stekel had originally been a patient of Freud himself, and later became one of the leading figures in the circle that gathered around Freud

---

*However, Burt, who perhaps knew more than Neill about such things, turned out to be right. The book was eventually acknowledged to be by Hermine von Hug-Hellmuth, a pioneer in child analysis, who, on the most charitable interpretation, had re-worked her childhood memories in the light of the psychoanalytical theories of the 1920s.

in Vienna at the turn of the century. It was Stekel who had proposed that a small group meet once a week in Freud's waiting-room, forming what later became the Vienna Psychoanalytical Association. There Freud, Stekel, Jung, Adler and others – with the aid of cigars and black coffee – read papers, exchanged case material, and criticised each other's theories. Stekel was noted for his extraordinary ability to understand intuitively his patients' unconscious emotions, and for his pioneering work with dream symbolism. Even Freud, who was extremely spare in his praise of colleagues, acknowledged that Stekel had the edge on him in the interpretation of dreams, and had influenced his own work in this sphere. However, like many of Freud's colleagues – notably Jung and Adler – Stekel eventually quarrelled and broke with Freud. Stekel had many qualities which endeared him to the other members of Freud's circle: he was an excellent musician, a poet, a talented and fluent – if sometimes careless – journalist, who was, in the eyes of Freud's colleague and biographer Ernest Jones, 'a very agreeable companion, light-hearted, and very amusing'. But many of his fellow-analysts believed that he had no scientific conscience at all. He did indeed confess to making up some case histories, and Freud was deeply upset by what he called 'his far-reaching lack of self-criticism and truthfulness'. Some of the group felt that his interest in sexuality was dubious, and that he displayed a near-pornographic fascination with case material. After their split, Freud turned against Stekel, and by the time Neill came to know him in Vienna, Freud was declaring his former colleague and patient a case of 'moral insanity'.*

When he came to Vienna Neill was reading Stekel's *Conditions of Nervous Anxiety and their Treatment*, was impressed by what he read, and decided to call on Stekel. He found him 'a charming man with a big pipe in his mouth'. Evidently he was not the kind of figure Neill had imagined him to be: 'There wasn't a trace of authority about him,' he wrote shortly after his first visit, 'and I am sure children love him. . . in talking with him I found a great interest in education, and a great belief in freedom for the child. But what I liked best about him was a delightfully boyish conceit about how he had mastered the English language in a few months.' He decided that Stekel was a 'man of much experience, of broad mind, of humour.'

Neill was especially impressed by Stekel's belief, expressed in his book, that 'the consciousness of guilt is the chief cause of all neuroses and psychoses'. In his review for the *New Era* Neill considered the implications of Stekel's view: 'To me the book says, "Yes, guilt causes neurosis." We must therefore abolish what causes guilt, namely a conscience given from without. Moral education is the sin against the Holy Ghost, for it gives a child a conscience.' Neill was also interested in Stekel's concept of 'pleasure without guilt', which Stekel believed to be the guiding principle of every

---

*One of Stekel's favourite phrases that Neill recalls, possibly in answer to this kind of charge from Freud, was 'A dwarf sitting on a tall man's shoulder sees further than he does.'

neurotic. 'I am inclined to think it is also the guiding principle of every child,' Neill observed at the time. He went on to read another of Stekel's books, *Onanie und Homosexualität*, which he felt to be the only book dealing with masturbation that was 'sane and helpful'. Masturbation was a topic to which Neill was to return frequently; his basic thinking about it was substantially influenced by Stekel, who took the view – rare among the early Freudians – that masturbation was inherently harmless. But Neill was not only interested in Stekel's ideas, though he did read many case histories and dream analyses as a result of this meeting. Stekel had said in his book that analysis was too long, and that it could be effected in a period as short as three months. This, Neill said, appealed to his Scots thrift, and he persuaded Stekel to take him as a patient.*

His real reasons for doing this can only be guessed at. Neill had been interpreting the dreams of many of his pupils and students, and may well have thought it useful to see at first hand how an acknowledged expert used this technique. On a more personal level, Neill had been compelled to break off his analysis with Homer Lane when he moved to Germany. He might well have thought that Stekel, who was especially skilful in dealing with his patients' repressed emotions, could be of help to him here. Gustav Mattson remembers that 'in some ways Neill was somewhat, shall I say, buttoned-up'. It was now some time since he had been involved in a significant relationship with a member of the opposite sex – in Hellerau he 'had his flirts', Willa Muir recalls, but there does not appear to have been anything deeper. Stekel, as it turned out, had an explanation for this, telling Neill that he was 'still in love with his sister', an idea that Neill referred to in his later writing. Neill also wrote later that he received Stekel's thoughts with his intellect only, 'and in the absence of emotion the interpretation cut no ice'. Again this was a later judgment following a different type of analysis, and may have been no more accurate than his assertion that Lane's private lessons 'did not touch any emotions'. Neill was certainly impressed by Stekel's ability to interpret the symbolism of his dreams, though he sometimes denied his interpretations.

Whatever doubts Neill may have had, either at the time or subsequently, about the value of his analysis, he certainly took to Stekel as a man, and became friends with him. It was very probably through his friendship with Stekel that Neill met and talked with three other eminent analysts, Siegfried Bernfeld, Alfred Aichorn and Otto Rank: he spent an evening in Vienna with Aichorn, telling him about Homer Lane. And his encounters with Stekel encouraged him to steep himself in analytical case histories and dream analyses.

Around the time he moved his school to Austria, Neill wrote the last of the 'Dominie' books, *A Dominie's Five*. This time the format was different: the book consisted almost entirely of a story for children, which

---

*Neill later told a friend that Stekel would often break off his analysis to talk to the postman when he arrived with the mail. 'I got very cross, and said if I was paying a guinea a time, he shouldn't give half of it to the postman.'

he had developed with his English class at Hellerau. In this 'rattling story of machine guns and lions', Neill revealed his continuing liking for the 'penny dreadful' type of narrative, though he also had a serious intention in writing the story. The children themselves – the group included three now in Sonntagsberg, Geoffrey Carter, Derrick and Donald Boyd – featured as the principal characters, and were given a multitude of aggressive and criminal acts to carry out. Neill believed that if a child wanted to kill *in fantasy*, it should be encouraged to do so. In a postcript to the story, entitled 'And the Psychology of it all', Neill relates his purpose to Stekel's 'pleasure without guilt' principle. He also points to a less abstract issue concerning the tale: 'Where the story did good was in this: each child felt that he or she was loved. "Here is old Neill (father substitute) loving me so much that he makes me do brave deeds." ' Neill continued with these story-telling sessions for many years, often incorporating the children's suggestions or criticisms into the narrative in a very skilful and imaginative manner.*

As it turned out, it was fortunate that Neill had only signed up for a short course of analysis with Stekel. Around Easter 1924, problems began to arise in Sonntagsberg. The church next to the hostel had been built to celebrate a miracle, and had become a place of pilgrimage. In the pause between the hay and the corn harvests, men, women and children came from many countries to visit the celebrated spot. The families slept in the local inn or the fields, and bought their rosaries, breviaries, postcards and other souvenirs from the three local shops run by elderly women in the village. They attended Easter Mass – held this year by the Archbishop of Rome – and other services in the monastery. Neill, of course, had no time at all for religious worship, and was particularly hostile to the Catholic Church – he commented caustically that the pilgrimage 'docked four hundred years off purgatory'. One of Neill's pupils had stolen candles and a crucifix from a local shop. Around the church was a number of lichened and weather-beaten statues of the saints, on which a group of children now shone mirrors, creating the effect of a halo. As Neill remembers, 'There was much crossing of themselves by visitors, and when the children's trick was discovered, I wondered why we were not lynched, for the peasants were the most hateful people I ever came across.'

It was the villagers rather than the pilgrims that provoked this remark from Neill, and it is easy to understand the mutual hostility that arose. Willa Muir recalls that 'the village people, being Catholics who made a living from that holiness, looked on us all with great suspicion, since we were foreigners, aliens who never went to church and were certainly heretics if not altogether godless.' But it was not merely a question of belief. The villagers were not amused when one of the boys threw a snowball at a holy image in the village. They also had other grounds for complaint, though

---

*He showed the story to Stekel – indeed it is just possible that Stekel encouraged him to put on paper what had previously been purely oral. Stekel gave him an analysis of it which Neill thought delightful, but, regrettably, felt should not be made public.

the proposed remedy seems excessive in the extreme. Donald Boyd looks back on the incident: 'I went round the church steps on my scooter, and this upset the clergy very much indeed. They wanted me to climb up all the steps of the church, on my knees, and say a prayer of forgiveness on every step.' Neill, it appears, 'persuaded them off the idea', and hostilities intensified. Farmers and their wives threw broken bottles and crockery into the pond to stop the children bathing – they had apparently been scandalised by the sight of a girl of 9 in a bathing costume. Then the caretaker told Neill that the villagers were accusing the adults of indulging in illicit sexual relations. Not for the first time, the police were called in.*

On top of all this, Neill began to get inquiries about his failure to teach religion, and was told that he would have to employ a teacher for the subject in order to comply with Austrian law. Willa Muir remembers the final and most dramatic encounter between Neill and the upholders of Tyrolean law and order: 'One day a gendarme arrived with a fixed bayonet and a questionnaire for Neill to answer, a comprehensive document based on the official regulations for village schools enshrined in a *Schul-gesetz* dating back to the middle of the nineteenth century. All male pupils had to have so-and-so many hours of physical instruction weekly: the gendarme wanted to know what Herr Neill was doing about that? All female pupils had to have so-and-so many hours of domestic instruction weekly: was Herr Neill complying with that regulation? And so on. Neill refused to provide any answers or to accept the document.'

Neill was thinking seriously about moving his school when once again outside events forced his hand. In June 1924 the bank in which he had lodged all his savings collapsed. The school was hurriedly dismantled, and the children dispersed to their homes. The school cat, tucked into Willa Muir's woollen scarf, was taken back safely to its home in Hellerau, while Neill, together with Lilian Neustatter, set out in search of a country which would allow him to continue his experiment without interference.

---

*The philosopher Ludwig Wittgenstein also met hostility in the mountains around Vienna, when two years before he had been an elementary school teacher in the village of Trattenbach. The peasants refused to sell him milk because he taught them sums that were not about money.

PART TWO

Summerhill

CHAPTER 8

A School with a View

'Casting Out Fear' ought to be the motto over every school door.
The Problem Child, 1926

A. S. Neill, the Dominie, has brought his International School home,
and has set up at Summerhill, Lyme Regis. He is specialising in
problem children, and says that he wants boys and girls that other
schools find troublesome, lazy, dull, anti-social. He steadfastly
refuses to compromise. . .'Here is my school,' he says to parents,
'absolute freedom to work or to play. Take it or leave it.'

In placing this note in the *New Era* of October 1924, Neill was making it
abundantly clear where his interest lay. Ironically, at the precise moment
when he was formally setting up a school that was to create an enormous
stir within English education, he was signalling his intention to build up a
therapeutic community which had little to do with school in the recognised
sense. He had, as he put it, already 'left education for child psychology'
when he began the International School in Hellerau. Both there and in
Austria it had proved difficult to run his experiment along lines which
satisfied his ideas about child nature. England, he decided after a few
months, was 'still the freest country in the world'. No officials would be
coming along, with or without bayonets, to see if he had religious education
on the timetable; the people would, it seemed, be quite tolerant of his
unconventional community.

The climate of the 1920s seemed in many ways a propitious one to
start such a venture. The younger generation in particular were questioning
pre-war beliefs in the virtue of tradition, obedience and respect. It had been

the values inculcated by the 'Old Men' that had brought the nations to war, at the expense of 10 million lives and 36 million casualties. Authority had for many become a dirty word. The war had brought other changes too, notably the vote for women, although they only finally achieved full equality with men in 1928. Ironically, it was the work done by women in factories and offices during the war, rather than their fierce campaign for equality in the years preceding it, that had brought them the franchise. Many careers, for example in the professions, were now in theory open to them, as was higher education.

Reflecting these advances, a new frankness among women superseded the pre-war tendency to evade or gloss over 'difficult' topics. Vera Brittain, in *Testament of Youth*, looked back some years later at these changing attitudes:

> We were now sophisticated to an extent which was revolutionary when compared with the romantic ignorance of 1914. Where we had once spoken with polite evasion of 'a certain condition', a 'certain profession', we now unblushingly used the words 'pregnancy' and 'prostitution'. Amongst our friends we discussed sodomy and lesbianism with as little hesitation as we compared the merits of different contraceptives, and were therefore theoretically familiar with varieties of homosexuality and venereal disease of which the very existence was unknown to our grandparents.

Much of this new freedom was due to the determination of Marie Stopes, whose book *Married Love* created a sensation when it appeared in 1918. She argued that women should be encouraged to delight in sexual passion, that men should recognise that women had such desires, and treat them with greater understanding. In an attempt to help such a transformation of the relationship between the sexes, she opened the first birth control clinic in England.

Part of the change in morals and attitudes came from the increasing interest in the ideas of Freud and his co-workers, described as the 'New Psychology'. Edwin Muir, while staying with Neill shortly after the return from Sonntagsberg, and browsing amongst his psychology books, wrote to a friend: 'Certainly it seems more clear to me than ever that if we are to have any revaluation of values, it must come from a study of psychology, conscious and unconscious.' The literature which might help to bring this about was now becoming available. Freud's own *Introductory Lectures on Psychoanalysis* appeared in translation in 1920; the works of Edward Carpenter and Havelock Ellis began to be read more widely; and a number of popular books about psychology sold in large numbers – W. H. Rivers, with his *Instinct and the Unconscious*, was one of several who helped to bring the ideas of the analysts to a wider audience.

Yet the period was a transition rather than a total revolt from the Victorian and Edwardian years. Not everyone was as determined as the 'advanced' men and women to demonstrate their 'emancipation'. There was, in any case, still an astounding measure of ignorance, confusion and unhappiness amongst the population as a whole, as the letters written by people of all classes to Marie Stopes indicate. Most expressed guilt at daring to mention topics such as sexual intercourse or birth control. Their language was evasive: women's periods were called 'colours', intercourse referred to as 'connection', sex organs labelled as 'things'; a wife spoke approvingly of her husband who never 'worried' her more than once or twice a month. Even Marie Stopes herself believed sex should only take place within marriage, and that not to marry was to 'flout nature'. To one London mother, who wanted to know if her son should refrain from any 'indulgence' until his marriage, she wrote: 'Healthy exercise, plenty of cold water cleanliness, keeping his mind off the subject, and knowing that his women folk expect him to keep straight until his marriage, are sufficient to keep a well-bred man clean for his wife.'

There was also plenty of resistance in high places to open discussion of sexual matters. *The Times* refused to print an advertisement for a meeting to be addressed by Marie Stopes, on the grounds that 'it was not considered by the Management to be suitable for insertion in *The Times*.' The Catholic Women's Guild declared that her book would lead to 'race suicide and moral degeneracy'. The Ministry of Health threatened to dismiss any doctor or health visitor who gave advice on birth control, so that most people had to obtain contraceptives surreptitiously. Homosexuality was looked upon as either a perversion, an illness or a crime, and practising homosexuals could be and were sent to prison – 'I thought men like that shot themselves,' George V was supposed to have remarked, when he heard that someone he knew fell into this unlucky category. The same applied to lesbianism: Radclyffe Hall's sensitive novel about the subject, *The Well of Loneliness*, was suppressed; a journalist writing in a popular newspaper declared that he would 'rather give a healthy boy or girl a phial of prussic acid than *The Well of Loneliness* to read'. While the works of Freud and his fellow analysts did bring the chance of a new understanding of the nature of infantile sexuality, and the importance of a child's early years, many adults were still greatly inhibited in what they discussed with their children. It was still unusual for children to be given the true facts about reproduction. Masturbation was even more of a taboo subject – it was known as 'the secret vice' and referred to as 'abuse'. Children were told it could lead to blindness, baldness, impotence or consumption. In most girls' schools facts about menstruation were never mentioned; in a few schools, such as the convent attended by the writer Antonia White, girls were even forbidden to look at their own bodies. Many traces of Victorian prudery remained, as Neill was soon to discover.

Lyme Regis is a small, hilly and attractive town in Dorset on the south coast of England. It was Henry Handel Richardson and her husband, George Robertson, whose second home was in the town, who found premises for the school. The house, built early in the nineteenth century on 'Summer Hill', was originally called Pine Crest, and stood on the hillside above the town on the road to Charmouth. It had a view across Lyme Bay which, from the top storey, provided a glimpse of The Cobb, the famous grey-stone sea wall which encircles the harbour. It was an attractive three-storey building with a basement, a rather grand portico entrance, shutters on the windows, a smallish garden with a larger field behind, and rambling outhouses. It had fifteen rooms, providing ample space for Neill, Lilian Neustatter and the five children they had brought back from Sonntagsberg. Conditions were very sparse, and at first they had to improvise with tea chests – they had been forced to leave £100 worth of furniture in Austria. There was no money to spare: Neill recalled later that they would stand looking at an ironmonger's window in the town, wondering if they could afford a spade. Setting up the school was a tremendous struggle: at one point it was saved from closure by a gift of £300 from an Australian sympathiser. In order to make ends meet it was necessary to take in paying guests during the school holidays, and for three years Lilian Neustatter worked without a break. Neill recalled later her determination that they should succeed: 'Her optimism and energy were so great that neither of us ever thought of failure.'

The writer Ethel Mannin, who plunged with gusto into many of the new ideas and movements of the 1920s, quickly became an ardent supporter of Summerhill after she came to hear about Neill through one of his books. In her book *Confessions and Impressions*, published in July 1930, she set down her recollection of her very first visit to the school in Lyme some five years before:

> The gates were painted black and orange, which I thought encouraging. I hardly knew what I expected. There were a great many 'noises off', yells and whoops and shrieks and laughter, but nothing in view except a disconsolate-looking hen walking across the untidy lawns. The front door, also painted black and orange, was open and I saw into a whitewashed hall with wildly futuristic paintings on the walls, and cocoanut matting on the stained boards of the floor. Finally a black-haired, stockingless, sandalled young woman came round a corner. . . . She showed me into a big room with more whitewashed walls and futuristic paintings, all discs and angles and cubes and distorted perspectives, in the German vein. . . .There was a grand piano in the room, and on it wild flowers in glass jam-jars. There were also rickety looking bookshelves overflowing with books of all descriptions, English and German, novels, poets, works on psychology and psycho-analysis. There were basket chairs with orange cushions, and on the bare boards of the floor Persian rugs. . . .Through the windows a great cedar tree reached its arms out over a tennis lawn, and beyond it the sea, the colour of light merged in a shimmering opalescence with the sky. Whilst I looked about and waited, and wondered, two boys and a girl, all hatless and in riding breeches, rode up on ponies and dismounted at the crumbling steps leading up to the front door. . . . Presently other people drifted in, members of the staff; there were no introductions and nobody seemed surprised to find a stranger in

their midst; being there one was accepted without question. . . . It was all very casual – a simple, comfortable, friendly sort of casualness, infinitely refreshing.

After only a few months in England Neill started to write his next book, on the subject that now preoccupied him. *The Problem Child*, published in 1926, represented a new departure in several ways. Gone was the Dominie figure, the self-portrait whose humour and earthy Scottishness tended to distract attention from the serious arguments contained in his earlier books. The *Teacher*, reviewing his previous book *A Dominie Abroad*, judged that 'Mr Neill is certainly the most popular writer on education today'. In so far as that popularity was based on the self-deprecating humour and wry pungency of his style, some readers may have initially been disappointed with the new book. It was more serious, more controlled in its argument, and more confident in its purpose. Neill aimed to show parents where they had gone wrong. It was, he argued, their failure to understand children's motives, and in particular their unconscious wishes and needs, that caused them to make their children unhappy. The problem child was the child who was unhappy, at war with him or herself. This in essence made his job as a psychologist rather than an educator a straightforward one: 'The only curing that should be practised is the curing of unhappiness.'

The book is also significant for Neill's first substantial reference to the motivating force behind his work. He admits that

> in propounding a gospel of freedom for the child I am conscious that the foundation of the gospel is subjective. My interest in freedom began as a protest against the authority of my childhood. Rather it began as an over-protest, but after years the over-protest has become mellowed. It is probable that I now value freedom for its own sake, not as a protest against authority.

If Neill felt that he had overcome the malignant effects of his childhood, and could now look at matters more objectively, his words and actions belied such a judgment. Indeed, this apparent failure could often be his greatest strength. In dealing with a 'problem child' he was able, both intuitively and intellectually, to return to his childhood, to see the child's neurosis or anti-social behaviour through the glass of his own unhappy early years in Scotland, and to find a way through to that child's inner compulsions.

Gradually, and especially after the publication of *The Problem Child*, the school began to attract attention, and also pupils. Neill took in thieves, liars, bedwetters, children with temper tantrums, others who lived fantasy lives. Several who came had suffered from the harsh regime of the English public schools. In 1925, in a letter to the *Evening Standard*, the ex-headmaster of Eton, the Reverend Lyttleton, wrote: 'Children go to school impressed with a belief that they have a right to be happy, that God will give them a good time. This is the perversion of the true religion, self-denial and obedience.' Eton and Harrow supplied one problem child each while Summerhill was in Lyme. Other children who came had been abused, neglected and even abandoned by their parents, or were suffering intense jealousy of a brother or sister. Neill also, at least for a while, took in a few children who were not simply 'troublesome, lazy, dull and anti-social', but who suffered from physical defects, or who were mentally handicapped in some way. He also took on one pupil who provided another link with Homer Lane. Olive Lane, one of the 'infants' at the Little Commonwealth, had been adopted by Lane in 1914. On his death, and at his request, she was informally re-adopted by Neill and Lilian Neustatter and remained with them as a pupil for many years, free of charge

As the numbers increased, Neill took on a number of 'housemothers', whose job he considered to be even more important than that of the teaching staff. They were often young women wanting to gain experience working with children, or students of child psychology, or, later on, ex-pupils who felt unready or unwilling to leave the school. One of the first, Klares Lewis, had originally come as a paying guest, many of whom came back every summer. Another was Joan Jennings, whose future brother-in-law was already a pupil there. As she recalls, the pattern of the house-mothers' lives was almost as unplanned as that of the children: 'Staff – if such we were – just got on with things. There was no timetable – I read stories to the younger ones, took "runs" when it was too wet to play hockey, cooked the evening meals, washed up, went riding and swimming, and tried to chase the kids to bed.' There would also be trips to the local cinema in the assembly rooms on the sea-front, a woman pianist providing the accompaniment to the silent films of the day. Adults and children would go for walks over the hills above Lyme, or down to Monmouth Beach next to the Cobb to swim. A few took lessons from the local riding school in Uplyme. And on warm summer nights they were allowed to sleep out in the garden.

Neill's aim was to create a setting in which the children could find a release for their emotional problems by being allowed and even encouraged to work through their fantasies, act out their aggression, talk about their fears. Although he argued and believed that it was this kind of freedom which was the principal cause of change in a child's behaviour, there is no doubt that his own personality had an enormous amount to do with his success in dealing with the 'problem children' at Summerhill. 'I am the man who allows him to be free,' he wrote in *The Problem Child*:

> I am the Daddy that Daddy should have been. The boy is not really loving me. A boy does not love; he wants to be loved. His unspoken thought is: 'I am happy here. Old Neill is rather a decent sort of chap, never butts in and all that. He must be jolly fond of me or he would butt in and order me about.'

Many of the first Summerhill pupils speak positively of the warm, undemanding benevolence that emanated from 'Old Neill'. Some of this they ascribe to his manner and appearance. Brian Anscombe, Neill's tenth pupil, recalls his arrival in 1925, when he was 10 years old: 'I was told I was going to be met at Axminster, a little junction near Lyme Regis. There were only two people on the platform: one was the porter, the other a rather nondescript looking fellow in an old raincoat. That was Neill – quite unlike my preconceived notion of a headmaster.' Teddy Raw, who came a year later at the age of 7, and virtually lived at Summerhill for twelve years, had experienced problems both at home and school. 'I had been at several schools already, and was highly suspicious of everybody. Neill was never threatening in any way, and was always very kind. For a long time I thought that what ever he did was right.' Donald Boyd was one of many who perceived Neill as different in a particular way from other adults: 'I saw him as a personality who had no age: he was neither young nor old: he was always Neill.'

Neill's Private Lessons (PLs) with the children at Summerhill differed not only in his relaxed, informal and 'unprofessional' manner from those offered by conventional analysts: in his case 'patient' and 'analyst' had a relationship outside the hours of 'consultation'. Neill was criticised for living with those he was treating, but he saw no other way. He recognised that the children often transferred their love or hate of another adult on to him, and that such a 'transference' needed extremely careful handling. Diana Fishwick was another of the early Lyme pupils; her parents apparently failed to explain to her why she was being sent to Summerhill. When she first arrived, she kicked Neill for an hour, but he refused to react. Another girl, who had been thrown out of her previous school for infringing the rules, kept up a similar barrage of kicks and bites for three hours. Neill managed, with difficulty, to keep his temper, and eventually she quietened down. She was, he felt, essentially a lover of law and order, who had revolted against the rule of her parents and teachers, and was expressing her frustrations to him. Psychology, he wrote later, 'is the art of having infinite patience, the art of being able to wait and wait and wait.'

Neill was able to adapt his approach to the individual concerned, and this sometimes required a less passive reaction on his part. Johnnie Collier, another pupil at Lyme, recalls one such incident: 'One boy had a temper rage, which he was very prone to, and he had a knife. He was in the workshop, and Neill went up to him and said quietly, "Give me the knife, Peter," and he did.' Another time the same boy was threatening other children with a hammer, when Neill came in: ' "Chuck it, my lad," I said sharply. "We aren't afraid of you." He dropped the hammer and rushed at me, biting and kicking me. "Every time you scratch or bite me," I said quietly, "I'll hit you back." And I did. He very soon gave up the contest and rushed from the room.' In Johnnie Collier's view, 'Neill's charisma arose partly through this sort of incident. You felt that in some sense he was magical.'

Such firm action from Neill was, though, a fairly rare occurrence. Normally he would, as he wrote in *The Problem Child*, 'sit still and approve of all the things that a child disapproves of in himself.' Roger Anscombe recalls: 'He was terribly good at entering into their fantasies without intruding.' Outside his Private Lessons, he tried to make sure that other members of the community, both adults and children, took on the mantle of authority. Joan Jennings remembers one problem that arose, as it did throughout the life of the school: 'The bedtime was fixed by a general meeting of kids and staff, but it was not always adhered to. Neill would not dream of enforcing anything, but no objections were raised if we rather "in-between" people tried to lay down the law. . . for the sake of peace and quiet in the evenings for the adults. Neill's theories about freedom didn't stop his resenting the occasional din, and I was several times asked to go and "shut up" the bigger boys who were refusing to settle down to sleep.' It was a cornerstone of Neill's philosophy, which he articulated again and again, that just as adults should not be 'moulding' children, a child could behave as he or she liked in Summerhill, as long as it did not interfere with the rights of others.

It was, of course, part of the function of the *Schulgemeinde*, as the weekly meeting in the lounge was still called, to define in practical ways the limits of freedom, by making and attempting to enforce the rules agreed upon by the community. Neill, like Homer Lane, believed that the mechanism of self-government was a way of allowing problem children to transfer their emotions on to the community, rather than on to him. Indeed, in these early years, the children held a tribunal to make laws and punish offenders without Neill being present, though he and everyone else attended the general meetings. At Lyme it was difficult for the adults not to play a major role, as the oldest child, Derrick Boyd, was still only 12. Sometimes Neill went so far as to *encourage* children to break the rules. One boy, who had been thrown out of one of the most prestigious English public schools, was constantly in trouble at Summerhill. After six weeks he asked Neill for permission to go into the town by himself – the meeting had previously decided that pupils should only be allowed to go 'down town' in twos. Neill pointed out that, as he didn't make the rules, he couldn't give his permission to go, but suggested that no one would notice if he sneaked off by the back door. The boy refused to break the rule, and decided to wait until he could find someone to accompany him.

Neill's patience and self-effacement at meetings were in contrast to the attitude of Mrs Lins,* as Neill admitted many years later: 'In her heart she never really liked self-government: it was cumbersome and slow, and often she would want to act with her usual energy and quickness, when I held that a matter was a community one and should be dealt with communally.' This impatience, together with standards of order and cleanliness which were quite at variance with Neill's lack of interest in such matters, provoked her on occasion to act against the accepted procedures. Mervyn Corkhill, who came to Lyme in 1925 as a pupil, remembers the effect she made: 'She used to get up at the meeting when she saw toffee papers and ice-cream cartons strewn around the place, and say, "We must clear up."

---

*At Summerhill, Lilian Neustatter was initially known as Mrs Lindesay – a family name – until the children shortened it to 'Mrs Lins'.

When she said that, everyone went out and did it. She was almost like a House of Lords that overruled everyone else.'

It was Mrs Lins who handled the money side of Summerhill, and who therefore bore the brunt of what was to prove one of the most intractable problems over the years: defaulting parents. A few paid no fees at all; many others fell seriously behind with their bills. Neill, despite his perennial poverty, was extremely generous and kind-hearted towards such parents. Often it was those with the most difficult children who were guilty of late or non-payment; yet he was loath to remove a child as long as he or she was getting help from Summerhill. Some parents evidently took Neill's charitable attitude for granted: when one who had not paid for several terms received an account, she wrote back saying it was like getting a slap in the face from Jesus Christ. Mrs Lins did occasionally get angry with such parents, but in general she adopted the same attitude as Neill, and was sometimes the first to suggest that payment should be waived or postponed.

Mrs Lins was, in most respects, truly the ideal partner for Neill at Summerhill. Larry Collier, another pupil at Lyme, speaks for many in his admiration of her qualities: 'She was fantastic: oozing culture, a good housekeeper, always absolutely unflappable. She had a terrific adoration for Neill, and great respect. She thought he was the Messiah, and gave him unlimited support. It was a great team, and created a quite exceptional domestic atmosphere.' Greta Sergeant, who came to Lyme as a house-mother, remembers another side to her personality: 'She was a mother to everyone, staff as well as children. You could talk to her about everything: she listened and understood.'

Her width of culture and tremendous organising skills were a rare combination, providing a stabilising influence for many children and adults. If the school had no timetable, she certainly did. Her mornings were spent supervising the breakfasts, sorting the children's clothes, dealing with rou-tine administration tasks, and teaching a couple of lessons. Lunch would be taken promptly at one, she and Neill eating in the kitchen while the maids took the children's food into the dining room. Her afternoons would consist of a short rest, a walk down the hill to the shops, a brisk turn by the sea, and a light tea and a game of tennis on her return. And in the evenings, after the meal was over, she would invite staff and some of the older children into her sitting room for some musical entertainment, when she would play a little Chopin on her shiny black grand piano.

Roger Anscombe remembers that 'she had a marvellous way of making you feel that this was home. She was terribly good at giving these occasions great warmth, and keeping them going if they were flagging.' 'On the other hand,' he recalls, 'she could be extremely unreasonable at times. She used to get terribly irascible if anyone started fooling about. Sometimes Neill used to quarrel with her, and say, "No, no, you shouldn't have said that." She would say, "Yes I should." "No, I'm not having that," he'd reply.' Such open disagreement between the two was rare, for however much he relished a public debate, Neill disliked conflict of a personal nature, and would go to considerable lengths to avoid it. This was more than simply a determination not to be authoritarian: he seems to have been incapable of coping with emotionally charged situations in which another adult was involved. Roger Anscombe remembers an incident which highlighted this: 'Three of us had composed an obscene letter to one of the housemothers, who had told Mrs Lins of the episode. We got out of the school and went down to the sea, but then decided we should come back and face the music. Mrs Lins tore us off a most terrible strip, telling us that what we had done was disgusting. I sensed that Neill was not 100 per cent behind the scolding; that Mrs Lins was almost saying to him, "Come on, you lam into them," and that he was saying, "If anyone thinks I'm going to come the heavy father, they've got another think coming!" '

Neill admired Mrs Lins greatly, and could even be provoked to uncharacteristic anger in her defence, as Johnnie Collier recalls: 'There was one boy who was very offensive to her, and just couldn't get on with her at all. Knowing that she was Australian, he would say things like, "I'm glad my mother doesn't come from a convict settlement." Neill got very indignant with him, and told him that he couldn't talk to Mrs Lins like that.' But his admiration for her energy and courage, and his gratitude for her patient and dedicated support, were clearly diluted with a certain amount of apprehension.

Yet in 1927 he and Mrs Lins agreed to put their relationship on a different footing. 'They just went out one day and came home saying they were married,' Joan Jennings remembers. There was no celebration, and no one from Summerhill witnessed the ceremony at the registry office. Parents were informed in an end-of-term note: 'P. S. Neill and Mrs Lins have married.' There were a number of reasons for this decision. One was to do with nationality. Because of her marriage to Otto Neustatter, which had now been amicably dissolved, Mrs Lins was technically an alien, and had to register with the police. She resented this, and was glad to be able to revert to being a British subject. Another factor, according to her son, was her desire to present a respectable front to the outside world. She insisted that, until her divorce came through, Otto Neustatter should only visit the school under the fictitious name of Professor Altdorf, a supposed 'old friend' from Germany. She liked to maintain this fiction even though most people at Summerhill knew exactly who he was. This desire for the trappings of respectability was only a matter of form, for, as Wally Neustatter remembered it, she and Neill 'led their separate lives'. When they eventually found time for a delayed honeymoon, they went in a foursome, with Otto Neustatter and his wife Helen, and this became the pattern of many subsequent holidays. Neill later wrote: 'Violent passion was not for me and that is why I came to marry a woman older than myself.' But the cause and effect were not as straightforward as this. The question of Neill's capacity to achieve a satisfactory sexual relationship was neither posed nor answered by his marriage. This situation seems to have suited Mrs Lins: asked once what she thought an ideal husband should be, she replied: 'I'm married to one.' There is, though, some evidence that Mrs Lins could sometimes feel overshadowed by Neill. On his return from an extended lecture tour, Neill was told that she had been 'a different person' while he had been away, 'full of beans and initiative'.

Alongside her practical qualities, Mrs Lins, though she had no training, clearly had ability as a teacher. She taught shorthand and typing, History, German and English. Her lessons were often little more than conversations with a small group of children. Johnnie Collier recalls her approach: 'She was a very good raconteur. She used to read books with the class, and stop and discuss things. There was one about a man who worked his way from Australia as a steward, and she would stop in the middle to talk about her own experience in relation to the book.' She taught German by bringing food to the classroom, and getting the children to ask politely for the items they wanted. She could also be humorous, as a later pupil, David Newton, recalls: 'Once she asked another boy and I to write down every word that rymed with "muck", so of course we wrote "fuck". "Take a year's holiday," she said, "and I'll arrange for you to have some PLs with Neill." ' Vanji Collier especially remembers the atmosphere of her lessons: 'We were always a little bit in awe of her: there was nothing she could do to us, but somehow we had this feeling that we had to listen to her. There was just that little bit of pressure.'

There was though no question of any child having pressure put on them to attend lessons – indeed, in some cases the pressure was in the other direction, as Roger Anscombe recalls: 'I found it terribly hard to believe that one didn't have to go to lessons. I thought I ought to, and did at first, until Neill said: "Why are you going to lessons? Who said you'd got to? I forbid it – unless you really want to." So I went to the ones I liked, and promptly gave up the ones I didn't.' Neill insisted that children should be allowed to pursue their own activities for as long as they wanted to. Many stayed away from lessons for months, and in a few cases years, often in reaction to their previous experience of school. Diana Fishwick followed a typical pattern: 'I had been at Sydenham High School, but didn't really understand what I was taught there. I went to Summerhill at about 11, and for six months I did nothing. Then I wanted to learn, I enjoyed lessons, and got better scholastically.' She stayed little more than a year at Summerhill: as was to happen frequently, much to Neill's annoyance, some parents would remove their child from the school as soon as they showed signs of being 'cured', or of making normal academic progress.

Because he gave lessons a low priority, Neill was not concerned with hiring teachers with outstanding pedagogic gifts or conventional qualifications. Essentially he wanted people who would like and be able to get on with children. At Lyme his first teacher, George Corkhill, fitted this mould perfectly. A tall, quiet and courageous man, he had been a conscientious objector in the war, and had spent some time in Dartmoor prison for his beliefs. Later, when his pacifist views became known, he was sacked from his teaching post. He promptly took the headmaster to court, secured reinstatement and an apology, and then resigned in protest at his treatment. He had a degree in science, but had also taken an MA in psychology in 1911, the first year it had been a recognised subject at university level –

'*They* didn't know anything about it either,' he liked to remark. According to his son Mervyn, he had no interest in money or possessions: 'As long as someone put meals in front of him, and he had enough for a packet of Woodbines, he was fine.' Unobtrusive, naïve – he once found lodgings for a group of Summerhill boys in the middle of the red light district in Munich – and rather unimaginative, he was liked immensely by the children. His science lessons could be very unconventional. 'He used to help us get involved in all sorts of experiments,' Teddy Raw recalls. 'If you wanted to try something a certain way, he'd always let you, sometimes with startling results. Things would blow up periodically.' 'Corks' – as he came to be known – let the children make lemonade with citric acid, soap with fat and soda, water gardens, fireworks, glass and stink bombs – and once even Irish stew. He was to remain at Summerhill for the rest of his working life, providing Neill with a valuable right-hand man who could in his absence deal with any situation that arose. He was the kind of man, one later pupil observed, you could wake at two in the morning without any inhibition. 'Good stolid old George, never ruffled', was how Neill saw him.

Bronwen Jones had returned home with Neill and Mrs Lins from Austria, and re-joined them at Lyme Regis to teach maths and science. A later pupil remembers her as 'extremely plain, but the jolliest lady of them all'. Her flair for practical subjects such as photography and astronomy fitted in with Neill's desire to have an 'out and out "doing" school'. Children enjoyed her lessons about refractive indexes or the planets, and Neill admired her temperament. 'She was equable. . . .I cannot even recall her losing her temper with adult or child. She was one of the few balanced people that schools and life need.' The third adult to be part of the original staff at Lyme was George Corkhill's wife, Angharad – 'Mrs Corks' as she inevitably became. Brought up in a Welsh farming community, she fitted less easily into the Summerhill community: she was very religious, forceful enough to be clashing with Mrs Lins most of the time, and had considerable reservations about the school. Despite this, she remained there for many years, and played an important part as matron and housemother. As Neill had found at Hellerau, it was no easy task to find staff who were in sympathy with his ideas, were stable enough both to handle the emotions of 'problem' children and cope with substantial freedom for themselves, and were yet prepared to work for the £4 a month which he paid all the adults in the early years of the school.

A few of the problem children that Neill took on at Lyme were too much even for him to handle, though he was interested in trying to effect a cure for them. One girl, for example, had sleepy sickness: 'She was completely dopey, and dribbled a lot, and it was disgusting to have to eat with her,' one pupil remembers. In May 1927, Neill wrote: 'she is improving a bit. Most interesting material I am on to now. She has the phantasy that she is a princess stolen from a palace and made ugly by a gipsy. Her sleepy sickness may be a waiting till the prince comes along to wake her with a kiss. I took up the Sleeping Beauty tale with her yesterday and today she has been asking all the boys to kiss her. Even John. . . much to his alarm and indignation.' Another pupil was mentally handicapped, and would wander around Lyme pretending that he was a horse or car. 'There goes his father's conscience,' Neill remarked to a visitor.

Although the local people showed none of the hostility that Neill had come up against in Sonntagsberg, there was inevitably some lack of understanding about what went on at the school, and why. Dorothy Bailey, who worked enthusiastically for the school for four years, cooking, mending and washing, was a native of Lyme. She remembers that 'many of the townspeople thought they were a little mad', and that they expressed surprise that anyone should be prepared to work there. Neill did his best to keep in with the local shopkeepers, since he occasionally had to deal with instances of shop-lifting by Summerhill children. Later, he wrote disparagingly of Lyme as 'a class-conscious little town. We were outsiders; our dirty little youngsters were looked at down upper-class noses.' This memory conflicts with a statement he made in *The Problem Child*: 'It is to me delightful to think that only one inhabitant of Lyme Regis has ever had to complain about the conduct of my problem pupils.' This corresponds with the recollection of one of the housemothers, Greta Sargeant, that 'the kids behaved well in the town, and were liked by the local people'.

If Neill's experiment only caused a minor stir in Lyme Regis, it was having considerably more impact in the wider world. He was now being asked to lecture about his work to various groups and societies. In September 1924, just as he was settling in to Lyme, he was invited by the British Sexological Society to lecture on a topic of his choice. He decided on 'Sex Education in the School', but was careful to prepare the ground first, writing to the Society's secretary: 'Please tell me what sort of an audience I shall have. Members only? Naturally, if the general public comes to these meetings I shall have to study carefully what to say.' Neill's views about sex education had altered since he first started to run a school. In his Gretna days he was certainly uneasy about adult attitudes to sex. In *A Dominie's Log* he wrote: 'Most of us realise that there is something wrong with our views about sex. The present attitude of education is to ignore sex, and the result is that sex remains a conspiracy of silence.' However, his ideas about what should be done to break this conspiracy were, in comparison with his later standpoint, both more directive and more cautious. They also had a sentimental element, which may in part have been due to his relationship with Jessie Irving in Gretna. He declared in the *Log*: 'The ideal some of us have is to raise sex to its proper position as a wondrous beautiful thing. Today we try to convey to bairns that birth is a disgrace to humanity.' He decides that, if he had his own school free of state restrictions, the bairns 'would be encouraged to believe in the stork theory of birth until they reached the age of nine. At that age they would get the naked truth.'

This stork theory fitted ill with the rest of his burgeoning beliefs even then, and once he had discovered psychoanalysis Neill quickly abandoned it: 'I see now that the child should be told the truth about sex whenever he asks for the information,' he wrote in *A Dominie in Doubt*, during his stint on the *New Era*. Yet he was doubtful whether this could be done effectively, since most adults were, he felt, either embarrassed or shocked when it came to a frank discussion about sex with children. Just as Lane felt that a teacher needed to be analysed in order to be able to work with children in schools, so Neill now concluded: 'I cannot see a way to a good sex education unless every teacher and parent has discovered his or her own sex complexes.' By the time he came to write *The Problem Child* his thinking had moved further in a libertarian direction. After five years' experience in Hellerau, Sonntagsberg and Lyme, he had seen enough evidence of adult handling of the issue to write with feeling: 'I have never yet had a pupil who did not bring to school a diseased attitude to sexuality and bodily functions.' From contemporary evidence of adult difficulties and inhibitions concerning sex, not least the thousands of unhappy letters written to Marie Stopes, it is clear that this was not one of his provocative remarks designed to shock or stir up a debate, but a straight account of the sexual problems which children in this period brought to Summerhill.

Neill's efforts to help and enlighten them meant that he went further than some of the champions of freedom of the day. He now believed that children should not just be told the truth about reproduction, but that issues such as masturbation should also be brought out in to the open. Although he believed that Marie Stopes's pioneering work could 'only have a beneficial effect on the new generation', he was certainly not in sympathy with her highly moralistic advice on what to do about such 'indulgence'. It appears that he himself experienced considerable guilt about masturbation as a result of his parents' attitude to sex, a fact that was uncovered during his sessions of psychoanalysis. So he was speaking from personal experience when he argued, echoing Stekel, that masturbation was not harmful in itself, but because of the guilt which was associated with it as a result of adult moralising. He believed that 'If a wise mother paid no attention to her child's first exploration of his lower body I am convinced that masturbation would have no allurement for him. The *Verbot* fixes the interest.' He found that 'by destroying the feeling of guilt one can make a child happier. I know cases where the destroying of the conscience about masturbation cured the patient altogether.' He suggested that people should 'face the facts without prudery and hypocrisy. Let us abolish the dangerous *Verbot*. The world will be a better place, for there will be fewer self-haters in it. I write it without blasphemy – that a child is nearer to God in masturbation than in repenting.'

This last remark was precisely the kind that persuaded some people that Neill was a dangerous iconoclast. In fact, though his opinions were radical for the time, it was the pungent and provocative style as much as the content of his remarks that often produced the impact. It was also true that he tended, in public at least, to focus his attacks on institutions, attitudes and ideas rather than personalities. *The Problem Child* is full of aphorisms such as 'The most neurotic children are those who have had a religious upbringing.' Neill reserved some of his most withering remarks for the religion which, in its Calvinistic guise, had brought him much misery and anguish as a child. And it may well have been his stance on this question which brought him during the Lyme period an invitation to lecture in Cambridge to an interesting and prestigious body.

The Heretics had been formed in 1909, when the university vice-chancellor had complained about 'the conspiracy of silence facing boys coming to the University, who had already been made aware at school of the objections to the orthodox system of religion'. Membership of the Heretics implied 'the rejection of all appeal to Authority in the discussion of religious questions', and among the honorary members were Shaw, Bertrand Russell – who had been involved in its founding – Rivers, and other Cambridge figures such as G. Lowes Dickinson, Maynard Keynes and F. L. Lucas. Before the war the speakers had included Shaw on 'The Future of Religion', Russell on 'Religion and Science' and Rivers on 'The Primitive Conception of Death'; afterwards had come Rebecca West on 'Emotional Education', Lytton Strachey to speak on 'Art and Indecency', Marie Stopes on 'Birth Control', Freud's disciple Ernest Jones on 'Narcissism', E. M. Forster on 'Anonymity', Henry Morris on 'The Tragedy of Education', and Russell and his wife Dora on 'Industrialisation and Religion'. Neill may have received his invitation from one of the society's committee members, Rolf Gardiner, an enthusiast for the works of D. H. Lawrence whom he had got to know in Hellerau. The precise date and topic of his lecture are not recorded, but the invitation itself is some mark of the seriousness with which, at least among reformers, his ideas were now being received. Not long after this his work was given further recognition: he was invited to join a radio discussion chaired by the psychologist Cyril Burt, and to be a guest at a Foyles Literary Luncheon.

The kind of men and women belonging to such dissenting groups as the Heretics and the British Sexological Society were certainly receptive to his libertarian and anti-clerical opinions. Among professional people the reactions were mixed. Certain analysts found a lot to admire in Neill. One of these was Jack Flugel, who had written *The Psychoanalytical Study of the Family* while Neill was at Lyme. Flugel was especially interested in the influence of Freud's views on the family and education, and was one of the first, together with Ernest Jones, to bring Freud's ideas to an English-speaking audience. It was at informal gatherings at Flugel's house in London that Neill began to meet other psychologists, analysts and their associates and friends. The Freudians themselves were in disagreement over certain issues. Neill was one of those who, from observation as much as from intellectual conviction, believed that adult neuroses could be put down to experiences in early childhood. In this he followed Lane, who saw the problem beginning in the very early weeks, with the mother's attempt to wean her child before it was ready for it. But Freud, though he had at first emphasised the crucial nature of the early years, in 1897 did a *volte-face*, with the result that such a view became a heresy in analytical circles. Neill was therefore moving *against* the professional tide when he asserted that the way a parent treated the young child was crucial to its later psychological well-being.

The Freudians were also divided about the validity of Neill's work at

Summerhill. Analysts would turn up at his lectures to tell him of the faults
in his theory and practice. One of them, Barbara Low, believed that 'in the
deepest recesses of the human soul are some of its profoundest emotions,
reverence, fear and shame'. Given Neill's conviction of the innate goodness
of children, it was predictable that she should be critical of him. Other
Freudians felt that he was misusing Freud's ideas, or practising them in a
decidedly unprofessional manner, and refused to recommend Summerhill
to their patients. Stekel remained in friendly touch with Neill, and sent him
copies of his books when they appeared; but he took issue with him over
his belief that the child was born good. Flugel's admiration was mixed with
reservations about Summerhill, though he was happy enough to leave his
daughter there for six weeks during these early years. But one woman who
did evidently approve wholeheartedly of what Neill was doing was Alice
Hutchison, a London psychologist, who was responsible for supplying him
with several of his early pupils at Lyme.

Neill wrote later, in connection with the founding of Summerhill:
'Freud showed that every neurosis is founded on sex repression. I said: I'll
have a school in which there will be no sex repression. Freud said that the
Unconscious was infinitely more important and powerful than the Conscious. I said: In my school depth psychology will be the main thing.' Yet
he was no out-and-out Freudian: at the time he saw a great deal of point
in the theories of Alfred Adler, another of Freud's co-workers who had,
like Stekel, broken from the founder of the movement.* In *A Dominie in
Doubt* he recalled an incident from his own childhood, in which he had
taken delight in hitting some cattle with a cudgel, and observed:

> Freud would say that in this way I was releasing sex energy, but I
> think that the infantile sense of power was at the root of my
> cruelty. . . .Our task is to provide the opportunity for a boy to wield
> his power. We suppress it and the lad shows his power in destructive
> instead of constructive activities.

By 1926 his work had reinforced his view that 'too little importance is
attached to the power theories of Alfred Adler'. Delinquency, he believed,
was 'trying to express power that has been suppressed.' He had found that
'the anti-social boy, the leader of a gang of window breakers, becomes,
under freedom, a strong supporter of law and order.' Again, the strong
influence of Lane is evident.

Neill's ideas were to some extent getting a more sympathetic hearing
among parents and teachers, who bought *The Problem Child* in large
numbers. Harold Dent, who was teaching in a grammar school in the early
1920s, recalls that 'his views, and especially those relating to the necessity
of freedom for pupils (and teachers), were an inspiration to a small minority

---

*Adler, like other analysts, was considered suspect within the field of academic
psychology. When he was in Cambridge in the 1920s, the small Psychology Faculty
refused to allow him to address the students, on the grounds that his English was too
poor; the students countered this by arranging the meeting themselves, and excluding the
staff from it.

of teachers in state schools, especially men recently returned from war service'. For those who were not so enthusiastic as to be inspired, Neill certainly provoked them to think about their work with children. Amabel Williams-Ellis, reviewing Neill's five 'Dominie' books in the *Spectator* in October 1924, found them 'as readable as they are contentious', and noted that they 'are having a very distinct effect upon education both in the "crank" and in the primary school. Nearly all the more alive and up-to-date teachers in Britain have read and argued about his notions'. Neill's contentiousness is in evidence in a brief correspondence that followed this review. A reader wrote to suggest that Neill and others could profitably look at the ideas of a man whose work was then unknown in Britain, Rudolf Steiner. In particular he mentioned Steiner's view that self-government was harmful for younger children, 'because it tends to make them adult in their conception of life when they are, after all, still children, and deprives them of that reverence for authority which, as Dr Steiner observes, appears transformed in later life as the capacity which can only be inadequately described as the power of conferring blessing'.

Steiner, who had founded his Anthroposophical Society as a breakaway from the Theosophics in 1913, evolved a system of education which reflected his belief that children in their lives recapitulate stages of cosmic evolution. Neill was familiar with his ideas, and recognised their originality. In Germany he had seen some Steiner pupils working in Eurythmics, one of the activities held to be of especial significance in Steiner's system. However, Neill disliked much of the practice, principally because Steiner *had* a system. The reference in the *Spectator* letter to a child's need of 'reverence for authority' was sufficient to provoke Neill to a reply in which, as he did so often in defence of Summerhill, he presented himself as just an ordinary fellow, letting children get on with their lives:

> My chief interests in life at this moment are children, inlaying ornaments, fox-trotting. . . . I might well evolve a theory of education and life from these interests, but I am held back by the suspicion that next month my interests may be painting, gardening and detective stories. In other words, my interests express my complexes. If I evolve theories about education they also express my complexes, or shall I call them my limitations? I think that Dr Steiner is in a similar position, or should be. He has an adult theory of life, of good and bad, of higher and lower. It is obviously right for him, but it isn't right for me. How, then, can anyone be sure that it is right for children? Steiner guides children. I don't try to. I don't know where they are going. . . . I believe that a child does not require to be led; that left to himself he will evolve a social and personal conscience for himself.

The three years that Neill spent at Lyme Regis marked a change in his reputation, from an eccentric, pipe-smoking dominie who wrote humorous books, to a more serious, zealous and – to some people – dangerous proselytiser, 'a seducer of children's minds'. Ethel Mannin, in her book

Confessions and Impressions, published in 1930, recorded her first meeting with Neill some five years earlier. It is a portrait that shows him neither as fierce and dismissive as some of his public polemic might indicate, nor so quaintly loquacious as might be expected from the self-portraits in his 'Dominie' books:

> I have a vivid picture of a tall, thin, slightly stooping figure, with a clean, clever, sensitive face. . . . He wore grubby white flannels, an old and sagging tweed coat, and a gay, careless sort of tie – and sandals. . . . His long fingers were stained. . . from the metalwork which is his recreation from child psychology. He gave the impression of shyness, and one felt that he hoped he wasn't going to be asked a lot of tiresome questions. We talked for a bit and he dexterously kept the conversation from children, psychology and education.

What Ethel Mannin on her first visit to Summerhill diagnosed as shyness, others who were there on a more permanent basis saw in a different light. To a pupil such as Vanji Collier, who was one of the few at Lyme not to be sent there as a 'problem' child, Neill appeared as a benign but distant figure, as often as not absorbed in one of his own activities: 'He was a very quiet, silent man, who just got on with his own work. He was very practical: he made brass ashtrays, he painted, he mended things, he gardened. If you came up to talk to him, he would talk to you; but he was quite happy to carry on regardless, and we accepted this.' Others got to know him better through their private lessons, where his combination of authority and reticence made a strong impression: 'To a very large extent he understood, even if he couldn't verbalise it much,' Roger Anscombe remembers. Many were impressed by his apparently infinite patience, his capacity to tolerate constant invasions of his privacy. Donald Boyd remembers: 'He had that generosity of giving himself to anybody who seemed to need it. He was able to give to all and sundry in ways that were important to them, but not to him.' His patience often astounded the housemothers at Lyme: 'He was always available to any of us, but especially his kids,' Joan Jennings remembers. Greta Sergeant feels that: 'He was a true Christian if ever there was one. He was kind, considerate and unassuming, and would never hurt anyone.' She recalls that he was liked even by those who disagreed with his ideas: 'People would come to visit with a negative attitude. When they left they hadn't changed their opinions about bringing up children, but they liked Neill.' This was to be a useful asset to Neill in his efforts to get his controversial ideas accepted.

The Problem Child was well received and widely noticed. Ethel Mannin reviewed it ecstatically in *Nursery World*, calling it 'one of the wisest and sanest books that has ever been written about children'. Other papers, such as the *Manchester Guardian* and the *Daily Herald*, thought the book would be of tremendous value to parents; and even a professional paper such as the *Medical Times* declared it 'a remarkable book'. It sold well, and after eight years was in its fourth edition. Its success resulted in a gradual increase in the number of families who thought Neill could do something for their problem children. In 1927, when the lease on the Lyme building expired, it was clear that new premises would have to be found if the school was going to expand further. Joan Jennings had taught Neill to drive, and one day in the spring of that year she, Neill, Mrs Lins and her son Wally set out in his snub-nosed Morris Cowley on a house-hunting trip. After a trip along the south coast during which, Neill recalled, 'we saw some beauties going for around £20,000', they carried on up the east coast, until they reached the small town of Leiston in Suffolk, two miles inland from the sea.

Here Neill was to live and work for the rest of his life.

CHAPTER 9

Pioneers and Parents

Pioneering is a washout, man. I am getting weary of cleaning up the mess that parents make.

Letter to Bertrand Russell, January 1931

To most of those involved with Summerhill, the 1930s represented a kind of golden age, a time when, as Neill argued, the school stopped being an experiment and became a demonstration – that freedom worked. Parents began to send their children to Summerhill because they believed in Neill's ideas, or shared his ideals for a better society. Many of the adults Neill took on to his staff were hostile to coventional schooling, and committed to his vision of the possibilities for good in children. Summerhill became an informal meeting-place for many of the artistic, literary and scientific intelligentsia. The press discovered Neill, and came eagerly to look at and write about what, almost without exception, they called the 'do-as-you-please' school.

Outside his school, Neill was in demand as a lecturer, not only in Britain, but in several European countries. A lecture tour he made in South Africa brought him into conflict with both church and state, and stymied his attempt to open a branch of Summerhill there. Visitors came from all over the world to ask him questions, and to observe the system of self-government in action. They returned to their own countries shocked, impressed, bewildered, inspired – but rarely indifferent. Neill's books began to be translated, and he added to the list two further titles which encapsulated his theory and practice. And, in the period between the beginning of the Spanish Civil War and the start of the Second World War, Summerhill became a focus for left-wing activity aimed at combating the rise of fascism.

In fact, the decade brought troubles and satisfactions of many different kinds, which were not always reflected in Neill's dealings with those immediately around him, or the wider world. One close family friend of this period observed: 'Everything he spoke of was pessimistic, but every action showed he was optimistic about the future.' Neill was certainly inclined to grumble about a number of things – especially money, of which he had little. Frequently he would rail against certain *categories* of people, in particular school inspectors, parents, 'moralists', 'high lifers', authoritarian teachers, Catholics – in other words, any group that in his view had been responsible for damaging the lives of children.

This fierce determination to be 'on the side of the child' gave him the energy and the courage needed to begin and continue a venture such as Summerhill. But it also contributed to a tendency to argue matters out in simplistic terms, to see any person associated with authority as inherently evil, destructive or malignant. Inside Summerhill, it was this which caused him to make some serious misjudgments about the role of parents, with unfortunate consequences for certain children. To many outside Summerhill, his absolute refusal to compromise in his dealings with children was one of his most admirable qualities; yet at the same time it resulted in a degree of isolation for Neill, which in turn influenced the way in which he perceived and dealt with people and issues in the wider community.

It was about the time he moved the school to Leiston that he found some potential allies to lessen his isolation. In September 1927 Bertrand and Dora Russell opened Beacon Hill, a small school in a wild and secluded spot on the West Sussex Downs. Russell, already an eminent philosopher and mathematician, was highly critical of conventional schools, on the grounds that they moulded the child in a way that crushed its spirit. In 1917 he had written, in *Principles of Social Reconstruction,* of the need for adults to have 'reverence' for the potential of the child. 'In education, with its codes of rules emanating from a Government Office, its large classes and fixed curriculum and overworked teachers, its determination to produce a dead level of glib mediocrity, the lack of reverence is almost universal.' In contrast, his ideal educator would find in every living thing, but particularly in children, 'something sacred, indefinable, unlimited, something individual and strangely precious, the growing principle of life, an embodied fragment of the dumb striving of the world'. It would be the educator's task to help the child in its own battle: 'he would equip and strengthen it, not for some outside end proposed by the State or by any other impersonal authority, but for the ends which the child's own spirit is obscurely seeking'. The man who can do this would, he felt, be able to 'wield the authority of an educator without infringing the principle of liberty'.

These libertarian ideals were certainly still grossly at odds with the attitudes to be found both in the British public school system, and in the state schools in which Neill had served his apprenticeship. Though a few small changes were beginning to be made, some of them in reaction to the war, the overwhelming majority of schools provided an experience which would have been anathema to anyone with sympathy for the aims and practices of the educational pioneers. At about the time Neill started his school in Lyme, Christian Schiller, then a young inspector, was working in slum schools in Liverpool: 'What I found was horrifying. At one school there were 86 children in a single class, fully a third sitting in a coal-hole. . . . Schools consisted of long halls in which perhaps five classes, each one of them with more than fifty children in them, occupied the same four walls, so that the accent was on strict conformity, silence and absolute obedience if chaos was to be kept to a minimum.' Though the payment-by-results system had been formally abandoned many years before, it might just as well have been in force for all the difference it made to the education of many children.

Russell and his second wife, Dora, had two children coming up to school age. She too was unhappy about existing schools, in particular their rigid timetables and intense competition. She was active in various move-ments for reform, but found that even the pioneer schools, though certainly more humane places than conventional public or state schools, did not go far enough: 'Nearly all the new type of schools, though outside state jurisdiction, were in tune with the established beliefs, psychology and cus-toms as to conduct and class; they were not seeking to upset the social system.' In the belief that there would be other parents 'like ourselves who desired radical changes in education', she and Russell decided to start their own school. The idea, as the first prospectus made clear, was to produce 'not listless intellectuals, but young men and women filled with constructive hopefulness, conscious that there are great things to be done in the world, and possessed of the skill required for taking their part.' There was to be no corporal punishment; attendance at lessons was to be voluntary; there was to be frank and full discussion about difficult topics such as sex and religion; and both the rules and the timetable were to be decided upon by a School Council.

In preparation for opening the school, the Russells did some homework on the ideas of certain pioneers. One of their children spent some time in a Montessori day school in London. Both were taken for a half-day to the open-air nursery school in Deptford run by Margaret McMillan, while their parents talked with its creator, and observed the environment which she had created, aiming to allow children room to move and play. The Russells studied the theories of psychologists such as Freud and Adler, and the educational ideas of Piaget, Froebel and Pestalozzi. And, in 1927, Russell arrived in a Minerva limousine to stay for a week at Summerhill. The staff 'sat at the feet' of the two men as they discussed the problem children at the school. Though the great mathematician dropped in on some lessons, there was disappointment that he missed one in particular, as Neill wrote in a letter of 26 May just after the visit: 'I have it on my conscience that I docked you of that Maths lesson. Especially so when I learnt that Mrs Barton [Jonesie] was annoyed at me for not bringing you in. It transpired that she had a specially brilliant lesson that day. I think therefore that you'll have to come back again . . . bringing your wife next time.'

One night, when he and Russell went for a walk together, Neill defined the difference between the two of them: ' "Russell," I said, "if we had a boy with us now you would want to tell him about the stars while I would leave him to his own thoughts." He laughed when I added: "I maybe say that because I know damn all about the stars anyway." ' Neill was certainly right to see a fundamental difference in their attitude to children, despite the fact that he and Russell shared many views about the deficiencies of conventional schooling. The difference had first become clear when the two men had initially made contact by letter the previous year. But to some extent it was obscured by two qualities in Neill which were to be a source of amusement, puzzlement and irritation to many involved with Summerhill: a streak of mild if harmless snobbery, which allowed him to be impressed by titles and eminence; and a very Scottish respect for learning, which sat somewhat uneasily with a genuine hatred of 'book learning'. When Russell sent Neill a copy of his *On Education,* at about the time *The Problem Child* was being published, Neill wrote back saying that it was 'the only book on education that I have read that does not make me swear. All the others are morals disguised as education.' He ignored the fact that he had made similar comments on earlier books by Edmond Holmes, Norman MacMunn and Caldwell Cook during his *New Era* period. Here he confesses himself impressed by Russell's knowledge: 'To me the most interesting thing about your book is that it is scholarly (nasty word) in the sense that it is written by a man who knows history and science. I am ignorant of both and I think that my own conclusions come partly from blind intuition.' Only in a very tentative manner does he point to a difference between them: 'Possibly . . . I attach more importance to emotion in education than you do.'

This was indeed a crucial difference, and one that was underlined by Russell in a letter to H. G. Wells a year after his visit to Summerhill. In trying to persuade Wells to help raise an extra £1000 a year to keep his and Dora's school going, Russell wrote:

I believe profoundly in the importance of what we are doing here. If I were to put into one single phrase our educational objects, I should say that we aim at training initiative without diminishing its strength. . . . You will realise that hardly any other educational reformers lay much stress upon intelligence. A. S. Neill, for example, who is in many ways an admirable man, allows such complete liberty that his children fail to get the necessary training and are always going to the cinema, when they might otherwise be interested in things of more value. Absence of opportunity for exciting pleasures at this place is, I think, an important factor in the development of the children's intellectual interests.

The distinction is clear: while Neill aims to release the emotions, Russell wants to train the mind. In anyone else Neill would have attacked this attitude, since it falls clearly into his category of 'moulding' adults at work. In the *New Era* days he had several times criticised the 'high lifers' of the progressive movement for placing Shakespeare above Charlie Chaplin, and trying to force their cultural values on children. Yet there is no direct evidence that Neill was overtly critical of Russell in this sphere.*

Neill certainly kept in touch for as long as Russell stayed with the school. When he left in 1931, Neill found in Dora Russell someone who was able to give him rather more practical support, and whose ideas were closer to his own. Like Neill, she was critical of other progressive schools for limiting self-government to older children, feeling that an undesirable deference to authority might have become ingrained by that age. She believed that 'a child going on the rampage at the age of four or five would do less harm to himself and to others than in adolescence, while in so doing he would at the same time begin to evolve his own self-restraint and control.' Under the influence of Margaret McMillan, she placed much emphasis, as Neill did, on the child's need for free play. Over the next few years, when she ran the school without Russell, she aimed to let the children express themselves through unorganised play as well as through drama, art and movement. Though at first she felt unable to go all the way with Neill's libertarian ideas – 'it seemed to me that he might be too much concerned with a negative revolt against what he now condemned, rather than with a positive statement of what should be put in its place' – after a few years she came to the conclusion that his approach was a necessary one, since 'the gulf between the old and the new was too wide to bridge by compromise'. By the middle of the 1930s, Neill was telling her that he and she were 'the only educators'.

By this time it was clear that, despite the superficial similarities between Summerhill and other 'progressive' schools, Neill's aims and practice set him apart from almost all the other pioneers whose work could be placed in the New Education movement. Just as he tended to label state schools 'barrack schools', so he saw almost all his fellow-pioneers outside the system as running 'compromise schools'. His attitude to one of the earliest of such schools was thoroughly typical. Bedales, set in the middle of exquisite countryside on the Hampshire Downs, and having the use of 150 acres, had been founded in 1895 by J. H. Badley, in reaction against the harsh discipline and narrow curriculum of the public schools. Badley had taught for a while at one of the most celebrated, Rugby, and had also had a spell at what is recognised as the first of the progressive schools, Abbotsholme in Derby.

Abbotsholme itself was founded by Cecil Reddie, an autocratic character who saw the public schools of the day as 'steam-driven factories for turning out by the dozen hastily crammed candidates for examinations'.

---

*However, one Summerhill teacher later recalled that Neill returned from a visit to Beacon Hill declaring it to be 'all highly moral'. A parent recalls a party of Summerhill children visiting Beacon Hill and being shocked by the pupils' behaviour – they thought the school was 'too free'.

He was opposed to book learning, and made the curriculum both broader and more practical; he also introduced sex instruction, an unheard-of practice during the Victorian period. However, Reddie's personality dominated the life of the school, in which both pupils and staff had every minute of their lives organised for them. He wrote, and had printed on hand-made paper, numerous documents, with such headings as 'How Should We Begin the Day?' and 'What are the Advantages of Haymaking?' He encouraged the boys to do a great deal of outdoor work, such as navvying, gardening and bringing in the harvest, and insisted on retaining outdoor earth closets to which they went in teams (with a special trophy for the one to use the facilities with the most 'efficiency'). He was one of the first to try to break down the formal barriers between pupils and teachers, all the while insisting on a number of bizarre rules which seem calculated to achieve the opposite effect – he insisted, for example, that children's socks should be marked Left and Right, and caned any boy who got them mixed up.

Reddie was also a sexual puritan, and opposed co-education, which was just beginning to be discussed in England. He also disliked his staff to be married, and it was this that led Badley to break away and found Bedales. Badley took with him many of the features of Abbotsholme, but he was not an autocrat like Reddie. Among other changes he instituted a system which allowed the younger pupils to have the right to attend school meetings, rather than, as at Abbotsholme, be under the control of their seniors. Badley, like Neill, believed that children learn only when they wish to learn: 'Every child is an individual marvel,' he wrote, 'gifted with unique capacities, ready to respond to those who trust them and to those who have no fear of giving them freedom.' Yet under his guidance, which was still somewhat severe and very puritanical, Bedales exhibited many of the features which Neill had spent so much time condemning. Badley himself neither smoke nor drank, and was known to everyone at the school, staff and children alike, as 'the Chief'. Corporal punishment was used in the early years, and Badley himself was prepared to wield the cane. Staff were addressed as Sir, Miss or Mrs; and religion remained a pervasive influence, the Sunday evening service being seen as a key moment in the week. Girls arrived in 1898 – one story has it that Badley only allowed them to come because his wife refused to marry him unless he did so. They had to abide by a rule of 'no corsets and hair parted in the middle'. Solemn emphasis was put on boys and girls being 'comrades' together: sexual feelings were implicitly dismissed as 'silly', or at best as something which could safely be set aside until adulthood. Not surprisingly, when he spent a few hours at the school while he was on the *New Era*, Neill was dismissive of the quality of the freedom at Bedales. He asked Badley why he didn't cane girls as well as boys; and when Badley asked him as he was leaving what he thought of Bedales, he replied: 'A poor place, I didn't hear a single damn all day.'

Other progressive schools also failed to come up to Neill's required standards of child freedom. Nicholas King Harris took over as head of St

Christopher School from his parents, Lyn and Eleanor Harris, who had run the school jointly for nearly thirty years from 1925. 'My father used the phrase "ordered freedom" in an ad in the *New Statesman*,' he recalls. 'That phrase really got Neill's goat. He thought it was a contradiction in terms. Every now and then he attacked the concept in an educational journal, and we knew who he was getting at!'

One school whose practice Neill did seem to approve of was The Malting House in Cambridge, which opened in the autumn of 1924, at the precise moment that Neill was starting Summerhill at Lyme Regis. The school was the idea of Geoffrey Pike, an unorthodox, restless man of Jewish origin, who had been severely bullied at his public school, Wellington College. Pike, like the Russells, set up the venture originally to provide a schooling for his own son David. The Malting House took in children from 2½ to 8, most of them from university families, with very high IQ scores. It was said that the ten most difficult children in Cambridge were sent there; some of the pupils were certainly of a kind with which Neill was also having to deal in Summerhill. The school was set up as a very careful experiment, in which children would not be led by adults, but would be free to follow their own interests. They would come to read only when they themselves felt they were ready, and would be encouraged to learn through inquiry and experiment and the use of fire, water, earth and tools. They were given considerable freedom to choose their own activities, which, together with their day-to-day conversations, were noted down unobtrusively by a research assistant.

The director of this 'experiment' was a young psychologist called Susan Isaacs. Two years after she started she wrote about the purpose of her work, and the methods used:

> The key to the school is the growth of the children, and its methods must be based on direct observation of the children themselves. One of the most far-reaching changes of thought in human history is the modern view of the freedom of children as the basis of education. This is the great experiment of our age. Merely to give a vague and general freedom is, however, not enough. We must also observe what children do under free conditions, and study the laws of growth, so as to be able to meet their needs in detail.

It was the material that she gathered at the school which was later to have a significant influence in the liberalisation of state primary schools.

Neill's own experiment was of course infinitely less scientific. Yet, though he does not appear to have visited The Malting House, he clearly would have found much in common with Susan Isaacs, even if his style was substantially different from hers. One teacher who taught at the Cambridge school believes that Susan Isaacs, when she later moved in to teacher training, sent her students to Summerhill. 'I always heard her speak of Neill's work with respect,' she recalls. 'She may have disagreed with Neill on this or that issue, but I'm certain she had a very real respect for him, and would have sympathised with many of his beliefs and many of the features of his school, even if not *everything*.' Susan Isaacs wrote disapprovingly of 'the theory that the little child needs, and can make use of, complete and absolute "freedom" ', which may have been a reference to Neill; and there was certainly a discernible element of overt adult control at The Malting House which Neill would not have found acceptable. Yet Neill, while later berating Freudians for 'doing little to alter society so that it may give both children and adults a freer, happier life', agreed that he was being unjust to some 'who are applying their knowledge practically in education. Women like Anna Freud and Susan Isaacs are earnest workers who are a long way outside the consulting-room and the individual treatment.'

There was only one school other than Beacon Hill which gained any real approval from Neill, and that was Dartington Hall. Dartington was, like Beacon Hill, started because its founders were looking for a suitable school for their own children. Leonard Elmhirst was a Yorkshireman with an interest in land problems, who had spent some time in India at the invitation of the poet Rabindranath Tagore, working on rural reconstruction in Bengal. Subsequently, in America, he met an heiress, Dorothy Whitney, whose children had been attending an experimental school in New York. Together they bought a beautiful wooded estate by the River Dart near Totnes in Devon, intending to use it for a programme of rural reconstruction, which would also allow 'scope for a full life for everyone connected with the enterprise'. The school, which opened in September 1926, was seen as a part of the wider community on the estate, though it remained formally a separate venture open to outsiders. Great emphasis was put on arts and crafts activities, on giving children scope for adventure, on 'learning by doing', and on allowing children to plan their own work. There was no corporal punishment, and, gradually, a considerable measure of self-government.

In July 1931 the Elmhirsts appointed as head Bill Curry, who had earlier been in charge of a well-known American progressive school, Oak Lane Country Day School in Philadelphia, and had taught under Badley at Bedales. Small, bald, and a man of great force, he was passionately interested in questions of democracy and world government, and was a friend of Bertrand Russell, who may have first introduced him to Neill. Neill found Curry a strange, very shy but likeable man, and developed an affectionate friendship with him over the years; 'We have the mutual effect of cheering each other up, even when the pubs are closed,' he told Curry. Their friendship survived Neill's envy of the facilities available at Dartington. In January 1931 Neill wrote to Russell: 'When Elmhirst needs a new wing he writes out a cheque to Heals. . . Heals! And here I am absolutely gravelled to raise cash for a pottery shed.' Three months later he grumbled: 'Elmhirst is opening his kindergarden in September and he will rope in all the bloody people with money and complexes.' And the following spring: 'Poor old Elmhirst has become the super-father-complex hate symbol. . . vulgar wealth. . . pah. Wish he'd divide out.' He put another of his many variations on this theme in a letter to Curry the following year:

'When a bloke like me has to think for six months before he can buy a radiogram for dancing, he. . . well, I needn't finish.'

Far from resenting Neill's grumbles, Curry invited him down to talk to the estate staff, the school's staff and some of the older children: 'It would be a good thing for me to have a really radical blast, it would make them all think me quite mild by comparison,' he told Neill, and added that he had spent the previous weekend with a group that included Russell, who had mischieviously suggested 'that I should get the place untidied a bit before you come'.* Neill's visit, and the two meetings he addressed, caused a stir in Dartington. They also gave Neill a chance to think about more important differences between his school and Curry's. A few days after his trip he wrote to Curry who, like Badley at Bedales, had asked him for his opinion of the school, soliciting his view of the Dartington prospectus:

> Last weekend I couldn't take it all in, and the fact that I was a guest kept me from criticising, even to myself. Now I can see you all in a better perspective. My one important criticism is that you're not making psychology nearly important enough. What is happening to your kids' anal eroticism, hate, destruction, parental complexes, masturbation guilts? My dear lad, I fear me they're repressing them. You have a few problems of discipline, but damn it all you ought to have fifty a day. . . . I learned something important last weekend, that the fault of DH doesn't lie in its wealth, as I supposed. The fault lies in its poverty of ways and means for living out primitive instincts. Your gangster age ought to be in dirty hovels, moving up gradually to the swagger rooms all pupils now have.

He also felt that Dartington had no focal point, and that it was too large: 'If you had a weekly self-government meeting you'd find a helluva difference in social spirit. Your life would bring you grey hair soon.' Despite his criticisms, Neill acknowledged that Curry was essentially an ally: 'our schools may differ, but you and I have much the same standpoint,' he ended.

During this period Neill used his friendship with Curry and the Russells to air his grievances about authorities in different shapes and sizes. One meeting at which both Dora Russell and Curry were present provoked Neill to real fury. In October 1932 the New Education Fellowship met in Tavistock Square in London, to set up a new association for progressive schools to provide mutual help, advice and information, and resources. Though he still wrote occasionally for the *New Era,* Neill had never joined the NEF – 'I could not see it going the way I wanted it to', he wrote at this time. He was indeed chary of joining *any* group, and told Curry after the meeting: 'Say, man, I rather regret joining that *Bund,* I don't care much for

---

*The Elmhirsts had visited Summerhill during its last months in Lyme, and were, according to their diary, 'horrified at the mess and disorder and seeming chaos'. Their reaction is not surprising in view of Leonard Elmhirst's remark to an estate agent when he was looking for a place in the country: 'We're going to have a school, so it must be beautiful!'

the job of trying to make that bunch of sad faces laugh.' He agreed to go to a follow-up meeting the next month, 'but without enthusiasm'. The meeting was chaired by Clifford Allen, a close friend of Russell's, whose pacifist beliefs and work for the No Conscription Fellowship had caused him to be in and out of prison during the war. His position on educational freedom is shown in a letter he wrote to Curry some months later, when he was attempting to outline the reasons for his support of another pioneer, Kurt Hahn, the founder of Gordonstoun School:

> I am sceptical of freedom for growing persons carried quite to the lengths which, so far as I can make out, would be favoured in different degrees by Neill, you and Dora . . . I am fairly confident that he [Hahn] is more likely to produce children of the dynamic outlook on life and a high standard of value than the more extreme freedom of some of the other schools.

Dora Russell wrote to Neill just before the NEF meeting: 'I shall go in order to put forward a libertarian basis for such an association of schools, or else to have no association at all. I would like to have your help there.' Evidently, as she recalled later, Neill spoke his mind:

> Allen was trying, as he always had done at the ILP, to reconcile opposing points of view. A. S. Neill and I were regarded as so far to the left, educationally speaking, as to be almost beyond the pale. It was said that we might be admitted to the organisation, though there were some members who would definitely not wish the names of their schools to be set beside Neill's and mine. I found this very funny, and remarked that possibly Neill and I might return the compliment and refuse open association with them.

Neill clearly didn't take this hostility so lightly, as he wrote to Curry after the meeting:

> I've told Mrs Ensor that I'm chucking those bloody meetings. You and I and Dora Russell talk a different language from them. We're the only ones who make child psychology the basis of our job. I can't waste my time going to town to hear a lot of bilge about self-government and Montessori etc. Besides, Allen is definitely against the left wingers, always tries to shelve me as a bloke who deals with abnormal kids. . . . The atmosphere of that room makes me sick, rouses all my old complexes about teachers and their 'damned education'. I get led on to say things I don't want to say. . . . Well, well, count me out, sorry to leave you and Dora to educate the bunch of them, but I simply can't go on with it.*

---

*David Wills, another influential pioneer worker with problem children, recalls how Neill's absence from a conference on self-government later in the 1930s caused Dora Russell some concern: 'She kept running around moaning "What's the good without Neill? Why isn't he here? We might as well go home if Neill isn't coming." ' At the same conference children from different schools came up on to the platform to discuss the issue

Curry was distressed that Neill had deserted the association. He tried
to explain that Allen was not necessarily against him, as he seemed to
believe, but that he felt that the way Neill put his arguments put people's
backs up; they might have been converted if the same thing had been said
in a different way. Neill, however, was not to be wooed back: 'I am willing
to be shot at dawn for you, but don't ask me to come to that meeting,' he
told Curry the following summer. In January 1934 he formally resigned
from the new group, and refused to be persuaded by 'a strong letter asking
me to reconsider'. The incident highlights the fundamentally practical side
of Neill's nature, his preference for action rather than talk, as well as his
inability to trim his ideas or style for the sake of some larger, collective
purpose. He now saw very clearly that the schools coming under the NEF
umbrella had only one thing in common, a dissatisfaction with conventional
schooling. They might agree that children should have freedom, but their
definition of such freedom differed. Just before the divisive meeting, Neill
touched on this subject of unity among the progressives in a piece in the
New Era in October 1932:

> Among us is just as much professional jealousy and hate as among
> Freudian and Jungian analysts. The bee in my bonnet is not of the
> same breed as the bee in your bonnet. Your bee may be the Dalton
> Plan, or the Higher Life, or Literary Style, or the Long Stair, while
> my bee is self-government and freedom from moral teaching. . . .
> This is our weakness as a body of pioneers; we are all at sixes and
> sevens. We can of course form a body that will have its major Right
> Wing, and its minor Left Wing, but possibly at this present moment
> this Left Wing would contain only Summerhill and Beacon Hill.

Neill did set considerable store by the two other members of his
potential 'Left Wing'. In February 1931 he wrote to Russell, alarmed to
hear that Beacon Hill might have to close,

> for then I'll stand alone against the four winds of respectability. So
> far I have felt a vague protection in the idea that B. Russell was
> there to point to as a defence. . . . 'He's a well-known bloke,
> philosopher and so on, you know; *he* believes in freedom and shit
> etc.' And now all I will have will be poor Elmhirst, who couldn't
> shock an unmarried mother, and Faithfull, who shocks all and goes
> bankrupt.*

---

of self-government. Wills remembers 'some very proper young persons from St
Christopher's' being amongst the speakers: 'But the child who carried the house and
wiped the floor with the other children was a girl of about six from Beacon Hill. This
precocious little minx, in tones of withering contempt, said to the St Christopher
children: "*You* lot don't know anything about self-government. That's just the adults
letting you play at it and pretending you're deciding things. You try deciding something
they don't like and see what happens." '

*Theodore Faithfull was the head of another pioneer school, Priory Gate in Norfolk,
who, like Neill, drew on Freud's ideas.

Neill took delight in speaking his mind to Russell, having quickly got beyond the formality of addressing him as 'Mr Russell'. There is an element of mischievousness in their correspondence, as Russell with dry wit and Neill with warm humour compare notes on the inadequacies of fellow-pioneers, government departments, parents, inspectors and visitors.

In December 1930 Neill looked ahead with some trepidation to the outcome of the deliberations of a new Committee on Private Schools, which seemed likely to recommend more stringent rules and regulations for schools outside the state system. He told Russell of his fears:

> They will call in all the respectable old deadheads of education as expert witnesses (Badley and Co.) and unless men of moment like you make a fight for it we (the out and outer Bolshies of education) will be ignored. Then we'll have to put up with the nice rules advocated by the diehards. Can't we get up a league of heretical dominies called the 'Anal'-ists?

The week before, he had outlined his apprehension in more serious and graphic terms:

> 'You and I will have to fight like hell against having a few stupid inspectors mucking about demanding why Tommy can't read. Any inspector coming to me now would certainly be greeted by Colin (aged 6) with the friendly words, 'Who the fucking hell are you?' So that we must fight to keep Whitehall out of our schools.

In April 1931 Neill and Mrs Lins decided to do some walking on the South Downs, and Neill suggested that they might call in at Beacon Hill 'and enjoy a blasphemous conversation on parents'. Russell replied that he and Dora would be 'overjoyed' at the prospect, and afterwards wrote to Neill: 'Your visit here was a bright moment to us both. There are so few people to whom one can talk without tedious explanations.' Neill replied the next day: 'Yes, we said the same about you two . . . how fine to talk to people you haven't to explain and defend with'; and some months later he told Russell: 'Wish we could have a yarn again. You are one of the few people I like to talk to and hear talk. The other educational blokes and blokesses are simply not there. They have ideals, bless em.'

The arrival of Beacon Hill and Dartington Hall produced a surge of interest in the more libertarian progressive ideas. Neill, Curry and the Russells found themselves referring to each other interested teachers, parents and visitors, and comparing notes on their virtues and deficiencies. Neill was grateful to be able to pass on some of the increasing numbers descending on the school, as he confided to Curry in December 1932: 'Fact is that crowds of people come round asking for jobs, and to get rid of them I say sweetly, Now there is Dartington Hall. What about applying there? Sometimes I send them on to Beacon Hill; most of them I send to hell; but not audibly.' Yet Neill was both patient with and helpful to many who were looking for a job, especially any who he felt were 'genuine cases who want the new ideas and hate the old schools in which they teach.' But he confessed to becoming weary of being asked the same questions again and again, of having to explain his ideas afresh to each new visitor.

It was no doubt in part to answer the increasing questions that Neill wrote his second 'Problem' book. *The Problem Parent* was published in 1932, and opened with an epigrammatic flourish: 'There is never a problem child; there is only a problem parent. That may not be the whole truth, but it is nearly the whole truth.' Neill had decided after completing *The Problem Child* that he was not really attacking the matter at source. 'Parents have never had the chance to understand their children, because understanding children is like understanding astronomy or surgery, a skilled profession, and only recently a skilled profession, because before the present Freud era psychology was groping for the truth in human consciousness.' He had come to realise, he said, 'that parents, like children, need sympathy and understanding, not blame or contempt'.

However, Neill had up to now shown little sympathy with parents, in particular when they made clear their opposition to his ideas about the way children should be brought up. Although he met no great hostility from those whose children he taught in Gretna, his experience there clearly shaped his views about the power of the home influence. 'Anything I say will surely be negatived at home; my word, unfortunately, is not so weighty as father's,' he wrote in *A Dominie's Log*. He was acutely aware of the position of his young pupils, caught between two conflicting philosophies. Even before he began Summerhill he believed, as he noted in *A Dominie in Doubt,* that 'To the teacher the parent is the enemy.' And once he had his own school he confessed, in *The Problem Child*: 'I grant I cannot write dispassionately, for I have a grievance against the parent.'

Inevitably then, although Neill's stated aim in *The Problem Parent* was to help them understand the new psychology in relation to their children, a great deal of the book was highly critical of parents. This was commented upon by the *New Era* reviewer who, while suggesting that every parent should read it, felt that Neill's manner of dealing with them might prevent the book from getting through to those who needed it most: 'For the problem parent was originally a mishandled child – so the vicious circle goes on and, if he is to be freed, he needs the same gentleness in the presentation of his problem as does the child.' Neill may have been influenced to some degree by a view expressed by Bertrand Russell. After he had read the manuscript, he told Neill that he 'should have laid even more stress than you do on quarrels between parents as a cause of problem children'. Parents, Neill argued, were trying to create children in their own image, using them as compensation for their own failures, or feelings of guilt and jealousy. Their tolerance and imitation of the harsh discipline of the school system was the cause of unhappiness in their children. Parents were trying to impose a code of behaviour that took no account of the true nature of a child; instead they should be 'playmates' to their children. Neill criticised them for demanding gratitude and love from their sons and daughters, arguing that 'No child can love; he can only want to be loved. No child can be grateful, for his interest is in the thing given, not in the giver.'

One of the principal causes of unhappiness in the children he had dealt with concerned sex. Boys and girls, he argued, especially those from single-sex schools, came with an unhealthy attitude to sex, which they had learned in the home. Much of this derived from the fear or anxiety which adults felt about infant sexuality, and a child's natural desire to find out about its body. Punishment, Neill wrote, showed how much self-hate there was in adults, a feeling which many parents unconsciously transferred to their children. He concluded:

> Oh parents, I know that you need sympathy and understanding, but I am so weary of you. You are the problems. I try to help some of the children that you make problems, and they become happy and efficient children, but you have no school in which to learn. You go on misunderstanding and undoing my work. You waste my time with doubts that belong, not to your anxiety about your children, but to your anxiety about yourselves. You are all problem children, and the greatest need in education today is the setting up of schools for problem parents.

Neill's hostility to parents had repercussions outside the school, as the child psychologist John Bowlby remembers: 'Working in child guidance clinics in the late 1930s, and seeing parents making things difficult for children, one was accused of "blaming" parents. I myself didn't – but to some extent the comment came as a result of Neill having done so. One was equated with Neill, and it took a long time to live down.' Bowlby visited Summerhill in 1929, during 'a bit of a reconnaissance around progressive schools': he had taught for a while at Bedales Junior House – which he remembers as 'prim Montessori' – and at Priory Gate in Norfolk.* He was interested in Summerhill because he felt that 'Neill's idea that a child was essentially good struck a chord'. He concluded that his methods were particularly 'suitable to disturbed children, especially those who had experiences similar to his own'. Yet it was not very long after Summerhill was established in England that certain families began to send their children to the school because of a *positive* belief in Neill's ideas, rather than because they needed someone to help with a problem child.

The scientist J. D. Bernal and his wife Eileen were among the first to take this decision. They heard of Summerhill through a young woman running a nursery school in Cambridge, 'as nearly as she could on Neill's kind of lines'. Eileen Bernal recalls her first taste of Neill's attitude to parents, when she went to visit her 5-year-old son Michael shortly after he had started at Summerhill. 'He met me at the gates, and said: "You sent me here because you thought I was a problem child, didn't you?" I said: "I don't think so." So he said: "Well, you know most people do; but the

---

*At Priory Gate Bowlby came across a gifted teacher called John Alford, who had been analysed and influenced by Homer Lane. Alford became his 'guide and advisor', and it was through him that Bowlby was introduced to Lane's ideas, which he acknowledges had a significant influence on his later work with children.

truth is that it's the parents who are the problems, not the children." ' Her very first glimpse of Summerhill provided her with an indication of Neill's priorities: 'I arrived at this very ramshackle house, and just walked in, because nobody answered the door. I was directed to Neill's study, and he asked me in. I had hardly said hello when there was a knock at the door, and a little girl came in and said, "You haven't forgotten me, have you, Neill?" So he said, "No, I'll ask my visitor to wait." He then excused himself to me, saying, "I have an appointment with Evelyn, to discuss with her how she is to liquidate her sister. I'm afraid I shall be about a quarter of an hour, as we shall be walking round the grounds discussing it." I thought, This is Summerhill as I expected it. Later, I told him why we wanted to send Michael there, and I remember him telling me: "You're much too keen on education, you know; I don't think it's really a suitable school for your child." This rather took me aback, because although I certainly valued education, at the age of 5 you consider children's happiness first, and this is what had attracted us to Summerhill. In the end I overcame Neill's objections.'

Gradually, a number of middle-class families, many of them members of the intelligentsia, or involved in the arts or left-wing politics, began to support Neill's school, seeing it as the ideal place in which their children could grow up. Brendan Williams recalls why he sent his two daughters Branwen and Evelyn to Summerhill in 1931: 'I wished them to spend their childhood at a place where they would be free from all compulsion and from all indoctrination, whether religious, ethical or political (of whatever colour), and where they could study if they wished to, and if not, not.' He and his wife Jennie were given the same message as the Bernal family: 'Neill warned me that if I wanted the kids to be educated, I should not send them to him. But having successfully resisted education myself, that was no objection to me.' Other parents based their decision to support Summerhill on their feelings about their own schooling. Ivor Montagu, the son of Lord Swaythling, had been sent to Westminister, one of the foremost English public schools, where he felt that 'the ultimate evil and oppression to me was being expected to accept standards ready made, without right of challenge to them.' His generation read Neill, he recalled, 'in order to find in him the key to what we thought wrong in our own schools'. Neill's anti-authority stance was also part of the appeal: 'we were reacting against the Victorian horror – morally fortified by Biblical injunction and precedent – whereby the paterfamilias considered it not only his right but his duty to expect absolute obedience from his children, and unlimited gratitude.' In 1929 he sent his stepdaughter Rowna Ely to Summerhill.

In some cases, children came to Summerhill after disturbing experiences elsewhere. Gordon Leff, together with his sister Angela, attended a local Montessori school whose methods must have reinforced Neill's scepticism about his fellow-pioneer's philosophy. 'The school was nothing more than three old maids giving the ordinary kind of teaching, with one room filled with bricks. I was always very slow and found it hard to keep up, and tended to be very easily intimidated. When my mother discovered that

I had been tied to a chair for one whole day in order to keep my back up, and when I used to say as we approached the school, "Ssh, you mustn't speak too loud," she realised something was wrong. She got in touch with Neill on impulse, and wrote one of those effusions about wanting her children to grow up free and all the rest of it. Neill, being a very spontaneous person himself, wrote back saying, You sound the kind of parents we should have here.'

The Leffs, their son recalls, were 'part of the bright young things of the 1920s, when psychoanalysis was in vogue' – his mother was analysed as a wedding present. Neill certainly attracted to Summerhill many individuals who embraced with enthusiasm new ideas such as psychoanalysis, though their fervour was not always long-lasting. The novelist Leonora Eyles, who had worked on the *Daily Herald* under George Lansbury's editorship, sent two of her children, Billy and Merle, to Summerhill. Their half-sister Vivyan Volbach, who was educated in somewhat different fashion at Cheltenham Ladies' College, recalls the sequence of their mother's enthusiasms: 'They changed awfully often. At one time it was spiritualism, with table-tapping in the kitchen. Then it was the Single-Tax Movement. Then the Labour Party. Then it was Methodism, and then Liberal Catholicism. Then it was Anglo-Catholicism – and at one time in all this muddle it was Neill and Summerhill!'

Another great enthusiast was Ethel Mannin, who heard about Neill on the cross-Channel ferry while talking to the psychologist Beryl Sandford and her husband. She had as a child gone through unhappy experiences, initially at a strict private school, and later at an ordinary 'board' school. Like Neill she had experienced guilt and fear about sexual matters, and had inwardly rebelled against the force-feeding of the state system. She was anxious not to have to put her 5-year-old daughter Jean through a similar experience; Neill's ideas came as a revelation to her. 'It seemed incredible that there really was another person in the world with the same views about the futility of education that I had. . . . It all sounded too good to be true. . . . As soon as I got back to London I bought a copy of *The Problem Child*, and was so excited about it that I wrote to Neill at once and said that my heart went out to him. He replied courteously that he was glad of that, and wouldn't I come and see his "group".' Her visit convinced her that Summerhill was the place for her daughter.

Ethel Mannin rapidly became one of Neill's most fervent advocates. Neill was grateful for her support, and welcomed her as an outspoken ally and friend who could help publicise Summerhill. In 1931 he wrote a prefatory letter to her book *Common-Sense and the Child*, which was sub-titled 'A Plea for Freedom'. Neill expressed his pleasure at the thought that 'your terse pen will spread the much-needed news of freedom'. While correcting the proofs he complimented her on her achievement: 'It is a very good book, child, most sane and direct. God help it to convert its thousands . . . and to send a few of em on to us.' But he also expressed slight doubts, mixed with his evident pleasure, at her praise of his work: 'You really are too good to me. . . as if I were better than Freud and all of them.' He voiced the same misgivings more explicitly in a letter to Bertrand Russell the following day: 'I am not certain whether Ethel's recognition of me as a Plus Four Christ will ruin my school or make me a millionaire. Did Mary Magdalen's Daily Mail articles JESUS BEHIND THE SCENES make any converts for the saint? I think not.'

Another supposedly emancipated Summerhill parent during the Lyme Regis period was the mother of the four Collier children, Larry, Vanji, Johnnie and Gerry. Her own father had been a great friend of Bertrand Russell's grandmother, and her older sisters had played with the young Russell during his isolated upbringing in Richmond Park. She too suffered a very strict Victorian upbringing, and was determined that the experience would not be repeated with her children. 'She was I suppose the freest parent there has ever been,' her daughter recalls. Her son Larry confirms this in connection with the sexual activities of her children: 'Her attitude was, As long as you come home and do it in my house, that's all right – but I don't want you gadding about.' A striking red-headed woman who wrote poetry and romantic novels, she heard of Summerhill during the 1926 General Strike, immediately hitch-hiked to Lyme Regis (characteristically getting a lift in a Rolls-Royce), took a bungalow in the town, and enrolled her four children as the first Summerhill 'day' pupils. Neill had his first *non*-problem children.

One young boy had the opportunity of sampling the entire 'Left Wing' of the pioneer schools. Nicky Malleson, the son of Joan and Miles Malleson, went to Beacon Hill in 1926 when he was 3, after two years moved to Summerhill, and two years later moved on to Dartington Hall. Miles Malleson, a friend of Russell's, was intimately involved in many of the reform movements of the day. Later known principally for his character parts in British films, he was a theatre director, playwright and pacifist, and wrote an anti-war play called *Black 'Ell*. One of the groups of which he was a leading light was the Men's Dress Reform Society, a movement which in the 1920s favoured what was known as 'rational' dress. The popular imagination tended to see this as consisting of Boy Scout shorts, open-necked shirts and sandals, and to associate it, with some justification, with vegetarianism and pioneer schoolteachers. Neill himself certainly favoured casual dress, though he never quite took rationality to such extremes. In hot weather he would, especially when visitors came, go shirtless. He rarely wore a tie, except occasionally when lecturing – and even then he was likely to remove it during the evening. 'He wore corduroys when they were ploughman's garb,' one family friend remembers. This was not merely for comfort; he was quite conscious of the impact of his clothes, and affected a ruggedly unconventional look, with an emphasis on thick coloured jerseys, heavy woollen socks of vivid hue, heavy shoes, and, for many years, a long, bright orange overcoat.*

---

*Sandals were not a possibility for Neill: the condition of his feet forced him to have special square shoes made, giving the impression when he walked that he was pigeon-toed.

Others in Summerhill also tended to dress unconventionally: many of the men wore shorts and sandals; and until she was into her seventies the cook, Mrs Piercey, favoured beach pyjamas for her leisure moments. Mrs Lins, however, set a rather different tone. Although she was one of the first women to wear trousers, her usual style of dress consisted of a long skirt with pleats back and front, and plain casual cardigans. She nearly always wore the same clothes; her nails were carefully manicured; her wavy hair was cut short and worn in a hair net; and she wore powder and a little make-up. Yet though her clothes were more 'sensible' than those of some of the other adults in the school, it was she who was chiefly responsible for the 'advanced' nature of the food in Summerhill – another area of life that received the attention of the reformers after the war. A Summerhill prospectus for the late 1920s declared: 'The school diet follows the principles of the New Health Society, i.e. chiefly those foods with vitamin values are given.' In Germany Mrs Lins had studied the ideas of the Swiss dietician Dr Bircher Benner. As a result the children had a spoonful of raw chopped cabbage or carrot with their lunches, were given plenty of fruit, raw greens and wholemeal bread and, when constipated, a bowl of muesli made up of soaked oatmeal, grated apple, prunes, chopped nuts, brown sugar and cream. There were vegetarian dishes for those who preferred not to eat meat. Even natural medicine was practised in a small way – Jonesie, a herb enthusiast, made infusions of tansy gathered from the hedgerows, which was given to children suffering from threadworm. At the time almost all these ideas were labelled as 'cranky' by the mass of the population, who were either amused or hostile to such practices.

There were other links between Neill and the social reformers of a more predictable kind, in the sphere of sexual reform. Jack Flugel, who wrote a book about *The Psychology of Clothes*, was another advocate of 'rational' dress, as was Norman Haire, with whom Neill now became acquainted. A flamboyant Harley Street gynaecologist and obstetrician, Haire took a delight in talking frankly about sex, and was an untiring organiser of conferences and writer of books on issues such as Sex, Birth Control and Marriage. He started the English section of the World League for Sexual Reform, which held a Congress in London in September 1929. Though Neill himself, with his dislike of such occasions, was almost certainly not present, many of his pioneering friends and acquaintances read papers, including Dora Russell (who acted as the League's secretary), Ethel Mannin, Barbara Low, Ivor Montagu, Jack Flugel, Bertrand Russell, and Miles Malleson.

Some of these public figures were among the increasing number of visitors who came to Summerhill as Neill began to establish himself as a national figure outside the world of education in the late 1920s and early 1930s. Pupils recall Miles Malleson's chinless profile in evidence at the Saturday night dances which followed the weekly general meetings. Jack Flugel boarded his daughter Erica at the school for a period while he lectured in America. Ethel Mannin was a frequent visitor, staying in Lyme in a cottage down the hill: Joan Jennings recalls being sent to chat with her while Neill finished off some artefact in his workship. Eric Dingwall, the official investigator of the Society for Psychical Research, was remembered as one of the more eccentric of the regular visitors: 'He wore shorts and behaved a bit like a grown-up boy scout,' one pupil remembers. 'He would spend hours on rubbish tips, on the beach, at the back of garages. Neill sometimes regarded him as a bit of a time-waster: "I wish to God that man would let us know when he was coming," he was heard to complain.' His workshop was a very useful refuge if he wanted to keep away from un-welcome callers. Once he was discovered hiding behind a tree from a troublesome parent. One method of stemming the tide of visitors he out-lined in a letter to Curry, in the summer of 1934: 'I'm lying to all the visitors who write asking to see me. I write a letter and sign it with the name of an imaginary secretary saying Mr Neill is in Scotland.' In June 1933 he told Curry: 'Am full to the neck with visitors daily and am a dry sponge now.' In May 1931 he told Russell: 'This week I have had three damn fool women each day, telling them the same old lies about the school. . . . Limp as a rag.' However, there was an ambivalence in his attitude to visitors which was to become more evident at a later stage.

One person whom Neill would have been quite delighted to see at the Summerhill front door was the man who gave the final paper at the 1929 World Congress. Bernard Shaw chose for his paper the title 'The Need for Expert Opinion on Sexual Reform', and proceeded to offer it himself, on the grounds that 'the theatre is continually occupied with sex appeal . . . as a costermonger has to deal with turnips; and a costermonger's opinion on turnips is worth having'. In 1928 he had been interviewed about his views on education for the *New Era* – an idea that Neill must have wished he had thought of during his co-editorship of that journal. In his flat over-looking the Thames, Shaw spoke approvingly of the experimental schools; declared that education 'must be brought into line with the nature of the child'; repeated the dictum from his *Maxims for Revolutionists* which Neill was to quote so frequently, that 'the vilest abortionist is he who attempts to mould a child's character'; and concluded that 'the great test of a school would be to tell the children that they might go home if they wished'. Elsewhere he had characterised his own schooling as 'dragging a child's soul through the dirt', and declared that children should spend most of their time at play. In a letter to *The Times* he wrote: 'All children should be tirelessly noisy, playful, grubby-handed except at mealtimes, soiling and tearing such clothes as they need wear, bringing the joy of childhood not only into the house but dust and mud as well.'

However, the nearest that Shaw came, educationally rather than geo-graphically, to seeing Summerhill was when he visited Dartington Hall with Lady Astor, and Beacon Hill in the company of his fellow-Fabians Beatrice and Sidney Webb. Dora Russell remembers the day: 'Just before tea the children were apt to be at their wildest. They found this tall, bearded visitor most attractive. As Shaw muttered, "Let's get out of here," I hastily led the way into the staff dining room, where I dispensed tea. . . . Shaw remarked on what good wholemeal bread and butter we had. He and Beatrice Webb then began to lecture the staff and myself on the care and education of children.' As this incident showed, Shaw was not at ease in close proximity to children, and believed that adults could not live comfortably together with them. It is therefore not surprising that, when Neill sent him a copy of the Summerhill prospectus when he was setting up the school in Lyme, Shaw merely sent back one of his customary postcards, saying: 'Very interesting. I hope I live long enough to see how it turns out.' However, though he lived for another quarter of a century, he never did go and see how Summerhill had turned out. Neill had to content himself with Shaw's postcard, one of the few pieces of correspondence he kept until the end of his life.

CHAPTER 10

One of the Gang

You can only give a child love if you have remained a child yourself.
That Dreadful School, 1937

With the help of an unexpected loan from friends, Neill and Mrs Lins were able to take out a mortgage of £3,250, and buy outright a large Victorian house near Leiston railway station, into which they moved in the autumn of 1927. Built as a 'gentleman's home' by an industrialist, it had once been used as a girls' school. It was situated in 11 acres of ground, with beautiful lawns, gravel paths and a duck pond, and a huge copper beech tree in front of the house. The house itself had large windows and spacious bedrooms, with doors made of oak and pine panelling. Because of their poverty, Neill and Mrs Lins had to improvise in adapting the house to the needs of their community. The squash court was eventually converted into a theatre, and Neill was able to secure the tip-up seats which were just being replaced in the cinema in nearby Aldeburgh. Staff and older children helped to build a sanatorium, for no more than the price of the cement and some timber. To provide sleeping quarters for the older boys, a group of railway carriages was brought in from the nearby station, and wood-burning stoves put in for heating. The furniture in the staff room was equally primitive, consisting of seats taken from cars no longer fit for the road. A short distance from the house, and still within the grounds, stood a Cottage, which was used as a separate 'home' for the youngest children. The house itself was called 'Newhaven', but, despite the flatness of the surrounding Suffolk country-side, Neill and Mrs Lins preferred to bring with them from Lyme the existing name of their school – a name that had also been attached to one of Mrs Lins's many homes during her Australian childhood.

In 1937 Neill wrote another book, giving it the ironic title *That Dreadful School.** He wrote it partly to counter some of the wilder ideas about the school that had become current, giving it the reputation of being 'a gathering of wild primitives who know no law and have no manners'. The popular press, which had discovered Summerhill at the beginning of the 1930s, was in part responsible for this image. The *News Chronicle*, for instance, ran a story on 10 August 1932 headed: 'School without Rules', beginning with the statement: 'A school where pupils do just as they please is to be found in the heart of Suffolk.' Ironically, Summerhill very often had a good many *more* rules than other schools, though they changed frequently, were often broken, and on a number of occasions abolished altogether. What intrigued reporters and visitors who came to see the school was the fact that the children not only seemed to be capable of governing most areas of their lives, but of doing so in a manner that was open, just and sensible. Not only did Neill have exactly the same rights as even the youngest child at Summerhill, but he seemed to be able to stay in the background during the meetings, and to be treated by the children with no more or less respect than anyone else present. He explained the basis of his attitude in *That Dreadful School*: 'The school that has no self-government should not be called a progressive school at all. . . . You cannot have progression unless children feel completely free to govern their own social life. When there is a boss, freedom is not there.' He saw self-government as an invaluable opportunity for children to learn practical civics: 'one weekly general meeting is, in my opinion, of more value than a week's curriculum of school subjects.'

Once the school moved to Leiston and grew in numbers – by 1934 there were some 70 children – the structure of the meeting changed. It became the custom for a child to take the chair. As an increasing number of rules were formulated, officers with different functions were appointed: a Bedtime Officer, a Down Town Officer, a Bicycle Officer, a Climbing Roofs and Out of Bounds Trees Officer. A system of fines for misbehaviour was introduced, the most regular being loss of pocket money or second helpings at meals, or missing a visit to the cinema. At different times a jury system, an elected government and a tribunal structure were tried, the impetus for change usually coming from the children themselves. Shortly after the move, Neill was disturbed to find that the meeting was spending hours wrangling over identifying transgressors of the law, in a state of great noise and confusion. He then decided to abolish it altogether, to the delight of the children, and for a term there was no government. Although the more necessary laws were kept, the adults eventually felt that some form of government was needed, and called a meeting at which a new form was hammered out.

---

*When he finished writing it he was stuck for a title, and offered a prize of 2s 6d for the best suggestion. Ruth Allen, one of the housemothers, came up with the winning idea.

On a few occasions, Neill used the device of abolishing the rules altogether, usually declaring himself Dictator, or appointing one of the staff or even an older child to the position. His aim was to show the children how a community needed certain laws to protect the individual, or, once or twice, to breathe a bit of life into a system that appeared to him to have gone a little stale. These dictatorships varied in their length and effect. Rowna Ely recalls what must have been one of the shortest, following an incident in which she and other children had raided the larder. 'A meeting was called in the hall the following evening, and Neill decided that all rules were to be abolished. Everyone went haywire, beds were turned over, things thrown over the bannisters, kids running everywhere, staying up all night. We were all so exhausted by the next evening that we begged Neill to put all the rules back. I guess he knew what he was doing.' During one period of a fortnight's dictatorship, he introduced some very severe laws, since in this instance it was the children who had elected him dictator, and he thought they should know what a dictatorship could really be like. Lionel Elvin and his wife, who were regular visitors at the time, arrived near the climax of the fortnight, as he recalls: 'One week-end when we were there, and Neill wasn't, we heard the sound of breaking crockery. When we asked in the staff room what it was all about, we were told: "Oh, that's the revolution Neill wanted. He's gone away specially for the week-end hoping that it would break out." '

Neill's instinct for doing the right thing at the right moment seems to have been immaculate, as is clear from another such episode in the mid-1930s, remembered by Roger Anscombe: 'At one time there were a couple of really anti-social children needing to work out their aggression, and this affected some of the other children. Before long a state of anarchy reigned: no rules were being kept, and the officers were in despair. Neill suddenly announced that as democracy had obviously failed he was pronouncing himself dictator, and we had only ourselves to blame. At first everyone laughed, but when they discovered there were very strict restrictions on mealtimes, how many times you could go to the cinema or down town, within a fortnight there was gloom and despair. Then there was a rebellion – but Neill said it would get worse still. Finally a deputation was sent to ask him to consider relaxing all these restrictions, but he said he wouldn't do that, we were finding what it was like to live under a totalitarian regime. At the right moment he said he would be prepared to have a meeting to listen to what was being said, and he would then outline his conditions for stopping to be dictator. If the conditions were not accepted, then the dictatorship would be stepped up. There was quite an argy-bargy at the meeting, and at one stage Neill said: "Right, dictatorship it is," and got up as if to go out. Finally he won the day, and we went back to self-government, having agreed to take responsibility for ourselves. It was brilliant.'

Neill could sit in a meeting for ages without saying a word, and then intervene in a way that would transform the situation. Lucy Francis, who came expressly to work with the younger children, and was later Neill's unofficial deputy, recalls one such moment. 'I remember at one meeting he suddenly said, "It's getting so boring, it's nothing but rules." They started to run through them all, to see if they could scrap any. But one kid said, "No, no, we must keep that one." And another said, "No, no, we must keep that one." And then Neill said, "I propose that we scrap the whole lot and start again." And very surprisingly this was accepted. But when the meeting was over, they had this great emotional reaction, and went to bed with their private, precious possessions – bicycles and things – because they didn't feel they could live without rules. And they kept going to Neill and saying, "This is terrible." And he said cheerfully, "Oh, I think it's marvellous." So finally, at another meeting, they voted to make Neill a dictator. But that didn't help them, because as a dictator he just didn't dictate any rules.'

Though Neill could certainly act as a catalyst in this way, there is general agreement amongst Summerhill pupils and staff that he rarely attempted to manipulate the meeting, to get his own point of view or proposal carried. He did though sometimes take a delight in setting the tone of a meeting, as another early pupil, David Barton, recollects: 'He was for ever experimenting, in a rather formal kind of way, to test the kids' reactions. He would be deliberately obstreperous and get fined, or play up a bit and be told to shut up by one of the kids who was chairman.' Several times proposals that he put forward, not all of them by any means light-hearted, were rejected by the meeting. Daphne Oliver, an early pupil who subsequently became a housemother, remembers one of the less serious instances: 'At the beginning of term the first thing that he always brought up in a meeting was that he should be paid two shillings for each bed that he had mended during the holidays. He was always voted down.' Sometimes he could find himself in a minority of one, as Ruth Allen, a housemother in the 1930s, remembers in connection with one problem girl, who had a spell of window-breaking: 'I remember a brick coming through the staff-room window when I was having tea. She broke so many windows it was brought up at the general meeting. Neill said he couldn't put the money on the parents' bill because they wouldn't have enough to pay. It was suggested that the school should go without tea for a time, to cover the cost. I think the idea was carried; Neill voted against it, because he liked his cup of tea.'

Once Neill himself was brought up at the meeting, though for an offence which was quite unintentional. The incident, as told by Teddy Raw, highlights not just the sort of justice that could be dispensed, whoever the offender was, but also the kind of pressure that Neill had to endure as a matter of everyday living. 'The staff saved up and bought this very old car of the sit-up-and-beg type, with a wooden steering wheel. We had a char-acter who needed someone to lean on, and he leaned on Neill. All the time. All day. Whenever Neill failed to avoid being seen. One day Neill was in his workshop, doodling on his lathe, or something similar, when Bruce appeared. Bruce kept on asking questions, and Neill switched himself off, saying "Yes", "No", and "Mmm", as seemed appropriate, without taking too much notice of what Bruce was saying. Eventually Bruce went away, and Neill carried on with whatever he was doing, and without any recollection of the rather one-sided conversation. Some time later Bruce was seen with pieces of car, and other parts were also found lying around. Then the staff couldn't find their car, until the stripped chassis was discovered behind the garage. Bruce was apprehended, and promptly and indignantly said that he was entitled to do as he liked with the car, as Neill had given it to him. At the next weekly general meeting, Neill was charged with giving away the staff car, and after a trial was found guilty, although it was accepted that he had not realised that he had done so. He was fined five shillings.'

At times, there were moves to deprive the younger children under 11 of the vote at meetings, but they always spoke out in protest, and the proposal was never carried. Very often quite small children got their own way, or understood the value of the meeting as a sanction against anti-social behaviour. Kerstin Barton, who came later as a housemother, recalls a night when she was giving baths to the Cottage children. 'I was fed up, they were being so slow, and I stamped my foot at Storm, and said: "For Christ's sake get in to that bath!" He can't have been more than 4, and he just looked up and said, "You stamp once more at me, and I'm going to bring you up at the Saturday meeting." ' Inevitably, the younger children tended to look up to the older children, and to some extent were influenced by them. Just occasionally this influence came about through the intentional lobbying of the older children. Johnnie Collier remembers this happening as a result of an incident on Bonfire Night: 'I and some of the other older ones found some seed potatoes in the hockey field. We stuck halfpenny bangers in them and hurled them towards the bonfire, where they exploded amongst the staff, the girls and the little kids. Cyril Eyre, a young maths graduate who had recently come from Oxford to teach at Summerhill, was outraged at this anti-social behaviour, and charged us at the meeting. Neill backed Cyril up, and they both waxed very wrath. But one or two of our number primed a lot of little kids before the meeting, and we got off on a vote. We were jubiliant at our acquittal, and our victory over the new teacher.'

Such direct division along adult/child lines was unusual, as another teacher of the period, Leslie Morton, remembers: 'The staff were very much part of the meeting – there used to be many arguments amongst them, very heated and involved, and not always on the same side. I don't remember staff versus children situations, although this could happen. But staff differences could be most ferociously argued out.' In February 1933 Neill mentioned such a division in a letter to Curry: 'Tonight at our meeting I hear there is to be a helluva row about food chucking in the dining room. Some of the staff say the staff should join in, others say no. Kids also divided.' At one time, an individual charged at the meeting could call on another to be their 'advocate'. Here again, no special distinction was made between adults and children – as Teddy Raw found to his cost: 'I was charged with stealing some money. Though I was a villain in many ways, I hadn't done it that time. I was asked if I wanted someone to represent me, and in a flash of inspiration I said I would have Neill. He looked a bit

'Allie' Neill, aged 3, with his mother Mary: 'She was a snob and she made us snobs'

The Kingsmuir dominie and his 'bairns', about 1900. Neill (back row, far right) was by now a pupil teacher under his father; three of his younger sisters, May (second row, fifth from left), Ada (second row, seventh from left) and Hilda (front row, second from right) also attended the village school

Kingsmuir and some of its inhabitants, before the First World War

Willie Neill, the bright hope of the family, and a hero to his younger brother

Neill in 1912 at the Inter-University Conference at St Andrews University (middle row, far left), where he talked journalism with J. B. Salmond (back row, far left), and drank champagne with Walter Elliott (front row, far right)

(above) One of the pictures of Neill which Jessie Irving kept until her death

(left) Neill's fiancée from Gretna, Jessie Irving: 'The gulf between our interests was too great'

Neill (top left), the aspiring journalist, and three of his literary mentors:
J. M. Barrie (bottom left), G. B. Shaw (top right) and H. G. Wells (bottom right)

Second Lieutenant A. S. Neill (right), Royal Garrison Artillery, May 1918:
'I thought of being a conscientious objector, but hadn't the moral courage'

Neill was among the rescuers on the day Gretna has never forgotten

(left) Homer Lane: 'The first man who said we don't know a damn thing about children'

(right) John Russell, head of King Alfred School in London: 'He was a lovable old God, but nevertheless God'

Neill (centre back with white trilby) and some King Alfred pupils on a river boat trip, 1918-19. Wally Neustatter stands between the two women in white

Lilian Neustatter (left) and her novelist sister Henry Handel Richardson (centre) shortly after they arrived in Europe

(above left) Beatrice Ensor, Neill's co-editor on the *New Era*: 'The more outrageously I attacked pedants and schools, the more delighted she was'

European beginnings: (above right) the International School in Hellerau, Germany, and (below) its second home on Sonntagsberg, Austria

(above left) Edwin Muir in Vienna during the time he stayed with Neill, 1923-4: 'Edwin had a mysticism that was beyond me'

(above right) The young Willa Muir as Neill first knew her, at St Andrews University, 1910: she thought Neill's practice with children 'almost infallible'

Wilhelm Stekel, Neill's analyst and friend: 'His analysis touched my head, but never my emotions'

Summerhill at Lyme Regis, Dorset, 1924-7

Neill with a group of staff and children at Lyme, 1925

Neill and Mrs Lins in the early years at Leiston: 'Her optimism and energy were so great that neither of us ever thought of failure'

Neill's allies on the left
wing of the progressive
school movement: Bill
Curry (left), head of
Dartington School; Dora
and Bertrand Russell
(below), who started
Beacon Hill School in 1927

Neill, George Corkhill (standing, second from right), and Summerhill children on a camping holiday in Scotland, 1932

Neill at work – as craftsman . . .   as labourer . . .

as storyteller . . .

and writer

Neill at play –
(left) escaping
from visitors on
the golf course;
(below) taking a
leading role in
his own play, *One
of the Family*
(centre, with
glasses)

Many politically active parents sent their children to Summerhill:
J. D. Bernal (above left), Ivor Montagu (above right), Miles Malleson (below left),
Ethel Mannin (below right) here with her daughter Jean

(above) Summerhill at
Ffestiniog, 1940-5

(left) Ena Wood, Neill's
second wife

opposite
Neill's daughter Zoë: (top) on
the cover of *Picture Post,* and
(bottom) with Neill: 'Watching
her makes me convinced I
don't know a thing about kids
or human nature'

PICTURE POST

THE CHILD WHO NEVER GETS SLAPPED
(see inside)

Neill with his therapist and great friend Wilhelm Reich: 'I can't remember knowing so honest a guy as Willie'

Neill en route to the USA, 1948: two years later he was refused entry

Life in
Summerhill –
teaching . . .

attending
the weekly
meeting . . .

handing out
pocket money
afterwards

Henry Miller in 1969: 'I know of no other educator in the western world to compare with Neill'

Anti-Polaris protest on the Dunoon ferry, May 1961: Neill's night in prison came after he joined a similar demonstration in Scotland four months later

Neill receiving one of his three honorary degrees, University of Exeter, 1968

Neill in old age with his dog, Biscuit

reluctant, but agreed. And of course he lost. I was absolutely shattered: I thought, I'm innocent, and they've found me guilty, and Neill didn't get me off.'

Such a miscarriage of justice was a rare event, though it did tend to support Neill's view that his influence was no more potent than that of anyone else present. But how true was this claim, a pivotal one in his philosophy? It was not merely a matter of Neill's theoretical equality with everyone else. Nona Simon, who came to Summerhill at the age of 4, and was virtually brought up by the Neills, recalls: 'Most little kids would only vote with the majority, and you'd get just as much hero worship of the older children as of Neill. But he would affect the voting – he was an authority without having to say too much.' Branwen Williams takes a similar view: 'Though he would say that we ran the school, that he had no more say at the meetings than anyone else, I think in practice we still looked to him for a lead – certainly when we were very little. We used to outvote him occasionally, just to prove that his theories were right; but I think we were a little uneasy about it. So there was a subtle kind of guidance.' Cynthia Allen reinforces this idea: 'His very withdrawal from a conflict, his departure to his workshop or desk, made an impact,' she remembers.

There were of course a few areas in which it was understood and accepted that Neill and Mrs Lins had to have ultimate control. Most matters concerning health and safety, the hiring and firing of staff, and the law of the land were under their jurisdiction. Yet even here there was some flexibility, though the impact of the meeting was minimal compared to its power in other matters. Food was often a matter for intense debate; Neill more than once woke up a dull meeting by proposing that second helpings should be abolished. Often there were debates about which areas of the school should be out of bounds because of the risk to life and limb. Sometimes it was clearly difficult to draw satisfactory boundaries; and Neill was not always able to argue convincingly for certain measures. At one time he insisted that no child should be allowed to climb one particularly dangerous route up on the roof; yet he allowed them to climb the tall copper beech at the front of the house. This was arguably an equally hazardous challenge – and one child was lucky to survive when he fell twenty feet from the tree on to his skull. Neill argued, with little logic or consistency, that 'To ban tree-climbing would be wrong and futile, for it is the right of every child to climb trees.' In general though, the laws concerning safety were based on common sense, and were almost always adhered to.

There was, however, some division between Neill and Mrs Lins over certain decisions made by the meeting. She disliked, for instance, any form of punishment which deprived children of food – in her terms this was something akin to the withdrawal of love. However, since she often did not attend the meetings, it was difficult for her to argue against such a proposal. Her non-attendance caused annoyance, and she was often criticised at meetings. In many respects she was a law unto herself, regarding

Summerhill as a large family under her control. The school garden, with its fine trees, flowers and rose bushes, she called 'My Garden'. She forbade the children to pick flowers, and would chase off any whom she found straying on to her much-prized round lawn. The children were only allowed in the lounge on Wednesdays, Saturdays and Sundays, and if they were caught going up or down the front stairs, or in and out of the front door, she would fine them a halfpenny. Incurring her wrath was considered by some pupils to be more of a punishment than the financial one, as Daphne Oliver recalls: 'We used to dare each other to go down the stairs and out of the door while Mrs Lins was in the vicinity. That was considered the most dangerous thing to do in Summerhill.' Staff as well as children would come up against her assertiveness. Ruth Allen, a housemother during this period, remembers that 'she had a rather brisk way of saying, "Go and do so and so." ' Max Morton, one of the early teachers, saw her as 'a sort of matriarch. She was someone you couldn't help liking, but you also had to oppose her, because she was so dictatorial. She was very un-Neillish in that way.' The contrast between her and Neill was vividly demonstrated in one small incident recalled by David Newton, a pupil throughout the 1930s. 'Virginia Pilkington and I stripped a tree of its Victoria plums. Mrs Lins was furious, and expelled us. We went and appealed to Neill, and he advised us to keep out of her way for a few days. After that she was OK.'

Neill and Mrs Lins sometimes had to make difficult decisions about whether a disturbed or anti-social child should be allowed to continue at the school. Neill was loath to expel a child except in exceptional circumstances, and once took his problem to the meeting. Two children were leading gangs and doing a lot of stealing, and he called a general meeting to ask what should be done with them. The meeting recommended expulsion, and the two children were asked to leave. In this instance, Neill had almost certainly already decided on such a course of action and was simply looking for public support. At other times, he would deliberately go against the meeting, though not necessarily in public. Peter Byles, a teacher who came in 1928, remembers a time when 'the meeting took away one boy's gun and knife, but afterwards Neill gave the knife back, saying that there was no rule against that'. Such a gesture often had a powerful effect on the individual concerned, though it involved a risk on Neill's part, especially in the case of a disturbed child.

Although the proportion of problem children was less than it had been in the early years at Lyme, Neill was still taking in a number who were seriously disturbed. A few were violent, hysterical or incontinent; several were thieves or bullies; and one or two were mentally retarded. One boy cut the heads off some live chickens on the day of his arrival. Another refused to wash for weeks on end, even when Neill and Mrs Lins offered him their bathroom. One older boy threw Neill from the top of the stairs to the bottom. A girl once hurled a golf club at his head. Theft was a common occurrence: one boy stole Neill's wireless and sold it in Leiston, another did the same with his seven-guinea mackintosh. It may have been this occasion which Ruth Allen recalled later: 'One of the teachers told me that Neill was in a furious temper because somebody had been selling his clothes down town. I went into the kitchen and said, "Neill, I hear you were in an awful bate this morning because somebody has sold your coat." He said: "Oh well, I was for a time, but then I thought, I've got two coats." ' Neill's temper, rare in itself, never lasted for long.

Often it was the community's patience and tolerance, as well as Neill's, which were tested. One boy, who arrived at the relatively advanced age of 17, from a private school in Oxford and an 'impeccable' background, was preoccupied with his own cleanliness. Rather than join in any school activities, he spent his days with the local railway men, helping them to load coal. He would return briefly for his meals, his face and hands covered in soot. Neill made it clear that no comment should be made on his condition while the boy was working through these difficulties. After a few weeks he exhausted his interest in coal, lost his obsession with cleanliness, and started to attend lessons.

Though he placed an increasing emphasis on the influence of the environment in allowing a child to overcome its problems, Neill still made use of Private Lessons, and indeed spent a considerable part of his time in this kind of curative work. The PLs were essentially relaxed conversations, in which Neill encouraged children to talk about themselves, their anxieties and fears, their feelings about school or home. Whatever the content of these talks, Neill relied greatly on the child's capacity to accept him as a *friendly* adult, in contrast to certain teachers and parents that some of them had previously encountered. Brian Anscombe remembers: 'He'd try to get you to talk about yourself, but you could sit there and say nothing if you felt like it. It was quite a pleasant experience just talking to somebody like Neill.' The PLs were by no means always serious occasions, as Johnnie Collier recalls: 'Neill gave me one PL, when I was about 7. He told me a story about my having a penis which stretched all the two miles from Leiston to Sizewell. I was highly delighted and greatly amused.' Sex and reproduction were often among the topics discussed, as was religion: Neill used anecdotes or word games to bring children's fears or misconceptions out in to the open. Frequently he traced the child's problem back to the attitudes of its mother or father, and encouraged the child to express its feelings. Edna Raymond was one of many who had this experience: 'My mother was an extremely dominating woman. Neill told me in a PL that I hated her. That was quite a revelation, something that one would never dare admit then. It was also quite a release.' To assist in these discussions, Neill had a series of dolls made – one for father and mother, one for little sister, one for little brother. He would present the appropriate one to the child, and await developments.

Though the PLs were undoubtedly an enormous benefit to many children, they could also be uncomfortable occasions at times. Although they were voluntary, Neill did sometimes hold them without warning whenever he found a child on the potato patch, the golf course or in his workshop. Some children tried to resist Neill's probings, or, as his technique became better known, to evade his questions in more devious ways. Daphne Oliver, who came to Summerhill after being expelled from another school, recalls: 'I didn't like his PLs at all. I always felt very uncomfortable, and told him the most terrible lies. I was afraid that, if I told him the truth, he would tell *me* the truth, and I was a bit nervous about that.' Anne Forbes offers a similar recollection: 'He was always keen to hear one's dreams. I remember getting a bit crafty after a while: I got to realise the things that figured. If you couldn't remember a dream you made it up, and Neill was delighted with it. After ten minutes of "I say poker and you say what comes into your head", we ended up giggling, and that was that.' Neill found some children easier to work with than others, as Larry Collier recollects: 'He always maintained that I was an impossible person to analyse; he didn't think I was a very warm subject. But I found him rather aggressive, and his insistence on sex and masturbation a bit peculiar. I was a very late developer sexually, and this didn't touch me very much.' Cynthia Allen, another early Leiston pupil, was even more unhappy about such sessions with Neill: 'I was very embarrassed by his rough and ready questions, and by being told the most surprising things about my own nature. I never found them the slightest help, they just gave me a fresh load of things to worry about. Once I was ill in bed, and he gave me a PL on penis envy. I was never ill again after that unforgettable experience.'

Though Neill's intuitions about children's problems often seemed to border on the miraculous, it was not only the children who felt some unease about his methods. Beryl Sandford trained as an analyst and, after reading Neill's books, decided even before she became a parent that any child she had would go to Summerhill – which her son David did in 1931. Observing him with a professional as well as a parental eye, she felt that 'Neill was a genius with delinquent children. . .but his PLs were a bit suspect. He would give the child a pillow, and say Bash it. He didn't realise that he could add to their anxiety, and that he might not be able to put the pieces together again.' Roger Anscombe, looking back from the perspective of a psychiatric social worker, recalls: 'I don't think he did it in quite the way it should have been done. But you can't really blame him for that, because no one knew much about that sort of thing then. He could achieve a positive transference, but he didn't know what to do when he'd done that. I regarded him as the ideal father, but he didn't realise this. So he didn't know how to get me to react, to be angry with him but to find that it was all right.'

There were two startling and original ways in which Neill dealt with problem children. These were his use of rewards instead of punishment for anti-social behaviour, and his way of becoming 'one of the gang' by joining in with such behaviour – both derived from Homer Lane. Time and again in the early years of Summerhill, he responded to acts of theft by giving the child money – for a while 6*d* seemed to be the accepted token. Sometimes this treatment was handed out through the meeting: one persistent thief was compelled to steal something every day, or be fined his pocket money. Neill believed such a gesture should be aimed at the child's unconscious. 'He may think that I'm a fool, but what he thinks doesn't matter much,' he wrote; 'it's what he feels that matters. And he feels that I am his friend, his approver, one who gives him love instead of hate.' Neill sometimes approached the problem in a more roundabout way. On one occasion a boy tricked him into giving him some money for a supposed visit to his uncle, by imitating his voice on the phone with a call from a public call-box in Leiston. He had been a persistent thief before he came to Summerhill, and none of the traditional forms of punishment had made any impression on his behaviour. Neill tried something startlingly different. He went up to the boy's bedroom, told him that there had been another call from his family to say that the fare was more than they had thought, and that his mother had asked him to give the boy an additional ten shillings – which Neill then threw on his bed, and left the room.

There is no doubt that this type of treatment had a significant effect on some of the problem children, though the change in their behaviour was not necessarily as quick or dramatic as Neill sometimes made out in his books and lectures. Nor did it necessarily need to be Neill who offered the 'reward' – this could be done either by the school as a whole through the meeting, or by another adult. In January 1931 Neill confided to Bertrand Russell: 'At present I have a lad of six who shits his pants six times daily. . . his dear mamma "cured" him by making him eat the shit.' The boy had been beaten and expelled from a number of schools because of his incontinence: Summerhill, as for several other children in the early years, was a last resort. Neill asked Mrs Corks the matron to take the boy in hand on his arrival, as her son Mervyn remembers: 'Neill wanted her to reward him, starting with 1*d* or 2*d* in the morning, and increasing the amount as the day progressed. Towards the end of the week Neill's instructions changed: mother had to go along and see Colin and say, "Haven't you done anything yet? You're letting me down." He got very bored with this: he stuck it out for seven or eight days, and then it dried up, and never happened again. He left at 14 or 15, a damn nice lad.'

Neill's device of joining in with the anti-social behaviour of children also took a number of forms. At Lyme he once helped a boy to steal some chickens from the house next door to Summerhill, secure in the knowledge that they would soon fly back to their home. He mentioned an incident of a similar kind in a letter to Curry in February 1933: 'The past three days a gang of twelve-year-olds has rebelled against the government. They put up a notice for volunteers to join the gang, and I at once put my name down. The result: I've got the cook and maids on my neck, and it ain't pleasant.' Michael Bernal remembers an example of his reaction to a child's destructive behaviour: 'One boy was having a tantrum and tearing a mattress. Neill said nothing – he just picked up a china cup from the ledge and threw it on the floor. The boy stopped at once.' But his most famous 'gesture' of this kind came when he responded to a child breaking a window by doing exactly the same thing himself.

Here it is more difficult to separate fact from fiction, and for this Neill must take part of the blame. There were undoubtedly occasions, recalled by pupils, when Neill *did* break a window. One ex-pupil remembers a time when he went round the school breaking as many as a hundred, in response to one child's such action. On the other hand, it is also quite clear that he took a boyish delight in drawing attention to this element of his work, and in doing so exaggerated the number of occurrences, and perhaps on occasion the number of windows involved. Leslie and Vivien Morton are sceptical about the extent of his window-breaking activities. 'He was a canny Scot who hated destruction and damage. It happened a few times, but it was very much the exception. He certainly never broke a hundred windows or anything like that. That is the sort of myth he generated, and childhood memories can be very distorted.' Certainly Neill was never reticent about mentioning this part of his method in public. In August 1932 he was reported by the *News Chronicle* to have told an audience in Wales: 'I saw a lad in a temper break 24 windows of the school in one day. I pointed out to him one pane he had missed.' When, five years later, the same paper serialised parts of his book *That Dreadful School*, in which his views on window-breaking were set out in some detail, they chose to illustrate one extract with a photograph showing Neill and a group of Summerhill children laughing in front of a broken window. Neill, through his agent A. P. Watt, had insisted on seeing before publication any photographs to be used alongside his words, and retained the right of veto over any of which he disapproved. So it seems he was not unhappy to have this potentially sensational element of his work highlighted in this fashion. Neill could hardly be surprised at the comment of one newspaper photographer, who is alleged to have said in bewilderment: 'If this is a free school why aren't all these windows broken?'

Neill's skill in handling difficult children was not confined to the more overt actions of this kind. 'The art of dealing with children,' he wrote, 'might be defined as *knowing what not to say*.' Maurice Draper, who taught at Summerhill for two years in the late 1920s, remembers one example of this non-interventionist philosophy. 'There was an ex-public-school boy there who loved milk and sugar. Once he asked me to help him break into the kitchen, which I did. Neill looked in, simply said "Ah", walked out again, and did nothing.' Actions, Neill believed, were often more valuable than words. Daphne Oliver recalls how a group of girls received evidence of this: 'They were up on the platform above the back door of Neill's workshop, messing around with some water. When Neill came over from his workshop they poured water over him. He never twitched or anything: he just went into the house, got a bowl of water, went up on to the platform, and threw it all over them. Then he gave that little smile of his and went back into his office. They were astonished, and didn't say a word.' She also remembers a more serious occasion when Neill's timing, and his instinct for getting at a child's motivation, were put to the test: 'There was one terribly spoilt boy who wanted to get his own way all the time. If he didn't he used to threaten to do something really dangerous, and his sister used to panic. One day he got out on to a windowsill, and said to her, If you don't give me sixpence, I'll jump. She was very frightened, and asked someone to fetch Neill. He came into the room and asked the boy what he was doing. When the boy told him, Neill said, "Well, jump then." And of course he climbed back through the window.'

Knowledge of a child's home background, as Neill had in this instance, certainly helped him to decide if and how he should act or speak when dealing with problem children. One illegitimate boy who was there for several years was extremely difficult to handle: he was a potential danger to other children, and with adults would one moment be clinging, the next spitting in their face. He would talk endlessly about his father – to which Neill responded by telling him that Jesus was illegitimate. Another girl, whose father was dead, had stolen some money, though she had made no attempt to hide it. Lucy Francis, a teacher during the 1930s, remembers how Neill handled the matter: 'He took her in to the kitchen while he was having his lunch and he said to her, "Well, where's your Daddy?" – he could do something "cruel" like that – and she said, "I don't want to talk about it. You know he's dead." And Neill said, "Would you like me for a Daddy?" "No!" "Are you sure?" "Yes." And Neill said, "All right. If I give you a penny, would you like me for a Daddy?" "Oh yes, I would!" And she skipped about, as gay as a lark.' At the time it was by no means accepted that stealing money was a child's way of 'stealing love'; but Neill was quite convinced that such behaviour showed that a child was starved of love and affection. He did however try to distinguish between this kind of theft, which he saw as neurotic and requiring action, and a normal child's acquisitive urge or desire for adventure, which he considered natural, and which he felt they should be allowed to live out, up to a certain age.

Much of Neill's success in helping children with their problems derived from his markedly unsentimental way of coping with potentially distressing situations. Gordon Leff remembers the night he and his sister and brother arrived at Summerhill in 1934: 'We were put in a room with a little girl who had a cleft palate. Neill came up just to see how we were, and the girl was able to make it clear that she had no blankets. Neill had one of those engineering catalogues, and he said, "Here, you can cover yourself with that." ' He had a strong sense of fantasy which appealed to many children, and which he could sometimes convey in both brusque and humorous fashion. Once, a slightly retarded boy had been told by another child at Summerhill that Neill wanted him to get a pot of striped paint from the hardware store. He duly went on the errand, and then came back to Neill, saying that the shop didn't stock such an item. Neill immediately said: 'You damn fool, it wasn't striped paint I wanted, it was tartan.'

Neill was continuously anxious about the reputation of Summerhill in Leiston, and his feelings were transmitted to both adults and children. As a result, the meeting made a number of rules about behaviour 'down town', the most notable being the proposal by a girl of 11 that swearing should be confined to the school grounds, since 'The townspeople don't yet know that swearing doesn't matter'. There was something of a siege mentality in the school in these early years, according to David Barton: 'Neill had this horror of being closed down like Homer Lane. At meetings he would say that there was a real danger that this could happen. Before the war this was a realistic feeling: the local church was really rather hostile, and so were the local bigwigs. We had to be very conscious of the town, careful of kids going into Leiston without a tie.' Often it was the children who were most jealous of the school's reputation. Leslie Morton was once brought up before the meeting for wearing shorts in the town that were considered too brief. One left-wing teacher was criticised for refusing to stand up during the National Anthem at the end of a film show in the local cinema, thereby 'letting down' Summerhill in public. (He refused to change his behaviour.) Liz Hall, a housemother who came a few years later, recalls the behaviour of the younger children: 'The kids were so easy when you took them out. I can't keep discipline, but I've taken 40 kids on a bus to Aldeburgh with no anxiety. One time the whole lot thought they had been disgraced because a woman dropped a bag of sweets, and a little girl darted forward and said, "Bags I!" Another time I took them down to the barber, and he said: "They think they're in church, don't they." Once in Leiston I said something like "My bloody foot hurts", and they gasped: "Swearing down town!" '

Inevitably, there were a few incidents which served to intensify any hostility felt towards Summerhill by local people. Rowna Ely remembers making coins in the metal shop and passing them off in the town for chocolates and cigarettes. 'I don't remember any police arriving. But after a meeting in the hall, with Neill as judge, we were sentenced to three weeks without pocket money or visits to the pictures, until we had paid back the forged money.' Neill was terrified at the prospect of visits from the police – another type of authority figure with whom he never felt comfortable – but occasionally had to endure them. Once the altar cloth was stolen from the local church and, when the police turned up at Summerhill, Neill was happily able to deny all knowledge of the theft. Mervyn Corkhill remembers the sequel: 'One of the international pupils from Scandinavia had come three or four days before. I saw a fantastically beautiful carpet on the floor of his room, and commented on this to Neill as he came through the back door at that moment. He was speechless, and then said to me: "Shut the bloody door, Mervyn!" There was a hell of a stink. Neill and the police came to a gentlemanly agreement that if the boy was put on the next boat to Sweden the incident would be forgotten.' Though Neill would not necessarily have taken such a drastic step himself, the boy's father preferred the incident to be hushed up, and so he left.

This was not the only kind of incident which caused Neill anxiety. Attempts were made to interest local people in the school – for example, by inviting them to the regular Saturday night dances. A number of Leiston inhabitants also worked as domestic staff within the school. Yet it was still hard for Neill to demonstrate to some members of the local community the kind of school he was running. Summerhill was, at different times, known as 'the Home school'. In July 1934 Neill was sufficiently concerned about the matter to write to the *Leiston Observer*:

Dear Sir, Prospective parents of Summerhill sometimes make casual enquiries about the school from Leiston and Aldeburgh citizens. Sometimes they get good reports, but sometimes they are told that Summerhill is a school for imbeciles. Hitherto, I have paid no attention to these reports, but when an enquirer the other day was told the imbecile story in Aldeburgh I decided to make the matter public. Summerhill brings quite a lot of money to Leiston and some to Aldeburgh, without taking any money from these towns. We live on good terms with most of our neighbours, but if some of the neighbours persist in continuing the imbecile libel I fancy that legal action could be taken. I should not need to tell the local public that Summerhill does not deal with imbeciles. A school that is visited by enthusiasts from all parts of the world, a school that has produced a famous golfer, a famous cinema-star, and a rising authoress, a school that is known to be in the van of modern education, should not require to be explained to people living at its very doors. Summerhill of course does sometimes get 'problems', but only problems that can be made good citizens by proper treatment. But because we can cure children who have been ruined by ignorant treatment, we do not deserve to be libelled by ignorant busybodies.
Yours sincerely, A. S. Neill.

Neill once said he wished he could have two schools: one for the problem children, where they could freely act out their aggressions and fantasies, and another for the normal children, where the facilities could remain relatively unscathed. At one point he did make some effort to make his analytical work rather more separate from the rest of the school, as he told Curry in a letter of October 1934: 'I'm going to build a special outhouse for my analysis work, with all sorts of symbols in it. I need it badly for the younger kids, but can't afford it yet.' Though he never managed to find the money for a new building for this purpose, he did make some progress with the idea. In January he reported to Curry:

> I've begun a play analysis room for the smaller kids, but am handicapped by a lack of proper, or rather improper material. You should have seen the salesman in Abbott's Toy Shop when I asked him where I could get a doll with an unscrewable penis. Finally, he suggested Paris.

One project that might have proved useful to him was Sun Lodge in Aldeburgh, a small boarding school for disturbed children opened in the mid 1930s by Mrs Lins's son Wally, by now a psychiatrist working in London. The first child to go there, a boy of limited intelligence whose speciality had been to make forks stick upright in girls' heads, was transferred from Summerhill; but the others, though suggested by Neill, did not attend his school. The school in fact closed down after a fairly short life.

At times Neill found that his dealings with an individual child conflicted with the self-government of the weekly meeting. Occasionally he felt bound not to reveal information given to him during a PL, even if a child told a completely different story in public, and perhaps got away with breaking a rule. In the same way, there were times when he suggested that a particular incident or child's behaviour was best dealt with in a Private Lesson rather than by the meeting; occasionally the meeting itself would propose that Neill should handle the matter in this way. In general there was acceptance of the idea, and many children, according to adults present, showed remarkable sensitivity in knowing which cases might be appropriate for this kind of treatment. There could, however, be dissent on occasions, as Johnnie Collier recalls: 'A very well behaved and respectable girl came to the school, and was discovered to be a kleptomaniac. Once she stole a watch from a Swedish boy, and Neill somehow let it be known that this ought to be dealt with psychologically. There was quite a furore about this, as a lot of us thought this was favouritism – when *we* stole something it was brought up in the meeting.'

Yet Neill, for obvious reasons, tried hard not to show favouritism towards any child. There was some feeling that he preferred the company of the more extrovert 'gangster' type of child, but this was by no means obvious, and he seems generally to have succeeded in being seen to treat all children in the same way. With Mrs Lins it was a different matter. Many pupils recall her decided preference for the girls, some of whom were allowed up to her room in the evenings when boys were excluded, or given special items of food when she felt it was required. Yet she also went out of her way to show affection towards some of the least appealing problem children. One slightly imbecilic boy would lean heavily against her while they sat listening to records in the sitting room, but she never pushed him away. Vivien Morton recalls: 'She allowed some of the more repulsive problem children to comb her hair or fondle her, and would take it without flinching. One boy particularly liked to sit on the arm of her chair and comb her hair: she allowed him to turn the comb on to his greasy forelock and then back to her elegant shingle.' Her broad support for Neill's approach to matters such as theft was evident in the kind of incident recalled by Rowna Ely: 'When she was reading to us, we used to pick the green packet of cigarettes out of her jacket pocket and extract three or four tiny gold-tipped cigarettes from the box, and then slip it back. She didn't say a word, and always had a good supply of them there.' These reading sessions in the evenings were part of the security she engendered, and were greatly liked by the children, who would gather round in her room to hear stories by R. H. Mottram, Richard Hughes and – perhaps at Neill's instigation – J. M. Barrie.

Neill's own, more original story-telling sessions were by now a familiar and much-cherished part of Summerhill life. As with *A Dominie's Five*, which had originated in Hellerau, the children were always the main characters in these stories. Neill used them as a complement to the meetings and PLs, as part of his 'psychology of approval'. He assigned roles to the children which he intended would touch on their fantasy life. If they were shy or withdrawn, he would give them the most horrendous or courageous exploits to perform; those whom he saw as virtuous or assertive were usually made the villains of the tale, to be outwitted by the hero or heroine. He always gave himself a role in the story, in which he would become an object of ridicule or contempt for his qualities of cowardice, laziness or greed. One of the most popular characters was Pyecraft, a bulky and genial millionaire who had featured in *A Dominie's Five*, and whose wealth allowed the children to have a variety of extraordinary adventures. Pyecraft was a key figure in one of the children's favourite stories, *The Last Man Alive*, an idea that Neill had first tried on children in Gretna. In 1938 Herbert Jenkins published it in book form, with illustrations by a Summerhill pupil, Sonia Araquistain. The story reflected Neill's taste as much as any of his readers or listeners: it drew on the 'penny dreadful' style of narrative, Neill's interest in the mechanics of how things work, his reading of the early science fiction stories of Wells, his more recent interest in the dialogue of the Hollywood gangster movies, and the detective stories published in *Black Mask* and other American 'pulp' magazines.*

The stories often had a powerful effect on children. Jean Allen, a timid girl who featured in *The Last Man Alive* as a bold and fearless character, remembers their impact on her: 'He seemed to find new stories all the time. They were absolutely marvellous, and so convincing. I got so excited I used to have to sit there with my fingers in my ears, taking them in and out at will.' Neill would encourage the children to comment, criticise or interrupt as he told the story, breaking down the normal barrier between narrator and listener. Lucy Francis recalls how one 5-year-old responded: 'As Neill went on with the story, this boy got up, and very slowly took a step forward, his eyes fixed on Neill all the time. And then he did it again. And again. And at last he was right up against Neill, staring at him, entranced.' Sometimes the stories were so real to the children that it was hard for them to distinguish between fantasy and reality. One American visitor, Ilse Reich, was included in the story as the bringer of important papers, which certain villainous characters were trying to steal. 'The story ended with all of us victoriously defending the papers and chasing the enemy away', she remembers. 'The spell which Neill cast over us left an indelible impression, and was so real to some of the children that two little girls whose room was next to mine came up to me that same evening, and in a conspiratorial way asked me whether I really had those papers in my room.' But sometimes Neill misjudged the ability of a child to cope with his fictional deeds: a 9-year-old boy that he made steal some gold in one story came to him later in tears, saying that he had never stolen the gold.

What precisely was the secret of Neill's story-telling gift? Gavin Campbell, a pupil of a later period, remembers his technique: 'He would present each of us with our good sides and possibilities, as well as our defects. You knew that any criticism or danger would be followed or accompanied by reward or safety. The stories were immensely complex, and he had an

*In 1927, Neill wrote a fan letter to the relatively unknown Erle Stanley Gardner, complimenting him on his Ed Jenkins stories in *Black Mask*.

infinite capacity for remembering what had gone before. It all happened so easily: children, even neurotic ones, would be warmed and lulled.' Neill clearly took enormous delight in telling these stories, being able at one and the same time to provide emotional help to children and to indulge his own taste for manipulating an audience. Bill MacKinnon, a fellow-Scot who joined the Summerhill staff after the war, remembers the way Neill cast his spell: 'He was one of the best raconteurs that I've ever met. He could fill you with the greatest sense of anticipation when he was about to embark on a story – you could feel it in the others too. A kind of glow emanated from him. He had a most expressive face. It wasn't just the twinkle in his eye, or the way he pursed his lips or angled his head, that made his stories so funny, but the complete control he had over his features. He could say the funniest things with an absolute deadpan face that had you in uncontrollable laughter; but he just carried on, knowing he had you exactly where he wanted you. He had this indefinable something that could hold an audience; yet he never exaggerated for effect.'

What was the explanation for this extraordinary ability which impressed so many adults and children at Summerhill? There are some interesting parallels between his technique, and that of the literary hero of his youth, J. M. Barrie. 'What is genius? It is the power to be a boy again at will', he had written in *Tommy and Grizel*, the sequel to Neill's once favourite book, *Sentimental Tommy*. Parts of this second book were written in London's Kensington Gardens, where Barrie met and befriended the Llewellyn Davies boys, who provided him with the inspiration for *Peter Pan*. Barrie, who had none of his own, was much more at ease with children than with adults, and had a childish delight in stories and games of fantasy, especially when they involved pirates, hangings, murders, desert islands and other primitive elements. He evolved the tale of the 'boy who never grew up' through a series of story-telling sessions with the Llewellyn Davies boys in Kensington Gardens, which he wrote of in another of his books, *The Little White Bird*:

> I ought to mention here that the following is our way with a story: First I tell it to him, and then he tells it to me, the understanding being that it is quite a different story; and then I retell it with his additions, and so we go on until no one could say whether it is his story or mine.

Sometimes Barrie would pretend to forget what came next, and would ask the children to help him out. The method was not the same as Neill's, but the quality of the *rapport* with children was similar, though Neill's capacity for 'flinging off the years and whistling childhood back' was totally different from Barrie's whimsical and self-indulgent sentimentality.

Even though Neill tired of Barrie's fiction after his early admiration for it, he remained extremely interested in the Peter Pan story for many years. At university he had reviewed *Peter and Wendy*, Barrie's prose version of his highly successful play. In the *Student* Neill called it 'the sweetest story ever written', and praised it as 'a song of childhood, a song of innocent joys and delicious make-believe'. He thought the author 'rather hard on poor grown-ups, but he has so delicate a touch of irony that we all forgive him'. He concluded approvingly: 'The story is told in a charmingly child-like style: Barrie can be a boy again at will.' Neill returned to this phrase of Barrie's in many of his subsequent writings and, after his discovery of Freud, formulated the idea in terms of his own work. In *The Problem Parent* he wrote: 'Every successful teacher is a child at heart; he can enter into the work and play of children because he is at their emotional level of development. . . if the day comes when I find myself growing up I shall give up schoolmastering.' Homer Lane was an effusive admirer of Barrie's plays, especially *Peter Pan*, and in later years Neill said of his former analyst that 'like Barrie he never really did grow up. . . .Yet it was this Peter Panism that made him the creator of a new way of treating sick people.'* Neill himself even used the story in his treatment of his first problem child, Derrick Boyd, labelling his Unconscious 'Peter Pan', and saying, whenever the boy behaved in an objectionable way, 'Good, Peter, my lad!' He found the story – in which Peter is 'so full of wrath against grown-ups, who, as usual, were spoiling everything' – of considerable use in treating what he saw as 'a beautiful example of the Oedipus Complex'.

One of Peter Pan's most passionate outbursts concerned a particular aspect of the growing up that he so dreaded: 'I don't want to go to school and learn solemn things,' he tells Wendy; and, talking of the mother that he no longer misses, 'perhaps she would say I was old, and I just want always to be a little boy and to have fun.' There was without doubt a lot of Peter Pan in Neill, who had his own bitter and deeply entrenched reasons for being 'full of wrath against grown-ups'. In Summerhill he created his own version of Barrie's Neverland, in which children would be allowed to live out their fantasies, to experience the kind of carefree and guiltless childhood which Neill himself was never allowed.

Neill could, by general consent, work wonders with disturbed children, with his extraordinary blend of gruff humour, intuition and patience. But many who were with him at Summerhill felt that he was less capable of understanding the needs of 'normal' children, that he was most in tune with those whom he saw as being fellow-sufferers from the oppressive 'moulding' of adults that led to inhibitions and neuroses. Neill himself provided support for this view in a remark he made to Beryl Sandford, whose son went to Summerhill in 1931 at the age of 5: 'He was a genius with delinquent children,' she recalls, 'but he said he wasn't interested in children who hadn't got difficult problems. "I find ordinary children so damn boring," he said. "David hasn't broken a window yet." This worried him.' Anne Forbes, who went as a pupil in 1934, gained a similar impression: 'He was always disappointed in me because I didn't go wild when I came there. I used to watch him and think, Wouldn't you love me to break

*In his biography of Lane, David Wills records the following: 'Lane, in conversation with Barrie, asked him what a certain girl in one of his plays was supposed to represent. Barrie replied, "I don't know, but I think you do, and I don't like it!" '

a window, and I damn well won't.' An echo of this is found in the critical remarks made by another 1930s pupil, Cynthia Allen: 'Neill was only interested in fitting problems to his psychological theories, not in listening to our worries. Child psychology became his over-riding interest, and an introspective attitude was rife throughout the school. Quite small children could be heard analysing the behaviour of their companions, diagnosing mother fixations, father complexes or, in the case of thumb sucking, pre-mature weaning. I don't think he was especially interested in children except as an extension of his own experiences. We were the victims of his working out of his theories.'

One theory for which Neill was often criticised was his belief that children needed to come to Summerhill at the earliest possible age if they were to benefit fully from the environment there. He convinced a number of parents over the years that their children should be allowed to be away from home for several weeks on end at the age of 3, 4 or 5. For some children this caused bewilderment as much as any other feeling, as Peter Russell, who came in the mid-1930s, remembers: 'I was 5 years old when I came to Leiston. I didn't know much about schools, but what I did know was that schools had a steeple on them. There was no steeple at Summerhill, and for quite a time I was convinced that there was some terrible mistake. Occasionally I would ask a grown-up when I was going to school.' To others it was a move that caused acute distress. Howard Case was one parent who regretted sending his children there so young: 'It was like a death, but we believed in Neill so implicitly that we said that's how it must be. Donald, who went at 4½, was absolutely shattered; he used to run around in misery after his older brother, Peter, and watch every train in the hope that we would be on it.' Evelyn Williams went to Summerhill at the age of 3: 'My parents thought that it would be a kind of home for me. If you had to leave home at an early age, you couldn't have a better place to go to. But I felt a deep sense of loss, which I think marked me for life.' She developed a private language of her own, which only her sister Bran-wen, who was then aged 5 and had herself been at Summerhill for a term, could understand. The Williams children were at least prepared for their going to Summerhill, which was more than could be said for two other girls who arrived during the same period, Cynthia and Jean Allen. Their aunt Ruth was already at the school as a housemother, but that did little to soften the blow. As visitors they stayed with their mother for a weekend near Summerhill, and on the Monday morning the news was broken to them, as Jean Allen recalls: 'My mother was thrilled by the place; she thought it was "all so right", and left us there on the spot. I was six and a half. It was the most shattering experience that could happen to any child. I haven't really got over it.' One later pupil, Amarylla Stracey, who went at 4, observed in similar vein: 'It knocks the stuffing out of you: you can't understand why your mother has sent you away.' Another pupil, John Tooke, recalls: 'I resented being sent there at 5: I wondered where my parents were.'

In the case of the Allen sisters, Neill had told the mother during that weekend, 'If you don't leave them now, you never will.' He also persuaded other parents to send all their children to the school. Gordon Leff was 7 when he arrived, and his sister Angela 6; his brother Louie was however only 3½, which his brother in retrospect feels was a mistake: 'Neill, in the doublethink of the time, said to my parents that if he stayed behind he would be an only child. But it was clearly much too disturbing for him at three and a half.' Though it was to some extent the accepted idea in the middle classes that children should be sent to boarding school at a relatively tender age, Neill was hardly the person to accept a convention of this kind simply because that was what people 'did'. He seemed unable to appreciate that to take a child away from what was often quite a secure home could be seriously damaging to the child's well-being. He was never really able to modify his belief that a child's home was a poor substitute for Summerhill. Of course, his lengthy experience with children who *did* come from unhappy homes played a part in shaping this belief. The fact that he had no children of his own can also be put forward as part of the explanation. But, at a deeper, unconscious level, perhaps he just could not accept that a home where parents were in a position of authority could be equated with any kind of happiness or security. In this connection a remark recalled by Beryl Sandford may be significant: 'He was awfully proud that children stayed on in the holidays. "There you are, he likes me better than his mother," he would say. He never thought that might need some explanation; he was blind to the possible dangers of the arrangement.' He was never able to detach his view of parents in general from that which he had formed from his own during his childhood.

Although during the 1930s Neill took an increasing proportion of children from families who supported his ideas, this did not in itself exclude them from being problem children. On the other hand, if there was home support for what he was doing, he found that the child's reaction to the school would usually be different from that of those from homes that were hostile or indifferent to his approach. Neill found a pattern developing in most children's reponse to Summerhill, though the length of each phase could vary by months, and even years, depending on the child. The first phase involved the child repeating the behaviour it had followed prior to coming to Summerhill. In the second phase there would be a reaction, often violent, against their earlier behaviour, in which they would become destructive, anti-social, or spend the whole day at play in the school grounds. In the third phase they would adapt in some way to the ethos of the school, either by attending lessons of their own accord, 'finding their line' in the workshop, art room or theatre, or by becoming a more social and community-conscious being – or both. Of course there were exceptions to this pattern, and also, as Neill acknowledged, some 'failures', who never remotely looked like getting beyond the second stage. But there were undoubtedly many children whose changed behaviour reinforced Neill's belief in their capacity to make decisions for themselves, to follow their interests when left free to do so.

The question of the children's attitude to sex was one that Neill felt cut across definitions of normality. He certainly made every effort to alter the 'diseased' attitudes which he felt children brought from home, and which gave them guilt feelings about masturbation, nakedness and other sexual matters. For a while he and some staff and children bathed naked in the duck pond, though Neill made it clear that this was not acceptable to most outsiders. Maritza Clotworthy, a housemother at the time, recalls that 'Neill told the children they could run around naked as long as it wasn't in view of the drive, because then you might be shocking others.' Staff occasionally worked naked in the garden on a particularly hot day. Later there would be evening trips for nude bathing on the beach at Sizewell, though there was some trouble about changing into costumes on the beach. Until about 11, boys and girls sometimes shared a dormitory. There were rarely any locks on the doors of the bathroom, and many adolescent boys and girls, as well as adults, accepted nakedness as normal. Peter Byles recalls an incident involving a female psychologist who returned to Summerhill now and then: 'She always felt it was her home. I remember walking into the male bathroom, and finding her completely naked in the bath. "Oh, Corks wouldn't mind," she said.'

Neill and the other adults in Summerhill answered any question about sex that the children put to them, in the hope that this might remove feelings that it was a taboo subject. Mrs Lins told the children about birth, and the rearing of children; she was certainly not shy about discussing such matters. She once shocked some guests at a dinner party when, on being asked by her son Wally where babies came from, she provided the necessary information there and then. Gerry Collier recalls his earliest memory of the school: 'One of the pupils asked me to ask Neill the meaning of a couple of swear words – my previous schooling had rather limited my knowledge in this sphere. Neill gave me the meaning without embarrassment. I was a bit shaken; I had hardly heard a child use such words, let alone an adult.' Neill saw swearing as a sign of sex repression, and believed that the best course was to allow the child, at least within the school, to swear until they lost interest. On one occasion, during an outbreak of swearing amongst some of the children, he held an 'Obscenity Class', to which the whole school was invited to bring pencils and notebooks. Many of the younger children turned up, and Neill suggested that they write down all the bad words they knew. 'What shall we do now?' he asked them when they had finished. Someone suggested 'rude drawings', after which Neill asked for further ideas. As no one had any, the children became bored, and walked out of the class. The following week only one child turned up and, when he saw he was alone, hurriedly left the room. The level of swearing apparently diminished, at least for a while.

The question of the children's own sex lives was a more complicated one. By this time Neill believed that adolescents should be free to enjoy sex. He became interested late in the 1930s in the findings of the anthropologist Bronislaw Malinowski, who had found that the Trobriand Islanders in the South Seas had a free and un-neurotic attitude to sex – until the missionaries arrived and separated the boys from the girls. 'Malinowski's statement is shattering, final. External morality must always inhibit internal morality', Neill wrote. However, he did recognise that the parallel between Leiston and a South Sea island was not an exact one. He therefore made it clear to the children that, while he personally didn't see the sex question as a moral issue, society in general still did, and would be quite likely to force Summerhill to be closed if it were known that he encouraged this particular freedom. He refused to provide the children with contraceptives, on the practical grounds that he would be going against the wishes of most parents if he did so. He also mentioned the legal point that the age of consent was sixteen, no doubt remembering that Homer Lane had fallen foul of the authorities over sexual matters.

Neill was therefore caught between what were still very advanced beliefs, and the realities of having to live in a world that did not share them. It was not a happy position to be in, as Cynthia Allen recalls: 'Despite all his doctrines about the need for people to have free, happy, fulfilled sex lives, there was nothing terrified him more than the thought that we might have just that, and fill the school with unexpected little additions.' Inevitably, even during the Lyme period, children did occasionally sleep together, though most were cautious about complete sexual intercourse. Michael Bernal remembers his motive for caution: 'I had a girl friend at Summerhill, but never fully made love to her, though we had intimate relations. It was a combination of being a bit shy still, and realising that it could have bad results which would harm the school.' At the time contraception was considerably less safe and less socially accepted than it became later. 'I'm amazed there were no illegitimate children at Summerhill,' says Elna Lucas, a housemother who was there during the 1930s. Anne Forbes takes a similar view: 'I don't know how Neill got away with it, it was more by luck than good management. Everybody had affairs with everybody else, but I think most of them were heavy petting. It was before the time of the pill, and we were all frightened of pregnancy.'

Older children often shared a bed together, sometimes for a whole night, and it was considered quite natural for an adult to come in and sit on the bed to talk to a couple. Roger Anscombe feels in retrospect that such tolerance had its own dangers: 'It was asking a bit much of children, though they did their damndest to comply. Neill himself was rather fond of quoting the remark, "An erect penis has no conscience." ' Neill knew in broad terms the kind of sexual activity that was going on, but seems to have been determined to keep himself uninformed about the detail, shutting his eyes to as much as he could, unless he fell over it. Mrs Lins, however, adopted a more interventionist role. She would patrol the corridor by the girls' bedrooms, and if need be turn on the lights and eject any boys she found there. Affairs between staff and pupils, though rare, seem also to have been tolerated. One very susceptible young teacher who came in the 1930s had a series of affairs with staff, parents and visitors. According to one pupil, though this is doubted by certain adults on the staff at the time, he didn't stop there: 'He proceeded to have affairs with every girl in the school, including me. I was very thrilled, as I was a very square teenager, and no one had cast an eye my way before. I think each of us lasted about three months, and then he passed lightly on. We were all grinding our teeth in hate at each other. He certainly cut a swathe through the young females of the school.' Such relationships were not uncommon in progressive schools of the time, as well as other closed communities. Neill, however, never went as far as one contemporary pioneer working with problem children, who was reputed to encourage the older boys to sleep with his wife as part of their therapy. Nor did he follow the dangerous example of another 'progressive' head, who slept with a number of the older girls in his school.

Inevitably, this open attitude to sex did reach the ears of some in Leiston. At one time young men in the town were invited in to the Saturday night dance, and some took an interest in the older Summerhill girls. There were occasions when an outsider found his way into a girl's bed, as Evelyn Williams remembers: 'There were one or two outsiders who were allowed to carry on like this, and I don't think this should have been encouraged. It's no good turning the boys out of our dormitory if there's some man sleeping with a girl a few doors along.' Neill certainly knew about such incidents, as he told at least one visitor in later years. It remains unclear why he didn't take some steps to prevent this happening, although his dislike of personal conflict may have played a part. Such incidents did increase the possibility of a local scandal, or at least of giving the school the kind of reputation which he feared. Evidently this did happen to some extent, as he himself remembers: 'One youth of about seventeen hung about our gates for a time, and when I asked him what he wanted, he replied, "A free fuck." '

CHAPTER 11

Hearts not Heads

Whatever did we learn at Summerhill?
No maths, no hangups; how to play *Dear Brutus*.
It wasn't doing barbola on the mantelpiece
with red-hot pokers, breaking windows all day
or maidenheads all night – though you'd think so
to hear the critics. And did Neill set us free?
You never know with voluntary lessons,
they crouch there in your path like friendly enemies,
you pat them or you sidle past, knowing
you can't play truant when you're free already.
School government was on our hunkers, noisy,
fizzing, seesawing, Neill won, we won, no one won
while the long shadows gathered on the chintz.
We were Hitler's autobahns in reverse,
anti-Stakhanovites, our trains would never
run on time. 'If I create a millionaire'
cried Neill 'I've failed!' But capitalism
slid on its way despite our lost repressions.
We tinkered in the workshop, made toy guns
but never robbed a bank or even knew
half Europe had been robbed. Now if you ask
what I think of it I honestly don't know,
    it was great but I
    honestly don't know.

from 'School's Out', by Edwin Morgan,
written for *Glasgow High School Magazine*, April 1973

The publication of *That Dreadful School* provoked a debate about Neill's vision of child nature which exemplified many that were to take place in subsequent years. The book was widely reviewed, and generally welcomed as a clear and vivid account of Summerhill at work – and at play. The *Observer* reviewer commented: 'Mr Neill is probably the boldest among the pioneers of free education in this country. His courage and benevolence are unquestionable.' The anonymous reviewer in the *Listener*, who disagreed with Neill about the innate goodness of children and their ability to dispense with a framework of discipline and routine, nevertheless thought the book 'should be read by those who have only heard of Mr Neill and have condemned him on hearsay, as well as his disciples'. Neill's tendency to polarise opinion was also reflected in the *Daily Herald*, where the reviewer wrote of the book: 'It will shock many and annoy many more. It will provoke scorn among the diehards and sympathetic interest among the progressives.' The *TES* reviewer came down firmly in the former category, devoting less than a hundred words to the book, and using all of them to scold Neill for supposedly setting out to shock grown-ups in a childish manner.* Other reviewers criticised what they saw as Neill's dogmatism, his superficiality, and his infuriating habit of generalising in a highly unscientific way. Yet most acknowledged the significance of his work, and the courage which he had displayed in running Summerhill. Michael Roberts, in the *Spectator*, summed up the viewpoint of several in suggesting: 'If parents and teachers care to read this book and think about their own reaction to it, they may learn much about their own half-conscious aims and jealousies.'

Summerhill was already by this time well known in professional circles, and there had been one or two articles in the popular press about the school. Yet it was really only from this point on that Neill found himself at the centre of popular attention, and his ideas beginning to be considered of relevance to ordinary children. The *Observer* noted: 'Mr Neill seems to be collecting more and more evidence in support of the theory that children, given freedom from restrictions, threats, punishments, sexual misinformation, and other manifestations of adult neurosis, develop spontaneously a strong social and community sense.' Even in Scotland, which was less receptive to such ideas than England, Neill's book received serious attention: a lengthy review in the *Scots Magazine*, for which Neill himself had written an article some six years before, concluded with the assertion: 'It takes courage to read it properly, and to confess at the end that you missed much by not having had the chance to be educated yourself at Summerhill.' In England the book was serialised in five issues of the *News Chronicle* in April 1937, with an introduction that suggested to the readers: 'Perhaps you don't agree with A. S. Neill, the most criticised teacher of our times. But here he tells for the first time the story of Summerhill. Every parent,

*The interest shown by the *TES* in Neill's ideas may be gauged by the amount of space devoted to other books in the same issue: *Changing Eton* received double the coverage, while *Roadsense for Children* was given six times the amount of column inches as *That Dreadful School*.

everyone who has anything to do with children, must read it.' On the whole the treatment of what the paper called a 'Remarkable Series about Britain's Strangest School' was restrained. This may partly have been because of Neill's right of veto over the use of illustrations to accompany the serialisation; and partly because the *News Chronicle*, with its left-wing stance on many issues in the later 1930s, would have been more in sympathy with Neill's ideas than the rest of the popular press, with the exception of the *Daily Herald*. The serialisation provoked some response among the readers of the paper. One man from Berkshire wrote in ironical manner about his repressive schooldays: 'Once, when tapping out my pipe on the form-master's desk, he leaned over and scowled at me in a threatening manner. I was terrified, and the beginning of a malignant inhibition was formed.'

A woman from Sussex found rather more to admire in the book: 'Many of the remarks. . . must strike any impartial reader by their common sense,' she wrote. But she was more doubtful about the voluntary lessons: 'Probably it is a mistake to compel a child to learn passages of Shakespeare by heart. But surely he should be encouraged to seek knowledge and to love it for its own sake?' It was this issue, relating to Neill's belief that children should be free to decide what and when they should learn, which was taken up by the reviewer in the *New Statesman and Nation*. Professor C. E. M. Joad was head of the Department of Psychology and Philosophy at Birkbeck College, London, and later a panel member on the popular radio programme 'The Brains Trust'. Joad thought the book 'enormously exciting', and declared: 'Mr Neill, I have not the slightest doubt, is a genius. He is doing experimental work of the greatest social value, and he ought to be provided with an endowment by the Board of Education.' On the other hand he parted company, as did so many others, with Neill's idea that children are by nature virtuous. He also suggested that

> whatever we may think of their moral characters, children are
> intellectually lazy and averse from effort, and need compulsion in
> order to do unpleasant tasks. Now not even a man of Mr Neill's
> genius can make the multiplication table interesting or amusing. In
> point of fact Mr Neill does not try; he does not teach at all in the
> ordinary sense. If, therefore, one disapproves of compulsion and
> dislikes competition, the multiplication table will not be learnt; nor,
> indeed, will anything else that requires discipline and effort. . . . Is it
> not, it may be asked, a little hard on the child not only to saddle it
> with the responsibility of deciding every moral question with its own
> unaided resources, but to throw it upon these same resources for the
> filling of every unoccupied hour? Adults cannot do these things: why
> then should children?

Neill immediately took issue with Joad, in a letter published the following week in the *Statesman*. He thought it

a good review, a fair review, a flattering review. . . surprisingly enough, for friend Joad believes in square holes, while I live in a round one. His is an intellectual approach, while mine is an emotional one. Thus he cannot grasp the difference between freedom and licence because he presumably is occupied with philosophical ideas of both. He thinks about children; I live with them. . . .We daren't dogmatise about human nature; all we dare do is discover what it is.

Having put the eminent philosopher in his place, Neill went on to argue that Joad was 'dogmatising without sufficient observation' in his remarks about children being intellectually lazy:

All or nearly all children are lazy when faced with the Old Men's tasks of learning Latin or Maths, but adults are lazy when faced with things that do not interest them. I spend hours at my lathe, but I am a lazy devil in tidying up afterwards. Life itself compels 'free' children to do a thousand things that they don't want to do.

Joad's scepticism about children's capacity to motivate themselves and to use their own resources without adult prompting reflected the doubts felt and expressed by many educators, psychologists and parents about Neill's wisdom in leaving children to fill 'every unoccupied hour'. How then did the Summerhill pupils cope with this apparently onerous responsibility? In his *New Statesman* review Joad referred to a conversation alleged to have taken place at an 'advanced' school. 'Do you have to work?' one girl pupil was asked. 'No we don't have to go to lessons.' 'Do you play games then?' 'No, we needn't play games unless we want to, and practically nobody does.' 'What *do* you do then?' 'We just lie about in the woods and develop.' Was this the pattern of the children's lives at Summerhill? How *did* they make use of the freedom to choose their own activities? Did the kind of adults that Neill chose to work with him provide a genuine test of his theories about a child's inherent desire to learn?

Neill's stated aim was to fit the school to the child rather than the child to the school. He was not interested in getting the best qualified staff, nor finding teachers known to excel in a classroom. He was looking for men and women who liked children and would not need to demand respect from them; who would be able to cope with them leaving or not even attending their classes if their interest was not held; who would accept the concept of equality between adults and children inherent in the system of self-government; and who would, as Neill pointed out to one hopeful applicant in 1931, be prepared to work 'for board and lodging and maybe enough to buy the daily dose of Woodbine'. Neill alone was responsible for deciding on the suitability of adults to work at Summerhill. Given the casual and unsystematic way in which he made his appointments, it was astonishing that he found so many who *did* fit his requirements. Though he advertised occasionally in the *New Statesman* or the *Times Educational Supplement*, he refused to look at any references, preferring to trust his own judgment. He would often advertise at the last moment, and appoint the first person to apply or come for an interview. He occasionally asked Curry for his opinion of an applicant who had been passed on from Dartington, or gave his own of someone going in the opposite direction.

Those to whom he did give jobs were sometimes taken aback at the informality of the interview. Peter Byles was interviewed on the beach at Lyme, where Neill and Mrs Lins, who were on holiday there, invited him for a swim and a picnic: 'I was amazed at this lean, ordinary, friendly Scotsman and this motherly, understanding Australian accepting me as a new acquaintance, as if it were the most natural thing in the world. We chatted, and then they said, "Can you come next Thursday?" ' Leslie Morton had also expected an interview of a more formal kind when he arrived in Leiston in 1927: 'Neill threw me right off guard by asking, "What made you take up teaching?" I could only say, "For want of anything better to do." At least it was honest. He offered me the job with little more ado.'* Often staff were taken on at the last moment, or sometimes almost by chance. Cyril Eyre, having read some of his 'Dominie' books, had written out of the blue to Neill during his last term at Oxford: 'When the maths teacher resigned they searched frantically for this letter from this fellow in Oxford, which had been lost. I was then summoned by a postcard from Neill, "Can you come and see me?" '

Some adults who taught at Summerhill were not so much appointed as absorbed, happening to be on the spot at the right moment. 'There was always an enormous quantity of odds and ends of people there,' Max Morton, who came in 1932, recalls 'a lot of Scandinavians, and quite a lot of Australians and New Zealanders. They used to just drift in, and no one would turn them away. They'd come along and find a bed somewhere, and then gradually they would take on some job – the women as housemothers, the men perhaps working in the grounds.' Some visitors also found their way on to the teaching staff, temporarily or permanently. Geoffrey Cox, a Rhodes Scholar up at Oxford, came as a paying guest during one vacation: 'The history master was away, and I took some very elementary lessons, simply because Neill said, If you'd like to take the class, please do.' Tom Hackett was taken on as an art teacher by 'wriggling my way in'. Living in Aldeburgh and in his mid-20s, he first visited Summerhill for the Saturday night dances: 'Soon I went there as often as I could. Nobody told me not to come, and after a while I was given a vote at the school meeting. Then, when Neill had a gap, he offered me the chance of being in charge of the art room.' Sometimes former pupils returned for a visit and found themselves drawn in, as Brian Anscombe remembers: 'I came back for a bit of a holiday after failing my radio exam. Neill let me teach a bit of magnetism and electricity to some of the older boys in exchange for my keep and a bit of pocket money.' Later, girls who had been pupils came back or stayed on as housemothers.

*Perhaps Neill recalled his own father's reason for pushing him towards teaching – 'It's about all he's fit for.' Leslie Morton believes Neill saw an opportunity to save on travel expenses by appointing the nearest applicant, and the first to be interviewed!

As it happened, Neill did quite unintentionally attract several highly qualified adults in these first years at Leiston – partly because the severe unemployment of the period had produced a surplus of teachers in the country. Leslie Morton and Peter Byles had first-class degrees from Cambridge, as did Cyril Eyre from Oxford, and the man he replaced, Richard Goodman, another Oxford graduate. Bronwen Jones also had a degree, as did George Corkhill. Yet Neill was quite uninterested in these bits of paper, as Vivien Morton found when she came to Summerhill in 1933: 'I'd read all the books at the Institute of Education in London, and came armed with my first-class degree and certificate, and recommendations from academic staff. Neill wouldn't look at them: "Let's see how you get on with children," he said.' The standard of paper qualification was such that when Leslie Morton's brother Max came in 1932, he discovered that his second-class degree made him almost the lowest qualified of the teaching staff. He also found, as others were to do over the years, that Neill was not concerned to make use of his specialist knowledge: 'I was a historian, but I never taught history at Summerhill, because Mrs Lins did that. I did some English, and even a bit of Latin at one time, and maths, and gardening – none of which were my subjects.' Neill improvised with the adults he had, and was prepared to take considerable risks in matching people to subjects. 'Corks', who was taken on to teach chemistry, took over the pottery classes, learning with the children as he went along. Erna Gal, who came as a music teacher, had to take over some French classes, taught some Latin, and also did some embroidery and sewing. Ulla Otte, who arrived later during the war, started as a domestic help in the kitchen: 'I am the world's worst cook,' she recalls, 'so one day when Neill passed me he pulled my apron strings and said, "I want a word with you." I feared he would give me the sack. Not at all. He told me he had heard that I could make dolls and clothes and he wanted me to set up a new handwork class – the previous teacher had died some time ago.' Her classes were to last for twenty years.

In later years Neill was to complain a great deal about his 'problem teachers', who treated Summerhill as a refuge, and used it principally as a place where they could try to come to terms with their own problems. Even during this time he spoke of the difficulty in getting the type of person he wanted, a matter he raised in a letter to a fellow-pioneer Paulus Geheeb in April 1938: 'Alas, I can't help you to get a teacher. I find it so difficult when I need one myself, and too often the type who wants to teach in an advanced school is the introverted man who is really wanting to come as a child.' As will be seen, the question of Neill's relations with his staff was a complex one, and bound up with Neill's own difficulties in relating to adults. Yet it was certainly true that many of his staff, even during this early, less troubled period, had reasons other than purely pedagogic ones for joining Summerhill. Tom Hackett, for example, recalls: 'I was only too anxious to get away from my standing-on-the-corner type of background. I leapt at the opportunity – my mother used to fuss when I got in late at night. It got me away from my orthodox home.' Peter Byles found that he had been unable to keep discipline at the school he taught in after leaving university: 'I cracked up, was invalided out, and had a proper nervous breakdown. I wanted something to do to get myself back to health.' Ruth Allen recollects: 'I had such a very Victorian upbringing, I suppose it was a kind of rebellion that took me to Summerhill.' One young Oxford graduate locked the lavatories from inside and climbed out of the window. When Neill reported this incident in the staff room, the man owned up, admitting that he'd been wanting to do that all his life, and had now found somewhere where he could.

Neill actually gave PLs to certain adults, though this was not always a casual arrangement. Indeed, at one time he found that it was beginning to interfere with his work with children, as he indicated in a letter to Curry in January 1936:

> Have a few women in training college here, teachers all wanting analysis. I took on three, and have regretted it ever since. The others are jealous etc. . . .Owing to taking on adults, I've been neglecting the kids. I have enough of them needing attention as it is.

Nevertheless, he was able to help a number of the adults in different ways. 'My father disappeared when I was three, and so Neill was really a father substitute,' Cyril Eyre recalls. 'I was a repressed young man to whom he opened up a new world. I loved and revered him.' Tom Hackett had similar feelings: 'My father died when I was two. All my other father substitutes failed me. Neill never criticised me; he was the only one to accept me for what I was.' Maurice Draper remembers: 'He gave me PLs for a term, and got me to talk about my life, God, my family and how I hated my father.' Ruth Allen recalls: 'I hadn't heard about psychoanalysis, and was very wary of revealing anything. The PLs were useful in undoing some of my repressions.' Peter Byles was another of Neill's 'pupils': 'After some weeks I got depressed, feeling I was teaching the children so little and not justifying my existence. Neill reassured me, saying "The kids like you, and that's all I want." After a few PLs I began to cheer up, and began to live in a new way.' He found Summerhill a 're-education', and stayed for five years. Ivor Cutler, who came to teach at a slightly later date, was another who felt the comfort of Neill's personality: 'He let you be,' he recalls. 'When you were with him you knew that you were allowed to be yourself, that you were approved of. His being around was enough. I loved him.'

The first impression of Summerhill was often a startling one for adults, however carefully they may have read Neill's books. Ruth Allen came in response to an advertisement Neill put in the *New Era*, saying he would take on students to study psychology. Her first glimpse of the school, on the day after the Silver Jubilee of George V in 1935, made it clear there was going to be plenty to study: 'Neill was away in Norway, so I was met at Leiston station by two girls. They took me in to the dining room where some of the staff were sitting at a round table – Paxton Chadwick, the secretary and art teacher, Corky, Vivien, and the woodwork teacher, George Parsons. A Russian boy was cycling round and round the table, and there was talk of going to the cinema. This boy suddenly pointed at me and said, "I will go to the cinema with *you*." Another boy, referring to the "God Save the King" banners up in Leiston, said: "I don't believe in God; I can't see him." I heard the most terrible crying and wailing coming from the hall. I found Mrs Lins comforting this girl who was crying her eyes out: she was briskly told to go to the cinema. I thought, "My goodness, everybody's emotions *are* floating about." ' This emotional openness could of course sometimes take violent form, as Vivien Morton, with no previous experience of children, found on her first morning: 'I was aged 21, and had been given charge of a group of 7-year-olds. I walked into the breakfast room, in time to see one of the worst problem children hurling a fork at one of the others. I was scared stiff, but thought that I must tackle the problem. The child was bad enough to have a room of his own, he was so aggressive to the other children. So that night, putting him to bed, I stayed talking with him. I discovered that he was terrified of the dark, and was letting out his aggression in the day time. I told him he could have his light on if he liked, and that I would stay with him until he went to sleep. I just went by instinct, and it worked. He made good progress, and soon he was quite good with the other kids.'

Neill wrote in *That Dreadful School*: 'Personally I do not know what type of teaching is carried on, for I never visit lessons, and have no interest in how children learn.' The *Observer* reviewer of the book described this as one of Neill's 'pleasantries'. Yet it was not far from the truth, and certainly represented the essence of Neill's attitude to what went on inside the Summerhill classrooms. He took virtually no interest in teaching methods, and gave no sort of guidance to his teachers as to what they should be doing. Staff meetings were held from time to time, but were devoted mostly to discussions of the problems of individual children; and even then the focus was on their behaviour rather than on their academic progress or deficiencies. Mervyn Corkhill attended one such meeting when he was an adult: 'Neill was discussing some child at length. One woman was feverishly knitting away. Neill stopped and said, "For God's sake why do you bring your knitting to staff meetings?" And she said, "It's to give me something to think about while I'm talking." I thought that just about summed up a Summerhill staff meeting.' Discussion was often inhibited by the presence of a problem child in the room. Even though the child might be asleep, Neill would avoid discussing children while he or she was there: 'You never know how the unconscious mind works,' he would say.

As a result of Neill's indifference to this part of Summerhill life, and the fact that attendance at lessons was entirely voluntary, the possibility of children learning was even more dependent than usual on the personality of the teachers. The teaching was in general rather orthodox, though sometimes eccentric – a combination that seemed to characterise many of the pioneering schools of the time. There was a good deal of flexibility in the content of some teachers' lessons. 'You didn't really teach anything,' Max Morton remembers. 'The children just came along, and you more or less did whatever they were interested in.' Pupils recall Dickens being read in art lessons, a teacher reading modern novels when the children became bored with geography, an English lesson with Richard Goodman turning into a domestic science lesson, ending with pancakes being tossed on to the beams of his hut. The informality of these occasions was reinforced by the fact that many of the lessons took place in the makeshift huts which in the early years at Leiston doubled up as the staff's living quarters. 'You didn't go to Max Morton's lessons to learn,' Daphne Oliver remembers. 'We just liked Max, and spent the whole time leaping about on his bed. There was another chap who came from Tahiti. We all adored him. He was a vegetarian, and had this little cupboard in his room full of goodies, which he'd give us to eat. He taught maths, and we used to draw things with a compass and colour them, pretending that that was lessons.'

By no means all lessons were so unorthodox or devoid of any real content, and many pupils were greatly enthused about individual subjects. Michael Bernal, who became a university lecturer, sums up the view of many of his contemporaries: 'Because nobody forced any subject on you, you never got put off anything. I always *enjoyed* learning, even if I didn't learn a tremendous amount. The fact that you could have a warm and close relationship with the teachers made you sympathetic to their lessons.' Several children found plenty of interest in individual subjects, which in some cases led them on to their later careers. Virginia Pilkington, who became a professional actress, recalls: 'I did a lot of English, and May Chadwick had an enormous influence on me. She gave me a great love of Shakespeare at an early age. She made him real rather than just a set book. She would go to the theatre in London, and then tell us about the plays she had seen.' Evelyn Williams didn't attend many lessons, but at 10 she started to draw, at 14 left to go to art school, and is now a well-established painter. Bobby Townsend, who went on to gain a considerable reputation as a furniture-maker, had been turned against learning by the beatings he had received at his two previous schools. He found that 'being left to your own resources is a sort of stimulus in itself. I know it was this which got me into the workshop, where I became fascinated in making things.'

Although there was a significant minority of children who chose only to go to a few lessons at this time, and a few who stayed away from them altogether for months – and, in one or two cases, years – the majority of children did attend classes in several subjects, though in most cases not as many as they would have had to go to under a compulsory system. Neill somewhat distorted the picture here by claiming, for instance, that one boy who later became an expert maker of precision instruments never attended a lesson while he was at Summerhill. This was Mervyn Corkhill, who remembers a different story: 'I did go to the lessons I was interested in, but I was a bit of a daydreamer, I always had an inventive thing going on in my mind.' Other examples of non-attenders which Neill publicised are confirmed by Summerhill adults and children: Max Morton, for example, remembers one group to whom Neill frequently referred in his books and lectures: 'There was a gang of girls who never went to lessons. They mostly came from convents, and let fly as soon as they got away from them. They just sat around and painted their faces.'

Those who rarely or never attended lessons had to find or create other activities. 'I was never bored, because I was always able to do things which seemed much more interesting than the lessons,' Mervyn Corkhill remembers. David Barton recalls that many children found plenty to do: 'We were forever active, building huts and earthworks, engaging in mock battles, following the latest craze, bicycling, building model aeroplanes or kites or catapults or bows and arrows.' There were often trips to the beach at Sizewell, cycle rides, or long walks in the countryside, ending with a picnic tea round a camp fire and a sing-song on the way home. There were also the dance evenings, and regular trips to the cinema in Leiston. Yet if the children's lives sometimes had an idyllic quality, this was certainly not due to any material comfort provided by Neill. He himself seemed thoroughly at home in the cold, dry Suffolk climate, and in the spartan conditions of Summerhill. It was symptomatic of his attitude that, if he felt cold indoors, he would put on an overcoat rather than a fire. But for others the severe East Anglian winters often made for a hard life. The children's rooms could get extremely cold – hot water bottles froze, water had to be squeezed out of the sheets. Some children wore jerseys as pyjama trousers, to keep off the cold at night; a few even went to bed during the day in order to get some warmth.

'Do we have to do what we like all day tomorrow as well?' one child is alleged to have asked Neill. The story is almost certainly apocryphal. Yet some children inevitably found it difficult to cope with the lack of adult guidance, as Evelyn Williams remembers: 'You could often face long hours of unutterable boredom if you didn't want to go to lessons, just sitting around and drinking coffee.' Gavin Campbell, a later pupil, felt: 'To some extent we were left too much on our own: it was rather like putting little boys out on the Greek mountainside.' Tessa Hutchinson, who went to Summerhill at the age of 2, echoes this sentiment: 'I lived almost like a wild child until the age of 9. I can remember being very hungry, and going out to learn what I needed to eat. Otherwise I just talked to people – it was very easy not to go to lessons.' In the evening the staff would mostly be in their rooms, or down at the pub in Leiston, a fact that caused at least one child some unpleasant problems. 'We were allowed to go to the cinema twice a week,' Jean Allen recalls, 'and from the age of six I sat through the most terrifying films you could imagine – I used to have to be taken out screaming sometimes. I remember sitting in the cinema with my eyes closed and my ears blocked, wishing it would end. I went on going because there was nobody at the school if you didn't. There was no supervision, or that's how it seemed.'

If some children found it difficult to organise their own activities, others were critical of the kind of stimulus given by the adults. Bobby Townsend, for example, believed: 'The teachers just weren't good enough. I remember the few times one really did organise activities and motivate the kids – and Mrs Lins was perfect at this – the response was great.' Geoffrey Cox, in his role of temporary teacher, had the impression that 'the children would have taken more intellectual interest if it had been held open to them'. He remembers that the teachers 'were all very committed to the idea that if children didn't turn up and didn't care to learn, it would all come right in the end.' Yet the staff were not always entirely happy with Neill's convictions on this matter. David Barton recalls an incident in 1936: 'When my age group was about 10, the teaching staff called a meeting, and told us that if we wanted to earn our living as adults at jobs we enjoyed, we should begin to take our studies more seriously. And so we did.'

This meeting must have taken place without Neill knowing about it. Staff had to tread very carefully with him on the subject of lessons, as Lucy Francis, who taught the younger children in the Cottage, discovered. Of South African origin, she had taught in conventional schools before coming to Summerhill: 'It used to sicken me to find classes of children forced to sit and not say anything. It wasn't natural,' she recalled. In her first job, having read and been affected by Neill's early 'Dominie' books, she tried to teach in a more humane way than was acceptable in the school. She clashed with an autocratic headteacher, who insisted that she caned children; as a result she found she could only teach in the way she wanted to by holding classes after school. She then taught for a while at Bedales, whose freedom she felt was bogus. It was eventually realised that her talents lay with problem children, and she was given sole charge of one very disturbed boy there. 'If you are angry you can come and do something to me,' was how she began her work with him. She subsequently took a course with Maria Montessori – 'a frightful boss – terrible to her students' she remembered – and eventually started her own primary school in Hertfordshire. Later she became secretary to the Golden Cockerel Press run by the artist Robert Gibbings, whose two children were at Summerhill for a while in the early 1930s.

She had wanted to visit Neill when he was in Austria, but had been afraid of being disillusioned; she had however visited the school during the Lyme years, and, when the Press collapsed during the Depression, she came to Summerhill, with no money, and a small child whose father she had refused to marry. She liked and admired Neill a great deal, as she told the artist William McCance in a letter written in May 1934: 'I've come to the conclusion that Neill is the only schoolmaster it's possible to work for and keep yourself intact and free at the same time. The longer one works for him, the more one respects and likes him.' She was, however, a very forceful personality, and soon earned the title Lucy 'Lady' Francis. It seemed to be tacitly understood that children would quite naturally attend her lessons, as she herself recalls: 'Before the war we were already getting a lot of 6- and 7-year-olds, even 5s. And they all went to lessons: they never dreamed of not going.' It was here that she did come into conflict with Neill. 'The only thing I used to get annoyed about was that he'd come round and talk to them and say Hello, and they'd say, "Show Neill what we've done in lessons," and he wouldn't look at it. And I'd say, "Oh, *Neill*! I wish you'd be interested in what they're doing. You seem to think that all children hate lessons!" '

Neill held firmly to his view that anything remotely resembling conventional book learning was likely to be harmful to children – an attitude that was later to bring him trouble. One of his most provocative observations appears in a chapter called 'The Learning Side' in *That Dreadful School*, where he stated:

> Only pedants can claim that learning from books is education.
> Books are the least important apparatus in a school. All that any
> child needs is the three R's: the rest should be tools and clay and
> sports and theatres and paints. . . and freedom.

His attitude was reflected in the lack of care bestowed on books in Summerhill, as Max Morton recalls: 'When I went there was a so-called library, which consisted of a number of books lying about the staff room. There were shelves, but the books weren't often on them. Children could go and borrow them if they wanted, but no one really encouraged them to do so. I gathered them up, amassed a few more, catalogued them, and made a library in the room where I did my teaching. But no one said, "That's a good idea," or anything of that sort.'

If books were of such little importance, how then were children at Summerhill to pick up 'the three R's' which Neill accepted they would need? He was adamant that children should and could pick up reading skills when the need arose, and that they themselves were the best judges of when that moment had come. However, his behaviour on some occasions went against his own principles about the evils of adult 'interference'. One member of staff recalls: 'I noticed half a dozen times that when Neill saw a child sitting reading, he would snatch the book from his or her hands, declare it confiscated, and order the child to "go and *do* something".' It was because of this sort of attitude that certain parents who were anxious about their child's learning progress felt unable to approach Neill on the subject, though they sometimes expressed their anxieties to other staff. One parent who did disagree with him over the question of the importance of reading received a very unsatisfactory answer. Betty Tucker recalls: 'Neill asked if I would be worried if my child didn't read until much later (actually he was already reading). I answered that, as life was, yes, and what would *he* do. He replied: "Oh, but mine would!" '

The emphasis in Summerhill on 'tools and clay', 'theatres and paints', can be traced directly to Neill's own preoccupations. Just after he started Summerhill he discussed the question of adult 'direction' with Bertrand Russell, and confessed: 'I find myself supplying environment according to my own interests. I buy clay for modelling, wood, brass, chemical apparatus. Another man might buy Latin books or gardening tools.' Although he made a clear theoretical distinction between academic and creative work for children, in practice he found it extremely hard to accept that children's tastes might differ from his own. His liking for drama, however, ensured that children had plenty of scope to write and act in plays. He also held regular Sunday night sessions known as 'Neill's spontaneous acting'. This was a tradition carried on from the evening get-togethers at Sonntagsberg and Lyme, which continued for a while in the lounge at Leiston. (After some time the squash court was made into a theatre, and the sessions continued there with better facilities.) The children would be invited by Neill to make up a sketch or a charade on the spot, or to improvise from suggestions he gave them, such as 'Step in dog dung on the street' or 'Open a telegram that tells you your mother or father is dead'. Sometimes parents and other visitors would provide an audience at weekends, when the performance was occasionally less spontaneous. Edna Raymond remembers one particular sketch: 'Neill was the psychiatrist, and Betty Muller, who was 6, was his patient. He gave her some clay, and told her to fashion something out of it. She made a man and a woman, and then a bed, and put them in it. Then Neill asked her, "Is that Mummy and Daddy in bed?" And she said, "No, it's Mummy and Uncle John." That was quite something for that time: he wanted to shock the grown-ups.'

Neill saw these sessions as a form of therapy, which would both help the children's confidence and encourage their creativity. In that sense they complemented the work he did with individual children in his PLs – indeed the dialogue echoes some of the conversations during PLs that Neill noted down in his books and articles. Yet it was not just the children who got a great deal out of the spontaneous acting. These sessions of playful improvisation brought out Neill's own inventiveness, his sense of the absurd and his rough and ready humour, all of which combined to make him extremely adept at encouraging children to explore ideas and feelings. Over the years he tried out the same types of situations on many different children. One of his favourites involved a burglar cracking a safe, and being discovered by the owner of the house – played by Neill. A visitor in later years recorded one of these sessions:

> *Neill*: Now, here is a story I want you to act out. You are a burglar trying to crack a safe, and while you're doing it, I'm the owner of the house, and I come on the scene and speak to you. I want to see you react. Now think about it before raising your hands. Okay, you first.
>
> *Lou*: Where's the safe, Neill?
>
> *Neill*: In the middle of the room. Go on now.
> (Lou works on the safe.) You're not very good, are you? Why don't you learn your trade?
>
> *Lou*: Oh, it's you. (Continues working on the safe.)
>
> *Neill*: Now, look. Would you continue working on the safe after the man of the house finds you?
>
> *Lou*: But I know you, Neill.
>
> *Neill*: I know, but you're not acting, lad. Oh, God! Someone else try acting now. I'm not Neill. I'm the owner of the house, you chumps.
> (An older boy starts working on the safe.) Not bad. Oh, stop it, man. You're a bungler. I can open. . .

Brendan: Look, mate, I'm trying to open this safe, so will you belt up?

Neill: Do you know who I am?

Brendan: Look, mate, belt up. Two thieves can't crack a safe at the same time.

Neill: Oh, I see. That's rather good, but that happens to be my safe.

Brendan: Oh, really? (Smiling very weakly.)

Neill: That's right. (Brendan jumps out the window.) Okay, next. (Pause.) Not bad, not bad, but this is my house.

Clancy: Stand aside while I go on with my work, will you, Bud?

Neill (Picking up imaginary telephone): Police? This is Sir John Brown, 64 Lindale Gardens. There's a burglar in my house.

Clancy: Who me, a burglar?

Neill: Who are you, then?

Clancy: I'm a crack safer. I mean a safecracker.

Neill: Oh, I see. Excuse me, officer, he's a crack safer, not a burglar. Okay, good. Now stand over there and crack up. Next.
Hey, what are you doing in my house?

Scott: Okay, stick 'em up. Come on, move over. Now, open that safe.

Neill: Good, good. The only one to think of that. He's all right. Make a fine burglar once he leaves Summerhill. Okay, anyone else? Go on, Myrna, have a go. Rather unusual profession for a lady, isn't it?

Myrna: You! It's no good, you're not going to stop me now. I've been looking for this for years.

Neill: For what?

Myrna: You can call the police if you like. I'll plead insanity.

Neill: Well, go on. I'll plead insanity too, and they'll can us both. Okay. Next.
(A little girl of 8.)
You're not very good at your job, are you?

Lisa: Oh, good evening.

Neill: Good evening. What are you doing in my house near my safe?

Lisa: Well, you see, I'm a safe inspector. I'm just inspecting your safe.

Neill: Oh? Don't you think it would be a good idea for you to ring the bell, and come in through the front door?

Lisa: Well, no, sir. You see, we're trying to see people's reactions to burglars, so I dressed up as a burglar to see how you'd take it.

Neill: Well, very nice. Is the safe all right?

Lisa: Yes, quite. Well, goodbye.

Neill: Before you go, do you mind emptying your pockets?

Lisa: Oh, ha ha, yes, of course.

Neill: The other one, now. There is still a fiver in there.

Lisa: Oh, yes, how foolish. Well, goodbye.

Neill: Goodbye. Now, that was wonderful.*

The building of the theatre resulted in a real flowering of interest in the writing and performing of plays, in which Neill himself was undoubtedly the moving spirit. He never lost this passion for the theatre, which had begun when he saw some of the great Victorian actors, and been fuelled during his spell as student theatre critic in Edinburgh. At Summerhill he wrote plays for the end of term shows, which soon became a Summerhill tradition. David Barton recalls: 'He could generally be relied on for a play. His were never like as good as some of the best written by other staff or kids. But he would make a great song and dance about his having the dramatic unities and so on. Again, he was helping to stimulate others in this way.' Bill MacKinnon remembers the effect on others in the school: 'He didn't go round telling others to write, but because he wrote, kids at all levels as well as staff wrote plays. There would be eight or nine every term. He encouraged the use of imaginative props and scenery and lighting, and made money available for them.' When his interest was engaged in this way, he could exhibit a flair for organisation that was rarely evident in other spheres: 'It was he that got the producers together, worked out times, put up the rehearsal rota, all in a quiet, unobtrusive but very efficient way.' He himself also took part in the plays and sketches, usually assuming a comic role. 'He was an excellent actor, but his secret lay in underplaying the part,' Bill MacKinnon remembers. 'He was a joy to play with on the stage.'

Neill laid down two rules in relation to the plays to be performed: only those written inside Summerhill were eligible, and staff could only contribute if there was a dearth of children's plays. In this he was reacting against the conventional practice of schools doing productions of Shakespeare or other established dramatists. And he was now free to do what George Saintsbury had forbidden during his university days – to poke fun at The Bard. He reworked *Julius Caesar* to give it an American gangster setting. He rewrote *Hamlet* in the style of Edgar Wallace, with Freud as 'psychological adviser'. Johnnie Collier remembers a characteristic moment during rehearsals: 'A gay discussion developed on how to signify Ophelia's drowning. Someone came up with the idea of flushing the toilet next to the lounge. This whole discussion reduced Neill to uncontrolled mirth, the only time I saw him laugh in that way.' These skits were certainly appreciated by some children, but Neill sometimes misjudged his audience, forgetting that some had never read a word of Shakespeare. When one boy was asked in an English lesson who Hamlet was, he answered: 'A chap in Neill's play.' For this Neill was of course partly to blame himself. Yet he was not alone in his criticism of the use of Shakespeare in schools. The point was raised by Beatrice Ensor in her *New Era* interview with Shaw in 1928, in connection with Shaw's refusal to have school editions of his plays pub-

*Reprinted with permission from *Summerhill: A Loving World* (Macmillan), © 1963, 1964 by Hert Snitzer and Thomas Bohen.

lished: 'People loved Shakespeare at one time, he said, but Shakespeare became a school "subject", and was forced upon children, and now he is loathed.' Neill himself believed 'it was wrong to make them do classical plays which are far divorced from their real fantasy life. They do not want a story of Elsinore, they want a story of their own environment.' Again, he was influenced by his own experience: 'Many people read Shakespeare for pleasure; the only time I've read him was for examinations,' he reflected later. It was an experience that gave him an irrational dislike of Shakespeare that sometimes got him into difficulties. On one occasion the children *did* want a story of Elsinore – or in this case Burnham Wood – as Vivien Morton recalls: 'We read *Macbeth*, and the children liked it so much they said, "Let's do it for the end of term." I did my best to dissuade them, saying how much Neill hated people having to do Shakespeare, just like any other school. "We don't *have* to do it", they said, "we *want* to do it." I told Neill, and he said, "Oh lord! Well, we can't have it for the official end-of-term show, I'd be too ashamed. We'll have it the day before." The children of course all wrote home, and their parents came a day early.'

However antagonistic Neill was to Shakespeare, it was as nothing to his feelings about the church and religion. He once told Robert Graves that he stropped his razor on the Bible to show what he thought of it. 'Thank God I am an atheist!' was how he liked to summarise his feelings. His view was that children had no natural interest in religion, and should be protected against those who wished to impose their beliefs on them. Yet it seems that he was mostly able to restrain his feelings on the subject within the school – though he made up for this in his books and lectures. Religion was neither a timetabled subject at Summerhill, nor a topic that was mentioned very often. Teddy Raw recalls: 'There were a few children who wanted to go to church, and they did, and nobody made a point of it. On the whole people didn't go, but no one made fun of those who did go.' Cynthia Allen remembers going with two friends to a Sunday morning service at the local church for 'an adventure', and being welcomed by a member of the congregation, who then asked them into her pew the following Sunday. 'We attended for about three Sundays, and then the good lady decided to call on Neill and say how pleased she was that some of his little heathens had turned to religion.' This was of course a poor move, and what Neill said to his visitor was not complimentary to the church or anyone connected with it. Neill, though, reserved his most hostile remarks for the Catholic Church, though it seems his feelings were also mixed with some fear: Brendan Williams recalls his reaction to the opening of a Catholic Mission in nearby Aldeburgh: 'This put the wind up him. He feared that they would somehow learn that he had two children at the school born of a father who had been a Catholic, and that they'd descend on him. He asked me for a letter he could show them, asking them to go away, which I gladly supplied to him.' Similar feelings could be aroused by simply being in a church, as Virginia Pilkington remembers when Neill gave her away at her wedding: 'He went completely to pieces, he kept saying, "What am I going to do?" And I'd say, "It's all right, you don't have to do

anything, just walk quietly down the aisle." He was quite panic-stricken.'
The fearful religion of the 'kirk' had marked him for life.

Although he talked about the value of self-motivated learning, Neill
found it very hard to accept idleness in children. Gordon Leff remembers
standing with his brother and sister watching some of the older children
on a bench outside the front door of Summerhill: 'Neill would come along
and, with an intensity that was certainly not simulated, say: "Come on,
you louts and loutesses." He hated people being idle, he was quite clear in
his own mind that freedom was quite the opposite of just sitting around
and doing nothing.' He was certainly rarely idle himself, even during the
holidays, when he spent hours digging the garden, mending beds, breaking
up bricks to fill in the holes in the drive, scything the grass – grumbling all
the while at the lack of help he was getting from all those around him.
Johnnie Collier remembers a day when Neill was trying to get some children
to dig potatoes, and called him 'anti-social' for preferring to organise a
hockey game. In spite of himself, he retained some distinctive marks of the
work ethic of his childhood, as one member of staff remembers: 'With
some kids who had been idle for five or six years, he'd say, "Come on and
help, you lazy lot!" And then he'd come indoors and say, "I was never
allowed to do that, I was *working* when I was fourteen." '

In contrast to drama, music in Summerhill was much less determined
by Neill's own tastes and attitude. There was as yet no music teacher, and
so no formal lessons: children made their own music, or experienced it as
part of the social life of the school. In the evenings the older children would
crowd into Neill and Mrs Lins's sitting room, to listen to records on an
expensive radiogram donated by a rich parent. While the children's taste
tended towards jazz and popular dance band music, Neill's own had been
largely shaped by his time in Germany and Austria. To his abiding love for
Wagner's operas he had added a liking for Strauss waltzes, for Chopin,
Ravel, Bartók and Stravinsky. He was also passionately fond of *Der Rosenkavalier*, in particular the celebrated trio from Act Three, and would play
over and over again his recording of this part of the opera. The conflict of
tastes sometimes caused disputes, as Neill acknowledged: 'Sometimes I lay
down the law and say that since it is my room I'll play what I want to
play. The *Rosenkavalier* trio or the *Meistersinger* quintet will clear the
room of half the occupants, and a Brahms symphony will clear the room
of all the occupants.' Similar difficulties arose over the weekly dance evenings. The Summerhill *Joker*, an irreverent broadsheet put together by the
pupils, noted at the end of the decade in their 'It is Whispered' column
'that Neill is a fascist at heart, because he so strongly desires us to buy and
dance to Nazi dance music.' Neill's desire to show off his dancing skills to
the sound of foxtrots and tangoes was resisted by the children. Eventually,
after much discussion at the meeting, a rule was agreed whereby every
third record played on these occasions should be one of Neill's own.

Neill rarely took part in games and sport at Summerhill. His principal
concern was that those who excelled in sport should not, as in the public
schools, be made into heroes. He found that the younger child had no

interest in team games: 'Not having reached the cooperative stage, they should not have games organised for them,' he wrote. 'That comes naturally at the right time.' The only marginal effect Neill's sporting preferences had on the children's lives was in the rather surprising field of boxing, which he thought 'excellent training for any boy'. His friendship with J. B. Salmond at university and after had given him an interest in the sport, and a certain amount of skill: 'You could see it in the way he squared up playfully to the kids; there was a touch of the technique there,' Bill MacKinnon recalls. For the older children any organised sport depended on their own enthusiasm or that of individual adults. Corks was a ferocious and quite skilled hockey player, and for many years this was the principal winter game. The school hockey team consisted of a mixture of children and adults, so that their opponents were invariably adult teams from the area. In summer the main sport was tennis. Again Neill's influence was nowhere to be seen – though he did once venture on to the court when he decided he was not fit enough.* Golf was one of the few games in which Neill took a positive pleasure, though he professed to be no good at it, and not to care whether he won or lost. It did indeed seem above all to be a recreation; on more than one occasion he took what he called 'a golfing holiday' in Scotland. In November 1937 he wrote to Curry: 'Have taken up golf, and all interests are subordinated to mashies and drivers. Ego ideal now Henry Cotton, not Freud.' Often he would take one of the children along as caddy, and was even known to have given them a PL while walking along the fairways of the local golf course. His most regular partner was described very aptly by one Summerhillian as 'Neill's favourite bore'. Rich, fat, red-cheeked and catarrhal, Watson – no one ever knew his Christian name – was a second-hand car dealer from nearby Aldeburgh. Early in the 1930s he sold Neill a Hillman Straight Eight for £75, and from then on turned up regularly on Saturdays. He was always in a different car, took tea with Neill and Mrs Lins, and talked endlessly about nothing but cars. He also attended the end-of-term functions, and sometimes the Saturday night meetings and dances.

On the golf course Watson kept up a monologue, while Neill just got on with the game. It was a strange partnership, and many wondered what each got out of it. 'Neill was a complete mystery to Watson,' Gerry Collier recalls, 'and I suppose this was part of the attraction. He couldn't beat Neill at golf, though he could beat everyone else. They complemented each other in a peculiar way.'

A further contradiction was to be found in Neill's attitude to public examinations. In *The Problem Parent* he derided them as being the method by which the Old Men 'who believe in discipline and subjects and Kultur' tried to keep control over the young. Yet, according to Cyril Eyre, who was not alone in this view, 'although Neill decried learning, he was tickled

---

*Neill listed tennis and cycling amongst his hobbies in the 1936 edition of *Who's Who*. Metalwork and dancing he listed throughout his life, but earlier entries had included painting and cinema-going. By 1949 golf had appeared on the list.

to death if his children got through O levels; he was absolutely delighted, particularly if he had taught them himself.' Neill had an understandable desire to show the outside world that Summerhill pupils could, if they wished, cope with this conventional kind of pressure when the moment came. But there was more to it than that, and the clue can perhaps be found in Neill's view of his own ability as a teacher.

If at all possible he tried to avoid taking classes. But, when he found problems in getting suitable staff, he was compelled to step in himself, usually to take English or mathematics. His English lessons were characteristically quirky and light-hearted, and were similar in both content and spirit to those he had given in Gretna, King Alfred and Hellerau. His aim was to test originality rather than knowledge, and to this end he gave the children some very idiosyncratic class 'exams'. In *That Dreadful School* he described the questions that appeared in one of these 'papers', adding his own gloss on some of the answers given:

1. Where are the following: – Madrid, Thursday Island, yesterday, God, love, my pocket screwdriver (but alas, there was no helpful answer to this one), democracy, hate etc.
2. Give meanings for the following: the number shows how many are expected for each: – Hand (3). . .only two got the third right – the standard of measure for a horse. Bore (3). . .club bore, oil well bore, river bore. Shell (3). . .seaside, 'That was Shell that was', undertaker's word for coffin. Brass (4). . .metal, cheek, money, department of an orchestra. . . .'The stuff that Neill is stingy with in his workshop' was allowed double marks as metal and cheek.
3. Translate Hamlet's To be or Not to be speech into Summerhillese.

These lessons, which tended to focus more on language than literature, were greatly enjoyed by many pupils. However, in later years, during a particularly bleak period, Neill had to step in to teach an exam class in English. Here he was clearly of little use to anyone who wanted to succeed. Wally Neustatter's daughter Angela, a pupil at the time, recalls: 'When we were doing *Twelfth Night* for O level and he was teaching English, he used to say: I don't know why you have to do all this nonsense. It wasn't very helpful.' A letter he wrote to the teacher whose class he had taken over during this period highlights his limitations:

I have been taking Eng myself with III and the new IV, finding it difficult after so long a period of rust. I've dodged the set books as much as I could decently do, for I have no appreciation of 12th Night . . . when today I criticised the dullness of Shakie's clowns Amarilla said: 'You seem to be trying to make us hate the play.' And Mr Hardy's poems I cannot rhapsodise about. Haven't tackled Mr Davies yet, only to compare a paragraph of, to me, ordinary prose with a par from the Van Goghish word painting of *The House with the Green Shutters*.

This glimpse of his approach to teaching underlines the way in which

Neill tended to see lessons in terms of his own likes and dislikes, rather than from the perspective of the individual child. This failing was even more apparent in his maths lessons. Here his technique was not much more advanced than that used by his father and other dominies during his young days in Scotland. Teaching, he once wrote, was a matter of 'putting a subject across the footlights'. Bryn Purdy, who taught for a while at Summerhill at a later period, defined his method as 'not even chalk and talk, but talk and talk. He would just sit and tell people things. He would hand out the compasses and pencils, and then say: "Now let's get on with the isosceles triangle," or whatever it might be.' Maths was one of the few subjects in which he had achieved any success in his own schooldays. As an adult he retained a genuine interest in it, being happy to while away train journeys doing mathematical puzzles. Yet he seemed unable to teach it effectively, except perhaps to a few children who were already extremely interested in or had a natural aptitude for the subject. Most of those he taught were extremely critical of his ability. 'He was the worst maths teacher in the world, absolutely hopeless: we used to take our knitting,' Angela Neustatter remembers. Another post-war pupil, Norma Harris, puts a view shared by many others: 'It was so much his own subject he couldn't see how it could possibly be difficult for anybody. He didn't get cross when you didn't understand; he just couldn't conceive that you couldn't. It just all flowed over him. If you looked at him as if to say, "What are you talking about?" he couldn't bring himself to explain in any simpler terms.'*

In later years Neill tried to deflect these criticisms: 'They used to tell me I was a bloody awful teacher, which wasn't true; I was a damn good teacher. These were the children who didn't want to go to lessons, but went because their parents expected them to go, and so they blamed the teacher.' This explanation cannot account for the large proportion of pupils who were critical of his ability as a maths teacher. Many of these were clearly *not* under this kind of pressure from home; and several found they made reasonable progress with other adults who taught the subject at Summerhill. In this particular case, blaming the teacher seems not unreasonable.

Yet, however much Neill exaggerated its presence, parental pressure *was* an issue he had to contend with. Understandably, many parents – even those most eager to give their children the kind of freedom Neill was offering – became anxious when they found, for instance, that their child was still unable to read after several years at Summerhill. In March 1927 Homer Lane's widow Mabel wrote anxiously to a friend about Olive Lane's position as a pupil of Neill's: 'I am not sure if his school is the best for her. She just loves it all but she cannot write a legible letter and is very much behind other children of her age and she will simply have to earn her living

---

*The message seems to have got through even to the younger children, to judge from one child's reaction to the publication of Neill's book *The Problem Teacher* in 1940. 'Is this a book all about what a silly teacher he is?' she asked a housemother, when she saw it on her bookshelf.

in some way.' The most vivid example of such pressure was to be found within Summerhill itself. Mrs Corks never totally accepted the Summerhill philosophy, despite spending the better part of her adult life there. Her son Mervyn Corkhill recalls her attitude to his particular problem: 'I was quite unable to read, and wasn't very interested anyway. Reading seemed illogical to me, mathematics was logical, and I had no problem with that. There was a bit of conflict between mother and father over the reading. My father said, Let's leave it, it will come. But my mother used to get me in a corner some times, and try bullying ways to make me read, which didn't do any good.' Maurice Draper remembers that 'he used to go to painting classes because his mother badgered him to.'

A few parents actually withdrew their children, either because they were worried about their progress in such skills as reading and writing, or because they felt they would have more chance of exam success elsewhere. Few were able to be as relaxed as Brendan Williams about such matters: 'Evelyn never took to her books, and never bothered to read until she was 9,' he recalls. 'I asked her then whether she would like to, and she thought she might. So I and my wife and Branwen took turns during the summer holiday to read through *Alice in Wonderland* with her, and by the time we had got to the end she could read perfectly well.' An example of more typical parental feeling involved another pupil, the son of a famous novelist, who was still not able to read at 13. Bill MacKinnon remembers Neill's reaction: 'This boy's mother took him to a psychologist, who said he was backward. The mother was in tears about this when she brought him back at the beginning of term. Neill asked me to assure her that he was *not* backward – that, for instance, he was an excellent film critic and a good artist with pen and paper. Eventually, when he did read, his mother wrote an ecstatic letter of thanks. Neill said: "You wait, she'll be asking us why he's not doing three A levels soon." And he was right.'

One of Neill's central beliefs, which he held in relation to all children, was: 'If the emotions are free, the intellect will look after itself.' This freedom, he believed, could best be found in play, and in creative activities. This was not simply a reaction against the 'over-education' of the mind which Neill believed to be a fault of the conventional schools; it expressed his own experience since his boyhood. Of all the activities which he initiated or took part in at Summerhill, he clearly found most satisfaction in those where he could use his hands. Though by now he had virtually given up his pen and ink drawing, he did during the early years in Leiston do a certain amount of painting, though of a somewhat bizarre kind. Some of the early staff recall a strange, brightly painted wooden construction displayed in the staff room, and abstract designs on the garage door – including a black and orange dragon, which Neill explained in terms of the good it had done to his libido to execute the work. Though he liked people to admire his work, he accepted that it was not in the same class as that done by children. Once, when temporarily in charge of the art room, he wrote to a friend: 'I couldn't do anything so good as they did; my painting was sophisticated, more or less conscious and stylised, while theirs were straight from the soul, and of course brilliant.'

There are also recollections of him scything the long grass that grew up every year in the grounds. He learnt the skill from a local man, and would apply himself for hours at a time, exchanging no more than the occasional word with anyone who chose to assist him. Evidently there was, in addition to the satisfaction of a job well done, a feeling of respite from the often exhausting mental work which filled much of his normal day. He seems to have experienced a similar absorption, and perhaps too his greatest satisfaction, in activities which he pursued in his favourite room at Summerhill – the workshop. Over the years his interests ebbed and flowed: sometimes it was photography or bookbinding, later woodwork or making jewellery, at other times again metal and brass work. 'My aim is to start a machine shop,' he told Bertrand Russell in 1931, with only a hint of frivolity. In Leiston he had a separate workshop from the one used by the children. There he had the use of a good lathe and a collection of hand tools, which he seemed to treasure more than anything else: his angry complaints about their disappearance or destruction became a feature of the weekly meetings. In the workshop he was a teacher in a much more informal way. Mervyn Corkhill learned a great deal from Neill in the workshop: 'In my early teens I looked upon him as really something in metalwork,' he remembers. Daphne Oliver went to few lessons, and spent most of her four years at Summerhill in the art room and workshop, producing quantities of brass ashtrays and bowls, raffia table mats, lino cuts and various wooden objects. She recalls her first meeting with Neill, and his teaching 'method': 'I wandered into the workshop and saw him beating brass. He gave me a bit and showed me how to do it. But we never used to speak to each other there, except to ask for certain punches, or whether I had got the roundness right.'

Neill and his fellow-teachers in Summerhill were not, however, the children's only sources for learning. Any visitors with a skill or some interesting knowledge were encouraged to put in some time with the children. Johnny Rust, the welter-weight champion of South Africa, whom Neill had met during the 1930s, came during the summer holidays, and was encouraged by Neill to teach the children the rudiments of boxing. Some visiting 'experts' were Summerhill parents, who would be cornered when they came to the school. C. H. Waddington was one who was received in this way: a specialist in animal genetics, his son Jake attended the school for a while. Another frequent visitor was 'Sage' Bernal, who talked on the nutritious value of rosehips, changing the world's climate, the future of space travel, the idea of draining the North Sea and making it into arable land, and sundry other topics. Once Bernal brought with him the distinguished American anthropologist Gene Weltfish, who talked about her time with a tribe of Pawnee Indians, the subject of her book *The Lost Universe*. A teacher from Gandhi's school gave a talk on India and its hopes for the future. One of the more exotic visitors was Verrier Elwin, who lived among a primitive people in India, where he ran a leper colony.

His work had led him to believe that 'these wild and glorious children of the forest' should not 'be cramped into a town-made syllabus; they were not made for examinations'. He argued against them being forced to go through an education that would both destroy their culture, and make them servile. He had heard about Neill's work and, when he visited England, asked to see Summerhill in action. Ethel Mannin acted as his escort: 'He had an immense success at the school,' she remembered. 'After the evening meal all the older children crowded into Neill's room to hear him talk. . . . Neill made a few informal opening remarks from the depths of his armchair: This chap Verrier Elwin, he said, lived in a jungle in India with some very primitive people called Gonds. He supposed they all knew where India was on the map; this chap Elwin lived in the middle of it. "Now you go on, Elwin." '

Summerhill itself was a very primitive community – one visitor called it 'the bare minimum of a school'. The drab and austere physical conditions reflected the more puritan and frugal aspect of Neill's personality. In similar fashion, what the children learned at Summerhill was determined by Neill's own likes and dislikes to a much greater extent than he cared to admit. No child could really escape his influence, however free of adult 'moulding' he might claim they were.

Talking of Summerhill

ニイル
研　究

A LITTLE JOURNAL FOR THE
STUDY OF IDEAS AND WORKS OF
A. S. NEILL AND
OTHER EDUCATIONAL INNOVATORS

> Mr Neill hardly needed any introduction, as he was known over
> five continents. 'Is it five?' the chairman asked, turning to Mr Neill.
> 'I don't know how many continents there are,' Mr Neill answered,
> amid laughter.
>
> Report in *Cape Argus*, September 1936

'A stimulating visitor landed in the Union yesterday. Mr A. S. Neill, who
is to lecture on his educational methods, will certainly not meet with
indifference, and may easily start an educational commotion.' The *Cape
Argus* of 28 July 1936 was right in both of these predictions. Neill's
seven-week tour of South Africa caused a tremendous stir – and not just
amongst teachers. He managed to deeply offend the powerful Dutch Reformed Church, and forced members of the educational establishment to
speak out against him because of the hostility which his lectures aroused.
Yet he spoke to packed halls, and found a great deal of sympathy for his
ideas, especially amongst the younger generation of teachers.

He had been invited to South Africa by the Transvaal Teachers' Association. Since the publication of his first book, Neill had found more
interest in and enthusiasm for his ideas in South Africa than in any other
foreign country. His first lecture in Johannesburg City Hall seemed to
confirm this: the hall was packed, and 500 people were turned away. Neill
spoke on the provocative topic 'Should Schools Be Scrapped?', a question
almost never asked at that time. His answer was that – with one exception
– they should. After covering the issues which he had written of in his
widely read 'Problem' books, he repeated his view that the school system

'had the political aim of keeping people down', and of turning them into wage slaves. Summerhill, on the other hand, allowed children to acquire the art of dealing with people; 'they went through life spontaneously and without self-consciousness', he argued.

The pattern was set for the tour. Neill's teacher audiences mostly responded with sympathy and delight to his lectures, even when he made deliberately outrageous remarks. In East London, one eye-witness remembers, he began with the observation: 'I've seen all your schools here today, and they're simply dreadful'; at the end of the evening the applause was tremendous. In Pretoria he was asked what he would do with a child who played truant, and replied, 'Shoot his headmaster.' In another lecture, when asked why his boys and girls slept in separate rooms, he reminded the audience that Summerhill was a school, not a brothel. A man who heard him speak at Rhodes University College recalls that 'the interest was great' amongst the student body. A young teacher at his lecture in Kingersdorp remembers that 'his ideas created a great deal of interest among teachers in the Transvaal, although many were sceptical about the methods he advocated'.

By the time he reached Cape Town near the end of his tour, the *Argus* was describing him as 'the man who has called down on his head more thunderbolts from educational experts. . . than anyone else of his generation.' Part of Neill's skill as a lecturer, and the reason that he was not more reviled than he was, came from his ability to present himself as a simple, straightforward and humorous man of common sense – even when he was offering the most radical criticisms of established institutions or beliefs. His listeners often found themselves appreciating his iconoclastic remarks, even while not being in sympathy with his views about children. Indeed, it seems to have been the tone of his remarks almost as much as their content which eventually brought down the wrath of the South African Establishment on his head.

It was his comments about Christianity which got him into trouble. After one lecture he was asked if he practised Christ's teachings, and replied: 'We do not consciously follow Christ's teachings, but from a broad point of view Summerhill is about the only school in England that treats children in a way that Christ would have approved of. . . . In Summerhill we give children love and approval. I think that we are about the only true Christians in the world. . . outside Russia which, of course, is the only really Christian country left. That is why it abolished its churches.' On another occasion he was asked if he believed in the Bible, and used the occasion to criticise the Old Testament. He suggested that Solomon's proverb about sparing the rod and spoiling the child was 'a piece of foolish barbarity', and that 'only a mentally deficient person could believe all the Bible'. He said he believed that Christ was 'the greatest man of love I have read about', and that he found it strange that so-called believers showed so much hate in the way they ran their schools. 'I believe in the child, and the only Bible that any teacher should study is the good nature of the young child,' he ended. On other occasions he replied to attacks from Catholic members of his audience by asking them why children were beaten in Catholic schools.

About half way through his tour, the Free State Teachers' Union issued a statement, declaring that they had not invited Neill to lecture at Bloemfontein, and making it quite clear that they 'did not subscribe to his views'. The statement was greeted by members of the local Dutch Reformed Church as 'a timely warning against the foolish innovations in education that Mr Neill is advocating' in his 'sensational lectures'. In Bloemfontein, fourteen ministers of the church and two missionaries issued a signed protest 'against certain unsavoury, rash and more particularly disrespectful statements and views of this supposed educationist'. They then listed their specific objections to Neill: his 'blatant atheism', his 'mockery of Christ', his 'superficial view of sin', his 'condemnation of all knowledge and authority except his own', his 'heathenish conception of marriage', his 'twisting of well-known phrases to suit his own ends; for example, his analysis of Christ's love, which shows that he did not have the slightest conception of what he was talking about', and 'the way in which he encourages the degeneration of children by allowing them to smoke, swear and steal to their heart's content'. They concluded their protest by pointing to 'the striking manner in which Mr Neill contradicts himself: for example, by condemning all tradition and authority and then elevating the laws made by him and his 63 children to authority; his Freudian psychology which is mixed with all sorts of theories of psycho-analysis; his search after sensation, as his greater master G. B. Shaw has done before him; and the light-hearted spirit which has characterised his lectures.'

The University of Stellenbosch Council then cancelled the lecture which they had originally invited Neill to give under their auspices, because they were 'alarmed at the antagonism aroused by his extreme doctrines'. The Council outlined their reasons for the decision: 'As the Council does not approve of Mr Neill's theories of education, particularly in regard to religion and such matters, it would not be advisable to allow him to lecture under the auspices of the University. By having Mr Neill's lectures under the auspices of the University, it would appear that the University countenances or agrees with his views.' They added that 'no steps will be taken to prevent him from holding a meeting locally, and students can please themselves whether they want to attend or not.' The chairman of the Student Representative Council expressed his surprise that the lecture had been called off, and in a comment of breathtaking complacency suggested that the students would not have been influenced by 'such revolutionary ideas as expressed by Mr Neill. They have not yet stood the test of time.'

These events can hardly have taken Neill by surprise, though at the time he complained, with some justification, that he was being criticised by people who had never heard him, or had misunderstood his ideas. The Dutch Reformed Church was imbued with much of the spirit of Calvinism which he had been fighting against since his childhood, and many of his most fundamental beliefs and instincts derived from his experience of the Old Testament dogma of 'the kirk'. 'The Scots kirk element still has a strong hold in South Africa', he was told by one schools inspector. Calvinisn for Neill manifested itself in the beating of children, the hatred and fear of pleasure, the intolerance of dissenting opinion, the dislike of levity: 'Never try to be funny when there are Calvinists around,' he said towards the end of the tour. The cancellation of his lecture he took with apparent calm. In an interview with the *Cape Argus*, he said he thought the university was being narrow-minded, but that

> The younger generation is with me in looking for an education of love, not of punishment. That is what matters. It is significant that every hall in which I have spoken has been packed. There is a tremendous amount of dissatisfaction with present-day schools and their discipline and so-called education. There is no hope for future generations while the rule of the belt and cane is exercised over our children.

Neill nevertheless decided to answer some of the points made in the protest of the ministers and missionaries, 'to show how spite and hate will make men pervert an opponent's opinion'. Most of the attack he thought not worth a reply, but he defended himself on two counts:

> I never said God was a person like myself: what I said was that to me God was the deep Unconscious in man, the good life-force that was perverted by the moralists. I never mocked Christ. When I asked an audience if it could even imagine Jesus beating a child, someone asked me what I made of his scourging the money-lenders in the Temple. I replied that the incident made Jesus human and therefore more lovable.

He thought it 'interesting, if tragic, that my insistence on the love that Jesus gave has roused the Calvinists against me'. And in a letter published in the *Cape Argus* on 16 November, he invited his clergy and teacher critics to answer publicly some questions about their own attitudes:

> 1. Do you practise or believe in the punishment of children, and if so, how do you reconcile this with Christ's 'Suffer little children to come unto me'?
> 2. What would you do with a boy of twelve who stole?
> 3. Why does a teacher in a *backveld dorp* not dare to dance even on a weekday? Is dancing a sin?
> 4. Do you believe that the Unconscious exists?
> 5. Do you believe in telling a child the truth about birth? If you don't, why don't you?
> 6. How many of the critics attended a lecture of mine? I ask because a critic should at least know what he is criticising.
> These questions are asked seriously. I met so very many broad-minded and advanced teachers in South Africa, both Afrikaners and English, that I know the Orange Free State Teachers' Association are

not voicing the opinions of the majority of teachers. It is right that the moderns should hear the opinions of the conservative.

Despite the hostility from on high, Neill was sufficiently encouraged by his grass-roots reception to pursue a plan that had been forming in his mind before he arrived in the Union. One of the purposes of his tour was to explore the possibility of opening another school there. Before he returned to England this plan became known, and received a mixed reception. At the end of their formal protest, the ministers and missionaries asked 'Will our poor country have to put up with this poor importation?' In Kroonstad there was a debate in the council on the question of whether Neill should be invited to open a branch of Summerhill in the town. One councillor argued that it would be 'the finest attraction Kroonstad has ever had', but another spoke against the idea: 'I would not like to see the greater part of Mr Neill's teaching applied to my children. His methods, like some of the children at his school, are abnormal.' The meeting agreed to make the invitation, but Neill, perhaps unhappy about the idea of becoming a municipal showpiece, turned it down. He declared himself grateful to the citizens of Kroonstad for showing they lived in 'a broad-minded town', but regretted that 'it would not be agreeable to set up a school in a part of South Africa where pre-psychological views seem to rule'. He was, he said, 'looking for a spot where my work will be appreciated, and where religion takes the form of living and loving, rather than suppression and preaching.'

Neill's intention was for Cyril Eyre and Lucy Francis to run the South African version of Summerhill, and for him to come over during the winter. He returned again to South Africa, and for a short while it looked as if the venture might get off the ground, as Cyril Eyre recalls: 'A number of Johannesburg Jews, who were his main supporters, got together and raised enough promises of money to finance the building of a school, and to guarantee its start. Neill came back absolutely radiant; he looked about ten years younger, and was full of it.' However, not surprisingly, there was plenty of opposition to the idea, and it was eventually shelved. According to Cyril Eyre, this was 'because of organised opposition from the Dutch Reformed Church, who persuaded the Afrikaaners to oppose it.' Neill later wrote to Curry, suggesting the decision was his: 'Almost sorry now I refused to start in Johannesburg, when some rich boys offered to finance a school. Almost.'

Would Neill really have been happy to open another school in a country based on a system of apartheid? Later he wrote: 'My knowledge of South Africa is scanty; it is based on my lecture tour there when apartheid was everywhere. I saw it as a crime against black humanity, but some of the professors and teachers I met took it as a good and necessary system.' At the time he thought the law between black and white 'fairly equitable' in a city such as Johannesburg, even though native teachers were not allowed to attend his lecture there. But he was disturbed to hear of stories from the outlying towns, 'stories of a farmer beating a native to death, being tried by a farmer jury, and getting fined five pounds, while a native who attacks a white man gets floggings and ten years'. He himself witnessed Boer policemen with whips chasing natives out of a park at closing time. He was taken down a gold mine in the Rand, and noted the poor working conditions of both blacks and whites, and the high number of deaths from tuberculosis and silicosis. 'Humanity must be mad', he observed. His hatred of Calvinism was reinforced when he was told that the church accepted apartheid on the grounds that the Bible consigns the black man to be a hewer of wood and a drawer of water. From the limited amount of contact he had with the black population – in Boksburg the mayor gave permission for 'native teachers' to attend his lecture – he was disappointed to find that 'their one idea was to get a white man's education in school subjects'. On the other hand, he does seem to have seen some possibilities for reform in education in South Africa. Writing at the very end of his tour, he observed that the country was 'very much alive about education, and, judging from my audiences, will tolerate the most extreme opinions'. He thought South Africa had 'none of the hide-bound tradition of the homeland, and it is forced to be alive to its modern problems'.

As his books began to find a substantial readership abroad, and he himself was invited to lecture, Neill increasingly referred to himself as 'a prophet without honour in his own country'. There was perhaps more truth in this in reference to Scotland than to his adopted England. Near the end of his life he reflected: 'The most aggressive questioners I have met in a life of lecturing were women in Scotland, teachers I guess.' In 1936 he wrote: 'I can get a packed hall when I lecture in London, Oslo or Stockholm, but the local papers in my own county seldom mention my name.' He also noted that six months previously in Norway he had found his audience 'one of the most appreciative. . . that I have ever lectured to. . . it showed an interest in modern education that no Aberdeen or Edinburgh audience would show'. These last two remarks, and others much more critical about the country of his birth, appeared in his book *Is Scotland Educated?*, written the same year as his trip to South Africa.

The book was part of a series commissioned by George Routledge & Sons Ltd, intended to cover a number of aspects of Scottish life under the heading 'Voice of Scotland'. The editor was the widely praised working-class novelist Lewis Grassic Gibbon, whose trilogy of novels *A Scots Quair*, and volume of essays and short stories written with Hugh MacDiarmid, *Scottish Scene*, had just appeared. Gibbon, whose real name was Leslie Mitchell, had been brought up in a similar environment to Neill, in the rural farming areas of north-east Scotland. According to his son, Daryll Mitchell, who later went to Summerhill, the novelist was a great admirer of Neill and his ideas about freedom for children. Gibbon described himself as a 'revolutionist', declaring that 'all my books are explicit or implicit propaganda'. He was determined to get the best writers, who would provide 'liveliness and controversy'. MacDiarmid, a fine poet, one of the founders of the Scottish National Party, and a long-standing critic of Scottish bourgeois culture, contributed to the series. He knew and admired Neill's work and helped Gibbon with the selection of authors and titles.

Neill took with relish the opportunity to put Scotland in its place. He confessed that he spoke 'as an outsider who has little opportunity of seeing what is really going on in Scotland' and that 'in thinking about Scottish education I have angry emotions'. He then expressed this anger in withering attacks on the 'deadness' of Scottish culture, the narrowness of family life, the repressiveness of the church, and the education system's obsession with knowledge. He called Edinburgh University 'a factory for mass production of degrees', and recalled with bitterness episodes from his life as a student there. He argued that 'it is impossible to have a free healthy education in a land that is kirk-ridden', and that 'Scots education is of no value whatever so far as anything that matters in life is concerned'. It was in essence a book into which Neill poured his frustrated emotions, as he tacitly acknowledged in a letter some years later, when he described it as 'a poor book full of pudding to hide my gross ignorance of Scotland.' He thought there was 'too much ASN in it' and only a 'few wee diamonds in the mass of blue clay'. The *New Era* reviewer agreed, suggesting that it was 'a pity he should sprinkle his pages with smart trivialities and reckless statements, as though determined to be "frank, fearless and provocative" at all costs.'

The book provoked little comment, and sold poorly. His message was however beginning to spread to other countries. In 1928 Seishi Shimoda, an art teacher in a primary school in Japan, made a visit of several weeks to Summerhill, having been lent a copy of *A Dominie's Log* by an English teacher in Tokyo, Eric Bell. The two men got on well, and Shimoda was greatly impressed with Summerhill: 'I was truly fascinated by Neill and his work. The fact that I found Neill was the greatest event in my life. How much I have learned from him and how much my mind has been opened by him is beyond expression. It is true that Neill has shown me a new light towards child psychology and education and brought me so many good ideas. I felt that it was my responsibility to introduce Neill's thoughts on education to the Japanese people and I devoted many years to translating his works.'

Shimoda became a professor of art at Tama Art College and director of the Iogi Child Institute, and wrote a book about Neill's life and work. His translation of *The Problem Child* appeared in 1930, *The Problem Parent* and an abridged version of four of the 'Dominie' books in 1933, and *That Dreadful School* in 1938. 'I feel most warmly about your great kindness in translating my books,' Neill later wrote to Shimoda. 'When the world is full of hate, and when it looks as if it is going to destroy itself in our time, it is good to know that in Japan even a small group of teachers and parents is seeking life for children.' In fact, in the militaristic pre-war years in Japan, the early translations did not sell widely; but they sowed the seeds for a wider interest in Neill's ideas at a later period.

In Scandinavia it was a very different story. In 1929 he was invited to speak at a conference in Elsinore, along with Piaget, Cizek, Montessori and Rabindranath Tagore, and to lead a discussion group on 'The Problem Child'. He made several visits during the 1930s, as his books began to appear in translation. Almost from the start he was treated as a celebrity, with notices in the press about his arrival, press conferences, and dinner parties held in his honour. 'When I come here they treat me as if I were somebody, at home I am bloody nobody,' he once remarked in Sweden. In Stockholm he met Adler over lunch – they had the same publisher. (He found the analyst 'charming', but felt that 'he was talking of surface things'.) One of those who remembers the impact he made is Gustav Jonsson, who later founded the Skaa Children's Village at Edeby, Sweden, and was subsequently to become the country's leading authority on child welfare. In the 1930s he was a young medical student training at a children's clinic in Stockholm, and specialising in child psychiatry. 'At that time quite a few of us were reading Neill's books, freshly translated into Swedish, and finding in them ideas which were also being bandied about here in Sweden, chiefly in intellectual circles and chiefly among women. I remember him as a brilliant lecturer who always drew a full house, and who spoke like an evangelist against authoritarianism in society and in favour of a free up- bringing. He was something of a performer, who could score points and make people laugh while putting across his serious theses on a new way of bringing up children.'

One of the many people who heard him lecture in Scandinavia was Elna Lucas. A young psychology student working with 'difficult' children, she was sufficiently impressed by Neill to come to Summerhill 'to study him and the place', and to stay on as a housemother. She recalls Neill's lecture in Stockholm in 1934: 'He talked about Summerhill, freedom, sexual problems, masturbation, stealing. He spoke in a lazy way, and with his Scots accent and his pipe in his mouth he was difficult to follow – but spell-binding.' In his tweed jacket, red tie and heavy walking shoes Neill cut a somewhat eccentric figure, an impression occasionally reinforced on visits he made to schools in Sweden. Greta Sergeant, after her spell as a housemother at Summerhill, acted as Neill's interpreter: 'Once he visited a school in Stockholm, and was taken in to a geography lesson. He went up to the map on the wall, pointed to Italy, and said: "This is London." The pupils stared at him in surprise. At Summerhill when he did things like that, they laughed and told him he was a silly fool.'

Sometimes his outspoken remarks caused offence. In a lecture in Oslo in 1935 he made his standard comment about religion, that it was danger- ous to teach it to children, and half a dozen headmistresses left the hall. 'My audience looked at me as if I had walked straight out of the pages of an Ibsen play,' he remembered. In Stockholm he berated an audience of teachers for coming to his lectures but not doing anything about changing the schools, which he labelled 'exam factories'. One teacher pointed out that those who controlled the schools never came to Neill's lectures. Neill later acknowledged the problems of the teachers who came to hear him speak: 'I feel humble and ashamed when I am reminded of their difficulties – large classes, barrack rooms, inspectors, codes, curricula: I feel a little mean talking to them, knowing that I have none of their difficulties myself.' On the other hand, it was precisely Neill's attacks on these elements of conventional schooling which he saw as being one of the principal reasons for his success with many audiences: 'I talk to their guts; I talk to them of really important things. . . of a world they missed and go on missing.'

Neill was also attracting large audiences in England. 'There are few people who have not read his entertaining and thought-provoking books on education, and he has hundreds of thousands of admirers all over the world,' reported one member of the audience, at a lecture he gave in the London School of Hygiene in the summer of 1933. The occasion apparently 'caused quite a little stir among the intelligentsia and semi-intellectuals' in London. 'The tiers of seats in the large amphitheatre lecture-room were filled long before the lecture was timed to begin and in the absence of police, people crowded onto the steps, in the aisles, on the high window-sills, huddled against the walls and in every corner and angle. The audience was even mixed up with the presiding committee. There was a whole row of scribbling pressmen.' The writer reacted to Neill's appearance in a way typical of many at the first encounter:

> Tall and lean, the 'Dominie' is not a very prepossessing personality at first sight. He looks dour and uncommunicative – his pipe, firmly held between his strong teeth, gives him the inward concentrated look of the man who keeps his own counsel and does not wish to discuss his affairs with anybody. This air of reticence indeed must be a deliberate cloak which he puts on to scare off the inquisitive, for there is a charm about Neill's books which attracts every amateur educationist who visits England from every corner of the earth.

Leila Rendel, who began the Caldecott Community, another self-governing school, found a different discrepancy in Neill: 'I was surprised, he was such a wholesome man,' she remarked after one of his lectures.

In his early lectures Neill had found it an ordeal facing audiences: he was anxious about drying up half way through, and relied on notes. But with his growing confidence in his ideas, and the establishment of Summerhill's reputation, he found he was beginning to enjoy himself, and developed a technique for holding an audience. If they seemed bored or hostile he would try out what soon became a well-worn opening gambit – taking off his tie, or telling the audience that they all looked dead, so he assumed they must be teachers. Once, addressing students in Cheltenham in a room plastered with No Smoking signs, he searched in his pockets for a cigarette, and then accepted one from the audience, explaining that he only smoked to be sociable. Such devices tended to soften the audience up for the hard-hitting remarks that followed; but they also had the effect of easing his own tension.

His reticent manner often belied the ferocity of his observations, which could shock some in his audience. Lois Child, who later became joint head of Dartington Hall, remembers hearing Neill speak at a New Education Fellowship meeting in London in the mid-1930s: 'He peppered his speech with expletives while urging the audience not to mind if children swore. I remember coming away thinking that freedom to swear at Summerhill was something that one caught – an infection rather than a response to an innate need.' Eileen Bernal saw Neill's desire to shock as an indication of his belief that his ideas had not been accepted: 'In a way he was far too modest, and so always on the defensive. So when he spoke at meetings he had a tendency to try to shock people, who weren't prepared to hear the free and easy way he dealt with any subject. For Neill to talk about masturbation in a perfectly open and objective way in a lecture on education was more than some people could take forty years ago.'

In 1934 Victor Gollancz published *The Modern Schools Handbook*, with an introduction by Amabel Williams-Ellis. The first half consisted of essays by those in charge of the better known co-educational schools – Beacon Hill, Bedales, Dartington, Frensham Heights, King Alfred, St Christopher and Summerhill. In his piece Neill observed:

> Our work has been appreciated by teachers and parents from all over the world; it has been cursed and libelled by thousands of people who never saw the school or its results; we have had unhelpful publicity in the form of newspaper headlines of the School-Where-Pupils-Kick-The-Headmaster type.

The public image of Summerhill differed only in degree from that of other pioneering schools of the time. Typical epithets used to describe Dartington were 'Bolshie', 'immoral', 'atheistic', 'crazy', 'dangerous', and 'nudist'. One famous but probably apocryphal story has been pinned to at least three of the pioneer schools. It seems that a visiting clergyman was received at the front door of the school by a naked girl. 'Good God!' he exclaimed. 'There is no God,' came back the instant reply. The Maltings House was known by some in Cambridge as 'a pre-genital brothel'. One boy was alleged to have come to school by taxi, and, when he refused to get out of it, been allowed to ride round in it for the rest of the day, after which his father received a substantial bill. A characteristic story in the *Daily Express* in January 1933 appeared under the heading 'Go-As-You-Please-Schools/ Abolishing Teaching/Revolt Spreads All Over the World/No Stupid Prohibitions', and went on to describe how 'in hundreds of pioneer establishments in Germany, US and England, the little citizen of the world learns to do as it likes instead of as it is told'.

Summerhill received more than its fair share of sensational and misleading headlines, and was consistently labelled the 'do-as-you-please' school in the popular press. The general impression created by these stories over the years was that the children spent most of their time running wild, swearing, breaking windows, riding their bicycles, being rude to the staff, and telling Neill what a silly old fool he was. A rumour developed that children were given so much freedom that they were permitted to hammer nails into the Summerhill grand piano if the fancy took them. Here, as in certain other instances, Neill was partly to blame, because of his tendency to describe his ideas in striking but potentially misleading terms. Such 'permissiveness' would certainly not have been tolerated at Summerhill, since the child would have been interfering with the rights of others, so undermining one of the basic tenets of Neill's philosophy. However, Neill was supposed to have once replied to a question 'What would you do if your son wanted to hammer nails into your piano?' by saying that his son's soul was more precious to him than a piano. By 1934 he was already having to deny that this happened at Summerhill, but before long the revised version had entered the mythology.

However, there is no doubt that certain newspapers deliberately tried to encourage children at Summerhill to behave in ways that would provide them with good copy. Gerry Collier recalls one particular visit: 'The journalist took photographs of the children smoking, they gave the very young children sweets, and persuaded boys and girls to walk about with their arms around reach other. He wrote something really ghastly: I've never really been able to read a newspaper with any confidence since.' Teddy Raw has a similar recollection of press behaviour during the early years: 'They came on several occasions, but there was one particular time when they wanted to take pictures of us throwing stones through windows, and kicking Neill's bottom. They seemed surprised and a little hurt when they discovered that we thought this to be an infantile idea.' After one visit the children brought the matter up at a meeting, and voted that such behaviour should not be allowed. The resolution had little effect.

It was understandable that Neill should have a jaundiced view of what he variously described as the 'yellow', 'gutter' and 'stunt' press. In *The Problem Parent* he wrote: 'With a daily Press that must be dishonest because it must keep people from thinking, it is small wonder that our homes are filled with lies.' Yet some papers during the early Leiston years provided quite balanced and sympathetic coverage – even to the point of the writer swallowing some of Neill's more outrageous assertions without comment. Often there was a conflict between the article itself and the way it was presented. A full-page piece in the *Cape Argus*, headed 'The Queerest School in the World', and illustrated with drawings suggesting general mayhem, gave a detailed and very fair account of both the aims and the atmosphere of the school. The writers, Roza van Gelderen and Hilda Purwitsky, were in fact not journalists but teachers from South Africa, and were evidently beguiled by Neill himself as well as finding much to approve of in his ideas:

> In the congenial environment of his own school, sprawling on a
> couch in his book-lined study, with his eternal pipe in his mouth,
> A. S. Neill emerges from his self-imposed silence as an intensely
> interesting personality. There is something indolent and
> unargumentatively confident about him. He is sure of himself and
> knows that he is right. Yet there can be few experts on any subject
> less ready to lay down the law on the topics they can well claim as
> their own.

Neill's determination to persuade the outside world of the value of his work ensured that the Summerhill door remained open to reporters, teachers and other visitors. In addition, however much he complained of their existence, Neill undoubtedly enjoyed putting on a show for those who were prepared to listen to his views. It became a tradition for visitors to attend the Saturday night meeting to observe the self-government in action, and for Neill then to take them across to the theatre for an hour or so of questions. Although the same questions came up again and again, Neill never seemed to tire of the ritual: 'he scorned visitors and at the same time courted them,' one housemother observed. Yet the sheer number of visitors was a real burden, and some of his resentment was certainly genuine. 'Every summer I become a kind of commissionaire in uniform,' he wrote, after Summerhill had been at Leiston for ten years. 'By the end of the summer term I feel like screaming if I see a strange car drive up.' Frequently he took evasive action when visitors approached: a piece of metalwork needed finishing in the workshop, some digging was required on the potato patch – and once he was discovered behind a tree in the grounds, hiding from a parent he particularly disliked.

Like Neill, the children preferred some visitors to others, and were less inclined to tolerate any who tended to act in the grand manner. Ethel Mannin, who some at Summerhill felt was rather taken up with her own importance, was nicknamed 'The Painted Lady' by the children. Another novelist not always accorded deferential treatment was Henry Handel Richardson, who after the death of her husband came to live in Aldeburgh in order to be near her sister. For a while she dined regularly at Summerhill with her friend Olga Roncoroni, who remembers the reception given to this somewhat forbidding and austere visitor: 'One boy would regularly come out, ostensibly to greet us, and then plant his feet over my newly whitened shoes. He would then proceed to plaster mud and dirt all over our shiny car. We said nothing, but smarted under the treatment.' Other individuals, especially those with something specific to offer, were given a more friendly welcome. When Bertrand Russell visited Summerhill at Lyme, the children were much more interested in his companion, a friend of Baden-Powell's, who brought with him little bits of meat and flour, and taught them how to cook the meat over a fire. They were, though, less tolerant of large groups descending on the school, as they did from about 1930 onwards. Greeba Pilkington, a housemother in the early days, remembers one occasion when they took their revenge on a coachload of teachers: 'The kids hated it, the charabanc load coming up to look at them. The dining table was laid out with a beautiful afternoon tea, everything on it. We had a big bell that was used at an emergency to summon people for a special meeting in the hall. Tony rang it. The visitors all trooped into the hall. They were very pleased and excited – a special meeting. And while they were out of the room the kids cleared everything off the table.'

Whatever Mrs Lins's faults were as a democrat, she was generally acknowledged by both staff and visitors to be an admirable hostess, thoroughly capable of making newcomers welcome in a way that Neill could never emulate. Her liking for company and her curiosity about people made them feel wanted, and on many occasions she would stand in for Neill when he did his disappearing act. Visitors would be met at Leiston station by a representative welcoming committee – a member of staff, one or two of the older children, and four little ones. Certain privileged visitors would be entertained to coffee in her room, where they sat and talked surrounded by her few possessions – a sofa made for her by a pupil, Bobby Townsend, a Benares table, a few Persian rugs and a portrait of her eminent novelist sister. At other times visitors would gather in Neill's room, but even then Mrs Lins tended to lead the discussions. According to Roger Anscombe, who came back as a teacher after his years as a pupil, 'she wanted to clear everyone else out of the way so that she could hog the visitor'. This was most likely to happen when the visitor was a celebrity or a titled person, since, by general consent, Mrs Lins was a snob. This trait was also evident in her attitude to certain children. One girl, the daughter of Lord North, came to school at the beginning of term in her grandfather's chauffeur-driven car. Mrs Lins took her under her wing, and allowed her the special privilege of coming to her room in the evening to drink soup if she felt at all indisposed.

Neill too was impressed by a 'name', though unlike Mrs Lins he made some attempt to conceal it. He was unable to resist referring to 'my friend Russell' and was liable to use the same label for any public figure whose path had, however briefly, crossed his own. George Lansbury, for example, on the strength of writing one short piece for the *New Era* while Neill was co-editor, was henceforth known as 'my friend Lansbury'. Like his erstwhile hero Barrie, Neill 'loved a laird', and was noticeably pleased when men such as Lord Saye and Sele and Lord Stradbroke visited the school, even though he went to some lengths to point out how they were really just as 'ordinary' as anyone else. 'He has no dignity at all, and his lineage dates back hundreds of years,' he observed with some amazement of one titled visitor. The interest in social status which he acquired from his mother never really left him, though his snobbery was mild enough, and certainly had no significant effect on his life or work.

One man of rank and wealth who appeared briefly at Summerhill just before the school moved to Leiston was Lord Sandwich, the ninth Earl of Montagu, who founded the Little Commonwealth, and was responsible for bringing Homer Lane to England to run it. He never showed any further interest in Neill's work, but others who had been involved with Lane did, seeing in Summerhill a place where the spirit of the Little Commonwealth lived on. E. J. Radclyffe, a journalist on the fringes of the literary world, was one of Lane's former pupils who turned up, playing the grand piano with some ferocity. Another who became a regular visitor was the anthropologist John Layard. According to Neill, he had been 'stuck in the midst of a negative transference to Lane when Lane died, and was left without a saviour, and tried me (I refused of course) and then Stekel.' Layard's own account, written in the early 1930s, tells a slightly different story: 'I was seeing a lot of A. S. Neill, who had also been one of Homer Lane's pupils, but who by now was getting a little sour about him, complaining that Lane had never been able to take a negative transference; I had got out in time not to discover that. He said cynically: "Better a live Neill than a dead Lane." I talked to Neill about my problems. I would have liked to have

worked at his school. He refused nicely ("You are too much of an individual"); he probably meant that I was too neurotic. He said that by far the
best analyst was Stekel. In the end I decided to go out to Stekel.'

However sour Neill may have been getting about Lane as a person, he
remained very enthusiastic about his ideas, and used Lane's notes as a basis
for a number of weekend seminars and evening discussions in his sitting-
room on psychology. 'We were constantly talking about Lane,' Leslie Morton recalls. 'Neill would tell stories about him, talk about his work at the
Little Commonwealth and his ideas: it was always in the air.' During these
sessions, which echoed Lane's own psychological talks to his study circle
in Regent's Park, Neill would range over a number of his favourite topics:
The Inferiority Complex, The Psychology of Theft, Masturbation, The
Psychology of Humour, Why Man Became a Moralist, The Psychology of
the Gangster, Crowd Psychology. 'People who loved Neill as a father would
attend, as well as older pupils,' Cyril Eyre recalls. 'They were very stimulating question and answer sessions. The staff were almost pupils on these
occasions: our repressions, inhibitions were free to be exhibited, the atmosphere allowed one to live out one's hangups'. On one occasion, when Neill
invited people to write down questions if they wished, one of the psychology
students wrote: 'Why do you always leave your top fly button undone?'
Neill's answer, though not his roar of laughter, went unrecorded.

If many who came to Summerhill looked upon Neill as a potential
'saviour', to some in the outside world he came over as a much less benign
figure. In 1936 he was asked by J. R. Ackerley, the well-known editor of
the BBC weekly journal the *Listener*, to review three books by headteachers.
Neill obliged in characteristically trenchant style, beginning with the hope
that he would 'find something new in such books, something big, something
beyond the little thing we call education but in our hearts know is only
learning'. He found *A Headmaster Reflects* by Guy Kendall well written
and sensible, the author likeable but limited: 'he does not appear to see
that our education is a class one deriving from our social system of exploiter
and exploited, that indeed our system is a branch of politics'. Neill was
more in sympathy with *A Schoolmaster's Testament*, by his fellow-pioneer,
Badley of Bedales: 'His analysis of the old type of public school is almost
shattering, and his description of the new school is thorough.' Neill, though,
emphasised the difference between Badley and himself by again berating
him for using corporal punishment, adding that 'his remarks about the
necessity of checking such things as smoking and swearing are unworthy
of a modern educationist. He is still the head, still the schoolmaster.' He
reserved his most severe comments for *The Headmaster Speaks*, a symposium of essays by twelve eminent public school headmasters, with a preface
by Lord Eustace Percy. After running through the deficiencies in the philosophies of those in charge of Fettes, St Paul's, Tonbridge and Repton and
other schools (only Hugh Lyon of Rugby escaped censure), Neill concluded:
'The truth is that most of these heads have nothing new or important to
say. Their psychology is pre-war; their outlook is that of a civilisation built

on class. . . they cannot see life and education because the old school tie is in the way of their vision.'

The editor of the *Listener* was Sir Stephen Tallents, known for his tendency to crouch over the paper 'with his busy blue pencil'. He refused to let Ackerley print the review. At the bottom of the galley proof Ackerley scribbled the words: 'Rejected by Tallents, with his famous remark: "I won't have all this cocking snooks at the bigwigs. I don't want misunderstandings with the bigwigs." ' When Ackerley conveyed this decision to Neill, evidently with expressions of frustration, Neill replied sympathetically: 'Dear Ackerley, I'm damned sorry. . . for YOU. To be unfree to work in your own way is simply bloody. Confidentially between ourselves, would it damage you if I got another paper to publish the review stating that it was rejected by the *Listener*? I'd like to. But only on condition that it doesn't hurt you in any way.' It appears that Ackerely preferred not to do this, writing 'Kill' across Neill's corrected proofs. Neill had to be content with a fee of three guineas, and a little more fuel to fire his belief that he was indeed 'a prophet without honour in his own country'.

CHAPTER 13

The Politics of Freedom

September 1, 1933   THE NEW LEADER

HOW I RUN A FREE SCHOOL

By A. S. NEILL

The only thing certain is that we must keep freedom for kids going until they shoot us at the dusk of civilisation.

Letter to Bill Curry, June 1940

'The truth is that I *wanted* to believe in the new order; I wanted to think that the new education in Russia was wonderful.' Neill was not alone in pinning his reforming hopes to the Soviet flag in the aftermath of the Russian revolution. In England the seizure of power by Lenin and the Bolsheviks in October 1917 encouraged many to believe that the collapse of capitalism was imminent. The principal doubt seemed to be whether it would be replaced by democratic socialism or revolutionary communism. Lloyd George's promise of 'a land fit for heroes to live in' had proved illusory: by 1921 there were 2 million unemployed, and substantial disenchantment amongst the young, the middle classes and the intelligentsia. The Labour Party, with its membership of 4 million, now emerged as a serious alternative to the Conservative government. In July 1920 a number of revolutionary groups were set up by the Communist Party of Great Britain, with the aim of establishing a native version of Lenin's dictatorship of the proletariat. As the Party's historian James Klugmann later wrote: 'Everything that we wanted and desired in the new social system, we "read into" Soviet society.'

During the 1920s and into the 1930s, there was tremendous enthusiasm in England for the social, sexual and political reforms set in motion by the Russians. Several Anglo-Soviet friendly societies were set up. Film clubs were founded, audiences watching with reverence the works of the new

Russian film makers such as Eisenstein. Shaw, who had sent Lenin a copy of one of his books, announced to his fellow-Fabians not long after the revolution: 'We are socialists. The Russian side is our side.' Politicians, writers and other members of the intelligentsia made pilgrimages to the Soviet Union. Wells invited himself to the Kremlin and talked politics with Stalin; their discussions were printed verbatim in a special supplement of the *New Statesman*. Ethel Mannin, visiting in 1934, called it 'the greatest experiment in the history of humanity', and concluded: 'Russia is the land of Youth, the country of Tomorrow. The hardships and privations so patiently endured by the generation of today are for the children at present growing up, that they may enjoy in their maturity the benefits of a classless society without any of these preliminary labour pains.' Writing later in *The Age of Illusion,* Ronald Blythe observed: 'The new Soviet Union, mysterious, vast, and seemingly unsullied, became the land of hope. An acceptance of Marxism appeared not only ideal but plain common sense.'

However, with the rise of Stalin in the late 1920s, many of the reforms were halted and then reversed, as a new and rigid bureaucracy developed. In 1930 Stalin ordered a mass liquidation of the Russian peasantry, and in succeeding years carried out a ruthless purge of opponents by a policy of murder, imprisonment and forced labour. The enormity of the events taking place only slowly became known in Britain: people seemed only to hear what they wanted to hear. Leonard Woolf, who was in touch with dissident Russians as early as 1931, remembered that 'a realization of the truth came only gradually by personal experience, by knowing some insignificant individual caught and crushed in the inhuman machinery of the Soviet state'. Stalin's 'show trials', in which former Bolsheviks confessed to crimes they had never committed, were still a matter for dispute. Stephen Spender, writing later of his decision to join the Communist Party in 1937, argued that 'one ought to realise that at the time it was not at all certain that they were innocent, despite the grossness of some of the accusations made against them and the extravagance of their confessions.'

A similar pattern characterised the educational reforms made by the Bolsheviks. Almost immediately after the revolution a number of measures were agreed on which aimed to transform the school system. In 1918 the Council of People's Commissars issued decrees stating that religious instruction was to be forbidden, grading and examinations dispensed with, uniform abolished, co-education to be made compulsory, punishments and homework to be prohibited, hierarchical distinctions between teachers done away with, and equal pay introduced. Lenin's wife Krupskaya, herself a former teacher, was in the vanguard of those pressing for these radical changes. She was also a believer in pupil participation: under one of the decrees, children over 12 were given the right to become members of the school councils which were to administer the schools. Self-government, according to another official document, was to be 'a means by which the pupils may learn to live and work more intelligently'. To finance these reforms, relatively large sums were voted for the education and care of children.

For a short while there was intense and open debate in Russia about these new ideas. Anton Makarenko was the head of a secondary school when the Bolsheviks ousted the Tsarist regime: 'After the October Revolution wide horizons opened before me. We pedagogues were fairly intoxicated by these horizons,' he wrote. This new climate prompted him to set up the Gorky Colony, in which he provided a home for the young thieves, vagabonds and murderers left homeless by the Revolution. There were in his work some similarities with what Lane had been doing a short while before at the Little Commonwealth. Makarenko allowed the boys to run their own affairs, and to form themselves into a work community, producing an astonishing change of behaviour and attitude in some of the most hardened delinquents. In similar vein, S. T. Schatzsky, a leading progressive educator before the Revolution, began an 'experimental station', where it was the children who decided what work needed doing, and how it should be done. As in the Gorky colony, the children held assemblies to make and enforce rules, and to discuss matters of importance. Formal subject teaching gave way to a system which encouraged children to organise their own studies, and to learn through play to develop their curiosity about the world around them.

All these changes brought great encouragement to pioneers outside Russia. Educationists from the West came to observe the experiment in action, and to report back on what they had seen. John Dewey paid a visit in 1928, and wrote in the *New Republic*: 'The Russian educational situation is enough to convert one to the idea that only in a society based on cooperative principles can the ideals of educational reformers be adequately carried into operation.' Dora Russell, in 1920 one of the earliest to visit, found that the ideas of Montessori were being taken up, as well as certain features of the English pioneer schools such as Dalcroze Eurythmics. Marion Richardson, a pioneer in art teaching, went in 1926, and was impressed by the freedom allowed in the children's art work. John Lister, another of the many observers, told a New Education Fellowship conference:

> The New Education debates co-education: it is axiomatic in Russia.
> The New Education debates self-government: in Russian schools self-government is practised to a degree that would be positively indecent to the Etonian mind. . . . New Educators debate constantly the question of corporal punishment: Soviet Russia has made corporal punishment illegal by national edict, and a teacher has been dismissed for even slapping a child. . . . Every Soviet school is an activity school.*

*Lady Astor, who fostered and financed the experimental outdoor nursery school run by the Macmillan sisters in Deptford, was less happy than some with parts of the new system. In company with Shaw she secured an interview with Stalin in the Kremlin in 1931, and told him that the Russians didn't know how to treat children. They should, she said, be allowed to get dirty and play out of doors, instead of being cooped up in their spotless dresses in the state nurseries or collective farms. Stalin, according to Shaw, suddenly became stern, and replied, reasonably enough: 'In England you beat children, don't you?'

However, once Stalin came to power, the educational reforms vanished in much the same way as those in other spheres. Pioneers such as Makarenko and Schatzsky were absorbed into the bureaucracy. The schools reverted to a more formal, systematic and centralised approach, in which the needs of the state became paramount. Krupskaya and others protested in vain – Stalin threatened to make another woman Lenin's official widow if she continued to oppose his policies. The experiment was over.

Neill had little to help him build up a true picture of life in Russia. While in Gretna he wrote: 'I think of Russia with its darkness and cruelty, and I am appalled, a true democracy there will be centuries in coming.' By 1932, in *The Problem Parent*, he was describing Russia as 'the most wonderful country in the world'. He believed that the 'solution of the economic question is certainly coming from Russia's brave experiment, and it is probable that the solution of the moral question will come from the same quarter'. Neill's hatred of organised religion was clearly a major factor in shaping his roseate view:

> the only country that has a chance of making a new God of Love is Russia, for she is the only country that has seen that the churches have become the enemy of human progress and happiness. When a Russian village turns its church into a cinema or a reading room it is doing what Jesus Christ would have approved of and applauded.

In 1934 he described the democracy in Summerhill as 'more complete than any other democracy, with the possible exception of a Soviet village in Russia'. Writing in the *New Era* the following year, he outlined what he saw as the distinction between fascism and communism:

> Fascism is capitalism in its latest form: it seeks to make the workers subserve the interests of the folk who have possession. Russia's central government is something different. It works for the worker: it seeks to build up a new civilization of unexploited people. . . while Fascism will always need a strong central government to keep down the workers.

As late as 1937 he felt able to talk of Russia as 'a creative civilisation'. In that year he applied for a visa to visit Russia, and was turned down without explanation. From this time on, he began to have doubts about the 'brave experiment' which had seemed as if it might provide the basis of a new freedom for coming generations. But his disillusionment took a long time.

In *The Climate of Treason*, describing the growth of the Communist Party in Great Britain, Andrew Boyle wrote:

> As an outlet for youthful idealism, rebelliousness and confused anti-Establishment fervour, the new Communist Party managed to attract non-conformists of radical instincts quite unprepared in most cases to be ordered how to think and what to say by an uncompromising leadership drawn mainly from the working class.

Several of these non-conformists, attracted to Neill's vision of freedom for the next generation, came to teach at Summerhill. Leslie Morton, who had been eased out of a teaching job in a Sussex grammar school because of his support for the workers in the 1926 General Strike, admired Neill's refusal to indoctrinate children with the prevailing capitalist values. His wife Vivien Morton, daughter of the well-known Communist writer and speaker Tommy Jackson, remembers that coming to Summerhill was 'like walking into paradise'. For Cyril Eyre, who infuriated his tutors at Oxford by throwing up a very promising career as an atomic scientist, Neill 'opened up a whole new world'. Even Geoffrey Cox, who was not a communist, and quickly had some reservations about the school, was initially beguiled by the Summerhill way of life: 'My first spontaneous reaction was one of delight in its atmosphere of freedom and life. I felt myself to be in a marvellous sunlit place of freedom where people could try to be themselves.'

Several of these teachers came from Oxford and Cambridge, centres of left-wing activity which provided many Party members or sympathisers. Richard Goodman, a student poet and already a Marxist, had been the editor of the student magazine *Oxford Outlook* in 1932, the year in which a debate in the Union resulted in a majority support for a motion asserting that 'in socialism lies the only solution to the problems facing this country'. Ten years earlier, in Cambridge, Leslie Morton was active politically in the small university Labour Club. He and other undergraduates later became members of the Communist Party, but at this time were working to change Labour Party policies. Three others who belonged to this group were also attracted to Neill's school, and sent their children there. One was J. D. ('Sage') Bernal, a highly intelligent polymath of great imagination and originality, who specialised in physics and crystallography.* He visited Russia many times, and helped to found a communist cell in Cambridge, in an attempt to bring the Party more intellectual respectability. Bernal was introduced to the works of Marx and Lenin by another member of the Cambridge group, Allen Hutt. A distinguished newspaper typographer, a writer on Labour history, and for many years chief sub-editor on the Party newspaper the *Daily Worker* (on which both Leslie Morton and Richard Goodman later worked), Hutt sent his daughter Jenny to Summerhill in 1930. The third member of the group to send his child there, Ivor Montagu, was involved in the workers' film movement in the early 1930s, founded the Progressive Film Institute, and became an expert on film censorship.

Neill, then, found himself with a substantial proportion of Communist Party members on his staff – Cyril Eyre, Bronwen Jones and the art teacher Paxton Chadwick also belonged – and several parents who, if not actually CP members, were of a left-wing persuasion. Yet, despite his enthusiasm for the Russian experiment, Neill himself never joined. Johnnie Collier remembers: 'Neill travelled a not very serious political road, veering towards and then away from the Party. Sometimes he nearly joined, sometimes he was outraged by some report from the Soviet Union. He used to read Claud Cockburn's paper *The Week,* and was sometimes impressed by

---

*A bookshop assistant in Cambridge called him 'Sage', and the nickname stuck.

something he read there. My memory is that he once approached D. N. Pritt to get advice about joining.'*

Neill had some sympathies too with the Independent Labour Party, which, after the rise of the Labour Party, had become more of a refuge for middle-class socialists than the working-class movement it had set out to be. Fenner Brockway, one of the ILP leaders of the post-war years, recalls: 'There is warmth inside me when I think of Neill... we all admired his school, and had continued association with him.' Brockway invited Neill to write a piece on Summerhill, which appeared in September 1933 in the Party's lively weekly the *New Leader,* 'a propaganda sheet for the factory floor'. The previous year at the ILP Summer School in Monmouth, the *New Leader* had noted: 'Great interest was aroused by the visit of A. S. Neill, the famous author of *The Problem Parent* and the head of Summerhill School. His subject was "The Free School".'

Yet Neill did not join the ILP either. He never had any lasting enthusiasm for party politics. During his days as a young teacher he was mildly sympathetic to the Tory cause. In Kettle, during the 1906 general election, he helped the local party to distribute circulars – perhaps less as a result of conviction than because of his friendship with his landlord and the village minister, both of them Tories. In Dundee two years later, during a famous by-election, he threw a tomato at the successful Liberal candidate, Winston Churchill – principally, he later alleged, because the pretty daughter of the Tory agent had dared him to do so. He steered clear of politics at university, and it was only when he came to London and joined the Labour Party in 1913 that he briefly took a serious interest in party political matters. In Gretna, under the influence of Wells and Shaw, Orage, William Morris and Robert Blatchford, he declared himself a socialist. But once he discovered Freud and psychoanalysis, politics faded into the background.

Ultimately, as Larry Collier observes, 'Neill was obsessed with the politics of Summerhill. He may have been a socialist, but if by sticking his neck out for socialism he was going to jeopardise Summerhill's position, he wasn't going to risk it.' Even while the school was at Lyme, Neill was aware of the potential danger. Early in 1927 he received an 'offer' from the Teachers' Labour League – though what this was for is not clear. He told Russell that he would refuse it: 'The situation is awkward because the secretary Duncan is an old pupil of mine. I must, however, keep clear of all politics.' However, though he stuck to this principle himself, he accepted that others in Summerhill should not be compelled to do so. Cyril Eyre remembers: 'He didn't like people belonging to the Party in so far as it might get his school the reputation of being "red", but he didn't try to ban or dissuade them.' His attitude to the staff's political allegiances is clearly exemplified in a letter he wrote in 1935 to Curry, in connection with

---

The Week was a cyclostyled broadsheet, edited by Claud Cockburn – who wrote for the *Daily Worker* – and read by the intellectual middle classes. D. N. Pritt was a distinguished lawyer and Labour MP, dismissed from the Labour Party because of his communist sympathies.

Richard Goodman's application for a job at Dartington: 'Goodman was without punning a good man. Kids like his teaching, and I like his energetic part in community life. Very Left in politics, but that toned down after a time. I mean he ceased to show it in school life.' Yet some outsiders were not always able to see the distinction between Neill and his staff on such matters. Arthur Calder-Marshall, for example, in reviewing *That Dreadful School* in *Time and Tide* in April 1937, asserted: 'Though he gives no political instruction at his school, Mr Neill is a communist. The atmosphere of Summerhill is Communist, and it is obvious that his pupils would be most at home in such a society.'

Just as Neill was determined that children at Summerhill should be free to make their own judgments about matters of religion and morality, so he was concerned that they should be protected from any political 'moulding' by adults. Free education, he believed, must allow a free open mind. It was a matter that he had pondered on during his teaching days in Gretna, where he had an uneasy feeling that he was presenting a one-sided picture of the world to the village children: 'I want these boys and girls to acquire the habit of looking honestly at life,' he wrote in *A Dominie's Log*. 'Ah! I wonder if I look honestly at life myself! Am I not a very one-sided man? Am I not a socialist, a doubter, a heretic? . . . Do I teach my bairns socialism? I do not think so.' In *The Problem Parent* he was still equivocal about the issue: 'I hate giving children any propaganda, yet I think that the socialistic teacher is within his rights if he tries to undo the capitalist state propaganda by giving the other side of the question to his pupils.' By 1933, in writing for the *New Leader,* he was more sure of his ground:

> Now I can be comparatively free from lies in my school. I am free from the flag-waving lie we call patriotism, free from the church lie that man is born in sin. Many teachers cannot get free from such lies. The ideal is *no propaganda* in the school. Many socialist and communist teachers would not subscribe to this. They would substitute socialistic or communistic propaganda. I am all for a war cry of NO PROPAGANDA OF ANY KIND.

This remained his position for the rest of his life. Yet how far was he able to carry out this wish in Summerhill? Many of the staff took a very active part in local politics in Leiston. They were involved in starting up a local monthly newspaper, the *Leiston Leader,* which was bought by nearly half the inhabitants. Paxton Chadwick drew the cartoons, and Neill himself lent a flatbed duplicator for printing the first few numbers. Max Morton remembers: 'We had quite close relations with the working-class chaps in Leiston. Three-quarters of the population were unemployed, and were frequently defrauded of their legal rights. We helped to organise opposition to the dole cuts and the means test.' Activity intensified in 1934, when one of the hunger marches that characterised these years of mass unemployment stopped at nearby Saxmundham, and a well-attended meeting in the Leiston town square provided a valuable impetus to the local branch of the Communist Party.

The children seem to have been involved in some political activity. One visitor recalls seeing a teacher and some children making a banner with the slogan 'Up the Workers' upon it. 'We did a little bit, such as addressing envelopes, and delivering leaflets for a Communist meeting in a field in Leiston,' Cynthia Allen recalls. 'We had tea with Cyril, and were then taken down to the meeting. We couldn't follow it very well, except that at the end we sang the "Internationale' and "The Red Flag" around the fire, and were regaled with mugs of cocoa. This we thought frightfully good fun, especially as it was rather frowned on by Neill.' Neill did once intervene in one of their activities, when the staff got them to distribute copies of the *Daily Worker* – a paper that he himself liked, subscribed to, and had written for on at least one occasion. In the main though he confined himself to theoretical arguments with his staff.

There was perhaps less division between Neill and his Communist colleagues than he later maintained. Towards the end of his life he looked back at the political differences between them:

> I found it very strange having so much support from the Communist Party. I used to say, 'How can you believe in Summerhill and Stalinism?' They would say that Russia was surrounded by its enemies, it had to discipline its people, and that it was only a passing phase. That was a lot of balls.

Yet Neill confessed in later years that he had been slow to appreciate the real nature of Stalinism: 'For years I had a blind spot; I simply would not accept the stories of Stalin's mass murder by starvation of a million or more peasants who would not fit into his state farming scheme.' Certainly, in his *New Era* article of January 1935, he seemed to be advancing precisely the same argument as his staff about the need for a transitional period in the Soviet Union. Looking forward to a greater freedom for the people from central control, he wrote: 'Communism in, say, a hundred years, when it is not in fear of attack from an enemy system, should easily become decentralised.'

Several Summerhill pupils became interested in communism, and some subsequently joined the Party. They too sometimes found themselves in intellectual conflict with Neill. 'Most of us at some time became communists,' Gordon Leff recalls, 'but Neill couldn't understand this. "I don't understand how you can be a communist if you believe in freedom," he would say. We saw Russia in quite a different way then; it took a long time to see that it had become another tyranny.' Johnnie Collier remembers arguing with Neill over this question of loyalty: 'He never seemed to forgive me for not putting my support for Summerhill above my allegiance to the Party. I always felt this to be absurd; I didn't consider the two things were at all related. I didn't think of Summerhill in terms of allegiance.' He and other pupils who espoused communism continued to debate the matter after they had left Summerhill. David Barton, then a communist, wrote Neill a long and critical letter after the war, to which he replied:

You say I accept the newspapers as a father voice. I say that you blokes do it more effectively by seeing right in everything USSR does. Kravchenko may be a neurotic but ALL his book can't be a lie, yet most Party members dismiss him as a bloody Trotskyite.* You must know that Summerhill couldn't possibly exist under communism as it shapes today. . . see our kids salute any flag or portrait?. . . I want communism, i.e. a non-profit society PLUS what Summerhill stands for. . . independence of the individual. How you after a life at Summerhill can approve of the USSR telling musicians what they musn't compose, I dunno. . . . My new book. . . I fear will give the impression that I am an anti-communist bloke. So that when der Tag comes you may be commanded to shove me up against the Cottage wall and say Fire.†

Like other socialists of the day, Neill was involved in the fight against Fascism which, as Hitler and Mussolini rose to power, became the preoccupation of so many people during the 1930s. His three years in Europe had given him some glimpses of the Fascist mentality. In Dresden and Vienna he had witnessed the anti-semitism already visible in everyday life. In the mid-1930s he stood in a large crowd in the Tempelhof in Berlin, and listened to a speech of 'roaring hate' from Hitler. In Hanover he refused to give the Nazi salute to a troop of SS men, and had an uncomfortable moment while his passport was carefully checked. The nationalism inherent in such behaviour was anathema to him; his experience in Germany and Austria had convinced him of the importance of an internationalist outlook. Fascism, he recognised, was a philosophy that depended on a fear of authority, and for that reason alone was one to be opposed.

Given the outlook both of Neill and the teachers and parents involved with Summerhill, it was inevitable that the school should become the centre of a good deal of anti-Fascist activity. 'Finish with Dutt's *Fascism*, send it back, crowd waiting to read it,' Neill wrote to Curry in October 1934. 'Read *Hitler Over Europe* for a good analysis: top hole.' Books were a powerful weapon in the fight against Fascism, and the Left Book Club was the principal means by which people of many classes made themselves familar with the issues. Founded in 1936 by the publisher Victor Gollancz, the LBC had 6,000 members before it had published a book, 20,000 within six months, and nearly 60,000 by the spring of 1939; a significant proportion were school teachers. It published a number of polemical, up-to-date works by writers such as Arthur Koestler, George Orwell, R. H. Tawney, Leonard Woolf, André Malraux. The Club also issued a 'monthly choice'

---

*Victor Kravchenko, a Soviet official and member of the Party since 1929, defected to the USA in April 1944, in protest against Stalin's failure to grant political and civil liberties to the Russian people. His revealing descriptions of life inside Russia were published in *I Chose Freedom* in 1947.

†Neill claimed that the editor of the *Daily Worker* had said before the war that, if communism came to England, 'the first thing we would do is to shut Summerhill'. This seems an unlikely priority.

of which two of the many books were Leslie Morton's *A People's History
of England* and Allen Hutt's *The Post-War History of the British Working
Class*. The Club was Communist dominated, although Gollancz himself
was not a Party member. Neill met him only once, at a pro-China rally in
Ipswich during the LBC's heyday: Gollancz himself regarded Neill as 'one
of the great pioneers of educational reform, and as a leading fighter for a
liberal and humane approach to the individual.'

But Neill was prepared to do more than merely read about fascism.
During the 1930s many Jewish refugees came from Europe to England and
America, and a number of them found shelter in pioneer schools such as
Beacon Hill and Summerhill. Neill's precarious financial position made it
hard for him to be as much help as he would have liked, as he pointed out
in a letter to Curry in February 1937:

> Any use for a German teacher of about 50, an expert in brass
> repousse work? I knew him years ago in Dresden. He came to see
> me some time ago with a terrible story of persecution from the Nazis
> – he is no Jew, only pacifist – and implored me to take him on for a
> bit to escape the hell out there. . . . I pay him £1 a week, and ten
> shillings for his lodgings out. I simply can't afford to keep him: I
> have two handworkers already, loads of unpaid fees, rising prices,
> no I can't do it. I've little hope that you'll want him, damn little, so I
> won't try to shove his qualities on top of the basket. Where can I
> park him anyway? Know any anti-German organisations that might
> help him to stay in this land?

Two of the women who came to Summerhill in the late 1930s were
also able to escape from the Nazis with Neill's assistance. During a trip to
Norway Neill met Erna Gal, a talented Austrian musician, and invited her
to come and teach music at Summerhill. 'I was surprised but delighted,'
she remembers, 'because they wouldn't renew my visa in Norway: the
Nazis were already sitting in the passport office, and I had on my passport
the big J for Jew.' The arrival of Ilse Rolfe was even more dramatic. In
1939 she had been in a Nazi concentration camp for three years, along
with her parents; four years later her mother was to die in the gas chambers.
She was, by chance, already familiar with Neill's ideas: 'At one time in the
camp we had still been allowed to have books sent to us, and my sister
sent me *Is Scotland Educated?* I couldn't read English, but a fellow-prisoner
who spoke it fluently had heard about Neill, and translated it for me. Later,
I was called one day and told I could go, as a permit had arrived for me
to work in England, and the Gestapo were prepared to release anyone with
such a document.' Her sister had met Neill in Oslo, and asked him to find
her a job; Neill had duly applied for a permit, saying he could use some
domestic help, and had thus secured her release from the camp.

The political activity in Summerhill was naturally of interest to the
children there. Branwen Williams recalls: 'Although we were fairly isolated
from the local community, we were not isolated from what was going on
in Spain and Germany. I hadn't the faintest idea of what was going on in

England, but I had in Europe, and that was through Neill and others on the staff.' Activities intensified after the outbreak of the Spanish Civil War in the summer of 1936, which threw both individuals and political parties in Britain into such confusion. The fight between the Republican government and the forces of General Franco who aimed to overthrow it was, in Stephen Spender's words, 'one of those intervals in history in which events make the individual feel that he counts'. There was a feeling that the Civil War was a rehearsal for a future war with Hitler and Mussolini, who gave support to Franco; the Russians gave backing to the Republicans, amongst whom were many communist groups. The left espoused the Republican cause, while the government followed a policy first of neutrality and then non-intervention. Writers, musicians and working men joined the International Brigade to fight on the Republican side. Others were invited to choose sides: *Left Review* sent out a questionnaire to over 150 artists and writers, asking: 'Are you for, or against, the legal government and the people of Republican Spain? Are you for, or against, Franco and Fascism?' Of those who replied, 127 supported the Republicans, 16 – including Shaw – put themselves in the category 'Neutral?', and 5 – including Evelyn Waugh and the poet Edmund Blunden – opposed the government.

Though he made little explicit reference to Spain in his books and letters, Neill, had he been asked, would certainly have put himself amongst the Republican supporters. Several of those around him were involved in different ways in the war in Spain, or as active supporters of the Republican cause. Ivor Montagu, one of the initiators of the *Left Review* questionnaire, helped to produce *In Defence of Madrid,* a film made for the Communist Party and widely shown in Britain. During this time there was a burst of activity from left theatre groups, which specialised in short plays or pageants on social and political issues to the labour movement. One of the best known groups was Unity Theatre, in which Miles Malleson was closely involved: at least two of their summer schools were held at Summerhill. One man who came with Unity was the scientist J. B. S. Haldane, who wrote for the *Daily Worker*. He was one of many involved in programmes for medical aid to help the Spanish people; another was his fellow-scientist J. D. Bernal, who was also active in the efforts to promote a 'Popular Front'. Another parent, Jimmy Shand, broadcast on Radio Madrid as the Voice of Republican Spain, and financed a ship to take refugees to Mexico.*

Two Summerhill children, Frances and Martin Green, came specifically because of their parents' involvement in the Civil War. George Green was driving an ambulance for the Republicans, and decided to join the International Brigade. His wife Nan joined him in Spain to become an administrator with the IB, and their children's fees at Summerhill were paid by Wogan Phillips, an old Etonian gentleman farmer who was one of the early members of the Communist Party in Britain. 'It was the only place I could think of where having no father or mother around wouldn't matter,' Nan

---

*A wealthy dog-track owner, he once took a taxi from Marseilles to Boulogne to rescue three of his son's friends who fought on the Republican side.

Green recalled. George Green went missing on the last day of fighting, though his death was not confirmed for six months. Nan Green came back alone from Spain, and helped to organise meetings for Spanish Aid. A fête was held in the hockey field at Summerhill to raise money for this purpose. During one Unity Theatre Summer School an ambulance was paraded in the grounds. A converted Rolls-Royce, it was alleged to have come from the front in Spain, complete with the bullet-holes in its sides made by the guns of Franco's army. Neill and Mrs Lins also gave help to several refugee children, many of whom came to England after the bombing of the village of Guernica. Some came to tea at Summerhill, others played football against the boys there, and one or two, including the daughter of the Spanish Ambassador, were taken in as pupils without charge.

Though all these activities made it quite clear where Neill's sympathies lay, it seems he himself played very little direct part in them. In the same way, his letters of the time make only terse references to the increasingly tense international situation; usually he is more preoccupied with personal problems, or the 'politics of Summerhill'. In March 1938, in the week that Hitler marched into Austria, and with the British government maintaining their policy of non-intervention in Spain, Neill wrote to a friend: 'Austria and Spain seem so terribly important that it sounds silly to write about myself. We are all furious about Austria and still more furious at Chamberlain and Co, who are really Fascists.' His view about political developments in England became increasingly gloomy during the years immediately before the outbreak of the Second World War. In October 1938 he felt: 'Everything points to England going Fascist now', and the following month he told Curry: 'What a bloody world! I feel depressed, for with a castrated Labour Party, I see nothing ahead of us but some sort of Fascism.' He concluded that: 'This generation is doomed. . . it will have to go through Fascism before it comes conscious of what is going on in society.'

In September 1938, as the Munich crisis developed, the country appeared to be on the threshold of war. Trenches were dug in the London parks, 38 million gas masks were distributed, air-raid sirens were tested over the radio, the first home blackouts were devised, and preparations were made to evacuate children from the cities. The mobilisation of the British fleet, and the fact that the crisis had blown up with such speed, caused a tremendous psychological shock to the British people. Only a month before the Home Secretary had been walking in canvas shoes and open shirt on the beach at Southwold, just up the coast from Aldeburgh, with no apparent thought of a crisis. Summerhill's position on the east coast made it highly vulnerable to any potential attack or invasion – it was here that the first German raids had been carried out during the First World War. Neill was in considerable doubts as to what action he should take. Dora Russell had agreed to accommodate the school at Beacon Hill, and at the height of the crisis he wrote to her: 'Oh it is so difficult to know when to act. If this meeting ends in the usual double-cross of C. Slovakia we'll have respite from scare for a few months. Our present position is that if war breaks out we begin to come to you by cars and coaches. To do so now at big expense would be awkward if war was postponed.' When a few days later Chamberlain flourished his agreement with Hitler as a guarantee of 'peace in our time', few people were confident it would be so. A week after the agreement Neill observed: 'Chamberlain's criminality to C. Slovakia will make us more easy to attack in the future.'

The Munich agreement provided only a few months' respite from war. On 23 August 1939, Germany and Soviet Russia signed a non-aggression pact. 'Like most people in England I am perplexed and troubled: I do not know what it means,' Neill wrote that week. 'My Communist friends say that this is Russia's way of undermining Fascism, but it might as well be Russia's way of crushing British and French imperialism and capitalism.' Stalin's agreement to remain neutral if Germany became involved in war came as an immense shock to all on the left in British politics. There were rumours that the Communist Party might be outlawed and arrests made. Neill saw the danger to Summerhill, called his staff together, and persuaded them to call a halt to all political activities within the school. Mrs Lins, holidaying in America, hurried back, and was shocked to find trenches being dug in the school grounds. On 3 September Britain's ultimatum to Germany over her invasion of Poland expired, and she entered the war. On the same day the children returned for the new term.

CHAPTER 14

Wilhelm Reich

Love, work and knowledge
are the well-springs
of our life.

They should also govern it.

I wish I could give up the school for a year and come back to you.
Letter to Wilhelm Reich, November 1938

I was lecturing at Oslo University, and after the lecture my chairman said, 'You had a distinguished man in your audience tonight: Wilhelm Reich.' 'Good God,' I said, 'I was reading his *Mass Psychology of Fascism* on the ship.' I phoned Reich and he invited me to dinner. We sat talking till late and I was fascinated. 'Reich,' I said, 'you are the man I have been searching for for years.'

This meeting led to a friendship which had a momentous effect on Neill's intellectual and emotional life. Reich was already a highly controversial figure when the two men first met in the winter of 1935. Born and brought up in the pre-war Austrian Empire, after the war Reich studied medicine at the University of Vienna. He was a brilliant and energetic student; and after attending a lecture on psychoanalysis in his second year, he decided to devote his life to psychiatry. He had the rare privilege of being allowed to join the Vienna Psychoanalytic Society while still an undergraduate. He continued to study psychoanalysis in Vienna after graduating in medicine, at a time when Neill was battling with the Austrian authorities over his mountain-top school at Sonntagsberg.*

Reich did a great deal of work in the free mental health clinics which he had helped to found in the poorer parts of Vienna. He became convinced

*His first paper was on a topic that would have interested Neill: 'Ibsen's *Peer Gynt*, Libido Conflicts and Hallucinations'.

that the psychological problems of the working-class men and women who attended these clinics could be ascribed to the repressive attitude towards sex then prevalent. He hoped to be analysed by Freud himself; but, having apparently considered breaking his rule of not analysing any member of his own Viennese circle, Freud eventually refused to help him in this way. Reich took this as a personal rejection. He remained interested in Freud's ideas, but diverged on matters of technique: he was, for example, the first analyst to believe in the need to treat patients by interpreting their character rather than analysing their dreams and associations. This break with Freud, and other differences that arose between Reich and his fellow-analysts, led to his expulsion from the International Psychoanalytical Association in 1934.

Reich believed that this expulsion was principally due to his increasing interest in relating psychoanalysis to its social and political context. As a student in Vienna he had been part of a circle which found Marxism a topic for passionate discussion in the wake of the Russian Revolution. In 1928 he joined the Austrian Communist Party, and was one of the original founders of the Socialist Society for Sex Consultation and Sexological Research. He was actively involved with the Society's sex hygiene clinics, which gave free information on birth control, child-rearing, and sex education for children and adolescents. He visited Russia in 1929 and observed the new child-care centres and kindergartens, but disliked the moralistic attitudes about childhood sexuality, which he thought little different from those in capitalist countries.

In 1930 he moved to Berlin, and founded the German Association for Proletarian Politics, which campaigned for the abolition of laws against homosexuality and abortion, better housing conditions for the masses, reform of the marriage and divorce laws, and other measures. The growth of the Association alarmed the leaders of the German Communist Party, who feared that work in the mental hygiene clinics would divert its members from more explicitly political and revolutionary aims. Reich was officially excluded from the Party in 1933, the year he published his *Mass Psychology of Fascism* which so impressed Neill two years later.

For the next six years Reich lived in Scandinavia. First in Denmark and then in Norway he continued his work, but now on his own, building up a circle of patients and fellow-workers. He developed the technique known as vegetotheraphy. This attempted to break down neuroses by a combination of talk and physical treatment on areas of bodily tension, in which, he argued, these neuroses were contained. Reich believed that sexual repressions could only be overcome if a person's 'character armour' was pierced – an idea which owed a great deal to Freud's belief in 'defence mechanisms', and which Reich outlined in his most widely read book, *Character Analysis*, published in 1933. In an earlier book, *The Function of the Orgasm*, Reich had expressed his belief in the theory that sexual energy builds up in the body, and can only be released by the orgasm, involving the whole body. He believed that if this energy were not released, all kinds of neuroses would occur.

Neill corresponded with Reich for some months, started to read his books, and in November 1937 got Reich to agree to take him on as a patient. 'As you probably know I am called the most advanced child psychologist in the country', he wrote, 'but I realise that I can learn much from you, and I think it splendid that you are giving me the opportunity to come and do so. Your *Character-Analyse* is the finest thing I have come across for many years.' However advanced Neill may have been in his work with children, he was in a state of some turmoil in his emotional life, and this was causing him physical distress. He already had plenty of experience of mental stress leading to physical disorder. His breakdown while waiting to go to fight in France during the war was not the only example of this. Almost from the start of his career as a young teacher, during which he was inwardly rebelling against the system he was forced to serve, he had been severely constipated, and suffered from migraine headaches. The log-books of Kingskettle, Newport and Gretna show him absent through sickness rather more frequently than his fellow-teachers – and once he was taken ill on the train on his way to start a new term in Gretna. In *A Dominie's Log* he wrote: 'I have not used the strap all this week, and if my liver keeps well, I hope to abolish it altogether.' And in *A Dominie Dismissed*: 'I am quite sure that physical courage is primarily dependent on physical health. If my liver is out of order I tremble to open a letter.' He had evidently not shaken off the fears and anxieties of his youth, and worry and stress seem easily to have affected his physical health.

In 1929 he became seriously ill. For three months he had been suffering from pyelitis, a disorder of the kidney, which was now deteriorating rapidly. In addition he had developed lumbago, was suffering severe pain in his left side, and had poor circulation and infected urine. Orthodox medicine had no effect, and he became desperate. Showing signs of nervous stress about his condition, he went to Edinburgh for an appointment with a highly unorthodox practitioner. James Thomson, an angular red-headed Scot born in the same county as Neill, had built up an established nature cure practice, founding the Edinburgh School of Natural Therapeutics with his wife Jessie. A Fabian and a suffragette, she had opened a clinic in the house, to offer nature cure treatment to children of poor families. The Thomsons had a special interest in food reform, an interest shared by Mrs Lins; two years before Jessie had published *A Healthy Childhood*. Neill had met the Thomsons in 1923, when they had offered him a bed after one of his early lectures; he had become friendly with the family, and stayed there when he occasionally came north to visit his mother and father.

James Thomson recommended a drastic treatment along nature cure lines. Neill went on a wholly vegetarian diet – plenty of raw greens to eat, buttermilk to drink. For nine weeks he had manipulation and massage, exercise in the gymnasium, and hydro-therapy. Though his condition was serious, he retained his sense of humour, as one friend of the Thomsons, Sheila Chesters, remembers: 'Neill had a saintly, almost fragile porcelain look, with even his voice speaking as if from a distance. J.C., with his usual flamboyance, had seen a large harp going cheap at a sale, had bought it, and then insisted that his daughter should take it up to Neill. I remember the thistledown edition of Neill coming through the doorway; he stopped, looked at the harp, said gently, "Have I got to heaven?", and grinned wanly.' Thanks to the Thomsons, Neill remained firmly in this world. The treatment produced a remarkable change in his condition: the constipation disappeared, his urine cleared up, and his energy returned. More importantly, the kidney deterioration was halted, and Neill was restored to a state of reasonable health.

This episode convinced Neill that the unorthodox ideas of nature cure should be taken seriously, and for the rest of his life he returned regularly to the Thomsons when he felt in need of a 'cleansing' for his system.* However, the kind of self-denial demanded by the nature cure regime did not come at all easily to him – although since his student days he had regularly taken a cold bath in the morning. His natural inclination was to indulge his taste for rich and often unhealthy food, especially cakes and pastries. He smoked cigarettes, and in between them brought out the pipe he had adopted in imitation of Barrie, and the John Cotton tobacco for which he had a particular liking. He liked to drink beer, wine and liqueurs, but had a special liking for whisky; it was a mark of approval of a friend or visitor when Neill brought the bottle out of his cupboard. Yet he remained a moderate drinker, seeing whisky as 'a good servant at night but a bad master next morning'. His appetite was also tempered by what he had seen of the effects of alcohol in his youth when whisky was three shillings a bottle.

Neill's spells at the Thomsons' clinic left him feeling fitter and refreshed. They were enough to persuade him that the practices of orthodox medicine, with its drugs, and its treatment of symptoms rather than causes, were 'the equivalents of the cane, the moral lecture, the prison in education', since they failed to touch the deep causes of illness and behaviour. Yet it was a decided effort for him to resist temptations of various kinds between his visits to Edinburgh. Although he tried all sorts of ploys for giving up tobacco – such as leaving his pipe and his pouch in different parts of the school – he was never able to do so. Sometimes on his way up to Edinburgh he would stay with his sister Hilda, at Muirlands Farm near Forfar, and spend some while with a pumice stone trying to get rid of the nicotine stains on his fingers. With drink there were similar lapses. At the end of his tour of South Africa, during which he had too many drinks and too little exercise, he found his urine was like mud, and felt 'a dying man' as he boarded the ship; but a six-day fast quickly restored him to health by the time he arrived in England. As for his diet, Neill would for a while stick to the salads and other health foods recommended by the clinic; but then one day he would be discovered making his mark in a cake or a pie. Often he would rationalise his fall from grace by referring to his father's longevity on a lifetime's diet of white bread, potatoes and Scottish teacakes.

*In 1938, the Thomsons moved to larger premises on the outskirts of Edinburgh, where they opened the Kingston Clinic. Neill continued to visit there after J. C. Thomson's death, when the clinic was taken over by his son Leslie.

Neill was attracted from the beginning by Reich's attempts to link the 'soma' and the 'psyche'. Ostensibly he was going to visit him to talk about *The Sexual Revolution*, of which Reich had recently sent him a copy on its publication. 'Reich's latest book is fascinating but so difficult for me to read that I want to get it in English from him,' he explained to Constance Tracey, a Summerhill parent and friend who was already undergoing analysis with Reich. Yet Neill evidently had more pressing personal reasons for requesting 'a few talks' with Reich. Although Mrs Lins had wanted to accompany him, he made it clear that he wanted to get some 'perspective', and preferred to go by himself: 'I want to be entirely on my own, with no feeling of duty or responsibility except to myself,' he told Constance Tracey. He then referred, as he tended to do with some regularity, to the uphill struggle of pioneering work, suggesting that Mrs Lins 'has gone stale also, and we carry on with too much effort. Both get so discouraged by setbacks.' Reich, in agreeing to take Neill on for what were clearly going to be vegetotherapy sessions rather than discussions about his ideas, thought that the reason for Neill's staleness could be found in 'the contradiction between the tremendous pioneer needs and the complete hopelessness of our great time under which we are suffering.'

If that was how it seemed to Reich after just one evening's conversation with Neill, he was soon to get a more detailed view of Neill's problems, and to discover that by no means all of them were connected with pioneering. Despite his previous analyses, Neill was still not at ease in his emotional life. 'He couldn't demonstrate affection,' Gordon Leff recalls, 'he could only do it by a joke, or in the way that a cat might switch his tail against you. If you came to see him after you had left Summerhill, he was terribly pleased to see you, but he could only gruffly thrust out a hand, and not look at you.' This was a common perception of those who knew him in his school; many remember him as being remote, aloof, even brusque. 'I never saw him express any warmth, or put his arm round any child,' Tom Hackett recalls. Nona Simon, who was virtually brought up in Summerhill as a member of Neill's family, recalls: 'He just wasn't a warm person, or someone you wanted to go up and throw your arms around.' Yet others, such as Branwen Williams, saw him very differently: 'I think his dour mask belied his real character. He was a poor propagandist for himself, and had some difficulty in getting across the warmth that was in him.' Neill had very few close relationships with either sex, but a few people, in particular the more extrovert type of girl or woman, seem to have been able to get him to lower this mask, though it was invariably they who had to take the initiative. Virginia Pilkington was one pupil who got more of an emotional response from him than most: 'He was a very warm, tactile man, and would always put his arm round you,' she remembers. 'I was very emotionally attached to him, and I think he was fond of me, though I didn't realise until I had left how much.'

Neill undoubtedly found most difficulty in coping with the emotional demands of adults. Perhaps this was a necessary corollary of his acknowledged capacity to emphathise with children, that he never quite mastered the art of moving easily in the complex adult world. One view, expressed by Johnnie Collier, was that Neill was only comfortable in carefully structured situations or relationships: 'At home he was the one who was told what to do. When he was in an everyday situation with Mrs Lins, it was she who "managed" it. When he was teaching or producing plays, or holding a Private Lesson, *he* was in control. As long as the situation was "set up" in this way, and emotional uncertainty avoided, Neill could relax. Then a sort of impersonal relationship of equality could be achieved: he was neither arrogant nor timid, but warm and friendly.' There is plenty of evidence that, when he saw choppy emotional waters ahead, Neill did all he could to take evasive action. His policy of non-interference in the greater part of the running of Summerhill was certainly as much a matter of temperament and instinct as a consequence of his belief in freedom for the child. Indeed, it is hard to know where one ended and the other began.

Reich, then, had no simple task on his hands in taking on Neill as a patient. For two weeks around Christmas time 1937, Neill had ten or twelve therapy sessions with him. He returned for a longer period the following year, and paid his last visit as a patient in April 1939. Although he left no detailed record of these sessions, he did make occasional references to specific incidents in his letters and books. It appears Reich unlocked some violent emotions – later Neill referred to the 'terrible weepings and angers' that came out as Reich 'tore me to pieces on his sofa'. At first he resisted Reich's attempts to do something about his stiff neck. When Reich suggested that he was repressing a lot of hate and anger, Neill replied that he found it difficult to hate, and declined the suggestion that he should hit Reich to release some of this repressed anger. Then came a turning point, as Neill later related: 'Finally I got furious. I sat up and looked him in the eye. "Reich," I said, "I have just discovered something. I have discovered that I don't believe a bloody word you say. I don't believe in your muscle theory one bit. You are a sham." I lay down on the sofa again, and Reich touched the back of my neck. "Good Lord," I said, "the pain's gone." "Yes," said Reich, "and so has the stiffness." ' Reich was also able to loosen Neill's stomach muscles, a fact which enabled him to accept Reich's ideas more readily – and to read his books more easily. Later he pondered on this moment: 'I had found something very vital, namely that I was allowing my petty ego to stand in the way of my progress. It was one of the most important discoveries of my life.'

Neill confessed to Reich that he found it difficult, even shameful, to have to learn new things from a man some fifteen years his junior. There is a hint in this of a characteristic in his make-up which Reich alighted upon, and Neill accepted as a failing. After his first visit to Oslo Neill told Reich that he was 'very conscious of the Narcism (sic), and able to smile at its signs when they appear.' It was not the first time he had referred to this trait in himself, and he did indeed show signs of this type of vanity. In its mildest form it was apparent, at least for some while, in his rather studied attitude to his appearance. From a somewhat self-conscious dandyism before the war, this had now changed to a rugged casualness. It was also apparent that he consistently rated his talents in certain fields rather higher than others were prepared to. He was, for instance, thoroughly proud of his dancing skills: 'I can still dance as fleetly and as rhythmically as I did in Sonntagsberg with Sepp at the piano and Nushy Rott my partner,' he informed Angus Murray, his ex-pupil from Austria, a short while after his sixty-third birthday. He was equally sure, with rather more justification, of his theatrical talents; 'I act well,' he assured a friend. He was also convinced, in spite of his many critics among the pupils in Summerhill, of his effectiveness as a teacher of maths. When some of the more academically inclined pupils told him he was hopeless, he became quite upset. Yet those who noticed his vanities were amused rather than irritated or angered by them. Even before he went to Reich, Neill was able to disarm criticism by indulging in self-mocking comments on such foibles.

One of the crucial matters which emerged from the sessions with Reich was that of Neill's sexual problems, as is clear from the first letter he wrote to Reich on his return to England at the beginning of 1938:

> So far I am dead. No sex, no interest in work or play, just dull and depressed with frequent headaches. But already I feel a change coming. . . there are good signs. Less afraid of the wife, and more decided about making up my mind. . . .Thanks for much. I long to return again.

The matter on which Neill was hoping to make up his mind was also perhaps the real reason why he sought treatment with Reich in the first place, and why he preferred to go alone rather than take Mrs Lins with him. Neill clearly found it difficult to cope with the absence of sex in their marriage. Despite his confusions and inhibitions, he was clearly not uninterested in sex, and was capable of feeling passionately about women. For many years he had been the focus of attention of a number of young, often attractive and frequently adoring women, many of whom saw him as someone who could free them from the old morality. Cyril Eyre remembers: 'Neill represented freedom, in a time when there was still a terrible hangover of Victorian morals and pressures. For young women he was a torch bearer. He got a great kick out of this adulation, and knew he did – he didn't deceive himself about it.'

In general Neill remained faithful to Mrs Lins; but there was one exception. In the early 1930s Neill fell in love and had an affair with one of the young women who came to Summerhill. Later he described his feelings about having to keep the affair concealed:

> The miserable hole-in-corner business began. I had to lie, inventing trips to London to see my publisher or my agent. We stayed at out-of-the-way hotels, scared that someone we knew would enter the dining-room. On country walks we hid our faces when motor headlights shone on us. We registered at hotels under false names. It was hell, hell and damnation.

His misery increased when Mrs Lins eventually found out about the affair
with 'Helga' (not her real name):

> Weeks of wretched argument and cruel words. I thought of walking
> out and living with my new love. I didn't. . . .To have gone with
> Helga would have wrecked the school. . . . I loved Helga, but not
> enough to sacrifice my work.

In Neill's correspondence with Reich there is no reference to Mrs
Lins's discovery, so that almost certainly it occurred before 1936. Two
years later, however, he was still seeing Helga, though his feelings towards
her were vacillating. 'Helga was on the boat but I had no interest in her at
all. *So eine Gesichte!* [What a business!]' he told Reich in February 1938.
Three months later he wrote in a different vein:

> Helga has been down here for a holiday and I find myself as much
> in love with her as ever, and she with me. I have a wife and a
> school: she has a husband and a child. Hell! *Was kann man
> machen?* [What can one do?] I know that if I were free inside I
> should know *was zu machen, aber* [what to do, but]. . . .

In October he is again uncertain: 'I saw Helga in London and wasn't sure
of my attitude to her. We were on the streets all the time and had to talk
only.' The following month it appears to have been Helga whose feelings
had altered: 'About myself. . . I am always depressed. I want only Helga
but that is impossible. She has now got a sense of loyalty to her husband
and child. *Nichts zu machen, aber das Leben für mich ist sehr sehr leer*
[Nothing to be done, but life for me is very, very empty.]' Throughout this
period, when contact with Helga was sporadic, Neill speaks of his sexual
frustration: 'this sexless life is going to destroy me if I don't settle it soon';
'I have no sex life and feel damned discontented and often hateful'.

It was nearly three years after he went to Reich for treatment before
he was able to bring himself to raise the topic with Mrs Lins, by which
time the relationship with Helga appears to have changed to one of friendship only. 'I arranged things with my wife about having a free life,' he
wrote to Reich in August 1940, 'and thanks to you and your treatment
have ways and means of having a full life with full satisfaction, although,
alas, not with full love as I could have had with Helga.' This decision must
have come as a considerable relief to Neill. Apart from his sexual feelings,
his frustrations had clearly made him feel a bitterness towards Mrs Lins of
which he sometimes felt ashamed. In October 1938 he told Reich: 'I am in
a bad mood myself. Full of hate, hating my wife and feeling ashamed to
introduce her to visitors because she looks so old, and then feeling angry
at myself for feeling ashamed.' In *The Problem Teacher*, which he was
working on at this time, he wrote with obvious feeling: 'Married life is not
synonymous with love life, marriage is the greatest obstacle love can meet,
for marriage involves permanency, and love cannot be made permanent by
law: love should be free.'

One of Reich's injunctions to Neill in relation to sex was, 'Give yourself, let go.' On his return from his third visit around Easter 1939, imbued with a 'great feeling of power and potency', he seems to have made an effort to do this. His first attempt was, however, unsuccessful. That summer a young attractive Danish woman with a very strong personality and an unhappy marriage came to stay at Summerhill for a few weeks. Neill was greatly attracted to her and, to her embarrassment, told her he was in love with her. She was, however, already interested in someone else, and preferred not to get involved. However, he was soon able to report back to Reich in more optimistic mood: 'My own affairs go fairly well. My reflex is not as good as it was, possibly mainly because I have not "love" to perfect it. . . . I do not feel one bit neurotic'. He had, he told Reich, found 'an attractive friend'; and to a former pupil he remarked at about this time: 'Do you know, sex is a marvellous thing, I hadn't realised till now how lovely it is.' Neill could not have been given a more convincing demonstration of Reich's theory of the link between bodily tensions and sexual well-being. In January 1940 he wrote in gratitude to Reich: 'I know that I am infinitely more relaxed and less afraid than I was before I went to you. My headaches have gone away completely. I believe completely in your method.'

There is no doubt that Reich's vegetotherapy gave Neill considerable help in enabling him to express feelings which he had hitherto kept contained. 'I got more emotional release in a few weeks than I ever had with Lane, Maurice Nicoll, Stekel,' he wrote later of his time in Oslo. Part of that release clearly came from being able to recall long-forgotten childhood memories, and in doing so to experience again the emotions he went through at the time. It was almost certainly as a direct outcome of his analysis with Reich that Neill decided to set down a long and detailed account of his childhood and youth, which was later to form the first part of his autobiography, *Neill! Neill! Orange Peel!* For the first time, Neill was able to look with some detachment at the traumas of his childhood, and in particular at the nature of his relationship with his parents which, as analysts before Reich had explained to him, had been so crucial in leading him to the creation of Summerhill.

However, it was not merely the coming of Reich into his life that enabled him to write with such vivid candour of his childhood days. Neill's mother had died in 1934, at the age of 79. In November 1937, just as he was fixing up his initial series of 'talks' with Reich, he heard that his father, now living in retirement in Forfar, had for the first time in his life called a doctor to his house. While Neill travelled up to Scotland, his sister May was already at their father's bedside: 'He knew he was dying, and he arranged his own funeral and everything else,' she recalls. 'He had lost his speech, but he wrote everything out. The doctor had left him some pills to take, but he knew that Allie was on the road, and he said he wasn't going to take them until he came.' Ironically, Neill had by now achieved a position akin to the favourite son of the family – Willie had died at the age of 44, after spending years in a profession he never enjoyed. By now, Neill wrote, he had overcome his fear of his father, and had even come to love him: 'His ambitions for us had long since gone, and he accepted us as we were.' Neill's brother-in-law, Keith Fife, remembers Neill having long talks with his father on his visits to Scotland. 'Allie was devoted to his parents,' he remembers. 'Mr Neill also thought a lot of Allie; and he changed his ideas about education completely in later years.'

Whether Neill's father went as far as actually to approve of what Neill was doing at Summerhill seems doubtful. It seems more likely that both he and his wife were pleased and satisfied that their apparently good-for-nothing son had after all 'got on', even if the path he had chosen seemed a peculiar one to them. What is clear is that, while they were still alive, Neill was certainly unwilling and perhaps unable to make any substantial public criticism of his father. At times he even wrote quite benevolently of him, confining his severe criticisms to the system in which his father had been compelled to work. He dedicated *A Dominie's Log* to his 'former dominie', attributing his love of freedom to the 'free life' to be found in the Kingsmuir village school, 'where the bairns chatted and were happy' – a rather different vision of his classroom experience from that which he was to set down a quarter of a century later in *Neill! Neill! Orange Peel!*. Similarly, in 1931 he wrote a lengthy piece in the *Scots Magazine* entitled 'My Schooldays', some of which he later drew upon for his autobiography. The earlier version is considerably more muted in its criticisms; indeed, Neill seems to be almost approving of a system which meant that 'boys who were carving names on the desk learned unconsciously the multiplication table, or spelling, or the rivers of Spain'. He even went as far as to declare: 'I am glad that my school was a Scots village one.' And he ended the piece on a personal note: 'To my mother and father, both still alive, I owe so very much.' Yet not until they were both dead was he able to spell out in detail the very ambivalent nature of that debt. Nor was he ever really able to escape from the shadow of his father's authority, as he told the writer Edward Blishen in his later years:

> I'm in thrall to my father, and always have been. To this day I care what people say about me because I think of my father reading it, and so if they say anything bad about me, I would be sorry, because my father would think, 'He's no good, I was right.' And every time anyone says anything good about me, I feel like saying, 'There you are, dad.'

Immediately after his first trip to Norway, Neill started to apply Reich's theory to his own work, as he reported in *The Problem Teacher*:

> When the child is corrected morally he stiffens his stomach. I took that with a large grain of salt when I first heard it from Reich, but on examining the small children at Summerhill I was astonished to find that the ones who had been brought up without morality had soft stomachs, while the children of the religious and moral had stiff stomachs.

He elaborated on his discovery in a letter to Reich in November 1938, after his second spell as his patient:

> Your stomach theory is completely proved by the stomachs of the children here. The repressed ones have stomachs like wooden boards, but children begin to loosen up very quickly, and at once begin to be hateful and savage. They kill off their enemies (family ones) eagerly in the form of cushions and dolls, and I feel sure that their analysis should be only the active one of doing things without any attempt by me to make unconscious things conscious.

Neill's attempts to test the bodily tensions of the children in Summerhill received a mixed reception. Some were amused, others puzzled, a few anxious. Edna Raymond recalls: 'When he came round to prod your stomach you immediately tensed up, and then had a guilty conscience about it.' Neill incorporated his newfound belief into the technique he used in his PLs, as Jean Allen remembers: 'I had to lie on the floor, and he made me breathe deeply. Then he started prodding my stomach, which made me laugh – it struck me as being pretty silly anyway. Then he said, "Now breathe deeply, as though you're having sexual intercourse." Well, I was 13, and had never dreamt of having sexual intercourse, and I thought, What ever is he talking about? So I said, "You mean like this?" and I started panting. "That's right," he said. After that we talked, but it all struck me as being absolutely daft. I thought to myself, I can tell him what I want to without lying on the floor and having my tummy prodded.'

In Norway Reich had suggested to Neill that his attitude towards adolescent sex was an intellectual rather than an emotional one, masking a jealousy of youth. To some extent Neill accepted this analysis. But he resisted Reich's efforts to persuade him to actively approve, rather than merely tolerate, a full sex life for Summerhill adolescents. Though Neill now shared Reich's belief, he argued that in running a school he had to take into account the views of the world outside. He was also realistic enough to see that there was unlikely to be a rapid change in society's attitude to adolescent sexuality:

> When society has a love attitude to sex instead of a fear and hate one, the co-educational school will provide facilities for a sex life for children when they are biologically ready for it, but many wars and revolutions and social re-education will intervene before that time comes.

It was one of the few issues on which Neill compromised his beliefs, putting above them the one thing that mattered to him more – the continuation of his school.

Neill accepted Reich's analysis of social evils virtually wholesale, endorsing, for example, his view that sexual repression was planned and carried out by the capitalist class in order to emasculate the proleteriat, and make it servile to its masters. Here Reich simply synthesised two strands of Neill's own philosophy: the socialism that he had embraced first at

Gretna, and the views on sex and child neuroses to which he had come through his work with problem children. However, like many others subsequently, Neill found it much harder to accept that part of Reich's work which strayed into the realm of science and physics. Influenced by Freud's work on mental energy and the libido, Reich had formulated the idea that there was a tangible and benign form of energy discharged after sexual orgasm, which was present in the atmosphere, could be measured, and had health-giving properties. This energy could be trapped inside specially constructed boxes, known as 'orgone energy accumulators', and consisting of alternating sheets of various metallic and organic substances. A spell sitting inside these telephone-box-style objects could, Reich argued, help to cure both neuroses and diseases, including cancer.

Neill was initially less sceptical about this aspect of Reich's work than he later made out. For a considerable time, the correspondence between the two men dwelt upon Neill's efforts to make a box, despite shortage of materials, his uncertainties about matters of atmosphere, or the time required for a cure to take effect. Erna Gal, a friend of Reich's, remembers Neill's doubts about the accumulator: 'When Reich expounded the idea to me I believed it. At Summerhill I sat in there with a cut finger, and I imagined it working. Neill pondered on Reich's ideas, and often said to me: "I don't know whether to believe in this box business or not. I can't say yes or no, it may be the truth." ' The help that Reich gave Neill appears to have made him more ready to suspend any disbelief he might have had if these novel ideas had originated from another source.

When he first came across Reich's work, Neill thought the notion of character armouring the most important discovery in the field of psychoanalysis since Freud's uncovering of the Unconscious. It was this belief which, even before he started his analysis with Reich, prompted him to circulate a confidential letter to a number of his friends and acquaintances, in the hope of being of practical use to his new 'mentor'. To Curry, one of those who received the circular, he wrote: 'Will you help with this wangle? Just a letter to me dated last September, saying how fine R's psychology is, and asking if his books are translated into English. The letter I can take out to R. Be helpful.' The circular letter read:

Dr Wilhelm Reich, the psychoanalyst, fled from Germany to Oslo, where he has lived for the past few years. He has published many books on psychology, including his brilliant *Massen Psychologie und Fascismus*. It is possibly because of his attack on Fascism that the reactionary forces in Norway are now trying to get his permission to reside in Norway withdrawn at the end of December. His friends in England want to try to help him. We think that if the authorities in Oslo had evidence of his appreciation of his work, they might think twice before they put him out of the country. I myself am so taken with his new book on character analysis that I am going to Oslo to study with him in the Christmas vacation. I am asking as many well-known people as I can to write to him congratulating him on his

books, which are unfortunately all in German so far. If you happen
to know his work, please write him about it. If you haven't read
him, take it from me that he has struck something big and new in
analysis, using patients' bodily movements as a means to get at the
unconscious. . . .I'm asking for much, but the victims of Fascism
require much.*

Neill also made efforts to interest some of his scientific friends in
Reich's work, beginning with Bernal and Haldane, two amongst a younger
group of scientists whom he saw as 'modern in politics and more open-
minded than the psychoanalysts here'. Haldane found it hard to read
Reich's books and, Neill reported, thought his ideas 'too unorthodox'.
Bernal was sceptical, believing that Reich's experiments on energy were
infected with the atmosphere. Eileen Bernal recalls Neill's efforts to persuade her husband of the validity of Reich's work: 'Sage didn't have much
time for the orgone box idea. Neill was saying that there are inexplicable
forces which you can detect under the microscope, which are in the atmosphere; and these are what you get pouring in to you during your sessions
in the box. Sage tried to explain to him that he *had* seen objects moving
about in a random way on a slide, bumping into each other, but it was
simply the Brownian motion. Neill was rather quiet about that. . . he was
the most unscientific person you could imagine.'

Neill concluded that the 'general attitude of the Bernal group is that
your discoveries are nonsense. I daren't try any more of them.' He did,
though, make one more effort in the scientific world, this time with one of
his former literary heroes. Neill had already met H. G. Wells not long
before, and was disappointed to find him irritable and accustomed to
deference — 'a little man with a squeaky voice and an arrogant manner'.
Nevertheless, he was evidently prepared to endure another meeting for the
sake of his friendship with Reich. He asked Reich to send him 'a clear
account of *Bione* so that I can at least explain them to Wells without of
course giving away the inner secrets'. It was Ethel Mannin who had
arranged for the two men to meet. However, the planned lunch had to be
cancelled, as she and Wells had a violent quarrel over some comments
about Wells which she had made in her follow-up to *Confessions and
Impressions*.

Some time later, when Reich had settled in America, Neill tried Wells
again, this time without any outside help. In February 1943 he wrote to
ask him:

Ever heard of Wilhelm Reich? Discoverer of Bions and Orgones.
Doing cancer research in New York now. Opinion of him
divided. . . genius or mountebank. I am no scientist and can't judge.

*To this Curry replied: 'I must confess I have never read a word of Reich, but I am
always prepared to purge my mortal soul to save anybody from Fascism.' The circular
was not included in the published correspondence between Reich and Neill, and there is
no evidence to show whether it had any effect. Reich remained in Norway until the late
summer of 1939.

You are and could. . . .Orthodox science so far has been sceptical, but as it was with Freud and Darwin and Pasteur.

Wells agreed to see the first three issues of Reich's newly founded *International Journal for Sex Economy and Orgone Research*. However, he dismissed the material as 'an awful gabble of competitive quacks', told Neill that 'Reich misuses every other word', and that 'There is not a gleam of fresh understanding in the whole bale'. Neill was annoyed, and told Wells:

> Your Black Out letter might have been written by Colonel
> Blimp. . . .You apply the word 'Quack' to a man whom Freud
> considered brilliant, a man who has slaved for years in a lab seeking
> truth. . . .Your reputation is that of a man who can't suffer fools
> gladly. Apparently you can't suffer sincere research gladly either.

To which Wells replied briefly, 'You call me a Blimp, I call you a sucker.'

To his chagrin, Neill found that Reich was not entirely happy with his efforts to publicise his work in England, believing that few established scientists or psychologists would accept the validity of work so different from their own. Having provided Neill with material to give to Wells, he then scolded him for believing that anything could come of the approach. He told Neill that he did 'not believe in the goodwill of the academic authorities', and berated him for sending his work to Wells and others:

> I really don't care whether my work is known or not, I only care
> about whether what I described is true. I want you to believe what I
> am saying: I don't care. So please, do not send any journals and any
> books any more to anyone. Let people come to you if they wish to.

Even Neill's fervent support of Reich was tested by this apparent ingratitude: 'You really are a most difficult man to help,' he told him. 'You seem to think we are all a lot of damn fools. . . . I grant that my ignorance of science is a handicap: if a scientist like Haldane cannot read and understand *Die Bione*, who can?' He asked Reich, very reasonably, 'You seem to have a phobia that you will always be misunderstood, but why write books if everyone is to misunderstand them?' Reich was indeed extremely intolerant of anyone else's ability to judge his work, and quite convinced that his ideas would be unacceptable. Could Edison, the inventor of the electric light bulb, expect recognition from the manufacturer of gas lamps, his argument ran? Neill, however, clearly identified Reich's struggles with his own, pointing out to him: 'You and I are both ahead of our time (you more than I)'. He assumed, quite illogically, that if Reich could be so self-evidently right in the field of psychology, he must know what he was talking about in the scientific sphere.

The mixture of naïveté and moral strength in Neill, combined with the enormous personal debt which he owed to Reich, helped to sustain the relationship between the two very different pioneers during the war years, when some fundamental disagreements threatened to end their friendship.

But it was to need something more than a mere war to bring to an end what for Neill was probably the most significant relationship of his life.

CHAPTER 15

Disastrous Interlude

> I'd die I think if I hadn't the hope of a rebirth of civilisation in my
> time.
>
> Letter to Lilian Morgans, December 1942

During the months of the 'Phoney War' of 1939 and 1940, as the country
watched apprehensively while Hitler moved through Europe, Neill's moods
had alternated between apprehension, depression and a certain dogged
determination to battle through. Two weeks into the war he wrote to
Reich: 'It isn't easy to concentrate on psychology at a time like this when
one is apt to concentrate on essential primitive things like eating and safety
and sex. . . . From now on I guess I shall have to devote more time to
planting and digging than psychology.' This proved to be the case, though
now he could count on more help. The weekly meeting had decided that
everyone should put in a minimum number of hours working in the garden,
a break with the normal voluntary principle which Neill heartily welcomed.
'We have a works plan, and the kids are doing the garden nobly,' he told
a former student in October 1939. 'The *Stimmung* of the school is better
than it has been for years.' Neill frequently spent seven hours a day in
physical work, much of which centred around the construction of four
air-raid shelters in the grounds. Here he had the valuable help of one of his
parents, J. D. Bernal, an expert on air-raid precautions who was later to
advise the government about the likely impact of the war in the air. Bernal
came down to the school to advise on the construction of the shelters,
which were to be shored up by the method used in mines, and carefully
designed for easy access. Amidst the gathering gloom, Neill retained his

sense of the ridiculous, as is indicated by an entry in Ruth Allen's diary for
1 November 1939: 'I was out in the hockey field today with Rae [a pupil]
looking at the improvements which have been made to the air-raid shelter
there – Neill was at the entrance scooping out some very watery clay into
a bucket and coming up to empty it on the top. "You see we keep a cow
down there," he said confidentially to Rae, as the stuff went plopping on
the ground; and she chuckled with great appreciation.'

During these autumn weeks there was plenty to unsettle the occupants
of Summerhill. Lorries full of soldiers passed along the Harwich–Lowestoft
road which ran past the school – 'We seem to be short of everything except
soldiers,' one of the younger girls remarked. Searchlights from the neighbouring town of Saxmundham cut across the night sky. The blackout came
into operation and, though Neill had feared that some of his problem
children might act irresponsibly over the use of lights, he was delighted to
be told by the local authority that Summerhill had the best blackout in
Leiston. Aeroplanes were frequently heard overhead, as Ruth Allen's diary
entry for 9 November records: 'Neill and I sneaked off to play golf – I
enjoyed this very much for it was a lovely day and the autumn colours are
marvellous just now. Neill however was not so keen, as he was feeling
rather depressed: when we heard some loud booming noises he immediately
wondered if they were guns. An aeroplane then circled round and unsettled
him – we kept on hearing it but could see nothing. Always on the coast the
war seems so much nearer, it's like being on the boundary line.'

On 17 October, with the German raid on Hull, the air-raid warnings
began. The children were shepherded into the Summerhill shelters, complete
with gas masks stuffed with sweets. 'I feel frightened, I feel frightened,'
young Egan Bernal repeated out loud as he lay beneath his father's protective construction. Soon, however, the children treated the rush to the
shelters as little more than a game, and carried on their ordinary life with
relative unconcern. Autumn turned to winter, bringing a spell of abnormally
high rainfall followed by deep snow and freezing winds, which froze tins
of paint solid in the Summerhill art room. Then, on 11 May 1940, Neill
and the others heard over the radio that Hitler had invaded Holland and
Belgium. The sound of gunfire was now audible in Leiston, and four days
later the house was shaken in the early hours by a series of tremendous
explosions. 'We the grown-ups feel very tense,' Ruth Allen noted in her
diary. The tension increased with the news that Holland had surrendered
to Germany, and within a short while France too had capitulated.

Fears of invasion grew, but Neill, though he realised the position was
becoming more dangerous, was still unsure whether to prepare for evacu-
ation. Accommodation with Dora Russell was no longer feasible. On the
evening of the explosions he wrote to Curry: 'I've no intention of leaving
here, but there may come a time when the authorities evacuate all kids
from the area of the East Coast. I wonder if you know of any vacant place
round about Devon where we might retire to at a pinch?' Soon, however,
Neill was compelled to make a decision. The Garrett Engineering Works
in the middle of Leiston was being used for the manufacture of armaments,

and was therefore a potential target for the German Luftwaffe. Parents became increasingly anxious about the safety of their children – who for their part had decided that, if the invasion came, those with bicycles would ride off as quickly as possible in a westward direction! In June a series of air-raid warnings sent everyone down in the shelter again. In the English Channel thousands of soldiers were being evacuated from Dunkirk, leaving the Germans in control of the French coastline. Now the decision was taken out of Neill's hands, as the army decided to requisition the premises for their own use. After spending one more night in the shelter – for some their last at Summerhill – the children were sent home, and Neill started to look for premises in a safer area.

The tensions of war had resulted in the departure of two Summerhill staff in a manner that upset everyone there. After Dunkirk, aliens were forbidden to reside in coastal regions, and soon the government's policy of internment came into force. Although most of them were Jewish refugees or political opponents of the Nazis, all German subjects were interned. One of the local shopkeepers informed the police of Ilse Rolfe's presence, an act that caused great resentment in Summerhill. Neill spoke at the local police station on her behalf, but to no effect. At the tribunal hearing the judge, on being told that she had been at Summerhill, suggested that she had been mixing 'with the wrong sort of people', and she was sent for internment on the Isle of Man. Similarly, Antoine Obert, a young Austrian who had been at Summerhill as an odd-job man for four years, and had become a special favourite of Mrs Lins, was taken away, and later sent to Canada. This caused a lot of distress, and Brendan Williams took Neill to task over the incident: 'I suggested to him that the reason for him being taken into custody was the impression created by some of the staff, with their banners and demonstrations, and by some of the hangers-on. Neill explained that, since he believed in freedom, he could not logically interfere with the right of these people to act in this way.'

Eventually Neill moved to Ffestiniog, an isolated village in North Wales. Bryn Llewellyn, owned by Lord Newborough, was a large, handsome, but dilapidated house perched on the side of a steep hill just outside the village. It had become since the owner's death a doss-house for tramps and vagrants. Neill and his school arrived there to find the roof letting the rain in, the bare wooden floor caked with dirt, the hot water boiler broken, and doors, windows and lavatories in need of repair. For the first two months, until the electricity was turned on, Summerhill was lit by candle-light. One of the few material compensations for the run-down state of the house was the breathtaking view across the valley to the Moelwyn mountain range opposite. Yet Neill, never particularly interested in the visual aspect of his surroundings, found that the grandeur wore off very quickly. 'I never noticed the glory of the mountain colours after the first week,' he wrote later. Soon after the move he commented sourly to Paxton Chadwick: 'You talk about the view, but you can't shit on view.'

Though this was a comment that was characteristic of his outlook, it did reflect a significant increase in the burdens he had to carry. Not all of them were to do with the physical state of the premises, as he explained in a gloomy letter to Curry in November 1940:

> I have to mend doors, stoke fires, teach maths, cater, and worst of all interview all the damned officials who still think in peace terms. MOH an old man objects because I'm overcrowded, and evaded my query what he was to do about the thousands of kids who have bad air in shelters and tubes.

Understandably, many parents had sent their children to Summerhill at this time in order not that they should be free, but safe. Neill found it hard to turn down the requests of anxious parents, and for a while many children had to sleep in the corridors. He could in fact have easily filled the school twice over, and throughout the war he had a lengthy waiting list. Several children who came were disturbed, or had become anxious at being separated from parents vulnerable to the bombing raids which now became part of everyday life in the English cities. One boy, Martin Tucker, sent to Summerhill at the age of 9 because he had been upset by the air raids, was clearly affected by the separation, writing home: 'I don't go to lessons now because I am so home sick I cry nearly the whole time I am afley unhappy and unlucky to come here. . . I can't understand people who say this is a nice school it is so nasty being away from home.'

As he had done in Sonntagsberg, Lyme and Leiston, Neill had to guard the reputation of Summerhill in the local community. This was not an easy task. Ffestiniog was in a Welsh-speaking area, where the inhabitants were mostly bilingual and some of the older people spoke no English at all. Even in peace time there would have been *some* suspicion of the English intruders; in war time there was a great deal, at least initially. David Barton remembers the day a group of pupils arrived for the first term in North Wales: 'We walked down the street, and through all these rather quiet houses, and we saw the lace curtains being drawn an inch back, and noses appearing round the edge.' Norman Davies, then a boy living in a nearby village, remembers 'the local prejudice and strange stories about Bryn Llewellyn: that the children could do as they liked, that boys and girls bathed together, that they were allowed to smoke and swear, and call their teachers or elders by their Christian names. I don't think the local folk knew anything about the purpose and ethos of the school, and would not have understood it anyway.' He also recalls that there were other reasons for misunderstanding the nature of the new arrivals: 'Because the pupils looked so untidy, we thought they must be poor and underprivileged, and felt sorry for them.'*

The clash of cultures resulted for some while in open warfare between the Summerhill children and what they called the 'Town Ginks'. There

---

*The children's unconventional appearance had its effect on one teacher appointed by Neill. He travelled up in the same train as some of the children, looked in to one of their compartments, got out at the next station, and sent a telegram informing Neill that he had decided not to come to Wales after all.

were constant fights across the slate fence that separated the Bryn Llewellyn estate from the village land, in which a well organised standing army of stone-carriers and sling-shot men from the school did battle with the locals. However, peace did sometimes break out between the rival gangs, and individually many of the children made friends with boys and girls from the enemy ranks. There was also a more positive side to community relations. Neill had to hire a number of domestic staff to cook and clean, and some of these came from Ffestiniog. Sometimes there were conflicts, as Ena Wood, who initially came to help with the cooking in Wales, remembers: 'If you offended the Welsh domestics they very soon downed tools and walked out, but they soon walked in again.' Dora Williams, one of those taken on from the village, recalls very little dissension: 'We couldn't have been treated better anywhere else,' she feels. The domestic staff were invited to the dances and, at Neill's suggestion, some of the local children were also asked, so becoming better acquainted with the way Summerhill operated. Norman Davies also remembers one football match between Summerhill and his own village of Trawsfynydd, in which Neill acted as informal mediator. The Welsh side, in proper gear, beat Summerhill, who played in their ordinary clothes, and included two girls in their team, by 17 goals to nil. 'This didn't worry Neill's pupils, but it gave us great joy. As the players walked away from the game, Neill gently persuaded us that the game was to be enjoyed for its own sake, that winning was a side issue, and that winning and losing both had their particular lesson.'

However, Neill was not always as diplomatic as this. Later in the war, when he was able to make the occasional trip out of the area, he made some critical remarks about the Welsh community to a London journalist. On his return journey, just after he had re-entered Wales, he was appalled to hear that a group of angry Welshmen were waiting at Ffestiniog, apparently with the firm intention of beating him up. The encounter never took place, and may indeed have been a joke or a misunderstanding; but Neill spoke feelingly about the matter on his return to Summerhill. He denied having ever made these comments to the press – though the pupils recognised the comments attributed to him as being quite authentic and familiar. He was indeed liable to make such generalised and often unjustified comments, and was lucky that they didn't get him into more trouble.

If Neill tended to exaggerate the amount of conflict that took place between Summerhill and the villagers, this may have been because he felt in Ffestiniog that he had, as he wrote later, 'returned to the atmosphere of my native Scottish village'. There were certainly features of life there that would have brought on such associations, in particular the Welsh people's belief that the Sabbath should be observed. Here again, Neill's deep-rooted hostility towards any form of organised religion found early expression. After only a few weeks in Ffestiniog he wrote to Curry: 'It isn't easy for us here, for Wales is a very narrow religious place and we are looked on as atheists and sinners.' The Summerhill way of life was inevitably the cause of some bewilderment and disapproval in the village, but not everyone living in Bryn Llewellyn felt the same hostility as Neill did. Ena Wood, for example, remembers: 'I don't think we had any real difficulties, except for the pubs being closed on Sundays. By and large the Welsh people were very nice to us.' Later Neill himself echoed this view, ending a recollection of the 'misery of memory' of Wales with the comment: 'But the people were jolly nice to us.'

It was, though, quite impossible for Neill to look with any objectivity or tolerance on matters connected with religion. 'I never yet saw a religious community that wasn't filled with rotten hate and spite,' he wrote to Curry while in Wales. Yet there were enough incidents to fuel his prejudices. One of the local deacons came to complain about the Summerhill children playing hockey on Sundays – to which they responded by deciding at a meeting to switch the games to Saturday. Similarly, when the local children complained at having to attend church or chapel on Sunday at a time when Summerhill was holding its dance after the weekly meeting, Neill suggested that Summerhill invite them to attend. Several did come, as a result of which the gang warfare diminished considerably. One other clash with the local church provided Neill with an anecdote which he told often in later years. The story is true in essence, except for one detail: the offender was not Neill himself, as he later made out, but another member of staff. Tom Hackett recalls the incident: 'I was repairing a gate on a Sunday morning, hoping to keep the stray sheep out. One of the deacons from the chapel came along and said that I should know better than to be working on a Sunday. I replied: ' "I bet your wife's cooking your lunch for you now." '

Though Neill complained about the restricted life forced on him in Wales, it was never quite as bleak as he made out, and many who were there found a great deal to do and enjoy. There were outings to nearby Harlech and Portmadoc, and to Clough Williams-Ellis's extraordinary Italianate creation of Port Merion, where the school had access to a private beach. In nearby Blainau Ffestiniog, a small town further up in the mountains tucked around its slate quarries, there was a choice of films in three cinemas. One of these, the Forum, was also used for other purposes: celebrities came to give regular Sunday concerts, and once Sybil Thorndike and Lewis Casson, who lived in the region, offered a performance of *Macbeth* there. At Blaenau there were also dances, where some of the younger female staff were partnered by the older Summerhill boys. And – Sundays apart – adults and older children would visit the two pubs in the village, singing their way down the hill to the school at the end of the evening.

Neill himself never went to the pub, and seldom took part in the other outings, preoccupied as he was with the myriad of jobs that needed doing in Summerhill. Ben Morris, who later became a friend, remembers his first meeting with Neill in Ffestiniog: 'When I arrived there was nobody about; eventually I found Neill in a hayfield, wielding a scythe. "I take it you're Morris?" he said. "Yes." "Can you use a scythe?" "Yes." "Then use this one." ' Like many during the war, Neill became very 'land-minded', and spent hours in the extensive garden that stretched up the hillside beyond the house, weeding, pruning, scything, and digging the potato patch. During the war the government had mounted a 'Potatoes are Good for You' campaign, broadcasting potato pie recipes on the radio programme 'Kitchen Front'. Food never became particularly scarce in Bryn Llewellyn, but the staff had to plan carefully in order to feed a hundred people. Neill became interested in questions of soil and manure, and was delighted to be able to buy 20 tons of mule dung, for compost for the vegetables. He wrote enthusiastically to Reich about the ideas of Sir Albert Howard, who was critical of the use of chemical sprays and a great believer in natural compost:

> You will guess by all this that the war has converted me from a psychologist into a damned farmer. . . . not much difference between the two, for both waste time dealing with muck, yet it is better to fork farmyard muck than to sit and listen to psychic repressed muck.

Neill's feelings about his 'psychic muck raking' shifted back and forth while he was in Ffestiniog. For a while he lost interest in the individual analysis that he gave to children in his PLs, and pondered on the significance of this to Reich: 'It is possible that my analysis with you, by giving me freedom in the reflex, destroyed a complex which had been expressed in trying to cure the other fellow.' He thought too that he was having some success in following Reich's advice that he should 'let himself go': 'the time I had with you has changed me much. The effect is seen on the school. The atmosphere is happier because I am happier. I can take decisions easily now, but still can't be aggressive.' The weariness that he had sometimes shown in his work with children appeared to have vanished:

> Thank God, I think I have more interest in the children than I ever had. They are grand and clever and lovable, and I know that this system is the only one of any value in the world. They don't seem to need therapy of any kind, and that is the ideal education – to educate children in such a way that they won't need therapy later on.

Though this letter may well have represented Neill's true feelings, the implication that he was no longer having to deal with problem children was misleading. As at Lyme, some parents were content to leave their children with him whether or not they believed in his ideas. In addition, the war brought him a number of children with severe problems. One very disturbed boy was given a kitten to compensate for a baby brother, and proceeded to strangle it. Henry Stracey, a new member of staff, recalls another of Neill's fresh crop of problem children, and how he dealt with her: 'One girl of 11 arrived full of hatred. She had red hair, looked hideous, and had a father who was a fire-eating communist. She had the unpleasant habit of trying to knock people over by charging them from behind. Neill practised the Reich massage technique on her, and one day the expected reaction came. Neill allowed her to kick his legs raw as she screamed, sobbed and swore at him. Eventually she subsided. Two months after she started the treatment she became a social being, and a pleasure to be with, chatting amiably and laughing naturally. We were impressed.'

One group of girls caused particular problems for Neill. Once two of them remained behind during the holidays, broke into some of the other children's rooms, tore up their books and stamp albums, and defecated in their suitcases. On another occasion, two 8-year-olds festooned the front of the house with every available roll of toilet paper – in their case the meeting fined them the cost of a few urgently needed toilet rolls, and insisted that they roll them all up again. Yet another group of girls, aged 8 and 9, who had decided to run away to London, were skilfully dealt with by Neill, with the assistance of Ena Wood. Sonia Crampton, who came to teach art while the school was in Ffestiniog, recalls the incident: 'They got some food from the pantry and left early in the morning. Someone saw them in a field, and rang the school. Neill took Ena to a dip in the field, with just enough food for herself. She semi-stripped, and lay down. When the girls came across her, she said: "Oh, what are you doing here? I'm sunbathing." So they said, "We're running away." "That's funny," said Ena, "so am I." So they went on together, the girls becoming more and more tired. Ena guided them towards a village, and when they realised where they were, they asked to go to a café. Ena showed them the amount of money that she had, and they bought something small with the few coins. Then she said: "Poor Neill will be worried. Shall I just ring up and say where we are, that we're all right, but we're not coming back?" The girls agreed to this, and she rang Neill, giving him their planned route for the next few hours. They walked and walked, and suddenly saw Neill coming towards them in his car. They all rushed up and flung their arms around him, got in the car, and were driven back to Summerhill. Not a word was said. Previously they had been the ones who would break into the people's rooms and put treacle and soot over everything; but after that day they were awfully good.'

As at other times, Neill had to cope with a great deal of theft. 'Don't send me anything that's not food everything gets stolen,' Martin Tucker warned his parents in a letter. Neill maintained his belief that when they stole property or money children were stealing love. His refusal to take the conventional moral line on theft sometimes produced quick results. Norma Harris came to Ffestiniog at the age of 8, having previously been at a nearby Welsh primary school, where the head refused to speak English, and caned the children when they failed to learn. At Summerhill she and a friend stole a pound from one of the housemothers, and spent it in Blaenau Ffestiniog: 'I had never been so upset in all my life,' she recalls. 'I was frightened of Neill because I had had this awful experience with the previous head. I remember him talking to me about the theft before I had admitted it, and suddenly realising that I didn't have to be frightened of him. I admitted taking the money, and never stole another thing in my life.' Some of the new staff tried to put Neill's philosophy into practice. A pupil recalls Ena Wood leaving 2s 6d in her dressing gown pocket so that one boy who smoked 20 cigarettes a day could steal it to pay for them. Erna Gal, whose watch was taken on the first day in Wales, was later informed of the act by the thief herself. 'You didn't mind people telling you what they had pinched, because it wasn't frowned on at all, it was considered more or less natural,' she remembers. However, for some newcomers, as one, Joan Quarm, recalls, 'It was a bit trying to be told we must love the kids who stole our money and sweets, and looked us in the eye and knew we knew; but we had to do it somehow.'

Neill still sometimes allowed the meeting and the other adults to help with the therapy. One of the more remarkable judgments made by the children concerned a very disturbed child sent to Neill as a last resort. A highly confused girl, she had a passion for animals which sometimes took a bizarre form: once she punched a hole in a cat's ear in order to tie it up, on another occasion she took to wringing chickens' necks. She was famous for her rages, as Joan Quarm remembers: 'She used to throw crockery across the kitchen. I remember hiding under the table with a crowd of others, and cheering her on. We always encouraged her, as part of the therapy.' Neill discovered that she had been looking after an injured lamb from the nearby farm, housing it in the outside toilet. He returned the lamb to the farmer, somehow pacifying him about the incident, and then brought the case up for consideration at the meeting. The jury decided, after a long discussion, that the girl's punishment should be a present of a kitten, but that she would only be allowed to keep it if she looked after it properly. This girl also made considerable improvements in her behaviour but, much to Neill's irritation, was taken away just as the cure seemed to be having a substantial impact. To a parent who later wrote in appreciation of his work, Neill made caustic reference to this girl's case: 'It is very sweet to have appreciation from parents; they overbalance the father of ——, who attributed her improvement at S'hill to her keeping rabbits.'

However, during the war Neill seems to have had as much if not more problems with his staff than with the children. 'The kids as always are delightful; it is the adults who give trouble,' he wrote to Reich after two years in Ffestiniog. The war had compelled many of his staff to leave – Paxton Chadwick and Cyril Eyre had been called up, others had preferred not to come to Wales. It was of course extremely difficult for any private school to find suitable staff during the war, but Neill may have fared worse than most. 'His large heart was open, as was his school, to all who wanted refuge from the raids,' was one parent's explanation. Some of those who came clearly took advantage of Neill's inability to put his foot down. One newcomer brought his family along to have meals at the school, on the grounds that Neill was not paying him sufficient money. Another man parked his caravan on the front lawn, and settled in there with his wife and mistress. Probably the least conventional character of all was 'Sparks', who must have been the most versatile odd-job man on the market. Neill originally asked him to come only for a short trial period. He nevertheless arrived with stacks of luggage and a girl friend, and, dressed in his shorts, demanded in pronounced county tones: 'Is there a Concert Grand here? Can anyone play decently? I *must* have my classical music.' He played the zither, recorder, accordion and fiddle, and had a pleasing baritone voice. He was also a faith healer, and believed that he was likely to live for ever.

He and his girl friend wrote fourteen-page letters to each other every day. He was a vegetarian, and claimed to need only one meal a day; this consisted of a combination of nuts, soya beans, apples, slippery elm and mallam, which he would carry round with him in a rucksack. He was forever extolling the virtues of raw vegetables and fresh air, though he himself had an unhealthy look. The clue to this paradox was found when a pupil discovered him gorging himself with cream cakes in a café in Blaenau Ffestiniog, a disgrace that he was never quite able to live down.

Several of the adults who came to Bryn Llewellyn were conscientious objectors – though to Neill their main objection seemed to be to work rather than killing. 'I am fed up with their dreaminess and incompetence and negative attitude to life,' he complained in a letter to Reich. One CO refused either to teach or wash. Neill wrote sourly to Curry about 'refugees who can't hammer in a nail', and wondered if he should advertise along the lines: 'History master wanted, must be expert bogs cleaner, stoker, plumber etc.' Some of Neill's disgust arose from the staff's failure to assist him in the multitude of manual jobs that needed doing in the house and grounds. Joan Quarm recalls the staff's attitude to such tasks: 'Neill would be out in the vegetable garden alone, having made useless appeals to staff and children to help him dig for victory. The rest of us listened to records or went up to the village. We just didn't like heavy work. A large German-Jewish refugee, who was so overweight that I doubt if he would have been much use anyway, summed up our attitude. At one meeting, when Neill had been appealing for help, he said: "Mr Neill, you employed me to teach. I teach. I am a teacher. Had you wanted a gardener, I would not have applied." '

Some of the newcomers showed an equal distaste for teaching as for manual work. But two who did show some enthusiasm were Geoffrey and Troath Thorpe, remembered by one of the other staff as 'true Victorian elegants'. Troath Thorpe had trained as a Montessori teacher. She wore tweeds, smoked cheroots, and was the great-niece of the poet Swinburne. Her husband, a socialist and an atheist, had previously taught at University College School in Hampstead (which was overlooked by Neill's former school King Alfred). Stephen Spender was a pupil there, and remembers Geoffrey Thorpe as having 'the slightly shell-shocked dottiness of many who had fought on the Western Front'. This trait began to show itself in Summerhill, where for a while he taught history and art. A bright but weak man, his behaviour became noticeably strange, and in the end he had to leave because he saw everything double. Before that, as one of the Welsh domestic helps remembers, 'he used to walk around starkers, so it was eyes up, not eyes down'. One of his fellow teachers recalls being taken for a walk up the mountainside soon after she came, and being asked by Geoffrey Thorpe whether she had been beaten by her father. He then promptly burst into tears, crying, 'That's my trouble, I was never beaten.'

Many of the staff seemed more concerned with sorting out their own personal lives rather than working for the good of Summerhill: Neill told Reich that visitors often asked him 'Why do you have such normal children and such a neurotic staff?' Joan Quarm, who recalls 'being sillier than I ever was anywhere else', offers one explanation for the behaviour of some of the newer staff: 'The main problem was that we as adults imbibed the same air as the children and somehow reverted to childhood ourselves. If there was no guilt there was no sin. It was hard not to be children with the children, for Neill was the prototypal father-figure.' Yet by this stage Neill was less prepared than in previous times to accept this role with other adults. He made it clear that he was no longer prepared to give them PLs, pointing out that he was employing them to teach and not so that they could work out their problems at Summerhill's expense.

If Neill now found it now easier to take decisions, the results of this inner transformation were not always apparent. He did eventually manage to dislodge the *menage à trois* parked in the caravan on the front lawn. But at other times he appears to have returned to more recognisable behaviour patterns in his dealing with adults. Kirstie Ollendorff, who came to help with the cooking in Wales, remembers one incident at a staff meeting: 'One day Erna Gal said that she was not going to wash any dirty socks. I told her that she shouldn't be in Summerhill if she was not prepared to do as others did. We went on like this, back and forth, until Neill eventually said, "Oh, I'll do them." ' He also had difficulties in confronting the kitchen staff: 'I've just been called in by the cook to row the maids and it aint my job and I hate it and to hell with them all', he wrote in one war-time letter. Some of the Welsh kitchen staff took advantage of the war-time black market that flourished for items such as meat, butter, margarine, cheese, tea and sugar. They procured extra quantities for the school, for which Neill then paid an inflated price, yet only received the quantities allowed in the ration books. Although the surplus was quite openly taken home by the kitchen staff concerned, Neill refused to complain, using the argument that the food sources might dry up altogether if he did so. No doubt this was in part a rationalisation, but also perhaps a recognition that any attempt to complain was likely to be ineffectual. Gordon Leff remembers one brief encounter between Neill and 'Sparks' which highlighted Neill's inability to lay down the law: 'Sparks used to regularly oversleep, so that the boilers remained unlit in the mornings. We were walking with Neill to a maths lesson at about nine when Sparks emerged. Neill was as cross as he could be, and said: "Look, this is no good, you'll have to go." To which Sparks replied: "But Neill, I like the place, and I like you, and everything about it." "Oh get away," Neill said.' Sparks lived to oversleep for another day.

There were however other difficulties with staff which brought a very different reaction from Neill. 'I was 60 recently and wish I were twenty again,' he wrote to Reich in November 1943. Although he remained reasonably fit and active at a stage in life when many others were thinking of retirement, Neill began to show increasing signs of anxiety about the future of Summerhill – and sometimes with good cause. In Wales some of the newer staff began to be critical of his running of the school. In May 1943 Neill shared his experiences with Curry: 'Like you I found the staff business hopeless. I've had a run of pacifists who are no good at all, all negative, in the clouds, castrated and wanting to tell me how to run the school on Jesus lines.' One small group actually made a serious attempt to take over Summerhill. However, they made the mistake of talking about the idea to some of the older children, who informed Neill of their plan. Neill was understandably fierce in his determination to remain in charge, and the rebellion was short-lived.

One of Neill's fiercest critics during the war years was Robin Bond, a good-looking, very charming young man and a gifted teacher, whose presence inspired a burst of creative activity in the school. He took over the organisation of the end-of-term theatrical activities, and was also responsible for organising a London exhibition of the children's paintings and drawings. Held in the Arcade Gallery in Bond Street, it caused a stir in the art and educational worlds, and had the effect of launching one 17-year-old Summerhill girl, Ishbel McWhirter, on a successful career as a painter. Although Robin Bond had some differences with Neill on the question of children's art, his most severe criticisms were more personal. He criticised Neill for being incapable of facing up to adults. He also argued that Neill had moulded Summerhill to his own will, that his mind was closed, and that he was unable to accept criticisms. Neill was evidently disturbed by these remarks, though later he tried to make light of them, or to suggest that the fault lay with his critic. 'Poor Robin who must always kill what he loves' he wrote to one parent after the war; and in a letter to a pupil at about the same time, he referred to 'the worst days in Ffestiniog' as being when Robin Bond was 'working agnst old father Neill, and making some kids. . . critical of me'.

Yet there was some substance in Robin Bond's views, particularly in relation to Neill's ability to accept criticism. The resolution he had shown in founding and nurturing Summerhill in the teeth of considerable hostility and misunderstanding had now, after a quarter of a century, solidified into a less positive quality. Increasingly he tended to see differences in outlook and attitude on the part of other adults as an attempt to usurp his position. He betrayed signs of jealousy of other staff who appeared to have a particular skill in working with children, or who had become popular with them. Once, noticing one of the new teachers at the centre of a group of older children and younger staff, he remarked to another adult that he felt like the old bull being challenged by a younger one. The implied threat was to both Neill personally and to Summerhill, for like many others he was unable to imagine the school existing without him. 'Fancy thinking they could chuck me out of my own school!' he commented later about one group of rebels.

Yet his differences with other adults cannot merely be attributed to his own failings. Despite his inconsistencies of behaviour, he continued to believe that children should be free to develop in their own way at Summerhill, and not be over-influenced by adults. This was clearly a factor in his conflict with Robin Bond, as Neill made clear in a letter to Ishbel McWhirter after the young art teacher had left the school: 'Boys slaving to get theatre ready. Absence of Robin good for em, for they relied on his initiative, but now are tackling things on their own.' Though many pupils spoke of the encouragement they were given by Robin Bond, there were some who clearly echoed Neill's anxiety about his influence. Hylda Sims, another pupil of the time, remembers: 'Everyone went to his art lessons, but in a way he was too dynamic: it became a sort of elite, and people began to paint like Robin.' Anthony Jenkins, another pupil, felt the new teacher was 'like a Christ with disciples'. This for Neill would have been a sure sign of the adult 'moulding' against which he had fought for so long.

The large proportion of new staff that Neill had to take on in Wales, and the fact that many were so intent on working through their personal difficulties, brought a significant change to the spirit of Summerhill. It became a much less stable community, and also a more primitive one. The physical difficulties, and the anxiety generated by the war, meant that the quality of the children's lives depended more than before on the talents and commitment of the adults around them. This applied to the housemothers as much as to the teachers, and they too seemed to vary considerably in their attitude to the children. One parent who visited Ffestiniog several times felt that the group in which her 7-year-old son found himself 'lacked the most elementary care'. One new pupil, Ann Freshwater, who stayed for nine years at Summerhill, recalls of this period: 'The staff had different values and standards, so there was a confusing assortment of what was right and wrong.' Some housemothers were clearly able to provide greater warmth and security than others. One of these was Jenny Halliday, the daughter of Neill's sister May, who had come to the school just before the war, and married another of the staff there, Mahesh Desai. Another was Ena Wood, as Ann Freshwater recalls: 'She was a marvellous housemother, and stuck out above all the others: she kept us clean, put us to bed properly, and did things for us. There were many staff who didn't manage that.'

One group of children took the initiative in a different sphere, causing Neill yet again to demonstrate the irrationality of his attitude to book learning. A small number of academically able children who had spent their school life at Summerhill – Gordon Leff, Jenny Hutt, David Barton and Branwen Williams were amongst them – decided that the staff were not doing enough teaching. A meeting was held and it was agreed that an extra lesson should be put on the timetable at the end of the afternoon, and that the children should be provided with 'homework'. During this time, when one of the more able teachers left, some of the group went up to Neill's room, and stood over him until he agreed to write for a replacement. Before long they made it clear what their next aim was to be, as is shown by one classroom incident remembered by Geoffrey Thorpe's daughter Barbara, another pupil of the period: 'My father was a frightful old gossip, so he made history very interesting, and the boys encouraged him to digress. One day Gordon Leff said, "That's very interesting, but you can tell us that any time, and it won't get us through School Cert." My father was taken aback.' He was not the only one: Neill himself, Gordon Leff remembers, was 'at first incredulous that we should want to learn'. Their request had

come at the end of a turbulent few months, in which Neill found himself
in violent opposition with one of his new teachers, and subsequently with
others in the school. The conflict began with the arrival of a new teacher,
Stella Hagan, who had agreed to do some English teaching, but rapidly
found herself taking English literature and language, French (in which she
had a degree), geography and history. The children, she found, were vo-
racious to learn. 'Unwilling to wait until the official start to lessons, they
would drag me out of bed at seven, having already run my bath and rustled
up breakfast, which they carried to the classroom so as to lose no teaching
time.' This enthusiasm apparently extended into the weekends, when she
found herself giving 'quasi-lessons' in history, botany, politics, phonetics,
theatre and cinema. 'At meals, on the way to and from my room, while I
was bathing, while I was sitting in the staff room, when I was going to or
returning from the village, children would dash up with queries, which
very often developed into discussions in which other children joined. Sometimes these would finish in a classroom so that I could use the blackboard
for drawings or diagrams or sketch maps.'

Neill was unhappy about this development, and at staff meetings
accused Stella Hagan of forcing the children to have lessons. She argued
that it was they who were forcing *her,* an argument which was reinforced
when the topic surfaced at the weekly meeting. When Neill refused a
request from the children that they should have more lessons, they called
a special meeting, and carried the proposal by a considerable majority – in
one discussion Neill was the only dissenter. Neill's hostility turned to horror
when he heard that some of the children wanted to sit for the School
Certificate examination. Stella Hagan remembers that 'he refused point
blank to give anything so fiendishly un-Summerhillian even a moment's
consideration; but of course the children just called a General Meeting,
which tanked right over him.' Those who were intending to sit for the
exam, being unfamiliar with the procedures, then asked for a 'mock'. Neill's
refusal to countenance this was overcome in the now familiar way, and the
potential candidates sat a five-subject test under strict exam conditions
(except for the existence of a number of children with their noses pressed
to the window, absorbed by this unusual occurrence). They performed well
enough to be entered for the exam, and Neill put their applications in hand.
However, the saga was not yet over. Parents were asked to cover the cost
of books, and did so willingly; but money still needed to be found for some
basic reference books. Stella Hagan recalls that 'it took several highly
emotional staff meetings – with some of the staff reduced to tears by Neill's
fury – to get permission to order these. The bill came to £3 and a few
pence. Neill made a tremendous row over this "unwarranted" and "wan-
ton" expense.' Then when the children passed the exam, some with distinction, 'Neill did a complete volte-face, and made out that the whole
exam idea had come from and been sustained by him.'

Stella Hagan eventually left after another row with Neill, who became
angry about a booklist of English novels which she had compiled at the
children's request. 'I won't have this brainwashing and standardised cul-

ture,' was Neill's reaction. The whole episode highlights Neill's failure to see that children might want to make different uses of their freedom than those which *he* might think appropriate. He could acknowledge this failing in print, but was unable to overcome it in life. This was confirmed by a debate held some months after the examinations episode. It had become customary for Neill to initiate debates on topics such as 'What's Wrong with Summerhill?' or 'Is Summerhill Going the Right Way?' This time the topic, debated in Neill's absence, was 'Is Neill Anti-Academic?' Ishbel McWhirter recalls Neill's response to the meeting's decision that he was. 'He reacted with dismay and astonishment; he was rather upset. I think he saw himself as much more impartial.' This was hard for others to believe when Neill's own actions so clearly spoke for themselves. His hatred of idleness was such that there were moments when even lessons seemed a reasonable alternative.*

On the question of freedom in the matter of sex Neill was more consistent, as Erna Gal recalls: 'There were young lovers there, but Neill never said a word. I was sometimes worried when I went round to put the lights out and see whether they were in bed. Sure enough, they were – but with their girl friends. I went to Neill several times, and brought it up at the meeting. I said to him, "Is this all right that the young people are in bed with each other; I don't object personally, but are you going to do anything about it?" I was worried that something would happen one day. For Neill this was a difficult question, and he was not very willing to put his foot down or do anything, he didn't want to influence the children. He never ticked them off for it, he wouldn't do that.' One pupil who was there for a short time remembers that 'even for people like myself who were too young to take part, our actions and speech were full of sexual imagery. I remember one little girl, she was perhaps 10, walking round the school naked and shouting out, "Two Ryvitas and a half a crown for a fuck." I don't think anybody took up the offer.' Visitors were frequently taken aback at the amount of swearing at Summerhill, but perhaps none were more so than a group who arrived to find the 2-year-old son of one of the staff lying in his pram. One teacher remembers: 'Some of the visitors came up and gurgled and cooed at him in the usual way. He sat up, said, "Fuck off," and went back to sleep again.'

Publicly, Neill maintained that he knew of no pregnancies amongst the pupils. In private, he was anxious, and asked the parents of some of the older girls if they would give permission for their daughters to be fitted with a cap. Only one agreed to this, and some parents of older girls removed their children from the school, unable to accept the sexual freedom. Neill wrote to Reich pointing to the moral: 'any man who sets out in England to carry out the R theory of sex freedom would be likely to end

*A similar debate was held on the motion 'It would be good for humanity if all books were burned.' It was passed, but in amended form, the children deciding that it would be best to 'Burn all books except technical ones telling how to build houses and dig gardens'.

in being a martyr and a martyr only.' In his pragmatic way he observed that: 'Martyrdom for a cause isn't good enough, for it destroys other causes at the same time. . . i.e. the freedom from fear and moulding in small children.'

Neill's attitude to 'affairs' between children and staff is less easy to pin down – though one adult there at the time recalls that such relationships were looked upon as 'healthy'. There is no indication that Neill attempted to intervene when this occurred, as it did now more often than in the past. One new member of staff kept a diary at the time, and noted on one occasion: '—— has had a retrogressive series of semi-affairs; she started with a boy of 19, which was fairly normal except he was slightly undeveloped, didn't shave and had special hormone injections. At the end of last term it was a boy in the matric class, about 15; and now it's a boy in the class below that, about 14. Consequently she's very unpopular with all the girls.' Two of the teachers, a man and a woman, were having well-publicised affairs with a couple of the older children, and an ex-pupil in the forces often returned to Summerhill during his leave because of the sexual possibilities in the school. At least one parent, a close friend of Neill's, removed her child because she objected to this particular version of sexual freedom.

Some, though by no means all, of the difficulties Neill encountered in Wales undoubtedly arose because, as he explained to Reich, 'I have a double load to carry, having to do a thousand things I never had to do before. . . food, servants, children's clothing, etc. And settling the differences of opinion among the female staff, who all want to have things their own way.' The signs of old age which Neill had noticed and hated in Mrs Lins just before the war had increased, and almost from the moment the school settled in Wales her condition began to deteriorate. Before the fighting started she had remarked that, should another war come, she would just want to die. She had suffered a great deal from the tensions during the First World War, especially because of her divided loyalties between England and Germany. The anxiety of the 'Phoney War' and the upheaval of the sudden move affected her severely; after six months in Wales Neill wrote sadly to Reich: 'My wife is done out now, unable to do anything in the school. It is very sad to see one who has been so active become like a child again.'

The process of deterioration was a slow one, and immensely distressing for Neill. Mrs Lins had a slight stroke which paralysed one of her arms, her thoughts became disjointed, and she gradually withdrew from the life of the school. She would go for long walks along the steep mountain roads, allowing no one but her son Wally to accompany her; or wander round the school, saying 'Where's Mr Neill?' She would prepare herself for a bath, then wander naked down the corridor, forgetting where she had to go. At mealtimes she would take food from Neill's plate, believing that he was trying to starve her; and Neill would be too embarrassed to fetch any more. She began to hoard biscuits in her bedroom cupboard, resenting the fact that someone else had taken charge of 'her' kitchen. She would try to talk to the children, and be distressed at being unable to remember the words she wanted to use. She wrote letters to her family abroad which were totally incomprehensible. She also started to write an autobiographical novel, about a voyage on which she and Neill were embarking. She had to get help from staff to find a word in the dictionary, or to change the paper in her typewriter. The story began with a description of the boat on which she and Neill were taking their voyage, and of the people in it; it then moved on to depict one cabin, and then just the table in the cabin, the focus getting narrower all the time. Sometimes she wrote phrases over and over again: 'and there was the sea, and the moon, and the Captain'. Time became an obssession with her, and every evening she would come to Neill and ask him to wind up her watch. Neill told Erna Gal: 'She looks at that watch as somehow being connected with her death. If that watch stops, she would stop.' He would patiently wind it up for her, and bring her back upstairs to her own room. He spent a lot of time with her, talking, listening, holding her hand – a gesture of affection he had not previously made in public. To Reich he wrote: 'My wife fails fast and is most pathetic to see now. . . . It is a grim life to see one who was so energetic and capable go downhill like that.' Many years later he spoke even more candidly to one friend from the early Summerhill years, confessing that he had never lived through anything like the period following Mrs Lins's stroke, since, though she was unable to speak, she could 'speak with her eyes'.

Eventually, after she had a bad fall early in 1943, Neill was forced to send Mrs Lins away to a mental home in Harlech. For more than a year Neill visited her regularly in the home, a distressing occasion for both of them. 'Wife just the same, a shell of a woman,' he wrote that summer. 'Visiting makes her miserable and wanting to come home. Awful.' On 30 April 1944 she finally died, and was buried in Llanfairfechan some twenty miles from Ffestiniog. To Reich, who had sent his condolences, Neill wrote: 'It was a relief in one way, for life to her was a misery for three years, but I felt the parting keenly. Made me feel so much alone. You can't work closely with a woman for 24 years doing the same important work without feeling a strong bond.' For her grave Neill insisted on a simple stone, without any inscription on it. He then held up the proofs of his latest book, *Hearts not Heads in the School,* in order to write his own memorial tribute. The uncharacteristic display of sentiment at the end of his obituary was an eloquent acknowledgment of the debt that both he and Summerhill owed to Mrs Lins:

> Hers was a fine life, one of much self-effacement. Her memorial will lie in the lives of many boys and girls and adults who were helped by her, encouraged by her, loved by her. She left the world just a little richer, because she tried to do something new and important, just a little something to bring happiness into the lives of a few lucky children. . . and I do not mean only the children of Summerhill: I mean the countless children in the wide world who have had more happiness because their parents and teachers learned of the gospel of

love in education which it was her life work to forward. Memorial stones are temporal, but honest work touches the fringes of eternity, and that with children broadens out into a stream that flows on for ever. Her epitaph might well be: 'She belonged to tomorrow, to youth, to hope.'

CHAPTER 16

New Worlds?

If we are to continue with our dictator schools, then let the dictator be someone who knows something about child nature.

Hearts not Heads in the School, 1945

Ladies and Gentlemen,
I have chosen for my presidential address the subject of Truth. I want to make you ask yourselves the question: How much truth is in education? Or the cognate question: Are we living a lie?

I say we are. We have charge of the next generation and we are giving it the lies of our own generation. We are not doing this deliberately: we are doing it because we have never really thought deeply about education. We have not had the power to look ahead: our horizon has been a severely limited one.

Let us make this concrete. Today we see the nations arming to the teeth. At any moment the world may be plunged in an inferno of despair and terror and agony. It seems highly probable that millions of the children sitting in schools today will be killed. When the war is finished what is left of humanity will be faced with the herculean task of building up a new kind of civilisation. It will be one that will differ from the present one in many ways: its most probable form will be universal Socialism. Fascism cannot in the end win because it belongs to the old way of life, to profit and class distinction, and imperialistic conquest. It puts the clock back.

The pupils of our schools, those who survive, will build the new world. Are we doing anything to prepare them for this task? What

will our little lessons on school subjects do to help them to a new
life? Will their silly little examination successes help them to endure
the misery they may first have to face? Will that iniquity, home
lessons, help to make them conscientious citizens of a new world?

Teachers, if we really believed in truth we should stand together
and strike down this system of playing at education. We should train
the young to be citizens by allowing them to be free citizens now.

This was how Neill began his presidential address to the National
Union of Teachers in 1939. It was of course no more than a fantasy, which
he included in his new book *The Problem Teacher*, published in the early
weeks of the war. But the fact that he formulated such an idea was an
indication of an interesting shift in outlook on his part. Up to now he had
been preoccupied with the question of child psychology, and with running,
explaining and defending Summerhill. The imminence of war, and the
subsequent dislocation of social life, prompted him to give more consideration to the future of the state school system. Even while the conflict was
at its height, educators and politicians were beginning to plan for the
post-war world. In 1944 a new Education Act transformed the structure of
the school system in England and Wales: universal free secondary education
was introduced, church schools were absorbed into the state system, and
the school-leaving age was raised from 14 to 15. Neill, perhaps sensing that
his ideas might have more chance of serious consideration at a time of such
upheaval, joined in the debate.

His books and lectures had of course already made his ideas widely
known. Yet, as the threat of war grew, he felt this to be insufficient, and
resolved to do something different. In the early summer of 1939 he took
the step of organising the kind of event that he normally avoided if at all
possible: an educational conference. He invited teachers in East Anglian
schools to Summerhill, to discuss the idea of forming a new group who
would be prepared to 'make child psychology the centre of their interests
and activities'. Some sixty teachers came, a committee was formed, and
further meetings arranged. Any further progress was cut short by the
outbreak of war, but even before that Neill was doubtful about the future
of his idea. Some of the teachers admitted they were quite content with the
schools as they were; others were principally interested in structural
changes; and only a few seemed prepared to endorse Neill's idea of the
importance of child psychology. Although he could have hardly expected
a very different response, Neill was cast down by the clear gulf that existed
between himself and the majority at the conference:

> As the meeting went on I found myself sinking into a deep
> pessimism: I felt that some of the teachers were talking a language
> that I did not understand: to me they were emphasising all that was
> outer and unimportant in education. . . . I was disappointed not to
> find as many rebels as I had hoped to find. The reforms some of
> them wanted were small affairs, not touching fundamentals. I found
> myself wanting to cry out: 'The fundamental is the nature of the

child, and all this talk about size of classes and kind of curriculum is not to the point.'

Despite his uncompromising views, Neill was still aware of the kind of constraints under which most teachers in the system had to work. Some of those who attended his lectures pointed out to him the difference between his position and their own, a criticism with which Neill became familiar. He accepted that even those who welcomed his ideas could say to him:

All very well for you, but I have fifty kids to teach in a classroom. I can't study each individually, can't know their home and psychological history and complexes. I must keep them quiet, for the maths man is next door, and he won't have noise. Besides the parents expect their children to learn and pass exams. . . .Take away my desks and inspectors and local authorities and I also will pioneer. Today I am chained.

Neill saw the force of these arguments, and felt that 'the man or woman who carries on bravely struggling against authority and conventional education in a state school is more worthy of admiration than any of the state-free pioneers. They are the real hopes for the future.'

Because of his much greater freedom, Neill was able to generalise, to sweep aside as irrelevant disputes about methods of teaching or the structure of schools, and to speak his mind about headteachers, inspectors and education authorities. He was able to say out loud what many teachers could only say to themselves; he could be outrageous where they would have to be diplomatic or silent. Joan Quarm, then a young teacher in London, remembers the advice Neill gave her in the autumn of 1941, after she had attended a meeting in Conway Hall, where he had spoken about education to a packed audience: 'I had just endured a year of teaching in Walthamstow during the Blitz. The top of the school was rendered unsafe by landmine blast, there was a bomb crater in each playground, the caretaker and his family had been killed when a direct hit demolished their house, and we had a headmaster who wanted us to rap the children's knuckles because they weren't writing very well in classrooms without window glass, after nights in the shelters. In the pub after the meeting, I asked Neill what he would do if he had to teach for such a headmaster. He looked up – blazing blue eyes in a red face already topped by snow-white hair – and said without hesitation: "I'd shoot the bastard." ' Vincent Chapman attended a lecture Neill gave two years later at the College of Preceptors, one of a series of Saturday morning talks arranged by the honorary dean and Neill's fellow-pioneer, J. H. Simpson. 'This kind of event was rare in the middle of the war, and like an oasis in the desert,' he recalls. 'I was especially attracted by Neill's lecture because I had been appointed just before the war as one of the first remedial teachers in Essex. To hear Neill talk about a boy being allowed to break windows with a hammer underlined the wide gap of opportunity between the private and public sector.'

The 150 teachers present were apparently enthusiastic about Neill's lecture on the topic of 'The Difficult Boy or Girl', and formed a group to continue meeting. Their mood seems to have been typical of many of Neill's war-time audiences. The Conway Hall meeting, a success in itself, had been arranged because so many had been turned away from an earlier lecture by Neill. Early in 1942 he told Reich that 'when I lecture I get bigger and more enthusiastic audiences'; in 1944 he wrote, 'I lectured in London to a most enthusiastic audience (hundreds couldn't get into the hall) and felt happy and useful.' His contact with audiences not only put him in a more optimistic frame of mind, but also gave him some belief that his ideas were beginning to spread. In 1943 he wrote: 'Today freedom for children is growing, slowly, timidly, perhaps, but the idea of freedom has permeated thousands of homes and hundreds of schools.' He found that when he lectured to British troops 'they all appear to be with me'. He talked to a group of working mothers and was 'most agreeably surprised at their interest and understanding. Some of them had been spanking their children automatically, and were genuinely astonished to learn that there were other ways of keeping discipline in the home.'

Yet when the teacher unions, the political parties, the trade unions and other bodies began to publish their proposals for transforming the schools after the war, Neill found himself profoundly dissatisfied with most of their content. In February 1943 he told Reich: 'I am trying to get on with my new book, the one on the Future of Education. So many people are writing rubbish about it that I feel I ought to contribute my share of it also.' This 'rubbish' eventually emerged as *Hearts not Heads in the School*, though because of various production difficulties it did not appear until the autumn of 1945, after the war had ended.* When it finally appeared it received a mixed reception. *The Times* called Neill a genius; *John Bull* magazine headlined their review by Vincent Brome 'Mr Neill's Cock-Eyed College'; while the *New Era* reviewer asked: 'Is it ignorance, conceit or genius that makes this schoolmaster so unplaceable among his professional colleagues?' In the *New Statesman and Nation*, T. C. Worsley called the book 'dogmatic, sentimental and philistine', and pointed out to Neill that

> the planners of education he is addressing are not Summerhill
> trained, and they are more likely to be repelled than attracted by
> being addressed as if they were. . . . If I were a planner in search of
> enlightenment about modern methods I do not think I should be

*One reason for delay was the fact that the manager of the printing firm handling the book refused to go ahead unless Neill cut out what he saw as blasphemous and obscene remarks about religion and sex. 'My answer is: Go to hell,' Neill observed. 'I shall not tolerate censorship by any printer.' It is not clear if either side gave way. The published version of the book contains only one direct reference to religion, though the sentiment could well have caused offence. Writing of Summerhill, Neill explained that 'we consider religion dangerous and anti-life, just as we should not think of introducing children to sadism or anti-Semitism or Fascism or sexual perversion, because they, in another form, are anti-life.' On the other hand, Neill devoted a whole chapter to 'Sex and the Future Schools', and wrote with his customary frankness on the topic.

much impressed by the mixture of wild generalisations, chatty stories
and strongly held prejudices which make up this book.

The book was indeed a ragbag of familiar ideas and anecdotes, reflecting Neill's struggle to write it. But it did contain new thoughts of some
personal significance. While he was writing the book, Neill heard that
Russia had decided to abolish co-education, so that boys could be brought
up to be 'good fathers and manly fighters', and girls 'intelligent mothers
competent to rear the next generation'. It was for Neill an immensely
retrograde step: 'So many of us who have looked to Russia to lead the way
in politics and education must sigh, and decide to plough our lonely fur-
row,' he wrote. He felt the move would increase the ignorance the sexes
had about each other, and the likelihood of unconscious antagonism, leading to unhappy marriages and sex lives. He opposed the idea of trying to
force boys and girls to develop differently: 'It perpetuates the evil tradition
that the woman is the one who gives, the man the one who takes, a
tradition that makes a man ashamed to give himself.' He quoted disapprovingly some comments in *Pravda*, in which Russian children were being
reminded daily of the need to be 'disciplined, polite, clean'. For Neill all
this marked the final betrayal of the Soviet dream: 'It makes one inclined
to be pessimistic to see the only hope of a new civilisation regressing to the
infantile of civilisation, heading for a Czarist second childhood.'

The book's main interest lay in Neill's comments about the plans being
put out for post-war education. His remarks suggest that he already despaired of seeing any significant changes emerging from the debate. The
plans, he wrote, were 'mere skeletons and all the important organs are not
there'. He could find no reference to child psychology in them:

> They plan elaborate schools and labs, and apparently assume that
> education is a matter of learning and not of living. Oh yes, they talk
> about the school preparing the child for life and work. They do not
> declare that strapping and caning must be driven out of schools;
> they do not demand that every teacher must study psychology first
> and foremost. Their Plans might well have appeared in 1900 and
> been hailed by all Liberals then, for who does not want to see
> healthy schools full of facilities for learning and creating?

He went on to criticise the unions for

> planning pre-Freud schools in a post-Freud world, planning for
> consciousness only in a new world that is exploring the unconscious.
> These Plans do not realise that the child is the centre, not the school,
> that unless we are to treat children in such a way that they are
> happy, sincere, creative, no fine building is of any value
> educationally.

One of the points being debated was whether or not there should be
religious instruction; and the 1944 Act did subsequently lay down that
every school must include a daily act of worship and religious education in

its curriculum. For Neill, however, the more important question was whether Christianity was to be taught or lived:

> To be religious means to give out love, and no teacher can give out much love under discipline and punishment and moral teachings, for you can't love your neighbour as yourself if it is your job to cane him for putting out his tongue, or to lecture him for saying 'bloody'.

He also criticised the proposals for failing to deal with the question of the freedom of the child:

> Is his character to be moulded or allowed to grow freely? The Plans do not say, so that there may be freedom in the coming schools for any blustering bully of a moralist to warp child nature among splendid surroundings, with the walls all plastered with Old Masters, and Beethoven played during meals (which should be noisy as hell).

The best course, he suggested, would be 'to get a body of children together and ask them what sort of school they wanted'; but then he reflected that even this idea had its drawbacks, since 'being emasculated for years in their desk schools they would be likely to be sheep and mildly suggest that the desk school should remain'.

It was these kind of remarks, especially when they were delivered with some ferocity in his lectures, which convinced many teachers that Neill was totally out of touch with ordinary schools.* Neill himself acknowledged this risk for pioneers such as himself:

> We do tend to forget the world outside, and are apt to dismiss schools in general as out of date. We see all the bad things in the other fellow – his sadism, his stupid dignity, his dangerous authority – and we shut our eyes to the good work that is being done in many a school.

However, he argued that his view of the state system was shaped by the substantial number of letters he received from teachers, the overwhelming majority of which were critical of the system in which they worked. His correspondents were of course not necessarily a representative sample, since those teachers who were happy or even only moderately satisfied in their work would hardly have bothered to get in touch to tell him so. But Neill was also influenced by the comments and information that he picked up in his lectures to teachers. Lecturing in Scotland early in 1943, for instance, he was told by a number of parents in Kilmarnock that their children were being given the strap for making mistakes in spelling or talking in class.

---

*He was perhaps even less in touch with provision for pre-school children. In 1943 he had a letter printed in *The Times* about the gross mishandling of babies in nursery centres. He quoted four examples, and deduced from this that 'this barbarous attitude to children is nationwide'. Yet his criticisms were not ill-founded. During the war Lady Allen of Hurtwood visited many homes for children: in one, run by nuns, boys were caned for persistently wetting their beds. They were taken to the Chapel, for correction – where the cane lay across the feet of the plaster Virgin.

Such examples made it hard for him to be persuaded that there had been any real progress within the state system since he himself had left it more than a quarter of a century earlier.

And yet, even by Neill's standards, there had undoubtedly been changes in attitude and practice between the two World Wars. If many schools could with some justification still be labelled 'barrack', and many teachers 'moralisers' or 'moulders', a small but growing number of teachers and administrators were looking for a different way of working with children. In 1923 Henry Morris, who had just been appointed chief education officer for Cambridgeshire, noted that: 'The ambition of teachers is enlarged of late. No longer are they content to impart information. They would give and take with pupils. . . . For in the recent past Authority has given place to teaching, and today teaching gives place to conversation.' In 1931 the Hadow Report on primary education, produced by the consultative committee of the Board of Education, showed how the emphasis was beginning to shift away from 'what children should be' to 'what, in actual fact, children are'. The Report showed that the pioneering work of the 'progressive schools' had begun to impinge at least on the thinking in the public sector. The committee argued that 'the central consideration, by which the curricula and methods of the primary school must be determined, is the sum of the needs and possibilities of the pupils attending it'. They defined a good school as 'not a place of compulsory instruction, but a community of old and young, engaged in learning by co-operative experiment.' Education, they suggested, 'must be regarded not as a dead routine designed to facilitate the assimilation of dead matter, but as a group of activities by which powers are exercised, and curiosity aroused, satisfied, and again aroused'. The *Handbook of Suggestions for Teachers*, published every few years by the Board of Education, also reflected considerable changes in received wisdom: in 1927, for example, it was suggested that the teacher should 'aim at a discipline which arises naturally from a mutual understanding between himself and his pupils', and that 'Self-education should be the key-note of the older children's curriculum, just as free expression is of the youngest children's'.

Inevitably, much of this advice was not taken up in schools, for a number of reasons. Yet here and there changes of this kind were occurring, particularly at primary school level. The creative potential in children began not only to be acknowledged but actively encouraged, through the promptings of educationists such as Christian Schiller, who had a powerful influence on men and women who later became headteachers, administrators or school inspectors. 'Children move because they must, children speak because they must,' he told a group of primary teachers in the mid-1930s. 'They touch and explore and make, and this is how they learn and grow. . . .Children live only for the present, and our job is to help them fulfil to the full their present stage of growth.' Another influential figure, the art teacher and craftsman Robin Tanner, who spent many years as an inspector, was in a position to observe the extent of the changing attitudes: 'By 1939, there were few who failed to see that because no two children are alike and each has special gifts, it would be folly to attempt to instruct them *en masse*, instead of teaching them as individuals. The self-evident fact that children learn best when they see purpose in what they are asked to do – and are allowed to do it – was becoming more generally accepted'. In 1942 Henry Morris pointed to the 'decrease in child misery and increase in child happiness' that had resulted from reforms by teachers in primary schools.

In tune with this philosophy, the creative arts began to flourish in many schools, under the influence of other pioneers. Marion Richardson, as a young art teacher in Dudley High School, and later as a school inspector in London, fostered a movement which drew on the individual vision of children, and rejected the traditional idea of art as being the copying of inanimate objects, with nothing more adventurous than a pencil. 'Art cannot be taught, but in sympathy it can be shared,' she wrote. 'I see pictures, will you show me how to paint them – that is what the children are saying.' The work she inspired – and the exhibition of work done by Cizek's pupils which was brought to England by the Save the Children Fund in 1927 – persuaded many teachers to encourage children's creative abilities. Christian Schiller recalled that 'Throughout the country there was a sort of "underground" of teachers who. . . were working towards a single goal, not only through art and craft, but in every sphere of education.'

However, it would be wrong to suggest that these changes had led to a transformation in all schools. An inspectors' report of 1950 on the changes a head was making in a Hertfordshire secondary school makes it clear what a great distance there still was between Neill's views and those of the established authorities:

> The Headmaster is largely concerned with providing an environment which will allow the children to adjust themselves more harmoniously to one another and to adults. The Inspectors have asked the Headmaster to reconsider this point of view. They doubt whether the present staff is capable of understanding and implementing the Headmaster's philosophy. If he continues to adhere to this point of view he will send out children who are not well-mannered, not interested in a wide range of subjects, and not competent in basic skills.

Significantly, the report added: 'It might be legitimate in an Independent School to adopt his methods, but they could not be tolerated in a state school.'

Much of the more 'child-centred' approach, with its emphasis on creativity and on understanding the nature of the child, would have been welcome to Neill. Indeed, though it is virtually impossible to separate all the factors involved, it is clear that his own work at Summerhill, and his efforts to publicise what he was doing, contributed in all kinds of ways to a shift of this kind.* Eileen Bernal, for instance, recalls: 'I believe his

---

*The question of Neill's long-term influence is discussed at greater length in chapter 22.

theories were like manna from heaven to a number of young teachers of the 30s and 40s. Several times I met young teachers living in cottages in Cambridgeshire and the Isle of Ely, and their shelves were full of Neill's books. They lapped them up.' Leslie Jones taught in primary schools in Birmingham after the war. An enthusiast for Neill's ideas, in one school, where 9 of his class of 54 were on probation, he began a club for delinquents. By the time he left there no children were still on probation. R. F. Mackenzie, who taught before the war in the Forest School in Hampshire – and unsuccessfully applied for a job at Summerhill – remembers the hopes of a younger generation of teachers involved in the pioneer schools: 'We thought that dawn would broaden into boundless day. For some of us, A. S. Neill was the prophet of a new age.' Timothy Rogers, then still at school, read Worsley's review of *Hearts not Heads*: 'I became a bloody revolutionary then: Neill started me thinking and feeling, he gave me a different view of education,' he remembers. Yet despite the fervour with which many teachers embraced his ideas, such enthusiasts remained in a minority. Many of the significant changes were confined to a small, though influential, minority of schools and teachers. In the early 1950s such ideas were supposed to have spread much further afield; yet when the inspectorate received requests from foreign teachers to see the 'famous progressive schools' in England, they apparently found it difficult to find many that fitted that description.

The most tangible evidence of Neill's influence at this time is to be found in the schools which were set up by those directly inspired by his work. Ironically, one of the best-known, and possibly the school that mostly closely approximated to Summerhill, was founded in Scotland. John Aitkenhead, a young secondary school teacher in Ayrshire, read *That Dreadful School* and *Is Scotland Educated?*, and in the summer of 1937 went to stay for a fortnight in Summerhill: 'To say that it was exciting was an understatement: I was bowled over,' he recalls. 'One of the first things I saw was a kid building a dinghy. You could go to a hundred schools today where youngsters are building boats; but not in 1937 – it was toast-racks and toothbrush stands in those days. Here were boys and girls of all ages and of several colours and nations, living together and learning in freedom, helping to make the rules of their small international community. It was a new world in the context of schools, and to me it was intoxicating.'

John Aitkenhead returned the following summer: 'I might have waited for a chance to work at Summerhill, only the war came. Then Neill published *The Problem Teacher*, and I thought that this Scottish educator should have his philosophy practised in Scotland. So I put an advertisement in *The Times*, the *Glasgow Herald* and the *Scotsman* saying, with Neill's blessing, that there would be a school like Summerhill in Scotland, and would interested teachers, parents and capital please communicate with this number. There was no interested capital, and no interested parents, but there had to be a special delivery of mail for interested teachers. I could have staffed ten schools. That's the standing Neill's name had in 1940.'

With a small group of fellow-pacifists, Aitkenhead then set up a small boarding school in Kilquhanity, in the Stewartry of Kircudbright in west Scotland. Kilquhanity House was run on similar lines to Summerhill: it practised self-government, rejected all corporal punishment, and took children from many different countries. In other respects it differed from Neill's school. It took in between a third and a quarter of children paid for by the local authority, who for a variety of reasons had experienced failure in the state system. The school included a small farm which necessarily provided a certain amount of framework missing from Summerhill. Most significantly, children were expected to attend lessons.*

Another rural school started only a few months before Kilquhanity House was Monkton Wyld in Dorset. It was begun by a small group of Oxford graduates, including Carl and Eleanor Urban who, in 'sorting out our ideas in the 1930s', had been impressed by Neill's work. The school provided boarding places for children separated from their homes and families by the war. It was non-competitive, with a weekly meeting, and a very flexible timetable which allowed the children to organise their own work to a considerable degree. Children were free to call a meeting any day to discuss grievances and practical problems, the meeting being presided over by a child. Neill paid several visits to Monkton Wyld: one former pupil remembers him saying once to Eleanor Urban: 'There's something fishy about this school: everyone's working.'

Neill was also the catalyst for another pioneer who established a reputation for work with problem children. Otto Shaw was a petroleum technologist with Shell until, as he recalled, 'I read, by chance, a book on education in freedom by A. S. Neill. Reeling from the iconoclastic impact I read more by the same author.' He then paid several visits to Summerhill, and was impressed by the 'freedom, joy and contentment of the school'. This prompted him to bury himself in the psychoanalytical literature, make a study of delinquency, get himself analysed, and ultimately set up his own school, Red Hill in Kent. His aim was to cure highly disturbed boys and girls through psychotherapy, administered both by himself and other members of the staff. Like Neill, he was quite prepared to use unorthodox devices in his treatment – including rewarding children for stealing, a piece of 'trick psychology' almost certainly borrowed from Neill. Another clear influence was to be seen in the self-governing structure of the school: as at Summerhill, the community took on a therapeutic role by means of a court, in which delinquent behaviour was discussed and dealt with by the children and staff together.

Neill visted Red Hill and attended court meetings; he also referred people interested in working with problem children to Otto Shaw. He did the same in the case of another pioneer of the 1930s working in the same field. In 1930 George Lyward founded Finchden Manor, a school for highly

---

*During the school's early years, the debt to Neill was always mentioned in the Kilquhanity House advertisements, until Neill one day suggested they stopped using his name: it was their school, not his, he wrote to John Aitkenhead.

intelligent but emotionally disturbed older boys. He himself had worked in the public school system, and seen at first hand some of the emotional damage inflicted on children there. At Finchden he began by taking in a number of ex-public school boys, with the aim of allowing them to rediscover themselves, to lose the fear of authority which had been induced by their previous dealings with adults both at home and school. Though there is no direct evidence that Lyward was influenced by Neill in setting up his school, they certainly shared some common assumptions, and achieved similarly striking results. Lyward saw his boys as cases of 'arrested feeling development'. He thought little of any training or education which was 'divorced from the children's wishes, fantasies and needs'. Just as Neill argued that 'childhood should be playhood', so Lyward believed that his older boys should be allowed 'to have back their childhood'. His aim was to get them to respond to him 'as if we were both on the same side of the fence' – though, unlike Neill, he aimed to keep a certain formal distance by having the boys address him as 'sir'. Both Finchden and Summerhill were frequently seen as 'last resorts' by parents of other schools; and, like Neill, Lyward had some extraordinary successes in restoring emotionally crippled children to health. Yet despite their many shared beliefs, Neill and Lyward appear to have had a rather distant relationship: in later life Neill wrote to David Wills: 'One man I could never contact was George Lyward who gave nothing away about his methods.'

Neill was encouraged that a few like-minded people should set up their own schools in this way. Yet his physical isolation during the war, and his gradual realisation that the intensive debate on education was not going to produce 'a nation of Summerhills', made him yearn sometimes for a new kind of life, away from children and education. In December 1942 he wrote wistfully to Lilian Morgans, a Scots friend in Suffolk: 'Oh, to live only creatively, writing plays, novels, books, paintings, making things of wood and metals'. It was not the first time he had felt such an urge: in January 1935 he had written to Curry: 'I've taken to playwrighting, and have produced a damn good one I think. . . . I was tired of writing about psychology, and wanted to do something more creative.' The play was called *One of the Family*, in which an outwardly respectable middle-class family's life was disturbed by the arrival of a burglar in the household. It seems to have owed a little to both Shaw and Ibsen, rather more to Freud, and most of all to Neill's brand of humour. In this scene the burglar is disturbed by Dr Hanick, the part which Neill assumed when the play was tried out in Summerhill.

> *Dr H*: Mind if we have a chat?
> *Smith*: What about, the weather? A deep depression is –
> *Dr H*: Not descending on me, anyway. Why not talk about yourself?
> *Smith*: Okay, I'll try to be a guinea pig.
> *Dr H*: I don't want to probe into your character and I guess you
>   don't want me to. Have you the same attitude towards your
>   profession?

Smith: Profession?

Dr H: It must be rather a fascinating sort of life. You must meet, or rather I should say avoid meeting, some interesting people. Tell me, Smith, does it require any special talent, or are burglars born and not made?

Smith: Go on, I don't mind your laughing at me.

Dr H: I never laugh at anyone except myself. No, I am genuinely interested. What sort of sensation is it when you enter someone else's house? Possibly like learning to drive a car; the first few times a glorious adventure, but after that just mechanical and boring. Tell me, is burglary similar?

Smith: I don't know. I never tried it before.

Dr H: Really, this is most interesting. You mean you have branched out on a new line? Tell me, do criminals have a sort of grading? Does a crook begin by stealing milk bottles and gradually work his way up through pick-pocketing and forgery to company promoting and a title?

Smith: Go on, I can take it.

Dr H: I am so ignorant about it all. Now take the social side. Does the wife of, say, a cat burglar consider herself a cut above the wife of a pick-pocket? Possibly more of a climber.

Neill was not terribly encouraged by the reaction within Summerhill. Several people felt that it read better as a novel than a play. Cyril Eyre recalls that 'it had some good exits and entrances, but was a little naïve'. Neill later acknowledged that it wasn't a good play, but still maintained that the characterisation wasn't bad, 'and I like to think some of the dialogue was good'. At the time he thought enough of the play to send it to Maurice Browne, a producer and playwright who worked at Dartington Hall for a while, and whose production of R. C. Sherriff's famous anti-war play *Journey's End*, backed by Dorothy Elmhirst, had been highly successful in London in 1928. Three weeks later Neill wrote again to Curry, telling him of Browne's verdict: 'He sees a good play in it, gave me some valuable suggestions, told me to re-write it, and send it back to him.' It seems though that he never did re-submit the play, though whether this was because his enthusiasm waned or because, as he told Curry, 'to write a play in term time is impossible', is not clear.

In Wales it appears to have been Mrs Lins's death which prompted a fresh burst of creativity in Neill. He had, during her long and upsetting illness, got stuck after completing only three chapters of *Hearts not Heads in the School* – the first time he had experienced such a blockage, as writing usually came easily to him. After she died he finished the book, wrote another play, and turned his mind to further projects, conscious that the years were passing by. He yearned, he told Lilian Morgans,

> to write a long-planned Diary of an Ugly Woman, a psychoanalytic detective yarn, a life of G. D. Brown, lots of plays. . . in short a 50 yrs plan, and I am 59. Time is the most deadly enemy in the world.

In young years when we have time we are full of love and ambition and conceit and we do so little, and then when we feel inspired to do much Father Time steps in and says: 'Put your toys away, child, and come along.'

While the inspiration was upon him, he began with some eagerness on his new career as a biographer, and early in 1943 made a trip to Ayrshire to start to research the life of George Douglas Brown. For more than forty years he had had an obssession about *The House with the Green Shutters*, and knew it almost by heart. When it was first published in 1901 it instantly became his second most-loved book after *Sentimental Tommy*, and before long his favourite of all. Whenever he went to Edinburgh he would if possible call in at the National Library of Scotland, and read Brown's original MS written out on penny exercise books. Neill must have found, in the vivid and powerfully written story of life in a small Scottish community, substantial echoes of his own childhood – not least in the central relationship between the tyrannical father and unhappy son of the Gourlay family. Brown also made explicit his views about the harshness and futility of the strap, and the dangers of enforced book learning: 'Thereafter young Gourlay had to stick to his books. And as we know, the forced union of opposites breeds the greatest disgust between them,' he observed at one point. It was probably Brown more than Barrie that influenced Neill when he came to write *Carroty Broon* and *The Booming of Bunkie*: both writers, for example, use Scots dialect for their dialogue, but revert to standard English when using narrative or description. It was perhaps the book which Neill would have most liked to have written himself. As early as 1917 he admitted: 'When I want to feel humble I take up *The House with the Green Shutters.*'

One of the reasons which now led him to investigate Brown's life was his feeling, perhaps brought on after his own analysis with Reich, that the Scots writer had 'a hell of a lot of hate in himself which had to find expression in some way'. He found that the only existing life of Brown 'says almost nothing in too many words', and was astonished to find that a man he considered one of the great figures of Scottish literature should be the subject of so little curiosity. Through letters to the press and by other means he began to gather material; but before long he tired of the project. He felt that Brown's life had 'no highlights', that writing a biography was not after all creative enough, and that the material he had managed to gather was 'mostly dull, piddling stuff'. He passed what he had collected on to the Scottish novelist James Veitch, whose version of Brown's *Life* was eventually published by Neill's own publisher, Herbert Jenkins.*

Neill's desire to write something other than books on children and psychology fluctuated considerably, depending greatly upon his mood and

*In carrying out the research, Neill had some difficulty in separating fact from fiction. Edwin Muir had written an essay on Brown, in which he said that he was the illegitimate son of a servant girl. The official *Life* had said nothing of this. When Neill asked Muir for the source of his information, his friend replied, 'Why, *you* told me.'

his feelings about his own life and the outside world. In Ffestiniog he often
fell into deep depressions, feeling that the war would never end, or that if
it did it would be Hitler and the forces of fascism that would triumph. 'He
was quite certain we were going to lose the war,' Gordon Leff remembers.
'When the *Hood* was sunk in 1942, I remember his saying, "This is the
end." He used to say that regularly: he didn't think we would last out from
one year to the next, let alone win the war.' Such depressions sometimes
affected his physical health; and on one occasion he had to spend five
weeks in Scotland at the Kingston Clinic after a recurrence of his old kidney
trouble. Yet at other times he could find considerable satisfaction in his
way of life in the Welsh mountains, and would then feel more optimistic
about the future. In April 1942 he told Reich:

> I am in the best of health, full of work energy and not conscious of
> any tensions or anxieties, somatically functioning well too. Of course
> in these days there is the big anxiety about the future and the
> present. I think myself that Hitler won't last long although the
> pathological fellow will be the death of many yet.

One thing that he desired above all – and it was this that perhaps
enabled him to keep going during the most difficult times in Wales – was
to return to Leiston, where the climate was dry and the pubs didn't close
at nine. He was able to visit his old premises once a year during the war,
but found the occasions painful, as he told Lilian Morgans: 'I can't say I
enjoy visiting the old place and seeing its misery and forlornhood. Like
seeing it in a dream, for it now has all the intangibility of the dream
world. . . a never-never land I sometimes think. How long O Lord?' He did
acknowledge that his present circumstances made him idealise his former
home a little bit: 'Leiston and Sax sound paradise to me now, but I know
that if I come back for good they will once more become wee dull places
with windy station platforms and meagre shops. Paradise is only the creation of misery, a mirage.' But in the summer of 1945 his dream was at
last realised. On 8 May the church bells rang out in Britain in celebration
of VE day. In Ffestiniog there was a bonfire and a dance in the village hall,
at which Neill acted as Master of Ceremonies. Early in June he heard that
the soldiers were leaving Summerhill, and within another two months he
was back with his school in Leiston. It was, he wrote later, 'maybe the
most joyous day of my life'.

CHAPTER 17

The Problem Parent

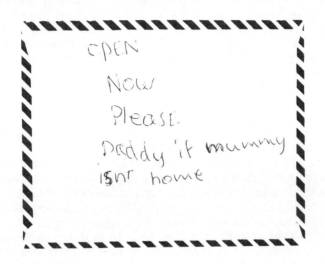

I could do whatever I wanted with him.
Zoë Neill

There was perhaps never any real doubt that Neill would eventually marry
again. But, as he observed to Reich, 'my wife has to be more than a success
with herself, and me. . . she has to succeed with herself, me, and the work.'
It was predictable that he should consider the needs of the school perhaps
more than his own feelings in choosing a successor to Mrs Lins. The
question of who that should be aroused both curiosity and tension within
Summerhill, and at one point led to serious division within the school. Part
of the difficulty lay in the fact that Neill had around him a number of
rather forceful women, not all of whom got on well with each other,
though they were each very attached to him. Some people, for instance,
felt that Neill's friend of long standing, Constance Tracey, might be keen
to fill the vacancy. Her daughter Suzanna remembers: 'My mother admired
and was fond of Neill, and thought he was a great man who had done a
lot for education. But Neill used to talk to her a lot about his problems,
and she found his depressions quite difficult to cope with.' Neill for his
part wondered if she would be quite the right person to settle in to the
work at Summerhill. 'To tell the truth,' he wrote to Reich, with whom she
had had analysis, 'I think that C would not fit into a community life easily.
I feel she tends to the autocratic in life and would clash with the system of
the majority rule, but maybe I am wrong.' Was he perhaps reminded of
Mrs Lins's tendency to ignore the power of the meeting and go her own
way?

There was also some feeling that Lucy Francis might be a possible successor. She had indeed been a crucial part of the school for many years in overseeing the lives of the younger children. But there were important differences in outlook between her and Neill. She was not entirely in agreement with Neill's views on voluntary lessons, and had made it quite clear without saying as much that she expected the younger children to come to lessons as a matter of course. Her temperament would also perhaps have counted against her. Kate Newman, who taught dance in Wales, recalls: 'She had this wonderful knack of getting lots of very nice people to work very hard for her. She was a power lady – you were either in Lucy's favour or you were not.' Neill had a number of disagreements with her, culminating in an occasion when he told her, 'This school is too small for both of us.' It was after this that she left Summerhill to open Neill's 'branch school', first in Sybil Hedingham in Suffolk, and later in West Hoathly in Sussex. The school was called 'Kingsmuir' after Neill's home village, and differed slightly from Summerhill in that it took in problem children paid for by the local authority. Though Lucy Francis ran it in a very different style from Neill, the two schools remained in close contact, and a number of adults and children moved between them over the years.

Contrary to what some in Summerhill assumed, it was this which was the principal reason for Lucy Francis leaving the school. On the other hand, it would have been difficult for her, having been Neill's unofficial deputy for some time, to stay on once Neill had made his choice. The matter at one time became a very fraught one, as Neill explained in a letter to Reich four months after Mrs Lins's death: 'Just off to Scotland to play golf, after a distressing time of disunion in the staff. Section against the lady in charge who happens to be very near to me in all ways. Tired of dealing with women; feel like having a male staff only.' Five weeks later the position appeared to have worsened: 'I am going through a most difficult stage,' he told Reich. 'Section of staff very much against my secretary who means a lot to me in every way. . . . At the moment the school is all divided and the rebels talk to old pupils and parents giving their side of the matter, and I have got to be careful lest S'hill goes to hell.'

The woman referred to as 'the lady in charge' and 'my secretary' was Ena Wood, and later that same month Neill announced that he and she were to be married. To some people this had seemed an inevitable choice for Neill to make. Though she had initially come to Wales to help with the cooking, like many other staff Ena soon found other work, becoming first a housemother and subsequently matron of the school. She had nursing experience, and had done more than anyone else to look after the ailing Mrs Lins. She was extremely practical, reliable and efficient, which could not be said for some of the other adults there at this time. A slim, dark and attractive woman, shy in many respects but very forthcoming in others, she had gradually become indispensable to Neill. There was inevitably a lot of resentment about Neill's decision, and considerable speculation about the motives of both parties. Gordon Leff remembers that 'there were people who thought that Ena deliberately insinuated herself, that she wasn't the genuine article and didn't really believe in it – and even if she did wasn't a fit person to be Neill's consort. In retrospect I think these people were wrong.' Erna Gal, who shared a room with her in Bryn Llewellyn, recalls that 'she fell really and honestly in love with Neill'. A few days after the end of the war, she and Neill were married in a registry office in London. Once again it was a quiet affair – 'we just sneaked off afterwards and had lunch with Jack Flugel and his wife,' Ena Neill remembers.

Once back in Leiston, Neill set about the task of putting his house in order. The army had left the place in a mess, and had, Neill maintained, done more damage in five years than the children had since he first took the house. He spent many hours making gravel paths, trundling wheelbarrows, wielding a pickaxe or scythe, mending beds. To Curry he wrote cheerfully that autumn: 'Great to be back in Suffolk. Had two months of heaving pianos about, and am still at it until the gang comes back after three months' hols. Christ won't they have some steam to let off!' In restoring the old house to a habitable state, Neill made one alteration which had considerable consequences. Until this time, he had not had any real private life of his own: Summerhill was both home and work, the children his 'family'. At 62 he felt it was time to change this. 'I want to live my own life in the few years left to me,' he wrote to Reich, 'for my life has been one long living for others.' He was also beginning to find himself less patient with the noise of the children around him. In an attempt to get at least some quiet and privacy, Neill had part of the main house partitioned off to make separate living space for himself and Ena. Occasionally he daydreamed 'of a quiet life in the country with a garden, a workshop and some hens and no post and no visitors'. Marriage, he decided, suited him; he began to put on weight, and confessed: 'I begin to look like a successful pork butcher.' He had, it seems, at last found emotional satisfaction too: 'We are very happy together and both have the fullest in love,' he told Reich.

Yet, predictably perhaps, the new set-up at Summerhill caused considerable difficulties almost from the time the school returned to Leiston. Neill's role of substitute father to so many of the children – and indeed to some of the adults – resulted in a great deal of hostility being shown to Ena. Resentment sometimes focused on petty matters, such as whether she should buy herself a new dress when Neill was pleading poverty and paying his staff such a low salary. There was a tendency on the part of some adults to treat her as a domestic servant, or at the most as Neill's wife rather than a person in her own right. She was thought to be too protective of Neill, and it was assumed that the idea of the new living arrangements was hers. Ena Neill herself believes that 'I was a mother symbol to the adults as well as the children,' and recalls that, 'they were for ever trying to get me out. They thought Neill was a soft touch, and they saw me standing in the way.'

There were also difficulties with the pupils, many of whom found it hard, unconsciously or otherwise, to cope with Neill's evident attachment to Ena. Branwen Williams recalls: 'My generation had some problems in sorting that one out. It was almost as if one of your parents had died and

the survivor had remarried.' There was a distinct division in attitude between those who had been at the school during Mrs Lins's era and the
more recent arrivals. One pupil from the pre-war days, Roger Anscombe,
remembers: 'It was perhaps a two-way hostility, not very conscious on
either side, but there all the same. Although Ena may not have been aware
she was doing it, she made us feel unwelcome – almost as if she were afraid
of us. She wanted to have Neill to herself, but we'd already got him, and
had been dug in for some years.' Norma Harris, who first came during the
war, recalls on the other hand: 'Most of the kids of my generation got on
with Ena: they hadn't known Mrs Lins, and didn't have any axe to grind.'

One of the most difficult problems facing anyone married to Neill was
having to deal with the many people who wanted to see him. Here again
it was a question of trying to keep home and work separate. 'I felt our
home should be our home,' Ena Neill says, 'and I was never very tolerant
of crowds of visitors. When he came over for his tea people would invade
us: they used to go round the front garden and photograph him through
the sitting-room window. It was pretty awful.' She also found it hard to
cope with the numbers of female visitors who made clear their admiration
of Neill: 'she hates it when my female fans come along and want to talk
to me at length,' Neill admitted to Reich. After a later trip abroad, Neill
wrote to Willa Muir: 'Ena spent a miserable time in USA with me, neglected
while my fans surrounded me. She vowed she would never go on a lecture
tour with me again. . . *gans richtig* [quite right].' Yet Neill, enjoying the
adulation he so often received, was not always as sensitive to Ena's difficulties as he might have been. At the start of that USA trip, the Neills
stayed in the New York apartment of Ellerie Fricker, a Summerhill parent,
who remembers: 'Many people called on Neill, but it took a long time
before people realised Ena was his wife. I remember saying to her, "We're
like a couple of maids, and he sits there like Lord Muck, with women
strewn at his feet." '

In the domestic sphere at least, Neill was clearly not an easy man to
live with. He expected to be looked after, to have his breakfast ready when
he got up, his post laid out. Yet he was totally uninterested in his physical
surroundings, and could be quite dismissive of anyone who concerned
themselves with domestic detail. He would extol the virtues of other people's houses, while showing no awareness of the efforts made by the women
around him to make his own agreeable. Ena Neill recalls one incident
which appears to typify Neill's attitude: 'Once he went to stay with friends
in Norway for three weeks. I decided to distemper and paint the sitting
room, and we had a good old clean-up at the same time. The room looked
lovely. When he came back he walked in and said, "Where's my mail?" So
we gave him the mail he needed to look at and he opened all the envelopes,
and the envelopes went one side and the letters the other. So we picked
them up and put them tidily, and then I went down town. When I came
back he had this biscuit tin full of rusty bed springs which he used for
mending the beds. He had tipped it into the clean chair, and all the rust

had gone all over the carpet and the chair, everywhere. But you dared not say anything.'

At Neill's age it might have been impossible for him to have a child of his own, but he was extremely keen to do so. Though careful not to show it in the school, Neill had always liked little girls more than boys, and wanted badly to have a daughter: 'My son is my work', was the way he explained his preference. When, little more than six months after their wedding, Ena showed signs of being pregnant, Neill was fretful enough to wonder whether she should see a specialist. But a few weeks later his hopes were realised, and it was confirmed that a baby was due in October. On the night of the birth some of the Summerhill chidren stayed awake to see who would be the first to hear the new baby's cry. Neill, as was customary, was not present at the birth: 'He wasn't the sort of person who gave you assurance in such a situation,' his wife recalls. The midwife, Valerie Bennett, remembers that he received the news of the birth 'urbanely'. In a hand-written scrawl across the bottom of a letter he had just finished to Reich, Neill wrote: 'A girl ZOË SUTHERLAND, healthy and big. Ena doing well.'

Neill was tremendously pleased and proud at Zoë's arrival, though he tried to disguise his pleasure. A few days after her birth he wrote to his former pupil Angus Murray: 'No special news to give you, for you don't know the new pupils at all. No news. . . except, oh yes, I became a father last week, a girl Zoë. Kinda late at 63.' Aside from his personal feelings, Neill was of course very interested in the *idea* of bringing up a child. From the moment Zoë was born, it was his firm intention that she should be brought up by what Reich called the 'self-regulation' method. This was no more than a logical extension of the philosophy that had led Neill to create Summerhill. In *The Free Child*, published when Zoë was 4, Neill defined the method:

> Self-regulation implies a belief in human nature, a belief that there is not, and never was, original sin. This belief is not new; many have held it and tried to practise it, in, for example, the kind of education called Naturalism and associated with the name of Rousseau, but it was applied only to the child's psyche, not to his soul and body together. Self-regulation means the right of a baby to live freely without outside authority in things psychic and somatic. It means that the baby feeds when he is hungry, that it becomes clean in habits only when it wants to, that it is never stormed at nor spanked, that it shall always be loved and protected. It all sounds easy and natural and fine, yet it is astounding how many young parents, keen on the idea, manage to misunderstand it.

Such a philosophy went against the prevailing wisdom as to how children should be reared. The timetable feeding of babies, as advocated by the New Zealand practitioner Truby King, and outlined in *The Mothercraft Manual*, was still the norm. It was a method that ensured that children created the minimum of disturbance in their parents' lives: 'Baby and mother should live by the clock', it advised. A few experts were beginning to suggest that the parents should follow the child rather than lead it – Susan Isaacs as the psychologist on *Nursery World* was one of these. Another was Benjamin Spock, whose highly influential book *Baby and Child Care* was published in America in May 1946, just six months before Zoë's birth. Neill described it soon afterwards as 'the best book on babies I have come across recently. . . . It is nearer to self-regulation than any book I have seen.' He was sufficiently impressed by Spock's work to buy up a number of copies, to sell to friends and others interested. He had, belatedly, come to realise the importance of a child's early years, and that the work he had been doing at Summerhill was essentially too late in a child's life. In his book *The Problem Family*, which he began when Zoë was 1, he observed: 'I feel like kicking myself for being so long in realising how much the sickness of the world is due to doctors and moralists who damage the child long before the teacher has anything to do with him.' In watching Zoë's development, he noticed that 'traits in child character that used to puzzle me I now recognise as being the result of early mishandling and parental ignorance'. In fact, Neill had been aware of this for many years in a general way, but it was only with a real-life example to hand that he seems to have appreciated its true significance.

During this part of Zoë's life, Neill compared notes with Reich, whose son Peter was born two years before Zoë. At first, in his letters to Reich, and to friends and members of his family, Neill was pleased and encouraged by his daughter's progress under 'self-regulation'. After only a fortnight he noticed that she was making her own timetable for feeding. At 7 weeks he wrote: 'Zoë flourishes and already is trying to bully us both. . .God help a poor father.' A month later she was 'fine and bonny and a bit too lively sometimes'. At 10 months he thought: 'Zoë is a darling. Taking a few steps now.' As she passed her first birthday he wrote that she 'walks about everywhere and is no trouble at all, a fine example of self-regulation'. Four months later 'she shows no sign of hate or destructiveness. It is a joy to watch her grow'; and he recorded her 'delightful happiness and cleverness and beauty'. She was, he decided, 'a bright kid', and felt that 'Ena has been an ideal mother for Zoë, and the result is just excellent. . . she hasn't made a single mistake in Zoë's case. The result is pure delight to me.' When she was 3 Neill called her 'our wonder child', and when he began *The Free Child* the following year he indicated what store he set by his observation of Zoë's growth: 'There are so few self-regulated babies in the world that any attempt to describe them must be tentative and conjectural. The observed results so far suggest the beginnings of a new civilisation, more profound than any new society that is promised by any kind of political party.'

Many of the visitors who were now beginning to return to Summerhill after the war were keen to see Zoë, and interest in her increased when she began to feature in the press. The *Daily Herald* sent their Fashion Expert Marjorie Proops down to report on the Neills' experiment, but this time in her role as 'an interested mother'. She found Zoë to be 'happy, healthy and uncomplicated, mentally and physically in advance of many children of her age', and decided that the parents had produced 'a lovely, lively creature, unselfconscious, never showing off'. She expressed her admiration for the Neills, and felt that Zoë would grow up 'happier and freer' than her own 7-year-old son Robert.

Letters from readers the following week make it clear that there was considerable sympathy for Neill's ideas on child-rearing. Some mothers, however, pointed out that Summerhill was not typical of the conditions in which most children had to be reared. 'Try the Neill way with three children and a kitchen the size of a postage stamp and see what happens. Order must prevail – or chaos,' wrote one. Another woman's comments show that the idea of following the child's needs had already gained some ground in England: 'Freedom, yes – but within the bounds of common sense. The pendulum has swung from one extreme to another, and children who were formerly expected to be seen and not heard are now encouraged to become the "little bosses of the household". Freedom should not degenerate into licence, or the rest of the family will suffer.' A third reader raised the sexual issue: 'Our own children have been told the facts of life, but a youngster with whom they play and rather admire has not. I am told that babies *do* come from cabbages because so-and-so says so.' One or two were totally dismissive, making a point that Neill was already familiar with: 'I see nothing to admire in the Neill way of bringing up a child. I consider their treatment of Zoë is just as deplorable as cruelty. They are failing to equip her for the world in which she is to live.'

The following month Zoë, unkempt, grubby and laughing as she romped in the Summerhill grass, featured on the cover of the famous weekly illustrated *Picture Post*, labelled as 'The Girl Who Never Gets Slapped'. The accompanying article by Susan Hicklin spelt out clearly and comprehensively what Neill and Ena were doing, and concluded:

> Whatever may be thought of the details of Neill's practice, the important thing for us is that we have here the beginning of a new pattern of upbringing. It is not by any means the most convenient way, but it is worth our while as parents to consider it in relation to ourselves and our children.

She found Zoë to be 'bright-eyed, strong-limbed and unafraid of people. Her movements have a steadiness rare in such a young child.' The only mildly critical note in an otherwise enthusiastic and sympathetic piece came at the end, when the reporter stated that Zoë 'has to do a lot of hard work settling her own problems', and that perhaps it was 'not so surprising after all that she clings so passionately to that bottle – the last shred of her babyhood'. The article was illustrated by some charming photographs, showing the 2-year-old Zoë cutting up her food, climbing unaided into the bath, scrambling over a heap of coal, perched in a tree, and being read to by Ena. Another picture showed her chalking pictures on her playroom floor, with Neill sitting nearby and watching her efforts. He told the *Picture Post* reporter that for him 'to watch her developing free and unhampered from the day she first opened her eyes is the crowning happiness of a lifetime'.*

However, Neill soon began to find that there had to be *some* adult interventions in Zoë's life. To Reich, who was having anxieties about aspects of his son Peter's behaviour, Neill wrote: 'Zoë, if too late up, owing to the exciting life here, is a problem next day, whining, ill-tempered. . . . I'd play the heavy parents about sleep if I were you. Self-regulation be damned sometimes. . . today is very cold; Zoë wanted to go out in her thin frock. Ena said no; must wear overalls. Anger, tears, but Ena insisted and put on the warm things.' To visitors and reporters he continued to enthuse about his 'wonder child', but in private he was not always so enchanted. Aged 63 when she was born, Neill often found Zoë 'too lively', and was not always in the mood to crawl around the floor with her twice a day, 'pretending to be a friendly lion what doesn't eat people'. 'I begin to feel my age now, and find it difficult to get up when Zoë makes me lie with her on the floor,' he told Reich when she was 1½; and to a niece who had just had a baby herself, he wrote: 'I wish you all the lovely joys of parenthood, especially the joy of being awakened at 3 a.m. on a frosty night.' When she was 3 he told Reich: 'Zoë grows big in every way, demanding reading lessons every day and far too bright for my taste, for she never lets up, simply goes on energetically all day till she gets tired.' This, he admitted, was 'the normal thing to do in life'. But it was evidently something of a strain on him physically to keep up with the demands of his self-regulated child.

It was not, however, Zoë's liveliness which caused Neill the most apprehension. He seems to have held to a naïve belief that a genuinely self-regulated child would remain uncontaminated by the 'neurotic' world outside, and would not pick up any ideas or values from children who had been repressed or over-indulged, or suffered in some way from adult 'moulding'. He concluded from his observations of Zoë that she had no innate hatred or aggression, and saw this as confirmation of his view that children were naturally good, and a refutation of Freud's ideas that aggression was inborn. 'She wants to give out love, to ask for love,' he wrote to Reich, 'and because in her environment she satisfies both wishes, she is no hate person.' But he was puzzled and upset when, aged 3, Zoë would say to him at bedtimes, 'Go away, Daddy, I don't like you'; and later, 'I wonder why I like Ena much more than I do you.'† He wondered if he himself was to blame: 'Maybe I am not a good father, distributing my love to 70 children?' Most of the blame though he put on the other children around Zoë, who frightened her with stories about wild animals and bloody

---

*Neill complained about the article the following year in a letter to one of his former teachers: 'No, it wasn't good, but no paper article ever is. I don't myself see what they mean by saying we went off the rails with Zoë, for after all, anti as the woman writer was, the article did give some idea of self-regulation.'

†Later, when a student tried out a questionnaire on a sample of Summerhill children, Zoë was the only one to refuse to answer the question, 'Who do you like best, your mother or your father?'

deaths, witches in her toy cupboard, or cows that would come to eat her up. Sadly he concluded that, even when he and Ena told her such stories were untrue, she didn't believe them: 'the word of the badly reared child of five has more weight than anything we can say.' He longed wistfully for an island on which only a select few self-regulated children could be reared; 'but even then I guess fears would appear. Prophylaxis has its snags I see.'

Neill was especially anxious that Zoë should not pick up or develop a negative attitude towards sex or her body, as Gordon Leff recalls. 'When Zoë was about 2, he told me with complete solemnity that if he should so much as move Zoë's hands from her genitals if she put them there, she would be ruined for life.' During her early years Zoë seems to have had few inhibitions about sex, happily telling people in the shops in Leiston that she came out of Mummy's fanny, that Daddy 'fertilised' Mummy, and asking who had fertilised them? At 6 she was in much closer contact with the other Summerhill children, and Neill was irritated when she asked him one day, 'Daddy, it is rude to say Cock, isn't it?' But he did feel it was necessary to give Zoë a rational explanation of the attitudes of those who disapproved of or were shocked by swearing, though one incident made him think that he should perhaps not go beyond explanation to prescribing behaviour. In *The Free Child* he described the episode:

> Some child taught her the word that the law will not let us print, and when we were interviewing a prospective parent, a conventional business man, she was trying unsuccessfully to fit some toy together and at each failure was exclaiming: 'Oh, f—— it!' Later we, quite wrongly I think now, told her that some people did not like the word and she should not use it when visitors were present. She said OK. A week later she was doing something difficult to accomplish; she looked up and said to our Language Mistress: 'Are you a visitor?' The lady replied: 'Of course not,' and Zoë gave a sigh of relief and cried: 'Oh, f—— it!'

Even when she was 8, Neill was still marvelling that Zoë should pick up the language of the apparently un-self-regulated children around her, even though by now she was clearly easing herself into a life in which Neill played a less central part. To Reich he wrote:

> She has little interest in grown-ups (including me) but enters fully into the group life of her pals. She has just come to me reciting a very obscene rhyme a boy taught her, and last week said she liked hymns and would like to go to church.

This particular request Neill clearly found very hard to take, commenting: 'Just shows how far a journey it is to a self-regulation world.' As with her earlier demands for reading lessons, Neill was in a familiar dilemma, caught between his intellectual convictions and his bitterly hostile feelings, developed first in his childhood, towards organised religion and book learning. Logically, Zoë's interest in hymns and church could be seen as proof that she was indeed regulating her self, and not being moulded by her father's views. Yet Neill managed to confuse ends with means, seeing her curiosity about a part of life he detested as representing a failure for self-regulation. There was still the implicit assumption that a self-regulated child could be protected from what he termed the hopelessly 'anti-life' values of those around her.

Despite these feelings, Neill never made any real attempt to push Zoë in any particular direction, or to impose his views on her. As she now remembers it: 'I wasn't academic, and never have been, but Neill never made any suggestion that I should go to lessons or anything. A lot of us were rather anti-social and didn't really go very often, but there was never any pressure or resentment that I felt.' Yet Neill did fret about her lack of interest in lessons, both to his wife and to friends, in his letters. Yet it was not just his philosophy of childhood that was responsible for this attitude, but the fact that he was totally unable to handle Zoë in any way that might remotely suggest the hand of authority. Ena Neill remembers that 'Zoë could practically twist him round her little finger from the moment she opened her eyes.' Zoë herself has similar memories: 'He was as soft as lights with me, I could do whatever I wanted with him, especially being the only daughter. I would always prime him up before asking Mum something.' Neill in fact often reacted in the worst possible way to his daughter's demands, by refusing them initially, and then being persuaded to change his mind by a few well-timed tears. 'He would hardly ever say no to her,' Ena recalls, 'and this was very difficult, because there are occasions when you have to. That was all left to me.' Roger Anscombe recalls one rare moment of intervention by Neill: 'He once got terribly upset because he'd taken Zoë down to the sea, and when she wouldn't come out, had smacked her. "Oh my God, what have I done?" he said.'

Neill's refusal and inability to act towards Zoë in any way that might so much as hint at adult 'moralising' was a source of both amusement and irritation to others at Summerhill. Jimmy East, who came as a teacher after the war, remembers another occasion when the family were bathing at Sizewell beach: 'Zoë was paddling, and Ena called her. She didn't come, and Neill was heard to say, "Zoë, you really must learn to do what you're told." This was felt to be really rather a triumph!' Unfortunately, Neill was unable to heed the very advice he had been giving parents for so many years, about the need to distinguish between freedom and licence. In an end-of-term circular about self-regulation which he wrote when Zoë was 3, he argued: 'Licence means spoiling, giving the child all the rights, and all babies will automatically take advantage of adult weakness in giving in to everything. There are occasions when one has to say "Don't".' Even if he sometimes saw the need to interfere with Zoë's freedom, he would leave the unpleasant task to someone else. Howard Case, a parent at this time, recalls: 'Neill would say, "Why do you let her run around in her best clothes?", but he wouldn't do anything about it. And he would blame Ena for anything that went wrong.'

Neill's role in bringing up Zoë during her formative years was in fact a very limited one. Daphne Oliver, who returned to Summerhill after the war to become a housemother, remembers the way he liked to play with her: 'Sometimes, especially at bedtimes, he used to get her over-excited. She was a very clever little girl, and Neill used to stimulate her brain a lot, with word games and things of this sort.' He did read stories to her in the evenings, but quickly grew weary of having to go through some of them over and over again, particularly 'one dreadful story that makes me feel murderous, Zoë's favourite: I have had to read it fifty times.' He certainly never gave her a bath or changed her nappy, though it was of course much rarer then for fathers to do such traditionally female tasks. In general he was able to preserve his image of a fond and gentle father.

The unusual circumstances in which Zoë was brought up, combined with Neill's inability to live up to his own precepts, caused considerable difficulties to arise between the Neills and the rest of the Summerhill community. Ena Neill confessed: ' I wouldn't ask for a child to be born in Summerhill again: the fight has too often come near to disaster.' Zoë's arrival inevitably caused jealousy among some of the other children, as Neill later acknowledged in a letter to one of his teachers: 'S'hill has been her enemy in a way – an only child with 50 brothers and sisters who take up all her parents' time and interests.' One post-war visitor, Harold Dent, remembers: 'In the evening Neill's wife brought downstairs a screaming infant, and Neill appealed to the school, assembled in the hall for a meeting, to moderate the noise they were making. They took no notice.' Vanji Collier remembers a visit she made as a parent: 'Zoë slept with her parents and the Cottage kids felt a bit pushed out. My son Storm and his gang told her that burglars were coming to burn down the house. She cried all night, and neither Ena nor Neill could calm her down. Neill came storming over to the Cottage, just like any irate and tired parent. It was most out of keeping.' Before this, Zoë had been bullied and frightened by certain older Cottage kids: toys and sweets were taken from her, and were broken or never returned. Eventually Ena and Neill decided that they would move as a family into the Cottage, which then became their permanent home. Zoë, from the age of 5, then attended the school over in the main house as a boarder, at her own request.

However, she clearly experienced great difficulty in coming to terms with the proximity of home to school, and Ena admits that both she and Neill 'made sad mistakes' in Zoë's upbringing. One criticism made by some adults was that they were wrong to try to treat Zoë as though she were no different from any other child in Summerhill. Liz Hall, a house-mother who looked after her a great deal, remembers the symptoms of Zoë's anxieties: 'She became ill with a horrible croup, and Neill and Ena took her back home. Later she came back to the main house, and at one point said to me, "If I get ill, they'll have to take me home." It was awfully difficult for her, and sad, because there was her home and her mother and father so near, and she had to share them with others.' Once she was in the main house, Zoë would sometimes not come home at all during term time: Ena would visit her at half term, like any other parent, and take her out to tea locally. It was a difficult existence for her, as she herself recalls:

'I think I probably didn't know Neill well from the family point of view. It seems to me there were great huge spans in my life when I didn't see him at all. I might have just met him at school, and said Hi, and run off.'

Neill's relatively advanced age obviously restricted the range of activities in which he could join with Zoë: 'I suppose to go fishing with him or something like that was not quite on,' she says. In some respects, Neill appeared to her as he did to most other children at Summerhill, a somewhat distant though kindly old 'gent', who dug the garden and took his dog for a daily walk. His age was clearly the cause of a dream she experienced while still one of the youngest in the school: 'I was always aware of the fact that he was an old man. I used to have quite horrible dreams when I was quite young. One I had involved a huge square of concrete. I dreamed that they had taken this up and buried Neill underneath it, and there was this red machine that was ticking away all the time, and he was alive under the concrete. I can see that machine in my mind now, and I remember waking up and crying and crying.' These nightmares prompted one housemother to try to persuade Zoë's parents to let her live with them, but Neill and Ena insisted that she should continue to be an ordinary member of the community.

Yet even in a community where there were markedly fewer barriers between adults and children, and an absence of the 'Them' and 'Us' syndrome, Zoë's position was an invidious one. 'We had a lot of problem children who used to make her suffer badly,' Ena Neill recalls; 'and some of the staff were absolutely dreadful to her.' As she grew up she became aware of having her loyalties divided, particularly where her own behaviour or that of other children was concerned: 'When something dangerous arose, or when people were really heavily anti-social, then I didn't like it at all, and I used to get quite cross. There was a line, and on one side of it was the school, but if anyone crossed it then it became personal, an affront to my father, or to both my parents, or to Summerhill. I remember having "I don't think we ought to do that" feelings.' Perhaps as an escape from these pressures, as a way of marking out her own territory, she became passionately interested in animals, especially horses. To Reich Neill wrote when Zoë was 4: 'Her identification of self with animals persists all the time; she wears out all her stocking knees and shoe points crawling on the floor as a zebra or a horse or a Bambi.' He observed that she seemed to be at home in both fantasy and reality; he would not acknowledge at this stage that her identification with animals might have a connection with her unenviable position in Summerhill as Neill's daughter. He suggested rather that it 'may be a flight from the wrongly reared human animals around her'. But she would also take flight from reality on occasions: often when she saw yet another group of visitors coming to see the model self-regulated child, she would disappear into the trees until they had gone.

When she was 12, Neill and Ena were forced to make a very difficult decision. For a year or two Zoë had been going through what in other children Neill termed the 'gangster' stage. Ena recalls her daughter 'never going to a lesson, smoking, swearing, and at times being completely anti-social, never going to a meeting, breaking bedtime laws, pinching, in fact being "one of the boys". Being charged in the meetings meant nothing to her and her group: they were at one time about as anti-social as they could be, and a headache to the community in general.' Ena felt that Zoë needed a spell away from Summerhill: but Neill found this proposal very hard to accept, although he was sorry that Zoë was involved with a group who were doing little that was positive. His resistance to the idea evidently went deeper than disappointment at the idea of separation. From his letters of this period to Reich and others, it is clear that Zoë herself was his principal reason for keeping Summerhill going. 'I should have been able to slack off at my age and have a peaceful old age,' he reflected in February 1950, 'but with a baby to work for I have to go on struggling until I die.' It was not however simply a matter of economic necessity. Neill believed that the only hope for a humanity now living under the threat of the Bomb lay in the coming generations, who would be reared to love rather than hate. Zoë was his representative of that generation: 'To hell with both their houses, east and west', he wrote during one Cold War crisis of the 1950s. 'I dislike the idea of my Zoë being made into cinders because of Lebanon or anywhere else.' And since Summerhill was his vision of how such children could be allowed to grow, how could the two be separated? Anxious about an apparent threat to private schools, he wrote to Reich in April 1949: 'I expect to be enquired into very soon. My fear is that I MAY BE TEMPTED to compromise so that Zoë can stay in a school of my making.'

Neill eventually agreed that Zoë could go to another school. Ena suggested they might send her to Kilquhanity House, but Neill was not prepared for her to go to any other British school. Before the war he had corresponded with Paulus Geheeb, telling him, as he had told Russell, that he was 'one of the few educationalists I have wanted to talk with'. A pacifist and an admirer of the poet Rabindranath Tagore, Geheeb had been involved with one of the first progressive schools in Germany, the Free School Community of Wickersdorf, which he helped to found in 1906. It was a co-educational community managed co-operatively by a weekly assembly of pupils and teachers. In 1910, together with his wife Edith, he set up the New Odenwald School, which had connections with the Dalcroze School in Hellerau while Neill was there. In the mid-1930s the Geheebs escaped from Hitler's Germany, and set up their school in Switzerland, under the name École de l'Humanité.

It was a strange choice for Neill to make, and no one, including his wife, seems quite to know why he made it. He had corresponded sporadically with Paulus Geheeb, and so presumably knew in outline how the school worked and what its philosophy was. Yet L'École de l'Humanité was significantly different from Summerhill. It had a religious tone to it. Above the doorway of each house in the school were portraits of representatives of German high culture such as Goethe and Schiller, who were seen as 'patrons'. The children had to rise at 6.30, take a cold shower, have an hour's rest after lunch, go for long walks in the mountains, and be in bed by 8.30. Neill was sending his daughter to the kind of place which he normally scorned for preaching the 'High Life'.

As Neill was away at the time, Ena wrote to the Geheebs in January 1959, and outlined the problem:

> Zoë is very healthy, quite a tall child and good-natured. Can be difficult but in the main is helpful and cooperative over everything, in fact just as a child of 12 should be. She is having a difficult time here in the school and feels it more now that she is older than in her earlier years and we would like her to be with understanding people to help her over this period.'

Two months later Neill confided to an old friend: 'It is too difficult for her here; as my daughter staff and pupils expect her to be perfect and the result will be a problem child if she stays here. But I hate to have to part from her.' In April, aged 12½, Zoë arrived for her first term away from Summerhill. 'I'm not quite sure why I went,' she says now; 'perhaps it was because I was a bit of a problem at Summerhill, though I never looked at it like that.' Her mother believes that 'she had made up her mind that she wasn't going, that was the beginning and the end of it'; and what followed then was 'a sheer battle of wills', between father and daughter.

As soon as Ena had left her in Switzerland, Zoë sent a letter to Neill, marked on the back with the words 'OPEN Now Please Daddy if mummy isn't home'. Inside she had written:

> Dear Mummy and Daddy, *PLEASE* COME AND TAKE ME AWAY FROM HERE PLEASE PLEASE. IM IN AGONY IM SO UNHAPPY I COULD COMMIT SUESIDE PLEASE Phone me to tell me the answer. Dont SAY NO PLEASE MAYBE YOU THINK ILL get over it But I wont, Im far too ill. They wont let me phone you so I do the best I can writing BUT PLEASE REALIZE your just about killing me.

A few days later Neill wrote to Edith Geheeb: 'Zoë's letters tear my heart and I long for the day she will write that she is happy with you.' He recalled the time when he was not much older than she was now, and was 'sent away to work in an office 100 miles away. . . and had many months of absolute hell with homesickness, so that I know what it can be'. He also quoted, with some embarrassment, one of his own statements about parents and children: 'Dear, dear, I blush to think that I once wrote that a child is homesick when it comes from a bad home.'

After a while, Zoë's letters home became more tranquil, though she was not finding the change an easy one, as she remembers: 'I hated it – God, was I homesick! The moral aspect of the École was never genuine to me. I had been brought up to feel and live life as it came. Nobody had ever preached to me about anything. Here in this other school I was being faced with a new and illogical set of ideas. . . . Too young to attend dances. . . no record players allowed. . . cold shower at 6.30 a.m. . . a minute's silence at mealtimes. Perhaps Neill and Ena hadn't told me enough about it, but it all seemed so false and stupid. Perhaps I had thought that because Neill was sending me there it was going to be like Summerhill. Or perhaps I just thought, if Summerhill suits me, why should I go to this other place?'

She seemed to her parents to have settled in when she returned for the summer holidays, and they noticed a real change. 'You have worked wonders,' Neill told the Geheebs; 'she is restful, happy, sweet to one and all. It is a delight that she so liked being with you, for it would have put us in a horrible position if she had not wanted to return.' Later, Neill told a different version of Zoë's return. 'I had a bit of sciatica, and she came and sat on my bed and told me about the school in German. She said: "I hate it, it's not freedom at all. You're a swindle, Daddy; you give other children freedom, but you won't let your own daughter be free." So I said, "You'll have to go back next term, because we've paid your fees." '

When Zoë returned to Switzerland the following term, she went through the same routine, crying and screaming on the first day, saying that she hated the school, and threatening to run away. Angela Neustatter, Wally's daughter, was there as a pupil, and wrote in her diary that night: 'Zoë was dreadfully homesick. I comforted her. Eventually it was agreed she should sleep just that one night with me.' The next day she wrote again: 'Went to comfort Zoë, who is very miserable.' Edith Geheeb wrote anxiously to the Neills: 'Zoë must. . . learn to face the difficult side of life. She must not remain so uncourageous, so possessed by fears and worries; otherwise, when something displeases her, she sees no answer except flight.' She implored Neill not to come on a visit, which by now he had decided to make in order to see the school for himself: 'We feel that Zoë would make hell really hot for you with her demand to be taken home again. For Zoë it would be seriously wrong, I may even say for her entire life, if she does not succeed in getting used to the École.'

As it happened, Neill had already left for Switzerland. Ena wrote a long and passionate letter to Edith Geheeb, telling her that she had tried to persuade Neill to leave Zoë at the school for a reasonable time to give her a chance to adapt to it:

> He says he loves her deeply and of course one knows how much he must love her, she is the only thing in his life that matters, but I try to say that he must bury his feelings about her and think only of what is good for her and her future now. It is hard not to have her around him and listen to her lively talk and sunny ways, I know so deeply how he must feel, but being with him all the time doesn't help the child to face what she will have to face in life.

She pointed out that it was 'going to be very hard for him to have to be really and truly firm with her, especially as she knows that her tears and entreaties tear him to pieces.'

Ena was right. Neill was greeted warmly by Paulus Geheeb, now nearly 90, and agreed to give a talk on Summerhill during his three days at the school. Angela Neustatter recorded his next move in her diary: 'Zoë suddenly announces that Neill is taking her home. It was a hell of a shock,

I felt very upset. As they were going, I burst into tears. Poor Neill.' Ena was extremely upset to receive an express letter from Neill telling her what he had done; she felt this was a tragedy for Zoë, and that she no longer knew how to deal with the situation. When they returned to Summerhill, Neill wrote to the Geheebs, telling them that Zoë had settled back there, and doubting if the École scheme would have worked: 'I don't think it was entirely the difference between our systems of education; I think that she felt so far away from home,' he concluded. To Helen Neustatter, Otto's second wife, Neill wrote shortly afterwards: 'The system is so different, so Deutsch. . . a teacher reads a sentence from Goethe or Nietzsche and the kids have two minutes *Schweigezeit* to contemplate it; as Zoë said, "All I contemplate is what is coming for grub." ' Later he spoke disparagingly of the Geheebs: 'Paulus was a man of 90, and a moralist. For some obscure reason he wouldn't have ping-pong in his school: it was all high life and uplift. His wife was running the school, but she was just an authority – there was no self-government. At the end I said I was taking Zoë home, and she said, "You're making a big mistake." I said, "I may be, but I can't keep a kid in a school if she's not completely happy." ' Looking back, Zoë herself feels that 'Neill was being true to his beliefs in taking me home.' Yet it was clearly his own happiness as well as Zoë's that prompted him to act in this way, and his later criticisms of L'École d'Humanité need to be seen in this light.

Years later, when comparing notes with Elna Lucas about their respective children, Neill remarked that he had never learned so much as when he had a child of his own. Many at Summerhill would not agree with him on that. Yet he did seem to have absorbed one lesson from his education in fatherhood. Having for years insisted that children should come to Summerhill at the earliest possible age, he suddenly announced to Reich, without any apparent awareness of his volte-face, that, at least until they were 5, infants 'need to be with their mothers for love and warmth'. Here Ena Neill clearly had some influence on him, though not as much as she would have liked: 'I thought it was terrible to take a child at 3½ or 4, but we had to agree to disagree on that. We did eventually change to 5, which I thought was still too young.'

It was a former Summerhill teacher who neatly summarised the feelings of many about Neill's performance as a father. On his way back from Switzerland with Zoë, Neill spent a night with Karl Waas, who had taught handwork at the school during the early 1930s. On hearing from Neill about his decision to take Zoë back to England, his host observed: 'Neill, a friend of mine wrote a book which I think I should lend you. It's called *The Problem Parent*.'

CHAPTER 18

Friends in Need

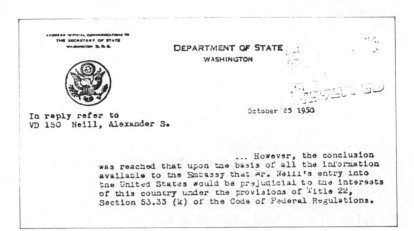

> . . .you are the only friend I have to whom I can let off steam.
>
> Letter to Wilhelm Reich, February 1950

In April 1942, Neill wrote to Reich from Wales:

> Let us be hopeful. Let us phantasy a little. . . daydream that Stalin is
> right and that Hitler will be smashed in '42. Japan can't stand alone
> long. Then in summer '43 a bloke called Neill crosses to New York
> to have a long talk (and a long drink) with old Reich, a talk about
> the new world and the work to be done in it.

Neill's phantasy took a little longer to materialise than he had hoped, but
in the summer of 1947, and again the following year, he was able to stay
with Reich in his home in Maine. 'I wouldn't have crossed the Atlantic for
anyone but you,' he told Reich just before his first trip to America. Reich
was equally complimentary in anticipating their next meeting: 'Matters of
utmost importance should be discussed and I know no one in Europe who
could listen better and understand better what is at stake at the present
time in the development of our work,' he told Neill. This time they were
to meet not as therapist and patient, but as friends and fellow pioneers. It
marked the growth of a warm, intense and lasting friendship which, despite
the fact that the two men were often in sharp disagreement over a number
of fundamental issues, affected Neill profoundly.

Reich was an extremely difficult and often intolerant man, who reacted
with immense hostility to any criticism of his life's work, and quarrelled
with almost all those who worked with him. He felt that his ideas were the

only hope for a sick humanity, and railed against all those who conspired to oppose them. In addition to the hostility he drew upon himself, he was also the subject of much uncritical admiration, and attracted disciples in many different countries. Neill himself, though an admirer of much of Reich's thought and practice, was certainly no disciple. This Reich recognised and valued, seeing Neill as 'my public conscience', and 'not only the important European connection, but more than that. . . an honest good friend'. He liked Neill's 'zest and zeal', and found, as did many others, that Neill enabled him to be himself. 'It is always invigorating to be able to speak out, without reservations and façades', he wrote to Neill; and later he confessed 'you are one of the very few to whom I can talk'. Two days after Neill arrived in Maine for the first time, Reich noted in his diary: 'Several hours of talk with Neill. He is still the same as ever. I could joke with him and be *simple*.'

Reich evidently enjoyed Neill's refusal to take him too seriously, and his ability to poke fun at him. The two men would go for long walks in the New England woods, when Reich would sometimes turn to Neill and ask him: 'Neill, am I crazy?' Each time Neill would reply, 'Crazy as a coot!', and Reich would smile with pleasure. 'I hope you aren't going to get solemn in your old age, Reich,' Neill admonished him in one letter. If he was not careful, people would soon be bottling holy orgone water, he told him. Neill could be playful with Reich and, perhaps partly because of his age, get away with it. 'I don't like to challenge the greatest authority on human nature in the world. . .', he wrote mockingly in one letter. Often he jokingly adopts the role of the heavy father to the younger man. When Reich had some heart trouble Neill wrote: 'Tut, tut, we can't have the ship's captain trying to navigate when he needs a rest. . .I think you neglect yourself a lot. As an old man I can lecture you about this, you being a mere youngster. . . . I feel like coming out now to boss you around and bully you into slacking off.' Reich summed up much of the warmth he felt towards Neill in a note he made in his diary after reading *The Problem Family* in manuscript: 'A very good book written by a child 64 years old; honest; playful; frank; full of love for children.'

When he stayed in Maine, Neill would sit with Reich in his cabin, drinking Scotch or Rye, smoking Chesterfield cigarettes and talking late into the night. For Neill it was a relief not to have to be giving out all the time, as he did for so much of the time in Summerhill. Reich also had the effect of pulling him out of the moods of depression which were now more frequent. 'You have no idea how much meeting you again meant to me,' he told Reich after his 1947 visit. 'You are a better tonic than your whiskey.' Problems in Summerhill over finance and staff, which were especially acute during the years following the war, seemed at times to overwhelm Neill: talking to Reich revived his spirits, and enabled him to see beyond his immediate landscape of unpaid fees and broken furniture. With him he could talk about and argue over political ideologies, sexual freedom, child-rearing, bodily and spiritual health. There was no need to *explain* or defend his work with children, since he and Reich shared so many assumptions about the cause of society's ills, and how they could be cured. And Reich's energy and optimism had the power to lift him out of his gloom, to rekindle his waning enthusiasm for his work at Summerhill. 'Ena says I look years younger and happier since I came back from Maine,' he wrote, on his return from his first visit to Reich.

Yet the inspiration that Neill gained from Reich did not blind him to the potential risks involved in any closer association. His attitude towards Reich was compounded of idolatry and canniness, of gullibility and shrewd common sense. Later Neill told an American friend: 'When in Maine Reich said: "Neill, I'd like to chuck the whole bloody business and come and teach in Summerhill," I replied: "Reich, I wouldn't have you within yards of my brats. You'd scare them." ' He reacted in similar fashion to a proposal which Reich put to him in February 1950. Reich had for many years nurtured a belief that a healthy society depended on a change in attitude towards children and adolescents. After his son Peter was born in April 1944, he told Neill: 'I assure you that after 25 years of intensive and extensive psychiatric work I am discovering for the first time, like a new student of psychiatry, the real nature of a new-born baby.' His observation of his own son's development led to a scheme for setting up an Infant Research Centre. Believing that 'the safeguarding of the natural self regulatory principles in newborn babies is of paramount importance', he saw the centre's task as being 'mainly to study *healthy* children and the prevention of armouring from birth onward'. To this end, Reich planned to build a children's home with a small hospital attached to it, and suggested to Neill that, 'of all people, you and Ena of course would be the choice to be entrusted with the directorship of such a children's home which would be devoted to the natural scientific, orderly study of the natural principles of self-regulation from birth onward.'

The offer caught Neill at a particularly despondent moment – for the first time in his life he was lying awake and worrying about finance and the future. His work, too, was getting him down: 'I see clearly that my interest in Summerhill is less than it was when we were building it up, when every new child was an interesting case.' An ex-parent, perhaps sensing Neill's disenchantment, sent him a telegram from Copenhagen, suggesting he move himself and Summerhill to Denmark as an International Scandinavian School. Though he immediately turned down the idea, he thought it 'a charming offer', and he admitted to Reich that: 'It is fascinating to dream of the possibilities of our being in charge of an Orgonon kindergarten.' When Reich pressed him further, Neill set out the pros and cons of moving to America:

Pros
I am learning and doing nothing new dealing with un-self-reg. kids.
USA has more self-reg. kids than England has.
To work with and near you would be a great delight and tonic.

Cons
I'd feel bad leaving so many kids here with no one I know capable
of carrying on S'hill as I'd like it carried on. And all old pupils
would feel I had left them in the lurch, for they assemble here thrice
yearly at end of terms.
Here I am known, a man of some importance, acknowledged to be
the leading pioneer in Britain. In USA I'd begin as a nobody.
I dunno the snag I'd meet in the way of opposition from church or
state.

In the end, Neill had the decision made for him by outside events, one
of which was a decision by a group of parents to form a society to raise
money to save the school. Later he told Reich of a 'con' that he had omitted
from his list: 'I knew it could not be, knew that the danger would be that
I became your disciple.' This could indeed have been a danger, though it
was perhaps only some years after Reich made the offer that Neill became
fully aware of the fact. There was a strong element of hero-worship in his
admiration of Reich, which made him at times see his friend as a man of
infinite wisdom. Neill once referred to 'the gulf between the man of talent
(me) and the man of universal insight (you).' He was impressed by Reich's
ability to combine intellectual brilliance with practical skills: 'You
think. . . and do things: I do things. . . and can't think. This isn't false
modesty; it is a real pain not being able to explain what I see to be truth
in children and adults.' From the start Neill was bowled over by Reich's
books, even when he found difficulty in understanding them. In February
1949 he wrote disparagingly to Reich of Melanie Klein's new book *Contributions to Psychoanalysis, 1921–1945*, 'full of castration and anal characteristics and mother's penis and what not. To read her is like being in a
graveyard with open putrefying bodies; to turn to your *Function* is like
going out into a meadow in spring.' Reich's works had such a powerful
effect on Neill that he sometimes felt quite inadequate about his own
output. When in the summer of 1953 Reich sent him his new book, *People
in Trouble*, Neill wrote a fulsome reply:

> Troubled People? You've said it, brother. You have made me one of
> them. My first reaction was entirely subjective. My new book *The
> Free Child* is in the press. After reading you I felt like withdrawing
> it. Your brilliant analysis, your manifold experience, your power of
> deep thinking made me feel that my book isn't worth a dime, feel
> that it is shallow and ignorant and full of wrong thinking.

Neill was less admiring of Reich when he gave glimpses of that hec-
toring intransigence which so alienated many who came into contact with
him. One of the most interesting of the disputes between the two men arose
over Neill's decision to marry Ena Wood. Neill had told the staff that he
didn't believe in marriage as it was then, but that professionally he would
be 'in danger of extinction if I lived without marriage'. Reich wrote back
scathingly, telling Neill that he shouldn't give in 'to pestilent public opinion

in such matters'. It was his belief 'that you were actually married to your wife when you felt married. Whether you take out a certificate or not is of no importance at all.' He regretted not being in Summerhill when Neill made the announcement, so that he could 'shake the conscience of those teachers of yours who did not take the trouble to think a matter through.'

In reply Neill dropped any trace of deference to Reich's wisdom, and defended his decision with fierce but canny resolution. He suggested that there is not time and energy to protest against *everything* of which one disapproves, and that it is better to compromise on minor matters than on fundamental issues. 'To me the big thing in my life is my work, and I shall compromise always enough to keep that work from being stopped.' He agreed with Reich that a certificate in itself didn't constitute a marriage, but that 'your idea of a marriage or my idea is a *Nebensache* [minor matter] when those in power have the right to kill our work. And my work is not primarily sex reform; it is work with children.' He attempted, not entirely convincingly, to refute Reich's suggestion that he was bowing to public opinion:

> I have no intention of getting married on their terms; any marriage for me will be on my own terms, and I can use the word in my own way while they can use it in their certificated way. . . to publish MY version of marriage to all and sundry would mean the end of my work. If you say: To hell with your work; it is more important to be a martyr for the cause of free marriage, then we differ much. But I don't think you do.

He then suggested that Reich failed to take into account the nature of English society:

> We are ruled by the 11th Commandment. . .Thou shalt not be found out, and a man can remain a great public figure if he has a dozen concubines. . .and keeps the fact dark. So that when I shall introduce a lady as my wife I shall be o.k. because the outer forms are satisfied, whereas if I boldly introduce a lady as 'my lover,' I am in danger of disaster.

In reply, Reich acknowledged the force of some of Neill's arguments, and agreed that 'If I had a school as you have, I would have to take the attitude of the Education Department as you have to take it'. Though the rest of the letter is not quite as gracious as this, the fact that Reich was prepared in such uncharacteristic manner to see Neill's side of the matter is an indicator of the store which he set by Neill's friendship. He ended with a hope that 'A talk of a few hours will do away with many a misunderstanding'. Neill agreed that they could 'clear all that up in half an hour's conversation' and observed that 'even when we do differ it cannot touch the warm regard we have for each other'.

This warm regard, which was undoubtedly mutual, to some extent depended on the personal encounters which both men found so valuable. Neill recalled his departure from Maine at the end of his second visit, when

Reich threw his arms around him, and said: 'Neill, I wish you could stay. I have no one I can talk to as an equal. I cannot talk about myself and my problems to the doctors I am training.' Neill walked off with Reich's door key, because, he supposed, 'I wanted to open your door again many times'. Reich wrote to Neill a week after he had gone, expressing his sense of loss in a style quite unlike that of his usual abstract prose:

> When you left, there was quite a gap at Orgonon. There was no
> emperor figure, walking slowly and meditatingly up the road
> towards the lab, there was no one playing around with the lathe and
> envying me for having it; there was no one I could tease with Stalin
> and no one to pour drink into. Well, we shall have it again.

But they were not to have it again. In the summer of 1950 Neill made preparations for this third visit to the USA, planning to take with him, as he had in 1948, both Ena and Zoë. On 14 July he arrived at the US Embassy in London, and after a lengthy wait was told by the Consul that his application for a visa was rejected. No explanation was given, but when he returned a week later he discovered the reason for the decision. The Consul asked if he had ever at any time written in favour of Communism: 'I answered: "Yes, years ago when communism was love and progress I wrote in favour of it, but on the other hand, since it hardened into hate and dictatorship, I have written strongly against it." Grim silence on Consul's part'. He then asked Neill if he was a Communist himself: 'I said, "Politically no and never was, but in life I practised the communism of Jesus, sharing all with children and staff." At the mention of Jesus he gave a nasty exclamation of annoyance.' A few days later a visa was also refused to the poet Stephen Spender, who had been a CP member in the 1930s but had subsequently become disillusioned with communism. From this Neill concluded that anyone who once showed any interest in communism would now be considered suspect – including many present Labour Party MPs. A Danish student in Summerhill suggested that he shouldn't have patted the red dog when it was a puppy, to which Neill replied that he couldn't have known that the puppy would grow up into a wolf. He wrote to Reich of his frustration:

> I am so angry at being held up *for the wrong reason*. My line is
> children not politics and if I were shut out from USA because of my
> views on children and their love life and their freedom, I'd have at
> least the satisfaction of knowing I was being martyred for something
> I believed in. To be martyred for an alien creed, that I know would
> shut my school at once if it succeeded, is too much to bear.

The passage to which American officialdom seems to have taken exception appeared in Neill's *The Problem Family*, which had been published the year before. In it he wrote of his reasons for *not* joining the Communist Party:

> My work and interest lie outwith the boundaries of all political

parties. Their interest is mainly one of solving the economic problem, while mine is one of solving the psychological problem. Fundamentally I am a Communist, believing in a society in which there will be no class exploiting another, for only in such a society will the mass of children have the chance to develop in freedom, and I can do more to further that society outside than inside the CP.

This, it seems, was enough to contravene the McCarran-Walter Act, which allowed entry to the USA to be refused to anyone who advocated doctrines or was affiliated with organisations held to be subversive. In September Neill was given official notification of the ruling by the Consul in London: 'I regret to have to inform you that it is now determined that you are inadmissible under the Immigration Laws and regulations, and a visa may not, therefore, be issued to you.' Still not satisfied with the reason for the refusal, Neill pursued the matter both in Britain and America. He enlisted the help of Edward Moeran, a left-wing Labour Member of Parliament who had visited Summerhill and was interested in his ideas. Moeran persuaded the embassy to refer the matter to the State Department in Washington. In October James Auchincloss, a member of the House of Representatives who had taken an interest in Neill's case, received a letter from the State Department, telling him that 'upon the basis of all the information. . . Mr Neill's entry into the United States would be prejudical to the interest of this country'.

The decision was a devastating one for Neill, for he recognised that it meant he would never see again 'the only friend I have to whom I can let off steam'. Depression descended on him once more: 'I fancy my high day is over, Reich,' he wrote in October 1950. 'The stimulation I had looked forward to at Orgonon and its loss has affected me more deeply than I yet realise. More than ever I feel ALONE.' There is an intensity in his sentiments which transcends his ritual grumbling. 'For two years I had looked forward to great talks with you in Maine, and when that anticipation was shattered, I had no one to talk to, no one who could give me anything new.' Yet it was not just the originality of Reich's ideas that meant so much to Neill. As long as it was possible to meet and talk over the problems of the world, so Neill could draw on Reich's essential optimsm about humanity to sustain his own work. 'I think of you often, especially when I am in trouble and want to talk to someone who will listen,' he had told Reich. Now that opportunity had disappeared, and Neill was left to brood on his isolation:

> One horrid feature of not going to USA is that the feeling of standing alone becomes greater. In Orgonon the fact of being one of a crowd of people who are life-positive is enough to inspire, but here I never meet anyone with anything to give; they all want me to give to them. The result is that I dry up, exhausted.

Five years later he was still dreaming at night of being in the USA with Reich.

The extraordinary strength of Neill's attachment to Reich was reflected in the eagerness with which he accepted Reich's view of the relation of sex and politics to the social evils of the time. Writing to David Barton about the attitude of the Communist Party to the discussion of sex issues, Neill explicitly acknowledged his mentor: 'I go parallel to Reich here. We hold that the sickness of humanity is primarily due to castration via sex repression in babyhood, and that communists ignore this factor and concentrate only on the economic one.' In *The Problem Teacher* he related his friend's beliefs to the educational sphere:

> If Reich's analysis of society is right, and personally I believe it is, what harm is being done by the teachers' acceptance of conventional sex morality? The schools are producing not only wage slaves but sex slaves. . . .What is the use of smashing capitalism if we are to retain capitalist morality? Sex is the creative force in life and our revolutionaries hope to remake the world by ignoring it, hope to remake it by their heads alone.

Yet he was not always prepared to swallow Reich's ideas whole. He disagreed, for example, with his belief that the world could be usefully divided into those who were free and those who were 'armoured', and suggested to Reich that

> if a division is to be made it should be. . .those who warp babies and those who don't, and there are a lot of still armoured people who are *not* warping and destroying babies. I say that all who are against baby life are red or black or blue fascists and that politics don't make fascists; they only organise them.

Neill's view of the world outside Summerhill was often a simplistic one, and this was not helped by the fact that he had little experience of ordinary social life, nor indeed ordinary schools. His pessimism led him frequently to act as though he were more beleaguered in his citadel of freedom than he actually was. This tendency was aggravated by his friendship with Reich, who had faced much more hostile criticism than Neill ever had, first in Europe and then in America. How much of this was due to Reich's personality and how much to the originality and subversiveness of his ideas is a difficult question. There is no doubt that he provoked hostility amongst many people, even among those who were attracted to his ideas. Neill, on the other hand, inspired love and affection, even from those who were antagonistic to his ideas, or at least felt they were not being given a fair test in Summerhill. Most people who got to know Neill at all well found a kind, humorous and relaxed personality behind the apparently dour exterior. Reich, however, partly perhaps because he had been his analyst, brought out another, more aggressive side of Neill. As a result, at least in his private letters to Reich, Neill attacked in belligerent and sweeping terms anyone who seemed to be opposed to the Summerhill idea.

Neill was sometimes aware of this characteristic that he shared with Reich: 'We are both apt to think the world is gegen us [against us],' he told him in October 1951. And, though he was from time to time infected by Reich's undoubted paranoia, Neill could also be pragmatic and clear-sighted in many important respects. Admired for being uncompromising, he was shrewd enough to know in practice when compromise was necessary in order to keep a long-term objective in sight. This quality was evident in the support he gave to Reich during the final and tragic period of his best friend's life.

In 1947, while Neill was staying with Reich, an official from the Food and Drug Administration called at Orgonon, following two hostile articles on his work published in *Harper's Magazine* and the *New Republic*. The FDA were investigating Reich's use of the orgone accumulators, which had been represented in the articles as both a cure-all and a device for 'enhancing sexual potency'. Many years of harassment followed, during which Reich behaved in an increasingly paranoid way. He came to believe that he was engaged in top secret work, that he had the personal protection of President Eisenhower to back him up, and that planes of the US Air Force flew overhead to give evidence of such protection. He also believed he had developed the power to control the atmosphere and had identified UFOs from other planets. Attempts were made by the FDA to ban the sale of accumulators, but Reich refused to appear in court, arguing that no jury was competent to judge a matter of science. The FDA obtained an injunction allowing the accumulators to be destroyed. Subsequently Reich was indicted for contempt of court, after one of his assistants had shipped accumulator parts from one state to another, so breaking the injunction. Reich was eventually sentenced to two years' imprisonment and, after an appeal had failed, was taken from the courthouse in handcuffs to serve his sentence. His books, accumulators and other equipment were gathered together in New York, and burned in the city's incinerator.

As the situation grew more grave for Reich, Neill was at first puzzled, and then alarmed. Reich addressed him as 'Lt. Alexander Neill', believing that Neill was one of his lieutenants in his fight against the 'red fascist plague'. For a while Neill defended Reich vigorously against the growing rumours that he was mad. To one visitor who asked if this was so, Neill replied: 'Absolutely mad. The rest of us are all sane. . . hence the world of today.' He also assured Reich several times that he shouldn't worry about people calling him mad – he suggested that even if a few Freudians had thought him crazy, 'that sort of thing is a compliment from them'. Just before the verdict on Reich's case was announced, Neill offered to organise a letter of protest against the expected sentence. When Reich was given two years in prison, Neill did involve himself, with Herbert Read and others, in a letter of protest, which both the *Manchester Guardian* and the *New Statesman* refused to publish. He also, while he was in Norway with some of Reich's Norwegian friends, sent a telegram of support to Reich. A reply came back to one of the Norwegians, saying that Neill was 'unreliable'. The apparent cause of Reich's sudden rejection of one of his closest allies was a visit that Reich's son had made to Summerhill. Much influenced by his father at the time, Peter Reich told Neill that the planes flying overhead from a nearby US airbase were sent to protect him. Neill told him this was nonsense, and the boy reported Neill's comments back to his father.

It seemed that Reich had finally broken with Neill as he had with all his other close associates. Greatly sorrowed by the telegram, Neill wrote with commendable lack of bitterness to Reich:

> So our long friendship has come to an end because you consider me unreliable. . . . How very sad. Just at a time when you require every friend you can have too. . . I think you have suffered from too many people being afraid to challenge you in any way. . . .Often I have heard you say: Everyone is right in some way. Now I say to you that everyone is wrong in some way also. I say that you are wrong about Peter. He looks too anxious. I think he is trying to live a part. . . . He isn't Peter Reich; he is Peter Reich plus Wilhelm Reich. And, dear old friend, call this emotional plague or what you will. To me it is just plain truth. I wish you every success in your appeal against an unjust sentence. I wish you many years to continue your work. Goodbye, Reich, and bless you.

In fact, Reich did contact Neill again, writing him a brief note: 'Can you be patient for a while until I am free to talk to you? Do not worry. . . .' The letter which Neill wrote in reply summed up in passionate terms all that Reich had meant to him:

> Your short letter made me cry. It seemed to symbolise your loneliness, your misery in this abominable martyrdom, yet it conveyed your courage, your belief in your faith and work. Damn this 3000 miles separation. . . . Reich I love you. I cannot bear to think of your being punished by an insane prison sentence. You couldn't do it and you know it. I wish to God that you'd simply let some good lawyer take up your case from the legal angle. Why should anyone waste breath and time trying to explain to a judge and jury what your work is? They can't possibly understand. . . .The *Tatsache* [fact] is that you are being crucified fundamentally because you are the first man in centuries who has preached pro-lifeness, because you were the one and only man to assert the right of adolescence to love completely. The majority in USA, Britain, Russia, in the whole world are anti-life, so that you do not need to look for specific enemies like the FDA: they are only the shot that was fired at Sarejevo, not the basic cause of the attack on you. In any court your defence should be in big letters I AM FOR LIFE AND LOVE, not I am the victim of Russia or red fascism or anything else. . . .To think that the great man who had advocated rationalism all his life would now embrace irrationalism is a terrible thought. . . . Sorry to lecture you like this, but I am concerned about you, very much so. Get that lawyer and fight them with their own legal weapons, for your weapons are invisible to them. My love and concern and blessings. Neill.

All Reich's appeals against his sentence were rejected, and in March 1957 he began his two-year sentence in the federal penitentiary in Lewisburg, Pennsylvania. A parole hearing was due on 5 November, with the possibility that he might be released on the 10th. On 3 November he was found dead in his cell, after a heart attack. Six weeks later Neill wrote to his widow, Ilse Reich:

> That Reich later had some illusions I think right, but they don't do anything to lessen his work. We all have illusions, and maybe the greater we are the greater the illusions. . . . Last night I sat down to read the many letters I've had from Reich, but I had to give it up; too near the shattering blow, too sad at this stage. Later I hope to read them with some calmness. His death grows on one. . . .You say it might have been avoided. I doubt it, Ilse. Only if he had compromised with the enemy and he couldn't do that. I can't remember ever knowing so honest a guy as Willi Reich.

In Oslo Reich had suggested to Neill that he was bottling up his aggression and hatred in order to preserve his Christ-like placidity. Neill took this diagnosis seriously enough to refer to it several times in his correspondence with Reich. It is perhaps no coincidence that both Lane and Reich, the two men who had the greatest influence on Neill, saw themselves as saviours of a kind. Both were subjected to court cases as a result of their work, and died shortly after their sentence, Lane in exile, Reich in prison. In different ways they both identified with Christ, and contributed to their own 'crucifixion'. Reich was clearly interested in Christ as a martyr, as Neill discovered once in a social gathering he attended in Scandinavia. Elsa Bakke, a friend of both the men, mentioned her interest in Krishnamurti, and said that he was the most Christ-like person she had encountered. Reich immediately asked: 'If he is Christ-like, why hasn't he been murdered?'

Despite his life-long hatred of and hostility to organised religion, Neill was nevertheless interested in the teachings of Christ. 'Read and re-read the life of Jesus Christ,' he exhorted the readers of the *New Era* in 1920. He saw Christ as the first and last Christian, and argued that 'Freedom, like Christianity, has never been given a trial.' Some of the remarks he made about his own work with children, although ostensibly designed to provoke or amuse, do have an underlying sense to them. 'The narrow religion of Scotland made me a saviour of souls,' he wrote in *The Problem Parent*; and in *That Dreadful School* he explained: 'We do not consciously follow Christ's teachings, but from a broad point of view Summerhill is about the only school in England that treats children in a way that Christ would have approved of.' He also felt that Lane's idea of being on the side of the child, which he himself embraced so wholeheartedly, was an expression of Christ's idea of love. Yet, though Neill's sense of mission was certainly powerful, his feet were always too firmly on the ground for him to suffer a similar fate to Lane or Reich. At the end of the war he pointed out the reason for this to Reich: 'Our main difference is that you. . . demand

All or Nothing and are brave enough to stick to that demand. I cannot as long as I have a school.'

CHAPTER 19

Paradise Lost?

If I have to shut down I don't know how to live.
Letter to Wilhelm Reich, April 1949

'I think in Wales the old Leiston Summerhill became a dream for Neill: "How wonderful it will be when we get back to the old place, everything will be like it always was." I wonder if it was ever the same when he did go back, whether there wasn't a bit of feeling of anticlimax, trying to pick up the threads, and never quite being able to?' As Leslie Morton here suggests, Neill did find it hard to set Summerhill on its feet again after the war was over. Under the new Labour government elected in 1945, the immediate post-war years were ones of austerity and reconstruction. Much of Neill's pioneering spirit seemed to have evaporated, and during the 1950s the situation of Summerhill became increasingly precarious. Although Neill continued to enjoy the role of *agent provocateur*, he also seemed to become even more out of touch with educational developments outside Summerhill. His relations with his staff, already damaged by the experience of Ffestiniog, became increasingly fraught. He began to speak of Summerhill in terms of a life sentence; less than a year after the return to Leiston he wrote: 'Summerhill is like a prison; it is so difficult to get away from it.' Yet, though he thought occasionally of giving it all up, and indulged his regular fantasy of 'starting again in a new line', he seems to have realised that there could never really be a life for him beyond Summerhill: 'I should retire, but know that if I did I'd die,' he wrote in 1956, at the age of 72.

There was another discernible difference from the pre-war period.

Although Neill had drawn immense personal sustenance from his friendship with Reich, the effect on his ideas and attitudes was not always seen as beneficial by those who worked with him after the war. Vivien Morton, who returned to Summerhill for five years, recalls that 'a whole new and, to me, horrible vocabulary came in. People were classified as "anti-life swine" on very flimsy pretexts.' There was also a change in Neill's outlook on what constituted a humorous story, as Bill MacKinnon recalls: 'Reich's influence was a very strong and moralistic one. At the beginning of one term, when Neill had just come back from one of his visits to Reich's "intellectual health farm", I started to tell him a story which had a sex angle, though it was not one that was just sexy for the sake of it. I was staggered when he said that Reich had altered his view of that kind of story, and that he no longer found them funny. It was so unlike Neill I thought he was having me on.' Neill's faith in Reich's works was also to be seen in more concrete form. In April 1947 Reich shipped out an orgone accumulator to Summerhill. For a while Neill sat in it daily, often reading Reich's books as he did so; and others in Summerhill also made use of the 'Akku'. For a considerable period he was prepared to be convinced about the effectiveness of the accumulator in assisting bodily and psychic well-being. But he also found other uses for the device. At one stage he tried growing lettuces in it, 'with giant-like results'. It also appears to have had its uses as an alternative refuge to his workshop: in June 1948 he complained to Reich about the constant flow of visitors who 'muck up our lives. . . for instance, four times last week I had to come out of the Akku to deal with some new arrivals'. Others, too, used it as a refuge: Tessa Hutchinson recalls: 'I use to sit in the orgone box while he wrote. I just wanted to be around him, and he didn't know where else to put me.'

The most damaging consequence of Reich's influence, however, was that it reinforced certain tendencies already present in Neill. His anxieties about such outside 'threats' as school inspectors approached paranoia, and became a joke amongst Summerhill staff. Not only was he unable to maintain a clear perspective on the dangers facing Summerhill from without; he also increasingly saw conspiracies within his own walls. Unlike Reich, he could occasionally see this failing in himself, yet the perception was not enough to affect his behaviour in Summerhill. Divisions between Neill and his staff were also exacerbated by his reluctance to bring his criticisms into the open. Instead he would write in scathing terms to Reich about the adults around him: 'Some new ones sit with sneering faces'; 'I have at least half my staff today who have this neurotic attitude'; 'I simply can't be bothered talking to my staff'. He could also be quite indiscreet and slanderous when gossiping to adults and children. Richard Tolson was a teacher there during a time of in-fighting amongst the staff: 'Neill deplored but enjoyed it in a very human way', he recalls. 'He would shuffle into my room, bring out his quarter bottle of whiskey, and say: ' "I disapprove of drinking, but I know you don't, so let's have a noggin." He would sit and grumble about the staff, how dissatisfied he was with most of them − and I've no doubt he grumbled about us to others!'

In February 1949 Neill wrote anxiously to Reich: 'I can't bring myself to sack one of the teachers who has managed to get many kids attached to him emotionally by flattery, football etc. . . .the moment I can get someone better to take his place I shall try to be brave.' The teacher in question was Bill MacKinnon, a fellow-Scot who had taught for a while at Kilquhanity House before coming to Summerhill in 1946. His account of Neill's reaction to his work with the children in the school indicates how Neill's 'problems' with staff could be of his own making.

'When I arrived there were no playing fields, because the army had vandalised Summerhill. I and another teacher, Douglas Collins, played for the football team whose ground adjoined the school, so we were allowed to have the use of the field. There we played hockey, rounders, cricket, athletics and football. Since the children had been starved of games, it was little wonder that they took to these activities hook, line and sinker. To Neill this was a dangerous turn of events, but from his point of view worse was to follow. As the children became more skilful they wanted competition outside the school. Though at first they were soundly beaten, they gradually improved, so that soon they could lick the local state schools at football, and more than hold their own in hockey and table tennis played against youth clubs and adult teams. In spite of the fairly wide spectrum of games, football was the one that dominated the conversations amongst the kids – many of them were from London and supported one of the professional clubs there. Although I liked football, much of this talk bored me stiff. God knows what it did to Neill. From his point of view there was an imbalance in the school – drama was confined to one week a term, art was at a low ebb, there was no woodwork teacher – and yet there was all this games activity, both in the week and at weekends. When you consider that he disliked games in general and football in particular, he was really very tolerant of the situation. I sympathised with the quandary he was in.'

After some five years Bill MacKinnon felt it was time to move on. However, there was a big exodus of children who came to the end of their school years at this time, and he and his wife Käte, who worked with the younger children, were prepared to stay for a while, to help Neill through what they thought was likely to be a difficult period. 'I was always aware of the rather ambivalent feelings he had towards my role in the school. I was never a Reichian, and felt a bit uneasy about kids and the orgone chamber and the aura of mysticism surrounding it all. I also felt that kids should be encouraged to go to lessons, and if not, should not be *constantly* reminded by Neill that they were not required to attend. In private I made it clear to Neill that I insisted children should come regularly for at least half a term if they opted to attend, and that they should let me know when they could not come. Neill didn't disguise the fact that he didn't approve, but he never interfered; he would just pull my leg privately about his running a free school and employing an old-fashioned Scots dominie. However, it was rather a shock when he said to me that he'd be happy if I and other staff looked for new jobs, because of the financial position. I didn't let many people know of this suggestion, so that it did rankle a bit to hear

parents, friends, old pupils and staff being "disappointed and surprised" at
me for leaving "poor old Neill and the sinking ship".'

Another teacher at Summerhill during this period was amazed to learn
later that Neill should have considered sacking Bill MacKinnon, whom he
remembers as a loyal teacher, presenting no sort of threat to Neill. He was
also very popular with the children, as Neill himself was all too well aware:
if he sacked him, he told Reich, 'There would be a revolution in the school.'
Neill was increasingly unable to cope with situations in which another
adult played such a prominent role in the school; but he tried to mask his
jealousy by bringing forward other reasons why his alleged rival should
leave. Such feelings would help to explain the contradictory explanations
Neill gave for his dismissing staff. Sometimes, despite his belief that personality counted for more than pedagogy, it was the classroom performance
that was invoked: Tom Hackett remembers being told by Neill: 'Look,
you're a nice bloke, and the kids like you, but you're not a very good
teacher, are you?' At other times Neill employed the opposite argument.
One sacked maths teacher was told that he was a luxury because, although
he taught well, he was useless as a 'community man'. Of another man, who
resigned shortly after, Neill wrote: 'Kids like his lessons but don't find any
emotional contact with him.' He added, without irony: 'Touchy if Ena or
anyone asks him to do a job. . . mend a door, etc. His philosophy seems to
be. . . I came here to teach not to be an odd job man. Worrying.' In general,
although Neill argued that the needs of the children were his prime consideration, it is quite clear that in a number of cases it was his own anxieties
which moved him to get rid of certain adults. 'The established Jesus in
Summerhill doesn't want any rivals,' he confessed to Reich, in a moment
of wry but accurate self-criticism.

Ena Neill recalls that 'Some of the teachers were over nice to the kids,
but not wise with them: they turned out to be nice people but poor
teachers.' Yet the situation was sometimes clearly more complex than this.
Several potentially effective teachers who were sympathetic to Summerhill
became frustrated at Neill's total opposition to any new ideas. Jimmy East,
who came in 1949 and stayed for five years, recalls: 'It was not going to
change, it was no good me or anyone else thinking Neill would try anything
new. This could produce slight frustration, and I think he could have been
a little more flexible.' One young couple, Kay and Gavin Dunbar, who
were very committed to Neill's approach, hoped to provide different kinds
of stimulus on the arts side when they arrived some years later. Kay Dunbar
remembers the opposition they met from Neill: 'Gavin organised a poster
design competition; Neill nearly went mad: "We've never had any competition in fifty years at Summerhill," was his response. We had some
sympathy with his point of view, but it was a gross over-reaction. We
wanted to have a theatre group in for a visit, but this was apparently
against Summerhill "tradition". We wanted to run a drama club, but
Daphne Oliver and Neill dominated the school's drama, and because our
style was different we felt they were suspicious and felt threatened.' The
Dunbars, like other staff, felt themselves to be outsiders, unable to initiate

new ideas without stern resistance from Neill: 'One felt hampered and restricted. We were often told that we didn't understand the "Summerhillian way of doing things" – but there was no machinery to make you more Summerhillian. It was impossible to change any practice, or even discuss changes, however minor: Neill had set replies and anecdotes to support his viewpoint – it was like a religious sect.'

One of the principal difficulties for staff at Summerhill lay in the fact that, while the children were able to take part in a genuine and revolutionary experiment in self-government, they themselves were compelled to operate under very different working conditions. Neill was able to hire and fire at will, and to make key decisions about the running of the school without reference to others. At one stage before the war, some of the more politically minded staff wanted the structure of Summerhill to be changed into a co-operative one. Neill refused to do this, arguing simply that since he had started the school he wanted to be in charge of it. Since he was at the time urging teachers to press for self-government in their schools, he was conscious of the charge of hypocrisy that could be levelled at him. In attempting to defend his position, he fell back on his favourite technique of admitting the justice of the criticism – 'I grant that here you have the clinging to power of the Old Man' – and then avoiding any serious intellectual defence. The best he could manage was to argue that the staff had all sorts of other freedoms, and, compared with teachers in other schools, believed in the work they were doing. He admitted though that 'the future belongs to co-operation', and that 'the days of the one-man show are passing'. Yet he himself was never able to give up the one-man show in the succeeding years. When, during the post-war period, a close friend suggested that the staff might be given a greater stake in the school, Neill 'just growled'.

While Neill's controlling position seemed to cause little conflict in the pre-war period, in later years it gave rise to a significant amount of resentment and disillusion amongst many of the staff. Ena Neill herself admits that he made no pretence at running the school in a democratic fashion: 'He wasn't quite the despotic monarch, but you didn't go against him easily. He made it quite clear how things were to be done, and at staff meetings he could be quite forthright – sometimes a little too forthright. He was the boss, and that was it: he had the final say on everything.' Sometimes he used more devious means to get his way, as with the issue of the timetable. In the late 1940s two new teachers, Ray Hemmings and John Wood, felt that the fixed morning timetable was out of keeping with a system based on voluntary attendance at lessons. Ray Hemmings recalls the scheme they evolved: 'There would be no timetable, but we would still be subject specialists who would be in our rooms during the mornings, and anyone who wanted to could come along and start working with us. We worked this out in some detail, and presented it first to the staff. They were particularly uncomprehending of what we were trying to do, and Neill was very quiet, as usual. He suggested that the idea should be put to the weekly meeting, and the staff grudgingly agreed to this. Of course, there it was voted out. I think nobody could understand what the advantage would be, and perhaps they liked the security of the timetable. It was as though all this stuff like history and geography was something that had to be done, so let's do it in the simplest possible way, and then it's done. We don't want to bring this into the rest of our life – that seemed to be the feeling.'

On this occasion Neill took the unusual step of putting pressure on the children at the weekly meeting. He himself was *for* the timetable, and his emotional appeal to the children for its retention persuaded them to support the status quo. Bill MacKinnon recalls another occasion when Neill acted in this uncharacteristic manner: 'He called an evening meeting of the staff and older kids, after a discussion that morning in the staff room. Some staff – notably Leslie and Vivien Morton – were suggesting to Neill that less *emphasis* should be put on children remaining away from lessons. He seemed intent on making an issue of it and, unlike his usual patient and tolerant self, lowered the standard of the discussion with a blatant appeal to the kids. He said things like, "I have always been on the kids' side, and I will remain on their side." Of course they rose to the bait, on an almost "Follow, Follow" level. This was very unlike him: usually he approached everything in a logical manner and argued it out fairly.'

It was this type of episode which made life confusing for staff who wanted to establish a little bit more of a framework to the learning side, without necessarily cutting across Neill's fundamental philosophy of child freedom. Certain teachers, like Bill MacKinnon, managed to establish a system whereby if children started to go to lessons, they had to continue to do so for an agreed period. It seems that Neill was prepared to tolerate such an arrangement if he was not required to put his name to it publicly. Was this, as some staff felt, because he privately hoped the O level candidates would get their passes? Certainly Neill continued to demonstrate the ambivalence of his feelings towards the learning side of school life, as another post-war pupil, Richard Marcus, recalls: ' "I don't care if you go to lessons or not," Neill would utter at times of anti-social crisis, but he always added under his breath, "but I wish you would!" ' This remark highlights the struggle which Neill had to maintain what many considered to be a thoroughly anti-intellectual stance. For years he indulged in deliberately provocative attacks on the kind of traditional culture he had been subjected to at university. 'These children live free,' he remarked of his pupils in 1932. 'You find Dickens, Thackeray and Scott neglected on the bookshelves, but a volume of Edgar Wallace is worn out in a week by constant use.' Yet, though he claimed that books were the least important items in a school, he himself showed a considerable interest in them throughout his life. During the early 1920s, after his discovery of psychology, he bought and read a large number of books on psychoanalysis, psychology – and even education. He also had on his shelves fiction works by such writers as Barrie, Wells, Conan Doyle, Jack London, Rider Haggard, O. Henry, Stephen Leacock and W. W. Jacobs. In the 1930s his interest shifted to biography – lives of eminent Scotsmen such as John

Calvin and David Hume – and books on current political issues – Palme Dutt's *Fascism*, Arthur Koestler's *Spanish Testament*.

He also had a very Scottish love of learning, which he could not always conceal, and which would often show itself in his replies to writers who sent him copies of their books. One of these was George Ives, a friend of Oscar Wilde's, who wrote about *The History of Penal Methods* and *Obstacles to Human Progress*. Neill wrote to him in February 1949: 'My very warm thanks for the gift of your book which awaited me at Norman Haire's. It kept me completely interested on my train way home. Your erudition is wonderful; you seem to have read everything of importance and remembered it.' Gordon Leff, who became a professor of history, recalls: 'If you produced a book, although he would say he knew nothing about it because he wasn't "a bloody intellectual", he would nevertheless go on about it.' In March 1962 he sent Neill a copy of his new book *The Tyranny of Concepts*, prompting what became a standard reply to such gifts: 'But, laddie, I don't know what to say about it. I can see it is a brilliant analysis showing a hell of a lot of knowledge and deep thinking, but. . . . I am a one-track-minded chap with limited interests. . . .You are a scholar, I never was one, not even in my degree subject English.' Sometimes he would couch his alleged ignorance in humorous terms: 'Barton sent me a 63-shilling book on maths and so far the only bit I understand is his name on the cover,' he wrote in a letter to a war-time pupil, Peter Russell. Yet this 'non-scholar' would take some pains to point out that he had only failed to get a first-class degree at Edinburgh because of the need to do Anglo-Saxon. Similarly, despite his hostility to Shakespeare, he once returned to Summerhill in ecstasies when a visit to Northumberland provided him with the opportunity of handling an edition of the First Folio.

Within the school, however, Neill kept up his pretended dislike of learning, to a degree that aggravated many who came to teach there. Rosalind Tolson, who came with her husband Richard in the late 1950s, remembers: 'It was very difficult teaching at Summerhill, because the children knew that Neill saw lessons as peripheral.' A teacher who arrived a little after this remembers: 'There was an anti-intellectual atmosphere to an extreme degree, from the Neills, some of the staff and pupils: "You're so intellectual" was a term of abuse.' Another teacher, who had been sacked by Neill, put it in more emotive terms: 'How is the child to grow into anything worthwhile in an atmosphere in which the pursuit of any social or academic standards is actively discouraged, and mathematics and manners are treated as dirty words?' This particular man was clearly out of sympathy with Neill's aims, as was another who was sacked by Neill after six months. 'My first few days were a nightmare,' he recalled. 'I started with 14 pupils in my class, but on the second day they all walked out on me. There was nothing I could do about it.'

Here again Neill has to take some of the blame. Although he claimed that it was very hard to get teachers, his scrutiny of the potential candidates seemed to be as casual and haphazard as ever. Several staff came without his ever having set eyes on them. Jimmy East was one of these: he simply received a telegram from Neill saying, 'Pay £8 a month. Do come, if only for a term.' Liz Hall, the daughter of H. C. O'Neill, who had given Neill his first job with Jacks the publishers, came as a housemother after Neill had met her once – when she was 3! Richard Tolson did manage an interview before he was appointed, but before his arrival received a letter from Neill: 'Just tell me again what you can teach, I think you said history and English. Of course it is all trial and error, but as long as both sides know this it is okay.' Two students who helped Neill to make a path the day they arrived, heard him say at breakfast the next morning that they would be taking his classes for a couple of days, as he was off to do some lecturing. This was the first they had heard of the idea. His unbusinesslike method of taking on staff made him an easy target for practical jokes, as Ann Freshwater remembers: 'One day I wrote a note saying, "Dear Neill, Have decided to come and be housemother for you. Coming down on the 9.15 on Saturday. Please meet me, and make sure my bed is warm and dry. Love Maria Crump." I did it on the sort of paper you stick stamps on, to give him a clue that it was a joke, and from me – my father was a philatelist. But I discovered later that he had gone to meet the train, and had the bed made up.'

New staff were rarely given much help by Neill when they first arrived at Summerhill. Ray Hemmings's experience was typical of many. He was interviewed by Neill in the ABC café on Liverpool Street Station. 'All he seemed to do was mumble and shrug his shoulders,' he remembers. 'I had been teaching in a grammar school, was thoroughly fed up and frustrated, and disgusted by the way kids were treated. When I mentioned this to Neill, he shrugged and said, "What can you do?" But he asked very little about me otherwise. I guess he thought that if there was someone qualified to teach who felt that about the grammar school, he'd be worth the risk. So he took me on. But I can't remember him saying anything about the way one should teach or behave. I do remember him saying on my first evening at Summerhill: "We don't go in for suggestion here." That was the only introduction he gave to his method.' Jimmy East found his first encounter with Neill thoroughly frustrating: 'I had expected him to chatter away – after all, his writing is so fluent. But he said absolutely nothing. I racked my brains, and came up with one or two questions, like: "If I'm taking English, what sort of courses are you doing at the moment?" "I've no idea at all," he said. So I then asked him to show me around, which was rather futile since the kids were away. I hung about in the afternoon, and eventually asked for the train times. I had hardly exchanged a word with him, and this was a bit shattering.'

The consequences of Neill's casual method of recruiting staff were often unfortunate, and on one occasion potentially dangerous. In this instance, he took on the only person who answered an advertisement, and soon regretted his decision. Richard Tolson recalls the case: 'He was said to have been the worst teacher ever suffered by the kids at Summerhill. He was a complete (or rather incomplete) lunatic; Neill called him a bugger, and suspected him of sexual malpractice. Having been sacked by Neill, he

came down to a Saturday night meeting, which on the whole was sympathetic to him. I got very cross, and said, "This man should be forbidden
to come." I thought he was a menace to children.' Neill agreed – it was
said he had been hitting the children – but was wary of imposing such a
ban, as he explained in a letter to John Aitkenhead: 'Dunno what to do
about him, dangerous I think, kids say he nearly strangled a boy of 12 with
a rope. . . he said in fun, but I am in a hole. If I ban him from the place he
may murder one of the kids or me or anyone, he is just that sick mentally.'

Here Neill was facing a real dilemma, though even now he was obviously reluctant to intervene. He still found it hard to summon up the
'courage' required to tell staff to leave. Writing to a friend in America on
the subject of human weakness, he agonised over this failing:

> How much cowardice is in it? I have a gardener, a young man who
> did well for five years. Now he slacks all day, plays with the kids,
> fetches coal for able-bodied staff and the garden is a wreck. I'm
> paying out about £6 weekly for vegetables he shd have grown. I
> speak to him nicely as man to man, gently telling him I want the
> garden done. He doesn't react, and I kick myself for not having the
> guts of a Hitler or a he man who would kick him out on his arse.

Neill's 'cowardice' in the face of adults sometimes led to farce. Once he
decided to dismiss a housemother, but couldn't bring himself to let her
know of his decision: having hired a replacement, he then had two people
for one job at the start of the following term. Another teacher first heard
of her impending dismissal through a friend from outside Summerhill. One
long-serving member of staff was sacked annually by Neill, but simply
returned as normal in September, after which nothing further would be
said for a year. Even when he felt able to screw his courage to the sacking
point, Neill was hardly a model of decisiveness. Noel Olley, who taught
for a short while in the 1960s, recalls Neill coming up to him and saying:
'Would you be terribly offended if I fired you?' Neill claimed that these
difficulties arose partly because he identified too much with the teacher he
was dismissing, and wondered how *he* would feel in such a position. One
particularly fraught conflict led him to confide to a close friend: 'After days
of tiresome wrangling and mutual recriminations —— handed in his resignation. . . .I feel limp. I hate playing God; I see the other guy's viewpoint
and feel sorry for him.' Though there was some truth in this, it was also
true that Neill was loath to take on the responsibility of making a potentially unpopular decision.

Neill's determined resistance to change within Summerhill was paral-
leled by a refusal to open his eyes and ears to the changes in practice and
attitudes taking place in the mainstream of education. During the 1950s
and 1960s, a number of primary schools – notably in Oxfordshire, Hertfordshire, Leicestershire and the West Riding of Yorkshire – began to adopt
many of the 'child-centred' ideas which had previously been visible only in
a tiny minority of schools. Yet Neill continued to talk and write as if none
of these changes had occurred. If the pre-war climate had justified the

imagery of battle which he employed, for many who sympathised with his ideas his beleaguered stance no longer seemed appropriate. The qualities of certainty and single-mindedness which had helped him to set up and fight for his pioneering experiment seemed to have fossilised into a stubborn refusal to accept that any significant progress had been made in the direction he wanted. It was almost as if he needed opposition in order to justify the continuation of Summerhill, and was therefore unable to accept that at least some of his ideas were now considered less extreme, and in certain cases were being incorporated into the ordinary schools. He certainly rarely ventured outside Summerhill to discover what was happening in state schools, and on the rare occasions he did so he received a surprise. During the post-war period he only seems to have seen inside three – and one of these was the local primary down the road in Leiston. 'I liked it,' he admitted later, 'the kids were chattering away, they were all doing different things.'

One of his two other visits was to St George in the East School, Stepney, during the early post-war years. The head of this secondary modern school, Alex Bloom, had taken over a derelict building in a bombed area of dockland in the East End of London. There was a school council, and an absence of exams, marks and the still ubiquitous corporal punishment. Bloom himself was a very approachable figure, and children took it for granted that they were welcome in his study if they wanted to talk to him. This was still an unusually informal attitude for the time, and one that clearly impressed Neill favourably: 'I was delighted with the *Stimmung* [atmosphere] and the obvious love and approval of children,' he wrote not long afterwards. But he also felt that this was as far as any pioneer could go within the state system: lessons still had to be compulsory, religion still had to be taught, and neither of these, in his eyes, was compatible with true freedom. E. F. O'Neill, Bloom and others might be able to experiment in methods of teaching or ways of organising the timetable, 'but not in methods of living'.

His other visit to a state school occurred many years later, during the 1960s, when he went to Ravenhurst Primary School in Leicestershire, one of the schools in the forefront of the movement towards a more open and informal style of teaching and learning. Children there were given plenty of freedom to choose what they learned, and relaxed adult-child relationships were positively encouraged. Neill spent an afternoon at the school, where the children were quite used to visitors wandering around the classrooms and observing them at work. He was delighted to see drama work very similar to his own 'spontaneous acting', and was staggered at the quality of the artwork on the walls. As Bill Hazell, the headteacher at Ravenhurst, recalls: 'He was not very interested in the curriculum, but more in the children; he just sat down and talked with them – not *at* them – and they responded.' At the end of the afternoon he patted the head on the back, saying: 'You're doing a good job, laddie.' Ray Hemmings, who arranged the visit and accompanied Neill, remembers: 'It all made quite an impact on him. When we left he just said it was all very different; but you had to understand his meaning from his expression rather than his words.' A recollection of Ben Morris suggests that what Neill saw that day had at least a temporary effect on him: 'After the visit he admitted he was out of date; he saw that adults could intervene usefully.'

Neill did now and then attend conferences, notably the bi-annual Co-Educational Schools' Conference, but found little that he could agree with in the discussions that took place: 'I have to soft-pedal myself there,' he wrote to one of his few allies. 'Have to keep up the pretence that we are ALL advanced guys, for the alternative, *Summerhill is right and you are all wrong*, would not be polite nor mannerly.' In practice, he was quite capable of expressing his opinions on these occasions, as Kenneth Barnes, the head of Wennington School, recalls: 'One day, in a small group which included Neill, we were discussing personal relationships, and the relevance of Christianity to this aspect of education. Neill suddenly and passionately broke in with his favourite exclamation: "I don't know what you're talking about!" He went on to say, "That's not religion: religion is about hell-fire, nothing else." Another member of the group turned to him and said: "The trouble with you, Neill, is that you're not an atheist at all: you're a Calvinist standing on his head!" '

Neill of course disagreed with many of the ideas and practices of the progressive school teachers who attended these conferences. He could also be quite scathing in his private remarks about them, once labelling the conference 'a bloody funeral of men who died years ago but were not yet buried'. From one he came home 'depressed and hopeless', reporting that it had been 'a battle between me and the Bedales, Barnes, Lyward brigade, with men of woolly words in no-man's-land, saying damn all at great length. . . .You get nowhere, just words: if the buggers could only laugh a bit more, but they are so earnest.' Another year he wrote before attending: 'Yes, the programme is dull as hell, so I'm going just to try to fight that deadness the conf. always has. . . the programme is typically Bedales. . . and the new Dartington. . . . Compromise, respectability, religion. . . . Looks as if the holy ones. . . . Jacks, Kenneth Barnes etc. are to run the conf.' Almost everyone who came to these events he labelled a 'fence-sitter' or 'middle-of-the-roader'. Yet some of those he privately criticised in this way he would at other times claim as an ally. Kenneth Barnes remembers: 'Several times he said that I was the only one with whom he shared a common language. We were interested in kids, he said; the others were only interested in O and A Levels. He would get up and say to them, with his eyes narrowing over his eagle's beak of a nose: "That's not education!" In truth I had a foot in both camps, and he wasn't being fair to the others.'

Many of those attending these conferences felt that Neill had nothing new to offer. Bets would be laid on how soon he would get on to the topic of sex: 'It was usually pretty soon,' one conference veteran remembers. He was, some headteachers felt, unable to appreciate the uniqueness of his position, that if other heads ignored the expectations of parents their schools would quickly be empty. Because of this, there were times when Neill was neglected or isolated. The Aitkenheads of Kilquhanity House were two of the few who remained on his 'side'. Morag Aitkenhead recalls Neill's attitude on these occasions: 'He got very fed up with what was being said, and would sit there glowering, looking dour and grim. It was sad, when these bigger, more successful schools rather patronised Neill: "We've heard all that before, that's just Neill again," they'd say. Yet humanly he was streets ahead of them all.' Nevertheless, he couldn't always get his humanity across to others. After one conference Neill wrote in disgust: 'Note that I often sit alone and no one comes to talk to me there. Little bastards.' This was an exaggeration, since Neill always had a few friends or allies, or younger teachers keen to hear him at first hand. Yet at one time there was some pressure to exclude him. This was a cause of some embarrassment to Paul Roberts, the head of Frensham Heights School then in charge of organising the conferences. He voiced his discomfort to Bill MacKinnon on more than one occasion: 'Paul really liked and admired Neill, but the influence of others weighed heavily against him being asked to be a guest speaker. I, and I think others, wrote to him about the apparent neglect of Neill, and eventually he was invited as the conference's honoured guest – hopefully gagged in that role. But Neill never remained gagged: he could divert apparently innocuous discussions of A and B streams to something more basic. Whenever he spoke it was direct, and immediately divided the gathering into two camps.'

Yet some who attended these conferences welcomed Neill's iconoclastic presence. Nikki Archer, head of King Alfred School, recalls: 'The fact that he was dogmatic was one of his great strengths: he had a genuine humility combined with bossiness.' Roger Tilbury, from Dartington Hall, remembers: 'People would construct elaborate theoretical models about education. Then Neill would ask, "What would the kids think about that?" and the whole edifice would come crumbling down.' Nicholas King Harris, the head of St Christopher School, recalls an occasion when Neill was in his element: 'One year George Lyward was the principal guest. There was a fairly conventional headmaster from a boys' school there. His school was going co-ed for financial reasons, and he had come to learn what it was about. In his terms this was, "I know what you do with boys, you beat them; but what do you do with girls?" Neill took a special delight in raising issues which were totally beyond the ken of this poor man, such as Freudian approaches to sex. The man was getting more and more desperate, and Lyward acted as Neill's foil. I think they took great pleasure in provoking this chap.'

Neill's other means of contact with the educational world were his lectures. There were still plenty of teachers prepared to listen to his attacks on the system of which he knew so little, and to be provoked, delighted and unsettled. Charles Hannam was a student teacher at Cambridge when Neill gave a lecture there in 1949: 'In an environment where there was not much concern for education and considerably less for children, I was deeply moved by this large, craggy, uncomfortable man, who startled his audience by saying that he would not tolerate circumlocution and false politeness, and that his daughter had said, "Neill, I want to shit." A cluster of ladies walked out of the lecture, but as far as I was concerned Neill had gained an ally.' Michael Duane recalls a lecture Neill gave in Lowestoft in 1953: 'I was amazed to find that almost all of the 300 members of the local NUT branch had turned up: only the sick and the lame must have been left behind. The majority came to criticise, and only a few were sympathetic; but they listened in dead silence.' Len Marsh, a trainer of teachers, recalls two occasions when he invited Neill to lecture: 'He was a brilliant speaker. I had him down to talk to students and teachers in-service at St Paul's College in Cheltenham. The effect of Neill in Gloucestershire was electric. Later, at Goldsmiths' College in London, he made outstanding contributions in speaking to heads, post-graduate students and others. On one occasion in the common room he discovered the species Ph.D. Lecturer in Psychology. It was a memorable meeting, leaving the psychologists anxious and worried about their territory, and Neill more happily confident.' Neill complained regularly about having to continue lecturing in order to raise money for the school, about the size of his fees, the time spent travelling, and many other inconveniences. Yet he still relished the chance of playing to a large audience, and in his letters would record with considerable pleasure the size of his audience and the reception he received. At Glasgow University in the late 1950s his talk was, one member of the audience remembers, 'almost like a pop concert', and Neill returned in buoyant mood, with not a mention of the 'prophet without honour'. 'Just back from Glasgow where I had a great reception, treated like a prince I was,' he wrote gleefully to a friend. 'He really came alive when he lectured,' Ena Neill recalls, 'and you could see that it had given him something.'

Neill undoubtedly enjoyed the attention and applause that he normally received on such occasions, both during, before and after the lectures. He was particularly spoilt when he visited Scandinavia, as he did again in April 1947, in the middle of the post-war austerity. 'Sweden was paradise; shops with everything we haven't seen for years here. I drank too much Schnapps and ate far too much and enjoyed it all,' he wrote to Reich. He was also able in Stockholm to preach his gospel of freedom in a more appropriate setting than the usual town hall or training college. Greta Sergeant, his interpreter, remembers the occasion: 'The place that we had booked was too small for the crowds that had come to hear him. At the last moment we got the vicar to open up the church across the road. People surged across the churchyard, jumping over the graves; there was no chance to collect entrance fees. The church was filled to the last pew, people sitting on the altar steps and the steps leading to the pulpit. The vicar had said, "Mr Neill must not talk about religion or sex." When we told him this, Neill remarked, "What the hell shall I talk about then?" He knocked out his pipe and, smiling good-naturedly, entered the church. "I've always dreamed of preaching from a pulpit," he announced, and made his way there, climbing over people with his long legs and big feet.' Later Neill himself recalled the occasion, and the vicar's conditions: 'It sure cramped my style. It was an odd feeling standing in a pulpit with a large Bible on the desk in front of me.' The same evening, at a different venue, he was able to talk more freely to some of the audience, and to bring in the topics forbidden in the church.

Neill was also given another opportunity to reach a wider public. In January 1946 he confided to Ishbel McWhirter in a letter: 'Been asked to be one of 25 famous men to write a presentation book of essays to Shaw on his 90th birthday.' The compliment clearly flattered him: 'They'll be offering me a title next just to prove I am out of date,' he concluded gleefully. Among the eminent contributors were Max Beerbohm, John Masefield, Maynard Keynes, Sidney Webb, J. B. Priestley, C. E. M. Joad, Aldous Huxley, Gilbert Murray and H. G. Wells. Also on the list was J. D. Bernal, to whom Neill wrote in some uncertainty about the project's editor, S. Winsten: 'It may be some raw youth living next door to GBS out for a stunt; it may be Shaw's secretary. I am in the dark. Seems a bit odd to me, such a varied list.' In the essay he wrote for the volume, on 'Shaw and Education', Neill complimented Shaw on his early championing of the right of the child to 'find its own way' and to 'spend most of its time at play'. But he also criticised him for over-valuing learning at the expense of 'the doing side', and for being too keen on knowledge and absorption rather than creation. However, he also suggested that Shaw still had plenty to say to people in education today, though some of his remarks would be considered heretical still by many teachers and parents. 'His words are a clean, strong wind that could blow a few cobwebs out of those Training Colleges that see education as a matter of school method, and class-room discipline, and school subjects.' As in so much of his writing, Neill used the occasion to put over much of the essence of his own philosophy, while ostensibly writing on another topic.

Neill grew increasingly worried about Summerhill's future during these post-war years. In April 1949 he suddenly became alarmed when questions about private schools began to be asked in the House of Commons. They had been prompted by a bizarre incident in one which termed itself a 'free school', when the head had invited a cane merchant to visit the school, and then got the older boys to take the cane from him and beat him with it. Further details emerged about the school, and soon it was closed, technically because the inspectors found its lavatories unsatisfactory. Neill immediately interpreted the scandal as posing a threat to Summerhill, and began to imagine the worst possible consequences. Kenneth Barnes met him at a conference at this time: 'He turned to me and said, seriously not humorously: "How are your WCs, Kenneth? Look to them, or they'll close you down!" ' 'One question about sex in Parliament and any Minister will at once make urgent inquiry and of course take the side of reaction and anti-youth,' he suggested to Reich. Although he decided that he could count on quite a lot of supporters, he feared that 'if you get into the hands of the law, some little judge has the power to kill your work.' He also added in another letter a few days later, 'If S'hill were ended, on what front could I fight?' In June he finally had confirmation that he was to receive a visit from His Majesty's Inspectorate.

Neill's fundamental anxieties about authority were distilled into his attitude to school inspectors, which he traced back to his father's fear of such men: 'On Inspection Day my father had a violent headache, was as pale as a sheet, and stood very truly at the Judgment Bar,' he remembered. In *A Dominie's Log* he had imagined a wonderful world in which teachers would be allowed to report on the inspectors, and submit their criticisms of them to the Scottish Education Department. His early fears were reinforced by his unhappy experiences with officials in Germany and Austria. Nor was he likely to forget the events that led to Homer Lane's downfall. In October 1932 he poured out his feelings about outside 'interference' in a ferocious article in the *New Era*, addressed to the heads of progressive private schools, and written on the occasion of the publication of a Report on the Inspection of Private Schools.

> We know what we are aiming at, and no man is good enough to step in and tell us how to run our schools. If any inspector were to demand of me that I give up allowing children complete freedom to stay away from each or every class at will I should have to give an emphatic No, closing my school rather than compromising an inch.... I don't mind inspection of my premises and my food; I don't mind having a few inspectors down to improve their own education. But I refuse to accept any guidance whatsoever from any inspector whatsoever, any guidance in child psychology and education. We must not allow ourselves to take up a subservient attitude to the Board of Education. We must remain what we are, superior persons who are helping to advance the happiness of children. Don't let us be too modest. Let us form a select body of pioneers which will have for a motto *Hands Off Us!* We have nothing to learn from any Board of Education.

In answer to the obvious question about the need to root out bad schools, Neill came up with the curious notion that a list of supporters would be quite enough to stand as a certificate of a school's worth:

> I know that I could get an excellent list of supporters myself. Why should we suffer the trouble and dignity of inspection? There is no earthly excuse for inspecting, say, Bedales or King Alfred. Their history and their successes make inspection merely fatuous and ludicrous.

Although Neill feared that the Ministry would decide to close Summerhill he had few grounds for such anxiety in 1949. First, since the 1944 Education Act had not yet been implemented in full, the inspectorate anyway had no power to close a school. No appeals machinery was yet in operation, and their job was therefore confined to making a report. Second, as Neill soon discovered when friends of his made informal soundings with officials, the Ministry appeared friendly to Summerhill. This is confirmed by John Blackie, the Inspector for the Eastern Division of Her Majesty's Inspectorate, and the man responsible for arranging the Summerhill visit. 'I had a note from the Department saying, I'm sure you'll bear in mind the particular difficulties, the particular nature of this school when arranging your panel.' Third, the English inspectorate, even in the days of payment by results, had never been as formal or rigid as their Scottish counterparts. By this time the attitude of the Inspectorate towards schools such as Summerhill was likely to be one of curiosity rather than hostility.

The composition of the two-man team worked in Neill's favour. John Blackie was a forward-looking inspector, concerned that schools should become freer places for children, and that teachers should be more aware of the nature of their growth. His fellow-inspector, Dick Pemberton, who had been chief inspector for Suffolk before the war, was also likely, in a rather different way, to be sympathetic to Neill. He had already been to Summerhill just before the move to Wales, and Neill had got on so well with him that he had asked him to come back again as an ordinary visitor. Educated at Eton and Christchurch College, Oxford, he came from a country family, and was, John Blackie recalls, one of a dying race: 'He was the sort of person who doesn't exist any longer, and couldn't. I don't think he'd ever taught in a school in his life. He had a very patrician manner and voice; and was the kind of chap who looked like his own gardener. He wouldn't have cared if the dormitories were in a mess – his own house was exactly like that.'

Neill made some effort to prevent the visit. He contacted a high-ranking official in the Ministry who was a personal friend, asking him to use his influence to see that Summerhill escaped an inspection. His friend wrote back saying that no private school could be exempt, that Neill would find the inspectors were quite used to taking things as they found them, and that the visit was not likely to be the ordeal he feared. Although Neill was somewhat reassured by this, his deeply ingrained anxieties remained and as the inspection day approached there was a mild panic. Neill instigated a mass clear-up and fumigation, with staff and children collecting litter, tidying the rooms, and generally making the school a little less ramshackle than usual. 'Clear up, clear up, if only to save your school,' Neill exhorted everywhere. He also told the children that, if they were not attending lessons, they should just make themselves inconspicuous. He had another worry on his mind too, as Kerstin Barton remembers: 'He hadn't applied for a labour permit for me to work at Summerhill, and was terrified that the inspectors would find out. So he hid me.'

Neill was, John Blackie recalls, 'clearly and undoubtedly very nervous when we arrived. But he was quick to discover that we were not going to conduct the kind of investigation he had feared.' It was an incident during the first lunch break which perhaps gave Neill a clear indication of the inspectors' approach. John Blackie recalls the moment: 'We were walking across the lawn, and Pemberton said, "Yes, Neill, well I think this is rather a pleasant place: you know, it's *almost* as free as Eton!" Neill tottered at this, and said: "Well, I *have* written all about it in my books, you know." "Good God," said Pemberton, "I haven't read your books. You don't think I spend my time reading books on education, do you? Heaven forbid!"

This was the terrible inspector. From this moment on he and Neill became firm friends, and got on frightfully well.'

At the start of the inspection, Neill had made his ritual remark about the impossibility of inspecting happiness, and had been told by the inspectors that they would have a go at doing so. John Blackie remembers the children's response: 'The children looked at us as if to say, Clearly the enemy has now arrived. However, we were greeted very politely, and found them very easy to get on with, nicely mannered in the basic sense. They didn't have many graces, but they treated us properly, as people they were going to regard as their guest, and potentially as their friends. What you might conventionally call the "discipline" was very good indeed. The children were very proud of the school. Generally speaking it seemed a very happy place.' In their official report the inspectors decided that

> the children are full of life and zest. Of boredom and apathy there was no sign. An atmosphere of contentment and tolerance pervades the school. . . the children's manners are delightful. They may lack, here and there, some of the conventions of manners, but their friendliness, ease and naturalness, and their total lack of shyness and self-consciousness, made them very easy, pleasant people to get on with. . . initiative, responsibility and integrity are all encouraged by the system and. . . so far as such things can be judged, they are in fact being developed.

Neill had totally misjudged the perceptiveness and fairness of the 'enemy', whose approving comments about the atmosphere of the school and the apparent happiness of the children represented a significant justification of his work. The inspectors described Summerhill as 'an experiment of profound interest', and 'a piece of fascinating and valuable educational research. . .which it would do all educationists good to see.' Neill was sufficiently pleased with the report to include it in full in his next book, *The Free Child*, published four years later. He even had the grace to say that the report was 'fair, sincere and generous', although he felt that in one section the two inspectors failed to 'rise above their academic preoccupations'. This was in their summary of the educational side of Summerhill, in which they wrote: 'To have created a situation in which academic education of the most intelligent kind could flourish is an achievement, but in fact it is not flourishing and a great opportunity is being lost.'

In their report, the inspectors had described Neill as

> a man of deep conviction and sincerity. His faith and patience must be inexhaustible. He has the rare power of being a strong personality without dominating. . . .He has a sense of humour, a warm humanity and a strong common sense which would make him a good Head Master anywhere.

Many others were struck by these kind of qualities in Neill, in particular his ability somehow to be able to stand aside and simultaneously make his presence felt. John Aitkenhead, as a friend and fellow-pioneer, felt that

'The kind of magic Neill carried was almost by default, because of his trying not to make an impression. He was so quiet, so gentle, and so genuine, that what he did carried real weight.' Edward Blishen remembers him as a 'positive non-interventionist. If he came in the room and didn't do anything, something happened in that room, which wouldn't have happened if he'd not been there. Physically you couldn't overlook him, but it wasn't just his size, it was an emanation. His negativeness was the most positive you could ever imagine.'

Inevitably, Neill often presented a different face to those who came from outside Summerhill to the one he often showed within the school. The abiding impression he left on many who worked with him in the post-war years was one of persistent gloom and despondency: 'It's *terribly* difficult,' had become his favourite expression. One factor that undoubtedly contributed to his pessimism about the future of both Summerhill and mankind was his health. Shortly after the 1949 inspection both he and Ena had a breakdown, brought on by overwork. In 1953 he was ill in bed for several weeks with flu, though one of his regular visits to the Kingston Clinic revived his spirits for a while. In 1957 his arthritis returned, and two years later he developed sciatica, which kept him in bed for the whole of a particularly warm summer. 'I get so depressed and wonder if I'll ever be able to walk again,' he wrote to Constance Butler, a friend from outside the school. 'They say that pain ennobles. It sure doesn't. It drags one down to a lower level.'

Neill was also frequently dragged down by the financial position of the school. The £2,250 compensation he had received for the damage done by the army was soon used up, through the failure of certain parents to pay the fees. In 1949 the situation deteriorated to such an extent that Neill was faced with closure. He acted with uncharacteristic decisiveness. The worst defaulters were told their children would have to leave, and Neill cut down on his staff. Even this was not enough, and the following year a group of parents stepped in and formed a special committee to look at the finances. It was discovered that, if everyone paid the fees already set down, the losses would be covered. The move certainly helped to keep the school open, as Neill publicly acknowledged; but in private he confessed to a friend in America: 'Ena and I have been talking of coming over for good if Summerhill finances don't start to make ends meet. . . . Part of me, and of Ena, wants it to fail.'

The parents' committee remained in existence, and in 1957, when another crisis seemed imminent, it became the Summerhill Society. That autumn all private schools were to be registered, and a recent local inspection had shown the facilities at Summerhill to be well below Ministry standards. The Society aimed to raise funds to improve staff salaries and amenities, to publicise the school, and 'to form an organised body of opinion to support Mr Neill in his dealings with public authorities'. It was the kind of help which Neill could have done with some time before, though his own attitude to parents was probably the principal barrier to any such move. In particular, he might have found a use for some advice in dealing with the public authorities who took the shape of inspectors, and who were now threatening to pay him another visit. The seal of approval given by the previous members of the Inspectorate seemed forgotten, as he wrote in despairing terms to Bill MacKinnon in August of that year: 'I'll never feel free again and look forward with dread to the stiff inspectors and their likely demands of fire escapes, separate bogs for boys and girls. . . . Nay Bill, we've had it.' A few months later he wrote again with some of his old fervour: 'I'm determined to fight em if they insist on applying their grammar school standards to us.'

In March 1959 Lady Helen Asquith – nicknamed 'The Dragon' – and two other inspectors came to Summerhill. Once again Neill was surprised by the 'enemy's' performance. 'Lady Helen was nice and the two men with her also,' he observed. 'They saw every thing with sharp eyes and knew every kid by name.' Nevertheless, he felt that 'they were mainly interested in the learning side and their report will maybe slate much of it'. Lady Asquith herself recalls that 'Mr Neill was very old, though he remained a very impressive personality. The school had declined a good deal, both in number and in many other ways, so that it was really rather a sad and difficult visit for us.' The official report, which Neill acknowledged to be 'fair and friendly', found the school to be physically 'drab, Spartan and comfortless'. The inspectors were critical of much of the teaching, while recognising that the low salaries severely restricted Neill's choice. (One 15-year-old girl, they found, had studied the Tudor and Stuart period several times, but didn't think she had learnt any history later than 1688.) They took issue with Neill's belief that a child could pick up most of what it needed to learn for an external exam in the last couple of years of school life, and suggested that there needed to be more systematic teaching from an earlier age – a somewhat difficult goal to attain if lessons were to remain voluntary. They also noted that Neill had, against his inclination, taken a number of older children who had not fitted in to other schools, 'mainly because of the need to keep up numbers, but partly, perhaps, because he finds it hard to resist a challenge.'*

At the time of the inspection there were 44 children at Summerhill; by the autumn of 1960 the numbers were down to a mere 24. Many children left in order to continue their schooling at other progressive schools such as Kilquhanity House, or New Sherwood School in Surrey. Some parents hesitated to consider Summerhill because of Neill's advanced age – he was now 77. Others said that they would send their children to him if he would agree to make lessons compulsory in the mornings. Whatever Neill's deviations and inconsistencies may have been over the question of lessons, he was absolutely clear that this would destroy the basis of Summerhill. He refused to entertain the idea, got rid of his gardener, sold his car, and contemplated further staff cuts. He had visions of the numbers dwindling to five, the number he had begun with in Lyme some thirty-six years before.

---

*One or two had been sent by the London County Council: in trying to keep numbers up, Neill had had to go against his usual practice.

Just after his seventy-seventh birthday he wrote wistfully to Maritza Clotworthy, a former housemother from the early years in Leiston: 'Pioneering doesn't pay dividends, alas. Hardly any parents want freedom for their kids now.'

CHAPTER 20

Summerhill USA

VOL. 1 NO. 1   PUBLISHED BY THE SUMMERHILL SOCIETY   JULY, 1961

Neill States Views About a Headmaster For Summerhill, U.S.A.

SUMMERHILL SOCIETY FORMED

Election of Officers and Appointment of Working Committees Spur Plans for Summerhill School, U.S.A., in New York Area

AS A DIRECT OUTGROWTH of the interest created by publication of SUMMERHILL: *A Radical Approach to Child Rearing*, by A. S. Neill, the Summerhill Society has been formed in New York City. Its purpose is to establish a school in the United States based on the principles set forth in Neill's book.

NOTED EDUCATOR SPONSORS SUMMERHILL SOCIETY

THE PUBLIC RELATIONS COMMITTEE of the Summerhill Society, under the chairmanship of Rita Frankiel, has been contacting educators and other public figures, requesting them to become sponsors of the Society.

The support of such prominent persons is deemed extremely important in promoting

At a general meeting held in New York City at the Grosvenor Hotel, and attended by more than 140 supporters of the Summerhill, U.S.A. plan, a set of by-laws and a policy statement were adopted.

The following officers were elected: *President:* HAROLD H. HART, President, Hart Publishing Co. (publisher of Neill's book); *First Vice-President:* BENJAMIN FINE, Ph. D., Education Editor of the North American Newspaper Alliance, and former

> I have had hundreds of letters, mostly from USA, making me the
> saviour of humanity. . .God help humanity!
>
> Letter to David Wills, December 1972

On 7 November 1960, a selection of Neill's writings from four of his books was published in the USA. The new book was called *Summerhill: A Radical Approach to Child-Rearing*. Ten days later Neill wrote to a friend: 'No word yet how the book is selling in USA. I've had one phone call from New York, an actress who sat up all night reading it, and had to phone me saying how wonderful it is.' It was Neill's first intimation that he was about to be discovered by the American public. The book's success over the next decade brought him international recognition, and with it financial security. Teachers, parents and others bought it in their hundreds of thousands. His ideas became an inspiration to many involved in the 'alternative schools' movement that developed in England and America during the 1960s. Such fame and success brought Neill considerable satisfaction. Yet his status as the 'Father Christmas' of progressive education resulted in much uncritical worship, both of Neill himself and of his school. He was also bewildered and alarmed at what he gradually came to see as a misuse or misinterpretation of the 'Summerhill idea'.

Before the publication of *Summerhill*, Neill's ideas were virtually unknown in America. One of the very first to discover his writings was Angelo Patri, the principal of a New York public school and author of *A Schoolmaster in a Great City*, published in 1917. Shortly after its publication he sent Neill a copy of his book, and subsequently answered an appeal in the

New Era by sending him some money for his International School in Hellerau. The first of Neill's books to be published in America was *The Problem Child*, issued by McBride in New York. Neill later reflected on its fate: 'A paper said it was an obscene book, and McBride got frightened and stopped advertising it, so that the yearly sales were about two copies.' His next book, *The Problem Parent*, fared even worse. Neill's agent Peter Watt had submitted it to a different publisher, W. W. Norton, who had rejected it, partly on the grounds that he disliked what he called 'the medical parts'. Bertrand Russell happened to be staying with the publisher while he was reading the MS, and subsequently told Neill where he thought the problem lay: 'There are places in your book where you make sweeping attacks upon serums, vaccines etc. Americans who have lost their belief in their Maker have all transferred their powers of belief to anti-toxins. Your remarks will therefore offend precisely those who might be got to agree with the rest of what you say.' Neill looked again at what he had written, found only two references to vaccine, and concluded: 'I think myself that Norton was rationalising, for if he had approved of the book in the main he would have suggested cutting the offending passages. Why they offend him I can't think, for I attack the law and the church just as much.' Ultimately, he decided, 'I guess it was the masturbation that got his goat.'

Towards the end of the war Neill began to get letters from New York, as a result of some publicity in one of Reich's journals. It made him think that there might be scope for a lecture tour after the war was over. In 1946 the International Universities Press published *The Problem Teacher*, but the book hardly sold any better than *The Problem Child* had done, notching up a mere 140 copies in the first nine months after publication.

But by the time Neill visited Reich in 1947 and again in 1948, there were some glimmerings of interest in his ideas amongst child psychologists and radical teachers. One man already acquainted with his work was Bruno Bettleheim, who had come from Europe to America in 1939, and subsequently worked with severely emotionally disturbed children in Chicago. *The Problem Child*, he remembered, had 'a deep and immediate impact on all those concerned with psychoanalytically oriented education'. Bettleheim had been a close friend of Reich in Vienna, and was, he remembers, 'interested in seeing what good the application of Reich's ideas in education might do.' Another who knew of Neill's ideas was Paul Goodman, who in 1943 had been teaching in Manumit, a progressive school in the state of New York. It was almost certainly this experience which led him to read *The Problem Teacher*, which he reviewed for the *New Republic* in August 1945.* It was both a sympathetic and critical review: Goodman liked the 'breezy and playful atmosphere of immediate common sense, direct action and truth' in the book, and supported Neill's view that children who were

---

*It was through Neill's book that Goodman was introduced to Reich's ideas, in which he then immersed himself for a while. He subsequently had Reichian therapy, and later met Reich himself. Reich, in a letter to Neill, dismissed Goodman as 'one of those intellectuals who does everything only in the form or words'.

allowed emotional release of the kind possible in Summerhill could make their own kind of adaptation to society: 'Neill is not afraid of maladjustment because he is convinced that the unrepressed heart makes its adjustment and forces itself on the rest of us who are after all only sheep. He is a million times right.' On the other hand, he believed that Neill was wrong not to urge teachers to fight the state system from within, rather than assume that 'the revolution' could only come from those working outside.

In raising this issue, Goodman was of course speaking from a different cultural background to Neill. Many of the ideas associated with 'progressive' education had been around for longer in America than in England. Francis Parker's work at Cook County Normal School in the last years of the nineteenth century made it the centre for progressive experimentation for the whole country. He had begun his first lesson as a young teacher with the words: 'My idea of a school is that it is a place where we should have a real good time. I would like to know what your idea is.' The work of John Dewey and his wife at their Laboratory School in Chicago, and Dewey's subsequent writings about education, had directed attention to the question of the growth of the individual child, and the best conditions in which that growth could take place. From Dewey's work there arose a number of ideas which were taken up and used in American, as well as British, classrooms. In 1910 Helen Parkhurst evolved the Dalton Plan – named after the small town in which she taught – which was designed to allow a greater freedom for children to move around the classroom, plan their own work and learn at their own pace. It was a disciple of Dewey, W. H. Kilpatrick, who devised what came to be known as the 'project method', by which children were encouraged to develop a skill or pursue an activity based on their own interests, rather than the ideas handed to them by teachers.

By 1920 there were many schools – Country Day Schools, Park Schools, Open Air Schools – where the influence of such ideas could be seen. In the 1930s progressive schools were given an academic seal of approval by the results of 'the Eight-Year Study'. In this experiment 300 American colleges and universities accepted students without the usual entrance qualifications, from schools broadly recognised as 'progressive'. Compared with students from 'ordinary schools', they performed creditably both in academic terms, and in the measurement of initiative, width of interest and responsibility. The results of this research led to changes in many American schools and colleges. In 1918 the Progressive Education Association had been formed, and had gradually begun to influence the American public schools system. At the Eighth World Conference of the New Education Fellowship, held in the University of Michigan in July 1941, Dewey, as the Association's President, declared: 'A new social order must be built and a new type of education must be worked out as an integral part of this inclusive human order.' After the war progressive ideas came under attack, and attempts were made to restore the old methods in the schools. School reformers were considered suspect, university teachers with 'liberal' views thought to be subversive, progressive schools accused of encouraging lax behaviour and undesirable ideas in their students.

It was thus at a moment of reaction against the liberalisation of American schools, at a time when the country was entering the 'McCarthyism' period, that Neill first arrived in the USA. A letter to Reich written just before his first visit shows that he was aware of the general climate of opinion, and looked forward to trying to change it:

> A few lectures might get me a public over there. I have just had five lectures in the North of England, speaking to about two thousand people in all. Their enthusiasm was tremendous. I don't see why I shouldn't come to a 'less advanced' country and wake folks up a bit about schools and children.

Neill did make some impression, notably in his one public lecture in the New School for Social Research. 'Got a great reception in New York, crowded hall' he told one Summerhill parent on his return. 'Seems that they have nothing so advanced as S'hill over there.' But he met some difficulty through the difference in the two cultures: often his standard jokes fell flat, or his audiences laughed in places where no humour was intended. He was asked to make two radio broadcasts, and was furious when one radio station partly owned by a flour company cut out some critical remarks he made about the shortage of wholemeal bread in America. For a few days he was a guest of A. E. ('Tajar') Hamilton and his wife Eleanor, who ran a private elementary school in New York City which subsequently became a farm school for emotionally disturbed bright children. There Neill gave a series of seminars and consultations to a group of psychologists and psychotherapists, many of them followers of Reich.

His most public exposure came in an article in *Time* Magazine headed 'That Dreadful School', which explained in some detail Neill's ideas and how they were carried out in Summerhill. But in general, though a few seeds were sown, his first trip had made no major impact, a fact that after a few weeks Neill himself was beginning to realise. He wrote to Reich:

> I have moods about coming back to USA. I half hoped that my visit would bring me letters from colleges, schools etc asking me to come and lecture. None came. So I sometimes think: 'Neill, you are cheating yourself. USA doesn't really care a damn if you come or stay at home.'

At this stage he was probably right.

It was in order to see Reich rather than to attempt another shaking up of the American public that Neill returned the following year, this time with Ena and Zoë. Again his impact was a limited one, though he had another enthusiastic audience for a lecture at the New School of Social Research. However, the publishing world began to show interest again: in New York Neill signed a contract for the Hermitage Press to publish his next book, *The Problem Family*. He was also invited to lunch by an editor on the *New York Times* Magazine, who asked him to write an article on discipline. The piece, entitled 'Love-Discipline, Yes – Hate-Discipline, No', carried a muted introduction: 'An educator says we must not impose our wills on children but should guide them by affection'; and Neill's relative obscurity was underlined by his opening remark: 'I feel that, as a guest in the United States, I should explain who I am. I am a Scot who has had a self-governing school in England for almost thirty years.'*

This article elicited a good many letters from the general public – including one from a schoolboy who asked for 50 copies, 'so that I can send a copy to each of my teachers'. Neill's lectures were this time spread over a longer period. He went to several American cities, talked to student teachers, arousing interest, and sometimes incredulity. 'I found USA behind on kid nature,' he wrote to a former Summerhill teacher, 'and my message seemed to stagger lots of people, which it often doesn't here and in Scandinavia.' The *New York Times* paid him 200 dollars for a second article, which they then failed to use. 'The head guy stepped in and said: Nix to this red guy from England. Ours is a respectable family paper', was how Neill interpreted the rejection. Once again he became dispirited about making any significant impact in America: 'so far my book is being killed by silence', he complained to Reich.

Neill had aroused so little enthusiasm that no lecture agent wanted to take him on for his third visit in 1950, which anyway had to be called off when his visa application was refused. In that same year he came into conflict with Paul Goodman, in an episode which strengthened his feeling that the USA was 'not the place for me'. Neill had been asked by Alexander Katz, a draft resister and a friend of Goodman's, to write an article for *Complex*, a new magazine which aimed to relate psychoanalytical issues to society. Katz sent Neill's article back, saying 'we felt it was not up to the level of our readers who are rather well initiated in the field'. Neill replied with a scathing letter, telling Katz that his journal 'is in the past tense. . . Reich has killed psychoanalysis. . . the new era is a biopsychological one'. Goodman, as co-editor of *Complex*, then joined in the correspondence. He told Neill that some of his introductory remarks about self-regulation were crude propaganda, and not worthy of the 'progressive' academics who read the journal. What the editors wanted, he said, was concrete detail from Neill's own experience with self-regulated children. Goodman himself, who was very interested in questions of adolescent sexuality, wanted Neill's views on what he claimed to be 'a pressing issue in most of our homes', which was 'the witnessing, or not-witnessing (and participation, or nonparticipation, and what degree of participation or censoring) of children in the first years of the sexual intercourse of the adults.' This was presumably more of a pressing issue amongst 'progressive' academics, particularly those interested in Reich's ideas, than a matter for intense debate across the

---

*One person who already knew about Neill was W. H. Auden. It was perhaps Auden's interest in Lane that led him to ask their mutual friend James Stern to arrange a meeting in New York. However, they don't appear to have touched on the subject during their lunch together, since Neill later expressed surprise to hear of Auden's former interest in Lane.

nation. More generally, Goodman returned to the point he had made in his review of *The Problem Teacher* five years before: 'The bother with you, Neill (let me say it as a friend), is that you think that, theoretically at least, your revolution is over; or, to a degree, you are willing to let Reich do your thinking for you.'

Neill was extremely irritated by this letter, no doubt in part because of the rather supercilious tone of Goodman's remarks – 'You presumably do good work in education (I have no first-hand acquaintance with it),' he had written at one point. He pointed out to Goodman that his school had been going for sixteen years before he met Reich, and that he had written sixteen books 'answering a thousand questions that you or others might think of, answering not in theory but in actual practice. There is the difference between us, that you theorise while I practise.' He indicated that he had no interest in the sex question that Goodman had raised.* It seemed to him to be part of a much larger question: 'Is sex intercourse a private thing or is it potentially a communal affair? I don't see how we can know unless and until folks are completely free from sex inhibitions as animals are.' He then underlined the distinction between himself as a 'doer', and others, such as Goodman, who he felt were primarily 'thinkers': 'I don't understand your letter, Goodman. You are too learned, too clever for me. I am a very simple person who can't think abstractedly.' In answer to the point about his 'revolution being over', Neill commented:

> What revolution? If you do as I have done, stood as it were outside children for 30 years observing what children do when not under adult discipline, is that revolution? If I had the power to alter all state schools so that they fitted the child as I have seen the child, that would be revolution, but as I have 60 children out of a few million British children who are all being educated the other way, my 'revolution' simply doesn't exist. All I am is a kind of scientist observing.

Summerhill was published in America during the week that John Kennedy was elected President, a moment which to some seemed to herald a new era. The book's preparation had not been an entirely straightforward matter. Harold Hart, a publisher in New York, had written to Neill suggesting that a book which drew on four of his earlier works – *The Problem Child, The Problem Parent, That Dreadful School* and *The Free Child* – might find a market in America. Neill was so delighted with the idea that, to his subsequent regret, he gave Hart a very free hand indeed in preparing the book for publication. Ena Neill recalls that 'he was so excited by someone in America being interested at last that he didn't give enough thought to it'. He found the business of reading his earlier books 'shattering', and in January 1959 told Hart: 'I suggest that you do exactly what

---

*Nevertheless, he thought it worth discussing in an end-of-term circular to Summerhill parents in June 1950, and promised to raise the question at a conference in Maine in August.

you like with the MS while I write either a preface or an appendix saying how I differ or agree with what has been written before.' However, he soon discovered that he no longer agreed with some of his earlier statements, telling Hart: 'A lot is from my Freudian period of child analysis which I wouldn't use now, e.g. today I would never interpret – say – a phallic symbol in a child's picture or dream.'

More critically from his point of view, he was disturbed to find that, though Reich figured prominently in *The Free Child*, there were scarcely any references to his ideas in Hart's edited version. 'I shudder to see an Index without his name,' he told Hart, 'for. . . I cannot claim to have discovered that neurosis shows in stiff necks and stomachs. I must give Reich credit for that.' Hart, however, was not prepared to alter the MS: 'Reich was considered by establishment psychiatrists to be a little wacky,' he recalls. 'Since the book needed the endorsement of well-known psychiatrists, linking *Summerhill* with Reich would not have done it much good.' Neill had no legal power to compel Hart to restore Reich's name to its proper prominence in the book, nor indeed the energy to argue for long over the issue. His main desire was to see *Summerhill* published, as he made clear to Hart later when another dispute arose, this time between Hart and Neill's agent A. P. Watt. 'Cannot this business be settled amicably?' he asked Hart. 'All this talk about rights and copyrights is outwith my interest. It is all Greek to me. My only interest is to get S'hill known all over the world, a sentiment I know you share.'

Neill ran into further trouble with his publisher over the question of the book's 'sponsor'. This notion of having an eminent figure contribute a forward to a book was one that was more common in American publishing than British, and at first Neill was unhappy about the idea. 'Just say this book doesn't need a sponsor,' he advised Hart. Or perhaps he could supply his own? 'I could easily begin thus: "It gives me great misery to write a preface to this bloody book by that damn fool Neill." ' But when Hart invited him to suggest a name to act as sponsor, Neill had what he thought a brainwave. Just before this he had received a fan letter from the writer Henry Miller, who told him that he had read his books with 'jubilation', and that everything Neill said in them 'strikes me as absolute common sense'. In reply, Neill mentioned the question of a sponsor for *Summerhill*: 'I'd like very much to ask you if you'd do it, I'd be proud as Punch to be backed by a man of your stature; my doubt, however, is whether the publisher would agree on the ground that your name would frighten off all the people of – shall we say Dulles mentality, i.e. the guys who buy the books.' For once Neill's pessimism was warranted: Hart would not entertain the idea of a forward by Miller, whose books – notably the *Tropic* titles – were still banned in America. 'At the time, Miller did not have a very savoury reputation among all groups in the United States,' Hart remembers. 'As it was important not to saddle the book with adverse opinion, it was considered politic not to include such sponsors as might damage the venture.' Neill's reaction was to accept this judgment with sorrow, and bow to the business acumen of his publisher: 'You of course know the sale angle', he told Hart. The next candidate for sponsor was the distinguished anthropologist Margaret Mead, but it seems that she too was unhappy with the Reich connection. Neill later told Ilse Reich: 'Hart tried to get Margaret Mead to write a preface and she said: "This man Neill is a Reichian; I won't touch a book that mentions Reich." ' This rejection seems to have upset Neill almost more than the other problems arising from the book's publication: whenever he subsequently referred to Margaret Mead, he never failed to observe: 'She hates my guts.' What Neill felt to be the injustice to Reich of such behaviour often provoked him to make this kind of intemperate remark.

It was several months before Hart finally found a willing and suitable sponsor in the psychoanalyst and sociologist Erich Fromm, who had written such influential books in the 1940s and 1950s as *The Fear of Freedom*, *The Sane Society* and *The Art of Loving*. Neill was soon reconciled to the decision: 'Fromm's introduction is a Wow. Wonderful,' he told Hart when he had read it. He had good reason to be pleased. Fromm put Neill's book into the context of the reaction then taking place against progressive education, suggesting that it was not the *idea* of freedom for the child that was wrong, but the 'perverted' way in which it had been used. Parents and teachers, he argued, had confused real non-authoritarian education with 'education by means of persuasion and hidden coercion', which had debased the original progressive idea. 'The child is forced to swallow the pill, but the pill is given a sugar coating.' This system, Fromm believed, was a perfect mechanism for fitting children into modern industrial society:

> Our system needs men who *feel* free and independent, but who are nevertheless willing to do what is expected of them, men who will fit into the social machine without friction, who can be guided without force, who can be led without leaders, and who can be directed without any aim except the one to 'make good'.

Neill's system, on the other hand,

> represents the true principle of education without fear. . . . Neill does not try to educate children to fit well into the existing order, but endeavours to rear children who will become happy human beings, men and women whose values are not to *have* much, not to *use* much, but to *be* much. Neill. . . has made a decision between full human development and full market-place success – and he is uncompromisingly honest in the way he pursues the road to his chosen goal.

Fromm confessed to being 'greatly stimulated and encouraged' by reading *Summerhill*, and thought that it would challenge parents to rethink their approach to their children. He believed that parents would find 'that Neill's way of handling children is quite different from what most people sneeringly brush aside as "permissive". Neill's insistence on a certain balance in the child-parent relationship – freedom without licence – is the kind of thinking that can radically change home attitudes.' He was doubtful if the

Summerhill experiment could be repeated many times given the state of modern America, in which 'few parents have the courage and independence to care more for their children's happiness than for their "success".' Nevertheless, he was optimistic about the long-term chances of Neill's methods catching on:

> If it can happen once in Summerhill, it can happen everywhere – *once the people are ready for it*. . . . I believe Neill's work is a seed that will germinate. In time, his ideas will become generally recognised in a new society in which man himself and his unfolding are the supreme aim of all social effort.

This sober and sympathetic consideration of Neill's philosophy of 'child-rearing' undoubtedly helped to bring the book to the attention of the academic community, as did a publicity booklet which Hart sent out to coincide with publication. In this, leading educators, writers and psychologists spelt out their enthusiasm for Neill and his writings, often in eulogistic terms. A typical comment was that of Harry Elmer Barnes, who called *Summerhill* 'one of the most exciting and challenging books to appear in the field of education since Rousseau's *Émile*', and suggested that those 'who think John Dewey was "dangerous" should lock their doors and read this book.' Similarly, the psychoanalyst Benjamin Wolstein suggested that 'Summerhill could find a place in the great American tradition of progressive education, of which John Dewey is perhaps the best known exponent.' Sir Herbert Read placed Neill 'with Pestalozzi and Caldwell Cook among the great reforming teachers, bringing light and love into places (the home as well as the school) where there was once tyranny and fear.' Even Paul Goodman, putting aside his reservations about Neill, declared: 'If we ever get a human society, his name will be remembered.'*

When the publication of *Summerhill* was first announced, not one American bookseller was prepared to order an advance copy. But as soon as it appeared it caused a tremendous stir, as Harold Hart recalls: 'The polarity was evident from the start. When the book was first published, a postcard was placed in the fly-leaf to solicit the opinion of the reader. More than 25 per cent of these cards were returned – an unusual response, as any mail-order man will testify. But even more striking was the intensity of the feelings which these cards revealed. Many of the writers plainly stated that *Summerhill* was "the greatest book I've ever read", and "the most important influence in my life". On the other hand, I remember one woman who returned her copy for a refund on the ground that her husband had told her that either she or the book must get out of the house.'

Over the decade its sales gradually increased; whereas it sold a respectable 24,000 copies in its first year, in 1968 it sold 100,000, and the following year double that number. By 1970 it had sold two million, and was required reading in at least 600 American university courses. During

---

*One influential intellectual, Herbert Marcuse, was more sceptical of the basis of Summerhill. He later wrote to Neill, telling him that young people should not be given self-government until their twenties, when they were able to reason properly.

these years Neill received an enormous volume of mail from America – from teachers interested in visiting or working in Summerhill; from parents asking for his advice, or telling him how his book had changed their lives; and from children, many of whom wrote asking how they could escape from their own schooling to enjoy the freedom on offer at Summerhill. The view of Summerhill as a version of Utopia was reinforced by an ecstatic article in *Look* Magazine, which then had a circulation of 7 million. The writer, Chandler Brossard, visited Summerhill, where, he wrote, the children 'vibrate with joy and delight and fearlessness'. He noted that 'The feeling in Summerhill's classrooms is one of complete mutual participation and enjoyment on the part of teacher and children.' Coming to the question of how ex-Summerhill children cope in 'the world of jobs, competition and unhappy people', he reported – no doubt prompted by Neill – that 'they do exceptionally well. . . they have greater psychological mobility – a mobility that manifests itself in quite successful interpersonal relations as well as happiness and success in whatever job they have chosen, be it bricklaying or teaching chemistry.' Neill, he concluded, was 'a genius'.

One of the reasons for Neill's ideas being taken up in America lay in the growing criticism of the public schools. This was not confined to radical reformers and teachers such as John Holt, Paul Goodman, Edgar Friedenberg, Herbert Kohl and George Dennison, but was also being made in more 'respectable' studies, such as the documentary work *Crisis in the Classroom*. The author, Charles Silberman, wrote:

> It is not possible to spend any prolonged period visiting public school classrooms without being appalled by the mutilation visible everywhere – mutilation of spontaneity, of joy in learning, of pleasure in creating, of sense of self. . . . Because adults take the schools so much for granted, they fail to appreciate what grim, joyless places most American schools are, how oppressive and petty are the rules by which they are governed, how intellectually sterile and aesthetically barren the atmosphere, what an appalling lack of civility obtains on the part of teachers and principals, what contempt they unconsciously display for children as children.

In order to provide some real alternative to these 'grim, joyless places', a growing number of teachers and parents began to set up small schools of their own, variously labelled 'free', 'open', 'community' or 'alternative'. The movement experienced a particular surge of growth from 1968 onwards, when student protests spread across the campuses of colleges and universities.

Only a small proportion of these schools took Summerhill as their direct model. This minority, estimated at one in ten of the alternative schools, not only espoused Neill's views about self-government and voluntary lesson attendance, but replicated other features of Summerhill. They tended to be boarding schools, usually set in the countryside, charging fees, and catering principally for white middle-class families. Their aim was

normally therapeutic rather than educative, as for example at the Summerhill Ranch School in Mendocino, California:

> Educationally this school can be described as twenty-four-hour life
> tutorial, where students and staff learn in accordance with their own
> interests. . . our emotional development remains primary. Self-
> awareness, individuality and personal responsibility to oneself and to
> others here are most important. . . . . Many of us regain self-
> confidence and awareness here, both of which aid us in dealing with
> the impersonal real world.

Some of these schools were very isolated communities, tending to be
inward-looking and concentrating on personal growth, aiming to create a
family atmosphere as an antidote to the broken homes from which many,
though not all, of their children came.

A greater number of schools were started on the street or in the
neighbourhood of the big cities where the children lived. Their aim was
often more consciously political – or if it was not to start with, the adults
involved often found it impossible not to be drawn in to local political
affairs. Mabel Chrystie, who first taught in the country, was involved in
setting up the first of the 'mini schools', the First Street School in New
York, together with her husband George Dennison. She had wanted to
apply Neill's ideas to the urban poor, and much of the achievement of the
school – perceptively and vividly written up in Dennison's *The Lives of
Children* – was directly inspired by him, as well as the work of Dewey and
Tolstoy. In particular, the adults in the First Street School drew on Neill's
belief in the value of unsupervised play, the curative effect children could
have on each other when freed from adult interference, and the desirability
of allowing them to express feelings, even when this led to conflict.

Many of the adults working in this type of school were critical of the
neo-Summerhillian variety, believing the need for alternatives was greatest
in the down-town urban areas where the poor working-class families lived.
Nevertheless, many of them owed their initial enthusiasm to *Summerhill*.
Allen Graubard, in *Free the Children*, noted that 'the books of radical
school reform became a prime source of inspiration and support. One often
finds in talking to free school people about how they got started that they
say things like: "We read John Holt and then called a meeting," or "A
friend gave me copies of *Summerhill*, Herb Kohl and Joseph Featherstone's
articles on the British infant schools, and then I talked to some other
parents. . ." ' Phyllis Fleishman, director of the Play Mountain Place in Los
Angeles, was one who had exactly this experience: 'Our school just sort of
grew the way it grew and I read *Summerhill* along the way,' she wrote.

Many who started schools in this way had little or no direct experience
in education. Orson Bean, who founded the Fifteenth Street School in New
York, seems to have been typical of many in the way he began. In *Me and
the Orgone* he records the moment when, sitting with a friend in his
apartment contemplating a poster about world peace, the idea came to
him:

'If there's ever going to be a change in human nature, you've got to get to the kids,' I said. 'I think maybe I ought to start a school.' Carolyn walked out of the kitchen holding a panful of eggs. 'What do you know about running a school?' she asked. 'Nothing,' I said. 'But I can learn. Have you ever heard of the book *Summerhill*?'

In fact, this school lasted longer than most of those begun in this period, perhaps partly because it avoided taking in disturbed or anti-social children. 'We didn't have any A. S. Neill on our staff,' Orson Bean wrote, 'and we didn't want to become a therapeutic institution.' Others were less successful, as John Holt implies in looking back at the period: '*Summerhill* was a very influential book, but since it greatly over-simplified and sentimentalised Neill's thought and work, its influence was often short-lived. That is, people would read *Summerhill*, and rush out to start an alternative school, not understanding that human freedom is a more complicated and difficult matter than that book suggested.'

Many alternative urban and country schools which blossomed for a while in America later encountered difficulties which led to their closure. Sometimes the cause was money, sometimes a waning of enthusiasm; in some there was hostility from the community, in others divisions within the ranks of the founding group. These kind of problems often came into even sharper focus where there was an attempt to 'infiltrate' Neillian ideas into the state system. Moves to have Neill's ideas tried out in the public system often came from members of university faculties who had read *Summerhill*. A similar phenomenon occurred in Canada, where by the end of the decade the alternative schools movement, again partly inspired by Neill's book, had made some impact.

Neill's effect on people outside schools may have been more lasting than any changes he helped to bring about in the attitudes of teachers. Erich Fromm suggested in his introduction to *Summerhill*: 'The thoughtful parent will be shocked to realise the extent of pressure and power that he is unwittingly using against the child. This book should provide new meanings for the words *love, approval, freedom*.' Many parents did indeed react violently to Neill's book, as Barbara Leonard of the Association for Counselling and Therapy in New York reported only six months after its publication: 'To many of the parents I have counselled, the reading of *Summerhill* produced almost a catharsis. The shock was first negative, but the after-reaction was thoughtful contemplation and sometimes dynamic action in their own efforts to work with, live with, and grow with their children. . . . My experiences with *Summerhill* have been many, but my conclusions are always the same. It has an impact. It cannot be sloughed off. The response grows and grows, curiosity is aroused, and feelings break through.' Sometimes the effect was instantaneous, as one parent from California recalls: 'At the time I was a new mother and teacher. Somewhere deep inside I felt like Neill, but I had never put it all together before. The day after I read his book I had a guide forever.' Frequently the book led to total 'conversion', as in the case of this mother from New York, who was in revolt against her own strict upbringing: 'To say my life entirely changed after reading *Summerhill* would not be an overstatement. Neill has been the single greatest influence on my life and philosophy, and I do not disagree with a single statement he has made.'

Not all American parents read Neill's book with care, and many failed or preferred not to notice the emphasis he had put on the limitations of freedom: 'To let a child have his own way, or do what he wants to *at another's expense*, is bad for the child. It creates a spoiled child, and the spoiled child is a bad citizen,' he wrote. Many were unwilling or unable to follow this advice, with the result that their children were allowed to dominate the household, at the expense of the parents' rights. What was here justifiably labelled 'permissiveness' soon came to be linked with Neill's name, reinforcing the view often purveyed in the popular press that Summerhill was a place where the children could 'do as they pleased'. Even Bruno Bettleheim, who thought he was familiar with Neill's work, began to wonder if Neill was not to blame in some way for the misreading and misapplication of his ideas: 'I should have known better. But so persuasive were his enthusiastic followers, so insistent that their own exaggerations and distortions truly represented his educational philosophy, so convinced were they that they read him correctly, that even I was slowly swayed. Little by little I began to think of Neill as somewhat foolish in his all-permissiveness.'

One of the first to alert Neill to this situation was Harold Hart, who thought Neill should write a follow-up book aimed specifically at American parents, and concentrating on the topic which loomed largest in Neill's 'fan' mail from America: the question of freedom in the home. Neill was surprised at this development, telling Hart: 'it is a joy to hear from so many saying that they have changed their attitude to their kids. I don't hear from the type you mention, the idiots who practise licence.' Yet he also said: 'I half feared that this would happen. Every message becomes corrupted. . . Jesus, Freud.' In general he was unenthusiastic about the idea of writing a new book; his health was indifferent, and he had decided many years before that he had nothing new to say.

In the end Neill took Hart's advice, and *Freedom not License!* was published in America in 1966. A hack job undertaken reluctantly by Neill, it consisted of a selection of the huge number of letters he had received from the American public, together with the salient points from Neill's replies. Later Neill received a number of letters suggesting that he had 'cheapened' himself by agreeing to this 'agony column' format. A short while after its publication he confessed his misgivings about the end product to Henry Miller, who had written with his customary approval of Neill's works:

> I am trying hard to find a halo in the Christmas stores but they are sold out. Henry, it was sweet of you to say what you said about my new book. . . . I think the book lousy. Hart changed my glorious Miltonic English into Americanese, splitting all my infinitives with an

axe, in short making me into American journalese. And I feel a bit
ashamed of impersonating Aunt Mary of the *Washerwoman's
Weekly*, only I don't think she would have given the same answers.
Hart says the book is selling like blazes and I'll just have to content
myself with the flowing-in royalties.

This was not the first time Neill had confided in Miller, for by now
they had been corresponding for some years. To some extent, Miller filled
a gap left by Reich's death: Neill poured out to him his increasingly
despondent thoughts about the future of mankind, and gossiped with him
about staff, health and their respective children. Friends whose books he
admired – Miller, Reich, James Stern – often seemed to bring out the best
in Neill as a letter-writer, as if he were striving to show that he too had
some literary ability. In contrast to his normal terse, cryptic notes, the
letters to these men were often uncharacteristically lengthy and effusive.
Neill was delighted to be in correspondence with a man of international
repute, and disarmingly told Miller this: 'I fear I use you. . . Henry Miller?
Oh, a pal of mine. Good guy.' As with other writers, Neill's antipathy to
academic knowledge seemed to evaporate in the face of his friend's books.
He read Miller's *Tropic of Cancer* with delight: 'What a style you have,
man! And what erudition – you mention scores of writers I never heard
of,' he told Miller. Perhaps in an unconscious effort to restore the balance
a little, he sent Miller by the same post a book which he hoped he hadn't
read, George Douglas Brown's *The House with the Green Shutters*. It was,
Neill explained, 'the only Scottish novel I consider of any merit'. He then
dropped in for good measure his principal literary connection: 'By the way
the Scots dialect may handicap you; it didn't when my brilliant sister-in-
law by my first wife, the Australian novelist Henry Handel Richardson,
read it.'
    Yet, though Neill was proud to be able to boast of his friendship with
Miller, it was certainly based on much more than his fame – or notoriety.
In Miller, as in Reich, Neill found a fellow-rebel, and one whose iconoclasm
appealed to him enormously. His letters reflect an assumption of a shared
delight in shocking the world. During the lawsuit in America against Miller's books, Neill told him that in England 'things are moving. . . . I can
use the word bugger when lecturing, or shit, but not fuck or cunt'. Later,
in pondering which of his heroes he would have liked to have met, Neill
wrote: 'Dunno if I'd have liked to meet Jesus, certainly not that anti-life
guy St Paul. . . I always think of his going through life trying to hold down
an erection.' Neill also compared notes with Miller at a more philosophical
level. Shortly after his seventy-fifth birthday, he told his friend:

You puzzle me when you speak of God. . . .God the word doesn't
mean a thing to me, meaning that I can't visualise or fantasy any
Power that is external to me. Like Reich, I can see no purpose in
life. I guess that the godly argue that God slew millions of men in
two world wars and 4 million Jews in order to chasten his creations.

Neill also regretted that he and Miller should be separated by the Atlantic and only be able to communicate by letter: 'One of my boys defined masturbation as the pale shadow of sex and I think we can call correspondence the pale shadow of friendship.' Eventually the two men were able to meet, in a London restaurant in the autumn of 1961. After-wards Neill described his feelings to Miller: 'It was grand meeting you, Henry. Just exactly as I pictured you. Why must kindred souls have to live miles away from each other?' The feeling was mutual, as Miller made clear just a few months before his death in 1981, when he recalled that he and Neill 'immediately felt a kinship for one another – like brothers in mind and spirit'. Neill's warmth towards his new friend was certainly increased by the 500 dollars which Miller gave to Summerhill on that occasion, a gift he repeated a few months later. The money was not just a sign of friendship, but a token of Miller's approval of Neill's work. He had known of his school for some years, and had five of Neill's book before *Summerhill* was published in America. Miller himself had started, though shelved, a book which he described as 'a desperate appeal to save the children of this world – save them from the stupidity and cruelty of their elders'. Neill's work he clearly felt was fulfilling that very function. In his view, the education system was simply turning out 'dolts, jackasses, tame ducks, weathervanes, bigots and blind leaders of the blind'. He told Neill: 'Since reading you I feel I must make an effort to say something – to Americans – about you, your work, your aims. How we need you!' Two years later he was able in a small way to help spread Neill's ideas in America, by adding his own paean of praise to the publicity booklet sent out by Harold Hart to publicise *Summerhill*. In this he wrote:

> I know of no educator in the western world who can compare to A. S. Neill. It seems to me that he stands alone. The only possible revolution, the only worthwhile revolution, must be created not by politicians or militarists but by educators. Rimbaud was right when he said that 'everything we are taught is false'. Summerhill is a tiny ray of light in a world of darkness.

And in a copy of one of his own books which he sent to Neill, Miller wrote on the flyleaf: 'To Neill, the one true educator in all Christendom.'

When Miller first made contact with Neill in the summer of 1958, it was partly to ask if he knew of a school 'even remotely resembling yours' to which he could send his 13-year-old daughter. Neill said he knew of no such school; but within three or four years this was no longer true, as the American 'versions' of Summerhill began to get off the ground. The move-ment was given a boost by the founding in March 1961 of the Summerhill Society, which had as one of its aims the setting up of 'a Summerhill School based on principles set forth in A. S. Neill's *Summerhill*'. A detailed state-ment of policy, which outlined the desired philosophy and organisation of the planned school, took as its introductory message: 'We hold that when children are given a responsible freedom, in a climate of understanding and non-possessive love, they choose with wisdom, learn with alacrity, develop genuinely social attitudes, and grow to be non-fearful, warm, and loving human beings.' Harold Hart was made the first president, and a number of eminent sponsors – including Paul Goodman – agreed to support the Society. Sub-committees were formed, a set of bye-laws adopted, and a regular bulletin started. Neill's boat, it seemed, was well and truly launched.

Yet from the start Neill had some anxieties about the idea of an American Summerhill, as he told Harold Hart in a letter, part of which was printed on the front of the first of the Society's bulletins: 'I don't want to see an American Summerhill tied to my Summerhill. I want no disciples. If I have inspired anyone, OK; but he must move on to his own philosophy as I did.' Neill was, as always, sensitive to the potential threat to Summerhill of the actions of others over whom he had no control. He was soon alarmed by reports coming back to him from American friends and visitors. One told him of a film that was put out on the CBS network by the Summerhill Society, in which 'the word sex was, of course, never once mentioned, nor self-regulation, and what was quoted from your book could have easily earned a niche in the Columbia School of Education or, in your terms, in the *Times Educational Supplement*.' Others told of rumours that certain schools were interpreting Neill's gospel as licence rather than freedom. Before long, the Summerhill Society itself split over the question of whether its efforts should be put into founding more Summerhills, or in spreading Neill's ideas through existing teachers and educators. A lengthy and intensely bitter debate took place over the question of funding one particular school called Summerlane, run by George von Hilsheimer.

This issue became mixed up with the question of the use of the name 'Summerhill', and whether Neill was justified in asking American supporters not to use it for their own schools. Neill became increasingly bewildered and anxious as he received letters from various parties to the dispute within the Society, putting their case to him. Von Hilsheimer wrote:

> Summerhill is really not just the name of a school – at least in the US – it gives us something you didn't have, a generic name separated from professional educationalists (or whatever they call themselves now) and from 'progressive education'. We only use you to scare people away – so we can't see a problem. If you object, tho, tell us, and we'll say the devil inspired us or something.

The same week Neill had a letter from his Israeli publisher Dan Doran, who was in sympathy with Neill's attitude towards the use of the name Summerhill by others. He gave a graphic account of a meeting which had overturned the board of the Summerhill Society and voted to fund Summerlane. He alleged that von Hilsheimer and his supporters

> used lies, slander, melodrama, breast-beating and four-letter words to win the few uncommitted votes. There can be little doubt that they will continue to employ such tactics in order to realise their 'vision' of 'freedom here and now'; there is little doubt that they will go about it cloaked in your aura with the name Summerhill on the

banner. Unless they are stopped your name will eventually be dragged in the mud, and the hope of true responsible freedom will suffer a great setback.

Though Neill knew and trusted some of his correspondents more than others, he was careful not to rely on second-hand opinions in trying to assess the situation. To von Hilsheimer he wrote:

I am almost completely in the dark. When I get correspondents telling of your school I simply don't know what the truth is. One said there is only licence, promiscuous fucking among the adolescents with the ten-year-olds trying to imitate them. Another tale – yr young pupils using dope. How can I tell if the tales are true or if the writers are neurotic projectors of guilt?. . . . I know I have no monopoly of the name S'hill legally, but the bloody thing is what happens in America is attributed to my Summerhill, and I don't want to hold anyone's baby.

Warming to the defence of his school, he then took firm action, writing to the Summerhill Society:

The name Summerhill has for 40 years stood for something untarnished, for an uncompromising belief in freedom for children. I refuse to have the name used by men and women I have never seen, whose notions of freedom are divorced from mine. I was influenced by Homer Lane, Freud, Reich, but I didn't use their name in a school prospectus. Let your school founders stand on their own feet.

Neill sent a similar letter to the *Village Voice*, and found himself yet again in dispute with Paul Goodman. Goodman seemed unable to see the difference between an argument about a name and one that concerned ideas, and asked: 'Is it happy, or necessary, to have such a proprietary attitude towards one's contribution and influence?. . .Certainly nobody likes to be misunderstood, but I would rather risk that than suffer the illusion that "my" ideas are my Property.' In reply, Neill observed:

Paul Goodman is in the audience; he isn't a member of the cast. He doesn't know what dangers a school like mine has to meet. . . . Anything new, anything anti-Establishment can be killed by talk and bigotry and hate in general. I can defend my own school. Let the others stand up and protect their own schools.

He regretted that the Summerhill Society had ever been started, and saw no reason why it should continue. To Dan Doran he wrote: 'I can't carry on this business. It wears me out. . . .Take 40 years off my life and I can fight, but, since it isn't my battle ground. . . I haven't seen the enemy. . . it is hopeless.' He then withdrew from any further direct involvement in the dispute.

During the 1960s Neill was asked several times to visit America. Once he was woken in the middle of the night and asked if he would open a new progressive school in Los Angeles, but pleaded a shortage of teachers which meant he had to teach for most of the week. Although his excuse was genuine this time, he was becoming increasingly reluctant as he approached his eighties to undertake long and potentially tiring journeys. For many years he had also had a fear of flying. In April 1962 he did agree to go to America for a year to start the school which the Summerhill Society had hoped to launch; but privately he hoped that it would take so long to raise the money that he could back out on the grounds of old age. But there was another reason which held him back from crossing the Atlantic: he felt that Reich's death had left such a blank that no trip to the USA would ever be the same again.

However, in December 1968, Neill was rung up by Orson Bean, and invited to appear on the NBC *Tonight Show*, on which Bean was then guest-host. Now 85, he nevertheless decided to accept the invitation. This time there was no visa problem, and Neill spent an enjoyable week being entertained and feted, and visiting old friends in and around New York. As usual on these kind of trips, he made a strong impression on those who met him or heard him speak. 'A few minutes with A. S. Neill was all it took to know you were in the presence of one of the warmest and wisest men in the world,' was Orson Bean's enthusiastic recollection of Neill's stay. Neill visited his Fifteenth Street School in New York, which he thought 'okay, but coffined and confined by being in a city'. He went to see Ilse Reich in Connecticut, and gave a talk to the students of New Canaan High School where she was a teacher. On both these occasions, his listeners were enthusiastic to hear his ideas first hand, and heaped dollar bills on him to help with the Summerhill finances. On the television show he appeared before the largest audience of his life, some 15 million – 'he was the best guest the Tonight Show ever had', Orson Bean recalled later. And on the plane crossing the Atlantic Neill conquered his fear of flying with the help of two bottles of champagne, caviar and a brace of pheasant. Exhausted on his return, he noted tersely to a Summerhill parent: 'Summerhill is much better known there than here.'

The extent of Neill's influence in America cannot merely be measured by the sale of his books, or the number of schools which were set up or significantly modified as a direct or indirect result of his ideas. What is clear is that the beliefs which he had been practising for forty years caught a mood that suddenly made his ideas seem 'modern', and of intense relevance to a younger generation seeking to throw over the traditional values and beliefs. Yet how many individuals fundamentally and permanently modified their view of the world, or the way they behaved towards children, as a result of their exposure to Neill's ideas? Perhaps George Dennison's cautious view is the furthest it is possible to go. Looking back at the impact made by Neill and Reich in connection with self-regulation, he suggests:

Such men allied themselves with forces and powers they believed existed in nature. The everyday phenomenon that led them to their beliefs affected other people too, and look so much like influence that it's hard to know where ideology ends and human nature begins. I think that Neill has been extremely influential even in schools that don't remotely resemble Summerhill. I don't mean that you find many teachers adapting his attitude *in toto*, but that you find important modifications all down the line, in schools and out, that can be traced to Neill and other libertarians.

CHAPTER 21

Too Much, Too Late

MR. A. S. NEILL

For the degree of Doctor of Laws, honoris causa

Comparing his country to a well-bred but somewhat lethargic horse, Socrates declared that he was a sort of God-given gadfly, sent to tease it with doubts and questionings. In his many written works, from *A Dominie in Doubt* to *Talking of Summerhill*, A. S. Neill—"Neill" his pupils call him, but as a writer he does acknowledge initials—has always been the insatiable, provoking Socratic questioner, of others and himself, a grand talker and arguer. His very titles are a challenge— *The Problem Parent*, *The Problem Teacher* and *Is Scotland educated;* Who but a Scot would have dared to ask that?

> I don't much appreciate being a famous sod. . . I am all in favour of a Garboesque wanting to be alone.
>
> Letter to James Stern, June 1968

The success of the book in America, and soon after in Britain and other countries, had a dramatic effect on Summerhill, and on Neill's life there. The school was saved from almost certain closure by the arrival of a substantial number of American pupils whose parents had read and admired the book. The number of visitors increased dramatically and eventually got out of hand. Neill became a well known and widely admired public figure: he appeared on radio and television, had a number of honours conferred on him, and was seen as a major influence in the apparent spread of progressive methods and attitudes. Yet this public adulation seemed to bring him little real satisfaction. As he advanced into old age he became increasingly concerned about what would happen to Summerhill. His pessimism about the fate of mankind deepened, and his thoughts turned increasingly to his own death. On his eighty-fifth birthday he confessed to Henry Miller: 'I'll never dance, ski, run, play tennis again, and I don't care. But I do hate the idea of complete extinction, all gone, memory, love, work. Just a few ashes in a crematorium and a few books that will be forgotten soon.'*

---

*Shortly before this, he confided to Willa Muir: 'Odd, by the way, that the extinction of my sex glands does not bother me a bit, yet I did heave a sad sigh when a bonny American lassie recently wanted me to be the father of her child.'

Before long Neill encountered difficulties with the influx of American pupils: 'we have the nastiest little bunch of haters in our history, mostly USA kids whose parents didn't tell us they were sending them in despair,' he told John Aitkenhead. He found that some American children were less inclined to understand or accept the mechanisms of self-government than the English. This was highlighted when several of the older children who had come right up through the school left at the same time, and were replaced by a younger group. In 1967, as one teacher of the time, Barbara Grigor, remembers: 'There were so many new kids that their breaking out period was a body blow the community could hardly take – a punch in the solar plexus. Winded, but struggling to uphold its faith in freedom, the meeting would patiently explain to the wild ones that they couldn't go on behaving like this.' Often some of the more difficult children simply ignored the fines meted out for anti-social behaviour. When special meetings were called to deal with these persistent offenders, they frequently failed to turn up. Neill put some of the blame for this on their parents, in particular those who had not been candid about the nature or extent of their child's problems, which occasionally were severe. One child, who later died, was continually trying to start fires – it turned out she had a brain tumour, a fact the parents had not disclosed. Another girl broke a large number of windows on her very first day at Summerhill, and Neill sent her straight back to her parents. It was of course impossible for Neill to see most of the American children before they came as pupils to Summerhill. At the same time he did accept many applications with the minimum of discussion about the child's suitability. Victor Gregory recalls Neill's reply to his request for his three children to come to Summerhill: 'It was a no nonsense note – in the margin of an official announcement as to when school begins, the address and the tuition – stating simply "OK for the children to come, please have each one bring an eiderdown quilt along with their personal things." '

Neill's belief that self-government needed a leavening of older children was proved in one incident, when the activities of a small group led to the temporary overthrow of the normal procedures of self-government. Three boys had been persistently stealing food and money, and damaging people's possessions. The issue was brought to a head when they stole the school keys. A special meeting was called: Joshua Popenue, an American pupil who happened to be chairman for the occasion, remembers what happened: 'Everyone was furious and bloodthirsty. After hearing the usual denials, which by now were becoming an awful bore, one after another of the staff and kids gave hellfire speeches about how long we had tolerated these bastards, and how many second chances they had been given. Tempers were now raging hot. When the guilty kids tried to leave the meeting – which is always anybody's undeniable privilege – they were forced to stay and listen. For we all agreed: why should we obey the rules of courtesy and democracy that the school had made when these kids had been ignoring these rules and abusing them for months. . . .We had put up for a full year with bad behaviour of a kind that an ordinary school would not have put up with for a week. So some of the staff held these kids down. I and some others went through their pockets. And we found the missing keys. Then these kids started getting scared and confessed to all sorts of petty crimes done months ago.'

Neill was forced to expel the ringleader of this small gang, a measure he took with great reluctance. Even in the most difficult children he was often able to see some virtue; but there were times when he felt there was no other way out without causing great turmoil within the community. In May 1964 he wrote to a fellow headteacher about another boy who had to be asked to leave:

> —— is a nice kid but he can't keep his finger out of other pies, hence a nuisance to younger ones, not so much bullying them by hitting but annoying them till they get desperate. . . . Last term he tried to get into bed with bigger girls and they all told him to go to hell. Then the story goes that he made a hysterical girl of ten take down her knickers, also assaulted two other little ones. . . . Holidays, and hell let loose. The first girl, a clever, hysterical, bitchy kid, went home and told the parents. Result cables, phone calls to me. She was kept at home. Other parent a psychiatrist sent insulting cables about seduction. —— denied all. The other two girls tell me he never touched them, and there he was speaking the truth to me. Dunno abt [the first girl]. He swears nothing happened, but there must have been something. Over the phone the hysterical mother screamed: My daughter was raped. Oh, those bloody American parents. I've told the psychiatrist to take his damned daughter home if he thinks she is going to be raped. As Zoë says: Heavens, we all had bigger boys take down our knickers, but we aren't sex perverts now.

He then told of the boy's reaction to his expulsion: 'Poor —— wept bitterly when I told him he was going. . . he has a nice side to him. . . I parted from him with real sorrow.'

Neill still pinned his hopes in the large majority of cases on the curative effect of the community. Yet the new generation of children sometimes seemed to him both harder and more sophisticated: many of the older ones were less ready to stand either for his jokes or his now well worn psychological games. One 16-year-old boy was heard to say that it was time for another PL with Neill, and that he'd better go and say he masturbated while thinking of his mother, just to keep the old boy happy. Nor were some of the newcomers so prepared to abide by the community's decisions: bedtime rules were flouted with increasing regularity, and Neill himself would sometimes be shouted down at meetings. One new member of staff, Wilf Blakeley, wrote to a friend at this time:

> It seems to me that it's all well and good protecting children from parents and society, but the fines system is just not adequate to protect children from other children. The root of the problem is that

there are too many problem kids here and too many new kids. As
Ena says, 'It's just not Summerhill any more.'

Even Neill's well-tried formula for showing the children the need for rules
produced a different and more sinister reaction than usual, though in the
end it still appeared to have the desired effect. Prompted by Neill, two of
the older boys declared a dictatorship during one of the particularly intense
periods of law-breaking. This released a good deal of aggression in some
of the children. One 14-year-old boy, who liked to listen to records of
Hitler's speeches, gathered a group of younger 'henchmen' around him,
and insisted they call him 'Flag Master' and give him the Nazi salute. He
marched around in black boots, and carried out a form of military drill on
the hockey field. He also 'arrested' some of the younger children, and
ordered them not to eat anything for a whole day, or to run through the
woods while he set traps to catch them. The anarchy lasted for two days,
while small groups around the school furiously discussed the situation.
Eventually a special meeting was called, and the laws of the community
were reaffirmed. But the episode left a lot of bad feeling, and was later
looked back upon as a situation to which few people would want to return.
Neill had again made his point, but there was a strong feeling that this
time the device had misfired.

These instances were extreme examples of how the atmosphere of the
community had altered. There were other times when order prevailed, and
individual cases where Neill was still able to help a child with severe
difficulties. One such example was Stephen Schapiro, who at 6 had suffered
a road accident in Canada, had been in and out of hospital for five years
undergoing operations to save his legs, and had become both withdrawn
and incontinent as a result of his experiences. At one stage he was teased
by some of the Summerhill children, and barricaded himself into a tree
house: food was then sent to him attached to a rope. Subsequently, while
Neill took him for a walk, a special meeting was held, in which his problems
were discussed, and the other children's tolerance asked for. One year at
Summerhill enabled him to conquer his incontinence, learn to read and
write, and feel confident enough to be able to mix again with other children.
On his return to Canada he was able to catch up his lost years of schooling,
and attend a normal school once more. He wrote to Neill about this, and
Neill replied in the affectionate bantering style in which he often wrote to
children:

> Nice of you to write me, nice to hear of all the subjects you are
> studying. I am now teaching speling and i like kids to rite ritely and
> to have good gramer. . . . School as usual. Very full with many new
> ones you wouldn't know. . . but that big one Neill is still here. I keep
> telling him to leave but he won't. Well, Mister Schapiro, you sound
> as if you were happy. Good. . .Cheerio. Neill.

Neill could still operate effectively in the child's world. Although his
jokes were by now wearing thin, his PLs becoming stereotyped, his spon-

taneous acting less spontaneous, his enthusiasm for dealing with problem children waning, his personality still made its mark on new generations of Summerhill children. Amarylla Stracey, a post-war pupil, recalls that 'Neill had a magical way of understanding what was wrong with kids. He was incredibly perceptive.' Even staff who found fault with him in other spheres rarely criticised his handling of individual children. 'He had this extraordinary, almost instinctive way of dealing with them,' Jimmy East recalled; 'He just seemed to know answers suddenly and unexpectedly, out of the blue.' John Burningham, another pupil, remembers a characteristic example of Neill's skill: 'He was alarming in the way he could see through people. No matter what you said, you knew that he knew what the truth was. A couple of us had got hold of the key to the main food store, and for about a term we'd been taking tins of condensed milk and other items. One day I was in Neill's cottage and he was reading the paper. Suddenly he said, while fiddling with his ear lobe in characteristic style, "Oh Brum, some bugger's stolen the key to the food store: I don't suppose you know where it is, do you?" There was nothing else to do but go and get it straight away. I passed it to him, and he just went on reading the paper.'

Another pupil, Ann King, recalls a similar example of Neill's intuition, and the effect it had on her: 'He had this ability to turn a heavy situation into a manageable one, often with just a word. I was a thief for most of my years at Summerhill, and Neill must have known that it weighed heavily on my mind. One day he said to me, "Look here, Ann, you bloody thief, where are my scissors?" I'd never touched his scissors – but I didn't know that he knew that. Yet being innocent for a change allowed me to change roles without losing face. The pressure was released, and thievery became a manageable problem for me, until it left as naturally as it seemed to have come. Later, when I returned as an adult to visit, he said casually: "I see you've returned those scissors, you bloody thief. I found them down the side of my armchair." He never, ever forgot.'

There were also of course still many occasions when the community, either collectively or through individuals, played its part in helping the problem children to work through their difficulties. One pupil had been caught stealing at a famous public school, been publicly condemned and beaten before the whole school, and then expelled. When he was accused of a similar offence at the Summerhill meeting, he was astonished when, once a fine had been imposed, no one made any further reference to his delinquency, and some girls even asked him to dance in the normal way once the meeting was over.

Another pupil, Léonard Lassalle, recalls his involvement in a similar curative act: 'One morning I heard a little noise at my door, and through half-open eyes saw a boy who we knew needed to steal come in like a cat. Seeing me asleep, he took out of my jacket pocket all I had, put the wallet back, and left as swiftly as he came. I didn't want to give him a shock, so I let him do it – though had it been a year before I would have gone for him. A few days later he came up to me and said that he owed me £3, and gave it back to me. I said, "Oh, yes, thanks," and told him that I'd seen him that morning, at which he laughed.' These were the kind of incidents that reinforced Neill's belief in the strong sense of justice in children.

Though Neill had been grumbling almost since Summerhill began about having to work with problem children, by this stage of his life he had quite clearly had enough of being 'a curer of souls'. Yet there were still moments of elation when he could see the tangible results of his work. His contrasting feelings are clearly captured in two letters he wrote to Willa Muir. On Christmas Eve 1959, after detailing Summerhill's financial problems, he added: 'and worst of all I have had to revert to problems to try to make ends meet, and how I hate them! Nothing in them for me; I just know that my Etonian thief of 15 will raid the larder, go unwashed, pinch from shops, and, oh, how sick I am of all that.' But after his eighty-third birthday party in London he wrote: 'Had a great party on Friday, meeting tons of old pupils and was kissed by all the lassies. Wonderful feeling to be loved and I get a hell of a lot of it. In train coming back a very bonnie lassie came up to me. Six yrs ago she was sent by LCC as a problem, had tried suicide three times, face hard and voice harder, a model of hate all over. Anti-social for a year then a slow change, and after another year left a changed girl. Now at 20 she is soft and gentle and kind. Cases like that make my life well spent.'

Neill's relations with the adults in Summerhill continued to have their tensions. Again, this was by no means exclusively the fault of the men and women that he took on to his staff. There were indeed, as in earlier periods, certain individuals who were evidently quite unsuitable, for a variety of reasons. An exchange that took place between a Summerhill parent and child in the late 1960s highlights one of the more straightforward examples of a problem teacher:

> *Father*: What classes have you been to this term?
> *Son*: Well, none, really.
> *Father*: None? What about biology? I thought you liked biology?
> *Son*: Yes, but the biology teacher's been in court most of the term
>   for receiving stolen property.

Another man, appointed by Neill to teach science, argued that if children were not required to go to lessons, why should he be? One teacher, Neill felt, was emulating some of the American children, and encouraging licence rather than freedom. She was, he wrote,

> a damned good teacher, but I have a feeling that she is at the root of
> the anti-social behaviour of all the small kids. They obey no
> laws. . . .When —— was chucked out of a meeting for being a
> nuisance he ran to her and she wouldn't put him out. She is
> anarchical and the kids must feel it. She never says no to a kid, lets
> em do anything they like.

Neill was also disturbed by another new arrival in the mid-1960s, as he confided to a friend:

In his cups he is reported to have said: 'I don't believe in freedom for kids and only came here cos I want to go to USA and S'hill is an Open Sesame. . . . I hate the idea that he is here for his own bloody ends and not to support us all the way. . . . I may have misjudged him but he never talks to me, only about getting books, chalk etc. We'll see how he develops.

Neill found he had to dismiss several staff during the 1960s – indeed at one stage there came into existence what the staff called 'Hiring and Firing Week'. However, some of Neill's decisions provoked protests, sometimes from staff, sometimes from children. He was certainly capable of listening to the children's opinions when it suited him, and ignoring them at other times. One male teacher became unpopular with some of the older Summerhill girls, and when they complained to Neill, he dismissed the man. This greatly upset the other staff, who sent a deputation to Neill; but he refused to change his mind. Another teacher was asked to leave in the middle of a term, despite his obvious popularity with a significant number of children. It was evident that Neill's personal feelings as well as some deeply ingrained attitudes were as much to do with some of the decisions as the needs of the children which he so often invoked. For some this was particularly obvious in the case of one man, as a teacher of the time recalls: 'He was a gentle, devoted teacher, whom Neill got rid of because he was supposed to be "too Montessori". Yet I had the impression from what Neill said that it was really because he was homosexual.'

This was an issue on which Neill seemed unable to break away from the prevailing attitudes of earlier times. As early as 1926, in *The Problem Child*, he accepted that there was no sin in homosexuality. This was certainly a more tolerant stance than many took at the time; homosexuality was popularly reckoned to be a perversion or an illness. Neill related it fundamentally to the guilt feelings which he argued were aroused by masturbation: 'you masturbate with the other bloke and he shares the guilt with you and thus lightens your burden.' Yet this conviction seemed to be essentially an intellectual one; at other times he revealed the ambivalence of his feelings. On several occasions he claimed with pride that Summerhill had never 'produced' a homosexual. Nor, as happened on other issues, was his thinking likely to be modified by his friendship with Reich, who once refused to take a professional man for training because, as he put it, 'I don't want to deal with such filth.' Neill's attitude was quite different from this, but still implicitly disapproving: 'Rumour said he was a queer but what the hell anyway,' he told the writer Colin Ward in a letter in 1966, in referring to one of his fellow-pioneers of the 1920s, Caldwell Cook.

Neill was concerned about the possible harmful effect on children of a homosexual teacher. During the 1930s one man 'interfered' with one of the pupils in the woodshed; the boy went round telling the other children of this quick way to make a penny, and when Neill heard of the incident he sacked the man. Yet in later years, when the climate became more sympathetic to homosexuality, Neill retained more than a vestige of his anxiety. Gordon Leff recalls being present at an interview Neill conducted towards the end of his life: 'He was wanting to engage a new teacher, and this man came in to lunch while I was there. He was insufferable in many ways, and Neill afterwards called him a "besserwisser", a know-all. But during the interview he suddenly turned on him and said: "Are you a homosexual?" ' Ethan Ames, a pupil in the mid-1960s, recalls: 'I never heard Neill talk about homosexuality, but while I was at Summerhill I certainly felt it was wrong. Amongst the kids it was, as ever, very much nudge-nudge-wink-wink-homo-poof. My own feelings were very confused and guilt-ridden, but not resentful. I never made my gay feelings known to anyone while I was there.'

In one instance Neill's aversion to firing staff had unfortunate consequences. When Wilf Blakeley arrived at Summerhill he was very enthusiastic about the atmosphere, but after only a term found he had misgivings, as he wrote to a friend:

> There's a lack of culture in the school. And I think that we, the staff, are at fault. We don't communicate with the children, especially the older ones, to the necessary degree. . . .We don't know enough about child psychology. And I include Neill, too. We have problems with the children and we just have no idea how to cope with them.

Such criticisms soon came more out into the open, and eventually the new teacher, as he recorded in another letter, had a visit from Neill's stepson Peter Wood, who by this time had quite a central role in the school:

> Peter came in to see me and, with much effort, told me that 'they' (meaning I suppose he, Neill and Ena) thought it would be better if I left. His reasons were that although I was popular with the kids and a very good teacher, 'they' didn't think I fitted in to the school. A lot of staff pass through the school, and 'they' can feel when one isn't really suitable.

Michael Barth, one of the pupils at this time, remembers the sequel: 'Wilf had a large following among the kids, and when Neill told him he'd have to leave, the kids didn't like it much, and made out a petition saying that he should be allowed to stay. The petition was near unanimous, though it wasn't brought up at the meeting.' Libby Hall, one of that term's housemothers, remembers a slightly different version of events: 'Wilf was very anti-Ena, and got the kids to sign the petition. Ena was in tears, and Neill was very angry, but he wouldn't intervene.'*

The question of the suitability of the staff was raised in another manner, which brought Summerhill into the public eye once more in 1968. Again Neill feared the worst from his old 'enemy' the Inspectorate, and once again he was shown to have been in error in his judgment. The

---

*This episode was complicated by more difficult personal issues, that had no direct connection with Wilf Blakeley's suitability as a teacher.

previous November he had written to James Stern about a visit from two local inspectors:

> Everything wrong, not one word of praise. . . .Our premises won't pass the Ministry standard, and it would take a few thousand to put em right. We haven't got em, and it looks as if S'hill after 46 years is to have it. . . .We all feel as depressed as hell also very angry and disgusted. Two Establishment formal dead men my judges. To paraphrase Shaw. . . He who can does; he who cannot inspects.

He told Ben Morris, who had suggested that a group from Bristol University might make 'representations to the powers that be', that 'the whole set-up of freedom shocked their little souls. . . . But so long as I live I want to fight for S'hill's right to be odd man out.'

The inspectors were certainly much more severe than any of their predecessors. They gave Neill six months to bring his buildings up to Ministry standards, and asked him to recruit staff with more appropriate qualifications. They also wanted certain rules to be introduced, some of which went against his philosophy – for instance, no child was to be allowed to go to his or her bedroom during the day; no child, even with an adult present, should be allowed bonfires in the grounds. The new strictness had arisen because of a scandal at a private school a short while before, where the head had been given a five-year prison sentence on charges of assault and cruelty to pupils. Shirley Williams, who was then Minister of State at the Department of Education and Science, had been instructed to undertake an inquiry into the circumstances of this particulur case, and 'into the adequacy of existing statutory provision relating to proper standards of education and welfare in independent schools'. As a result, it was decided that all independent schools should be inspected within five years, and only those approved kept on the register.

Summerhill was due for inspection in June 1968. A month before the visit took place, a Summerhill parent, Robert Byng, organised a letter to *The Times*, 'in the hope of influencing public opinion and indirectly the Ministry to safeguard the continued existence of Summerhill'. The letter, published on 11 June 1968, outlined the position of the school for any who were unfamiliar with it, and concluded:

> Although many of Neill's ideas have been absorbed under the skin by modern educationists, can we afford to lose so vital a laboratory of ideas as Summerhill? In a world of increasing conformity it is surely to be hoped that regulations should continue to be administered with tolerance and even with latitude.

It was signed by a group which included Summerhill parents, education professors, distinguished writers, and others sympathetic to Neill: Ben Morris, Robin Pedley, J. D. Bernal, Robert Byng, James Cameron, Benn Levy, John Mackie, E. Maxwell Fry, Hugh MacDiarmid, Robert Morley,

Bertrand Russell, Lance Sieveking, James Stern and Julian Trevelyan.*

After the letter was published, Ben Morris told Neill: 'I would have been happier with a somewhat tougher letter, but England being England it is perhaps the gentle answer that opens doors.' On the day of its publication Neill blithely told *The Times*: 'I am not worried about the visit. When you are over 80 you cease to worry. But we are improving Summerhill with rebuilding now being carried out. I am willing to compromise on things like lavatories, but not on the fundamental aims.' The inspection itself he appeared to take more calmly than before, writing afterwards to Ben Morris: 'the four who came were okay but of course they had to do their routine re lessons and bogs. I don't mind their criticisms... quite a few just ones re bad teaching.' But one teacher recalls signs of the old panic: 'The whole school felt aggressive towards the HMIs. Afterwards there was a special meeting, and Neill told the school that they hadn't been polite enough. But it was not normal to be polite.' When the news that the HMI were not going to close the school was leaked in *The Times* the following month, Neill was bold enough to say that he had never thought the school would be closed because of its principles!

Neill had been irate at one of the suggestions of the local inspectors, that he should retire and close the school. The question of Summerhill's future was one that had been on his mind for many years. In the summer of 1946 he wrote to Reich:

> When at any time in London I happened to be in a blitz, my first thought was: If I am bumped off, what will happen to S'hill. Which means of course the old silly idea that no man can do our job if we depart. All the same, I can't find any man I'd like to carry on S'hill after my death.

Twenty years later he had made no progress: 'No one here big enough to follow the guy with the halo,' he told James Stern. From time to time he toyed with the idea of looking for a successor, though such efforts never seemed very serious. Essentially he could not envisage anyone else running the school while he was still alive, as he acknowledged in a letter in 1969, when he wrote: 'I carry on and hope to die in harness.' During the war Cyril Eyre was mentioned as a possible successor, though he himself was fairly certain that Neill would never give up the reins: 'It was talked about; I think he said I could stay on and take over, but that it might be years and years.' Later, Neill talked to Richard Tolson about the possibility: 'It came up several times. He was determined that another person, known to all of us, should not have a chance. I was flattered, but never took it seriously.' The idea was even broached to one man who at the time was still a student

---

*The original list contained friends of the Byngs known to the general public; some other public personalities – Marlon Brando was alleged to be prepared to sign the letter had it arrived on time; and a few names suggested by Neill – Bertrand Russell, Robert Morley, Derek Hart (who had interviewed him on television), Joan Baez, Henry Miller and – despite his Roman Catholicism – Lord Longford. Several of those approached refused to sign the letter.

at a college of education: Bryn Purdy had stayed on for a few weeks after his teaching practice, when Neill had asked him to help out with some teaching.

Once he seems to have felt that Zoë might involve herself: in June 1966 he wrote to James Stern: 'Zoë now 19 wants to help carry on when I am gone.' Neill arranged for her to visit the analyst Ola Raknes in Norway, a close friend of both Neill and Reich. Zoë herself recalls the reason for this: 'Neill felt it would help to give me an insight into problem children at the school.' The idea never came to anything at the time, not least because Zoë married a local farmer and started her own riding school and, eventually, a family of her own. Neill found this hard to accept at first, complaining incessantly about her joining the local 'huntin and shootin Tories'; but he did finally accept that she should go her own way.

Another man who seemed a possible successor once tried to get the position clear: 'I asked him directly, "Look, Neill, what's going to happen to Summerhill when you retire?" He looked me straight in the eye and said, "Laddie, you're talking about when I'm dead." And he never mentioned the idea to me again.' This particular 'contender' was Michael Duane, one of two men who created an uproar when they attempted to translate some of Neill's fundamental beliefs into action within the state system. Duane, with considerable experience as both a headteacher and a teacher trainer, had been appointed head of Risinghill School, a comprehensive in north London formed out of four existing schools at the moment he took over. Situated in a run-down area, the school took pupils from families of nine-teen different nationalities, a quarter of whom did not speak English. Many had been alienated from education by their previous experience of school, and several were on probation. It was, in other words, almost as unlike Summerhill as it was possible to be. Duane abolished the practice of cor-poral punishment, in the face of opposition from some of his staff. He introduced a school council which, though nothing like the Summerhill weekly meeting, gave the children the opportunity to express their views and take decisions in some areas of school life. He also made an attempt to talk to the children 'like reasonable human beings', making himself accessible to them in a way that alienated some of his teachers, who felt that he was too often 'on the side of the child'. After four turbulent years, during which Duane won the confidence of many local families and dra-matically reduced the numbers on probation, but incurred the displeasure of certain members of the London County Council and the inspectorate, Risinghill School was closed for good. Duane, though he applied, was never again appointed as a head.*

While this drama unfolded, Neill watched with dismay from the sidelines. Duane had first met Neill in 1950 when he attended one of his lectures. He later became a regular visitor to Summerhill, and a close friend. He recalls: 'Neill was wise enough not to send me any embarrassing mes-

---

*The fullest account of this complicated and celebrated saga is given by Leila Berg in her book *Risinghill: Death of a Comprehensive*.

sages of support, he knew it would be counter-productive. At the same time, what happened did upset him.' Neill however was not totally silent; in a letter he wrote to the *Guardian* in February 1965, he stated: 'Duane has done a great job, and the Risinghill incident shows that treating children with love and not with the cane is dangerous in this so-called Christian country.' He drew two particular lessons from the Risinghill story. First, that Duane's success in reducing crime amongst his pupils showed that freedom could be developed in places other than middle-class boarding schools. Second, that it was because he was a head that Duane had been able to get somewhere with his reforms; for ordinary classroom teachers in the state system the task was infinitely more difficult. Duane, he told a friend, was 'a bloody hero' to have done what he did: 'He has got more publicity for freedom for kids than all my books got. He is a good fellow.'

Neill also derived much pleasure in finding a practitioner who shared so many of his assumptions. 'Mike Duane looks in to see me every week-end,' he told another head. 'A joy to hae a crack wi' a body that goes all the way.' This letter was of course written to a fellow-Scot. After his experience at Forest School before the Second World War, R. F. Mackenzie had returned to Scotland and taken up the headship of a state school in the coalmining area of Fife. Like Neill, he was highly critical of what he saw as the narrow academicism of Scottish schools, of the examination system which 'like a Wellsian fungus throttles and chokes freedom of thought.' At Braehead School he tried to widen the horizons of children's learning, to shift the emphasis away from mental activity towards an encouragement of the children's creativity. He also attempted to do away with the tawse, but like Duane met resistance from some of his staff. He started a school council, though this was only partially successful. He took children out into the countryside in an effort to free their imaginations, and to allow them 'an opportunity for idleness' away from the rigours of the schoolroom. In trying to implement these reforms he met with opposition from teachers, parents and politicians. In 1970, as part of comprehensive reorganisation in the area, the school was closed.

Mackenzie admits to being inspired by Neill: 'I owed a great deal to him, because he showed that it was practicable. He didn't tell me anything I didn't *know*, but if it hadn't been for him I would have said, Well, it's all theory.' Neill seems to have seen in Mackenzie's struggles an image of how he would have had to fight had he stayed in Scotland. Soon after Braehead was closed he got into correspondence with Mackenzie, and touched on the reforms he and Duane were trying to carry out: 'Guys like you are the heroes who work inside the system, with all the handicaps that never touch me,' he wrote. This had been his feeling for many years. When E. F. O'Neill had encountered violent opposition to his attempts to liberalise his school in Prestolee, Neill had noted, in 1932: 'Reformation within the control of the State is almost an impossibility. . . .Only when a man is economically free of the State can he carry out his own ideas of education.' Mackenzie's relative failure to carry his experiment through confirmed Neill's pessimistic view of the possibilities for change in Scotland's schools: 'But laddie, if you are a pioneer you have a lifetime of fighting all the dead people who are in authority,' he told him. An article Mackenzie wrote shortly afterwards in the *Times Educational Supplement* provided Neill with further scope to lambast the educational establishment: 'Alas, you will have as much effect on teachers as I have. . . bugger all. I'll be surprised if there is a single letter in reply to you. . . .You and I can't contact the Establishment cos it runs away from all things emotional.'

Neill was taken aback when Mackenzie was appointed head of another Scottish school, Summerhill Academy in Aberdeen. For a moment he wondered if Scottish attitudes might after all be changing, but, characteristically, also looked for, and found, a possible snag to what seemed to be a hopeful development: 'I foresee a difficulty for you,' he told Mackenzie. 'If the Aberdeen lot are on your side you canna write any more books of challenge.' He recalled a visit he had made to a new school in Dundee years before, when he had said to the head he would like to see his workshop, and was asked what a workshop had to do with education. 'I fancy Aberdeen parents have still that attitude,' he wrote. When asked by Mackenzie for advice as to how to approach his new job, Neill broke his normal habit, and gave it:

> In yr place I'd ca canny [play safe] to begin with, not so much
> compromising as being as Reich used to put it a conscious
> hypocrite. . . .The worst snag is the parental belief in Leavings
> [Leaving Certificates] or today maybe O levels. Dunno how you
> evade that snag unless very gradually. . . . I think you are to have
> many a headache, but what the hell!. . . I am too far off state schools
> to give you any advice of any value. You'll wrastle through.

In fact, Neill's forebodings turned out later to be correct. In 1974 Mackenzie was suspended from his headship while the authorities investigated divisions that had come to light in the school. The staff had split into two camps. Some supported Mackenzie's attempts to abolish the tawse, to introduce a school council, to concentrate on the individual child, especially those opposed to the prevailing ethos of the school. Others openly denounced what they saw as 'the unusual and particularly permissive philosophy of the head teacher'. They drew up a code of conduct, which suggested among other points that pupils 'should obey the instructions of the head and staff without question. . . and communicate with teachers both politely and with respect'. 'The majority of pupils,' Mackenzie wrote later, 'needed neither a sanctuary nor a psychiatrist, only some ordinary care and affection and humour and support. The Summerhill story is the story of what happens to a group of teachers who try to help these pupils.'

Before the conflict came to public attention, Mackenzie kept Neill in touch with his problems, and in reply received fulminating support. In 1969 Neill wrote:

> Yr letter makes me sad for it told me that Scots education is where I
> left it over 60 years ago. You are in a hole, laddie. Got to support

your family so that you can't tell em all to go to hell, so that it means a pioneer, years before his time, has to compromise with all the bloody anti-life buggers. . . . I was silly enough to think that Aberdeen was advanced enough to appoint a rebel like you.

As Mackenzie's troubles deepened, so Neill's letters became more passionate. In 1970 he wrote:

'Man, I pity you in yr fight for the tawse abolition. Teachers and lawyers are the most reactionary bastards I know. All this talk about violence in schools but none about the cane strap violence of generations. . . . But it ain't only the teachers; battle axe Thatcher wd subscribe to all the profession's anti-lifeness.'*

In 1972, Neill replied to another of Mackenzie's letters in a spirit of gloomy admiration:

Man, that's a hell of a picter you paint of Scots dominies. . . . Makes it difficult to be an optimist about education. . . . You must feel lonely amongst the local teachers who are so anti-life. I admire your sticking to the state system. . . I ran awa from it.

In 1966, shortly after Michael Duane had paid one of his visits to Summerhill, Neill told Mackenzie: 'We three plus John Aitkenhead seem to be about the only rebels in the great scholastic Establishment.' There were of course others, working in different ways in all kinds of schools, and to many Neill was an example they could hold up to themselves, an apparently unstinting supporter of children's rights. One episode in 1971, however, underlined how careful Neill was and had to be in allying himself with outsiders. He had agreed – along with John Holt, Michael Duane and Leila Berg – to join the editorial board of a new magazine called *Children's Rights*. In one issue the editor Julian Hall, without consulting the board, published a 'communiqué' from a group known as the 'Children's Angry Brigade'. This, among other suggestions, urged children in school to 'unscrew locks, smash Tannoys, paint blackboards red, grind all the chalk to the dust'. Neill was understandably opposed to the publication of these statements in a magazine to which he had lent his name. He was, though, unsure whether to resign in protest, as he confided to one Summerhill parent, Howard Case, the head of a school for 'maladjusted' children in Hertfordshire:

I am in a dilemma. To resign hands a gift to the Thatcherites; to stay on without any control over what the young editors publish is bad. . . . The trouble is that so many of the advocates of freedom are sick, especially abt sex. . . . I don't want to play into the hands of the compact teacher majority that is anti-freedom and anti-life by announcing publicly that I sit on the fence re children's rights.

*Margaret Thatcher was at this time Secretary of State for Education and Science.

Here, as in many other instances where ideas were being debated, Neill tended to see an issue in simplistic terms: people were either 'pro-life' or 'anti-life', or fell into a category that was almost as bad as the latter, and seemed to be the only other position that could be taken up – 'sitting on the fence'. In fact, his letter in the *Guardian* the following day by no means put him into this undesirable category. He made quite clear his view that publication of the 'communiqué' would 'give the impression that the magazine advocates violence, sabotage and uncreative rebellion in general'. But he also stated unequivocally: 'I am all for children's rights. . . the right to reject the barbarous cane, the right to have some say in their lives and studies, the right to wear what they like. But sabotage is not the answer: it is negative, destructive.' He decided on balance not to resign; the editor was sacked; and the magazine came to an end not long after. A few months after the incident, Neill noted in a letter to Edward Blishen: 'Irritating if comic to read all that guff about kids not being ready for Children's Rights. No paper ever says that S'hill has had em for 51 years. Meaning that I have been retired into history.'

During the final years of his life Neill was offered and accepted honorary degrees from three English universities. 'Thirty years ago it would have seemed impossible: of late it has become inevitable,' observed *The Times* in May 1966:

> Some university, thumbing through its files for an eminent educationist to honour, was bound to pick up the name of A. S. Neill, headmaster of Summerhill and one of the real rebels and innovators in English education this century. Newcastle has got in first, and so tomorrow Mr Neill will be at last clapped into the ranks of the Establishment when the university gives him an honorary M Ed.

The idea had come from Brian Stanley, the professor of education and an admirer of Neill's work, who suggested that if twenty-four names were to be remembered in the history of twentieth-century education, Neill's would be one of them. At the award ceremony, the Public Orator called Neill 'the most venerable practising exponent of progressive education', describing his notion of child freedom as 'shamelessly provocative', but 'vastly successful in practice'. He also noted wryly: 'We must share Neill's regret that this distinction may mean that he has to start wearing a tie.' After the ceremony Neill wrote with undisguised glee to Willa Muir: 'I had a glorious time in Newcastle, sort of Christ with scores of students being received by me, only my hat didn't fit very well.' He then proceeded to bite the hand that fed him, continuing: 'Willa, how dead university teachers are, God, I met scores of em in both York and Newcastle. . . . Ay, the dead hand on all education is the university.'

The formal requirements of such an occasion did present Neill with problems. Two years later, dressed in a dinner jacket 'last used a century ago', and some trousers borrowed from a former pupil (his own had failed by six inches to meet round the waist), he was made a Doctor of Laws by the University of Exeter. Again a sympathetic professor of education had been the mediator. Robin Pedley had thought it appropriate to make the proposal on the grounds that the starting-place of Summerhill, Lyme Regis, was within the university's Area Training Organisation, and found that there was unanimous support in both the Senate and the Council. The Exeter Public Orator had clearly done his homework, observing that 'we can say that we have invited Summerhill's founder back to where he started, in order to demonstrate that a prophet is not always without honour, however belated, in his own country.' Finally, in July 1971, Essex conferred an honorary doctorate upon him.

Neill made fun of these honours, filling his letters with self-conscious remarks about becoming a member of the establishment. Even in his humorous moments, however, he found it hard to conceal his delight at this recognition: 'If yr next letter ain't addressed to Dr N you are out, see?' he wrote to one Summerhill parent just after the Exeter ceremony, signing the letter, 'I remain, Madam, Your obedient servant, A. S. Neill, MA (hons), M.Ed, LLD plus of course B.F.' To a friend he wrote: 'I think the san kids think that now I am a doctor they can come to me with their bellyaches.' Ena Neill remembers that 'however much he stuck his tongue in his cheek, the honours meant something to him.' It certainly gave him a weapon to use against any who still maintained that he was a crank; and it did indeed represent a significant gesture of recognition of the impact his work at Summerhill had made on the world at large. Yet in Neill's reaction could also be seen the vestiges of the feelings of the lowly young schoolmaster, trying some sixty years before to get into what was accepted as Society in the Scottish villages and provincial towns in which he lived. He had a similar ambivalence towards titles. As early as 1936, in *Is Scotland Educated?*, he asked in not totally humorous vein: 'Why is a title given to a man who makes a fortune out of cars and no title is offered to me?' His daughter Zoë recalls: 'People used to talk about putting his name up for a knighthood. When I'd say, "Wouldn't that be fun," he'd say, "Oh no, I'd turn it down." But that would have been the ultimate to him, to have been asked and been able to turn it down.'*

In talking about these awards, Neill often remarked that no Scottish university would ever think of honouring him in the way England had. This was not strictly true: in at least two Scottish universities an honorary doctorate was proposed, but rejected by the Senatus. One of these was Neill's own university, Edinburgh, and the question arose after an event in which he played an unwilling part, the election of a Rector in 1968. This was a post traditionally held by an outsider, usually a celebrity, who was elected every three years by the student body. Neill was persuaded to stand by Bob Cuddihy, a student in the university Labour Party whose brothers

---

*Shortly after the war he did turn down another offer, to stand as socialist MP for the Scots Universities by-election. 'I couldn't leave my valuable work to sit and listen for hours to speeches in the Westminster gas works. But I have a little regret that I couldn't be an MP and say living things about Education,' he told Reich in November 1946.

and sisters were at Summerhill. He adopted his by now traditional attitude of belligerent gloom, deciding in advance that he wouldn't stand a chance 'in a university largely of medicals who never read anything', and that he 'wouldn't get much support from the Senatus, which possibly never heard of me and certainly would hate my guts, for I'd be with the students all the way for freedom and the Pill.' His supporters mounted a vigorous campaign, enlisting a number of eminent names to back his candidature. At a fund-raising concert in Edinburgh, Hugh MacDiarmid gave an oration on Neill's position in the radical tradition in Scotland; and Henry Miller and others were persuaded to send a message of support. The candidates who stood for election were the television personality and writer Kenneth Allsop, Stephen Morrison, the first student to stand for the post, and Neill. Kenneth Allsop topped the poll with over 2000 votes, while Neill joined such distinguished former candidates as Julius Nyerere and Bertrand Russell by coming bottom, with 258 votes.

After the election was over, the new Rector received a telegram from the Neill for Rector Campaign Committee:

> DEAR MR ALLSOP WE CANNOT SUPPORT AS YET YOUR ELECTION TO RECTORSHIP AS WE SUPPORTED A. S. NEILL THE ONE MAN WHO STOOD FOR EDUCATIONAL ADVANCE. . . .WE SUGGEST WITH THE UTMOST URGENCY THAT YOUR FIRST ACT AS RECTOR IS TO PROMOTE HIS CHANCES OF RECEIVING AN HONORARY DEGREE FOR HIS TREMENDOUS GIFT FOR EDUCATION IMMEDIATELY. WE HOPE YOU ARE HAPPY AT DEFEATING THE GREATEST LIVING SCOT.

Kenneth Allsop replied with unerring courtesy and precision:

> Thank you for your telegram of non-congratulation. May I, mildly, ask you why you should assume that I derived some vindictive satisfaction from coming ahead of Mr A. S. Neill? Has it crossed your minds that, had it not been I, he would have been defeated by all the other candidates? However, let me add that your admiration for him is no greater than mine – otherwise I would not have sent my three children to a Neillian school.* I think your suggestion, despite its curiously offensive framework, is excellent and one I will enthusiastically endorse and recommend.

Meanwhile, the editor of the *TES* Scotland had the bright idea of asking Neill what he would have said if he *had* been elected. Neill sat down and wrote 'My Unrectorial Address', which was published even before Kenneth Allsop could give his official one. Neill told the students that they should stand on their own two feet, 'challenge all things and when they restrict your natural growth, reject them'. With evident relish, he suggested their job was to grow up, 'and all the courses on the faculties will not help you to do so. . . it is more important to get in touch with your emotions

---

*Neill would not have been at all satisfied with this description of St Christopher School, which he unfailingly labelled a 'compromise' school.

than the whole faculty staff.' It was a sustained diatribe which mixed together his feelings about his own student days, well-worn stories about Summerhill, and pungent remarks about the student protests then taking place on American and European campuses. It encapsulated virtually all the themes which had preoccupied Neill throughout his working life. As he might have predicted, it produced not a single reply in the columns of the *TES*.

At least two separate efforts were made to get Neill his honorary degree. R. F. Mackenzie approached one of the Law Lords, Lord Birsay, suggesting that, whatever Neill might publicly protest, he would be thrilled to bits to get a degree from his Alma Mater. He was told later that some of those responsible for considering the idea had said no, 'not under any circumstances'. Kenneth Allsop was amazed to learn that Edinburgh had not already conferred such a degree on Neill. Writing to him in April 1967, he told Neill that he had been delighted to make the recommendation via the Principal in person:

> I had by that time found that there was general enthusiasm among the student body that this should be done. As you know, the proposal was turned down. No reasons were given. By word of mouth, I'm fairly sure that it was suggested that you would, if offered it, turn it down (my reaction to that was that, even should that happen, Edinburgh presumably was stable enough to withstand such a snub) and also that your article in the *Times Ed Supp* was thought too derisive and disrespectful of the academic structure.

Allsop told Neill that he had wanted to do this 'small service' for him 'because I know the schooling system in this country, where it is at its best, is so because of your influence and teaching which has permeated even into the crustier quarters'. He felt that the university's refusal was 'mean-spirited and paltry', and offered to put Neill's name forward for consideration in the next Honours List. Neill, however, opted to remain a prophet without honour in his own university, and told the new Rector: 'If you don't mind I'd rather you didn't put my name forward again. I'd hate to have a degree from a Senatus that had to have a name suggested to them.'

If Neill was seen by some to be an instigator of student revolt, he was also looked upon as a champion of sexual freedom, both by sympathisers and opponents of his ideas. In 1961 he was accorded what he felt to be a big honour: an invitation to propose a motion in the Oxford Union 'That the Christian ideal of chastity is outmoded.' His opponent was Lord Longford, and Neill verbally licked his lips at the thought of doing battle with a member of the Catholic Church he so despised. In his speech he suggested that the ruling classes had corrupted religion by using it to confirm their own positions rather than to promote social reform. He argued that there were millions of married people who, having 'fallen out of love', were using each other's bodies immorally. And he attacked the church for condemning people's sexual behaviour without understanding why people acted as they do. He had, uncharacteristically, been confident that the motion would be

carried, and was rather surprised and dismayed when the students rejected
it by 302 votes to 227.* In opposing the motion, Lord Longford suggested
that sexual intercourse outside marriage led either to 'free love' or the
'callousness of adultery'. Twenty years later he looked back on the occasion: 'I remember the debate very well and the victory for chastity. Neill
was charming and dignified throughout. I am not sympathetic to "free
love" under any name, though I think that he called it something else.'
After the debate, the two men had an amicable conversation, during which
Neill tackled Lord Longford about the iniquity of the Catholic idea of Hell.
Lord Longford assured him that, of the two of them, Neill would be the
one to be better off in the next world, because he had done some good.

Neill's ability to get on with those with whom he disagreed fundamentally was also apparent, and occasionally produced unexpected results,
on some of the television programmes on which he was invited to appear
during the final years of his life. The church and the army were two
institutions which evoked some of his most bitter remarks. Yet he once
found himself in broad agreement with a bishop, and on another programme with the distinguished general Sir Brian Horrocks. He appeared
on the *Eamonn Andrews Show* with Henry Cooper, who told him in the
bar afterwards that he believed in beating his kids. 'I liked his unspoilt
personality and had a long talk about boxing,' Neill wrote afterwards. At
the other extreme, Neill was asked in the summer of 1968 to appear on a
BBC programme on the topic of The Permissive Society, with some fifty
other people. The supposed apostle of youth there found himself clashing
with some members of the younger generation dressed in the flowery jackets
fashionable at the time. Neill berated them for protesting on behalf of
things that he felt did not matter, such as the length of hair or the colour
of their clothes. Why weren't they protesting against the stupid education
system or religious indoctrination, he asked?[†]

Though he claimed to find these invitations a chore – and as he got
older they were undoubtedly a strain – the showman in Neill enabled him
still to relish such public appearances. He also took them seriously enough
to seek advice on how to be a successful interviewee from one of his former
temporary teachers, Geoffrey Cox, now deeply involved in the world of
television. In 1964 he even, temporarily, had visions of becoming a television personality, rather than simply an education expert. Prompted by a
letter Neill wrote in the *Guardian*, in which he had declared that he could
'see nothing in modern plays of any dramatic significance', the actor Robert
Morley invited him to appear on a programme to expand on his views.
Afterwards Neill wrote with ill-concealed glee to Bryn Purdy:

*The undergraduate magazine *Cherwell* noted in its issue of 25 February that Neill's
speech 'was not argued but put largely in the shape of a series of declarations, about
which he obviously felt very strongly. . .the aim of his speech was to show by example
that sex should be treated openly and not as a neurotic preoccupation.'

†Neill's reaction may have been coloured by a remark of one of the group who, on
seeing a short film about Summerhill, remarked that the headmaster was obviously
running the school simply to get money.

> I am now in the TV rat race. . . . .Today I have a letter from Robert
> Morley, saying he has arranged for us both to be on 'Juke Box Jury'.
> Says he must make me a TV star. . .Good for me to talk about
> things I know damn all about for a change.

Most of his television appearances, however, were intended to be occasions
on which he would express his provocative views about education and
children. Yet Neill would very quickly bring in other areas of life, and
would counter arguments about organisation or party politics with more
philosophical remarks about the happiness of a child, or the purpose of life.

Often he would move on to one of his hobby-horses, and few subjects
could get him going in the way that religion did. It was perhaps knowing
this that one producer invited Neill to make what turned out to be his only
trip to Ireland. Afterwards he described his impressions of the occasion to
James Stern:

> Flew to Dublin to do a live TV show, with 250 guests, all RC
> I guess. I had some nice battles with the priests and their hated
> religion. One said a child is born in sin and they beat a kid to make
> it good. I asked him if he saw any sin in a new-born babe and to my
> astonishment the audience applauded me. . . . I think I threw a
> spanner or two into their bloody hateful machinery.

He was interested to observe the large amounts of whisky consumed by
some of the Dublin priests in the bar after the programme, and wrote:
'Christ what a country. . . *verboten* are divorce and contraceptives; sequel
more drunkenness than I have seen since 1895 in Calvinist Scotland.'

While talking to the priests, Neill received several critical remarks
about an earlier film shown on the BBC programme *24 Hours*, in which
the Summerhill children had been shown bathing naked in the school's
pool; 'God seems to approve of drink but not of sex,' was his comment on
their reaction. The film had at the time provoked a number of calls from
viewers shocked by the nudity, an outcome that Neill himself had feared.
The most interesting part of the film showed a school meeting, in which
Neill argued that the cameras should not be allowed to film in the swimming
pool. His view was that most people were 'not ready to understand that
sort of thing', but he was outvoted by the majority: the children argued
that there was no difference between filming lessons and filming nude
swimming. Neill's anxieties would perhaps have been tempered by the fact
that this part of the film clearly demonstrated how the children were able
both to speak freely and outvote Neill.

While Neill's name and face was becoming familiar to millions through
these appearances, his books were also having considerable success in
England. Gollancz brought out an English edition of *Summerhill* which
received some ecstatic reviews.* The anonymous reviewer in the *Times*

---

*The publisher's reader was rather more cautious, reporting: 'A new book by Neill,
even if it says nothing new, is an event. Of course Neill talks some nonsense, and dodges
some difficulties in the most transparent fashion. But even his tricks and his nonsense are
endearing.'

Educational Supplement thought that 'for many years to come teachers will need to sit at the feet of this great educator'; while in the *Spectator* John Vaizey described the book as 'brilliant, wayward and stimulating', and Summerhill as 'clearly one of England's greatest schools'. Other reviewers, though less ecstatic, praised Neill's work, and his ability to be both readable and stimulating: 'His shock is of the quality of an electric shock – it puts back the thrill into dealing with children,' wrote one. The book very quickly went into a second edition, and Gollancz followed it up five years later with *Talking of Summerhill*, a version for the British market of the book Harold Hart had published in America under the title *Freedom not License!* By the end of the decade *Summerhill* had been translated into Norwegian, Danish, Finnish, Spanish, Portuguese, Hebrew, Italian, French and German.

While he was fast becoming an international figure through the sales of *Summerhill*, Neill was getting increasingly concerned with one matter of global importance: the Bomb. Two weeks after Hiroshima he asked Reich: 'What of the atomic bomb? How does it connect with your Orgone? Death versus Life. Inorganic versus Organic. Death always seems to win in science.' In subsequent years he often expressed anxiety about war in relation to Zoë: in 1948, when the Russians were harassing Tito in Trieste, he feared that atomic war might be near, and told Reich: 'Zoë's delightful happiness and cleverness and beauty make the picture terrifying for us.' On numerous occasions, at the first sign of increased international tension Neill expressed his alarm about a possible holocaust. The 1962 Cuban crisis, inevitably, brought out the familiar reaction, as he made clear in a letter to Brian Stanley:

> Last week all our fuss about eleven plus, GCE and Summerhill seemed of no importance when one of the K's might have pressed the button. We are all cocks crowing on our own little midden heaps, waiting for the farmer power politics to wring our necks.

On one occasion in 1961, when tension was at its height over the Berlin Wall, Neill was moved to act rather than simply express his anxieties. The Campaign for Nuclear Disarmament had recently been founded in Britain, and leading political figures such as Bertrand Russell, Michael Foot, Fenner Brockway, scientists such as J. D. Bernal and Ritchie Calder, and many others had joined thousands of protesters in the four-day march from Aldermaston Research Station outside London, held every Easter. Russell was amongst those who joined a group known as the Committee of 100, which favoured methods of civil disobedience – he himself was arrested in one sit-down demonstration in Whitehall. The Committee then organised a similar protest against the siting of Polaris missiles at the Holy Loch base in Scotland. Neill, now nearly 78, had been persuaded to join the Committee by Russell. As he happened to be on one of his visits to the Kingston Clinic, he decided on the spur of the moment to take part. Johnnie Collier, who drove him to the demonstration, remembers that he was doubtful whether the sit-down would do much good, but felt that he should make

the gesture. With others on the Committee, he sat down in the road at
Dunoon near the base, and was duly arrested. He was detained in a local
hall for eight hours, and then driven through the night to Glasgow Central
Police Court. There he was put in a cell with two others, where he stayed
for thirty hours. His belongings were taken away, and he had to sleep in
his clothes until his case was heard on the Monday morning. He was given
the choice of a £10 fine or sixty days in prison. Although he paid the fine,
he was disturbed that others on the demonstration, such as the pacifist Pat
Arrowsmith, elected to serve their prison term.

The following night he stayed at Kilquhanity School, where Morag
Aitkenhead recalls that 'he was touchingly childlike and upset when he
realised he couldn't go on with the Committee.' A few days later, in the
Scotsman, he explained why he was resigning from the Committee:

> Partly funk, of course, for if I am arrested again it would mean
> prison; partly shame at evading the issue. I cannot remain a sleeping
> (or sitting-down) partner while braver souls give up their liberty for
> the cause. I think now that one should remain on the committee
> only if prepared to give all. I cannot, not only because of my
> responsibility to my pupils, but also because I fear that the method
> of civil disobedience will not bring in enough recruits in the short
> time we may have.

He then criticised the 'establishment' for being indifferent or passive in the
face of the nuclear threat:

> The professions, the trade unions, the Churches should all be crying
> aloud for peace. . . .The fight for life seems a desperate one, but
> what is the alternative? To sit, as we do now, frightened to open our
> newspaper, trembling to read what one of the K's has said,
> wondering fearfully if any moment might bring unspeakable death.

But the following month, in explaining his resignation to a friend, the sense
of despair had returned: 'I felt and feel we can't do a damn thing to stop
the coming (sooner or later) end of mankind.'

Neill certainly didn't welcome unreservedly the huge increase in the
number of visitors who came to Summerhill as the result of his international
renown. He did, however, enjoy talking to those individuals who were able
to give rather than take. Edward Blishen, who dropped in occasionally
with a bottle of whisky, was one of several visitors who noticed this
preference: 'He liked free-ranging conversations, and had an enormous
desire to get away from the treadmill of the ideas and subjects which people
always discussed with him. He was the famous A. S. Neill, there was a
famous ground which people discussed with him, and he trudged round
and round it for ever. So you could always delight him by talking about
almost anything that wasn't part of that.' He would also still respond
positively to anyone with an apparently keen interest in Reich. The theatre
critic Kenneth Tynan, who had admired Neill's work for some time, spent
a day with him while gathering material for a book on Reich, and thought

Neill 'a man of perfect charity, in whom an immense tenderness was balanced by great shrewdness'. Neill made a similar impression on the writer Colin Wilson, who was doing research on Reich's life for his book *The Quest for Wilhelm Reich*, and who found him 'absolutely charming'.

Another very welcome visitor was the actor Robert James, who arrived on a more personal mission. He had been playing the part of the undertaker in *Dr Finlay's Casebook*, a popular television series set in the fictitious village of 'Tannochbrae'. Neill watched the programme regularly, and at one stage decided that he could make a better job of the script writing than the professionals employed by the BBC. Fascinated by Robert James's 'elastic face', he wrote a script which made him a central character, and invited James to give his opinion of it. The actor thought that it was a good idea, but not performable as it stood, and the story was passed on to the script editor with Neill's approval, but rejected. Months later, an episode with a theme not dissimilar to that written by Neill was shown, and Neill made a protest to the series author, A. J. Cronin. Subsequently he wrote to James: 'Alas, I can never hope to give you a part that would show your talent, not after my quarrel with Cronin.' Of the episode shown he wrote: 'I thought it terrible, unreal, without humour and all out of character. Man, they didn't give you a chance.'

Neill had originally written the Scots actor a 'fan' letter, and acted swiftly when he received a reply, as Robert James recalls: 'The next morning my telephone rang very early: "I didna ken we were both exiles doon here!" And so, on many occasions and over many years, I would be rung up and invited to account for the falling standards of the BBC in particular and the world in general.' Neill frequently invited his new friend to pay him a visit, but he was not able to do so until the last few months of Neill's life. 'I saw a signpost to Leiston and decided to set course for Summerhill at last. We floundered about in the grounds for a while, then a window opened and a lady – later to be identified as Mrs Neill – asked our business. I asked to see Mr Neill. Mr Neill was extremely busy and saw no one without appointment. Would I care to leave my name? Mr Gibson of Tannochbrae. Silence. Exit of lady from window. Arrival of outstretched hand of A. S. Neill. Closely followed by Mr Neill himself, of course, making us welcome.'

The ban on casual visitors had been made the year before. By 1970 between 60 and 100 visitors were turning up at Summerhill every week. Coachloads would draw up outside the school, their occupants would then wander round the house and grounds, intruding into the children's rooms, asking them about their sex lives, offering them sweets, drink or cigarettes. The children understandably resented those who behaved in this way, and in some cases reacted aggressively, bombarding them with snowballs or soggy toilet paper. Others took a more business-like attitude to the invasion, and began to sell the visitors souvenirs or refreshments, supposedly for the end of term party or the school building fund. 'Some visitors are so fanatically in love with the place that I'm confident we could sell them a packet of genuine Summerhill mud without difficulty,' observed one pupil.

In November 1971, with the numbers still increasing, and Neill un-willing to act, the children took the initiative, as Ena Neill recalls: 'One Saturday afternoon we had 280 visitors, a particularly disagreeable lot. They went upstairs into the children's bedrooms, opened their cupboards, looked in their drawers. The kids said, "You can't do that," but they just pushed them aside. Then they came to a meeting. You can imagine all that lot in our small hall. It had got to the stage where the children wouldn't discuss business in the school meeting: it was just superficial stuff, with all those cameras clicking and tape recorders whirring. That was the finish. The children asked for a meeting with Neill, and almost *en masse* they said, "It's either your school or your visitors, but not both. We can't talk about things we want to in front of strangers, and we want it stopped." We had a card printed, saying No More Visitors, and that was that.' A more public announcement appeared in the *New Statesman* a few days later: 'Summer-hill pupils, tired of being a zoo to 100 visitors weekly, made a Law: No more visitors, and I am too old and tired to give interviews. – A. S. Neill.'

Neill himself was in two minds about this move. Visitors were certainly proving a strain for him, and it became hard to retain any privacy, even in his own home. Yet talking about Summerhill was second nature to him now; answering visitors' questions in the dining room was almost as much a part of the Summerhill week as the meeting which preceded these sessions. Neill in fact tried to resist imposing a ban, as one pupil, Mikey Cuddihy, recalls: 'He argued that the meetings were a vital part of the running of the school, and that it was important for visitors to be able to listen in to the proceedings. Everyone except him voted in favour of the ban, and he stormed out of the meeting, almost in tears.' In this instance there seems to have been no play-acting on Neill's part, though afterwards he professed to be relieved at the decision.

Just before the ban on visitors, Neill suffered a heart attack, and had to spend a short time in hospital. His stay there concentrated his mind on the subject that had for a long while been uppermost in his mind. On his return home he wrote to Gordon Leff: 'I'm gey frail now and worry abt the future of S'hill. Maybe the Ministry will step in saying we have tolerated this school because of the outcry if we closed it, but now that the old man is dead we can't allow a school where the kids can play all day and get no education.' He hoped that, if this situation should arise, 'a few old pupils will write to *The Times* giving yr jobs and degrees. . . . I'll be a candle blown out but I want to help Ena carry on.' Ena Neill herself remembers: 'He thought at one time that Summerhill would close after his death. But he gave up running it about three years before he died, and he said: "You can carry on." I felt confident because he was still there, I never did anything without consulting him. It was his school, and I felt he shouldn't be left out of anything, or be made to feel that he wasn't wanted any more, because he very seriously was. So then he decided that when he died I would be capable of running it, and he said so.'

The pain and discomfort which Neill had experienced only occasion-ally before now became a permanent feature of his life. A body itch made it difficult for him to get to sleep. Soon he lost his taste for whisky. He found he could summon up no interest in handwork, and gave all his precious tools to the school workshop. In the summer of 1972 his auto-biography *Neill! Neill! Orange Peel!* was published in America, and in May 1973 in Britain, to warm and sympathetic reviews. They meant little to Neill, who had struggled to complete the second half at Harold Hart's request, and found no interest in looking back over the last thirty years of his life.* He threw a batch of reviews in the waste paper basket without showing them to anyone: 'In one I am a genius, in another an eccentric,' he wrote to James Stern. 'Just past caring.' John Holt remembers Neill in despondent mood when he visited Summerhill in the summer of 1973: 'My book *Escape from Childhood* had just appeared, and since it was a book that Neill and I might disagree about, I thought we might have some interesting talk. But soon after I arrived he said, "I haven't read your book, John. I can't read more than a page or two any more, I can't concentrate, as soon as I've read a page I've forgotten what's in it." He said that he was past the point of having any ambition, or of being disappointed because of not having achieved some ambition. He had no great hopes for British education, or education in general, or Britain in general, or for that matter the world in general.'

---

*The book had been rejected by three publishers, including Jenkins. The first half had remained in his drawer ever since he wrote it in 1939.

CHAPTER 22

The Message of Freedom

Yet, despite its limitations as a model for mass-education, Summerhill is one of the world's most powerful ideas, that is not likely ever to die. It has lived before Neill, although it has rarely been represented with such dynamic, charismatic power. It will outlast him – nuclear fission permitting – as long as men live and learn.

Fred M. Hechinger, in Summerhill: For and Against, 1970

Towards the end of his life, Neill became excessively gloomy about the influence of Summerhill on the world at large. He wrote or spoke as if his ideas had had little or no impact on teachers, parents and other adults who were shaping the values and behaviour of future generations. Yet in earlier years he had been considerably more optimistic about his achievement. In 1944, he wrote:

> I have no illusions about my own name: in fifty years it will be unknown. But the work Summerhill has done will go on. Without undue conceit I can say that it has influenced thousands of teachers and parents, and they in their turn will influence others.

Some ten years later, during the course of a dispute with Reich about different kinds of recognition, Neill wrote: 'I think of recognition in another way; I think of reaching as many as possible. . . . S'hill has had influence over half the globe simply because I wrote about it.'

What, then, has been the nature and extent of Neill's influence? Can and should the 'Summerhill idea' survive, or is it merely a product of a

particular time? How far was Neill's version of freedom for children dependent upon the peculiar mixture of skills, ideals and limitations which
made up his personality? In talking to many different people about these
issues, I have been offered a complete spectrum of answers to such fundamental questions. One schools inspector in England described Neill as
'one of the most influential educationists of this century', while another
asserted that 'he had no influence on state schools whatsoever'. It is self-
evident that everyone's answer will depend in turn on their own experiences, aspirations, sympathies and perceptiveness. It is equally clear that
Neill's philosophy and practice cannot simply be wrapped up in a parcel
labelled 'the Summerhill idea'. Perhaps, in putting forward some tentative
conclusions, it would be best first to look at those of his ideas which Neill
himself considered fundamental, and then to see in what regard they are
held some sixty years after he founded his school.

Absolutely paramount was his belief that children are innately good.
Of course he could not prove this assertion in any way that would be
recognised as scientific, just as those who believe the opposite cannot prove
that a child is born a creature of sin, or is inherently wicked in some more
secular way. Neill's importance lies in the fact that he made this statement
at a time when people were only just on the threshold of beginning to
understand the way that a child's mind worked. In place of the old authority, the subordination of children to a life of fear, ignorance, and stern
distrust, he offered them friendship, understanding, knowledge. In this he
was certainly years ahead of his time, anticipating many of the findings of
modern child psychology. He stuck tenaciously to this belief in the essential
goodness of the child, sometimes in the face of apparent evidence to the
contrary. Though he frequently and increasingly despaired of what he saw
as a sick society, he rarely gave up on any individual child.

David Wills, Homer Lane's biographer, suggested that 'Neill helped
people to get a "child's-eye view" of life, instead of expecting children to
see things through adult eyes.' Others working in education, psychology,
social work and psychoanalysis of course contributed to this shift of emphasis, but perhaps no one did it in quite such a dramatic fashion as Neill.
Whatever the unconscious motives for his determination to be 'on the side
of the child', the very fact that he was so consistently in that position forced
many adults to reconsider their attitude towards children. Leila Berg, the
children's book writer, saw Neill's impact across the generations in this
sphere: 'Our generation felt we knew best, and that it was our *duty* to
teach the child: you were made to feel you were ruining a child's life if you
gave in to him or her. Neill's idea of leaving the child alone, not pushing
your ideas on the child but following the child, was fresh air in the 1930s
and 1940s. But the younger generation are not so accepting of authority;
many of them are able to leave children alone without feeling odd about
such an attitude. In quite a large measure that is due to Neill.'

Another crucial part of Neill's philosophy was his conviction that
children are sufficiently self-motivated to want to learn, and are therefore
the best judges of when they should start to do so. Learning should be

based on specific need, as Samuel Butler suggested in his *Note Books* when he wrote: 'Never try to learn anything until the not knowing it has come to be a nuisance to you for some time. . . . A boy should never be made to learn anything until it is obvious that he cannot get on without it.' In Neill's view, a child would learn best if he or she saw a *point* to that learning, even if it took many years beyond the 'normal' age for such a connection to be made. This idea was certainly a startling and much-opposed one when Neill first started to propound it. That it is hardly less so today can be demonstrated by the fact that there is scarcely another school apart from Summerhill itself where such trust is placed upon a child's self-motivating potential.

Time and again, Neill made the assertion that 'childhood should be playhood'. The response to this idea has been more positive, not least because we have gradually come to understand both the learning and therapeutic potential of play, and to recognise it as a creative activity. Yet children's play is still heavily curtailed or controlled by the adults around them: few have been able to stand aside in the way that Neill could. It was perhaps easier to do this if, as he did, you saw childhood not as a preparation for later life, but as life itself. Such an idea remains subversive in our grossly competitive educational systems.

Neill once described self-government as 'the bee in my bonnet'. The weekly meeting at Summerhill was of course central to his belief in the goodness of the child, and his desire to demonstrate in practical form the boundaries of individual freedom in such a community. It was also an indication of the priority he placed upon social learning, on the importance of learning to live together – 'hearts not heads'. Children, he believed, have a natural sense of justice, and often have more wisdom in deciding how to deal with an offender than adults in a similar situation. There have been plenty of examples in Summerhill over the years to support this belief. Yet this feature of Summerhill has not been taken up in any significant way in other schools, despite the vogue for student participation during the 1960s.

Indeed, it seems that ultimately, on all these issues, Neill's influence has been much greater on individuals than it has on institutions, with the exception of that relatively small number of schools directly inspired by his work. His influence on individuals may not always have been a conscious one. As one English headteacher pointed out: 'I have no doubt that Neill will prove to have been a very important figure whose influence, directly or indirectly, extends to many teachers even when they, on the conscious level, dismiss his ideas as "hopelessly idealistic".' Others in England read Neill *because* of his idealism. Caught up in a system where ideals were difficult to put into practice, they found his books a tonic. The writer Edward Blishen, for example, who taught in state schools for many years, recalled: 'If I wanted to be relieved of anxiety, I would read Neill, and feel less anxious.' The poet Charles Causley, a headteacher in a primary school, believed that 'Neill's name, work, memory will always be a sort of ikon to me'. There were, he felt, several aspects of Neill's philosophy which could be of help to the practising teacher: 'His thought, his understanding of children, his tolerance, his ability to communicate his knowledge of the psychology of childhood without using teeth- and ear-cracking jargon, his sense of humour, I found immensely stimulating and encouraging through more than twenty-five years of very demanding classroom teaching. He was the only writer I ever read who sounded as though he not only liked but really loved children.'

Neill's most spectacular achievement at Summerhill was with problem children, and here he made a strong and lasting impression on many English teachers. One infant school headteacher remembers: 'As an assistant in my first teaching post I was encouraged by those in authority to punish severely all those disturbed children who were stealing, swearing etc. I rebelled and found many answers to my questions in Neill's books. . . .There are two boys in this school at present who are thrashed frequently at home by vicious step-fathers or "lodgers", and who are desperate for affection and understanding from their teacher. In my dealings with them I often recall how Neill has dealt with similar incidents.' Harry Rée, who as a professor of education in the 1960s had contact with many state schools, believes Neill had a significant effect on teachers' attitude to discipline: 'Many of my contemporaries, then in positions of relative power in state schools, had managed to modify the attitudes of traditional teachers, because they had been convinced by Neill that so often their approach was wrong. Many of us actually gave up caning boys, convinced by Neill of its uselessness.'

Neill perhaps made his greatest mark on the school system by showing teachers that it was possible to establish more relaxed and friendly relationships between adults and children. Robin Pedley, in *The Comprehensive School*, saw Neill as a seminal influence in this area of school life:

> More than anyone else, he swung teachers' opinion in England from
> its old reliance on authority and the cane to a hesitant recognition
> that a child's first need is love, and, with love, respect for the free
> growth of his personality: free, that is, from the arbitrary
> compulsion of elders, and disciplined instead by social experience.
> Today's friendliness between pupils and teachers is probably the
> greatest difference between the classrooms of the 1970s and those of
> the 1930s. The change owes much to Neill.

Such 'friendliness' is of course much more evident in the nursery and primary schools in England, and it is generally agreed that Neill's influence there has been greater than at the secondary level. Certainly the structure and ethos of most secondary schools, with their preoccupation with the needs of an outmoded and hideously uncreative examination system, cut right across the basic tenets of Neill's philosophy. The concern for results and status, the tendency to categorise children crudely from an early age as 'academic' or 'non-academic', 'able' and 'less able', the anxieties and pressures from parents – such factors make it an uphill battle even for those teachers who wish to follow through Neill's idea of being 'on the side of the child'. Philip Coggin, the head of a comprehensive school, observed: 'I don't find any general acceptance of this principle among my colleagues. A teacher will sometimes champion a child in an individual case, but the view of the child as a person with rights is still relatively rare.' Certainly secondary schools are all too ready to fit the child to the school rather than the school to the child, a fact evident in the apathy or hostility shown by thousands of adolescents during their later years of schooling.

Teachers sympathetic to Neill's ideas have inevitably found it difficult to translate many of them into action in circumstances very different from Summerhill. John Kirkham, a former secondary school head who also taught student teachers, suggested: 'Neill may have made students more human and honest, but he left them to find their own way to survive inside the whale, and few of them had any idea how to set about it. Some decided that schools were impossible. Those who are still teaching have, by and large, knuckled under and accepted things as they are, since they haven't the confidence to subvert the system from within.' This indeed has been the dilemma of many young teachers in England, some of whom expressed their dissatisfaction by moving sideways into related fields. Several educational psychologists, for instance, started as teachers, but finding they could not accept the traditional methods of dealing with children in schools, turned for inspiration to practitioners such as Neill. Others who wanted to continue in education found some scope for Neill's kind of approach to children through working in special units, truancy centres, intermediate treatment centres, withdrawal units, and other euphemistically labelled structures designed to cope with the casualties inflicted by the mainstream system. The favourable ratio of adults to children, the need to improvise, and to work out more individual learning programmes, has imbued many such places with a highly informal spirit, not unlike that which many identified at Summerhill.

Other teachers enthused by Neill's work, particularly in relation to 'problem children', have found considerable scope within the special schools, where there has been more freedom to experiment in handling children with special needs. Here Neill's direct influence has been considerable. Barbara Kahan, a former deputy chief inspector in the Home Office Children's Department, sees it as 'powerful and pervasive', and feels that a tangible result of his work can be seen in 'the general liberalisation of the former punitive approaches to disturbed and difficult children'. Some special schools, particularly those designed for 'maladjusted' or 'delinquent' children, have introduced a form of self-government. There are several variations especially within the private special schools, but most of them can be traced, directly or indirectly, to the work of Homer Lane, or later pioneers such as Neill and David Wills. Howard Case, for example, a Summerhill parent, was directly inspired by Neill in starting a meeting at his school for 'maladjusted' children, Epping House in Hertfordshire.

The idea of self-government has been taken up more readily in special schools than in the ordinary state schools. Few of the latter have introduced anything that remotely resembles the weekly meeting at Summerhill, where the children are given such real freedom and responsibility, and encouragement to discuss and make decisions concerning the behaviour of both adults and children. Many schools have introduced school councils, where pupils nominally have the opportunity to put forward their views about a limited range of school matters. However, such devices are invariably subject to the headteacher's control, and in practice rarely provide an opportunity for pupils to debate matters of real importance to them. Countesthorpe College in Leicestershire is one of the few state schools which has moved further than this. Its 'Moot', composed of all the staff, and any pupils or parents who wish to attend, makes all the major decisions to do with the running of the school. The system goes one step further than Summerhill, in that, through a staff selection committee, it can recommend new staff appointments. But it remains an isolated example of whole-school democracy: attempts to give some genuine responsibility to pupils are mostly confined to the efforts of individual teachers. Acknowledging their debt to Neill, many have allowed children some kind of informal forum for discussion within their own classroom, or encouraged them to argue out matters of dispute between themselves rather than accept uncritically the teacher's point of view.

Neill's impact on the system of teacher training in England has also been slight. From the 1930s onwards his books did occasionally appear on students' reading lists in certain colleges of education and university departments, often because of the enthusiasm of a particular lecturer. But in general he has been seen as background rather than recommended or compulsory reading, so that many students have had to discover his books through other channels. Sometimes his ideas have been deemed subversive: one student recalls being warned not to mention Neill during his course in 1949, as this could prejudice his chance of qualifying. In the 1960s there was renewed interest in Neill's ideas, and students often found themselves in conflict with their teachers as a result of their enthusiasm. Michael Montcombroux, for example, remembers 'a Neillian movement' among the sizeable body of mature students at a teacher training college in Oxford in the mid-1960s: 'Educational reformers such as Neill, Wills and Homer Lane were regarded as havens of sanity and humanity. Neill was the focus of our interest, and it was his ideas that kept most of us in teaching, despite the awfulness of what we saw in the state schools in which we did our teaching practice. Almost to a man we found that experience traumatic, particularly when we tried to slip in even a modicum of Summerhill theory. We would be criticised severely by both the school administration and the college staff sent to supervise our teaching stints. In educational psychology we sided with Neill's emphasis on personality against the orthodox behaviourism of Skinner – much to the chagrin of the college establishment and the detriment of our marks.'

It was through a combination of disillusion with the state system and the inspiration of Neill, or some of the American school reformers such as Paul Goodman, John Holt, Herbert Kohl, Jonathan Kozol and, eventually, Ivan Illich, that many such teachers attempted to set up or join one of the new 'alternative' schools established in England in the late 1960s and early 1970s. John Ord and Bill Murphy founded the Scotland Road Free School in Liverpool on this basis, declaring that they would not have started the school without Neill's example. They, and other free school pioneers, took on board Neill's practice of making lessons voluntary. Many of these schools, such as the White Lion Street Free School in London, saw the weekly meeting of staff and pupils as crucial to the aims of the school. Here again the inspiration was Summerhill, though the meetings varied in structure and content according to the school.

On the other hand, many working in such schools, while acknowledging their debt to Neill, were hostile to certain aspects of Summerhill. They were critical of its almost exclusively middle-class intake. They were unhappy with the autocratic way in which Neill treated other adults in 'his' school, preferring to work in a more democratic manner, and to involve all staff in decision-making. They were also, unlike Neill, very committed to the idea of working with parents, and in some cases to involve them in the running of the school. One school, Kirkdale in south London, which consciously aimed to be an urban version of Summerhill, was actually begun by parents, and subsequently run by a co-operative of parents and teachers. Durdham Park School in Bristol, another self-proclaimed 'urban Summerhill', involved parents in teaching the children. Almost all the alternative schools only survived for a few years, their demise hastened by the harsher economic climate of the 1970s, and the return to caution and conformity which in education characterised that decade.

Outside England, Neill's influence has been considerable, though only rarely has he made the kind of impact that he achieved in the USA during the 1960s (see Chapter 20). Perhaps he has had least effect where he would have liked it most, in his native country of Scotland. When William Ross, the former Secretary of State for Education in Scotland, officially opened Summerhill Academy in Aberdeen in 1968, he said in his speech: 'Summerhill is a name that is renowned, and if you mention it in any educational circles, they all know Summerhill. Nothing to do with Aberdeen, nothing at all; it's to do with a man called A. S. Neill. . . a man who spent his whole life experimenting in education, a man who made mistakes and admits he made mistakes, but a man who gained something of value and brought new values to old ideas of education, and I think he has done much.' Despite this cautious official pat on the back, Scotland has in general resisted the charms of Neill's beliefs. The tawse remains as a barbaric instrument of control by teachers. Many who have experience of the school system believe that it has changed little in essence since the days when Neill himself was a young teacher, even though the outward appearance may be more liberal. There are individuals who believe Neill has made some impact on the schools in Scotland: in 1944 a former member of His Majesty's Inspectorate declared that Neill had been more of an influence for good on the Scottish day schools than anyone else. Yet it would seem that Neill's real impact has been in the special (List D) schools where, as in England, there is more freedom to experiment.

Those who wished to adopt his ideas within ordinary schools experienced many of the same problems as R. F. Mackenzie in his reforming work in Fife and then Aberdeen. The position was especially difficult for the ordinary class teacher. Christine Meek, for example, who found Neill's books 'a revelation and a new hope', encountered some characteristic opposition while teaching in an Edinburgh school in the mid-1960s. As a new teacher, she wanted to establish a more human relationship with the children in her class, to relax the rule of the timetable, and to refrain from using corporal punishment. 'The mistake I made was discussing this with the children,' she recalls. 'Eventually I was asked by the headmaster to come and see him in his room. He referred to the familiarity of my class. "You see, Miss Meek, you must always remember that you're the teacher and they're the pupils, and your desk should always be between." I asked did he find the children cheeky? No, no, he could not say that, he just felt they did not have proper respect. They were too free in the attitude to myself and this, of course, reflected on other members of staff, who felt the rumblings of anarchy. I explained my thoughts on the matter – what I hoped to achieve. He smiled patronisingly and nodded. I spoke about Neill and Summerhill. He replied: "Look, lass, you're an idealist, but you're young and you'll mature out of it with experience. Just try to tone it down a bit, will you?" '

In contrast to Scotland, Scandinavia has always taken a keen interest in Neill's ideas, ever since they and he became known there in the 1930s. His books have been translated into Danish, Norwegian and Swedish, and his lectures invariably attracted large and enthusiastic audiences. One writer recently suggested that three factors had prompted Sweden to take up modern child psychology: Freud, the Second World War – and Neill. The comment was made by Kerstin Vinterhed in her biography of Gustav Jonsson, who spearheaded the development of child welfare in Sweden. Of the many institutions affected by Neill's ideas, Jonsson's famous Skaa Children's Village at Edeby, founded in 1947, is one of the very few to survive the growth of 'anti-authoritarian' institutions during the 1950s. A home for delinquent children aged 3 to 16, Skaa owed a lot to Neill, as well as to Reich, Freud and Lane. Several members of the founding group, mostly young women, had spent time at Summerhill, and considerable emphasis was put on the practice of self-regulation. Like Summerhill, Skaa attracted a great deal of controversy in its early years, though by his retirement Jonsson was acknowledged to be Sweden's leading authority on child welfare. 'I was often described as a Swedish "heir" to Neill,' he recalls, 'although I didn't really agree with this description: Summerhill's youngsters were different from ours – we had Stockholm children from the lower classes, who were in care because of anti-social behaviour.' Jonsson's anti-authoritarian methods provoked many people, some of whom sent him anonymous letters. 'In the old days there were more,' he remembers, 'and their content was coarser. Sometimes it was simply used toilet paper. . . .These days the letters are more proper, typewritten, and with impeccable grammar: "You, with your advice and moral pointers, destroyed a whole generation, which now finds itself irresolute and incapable of tackling its own child-rearing problems," is the kind of comment I receive.'

Other European countries have been slower to take up Neill's ideas, though when they have done so the effect has sometimes been spectacular. In 1969 a translation of *Summerhill* was published in West Germany, with the title *The Theory and Practice of Anti-Authoritarian Education*. Earlier in the decade one of the main German publishing houses had turned down a translation, having been advised by a number of 'experts', who had studied the book and held a conference on the subject, that Neill's ideas were at least fifteen years out of date.* It must have been one of the more costly errors in German publishing history: after three years the book had sold over a million copies. Its success was undoubtedly brought about by the student revolt of the late 1960s, which prompted many of the younger generation in Germany to challenge the country's traditionally authoritarian system of education. Summerhill was soon being called 'a holy place', and Neill's work there became a subject of intense debate in seminars and lectures in universities and teacher training colleges. Summerhill began to feature regularly in the daily and weekly press, as journalists from German newspapers and magazines joined the many pilgrims making the journey to Leiston.

Interest in Neill has been even more recent in France, though his ideas have had no discernible influence on the country's highly centralised and rigidly structured educational system. The interest has perhaps been at a more intellectual level, Neill being read and appreciated as a proponent of *la liberté*. His autobiography was translated in 1980, as *Neill! Neill! Peau de Mandarine!*. It was given a full-page review in *Le Monde*, whose reviewer thought the book 'wonderful', and wrote approvingly of Neill's 'pro-life' philosophy. At about the same time an abridged version of *A Dominie's Log* was published, renamed *Diary of a Country Teacher*, as well as an expensive folio edition of *The Last Man Alive*. Nor were sales of Neill's books limited to western Europe: at the beginning of the 1980s a translation of *Summerhill* achieved considerable success in Yugoslavia.

Japan was one of the first countries to have a translation of one of Neill's books on sale. His work has been known there for more than fifty years, thanks to the pioneering efforts of his translator, Seishi Shimoda. Though the early translations of *The Problem Child*, *The Problem Parent* and *That Dreadful School* sold few copies, there was a quickening of interest during the era of 'new education' following the Second World War. Further translations appeared, Shimoda wrote a number of books about Neill and his work, and in the 1970s a few Japanese families sent their children to Summerhill. In 1972 a questionnaire was sent to 600 members of the Japanese Society for the Study of Education, the Early Childhood Education Association of Japan, and the Japanese Association of Educational Psychology. The replies indicated a widespread familiarity with

---

*In 1930 Hilde Stekel, the analyst's wife, had expressed an interest in translating *The Problem Child* into German, but the project never came to fruition.

Neill's work among these groups, and considerable support for many of his ideas, particularly his emphasis on the individual child. In 1976 a Neill-Shimoda Society was founded by a group of teachers, psychologists and students; and two years later there began publication of *Neill Kenkyu*, a magazine which focused on the ideas of Neill and other educational innovators. By 1979 there were twelve of Neill's books in print – as opposed to five in England – and, according to Neill's most recent translator, Shin-ichiro Hori, 'Neill's books are attracting an increasing number of people, especially young teachers and students'. However, there would seem to be little opportunity for teachers to put much of Neill's philosophy into practice in Japanese schools, given the ruthlessly competitive examination system, and the firm hand kept on teachers in both the public and private sectors by the Ministry of Education. No doubt it is precisely because of the rigidity of the system that Neill's libertarian views have an appeal for many Japanese educators and students.

In Australia Neill's books became popular again with students of education during the 1970s. They came back into fashion after a long period of neglect – his 'Dominie' books had been on students' recommended lists in the mid-1930s. Neill was occasionally bracketed with figures such as Rousseau in the child development component of students' courses in colleges and universities. Part of the philosophy of many of the 'progressive schools' consisted of a belief in the 'natural child', due to Neill's ideas amongst others. A few who attempted to set up alternative schools were inspired by his thinking, but in general Neill's influence has been slight. Clive Nield, who taught briefly at Summerhill, ran a school along similar lines throughout the Second World War; while Preshil School in Melbourne owes a certain amount to Neill's work. As in other countries, some who have tried to put his ideas into practice have encountered stern opposition. One group of 17-year-olds, for instance, set up their own alternative school during the summer holidays as a direct result of reading *Summerhill*. Their action was thoroughly disapproved of by the official school authorities, and they were labelled 'dangerous rebels'.

However varied Neill's influence has been on the educational system of different countries, it may well be that he has ultimately had more effect on the thinking of parents than on that of teachers and other educators. He himself received an enormous number of letters from parents all over the world, who were interested in his views on child-rearing. The sales of his books, in particular of *Summerhill*, during the 1960s and early 1970s indicate how many people outside education took an interest in his ideas. 'I dread to think what my kids might have gone through if it hadn't been for Neill' was a characteristic parental reaction. Many found support from Neill in their efforts to provide their children with a different upbringing from their own. For some Neill reinforced views they already held; for others he provided authoritative confirmation for half-formulated ideas. The effect was often shattering and transforming – 'I had found the answer, the guide, the Eureka, the words which said it all', was how one parent recalled her feelings on first looking into Neill's *Summerhill*. Whether or not the child-rearing practices that followed a scrutiny of his work were actually those which Neill favoured, there is no doubt whatsoever that he caused a significant number of parents to look with more care and concern at the way they brought up their children.

It is of course impossible to measure in any precise way either the width or the depth of Neill's influence. He himself recognised that people, and the values which they were prepared to stand up for, are ultimately more important than institutions. In *Summerhill* he wrote:

> The future of Summerhill itself may be of little import. But the future of the Summerhill idea is of the greatest importance to humanity. New generations must be given the chance to grow in freedom. The bestowal of freedom is the bestowal of love. And only love can save the world.

However, Neill also recognised that new generations were coming into a world full of hatred and aggression, in which it would be increasingly difficult for his message of love and freedom to find an audience. Yet it still got through to many, sometimes in the most dire circumstances. During the Vietnam war, a priest ran a community home for youngsters whose parents had been killed or injured in the fighting there. They had lived off the pickings of war as pimps, prostitutes and thieves, and many had themselves been severely injured. A visiting worker from a British charity remarked on the quiet discipline of the place, and the complete openness of the children. He asked the priest how he had managed to create such an atmosphere in such conditions. 'It was very simple, really,' the priest replied. 'I read a book by an Englishman called A. S. Neill. I just put his ideas into practice here, and, as you can see, they work.'

CHAPTER 23

The Summerhill Child

> abilities that it teaches them. On this basis of evaluation it may be s
>
> 1. That the children are full of life and zest. Of boredom and apathy there was no sign. An atmosphere of contentment and tolerance pervades the School. The affection with which it is regarded by its old pupils is evidence of its success. An average number of thirty attend the end-of-term plays and dances, and many make the School their headquarters during the holidays.
>
> It may be worth noting at this point that, whereas in its early days the School was attended almost entirely by 'problem' children, the intake is now from a fairly normal cross-section of the population.
>
> 2. That the children's manners are delightful. They may lack, here and there, some of the conventions of manners, but their friendliness, ease and naturalness, and their total lack of shyness and self-consciousness made them very easy, pleasant people to get on with.
>
> 3. That initiative, responsibility and integrity are all encouraged by the system and that, so far as such things can be judged, they are in fact being developed.
>
> suggest that the

I'd be very disappointed if a Summerhill child became Prime Minister. I'd feel I'd failed.

Neill and Summerhill, 1969

Of all the many men and women touched by Neill's ideas, clearly none felt the effect of his work more powerfully and directly than those who were pupils at Summerhill. 'I hope that these free children will be pioneers in abolishing the drudgery of life,' Neill said once, when being taken to task for failing to prepare children for the 'real world' outside Summerhill. So what kind of people did emerge from the school he once characteristically called 'the least neurotic place in England and possibly the most sincere place in the world'? Does the 'Summerhill child' actually exist?

Neill made a number of statements over the years about Summerhill children which, if taken at face value, bear little relation to reality. 'They've no swank, no obsequiousness, they're absolutely open and frank and sincere,' he declared some ten years after Summerhill began. Later he was more specific, suggesting, for instance, that no ex-Summerhill pupil could possibly enjoy a pornographic film, or get excessively drunk. Such statements were self-evidently preposterous, since, apart from any other factor, Neill was certainly in no position to make a full and proper assessment of the personality and behaviour of those adults who had been at his school. His remarks should be taken as statements of hope rather than achievement, as descriptions of the kind of adults which he wanted to send out into society. Summerhillians, he hoped and believed, would be more likely than most to perform good deeds in a naughty world, and to bring up their own children in an atmosphere of genuine tolerance and freedom. As with Neill's influence in the wider sphere, it is of course impossible to determine in what way the lives of his ex-pupils have been affected by factors other than Summerhill. For some it certainly seemed in retrospect the most formative influence of their youth; for others it was a relatively minor experience, particularly for those who had several years' schooling elsewhere. It would be impossible for them, let alone an outsider, to unravel the different threads in their lives, in order to find which led back to Summerhill and Neill, which to Family, Class, Pre-School Environment, and so on. My own acquaintance with Summerhillians has been wide rather than deep, and certainly too brief to justify any attempt at an evaluation of their vices and virtues. However, in talking to and corresponding with them about Neill, I have in passing collected a variety of views about the 'Summerhill Child'. Some offered some general observations on the qualities which they felt Summerhill brought out in its ex-pupils; others commented specifically on what they themselves had got from their unusual schooling, and the way in which it prepared them for entering the adult world. Their subjective comments at least offer a set of perceptions about the effect of Neill's version of freedom for children, though they cannot hope to stand up as anything more than that.*

Despite his poorly concealed pleasure at the academic success of a small number of his ex-pupils, Neill was fundamentally more concerned with the kind of *people* that Summerhill children would become, than with their achievement or status: 'I am not principally interested in whether they are professors or bricklayers,' he wrote at the end of his life. 'I am interested in their character, their sincerity, their tolerance.' This latter quality, which Neill himself certainly displayed in abundance, was probably mentioned more often than any other as an outcome of being at Summerhill. It could of course take different forms, and was not always seen as a virtue. One of the parents of the early years, the novelist Leonora Eyles, complained that Summerhill had made her daughter 'too tolerant to people who behave badly to her and to others, but most especially to her: it is a lovely thing in her, a generous and serene thing. But it may give her unbearable burdens to carry.' Neill, however, took the criticism as a compliment, suggesting that 'No one can have too much charity'. Many ex-pupils spoke only of the positive side of tolerance, linking it specifically with a capacity to understand the reasons for other people's behaviour. Several saw this as coming from the self-governing element of Summerhill life, and in particular their own involvement in discussions about the behaviour of others. One man suggested: 'You learned to be tolerant because you were forced to grow up considering people as people, and understanding *why* they are unhappy or difficult. If someone was brought up at the school meeting,

---

*These observations are based on discussions with 80 former Summerhill pupils, some three-quarters of whom I interviewed personally. The 'results' are not dissimilar from those obtained by Man Bernstein, who, in the summer of 1964, interviewed 50 former pupils. His research was more statistical in nature: I have made no attempt to quantify in precise terms, preferring to leave individual ex-pupils to speak for themselves.

their reasons as well as their actions were discussed; and if they were punished, there was some attempt to make it logical.' This, many felt, gave them an insight into the motivations of others: 'It gave you a perception of people's characteristics, and made you see through a lot of situations'; 'It helped to create a tremendous feeling of sympathy with other people', were typical comments on this issue.

Yet certain ex-pupils felt that too much tolerance could have its drawbacks. One woman observed: 'You do learn to get on with people, but you also tend to justify negative actions, rather than do anything about them.' If to understand is to forgive, this may in part explain why Summerhill pupils have not been noticeably active in trying to change the world. There seems little danger of any of them attaining the ultimate failure of residence in 10 Downing Street, since none appear to have gone into politics, at least of the parliamentary kind. 'Summerhill people don't seem to be standing up for anything,' one woman noted. 'They fit into society quite happily, and that worries me.' This perhaps is an exaggeration, though it is supported to some extent by the view of one man, who suggested: 'Summerhillians are interested in their own lives, their families and kids, and in this sense I suppose they're rather inward-looking.' Yet several ex-pupils have gone into what are sometimes called the 'caring professions' – teaching, social work, medicine – which, in a less obvious manner than politics, can provide a useful base for helping others to challenge the status quo.

Neill, and others, have suggested that the freedom which Summerhill provided allowed his children to work through the kind of feelings which most are compelled to suppress at school or in their home, and that it is this suppression which often creates the drive to seek power, influence, wealth and status. This was linked by some to the self-government which formed such an essential part of Summerhill life. One man who was particularly active in that sphere remembers: 'It got entirely out of my system the desire to run anything. You have no wish to identify yourself with an institution or take on its importance. Summerhill allows you to rid yourself of these projections, which can otherwise be lifetime obsessions.' Often this resulted in a much less competitive attitude to life than shown by adults schooled in the traditional manner. One man observed: 'People have spent their childhood in desperate competition, and can't behave otherwise when they get older. So they spend their whole lives running desperately trying to prove that they are better than the next person. I've been very stuck when I've taken a job, and found people expecting me to be competitive, and to try to get a top job. At first they are wary of you, and then terribly puzzled if you appear just to want to do your own job well, and nothing more.'

Such a relaxed attitude to work might be seen as a sign of maturity, another quality which many felt was an inevitable result of spending your school years at Summerhill. Several ex-pupils commented on how much older than their contemporaries they felt when they left and mixed with children from other schools. 'At 16 I really felt I had something much better than others of my age as an upbringing,' one woman remarked. 'I felt I could cope easily with it all; I looked around at other girls and thought they were all so silly.' Others saw this maturity in relation to behaviour towards the opposite sex. 'I felt a lot older than my contemporaries, who had been to conventional schools and giggled over boys,' observed another woman. 'We didn't need to do that: boys were there and that was a fact of life. It's as if you grew up immediately; you weren't held back by misguided ideas about how you should behave.' Yet another recalled: 'I attended several strict schools after Summerhill. No one seemed to know anything about sex: it was regarded as something you did when drunk; otherwise it brought only jokes or smutty thinking.'

This feeling of being 'different' was experienced by many ex-pupils, and in some cases seems to have resulted in an attitude of Them and Us. 'We knew Summerhill was the right way, and others were wrong; that's how we were brought up,' remembers one woman. Another echoed this sentiment in a slightly different way: 'Life is a bit lonely, and I think in a way it's because of Summerhill, because I can't get on with ordinary people.' Yet another observed: 'When people say certain things I think, It's no good talking to you, because I'm on the other side of the fence completely. I don't agree with a word you're saying, and I don't have any of the problems you have, because I don't create them.' Such feelings of difference caused many Summerhillians to keep in touch with each other after they left, though whether they did this to any greater extent than those from other schools is impossible to know. Neill himself was aware of the problem, writing to one ex-pupil: 'More than most you seem to grasp the awful gulf between school and outside. It is true; I feel it often. . . . Here it is easy; we don't need to make contacts: once you leave you have got to live. All old Summerhillians feel it more or less, hence the London ones try to meet each other.' Several pupils preferred to stay on at Summerhill for a while, usually as housemothers, before making the break. 'At 16 I didn't feel able or ready to leave,' one recalled. For others the transition to the adult world could be a considerable shock. One man commented: 'It was like being cocooned in a hospital for a long time: you felt lost when you came out. There was an honesty at Summerhill that you never found anywhere else, and it really hits you on the snout when you get into the outside world.'

Neill's critics frequently suggested that, by allowing children the kind of freedom they had at Summerhill, he was failing to prepare them for the 'real world'. To one critic he replied that Summerhill *was* the real world, and he hoped his pupils would learn to be real, and remain so in the outside world. Whichever definition of reality one prefers, there is no denying the fundamental difference in values between Summerhill and much of the world outside it. Nor is it surprising that many ex-pupils found it difficult, at least initially, to come to terms with the larger community, where attitudes, expectations and behaviour could often be so markedly different from those they had been accustomed to at Summerhill. Yet several felt they had been able to develop a considerable measure of self-reliance, an inner strength that enabled them to face up to the real challenge of living in an adult society. 'Your life doesn't have to base itself on a structure,' was how one woman saw it. 'You have resources, imagination, you have a feeling that you can cope with change.' A man pointed out: 'People say you can't adjust to rules and restrictions. On the contrary, I think Summerhill teaches you this. You learn that there are laws in the world, and unless it's something which you morally believe should be changed for the good of mankind, you tend to say, Well, I can live my life more comfortably and happily if I stick to the necessary rules and do my own thing. I see far more people who have lived under authority feeling the need to break the laws.' Another man observed: 'It's often a lot harder disciplining yourself and making your own decisions, as we had to at Summerhill, than being given a rigid set of rules to obey. It seems to me that people sent to glass tower public schools live in a totally unreal world and are very lost when they leave. The Summerhillians I know are all very adaptable people.'

One of the more difficult questions to resolve is how the voluntary system of lessons at Summerhill affected ex-pupils' attitude to learning. Here there seemed to be a wide range of views. As with other schools, a few failed to achieve what would normally be considered functional literacy. 'I can't write, and I've had to be very devious about that,' one woman confessed. A man recalled: 'I was quite unable to read at Summerhill, and when I was young I was quite self-conscious about it. When I left I could muddle through, but I couldn't pick up a book and read it from cover to cover. I'm OK on reading now, but my spelling is atrocious.' However, neither of these two seemed to feel that this had been a major handicap, though others were less sure. 'In retrospect I think my education suffered a lot by being at Summerhill,' one woman suggested. 'There are a lot of things I don't know.' Others felt the lack of formal qualifications: 'Academically Summerhill failed me abysmally: I've still got a mini-chip on my shoulder about not having a degree,' another woman observed. One man remembered being 'terrified' at his lack of academic attainments when he first went to an employment office. Yet many of those who felt this way were clear that Summerhill was not necessarily at fault here. 'I would have liked to have had qualifications, but I don't blame the school for that,' was the comment of one noted former 'problem child'. 'Given the choice I would have still preferred Summerhill.' Others, while feeling some deficiency in the academic sphere, believed this was compensated by gains of other kinds.

Indeed, some ex-pupils saw the Summerhill system as being positively conducive to a real interest in work for its own sake. 'I always enjoyed learning, even if I didn't learn a tremendous amount,' one man recalled. 'I never got put off anything, because nobody made me feel it was boring by forcing it on me.' 'Even if you leave with a less solid education, there is no sense of being anti-learning,' said another. 'I can still enjoy learning, whereas I now meet a lot of people who are appalled at having been forced along a tight, academic path.' Yet another commented: 'I found it useful to be left alone rather than be told what to do in lessons. It suited me personally. I think you can be stifled with academic pressures. Despite all the things I lack, I came out with a free mind.' A similar point was made by another man in recollecting his move from Summerhill to a traditional grammar school: 'I soon saw how little I knew, how much I lacked all kinds of desirable acquisitions. But I did come with a greater freshness to the work, because I hadn't been doing it all the time.'

Several ex-pupils gave support to Neill's view that formal study can be left to a later stage in life, and that it is possible to 'catch up' if one is sufficiently motivated; for instance, in seeing for oneself the need for a specific qualification. 'When I left Summerhill I decided I wanted to study,' one man recalled. 'So I went to college and in a year got the exams necessary to take an art degree. I had hardly been to any lessons at Summerhill, spending hours in the art room. Strangely enough, although I loathed maths and was hopeless at it then, later when I needed it I enjoyed learning it, and went on to write a mathematical book.' Another remained at Summerhill until he was 19, when he decided he wanted to fly, and so set about getting the qualifications he needed to qualify as a pilot in the RAF. Often there was a break point at 14 or 15, when children who had spent many years at Summerhill moved on elsewhere in order to get qualifications. Others came back to formal study at a later stage: 'I was happy enough to go back to studying later,' one man said, 'and I suppose my Summerhill freedom has a lot to do with that. After all, ultimately it is better to be a bit ignorant or late learning than frightened all your schooldays.'

Given Neill's bias towards the arts field, and the emphasis put on creative subjects at Summerhill, it is not surprising to find that many Summerhillians chose careers in this sphere, nor that very few indeed have gone into business, commerce or industry. These two features apart, Summerhill seems to have produced as wide a range of chosen occupations as might be expected of a school with its particular middle-class intake. Among ex-pupils there are lawyers, artists, engineers, designers, salesmen, electricians, farmers, university professors, actors, antique dealers, cabinet-makers, writers, shopkeepers, musicians, van drivers, doctors, potters, housewives, charity workers, dancers, publishers, bricklayers, speech therapists and many other occupations. There are also now a few teachers, though for many years Neill was able to boast, with some glee, that Summerhill had never produced anyone who wanted to go into the teaching profession, thereby showing how well-adjusted they were.

In the last year of his life Neill wrote: 'I like to think that Summerhill children have a better chance of being pro-life than disciplined, moulded children have.' Some pupils echoed this hope in describing the way in which Summerhill affected their general outlook on life. One woman observed: 'Those who were there for a long time are optimistic in outlook, if they were happy enough to start with. Summerhill people have an acceptance of happiness as a norm, in a very simple kind of way.' Another woman summed up what many saw as the most positive virtue of Summerhill: 'You didn't have to be proving yourself all the time. If you got on with the other kids and had friendships that was enough. Nobody was saying, If you do this you'll be wonderful, and we'll reward you. You were all right, you felt approved of and liked, and this created a sort of optimism that other systems don't so readily. People who went to Summerhill believe that life can be good.'

Evidently individual temperament played a significant part in determining how one reacted to the freedoms available at Summerhill. There was some feeling that the school was more suitable for the extrovert type of child, though many who would not fall into this category appeared to have gained a great deal from being there. One woman, who described herself as 'an extremely introverted child', recalled the difficulties she experienced during her early years at Summerhill: 'Because of the way it was run, you felt great responsibility for your own actions, just at an age when children want and need to be carefree, and to be told what they can and can't do, at least to some extent.' Another woman, who admitted that she had 'absolutely no friends and have never been out on a date', suggested: 'Summerhill certainly did not bolster up my self-confidence, and shyness is quite a handicap.' Another woman, while feeling that her experience at Summerhill was much wider and more interesting than anything she had known before, said that 'later on I felt it had been no preparation for life, it didn't give one much of a start or much confidence. It made me very much more confused than I was to start with, and it took time to sort things out in my own mind.'

During his early years at Leiston, Neill once remarked: 'I want to raise people who know their own mind and can think for themselves.' His ex-pupils certainly showed plenty of independence in deciding where to send their own children to school. Although a minority did send them to Summerhill, a good many who thoroughly approved of Neill's ideas chose other schools, both state and private. There was a number of reasons for this. Some simply wished to be there as their children grew up, rather than send them away to boarding school. Others either could not afford the fees, or were against the idea of private education. But many also argued that their children had no particular *need* to go to Summerhill, since they were being brought up along 'Summerhill lines'. One woman spoke for many in defining her attitude as a parent: 'I think I have a very good relationship with my own children, which was affected by my upbringing at Summerhill and by Neill's views, this terrific thing that everybody is equal, no matter who they are.' Others felt that ex-pupils were noticeably loving and affectionate with their children, and tended not to manipulate them in the way many parents did.

It seems from the observations of his ex-pupils that Neill has failed to produce the hoped-for pioneers who would set about reforming society. What he has perhaps produced is a group of men and women who have been allowed more scope to develop as individuals than most people are given in their early years. He also gave them the right to have a say in the way their lives should be run, at a time when most children, both at home and at school, had no such freedom of expression or action. This clearly had a significant effect on most of those who went to Summerhill, though what they chose to do with the experience evidently varied enormously. Neill's greatest achievement, however, undoubtedly lay in his ability as 'a curer of souls'. A considerable number of adults now leading ordinary, unexceptionable lives, owe the fact that they do so to Neill. He himself in later life liked to argue that it was the environment of freedom rather than his individual work with problem children that was responsible for so many startling 'cures'. Many former Summerhill pupils thought otherwise, as did several of the adults who worked alongside Neill over the years. To them, it was Neill's humanity and understanding which produced the results. As one former problem child said, looking back over his time at Summerhill: 'I feel almost certain that, had it not been for Neill, I would have ended up in a mental hospital long ago.'

CHAPTER 24

Ending

I keep hearing an old bugger with a beard outside my office whetting his scythe.

Letter to Bill and Käte MacKinnon, May 1972

During his last months Neill kept up a façade of cheerfulness towards the outside world. Visitors to Summerhill often found him tired, but mentally still very alert. Donald Boyd, one of his very first pupils, recalls: 'He was just the same, cracking jokes; he was as kindly and as interesting then as he had always been.' Yet despite his often black humour and apparent stoicism, Neill had for years harboured a great fear of death, conditioned in part by the terrors of his childhood. In 1956, in one of his last letters to Wilhelm Reich, he confessed: 'I don't fear death; I fear ceasing to live, and of course the method of dying.' He found it difficult to face the fact that he would be unable to know what happened to Summerhill, or to Zoë and his grandchildren. But it was the process of dying that he most feared. 'He believed that death would be extremely painful and unpleasant,' Ena Neill remembers.

One of the very last letters he wrote, to an old friend, Nell Hutton, reflected his feelings about his own deterioration:

I have suddenly grown very old and think more of painkillers than schools. . . . Do I sound pessimistic? I often am these days; often things seem to be going backwards. Today's papers. . . Suffolk teachers demand to keep the cane. My fan mail shows the other side. It grieves me that I am not fit to answer it now, for I always did, so bugger old age and its pains and weaknesses, say I. I am now an empty shell with the A. Snail all dried up. Not self-pity, just raw fact.

Perhaps the only event to give him real pleasure during the last months of his life was the birth of his first grandchild, Amy, although even this was not allowed to pass without the familiar spell of pessimism. His daughter Zoë recalls: 'He was very worried when I was having Amy, he kept going on about women in labour, how awful it was, and looking terribly worried. But he was awfully pleased and proud when she was born.' When she was seven months old Neill described her approvingly as 'a smiling thing treated in a S'hill-Reich way by Zoë'. Perhaps for a moment he glimpsed the possibility of his ideas being taken through to at least some of the newest generation.

Almost immediately after his autobiography was published in England in May 1973, Neill's condition began to deteriorate. At the end of July he wrote to Gordon Leff: 'I put off going to hospital fearing that if I do I'll come out feet first.' He was eating very little now, and had to go into hospital in Ipswich because of trouble with his prostate gland. One visitor there was his nephew from Forfar, Sandy Fife, to whom Neill said: 'Other than my immediate family I have nothing to live for. All my friends have died; I don't want to live any longer.' But he also looked back to some of his happier moments in Scotland, when he had walked at low tide at Easthaven, looking for agates. Another visit brought to the surface a different memory from his days as a young teacher in Newport-on-Tay, as Margaret Duane recalls: 'On the day Michael and I came he'd had to have some drugs, and was rather woozy. I was holding his hand, and he suddenly looked at me and said, "Och, Margaret lassie, I should never have left you behind. I should have had the courage to think that you could grow with me." '

Neill then came home to Summerhill for a short while. He was now sleeping most of the time, and eating almost nothing. Though his ninetieth birthday was only weeks away, Ena Neill remembers that 'he'd made up his mind that he didn't want to be ninety'. In the middle of September he was moved into the Cottage Hospital in Aldeburgh. There, by his bedside, he kept a copy of the book that had stirred him so often, George Douglas Brown's *The House with the Green Shutters*. His fears about dying were eased a little by a former pupil and trained nurse, Rae Wylie Thomas, who tried to assure him that death need no longer be a painful process. His sister May visited him in hospital: 'The last time I saw him I kissed him goodbye, and he said in Scots, "Och, gie awa wi ye, lass." ' On Saturday 21 September he had a visit from his family: his son-in-law Peter Wood brought some champagne, and Neill played with his granddaughter Amy on his bed. The next day was fine and sunny, and he was taken in a wheelchair into the hospital's rose garden. When he was brought inside again he sat in a chair while the nurses made his bed for him. His doctor from Leiston, Alfred Burlingham, came in on his regular visit. 'Hello, Neill,' he said. There was no reply: Neill had died sitting in the chair, quickly, quietly and without pain.

He was cremated a few days later in Ipswich, after an emotional service attended by his family, friends and many former pupils and staff. The following day the children returned to start the autumn term at Summerhill.

Acknowledgments

In gathering material for Neill's life, I was helped by a considerable number of people in Britain, the USA and other countries where Neill made an impression. I would like to record here my deeply-felt gratitude to all these people. It would have been quite impossible to write Neill's life without their assistance; indeed, it would have been pointless to have tried to do so. Everyone's contribution was of value, even though many who helped are not quoted by name. I am especially grateful to a small number of people who, in addition to answering my endless questions as others did, offered hospitality to a stranger simply because of our mutual interest in Neill. Only a few were unable or unwilling to help. Should any of these have second thoughts, I would be glad to have their views or information to consider for any subsequent edition of the book.

I must give special thanks to Ena Neill who, despite her extremely busy life running Summerhill, found time to talk to me at some length, and provided me with valuable early contacts. Margaret Spencer was kind enough to read an early version of the MS, and to offer some most pertinent and valuable criticisms. Vera White persuaded me to stop researching and start writing. I am grateful too to Lilan Perera for typing parts of the final draft of the MS, to Elizabeth Rolfe for compiling the index, and to Jan Croall for researching some of the photographs. I would also like to thank Carol Gardiner, David Godwin and Stratford Caldecott at Routledge, and Wendy Woolf and Sara Bershtel at Pantheon, for seeing the book through to publication. The blame for the final result must of course be entirely mine.

Summerhill pupils

Cynthia Allen, Jean Allen, Ethan Ames, Brian Anscombe, Roger Anscombe, Juliet Balshaw, Michael Barth, David Barton, Shirley Beeton, Egan Bernal, Michael

Bernal, Michael Bolton, Donald Boyd, Gretel Boyer, John Burningham, Gavin Campbell, Jenny Caryll, Peter Case, Peter Catchpole, Mallory Clifford, Gerry Collier, Johnnie Collier, Larry Collier, Vanji Collier, Mervyn Corkhill, David Critchlow, Keith Critchlow, Mikey Cuddihy, Michael Davis, Jackie Elvey, Rowna Ely, Marianne Fall, Diana Fishwick, Nicholas Flowers, Anne Forbes, Ann Freshwater, Claudine Fricker, Frances Green, Martin Green, Norma Harris, Debby Hemmings, Jenny Hutt, Keith Horsfield, Tessa Hutchinson, Tim Israel, Caroline Jackson, Anthony Jenkins, Ann King, Barbara King, Hazel Knight, Léonard Lassalle, Gordon Leff, Karin Ann Lewis, Ishbel McWhirter, Richard Marcus, Daryll Mitchell, Diane Moscrop, Andrew Morton, Ralph Muller, Robert Muller, Angela Neustatter, David Newton, Daphne Oliver, Ruth Ann Pickup, Virginia Pilkington, Teddy Raw, Edna Raymond, Chris Reilley, Peter Russell, David Sandford, Irene Saunders, Veronica Saunders, Nona Simon, Hylda Sims, John Somerfield, Nigel Store, Amarylla Stracey, Suzanna Stracey, Barbara Thorpe, John Tooke, Philip Townsend, Robert Townsend, Martin Tucker, Sarah Vyse, Branwen Williams, Evelyn Williams.

Summerhill staff

Mark Abraham, Ruth Allen, Charles Arthurs, Dorothy Bailey, Kerstin Barton, Wilf Blakeley, Molly Brandt, Meredith Byles, Peter Byles, Bridget Callender, Maritza Clotworthy, Geoffrey Cox, Sonia Crampton, Ivor Cutler, Maurice Draper, Kay Dunbar, Jimmy East, May Edwards, Nina Elkan, Cyril Eyre, Claude Ferrière, Erna Gal, Barbara Grigor, Tom Hackett, S. F. Hagan, Liz Hall, Libby Hall, Ray Hemmings, Bernard Jackson, Joan Jennings, Peggy Johnson, Klares Lewis, Elna Lucas, Bill MacKinnon, Käte MacKinnon, Leslie Morton, Vivien Morton, Max Morton, Kate Newman, Antoine Obert, Kirstie Ollendorff, Noel Olley, Ulle Otte, Felix Phillips, Pam Phillips, Bryn Purdy, Joan Quarm, Kathy Reed, Ilse Rolfe, Greta Sergeant, Henry Stracey, Richard Tolson, Rosemary Tolson, Humphrey Truswell, Dora Williams.

Summerhill parents

Ann Ames, Eileen Bernal, Daphne Byng, Robert Byng, Josie Caryll, Howard Case, Mary Case, Sylvia Elvey, Mamie Fleming, Ellerie Fricker, Nan Green, Victor Gregory, Rose Hacker, Gwen Horsfield, Brian Innes, Eva Leff, Ethel Mannin, David Markham, Ivor Montagu, Dorothy Morton, Beryl Sandford, Norah Stucken, Betty Tucker, Vera Vivante, Brendan Williams, Jennie Williams, Courtenay Young.

Outsiders

Polly Allen, Betty Allsop, Nicholas Bagnall, Etti Bearman, Valerie Bennett, Fenner Brockway, Michael Burn, Constance Butler, Mavis Callow, James Cameron, Margaret Capon, Meriel Cardew, Len Cassini, Sheila Chesters, Hermione Cobbold, Margaret Cole, Cecily Cox, Elizabeth Craig, Bob Cuddihy, E. J. Dingwall, Dan Doran, Margaret Duane, Tom Eagle, Ruth Dudley Edwards, Michael Ensor, John Fairhall, Anton Felton, Michael Fodor, George Foulkes, P. H. Gaskill, Livia Gollancz, Robert Graves, James Greene, Derek Grimsdick, Erica Harper, Thora Harshaw, Nell Hutton, Robert James, Jack Jennings, Bernard Jones, William Kent, Richard Layard, Martin Lightfoot, Lord Longford,

Madeleine Lytton, Margaret McCance, Henry Miller, Edward Moeran, Edwin Morgan, Lilian Morgans, Robert Morley, Bob Osborne, Terry Philpot, Margaret Prideaux, Patrick Pringle, Ilse Reich, Gwylm Richards, Sally Rodwell, Rick Rogers, Olga Roncoroni, Hilary Rubinstein, Norman Sanderson, Renée Soskin, Erika Stekel, James Stern, Brenda Swann, Peggy Thomas, Leslie Thomson, Agnes Torrance, Kenneth Tynan, Stanley Uys, Dorothy Vaughan, Vivyan Volbach, Amabel Williams-Ellis, Elizabeth Wills, Colin Wilson, Barbara Wootton, Michael Young.

Education and Psychology

John Aitkenhead, Morag Aitkenhead, Mary Atkinson, John Bains, Kenneth Barnes, Leila Berg, Michael Birt, Edward Blishen, John Bowlby, Maurice Bridgeland, Julian Brotherton, Carol Burns, Peter Butter, Juan Campos, Charles Causley, Vincent Chapman, Dennis Child, Lois Child, Alan Clark, Arthur Clark, Fanny Cockerell, Philip Coggin, Muriel Colley, John Cross, Geoffrey Crump, Clive Davidson, Harold Dent, Michael Duane, Janet Duffin, Jack Eastwood, Lionel Elvin, Mona Elvin, Alex Evans, Christopher Exley, Winifred Fawcus, Mabel Fierz, Sonia Fodor, Anna Freud, Richard Freyman, Edith Geheeb, John Gibberd, Patricia Goldacre, Terry Gower, Tony Grainger, Fiona Green, Maggie Hall, Charles Hannam, Bill Hazell, James Hemming, Hertzmark, Jim Hill, Tony Hill, Robin Hodgkin, David Hume, W. A. Illsley, Brian Jackson, Walter James, Leslie Jones, Maxwell Jones, Barbara Kahan, Ros Kane, Jack Kerr, John Kirkham, Nicholas King Harris, Pat Kitto, Robert Laslett, Bill Lightbown, Ian Lister, Guy Love, N. B. C. Lucas, Tony Lynch, Norman McCaig, R. F. Mackenzie, Sybil Marshall, Naomi Mitchison, Michael Montcombroux, Ben Morris, Graham Morrison, Charles Morrison, John Morton, Mary Murray, Patrick Nobes, Raymond O'Malley, Brett Parker, Robin Pedley, Molly Pitts, Michael Pomerantz, Harry Rée, Paul Ritter, Timothy Rogers, Dora Russell, Arthur Smith, Eric Smith, Lydia Smith, David Snell, Reginald Snell, William Spray, J. H. Stamford, Brian Stanley, Campbell Stewart, D. Stratton, Kim Taylor, Robert Thomson, Roger Tilbury, Claire Tolley, Nicholas Tucker, Colin Ward, Geoff Watson, Anthony Weaver, John Wightwick, David Wills, Christopher Wilson, John Wilson, Nigel Wright, Jim Young.

Her Majesty's Inspectors

J. Allcock, George Allen, Helen Asquith, J. M. H. Berwick, John Blackie, John Burrows, Leonard Clark, Suzie Duncan, Ray Hopkins, David Hopkinson, W. T. John.

Neill in Scotland

David Adam, Margaret Adam, J. W. L. Adams, A. Alexander, John Anderson, William Bedborough, Harry Bell, Peggy Bell, Jean Clark, William Coutts, C. Hunter Craig, Elizabeth Craig, Mrs D'Arcy Sturrock, David Davis, James Dewar, Linda Dinnie, David Edwards, Jim Ewing, Marguerite Fairweather, Andrew Fraser, Caroline Hill, Barbara Johnson, Jim Kean, Christina Laing, J. W. Leng, Harold Leslie, Andrew Low, Alex McCracken, Agnes MacDonald, Fred McFarlane, Forbes MacGregor, David Miller, Margaret Moig, Rosamund Morton, Gladys Parker, Walter Roan, David Robertson, Flora Scrymgeour, James

414   *Acknowledgments*

Scrymgeour, Isabella Skinner, Alan Smith, Mary Stewart, Michael Swann, Elizabeth Sword, Jean Symington, James Wannan.

Neill in USA

Orson Bean, Bruno Bettleheim, Herbert Cogan, George Dennison, Eleanor Hamilton, Harold Hart, Lydia Hollowell, John Holt, Joseph Kirschner, Barbara Longbrook, Henry Miller, Pam Neu, Beverley Placzek, Mary Ann Raywid, Samuel Rosen, Iris Russell, Jeffery Salge, John Seeley, Sandy Stahl, Taylor Stoehr, Ruth Waller, Lois Wyvell.

Neill in Australia

William Connell, Pat Edwards, Suzanne Hewitt, Nicholas Hudson, Brian Pirkis, Merle Rankin.

Neill in Scandinavia

Stephen Croall, Gustav Jonsson, Christian Lindborg, Lillster Stenman-Kanold.

Neill in Japan

Shin-ichiro Hori, Koichi Shimoda.

Neill in South Africa

Violet Emmer, A. H. le Roux, Hilda Purwitsky, D. M. Rogers, Stanley Uys, Robin Whiteford.

King Alfred School

Nikki Archer, Diana Barry, Claire Epstein, Roderick Garrett, Patrick Harvey, A. Horton, Janet Livingstone, Peggy van Praagh, Eileen Wicksteed.

Neill in Sonntagsberg

Gustav Mattson, Angus Murray.

Neill's Family

Esther Bates, Keith Fife, Neil Fife, Sandy Fife, George Halliday, May Halliday, Angus Neill, Hamish Neill, Neill Neill, Helen Neustatter, Sheila O'Shaugnessey, Mary Peach.

Librarians and Archivists

Mary Ann Bonney, *Punch* Magazine; Charles Condie, A. P. Watt Ltd; Louise Fitton, University of Illinois at Urbana-Champaign Main Library; Andrew Fraser, Midlothian District Library; J. T. D. Hall, Edinburgh University Library; D. Herbert, Ministry of Defence; Diane Kerss, Bertrand Russell Archives, McMaster University, Ontario; B. V. Mennell, Exeter University Publications

Department; Charles Pettit, Dorset Library Service; Charles Seaton, the *Spectator*;
S. Sellgren, Suffolk County Education Office; John Shaw-Ridler, Essex County
Library; Robert Smart, St Andrews University Library; Ellen Dunlap, University
of Texas Humanities Research Center; Department of Special Collections,
Research Library, University of California; Robin Johnson, Elmhirst Centre,
Dartington Hall.

Copyright Acknowledgments

The author and publishers are grateful to the following people for permission to
quote copyright material: Edwin Morgan for an extract from 'School's Out', first
published in *The New Divan*, Carcanet Press, 1977; Herb Snitzer and Thomas
Bohen for the quotations on pp. 211–13, reproduced by kind permission of
Messrs Herb Snitzer and Thomas Bohen, © 1963, 1964 by Herb Snitzer from
Summerhill: A Loving World, Macmillan.

Sources

My principal source has of course been Neill himself, especially his autobiography *Neill! Neill! Orange Peel!*. Some details of sources have been given in the body of the book, where this seemed helpful; others are only mentioned here. I have deliberately avoided the academic paraphernalia of detailed references, preferring merely to list my principal sources for each chapter.

1 The Problem Child

Carroty Broon; Home in Forfar, a town guide, *c.* 1953; Kingsmuir School Logbook. Interviews with David Adam, Margaret Adam, Keith Fife, Neil Fife, May Halliday, Fred MacFarlane, David Miller, Sheila O'Shaugnessey.

2 Young Teacher

Logbooks of Kingsmuir, Kingskettle and Newport Public Schools; archives of Midlothian education authority. Interviews and correspondence: for Bonnyrigg School: Mrs. A. Alexander, Jim Kean, Mary Stewart; for Kingskettle School: James Dewar, Margaret Moig, Isabella Skinner; for Newport School: John Anderson, Mrs D'Arcy Sturrock, J. W. Leng, Andrew Low, Flora Scrymgeour, James Scrymgeour, James Wanaan; for Kingsmuir School: David Adam, Margaret Adam. For Neill as a young man: Elizabeth Craig.

3 Journey to Fleet Street

The *Student*, 1911–12; H. C. O'Neill (ed.), *Jack's Self-Educator*. Correspondence with Kenneth Barnes.

4 A Dominie in Doubt

A Dominie's Log, A Dominie Dismissed. 'Lochinvar', *Guide to Gretna Green*; V. S. Pritchett, *A Cab at the Door*; Robert Graves, *Goodbye to All That*; Christopher Martin, *English Life in the First World War*; A. J. P. Taylor, *English History 1914–1945*; James Cameron, *Yesterday's Witness*; Jon Stallworthy, *Wilfred Owen: A Biography*. For Gretna: interviews and correspondence with David Davis, Barbara Johnson, Agnes Macdonald, Forbes MacGregor, Gladys Parker, Walter Roan, Elizabeth Sword, Jean Symington; logbook of Gretna Public School. For Willie Neill: interview with Angus Neill. For Neill as a soldier: correspondence with William Coutts; archives of Ministry of Defence. Articles by Neill: 'The Lunatic', *New Age*, 4 February 1915; 'Psychoanalysis in Industry', *New Age*, 4 December 1919. Articles on Neill: *Punch*, 24 November 1915. Letters by Neill: *New Age*, 16 December 1915. Reviews of *A Dominie's Log*: Weekly Dispatch, 14 November 1915, The *Bookman*, December 1915, *TES*, 7 December 1915, *New Age*, 13 April 1916. Review of *A Dominie Dismissed*: *TES*, 7 December 1916.

5 Homer Lane

A Dominie in Doubt. On Homer Lane: Earl of Lytton, *New Treasure*; J. H. Simpson, *A Schoolmaster's Harvest*; David Wills, *Homer Lane*; unpublished notes on Lane by John Layard. On King Alfred School: chapter by Neill in Trevor Blewitt (ed.), *The Modern Schools Handbook*; Jonathan Gathorne-Hardy, *The Public School Phenomenon*; interviews or correspondence with Roderick Garrett, Patrick Harvey, A. Horton, R. E. B. Mullins, Muriel Rocke, Peggy van Praagh; KAS magazine, December 1918. Neill's play 'The Piper Passes' in *New Era*, July 1920.

6 The New Era

A Dominie in Doubt. Raymond Postgate, *The Life of George Lansbury*. Various pieces in *New Era* during his co-editorship, 1920–1. Review of *The Booming of Bunkie*, *TLS*, 9 October 1919. Reviews of *A Dominie in Doubt*: *TES*, 21 October 1920, *New Era*, January 1921, by Norman MacMunn. Review of *Carotty Broon*: *TLS*, 31 March 1921. On the new schools: W. Boyd and W. Rawson, *The Story of the New Education*; Robert Skidelsky, *English Progressive Schools*; Reginald Snell, *St Christopher School 1915–1975*; Gerard Holmes, *The Idiot Teacher*. On Lilian Neustatter and her family: Molly Neustatter, 'Henry Handel's Sister'. On Neill's family life: interviews with Keith and Neil Fife, May Halliday.

7 The International School

A Dominie Abroad, A Dominie's Five. Edwin Muir, *An Autobiography*; Willa Muir, *Belonging*; 'Memories of Edwin Muir', by Neill; Molly Neustatter, 'Henry Handel's Sister'. For Neill's visit to Holland: *New Era*, July 1920. For Neill's talk at Calais: printed collection of papers given at conference, published by New Education Fellowship. For Hellerau: *New Era*, January 1922, April 1922, April 1923; International School prospectus, Autumn 1921. For Sonntagsberg: Paul Roazen, *Freud and his Followers*; interviews or correspondence with Donald

Boyd, Gustav Mattson, Angus Murray, Erika Stekel; *New Era* January 1924.
Review of *A Dominie Abroad: Teacher's World*, no date.

8 A School with a View

The Problem Child. New Era, October 1924, July 1928, July 1929. Bruno
Bettleheim, in *Summerhill: For and Against*; Vera Brittain, *Testament of Youth*;
Jonathan Gathorne-Hardy, *The Public School Phenomenon*; Ruth Hall, *Marie
Stopes*; Ruth Hall (ed.), *Dear Dr Stopes*; Ethel Mannin, *Confessions and
Impressions*; Molly Neustatter, 'Henry Handel's Sister'; A. J. P. Taylor, *English
History 1914–1945*. Interviews or correspondence with Roger Anscombe, Brian
Anscombe, Dorothy Bailey, David Barton, Donald Boyd, Gerry Collier, Johnnie
Collier, Larry Collier, Vanji Collier, Harold Dent, Keith and Neil Fife, Diana
Fishwick, Joan Jennings, David Newton, Teddy Raw, Greta Sergeant.
Correspondence between Neill and Bertrand Russell, British Sexological Society.
Records of the Heretics Society, University of Cambridge Library. Review of
'Dominie' books by Amabel Williams-Ellis, *Spectator*, 4 October 1924. Review of
The Problem Child by Ethel Mannin in *Nursery World*; Leonora Eyles in *Daily
Herald*; other reviews in *Glasgow Evening News, Manchester Guardian, Medical
Times*, no dates.

9 Pioneers and Parents

The Problem Parent. New Era, October 1932. Lady Allen of Hurtwood,
Memoirs of an Uneducated Lady; Victor Bonham-Carter and W. B. Curry,
Dartington Hall; Jonathan Gathorne-Hardy, *The Public School Phenomenon*;
Ethel Mannin, *Confessions and Impressions* and *Young in the Twenties*; Molly
Neustatter, 'Henry Handel's Sister'; Bertrand Russell, *Autobiography* and
Principles of Social Reconstruction; Dora Russell, *The Tamarisk Tree* and
Tamarisk Tree 2; Robert Skidelsky, *English Progressive Schools*; Willem van der
Eyken and Barry Turner, *Adventures in Education*; Michael Young, *The
Elmhirsts of Dartington*. D. E. M. Gardner, letter to Ray Hemmings, in *Fifty
Years of Freedom*; article by Chris Griffin-Beale on Christian Schiller, *TES*,
19 September 1975; Bernard Shaw, interview in *New Era*, October 1928.
Correspondence between Neill and W. B. Curry, Bertrand Russell and Dora
Russell. Interviews or correspondence with Eileen Bernal, John Bowlby, Gerry
Collier, Johnnie Collier, Larry Collier, Vanji Collier, Maurice Draper, Erica
Harper, Nicholas King Harris, Gordon Leff, Ivor Montagu, Beryl Sandford,
David Snell, Branden and Jennie Williams, David Wills. Review of *The Problem
Parent: New Era*, May 1932; other reviews in *Glasgow Herald, Everyman*.

10 One of the Gang

The Problem Child, That Dreadful School. Andrew Birkin, *J. M. Barrie and the
Lost Boys*; Molly Neustatter, 'Henry Handel's Sister'. Interviews or
correspondence with Cynthia Allen, Jean Allen, Brian Anscombe, Roger
Anscombe, David Barton, Kerstin Barton, Michael Bernal, Peter Byles, Gavin
Campbell, Howard Case, Maritza Clotworthy, Gerry Collier, Johnnie Collier,
Larry Collier, Mervyn Corkhill, Geoffrey Cox, Maurice Draper, Lionel Elvin,
Mona Elvin, Rowna Ely, Anne Forbes, Liz Hall, Gordon Leff, Elna Lucas, Bill
MacKinnon, Leslie Morton, Max Morton, Vivien Morton, David Newton,

Daphne Oliver, Edna Raymond, Teddy Raw, Ilse Reich, Olga Roncoroni, Peter Russell, Beryl Sandford, Nona Simon, Nigel Store, Amarylla Stracey, John Tooke, Branwen Williams, Evelyn Williams. Interview with Lucy Francis by Leila Berg, extracts used in *Neill and Summerhill*. Correspondence between Neill and W. B. Curry, Bertrand Russell. Articles in *News Chronicle*, 10 August 1932 and 12 April 1937; letter in *Leiston Observer*, 24 January 1934; review of *Peter and Wendy* in the *Student*, 27 October 1911.

11 Hearts not Heads

That Dreadful School. Ethel Mannin, *Privileged Spectator*; Molly Neustatter, 'Henry Handel's Sister'; Herb Snitzer, *Summerhill: A Loving World.* Interviews or correspondence with Cynthia Allen, Ruth Allen, Brian Anscombe, David Barton, Eileen Bernal, Michael Bernal, Peter Byles, Gavin Campbell, Johnnie Collier, Mervyn Corkhill, Geoffrey Cox, Ivor Cutler, Maurice Draper, Rowna Ely, Cyril Eyre, Anne Forbes, Erna Gal, Tom Hackett, S. F. Hagan, Norma Harris, Tessa Hutchinson, Gordon Leff, Bill MacKinnon, Leslie Morton, Max Morton, Vivien Morton, Angela Neustatter, Daphne Oliver, Ulla Otte, Virginia Pilkington, Bryn Purdy, Edna Raymond, Teddy Raw, Nona Simon, Bobby Townsend, Betty Tucker, Brendan Williams, Evelyn Williams. Correspondence between Neill and W. B. Curry, Paulus Geheeb, Agnes Parker, Bertrand Russell. For Lucy Francis: interview by Leila Berg for *Neill and Summerhill*; letter to William McCance. For Bernard Shaw: *New Era*, October 1928. Reviews of *That Dreadful School*: *TES*, 20 March 1937; *Daily Herald*, 1 April 1937; *Time and Tide*, by Arthur Calder-Marshall, 10 April 1937; *Observer*, 25 April 1937; *Spectator*, by Michael Roberts, 30 April 1937; *Scots Magazine*, May 1937; *New Era*, May 1937; *New Statesman and Nation*, by C. E. M. Joad, 8 May 1937; *Listener*, 25 August 1937; other reviews in *Morning Post, News Chronicle*. Serialised in *News Chronicle*, 12–16 April 1937.

12 Talking of Summerhill

Is Scotland Educated?, That Dreadful School. For Neill's South African tour: correspondence with Violet Emmer, A. H. Le Roux, Hilda Purwitsky, D. M. Rogers, Robin Whiteford; articles in *Cape Argus*, 28 July 1936, 1 August 1936, 2, 16, 17 and 22 September 1936, 16 November 1936, *Cape Times*, 2 September 1936. Trevor Blewitt (ed.), *The Modern Schools Handbook*; A. S. Munro, *Leslie Mitchell: LGG*; Molly Neustatter, 'Henry Handel's Sister'; Willem van der Eyken and Barry Turner, *Adventures in Education*; John Walmsley and Leila Berg, *Neill and Summerhill*. Interviews or correspondence with Roger Anscombe, Eileen Bernal, Michael Birt, Peter Byles, Lois Child, Maritza Clotworthy, Gerry Collier, Larry Collier, Vanji Collier, Mervyn Corkhill, Maurice Draper, Cyril Eyre, Anne Forbes, Gustav Jonsson, Elna Lucas, Leslie Morton, Ena Neill, Angela Neustatter, Olga Roncoroni, Greta Sergeant, Koichi Shimoda, Teddy Raw. Correspondence between Neill and J. R. Ackerley, W. B. Curry, Lilian Morgans, Seishi Shimoda, David Wills. Articles in *Daily Express*, 10 January 1933, *Cape Argus*, 10 February 1934. Review of *Is Scotland Educated?*, *New Era*, May 1936.

13 The Politics of Freedom

Ronald Blythe, *The Age of Illusion*; Andrew Boyle, *The Climate of Treason*; Stephen Castles and Wiebke Wustenberg, *The Education of the Future*; Jon

Clark, Margot Heinemann, David Margolies, Carole Snee (eds), *Culture and Crisis in Britain in the 1930s*; Maurice Goldsmith, *Sage: A Life of J. D. Bernal*; Ray Hemmings, *Fifty Years of Freedom*; Anton Makerenko, *The Road to Life*; Ethel Mannin, *Privileged Spectator*; Hesketh Pearson, *Bernard Shaw*; Raymond Postgate, *The Life of George Lansbury*; Dora Russell, *The Tamarisk Tree* and *Tamarisk Tree 2*; Stephen Spender, *The Thirties and After*; A. J. P. Taylor, *English History 1914–1945*; Leonard Woolf, *Downhill All the Way*. For John Dewey: *New Republic*, November/December 1928. For Victor Gollancz: correspondence with Ruth Dudley Edwards. Interviews and correspondence with Cynthia Allen, David Barton, Fenner Brockway, Johnnie Collier, Larry Collier, Cecily Cox, Geoffrey Cox, Cyril Eyre, Erna Gal, Livia Gollancz, Nan Green, Tom Hackett, Gordon Leff, Leslie Morton, Max Morton, Vivien Morton, Ilse Rolfe, Branwen Williams. Correspondence between Neill and W. B. Curry, Wilhelm Reich, Dora Russell. Articles by Neill in *New Leader*, 1 September 1933, *New Era*, January 1935; Neill at ILP Summer School, *New Leader*, 12 August 1932.

14 Wilhelm Reich

The Problem Teacher. Beverley Placzek (ed.), *Record of a Friendship*; Ilse Reich, *Reich*; Paul Ritter (ed.), *Wilhelm Reich*. Interviews or correspondence with Jean Allen, Eileen Bernal, Edward Blishen, Sheila Chesters, Johnnie Collier, Cyril Eyre, Claude Ferrière, Keith and Neil Fife, Tom Hackett, May Halliday, Gordon Leff, Virginia Pilkington, Edna Raymond, Nona Simon, Leslie Thomson, Richard Tolson, Branwen Williams. Correspondence between Neill and W. B. Curry, Paul Goodman, Angus Murray, Wilhelm Reich, H. G. Wells. Article by Neill in *Scots Magazine*, 1931.

15 Disastrous Interlude

Molly Neustatter, 'Henry Handel's Sister'; Dora Russell, *Tamarisk Tree 2*; Stephen Spender, *The Thirties and After*; A. J. P. Taylor, *English History 1914– 1945*. Interviews or correspondence with Cynthia Allen, David Barton, Sonia Crampton, Norman Davies, Ann Freshwater, Erna Gal, Rose Hacker, Tom Hackett, Norma Harris, S. F. Hagan, Nell Hutton, Gordon Leff, Ishbel McWhirter, Ben Morris, Vivien Morton, Ena Neill, Kirstie Ollendorff, Joan Quarm, Ilse Reich, Peter Russell, Hylda Sims, John Somerfield, Henry Stracey, Barbara Thorpe, Martin Tucker, Branwen Williams, Brendan Williams, Dora Williams, Evelyn Williams. Correspondence between Neill and W. B. Curry, Claude Ferrière, Eva Leff, Ishbel McWhirter, Lilian Morgans, Wilhelm Reich.

16 New Worlds?

The Problem Teacher, Hearts not Heads in the School. Lady Allen of Hurtwood, *Memoirs of an Uneducated Lady*; Leila Berg, *Risinghill*; Trevor Blewitt (ed.), *The Modern Schools Handbook*; Victor Bonham-Carter and W. B. Curry, *Dartington Hall*; Harry Rée, *Educator Extraordinary*; Marion Richardson, *Art and the Child*. Interviews or correspondence with John Aitkenhead, Eileen Bernal, John Blackie, Carol Burns, Vincent Chapman, Cyril Eyre, Leslie Jones, Gordon Leff, R. F. Mackenzie, Joan Quarm, Timothy Rogers. Correspondence between Neill and W. B. Curry, Lilian Morgans, Wilhelm Reich. Article by Neill on *The House with the Green Shutters*, *Scots Magazine*, 1944. For Robin Tanner: 'The Dying Craft', *TES*, 19 March 1976. For Christian Schiller: talk by Robin Tanner, Goldsmiths' College, London, 4 July 1974. Reviews of *Hearts not Heads in the School*: *John Bull*, 12 January 1946; *New Statesman and Nation*, 12 January 1946, by T. C. Worsley; *Tribune*, 1 February 1946; *New Era*, February 1946.

17 The Problem Parent

The Problem Family, *The Free Child*. Interviews or correspondence with Roger Anscombe, Valerie Bennett, Leila Berg, Eileen Bernal, Howard Case, Vanji Collier, Jimmy East, Cyril Eyre, Erna Gal, Libby Hall, Liz Hall, Norma Harris, Gordon Leff, Guy Love, Elna Lucas, Ena Neill, Zoë Neill, Angela Neustatter, Kate Newman, Daphne Oliver, Bryn Purdy, Suzanna Stracey, Branwen Williams. Correspondence between Neill and W. B. Curry, Claude Ferrière, Edith Geheeb, Paulus Geheeb, Bill MacKinnon, Zoë Neill, Helen Neustatter, Wilhelm Reich. Articles on Zoë Neill: by Marjorie Proops, *Daily Herald*, 16 May 1949: by Susan Hicklin, *Picture Post*, 11 June 1949; by Ena Neill, *Id*, December 1960. Reviews of *The Problem Family*: *New Era*, January, 1950; *News Chronicle*, 17 February 1949.

18 Friends in Need

Beverley Placzek (ed.), *Record of a Friendship*; Paul Ritter (ed.), *Wilhelm Reich*; Charles Rycroft, *Reich*; Ilse Reich, *Reich*; David Wills, *Homer Lane*. Correspondence between Neill and David Barton, Wilhelm Reich. Correspondence with Edward Moeran. Letter from State Department, Washington, to James Auchincloss.

19 Paradise Lost?

Interviews or correspondence with Morag Aitkenhead, Helen Asquith, Kenneth Barnes, Kerstin Barton, John Blackie, Edward Blishen, Maritza Clotworthy, Michael Duane, Kay Dunbar, Jimmy East, Ann Freshwater, Tom Hackett, Liz Hall, Charles Hannam, Nicholas King Harris, Bill Hazell, Ray Hemmings, Tessa Hutchinson, Gordon Leff, Richard Marcus, Bill MacKinnon, Leonard Marsh, Leslie Morton, Vivien Morton, Ena Neill, Noel Olley, Greta Sergeant, Roger Tilbury, Richard Tolson, Rosalind Tolson, Leslie Thomson. Correspondence between Neill and John Aitkenhead, Constance Butler, W. B. Curry, George Ives, Gordon Leff, Bill MacKinnon, Ishbel McWhirter, Wilhelm Reich. Article by Neill on inspections: *New Era*, October 1932. Ministry of Education Reports, June 1949 and March 1959. Article in *Sunday Dispatch*, 18 August 1957.

20 Summerhill USA

Summerhill, *Freedom not License!*, *Summerhill: For and Against*. Orson Bean, *Me and the Orgone*; W. Boyd and W. Rawson, *The Story of the New Education*; George Dennison, *The Lives of Children*; Allen Graubard, *Free the Children*. Correspondence with Bruno Bettleheim, Herbert Cogan, George Dennison, Dan Doran, Eleanor Hamilton, Harold Hart, John Holt, Patricia Johnson, Henry Miller, Samuel Rosen, Ruth Waller. Correspondence between Neill and Constance Butler, Dan Doran, Paul Goodman, Harold Hart, Sandor Katz, Eva

Leff, Ishbel McWhirter, Henry Miller, Antoine Obert, Wilhelm Reich, Bertrand Russell, James Stern, George von Hilsheimer. Bulletins of the Summerhill Society. Review of *The Problem Teacher*: *New Republic*, August 1945 by Paul Goodman. Articles on Neill and Summerhill: *Time Magazine*, 25 August 1947; *Look*, 19 November 1963. Article by Neill, *New York Times Magazine*, 7 November 1948.

21 Too Much, Too Late

Summerhill, *Talking of Summerhill*. Joseph Popenue, *Inside Summerhill*; Bjarne Segefjord, *Summerhill Diary*; Bryn Purdy, 'Summerhill – Children Playing'; letters from Wilf Blakeley to Bryn Purdy. Correspondence between Neill and John Aitkenhead, Kenneth Allsop, Constance Butler, Robert Byng, Daphne Byng, Howard Case, Erna Gal, Gwen Horsfield, Gordon Leff, R. F. Mackenzie, Henry Miller, Ben Morris, Bryn Purdy, Wilhelm Reich, Brian Stanley, James Stern, Vera Vivante, Colin Ward. Interviews or correspondence with J. W. L. Adams, Morag Aitkenhead, Betty Allsop, Ethan Ames, Michael Barth, Lord Birsay, Edward Blishen, John Burningham, Johnnie Collier, Geoffrey Cox, Bob Cuddihy, Mikey Cuddihy, Michael Duane, Kay Dunbar, Cyril Eyre, Victor Gregory, Barbara Grigor, Libby Hall, John Holt, Brian Innes, Robert James, Ann King, Léonard Lassalle, Gordon Leff, Lord Longford, R. F. Mackenzie, Robert Morley, Ena Neill, Zoë Neill, Robin Pedley, Virginia Pilkington, Brian Stanley, Amarylla Stracey, Richard Tolson, Humphrey Truswell, Kenneth Tynan, Vera Vivante, Colin Wilson. Leila Berg, *Risinghill*; R. F. Mackenzie, *State School* and *The Unbowed Head*. Article in *Cherwell*, 25 February 1961; on the Committee of 100, the *Scotsman*, 19 and 22 September 1961; on the Newcastle degree, *The Times* 10 May 1966; on the Ministry inspection, *The Times*, 11 June 1968, 3 July 1968: Neill's 'Unrectorial Address', *TES*, 22 November 1968. Neill in West Germany, *TES*, 7 May 1971. Letter on Children's Rights, *Guardian*, 11 December 1971. Neill and TV appearance: unpublished discussion between Neill, Leila Berg, Michael Duane, John Holt, and R. F. Mackenzie. Reviews: *Summerhill*: *TES*, 13 April 1962; *Sunday Telegraph*, 15 April 1962, by Nigel Dennis; *New Statesman*, 20 April 1962, by D. W. Harding; *Spectator*, 10 June 1962; other reviews in *Daily Herald*, *Guardian*, *Observer*. *Talking of Summerhill*: *Guardian*, 17 March 1967, by Brian Jackson; *New Statesman*, 17 March 1967, by Harry Rée. *Summerhill* (paperback): *TES*, 29 November 1968. *Neill! Neill! Orange Peel!*: *Observer*, 20 May 1973, by Philip Toynbee; *Daily Mail*, 24 May 1973; *Guardian*, 24 May 1973, by Eric Midwinter; *TES*, 3 August 1973; other reviews in *Daily Mirror*, *Sunday Times* by Royston Lambert, *The Times*, *New Humanist* by Edward Blishen.

22 The Message of Freedom

Correspondence between Neill and Lilian Morgans, Wilhelm Reich. Interviews or correspondence with Leila Berg, Edward Blishen, Howard Case, Charles Causley, Philip Coggin, William Connell, Pat Edwards, Shin-ichiro Hori, Gustav Jonsson, Barbara Kahan, John Kirkham, Pat Kitto, Michael Montcombroux, Harry Rée, Sally Rodwell, Koichi Shimoda, David Wills. Robin Pedley, *The Comprehensive School*; R. F. Mackenzie, *The Unbowed Head*; Ray Hemmings, *Fifty Years of Freedom*. Visits to Kirkdale School, London, and White Lion Street Free School, London. For Scotland Road School, article by Carol Dix, *Guardian*, 18 June 1971; for Durdham Park School, article by Frances Farrer, *TES*, 3 February 1978; for Christine Meek, article in *TES Scotland*.

23 The Summerhill Child

Interviews with Cynthia Allen, Jean Allen, Ethan Ames, Brian Anscombe, Roger Anscombe, David Barton, Egan Bernal, Donald Boyd, John Burningham, Gavin Campbell, Peter Case, Gerry Collier, Johnnie Collier, Larry Collier, Vanji Collier, Mervyn Corkhill, David Critchlow, Jacquy Elvey, Rowna Ely, Diana Fishwick, Anne Forbes, Ann Freshwater, Martin Green, Norma Harris, Jenny Hutt, Anthony Jenkins, Léonard Lassalle, Gordon Leff, Andrew Morton, Ishbel McWhirter, Zoë Neill, Angela Neustatter, David Newton, Daphne Oliver, Teddy Raw, Edna Raymond, Irene Saunders, Veronica Saunders, Amarylla Stracey, Suzanna Stracey, Barbara Thorpe, Sarah Vyse, Branwen Williams, Evelyn Williams. Correspondence with Michael Barth, Shirley Beeton, Jennifer Caryll, Peter Catchpole, Mikey Cuddihy, Michael Davis, Frances Green, Debbie Hemmings, Keith Horsfield, Ann King, Karin Ann Lewes, Richard Marcus, Daryll Mitchell, Diane Moscrop, Chris Reilley, Peter Russell, Nigel Store, Martin Tucker. Phone conversations with Juliet Balshaw, Gretel Boyer, Mallory Clifford, Tessa Hutchinson, Timothy Israel, Hazel Knight, Ruth Pickup, John Somerfield, John Tooke, Robert Townsend. Unpublished interviews by Angela Neustatter with Michael Bernal, John Burningham, Keith Critchlow, Ralph Muller, Robert Townsend. Unpublished responses to questionnaire, sent out by Bryn Purdy, from Claudine Fricker, Diane Moscrop. Correspondence between Neill and Ishbel McWhirter. *Neill! Neill! Orange Peel!*; Leonora Eyles, *For My Enemy Daughter*. Man Bernstein, article on Summerhill pupils, *Id*, no. 14, March 1965.

24 Ending

Interviews or correspondence with Donald Boyd, Margaret Duane, Sandy Fife, May Halliday, Ena Neill. Correspondence between Neill and Nell Hutton, Gordon Leff, Wilhelm Reich.

Bibliography and Further Reading

Books by Neill

A Dominie's Log, Herbert Jenkins, 1916; Hart, 1975.
A Dominie Dismissed, Herbert Jenkins, 1917; Hart, 1975.
The Booming of Bunkie, Herbert Jenkins, 1919.
A Dominie in Doubt, Herbert Jenkins, 1921; Hart, 1975.
Carroty Broon, Herbert Jenkins, 1921.
A Dominie Abroad, Herbert Jenkins, 1923.
A Dominie's Five, Herbert Jenkins, 1924.
The Problem Child, Herbert Jenkins, 1926; McBride, 1928.
The Problem Parent, Herbert Jenkins, 1932.
Is Scotland Educated?, Routledge, 1936.
That Dreadful School, Herbert Jenkins, 1937.
The Last Man Alive: A Story for Children from the Age of Seven to Seventy,
    Herbert Jenkins, 1938; Gollancz, 1970.
The Problem Teacher, Herbert Jenkins, 1939; International Universities Press,
    1946.
Hearts not Heads in the School, Herbert Jenkins, 1945.
The Problem Family, Herbert Jenkins, 1949; Hermitage Press, 1949.
The Free Child, Herbert Jenkins, 1953.
Summerhill, Gollancz, 1962; Penguin, 1968; Hart, 1960.
Freedom not License!, Hart, 1966.
Talking of Summerhill, Gollancz, 1967.
Neill! Neill! Orange Peel!: A Personal View of Ninety Years, Weidenfeld &
    Nicolson, 1973; Quartet, 1977.

Essays by Neill

Sections on English Language, English Literature, Mathematics, in H. C. O'Neill (ed.), *Jack's Self-Educator: A Guide to Liberal Education*, T. C. & E. C. Jacks, 1916.
'Summerhill', in Trevor Blewitt (ed.), *The Modern Schools Handbook*, Gollancz, 1934.
'Shaw and Education', in S. Winsten (ed.), *GBS 90: Aspects of Bernard Shaw's Life and Work*, Hutchinson, 1946.
'The Man Reich', in Paul Ritter (ed.), *Wilhelm Reich*, Ritter Press, 1958.
'Freedom Works', in Julian Hall (ed.), *Children's Rights*, Panther, 1972.

Letters by Neill

Beverley R. Placzek (ed.), *Record of a Friendship: Wilhelm Reich and A. S. Neill*, Farrar, Straus, Giroux, 1981; Gollancz, 1982.
Jonathan Croall (ed.), *One of the Gang: Selected Letters of A. S. Neill*, Deutsch, 1983.

Books on Neill and Summerhill

Richard E. Bull, *Summerhill USA*, Penguin Inc., 1970.
Ray Hemmings, *Fifty Years of Freedom: A Study of the Development of the Ideas of A. S. Neill*, Allen & Unwin, 1972.
Joseph Popenue, *Inside Summerhill*, Hart, 1969.
Bryn Purdy, 'Summerhill – Children Playing: a Study of Summerhill School'; unpublished thesis, Padgate College of Education, 1963.
Bjarne Segefjord, *Summerhill Diary*, Gollancz, 1971.
Herb Snitzer, *Summerhill: A Loving World*, Macmillan, 1964.
John Walmsley and Leila Berg, *Neill and Summerhill: A Man and His Work*, Penguin, 1969.
Harold Hart (ed.), *Summerhill: For and Against: Assessments of A. S. Neill*, Hart, 1970; Angus & Robertson, 1973 (includes essays by Bruno Bettleheim, John Holt, Sylvia Ashton-Warner, Paul Goodman, Fred Hechinger, Erich Fromm).

Further Reading

Carol Adams, *Ordinary Lives*, Virago, 1982.
Lady Allen of Hurtwood, *Memoirs of an Uneducated Lady*, Thames & Hudson, 1975.
Maurice Ash (ed.), *Who Are the Progressives Now?*, Routledge & Kegan Paul, 1969.
J. M. Barrie, *Peter and Wendy*, Hodder & Stoughton, n.d.
J. M. Barrie, *An Edinburgh Eleven: Pencil Portraits of College Life*, 1889.
J. M. Barrie, *A Window in Thrums*, Hodder & Stoughton, 1890.
J. M. Barrie, *Margaret Ogilvy*, Hodder & Stoughton, 1896.
J. M. Barrie, *Sentimental Tommy: The Story of his Boyhood*, Cassell, 1896.
J. M. Barrie, *When A Man's Single*, Hodder & Stoughton, 1897.
Orson Bean, *Me and the Orgone*, St Martin's Press, 1971.
Leila Berg, *Risinghill: Death of a Comprehensive School*, Penguin, 1968.
Andrew Birkin, *J. M. Barrie and the Lost Boys*, Constable, 1979.

Trevor Blewitt (ed.), *The Modern Schools Handbook*, Gollancz, 1934.
Ronald Blythe, *The Age of Illusion: England in the Twenties and the Thirties, 1914–1939*, Penguin, 1964.
Victor Bonham-Carter, *Dartington Hall: The Formative Years 1925–1957, with An Account of the School by W. B. Curry*, Phoenix House, 1958.
W. Boyd and W. Rawson, *The Story of the New Education*, Heinemann, 1965.
Andrew Boyle, *The Climate of Treason: Five Who Spied for Russia*, Hutchinson, 1979.
Vera Brittain, *Testament of Youth*, Gollancz, 1933; Virago, 1978.
Vera Brittain, *Testament of Experience*, Gollancz, 1957; Virago, 1979.
George Douglas Brown, *The House with the Green Shutters*, 1901; Cassell, 1967.
Maurice Bridgeland, *Pioneer Work with Maladjusted Children*, Staples Press, 1971.
Michael Burn, *Mr Lyward's Answer*, Hamish Hamilton, 1956.
James Cameron, *Yesterday's Witness*, BBC Publications, 1979.
Neville Cardus, *An Autobiography*, Collins, 1947.
Stephen Castles and Wiebke Wustenberg, *The Education of the Future*, Pluto Press, 1979.
H. A. T. Child (ed.), *The Independent Progressive School*, Hutchinson, 1962.
Jon Clark, Margot Heinemann, David Margolies, Carole Snee (eds), *Culture and Crisis in Britain in the 1930s*, Lawrence & Wishart, 1979.
Alec Clegg (ed.), *The Changing Primary School*, Chatto & Windus, 1972.
John Coleman, *Childscourt*, Macdonald, 1967.
Maurice Cornforth (ed.), *Rebels and their Causes: Essays in Honour of A. L. Morton*, Lawrence & Wishart, 1978.
Bernard Crick, *George Orwell: A Life*, Secker & Warburg, 1980.
Valerie Cunningham (ed.), *The Penguin Book of Spanish Civil War Verse*, Penguin, 1980.
George Dennison, *The Lives of Children: The Story of the First Street School*, Penguin, 1972.
Lovat Dickson, *H. G. Wells: His Turbulent Life and Times*, Macmillan, 1969.
Janet Dunbar, *J. M. Barrie: The Man Behind the Image*, Collins, 1970.
Leonora Eyles, *For My Enemy Daughter*, Gollancz, 1941.
Sigmund Freud, *Two Short Accounts of Psychoanalysis*, Penguin, 1962.
Jonathan Gathorne-Hardy, *The Public School Phenomenon*, Hodder & Stoughton, 1977.
Robert Gittings, *Young Thomas Hardy*, Heinemann, 1975.
Robert Gittings, *The Nature of Biography*, Heinemann, 1978.
Robert Gittings, *The Older Hardy*, Penguin, 1980.
Maurice Goldsmith, *Sage: A Life of J. D. Bernal*, Hutchinson, 1980.
Allen Graubard, *Free the Children: Radical Reform and the Free School Movement*, Pantheon, 1972.
Robert Graves, *Goodbye to All That*, Cape, 1929.
Phyllis Grosskurth, *Havelock Ellis*, Allen Lane the Penguin Press, 1980.
Julian Hall (ed.), *Children's Rights*, Panther, 1972.
Ruth Hall, *Marie Stopes: A Biography*, Virago, 1978.
Ruth Hall (ed.), *Dear Dr Stopes: Sex in the 1920s*, Deutsch, 1978.
James Henderson, *Irregularly Bold: A Study of Bedales School*, Deutsch, 1978.
Gerard Holmes, *The Idiot Teacher*, Faber & Faber, 1952.
Ernest Jones, *The Life and Work of Sigmund Freud*, Hogarth Press, 1962.
Homer Lane, *Talks to Parents and Teachers*, Allen & Unwin, 1928.

'Lochinvar', *Guide to Gretna Green*, 4th edn, Nicholson & Cartner, n.d.
Earl of Lytton, *New Treasure: A Study of the Psychology of Love*, Allen & Unwin, 1934.
Norman and Jeanne Mackenzie, *The Time Traveller: The Life of H. G. Wells*, Weidenfeld & Nicolson, 1973.
R. F. Mackenzie, *State School*, Penguin 1970.
R. F. Mackenzie, *The Unbowed Head: Events at Summerhill Academy 1968–1974*, Edinburgh University Student Publications Board, 1980.
J. D. Mackie, *A History of Scotland*, Penguin, 1964.
A. S. Makarenko, *The Road to Life*, vol. 1, Foreign Languages Publishing House, Moscow, 1951.
Ethel Mannin, *Confessions and Impressions*, Penguin, 1930.
Ethel Mannin, *Privileged Spectator*, Jarrolds, 1939.
Ethel Mannin, *Young in the Twenties*, Hutchinson, 1971.
Christopher Martin, *English Life in the First World War*, Wayland, 1974.
Michael Meyer, *Ibsen*, Rupert Hart-Davis, 1967.
Ivor Montagu, *The Youngest Son*, Lawrence & Wishart, 1970.
Edwin Muir, *An Autobiography*, Hogarth Press, 1968.
Willa Muir, *Belonging*, Hogarth Press, 1968.
I. S. Munro, *Leslie Mitchell: LGG*, Oliver & Boyd,
Molly Neustatter, 'Henry Handel's Sister', unpublished MS.
Hesketh Pearson, *Bernard Shaw*, Collins, 1942.
Hesketh Pearson, *GBS: A Postscript*, Collins, 1951.
Robin Pedley, *The Comprehensive School*, Penguin, 3rd edn, 1978.
Raymond Postgate, *The Life of George Lansbury*, Longman, 1951.
V. S. Pritchett, *A Cab at the Door*, Chatto & Windus, 1968.
V. S. Pritchett, *Midnight Oil*, Chatto & Windus, 1971.
Harry Rée, *Educator Extraordinary: The Life and Achievement of Henry Morris*, Longman, 1973.
Ilse Reich, *Reich*, Elek, 1969.
Marion Richardson, *Art and the Child*, University of London Press, 1948.
Paul Roazen, *Freud and his Followers*, Allen Lane the Penguin Press, 1976.
Robert Roberts, *A Ragged Schooling*, Manchester University Press, 1976.
Bertrand Russell, *Principles of Social Reconstruction*, Allen & Unwin, 1916.
Bertrand Russell, *Autobiography*, Allen & Unwin, 1967–9.
Dora Russell, *The Tamarisk Tree*, Elek/Pemberton, 1975.
Dora Russell, *Tamarisk Tree 2: My School and the Years of War*, Virago, 1980.
Charles Rycroft, *Reich*, Fontana, 1971.
R. J. W. Selleck, *English Primary Education and the Progressives 1914–1939*, Routledge & Kegan Paul, 1972.
Bernard Shaw, *Prefaces*, Constable, 1934.
Otto Shaw, *Maladjusted Boys*, Allen & Unwin, 1965.
J. H. Simpson, *Schoolmaster's Harvest*, Faber & Faber, 1954.
Upton Sinclair, *World's End*, Laurie, 1940.
Robert Skidelsky, *English Progressive Schools*, Penguin, 1969.
Reginald Snell, *St Christopher School 1915–1975*, Aldine Press, 1975.
Stephen Spender, *The Thirties and After*, Fontana, 1978.
Jon Stallworthy, *Wilfred Owen: A Biography*, Oxford University Press/Chatto & Windus, 1974.
Wilhelm Stekel, *Autobiography*, Liveright, 1950.
W. A. C. Stewart, *Progressives and Radicals in English Education*, Macmillan, 1972.

Lytton Strachey, *Eminent Victorians*, Chatto & Windus, 1918.

A. J. A. Symons, *The Quest for Corvo*, Cassell, 1934.

A. J. P. Taylor, *English History 1914–1945,* Oxford University Press, 1965.

Henri Troyat, *Tolstoy*, Penguin, 1970.

Willem van der Eyken and Barry Turner, *Adventures in Education*, Allen Lane the Penguin Press, 1969.

Betty D. Vernon, *Ellen Wilkinson 1891–1947*, Croom Helm, 1982.

H. G. Wells, *Kipps*, 1905; Fontana, 1961.

David Wills, *Homer Lane: A Biography*, Allen & Unwin, 1964.

Colin Wilson, *My Quest for Wilhelm Reich*, Granada, 1981.

Leonard Woolf, *Downhill All the Way: an Autobiography of the Years 1919–1939*, Hogarth Press, 1967.

Michael Young, *The Elmhirsts of Dartington: The Creation of an Utopian Community*, Routledge & Kegan Paul, 1982.

Index